Hometown Memories . . .

Dust Storm Days and Two-Holers

Tales from the Good Old Days in Southwest and South Central Kansas
A TREASURY OF 20TH CENTURY MEMORIES

OTHER BOOKS FROM HOMETOWN MEMORIES
Claremont Tales
Taylorsville Tales
Burke County Tales
Catawba County Tales
Cleveland County Tales
Blue Ridge Tales
Foothills-Piedmont Tales
Memorable Tales of the Smokies and Blue Ridge Mountains
Caldwell County Tales
Albemarle Tales
Lincolnton Tales
Montgomery Tales
Lee County Tales
Rowan County Tales
Cold Biscuits and Fatback and other Richmond County Tales
Skinnydipping in the Mule Trough and Other Rockingham County Tales
Lunch in a Lard Bucket and Other Cabarrus County Tales
Rooster in a Milkwell and other Moore County Tales
It Always Rains When Old Folks Die and other Tales from Davidson and Randolph County
A Prayer for a Baby Goat and other Tales from Alamance County
The Mill Village and the Miracle Bicycle and other Tales from Gaston County
Wilmington Tales
Guilford County Tales
Asheville Tales
The Class of '47 Was Me and other Tales along the North Carolina Coast
The Elegant Tarpaper Shack and other Tales from the Heartland of North Carolina
Outhouse Spiders and Tin Tub Baths—Tales from the Blue Ridge Mountains
Wringer Washers and Ration Stamps—Tales from Forsyth County
Front Porch Stories, Back Porch Bathrooms —Tales from Alexander, Davie, Iredell, Rowan, and Yadkin Counties
Crank Victrolas and Wood Cook Stoves —Tales from Green, Lenoir, Pitt, and Wayne Counties
Mules, Mud and Homemade Soap —Tales from Anson, Stanly and Union Counties
Life in the Good Old Days in Alamance, Caswell and Rockingham Counties
Life in the Good Old Days in Catawba, Lincoln and Gaston Counties
Life in the Good Old Days in Buncombe and Henderson Counties
Moonshine and Blind Mules and other Western North Carolina Tales
Ain't No Bears Out Tonight and other Cabarrus County Tales
Two Holers and Model T Fords and other Randolph County Tales
Ham Biscuits and Baked Sweet Potatoes and other Montgomery, Richmond , and Scotland County Tales
Possum Hunters, Moonshine and Corn Shuck Dolls and other Tales from Wilkes County
Chasing the Ice Truck and other Tales from New Hanover County and Wilmington
Steam Whistles and Party Line Phones and other Tales from in and around Roanoke
Squirrel Gravy and Feed Sack Underwear—Tales from the Tennessee Mountains
Miners' Lamps and Cold Mountain Winters—Tales from Southwest Virginia
Cold Outhouses and Kerosene Lamps—Tales from Southeastern Ohio
Coal Camps and Castor Oil—Tales from Southern West Virginia
Brush Brooms and Straw Ticks—Tales from Northwest Georgia
Dust Storms and Half Dugouts—Tales from the Upper Panhandle of Texas
Lessons by Lamplight—Tales from Southeastern Kentucky
Frozen Laundry and Depression Soup—Tales from Upstate New York
Paper Dolls and Homemade Comforts—Tales from Northwestern Virginia
One-Room Schoolin'—Tales from Central West Virginia

Cow Chips in the Cook Stove—Tales from the Lower Panhandle of Texas
Moonshine and Mountaintops—Tales from Northeast Tennessee
When We Got Electric…—Tales from Northwest West Virginia
Outside Privies and Dinner Pails—Tales from Southwest Iowa
Milking the Kickers—Tales from Southwest Oklahoma
Rolling Stores and Country Cures—Tales from Northeast Alabama
Penny Candy and Grandma's Porch Swing—Tales from North Central Pennsylvania
Rumble Seats and Lumber Camps—Tales from Northern Michigan
Lye Soap and Sad Irons—Tales from Northwest Missouri
Almost Heaven—Tales from Western West Virginia
Hobos and Swimming Holes—Tales from Northern Wisconsin
Saturday Night Baths and Sunday Dinners—Tales from Northwest Iowa
Sod Houses and The Dirty Thirties—Tales from Northwest and North Central Kansas
Coal Oil Lamps and Cattle in the Crops— Tales from Northern and Mountain West Idaho
Morning Chores and Soda Fountains—Tales from The Texas Hill Country
County Schools and Classic Cars—Tales from Northeast Iowa
Wood Fire Saunas and Iron Mines—Tales from Michigan's Upper Peninsula
Kerosene Lamps and Grandma's Washboard—Tales from Northeastern Missouri
Picture Shows and Five Cent Moon Pies—Tales from North Carolina's Blue Ridge Mountains
    and Foothills
Corncob Fuel and Cold Prairie Winters—Tales from Eastern and Northeastern South Dakota
Filling Stations, Shine, and Sorghum Molasses—Tales from The Tennessee West Highland Rim
Down in the Holler—Tales from Southwestern Virginia
Monday Washdays and Outhouse Roosters—Tales from West Virginia's Eastern Panhandle and
    also Northwestern Maryland
Party Line "Rubberneckers"—Tales from Southwest and South Central Wisconsin

At Hometown Memories, our mission is to save and share the memories of days gone by…before they are lost forever. As of this publication, we have created 80 books of memories, and saved and shared over 20,000 stories and 10,000 pictures.
We hope you enjoy them!

Hometown Memories...

Dust Storm Days and Two-Holers
Tales from the Good Old Days in Southwest and South Central Kansas

A TREASURY OF 20TH CENTURY MEMORIES
Compiled and edited by Todd Blair and Karen Garvey

HOMETOWN MEMORIES, LLC
Hickory, North Carolina

Dust Storm Days and Two-Holers

Publisher: Todd Blair
Lead Editor: Karen Garvey
Design and Graphic Arts Editor: Karen Garvey and Laura Montgomery
Office Services Assistants: Laura Montgomery and Tim Bekemeier
Warehouse Manager: Tim Bekemeier
Assistant Editors: Monica Black, Lisa Hollar, Jodi Black, Greg Rutz, Heather Garvey, Brianne Mai, Reashea Montgomery, Hannah Pletcher, Cathy Elrod, and Tiffany Canaday

ISBN 978-1-940376-11-0 Copyright © 2014

All rights reserved by Hometown Memories, LLC and by the individuals who contributed articles to this work. No part of this work may be reproduced in any form, or by any means, without the written permission of the publisher or the individual contributor. Exceptions are made for brief excerpts to be used in published reviews.

Published by

Hometown Memories, LLC
2359 Highway 70 SE, Suite 350
Hickory, N. C. 28602
(877) 491-8802

Printed in the United States of America

Acknowledgements

To those Southwest and South Central Kansas folks (and to those few who "ain't from around here") who took the trouble to write down your memories and mail them in to us, we offer our heartfelt thanks. And we're sure you're grateful to each other, because together, you have created a wonderful book.

To encourage participation, the publisher offered cash awards to the contributors of the most appealing stories. These awards were not based upon writing ability or historical knowledge, but rather upon subject matter and interest. The winners were: Cecil A. Unruh of Hutchinson, KS; Doris Schroeder of Hutchinson, KS; Jim Gilger of Greely County, KS. We would also like to give honorable mention to the contributions from Marilyn Goracke of Phillipsburg, KS and Mr. Leslie Groves of McPherson, KS. The cash prizewinner for the book's cover photo goes to Arlene Schuler Grinnell of Longmont, CO (you'll find their names and page numbers in the table of contents). Congratulations! It was extremely difficult to choose these winners because every story and picture in this book had its own special appeal.

Associate Editors

Mary Ann Buller
Loretta "Rita" Casper
Naomi Chestnut
Mickie Gillette
Lorene P. Gnaedinger
Sister Irene Hartman
Bob Hessman
LuAnn Jamison
Frances Johnson
Francis "Frank" Moore
Nell Moore
Joyce Murphey
Roy F. Parker
Vernon Pauls
Marian Redford

Jane Keel Sapone
Dortha Schroeder
Lois Schroeder
Cecile M. Shoemaker
Rev. Allen Smith
Carroll M. Snell
Martina Stegman
Bernice Steinmetz
Ruby A. (Bare) Swanson
Marjorie L. Terrell
Clara B. Thompson
Joel Voran
Lavon Wiersig
Suzie Yunker

INTRODUCTION

We know that most folks don't bother to read introductions. But we do hope you (at least eventually) get around to reading this one. Here's why:

First, the creation of these books is in its fifth generation after we took over the responsibilities of Hometown Memories Publishing from its founders, Bob Lasley and Sallie Holt. After forty nine books, they said goodbye to enjoy retirement, and each other. Bob and Sallie had a passion for saving these wonderful old tales from the good old days that we can only hope to match. We would love to hear your thoughts on how we are doing.

Second—and far more important—is the who, what, where, when, why and how of this book. Until you're aware of these, you won't fully enjoy and appreciate it.

This is a very unusual kind of history book. It was actually written by 353 Kansas old-timers and not-so-old-timers who remember what life was really like back in the earlier years of the 20th century in Southwest and South Central Kansas. These folks come from all walks of life, and by voluntarily sharing their memories (which often include their emotions, as well), they have captured the spirit and character of a time that will never be seen again.

Unlike most history books, this one was written from the viewpoint of people who actually experienced history. They're familiar with the tribulations of the Great Depression; the horrible taste of castor oil; "outdoor" plumbing; party line phones; and countless other experiences unknown to today's generation.

We advertised all over Southwest and South Central Kansas to obtain these stories. We sought everyday folks, not experienced authors, and we asked them to simply jot down their memories. Our intention was by no means literary perfection. Most of these folks wrote the way they spoke, and that's exactly what we wanted. To preserve story authenticity, we tried to make only minimal changes to written contributions. We believe that an attempt at correction would damage the book's integrity.

We need to include a few disclaimers: first, many important names are missing in many stories. Several folks revealed the names of their teachers, neighbors, friends, even their pets and livestock, but the identities of parents or other important characters weren't given. Second, many contributors did not identify pictures or make corrections to their first draft copies. We're sure this resulted in many errors (and perhaps lost photographs) but we did the best we could. Third, each contributor accepts full responsibility for his or her submission and for our interpretation of requested changes. Fourth, because some of the submitted photographs were photocopied or "computer printed," their quality may be very poor. And finally, because there was never a charge, "fee," or any other obligation to contributors to have their material included in this book, we do not accept responsibility for any story or other material that was left out, either intentionally or accidentally.

We hope you enjoy this unique book as much as we enjoyed putting it together.

The Hometown Memories Team
August 2014

TABLE OF CONTENTS

The Table of Contents is listed in alphabetical order by the story contributor's last name.

To search for stories by the contributor's hometown or year of birth, see indexes beginning on page 441.

Dave Ackerman	360	Cleta Cornett	113
Jack Adams	63	Patty L. Craven	176
L. K. Adams	177	Maurice B. Creghead	251
Marilyn J. Albright	282	Evelyn Crockett	359
Rose Alderson	233	Glenda Crone	140
Nora Ellen Allender	242	Katherine Becker Cruz	387
Cathy Boles Amara	247	Pat Curtis	169
Carolyn Arpin	227	Joann Danley	125
Elma Ash	401	Dana Davidson	230
Kathy Ast	118	David G. Davis	105
Lolita Bonnie Baker	349	Marilyn Jean Davis	374
Thane Baker	417	Ruby Ashcraft Deaver	264
Chester I. Bare, Jr.	116	Merrill R. Deck	80
Calvin L. Barnhart	325	Arlie DeFreese, Jr.	272
Robert E. Barton	147	Robert C. Dick, Ph.D.	111
Gordon Beaushaw	373	Nancy Ashworth Douglas	288
Jennifer Isenhower Beaver	165	Diana Dry	65
Diane Berry	360	John H. Duncan	385
Richard D. Blackburn	35	Joan Irene Farney Dunn	301
Carol S. Blankenship	93	Verene V. Eason	280
Galen R. Boehme, Ph.D.	329	Brian M. Ede	283
Christiana Bongartz Bollig	377	Julane Ediger	36
Aliene Bolton	180	Susan Edmonston	59
Gwen Wilson Brooks	263	Jeanette Elder	218
Mary Ann Buller	331	Frances Elffner	131
Eugena "Jean" Burdorf	244	Melody Elsworth	225
Edna Irene Jacobs Butler	34	Barbara Engelhardt	136
Norma Caldwell	72	Flora Erickson	313
Barbara C. Campbell	269	Lesta Freeman Esser	362
Jim "Pete" Carmichael	43	Paula J. Etrick	31
Loretta (Rita) Casper	146	Gerold R. "Jerry" Falls	83
Wendel Chalfant	267	Helen Farney	234
Naomi Chestnut	35	Judy Farris	69
Joan Clayton	361	Elfreda Fast	150
Marie S. Clemence	42	Pauline Fecht	105
Estol Coen	346	Jana Sibley Finkbiner	74
Judy Schremmer Corby	429	Doug Fisher	371

Name	Page	Name	Page
Warrenetta Fisher	422	Leonard Hitz	238
Marie Fletcher	38	Lavona Hobson	336
Eleanor M. Fox	427	Roger Roy Hoffman	421
Roger G. Fox	145	Pauline F. Hoopes	179
Dr. Herb Frazier	177	Shirlee Hoopes	311
Peggy J. Gammill	430	Shirley Hoskinson	348
Larry L. Gates	147	Kenneth Howe	160
Garee Geist	108	Cyndee Huddleston	166
Linda Gering	48	Sister Teresita Huse	96
Jim Gilger	20	LuAnn Jamison	194
Mickie Gillette	62	J. R. Jenista	104
Clara Cottle Ginn	84	Frances Johnson	119
Helen Gilger Glenn	299	Lowell Wayne Jones	260
Lorene P. Gnaedinger	316	Terrence Keenan	68
Joan Goering	220	Elinor Keesling	248
Marlene L. Goertz	50	Aden E. Nettie Keim	339
Anna Jane Goetz	312	Shirley Kempke	49
Art Gomez	192	E. Earl Kendrick	434
Marilyn Goracke	21	Allan T. Kimmell	250
Don Graber	65	Alberta L. Kingsly	197
Maureen Grandon	398	Trulin Kinser	350
Juanita Grantz	53	Wilma Kinser	343
Arthur G. Green	154	Maxine Kirkpatrick	97
Helen Green	107	Dale Klenke	294
Laverne Griggs-Hiemstra	179	Kyle Klenke	124
Arlene Schuler Grinnell	25	Faye Klinge	247
Mr. Leslie Groves	22	Shirley Friesen Knackstedt	40
James M. Hall	401	Sue Knight	302
Howard Hamilton	363	Betty Elaine Koehn	261
Jim Hammeke	370	Peg Koehn	183
Albert Hanlon	180	Judy Konrade	121
Lottie Harder	51	Simon Korbe, jr.	335
John A. Harding	230	Arlys Kraus	311
Larry Harsh	173	Adolph Kuhn	114
Laura (Lorene Hunt) Hart	152	Elva Unruh Kunze	184
Sister Irene Hartman	130	Shauna Labo	270
Michael Hathaway	62	Alvera Lacey	406
Phyllis Hatltom	343	Betty J. Lehr	208
Marion L. Hearn	355	Colleen Lemman-Tarman	133
Charlene Heim	187	Larue Lennen	27
June M. Henderson	128	Delorse Lessenden	436
Vita M. Henning	392	Noah J. Lewis	194
Mary Hershberger	103	Donald C. Lipprand	259
Bob Hessman	282	Kenneth Lipprand	116
Jean Hicks	277	Brian T. Lohrenz	62
Gene Hirst	145	Anna Schlereth Looney	318

Name	#	Name	#
Lorraine L. Lovette	367	Vernon Pauls	48
Evelyn Mace	365	Marcketta Peak	156
Marita McBride	121	Jean Peintner	36
Olive Ann McCormick	378	Jacka Penner	149
Iris McIntosh	280	Walter Perrin	389
Mark McIver 3	10	Robert Peterson	298
Grace McLaughlin	281	Ivan Harris Phillips	266
Joyce A. McMannis	45	Jan Pinsince	155
Darlene McMillion	73	Earl Polk	144
Vernon McMinimy	264	Larry Popovich	151
Mardia "Dinky" Meece	205	Karen Poynter	51
Janice Merrill	112	Anna Mae Pracht	312
Bob Metzler	106	Jim E. Quillin	175
Larry Miles	281	Dorl Rader	433
Alice Kay Miller	396	Carla Rains	98
Liz Miller	148	Gertrude Raple	402
Siser Alvina Miller, O.P.	214	Galen Rapp	89
Rita Anne Mills	256	Beulah Gleeson Ratzlaff	153
John "J. W." Minor	119	Carol Redd	64
Carolyn Kay Mohler	366	Marian Redford	176
Francis "Frank" Moore	285	Marie Regehr	172
Milton B. Moore	79	Jean L. Regier	122
Nell Moore	35	Pat Reichenberger	394
Joyce Stark Morse	195	Sharilyn Reifschneider	188
Jack Moser	142	Elsie Reiger	287
Joy Kline Moser	380	Gwendolyn E. Rice	231
Joyce Murphey	137	Dorothy Richardson	240
Helen L. Murray	248	Charlotte Ringer	55
Jeri Myers	236	Kathleen Risley	171
Marion W. Nattier	159	Mary Ann Rix	150
Marlene Shirley Neufeld	126	Richard Robl	404
Peter J. Neufeld	91	L. Marlene Roe	30
Marilyn Newman	198	Letha Roets	280
Jeanette Unruh Nightengale	185	George Roets, Sr.	230
Helen Normandin	182	Alfred Rohr	314
Ralph E. Nutter, Sr.	222	Jolene Rice Roitman	403
Connie O'Bleness	315	E. Joan Rollins	437
Evelyn Olson	345	Galen Rudiger	99
Rebecca Otter	304	Icel Lee Russell	402
Karen Matthews Parker	382	Virginia L. Ryan	178
Roy F. Parker	76	Clayton Sadowski	321
Ken Patterson	319	Ruth B. Sanderson	410
Henry Pauls	200	Patricl Sandoval	253
Janice A. Pauls	211	Richard L. Sandoval	357
Melvin D. Pauls	191	Jane Keel Sapone	66
Nancy J. Pauls	184	Ruth Saranko	249

Name	Page	Name	Page
Mariella Sawin	274	Vera Jean Swafford	52
Loren and Arlene Schamaun	52	Ruby A. (Bare) Swanson	293
Larry Schlotfeldt	41	Betty Swendson	27
Esley Schmidt	401	Connie Taylor	289
Hildred Schmidt	351	Bill Temaat	295
Jane Keel Schmidt	338	Marjorie Terrell	108
Laura Ann Schrag	246	Lois M. Theis	33
Doris Schroeder	19	Georgia Thomas	305
Dortha Schroeder	42	LaVern Gregg Thomas	99
Esther L. Schroeder	110	Cecil Roger Thomas, Jr.	161
Gail Schroeder	311	Claire Ryta Thompson	296
Lois Schroeder	67	Clara B. Thompson	112
Shirley A. Schwarz	158	Lois Timmermeyer	334
Samuel Walter Scott	213	Sister Diane Traffas	347
Leah Sellers	100	Shirley Ummel	29
Earleta Selm	54	Howard L. Underwood	211
Lester Seuser	317	Doloris Ungles	110
Geri Shafer	108	Cecil A. Unruh	17
Cecile M. T. Shoemaker	70	Erlene R. Unruh	88
Beulah Simcox	202	Alice R. Uphoff	353
Helen Sindelar	101	Russell O. Vail	157
Marilyn Small	57	Pat Stapleton Van Dolah	412
Beverly J. Davis Smith	307	Douglas R. Van Horn	120
Clement A. Smith	71	Elinor "Skip" Vasey	408
Eleanor Smith	106	Jill Voran	425
Rev. Allen Smith	39	Joel Voran	28
Stanley J. Smith	115	Martha J. H. Wakefield	344
Jackie Carol Smith-Lamkin	217	Linda Walters	314
Jayne Smoot	405	Tom Walters	313
Carroll M. Snell	148	Ruby Waltner	210
Gerald Speer	407	Ann Warner	411
Dell Spurgeon	290	Mora L. Weber	308
Maxine Stapleton	415	Lavon Wiersig	215
Wilma Steadman	109	Beauford Wilkerson	414
Martina Stegman	250	Marian Williams	419
Bernice Steinmetz	81	Pat Williamson	107
Richard O. Stineman	138	Patsy Kaye M. Wilson	344
Carol J. Stone	326	Dorathe Wiltshire	231
Gregg A. Stone	61	June M. Winslow	163
Sister Cecilia Ann Stremel	288	Virginia C. Winter	310
Robert A. Strong	53	Rachel Witte	233
Martha Stroup	321	Jack Wolfe	47
Geraldine Stufflebeam	284	Barbara Woodman	144
Ellen Sullivan	280	Phyllis Yockey	87
Justine Sullivan	235	Lloyd H. Yoder	260
Margaret Surprise	37	Mary E. Yoder	341

Ellen Pulliam Young	286
Galen P. Yunker	232
Suzie Yunker	181
Index A (Year of Birth/Hometown)	441

The Tales...

True stories intentionally left just as the contributor wrote them.

Recollections: 1923-1946
By Cecil A. Unruh of Hutchinson, Kansas
Born 1923

Born June 19, 1923 on a farm seven miles south of Greensburg, Kansas in Kiowa County, I am the seventh of eight children to Jacob and Susie Unruh. Today I am the only living member of this family.

I can recall childhood events back to 1927 when I was five years old. That was the last year we harvested the wheat crop with a horse-drawn header. It took six horses to pull the header, which would cut the heads of wheat from straw and elevate them into a large hay wagon, pulled by two horses, which trailed alongside the header. When full, the straw in the wagon was pitched by hand into a large, neat stack and left to dry. Later in the season, the stacks were pitched into a steam-powered threshing machine, which separated the grain from the wheat straw. While my brother and I carried drinking water to the threshing crew, we were not allowed to get near any machinery.

The next year, Dad purchased his first tractor and combine, which was a great improvement for our bountiful wheat crop. Our new combine was not self-propelled, so a tractor was needed to pull it. After the second year of the bumper crop, a severe drought devastated the region, and the prevailing winds caused huge dust storms. By 1933, the country had fallen into the Great Depression. The market that sustained the farmer plummeted. Wheat was 25 cents per bushel, cattle were five cents per pound, and hogs were three cents per pound. There was a run on the banks, and many failed.

Our new president, Franklin D. Roosevelt, called for a four-day bank holiday, which restored stability. At the same time, the president initiated new programs to help the economy, including federal loans for productive farmers who needed assistance, the planting of shelterbelts (rows of trees) which prevented the wind from eroding the soil, and farmland management programs that encouraged crop rotation to further preserve soil nutrients. By 1938, the drought was over and we were once again able to plant and harvest wheat and other grains.

I am among the second generation of a group that emigrated from Ukraine to the United States and settled in Kansas. These people experienced difficult lives, but hard times on our Kansas farm were just a way of life for us. Our family was poor, but as farmers, we were resourceful and raised our own food. We had cherry and mulberry fruit trees. The summer garden produced potatoes, sweet potatoes, cucumbers, tomatoes, carrots, peas, green beans, cabbage, and radishes. The root vegetables were safely stored in an underground storm shelter, which doubled as storage for glass jars filled with pickled vegetables. Farmers needed their children to help with the farm work. Many farmers had as many as eight to ten children.

Our farm was modest, but we all worked

Cecil and his brother, Vernie

Unruh brothers and three grandsons

hard to make a living for the family. Each child had daily chores, including working horses, milking cows by hand, feeding hogs, feeding chickens, and gathering eggs. Since there was no running water, we children carried water into the home. There was no electricity either, but we had kerosene lamps to light the home. We would use the lamps in the early mornings to light the barn where we milked the cows. The cows would come into the dimly lit barn and find their places, where they would feed while we milked them.

Everyone in our family had important duties to accomplish. My mother and sisters prepared three meals a day on a wood or coal fueled cook stove. All cooking or baking bread required a well-stocked fire. One side of the stove had a water reservoir, which was kept warm by the resident heat. The stove also heated a heavy iron for pressing the cloths. The women stitched their own dresses, and used the wringer washer to do the laundry. They would crank a handle to agitate the clothes inside the washtub, and then the clothes were cranked through a wringer and hung outside on a wire line to dry.

Dogs were very important on our farm; however, they were never allowed to be in the farmhouse. In the summer months, they would sleep outside of the house. In the winter months, they slept in the cattle barn. When we got ready to do our work, the dog was always there waiting for us. Our dog worked with us all day getting cattle from the pasture to the farmstead. Cats were also important for keeping the farm free of mice. Every morning we fed our dogs and cats milk and leftover food from the kitchen table.

I remember Grade School District 26, which was a rural, one-room schoolhouse that also served as a church and a voting precinct. Each county in Kansas had a school superintendent. That superintendent was responsible for all schools in his or her county. When a child had successfully passed all eights grades, he or she was required to take a final test. They would need to go to another school district to take the written test and must have a passing grade to enter high school. Our school was located in the center of the district, ensuring that children would not have to walk more than a mile and a half from any direction. The district included children from no fewer than 14 farms. We carried tin lunch pails with an ad for Karo corn syrup on the side, complete with a wire handle and a lid that would seal the food. Mother would pack a peanut butter sandwich or a home-cured ham sandwich made with her homemade bread, an apple, and a homemade cookie.

Farm children were required to go to grade school eight months out of a year. The other four months they were needed to help on the farm. Two of my brothers and I walked to school every day. To get to school we walked across a wheat field into a cattle pasture until we came to a county road. The distance was one half mile. There we met four other children and walked with them on the county road for one half mile. At that point, we met four more children and all walked another half mile to our school. Once there, the boys would help bring in a supply of coal for the large stove, and would pump drinking

Loading wheat from the grain elevator
Vernic and Cecil Unruh

water from the well.

We began our school day by reciting the Pledge of Allegiance, which was followed by a brief prayer. Each December the students would prepare a Christmas program for our parents. My favorite teacher was Arthur Unruh (no relation) who taught us when we were in the seventh and eighth grades. I remember learning to play the harmonica in class with 18 other students. The schoolyard was large. It was supplied with a merry-go-round, a large swing, and a teeter-totter. On one side, there was room for us to play baseball.

After school, we walked back home and had a short rest period that might include a sugar cookie. Since we had evening chores, our teachers rarely assigned homework. Free time later in the evening might include checkers or Chinese checkers. After passing all eight grades, students wanted to continue their education at a high school. Dad bought a used Ford coupe, and we drove it seven miles to Greensburg High School for four years.

Worship was an important part of our upbringing, our minister was himself a farmer, and services were held on Sunday morning as well as Sunday evening. The Sunday Children would present a Christmas program.

The world changed abruptly for us on December 7 1941, when the Japanese attacked Pearl Harbor, and the United States was thrust into World War II. This was the beginning of a new era. World War II lasted from 1942 to 1945 and changed the world forever.

In conclusion: I have been the witness of more development then any generation in this world. 1941 for us began a great change. This change had no boundary, no limitations. An industrious age had begun. After World War II, farmers no longer needed horses for farming and new factories were being developed for making farm machinery. Agriculture colleges started development of hybrid grains. Factories were built to manufacture cars, jet airplanes, computers, laptop computers, and cell phones. The first cars had to be started using a hand crank, however today you only need to push a button from inside your house to start your car. In my lifetime, I also saw a biblical prophecy fulfilled. In 1948, Israel became a nation. Isaiah 60 reads, "I will again bring my people to their land which I the Lord have promised."

"Doing" the Dishes
By Doris Schroeder of Hutchinson, Kansas
Born 1933

Once in a while, I have decided it is almost as fast to wash the dishes by hand and have Hubby dry them than it is to rinse and load the dishwasher. It only takes a few minutes and then the dishes only have to be taken up once. Besides, there is a lot of companionship in "doing" the dishes the old-fashioned way.

In looking back, it is strange, but the best times of my life occurred when Mom and I were "doing" the dishes. When we lived on the farm, the REA had not yet come through our area, and we had no electricity. Therefore, suppertime was followed by heating a kettle of water on the kerosene stove, Mom getting out the dishpan and putting it on our little moveable cabinet. She got out another pan for rinsing, and began washing the dishes that I picked up from the large family table we had just eaten from.

Of course, all this water had to have been impelled outside at the pump a few feet from the house. This we had tried to do before it got dark because the lantern gave very little light. Besides, on the farm there was always a possibility that a wild animal like a raccoon or a skunk could be lurking in the dark. This was another item to look out for when Mom threw the dishwater out into the night!

Mom usually washed and I dried as we went over the events of the day. I would tell her what had happened at the one-room country school and she would tell me stories from her own childhood. The dim light of the kerosene lamp made shadows in our big family kitchen, and so some of her stories verged on being exciting.

It was unthinkable to stack the dishes and do them the next day. There was no room, and besides, we would need them in the morning. The glow from the coal stove in the middle of the room lent a cozy feeling as the shadows on the wall danced around with the events of the stories. Dad would sit at the large family table, sometimes doing some figuring while we talked. My little sister would be playing paper dolls cut from the catalog in the corner. I remember thinking how good it was when we were all home together like that. It made me feel secure.

When we went to both our grandmas'

Getting ready to "do" the dishes
Carol, Doris and their mom, Emma

houses on Thanksgiving and Christmas, the tables would be laden down with all kinds of wonderful food. Later, our mothers would congregate in the kitchens as they did the dishes and I could hear that they were having a good time visiting with each other. We children *almost* wished we could be in there, too, helping with the dishes.

These times continued when we moved back to town, at least the first two years when we lived in a little house on Eighth Street, and again when my family moved to Ford Street. Still, I always looked forward to helping Mom "do" the dishes.

A little later in life after John and I were married, Mom usually always invited us over for Sunday dinner along with someone else from church. It was always a treat. We women found that doing the dishes later was the best time to share our thoughts about different things. It is always easier to talk when you are shining a dish or putting something away. We talked about our children, what they did in school, and things like that. It was a time to "let our hair down," which means we sometimes talked of somewhat personal things.

Sometimes when we lived in the little house we built on 17th Street, I would invite our parents over for Sunday afternoon and they would play shuffleboard on our basement floor. Later, we had 4 o'clock lunch or "faspa" as we Germans call it. I usually had homemade zwiebach, lunchmeat, canned peaches or Jell-O, and my favorite—chocolate cake. No one left until we women would carry the dishes to the kitchen and "do" them. As was the custom of that day, the men usually sat in the living room during that time and the children would do their thing.

Later, when we built our present house, I thought it was so wonderful to have central air, a dryer, *and* a dishwasher. It does, however, seem like we lost something when we no longer stand by the sink "doing" the dishes.

There's a reason that God made us "work by the sweat of our brow!" When you have to put effort into something, it always becomes more meaningful. Now, if I can just get John to talk more while we are doing dishes, I have made it!

You, too, might try "doing" dishes sometime! You may enjoy it!

My Account of Black Friday
By Jim Gilger of Greely County, Kansas
Born 1924

This day in March 1934, was beautiful. The sun was shining, the wind not blowing, the temperature was very pleasant. I remember having the feeling that everything was all right with the world.

It was a daily chore of mine, after the school day, to bring our herd of cattle into the fenced in enclosure for the night. The herd of cattle grazed during the day on a quarter section of land that was covered with virgin grass, grass that had not been subjected to the plough. Our herd numbered about one hundred fifty, a mixed bunch of mother cows, calves, heifers, steers, two bulls, and although basically Herefords, were not a pure strain of beef cattle.

I rode a small horse called Sparky this evening. Sparky was a kid's pony belonging to a barber in the town of Tribune. My father agreed to keep the pony on our ranch. I remember being more fond of Sparky than any other horse, or other animal that I had ever known.

I had gathered the herd from where they were grazing and had driven them nearly a mile toward the enclosure, where they would be safe overnight, when I noticed a cloud rising over the northern horizon. At first, I had no idea whatsoever as to what I was about to experience.

The cloud was billowing dust, rising to an altitude of five thousand feet, or more, and moving towards me at perhaps thirty miles an hour. The herd was about a hundred yards from the fenced in enclosure, when I made the decision I must leave the herd and try to reach safety.

As a boy, I was an avid reader of western cowboy type tales. One of these tales told a horse could by instinct find his way in a storm. When the storm was upon me, I was perhaps half way between the herd and the gate to the enclosure'

The light went from full daylight to absolute darkness. The darkness was so intense I could not see the horse I was riding. This was when I learned a horse finding his way in a storm is pure myth. Poor Sparky was as lost as I was. He had turned around and we were among the herd again. Even though I could not see the cattle, I could hear them. I made the decision to turn Sparky in the direction where I thought the gate must be which was north. Another big mistake.

Instead of going north, Sparky and I were traveling west, away from the gate. The elapsed time was probably minimal, although it seemed an eternity. After this elapse of time, I was able to see the ground and recognized deep cut trails made by the cattle over the years on their way to the gate. I followed these trails to the enclosure, and then followed the fence to the house. At the age of nine, I am convinced God heard my prayers and guided me to Safety.

The Dust Storms continued for several years after this storm, which has become known as BLACK FRIDAY.

Hannah the Hen
By Marilyn Goracke of Phillipsburg, Kansas
Born 1945

"Hannah, Hannah," I would call out, and somewhere in a sea of white ruffled feathers and red combs would come a gentle singing, an answer to my calls. I could find Hannah almost immediately, with the rest of the chicken flock fluttering away. Hannah would continue to sing to me until I picked her up.

I've had a lot of people tell me, "Oh Marilyn, you can't make a pet out of a chicken, let alone have a chicken recognize a voice or even recognize its name."

I loved growing up on an Iowa farm. I loved being able to be outside in the fresh air and sunshine, running in the rain, and jumping in mud puddles. But, most of all, I loved being able to have the farm animals as friends. Heaven knows I had a lot of them. Spot the pony, Foxy the fox, Douglas the pig, Elmer the cat, and numerous cows that each had a name too.

Hannah's life started out as an ordinary chicken. A little yellow piece of fluff brought home from the hatchery with 90 other baby chicks. The baby chicks were housed in a "brooder house" that had special lamps to keep them warm. After three or four months the chickens were allowed to run free around the farm yard, returning to the chicken house at dusk to "go to roost" and sleep.

One afternoon, after getting home from school, I noticed a hen chicken laying on the yard. She seemed unable to get up and run away with the rest of the chickens. I went over to her and picked her up, noticing her right leg dangling loosely. Taking the chicken to the house for my mother to see, was told the chicken's leg is probably broken. I asked my mother if we could "fix it." Locating some Popsicle sticks, we taped the chicken's leg into place.

I couldn't allow the chicken to return to the chicken flock so a cardboard box was used to house my newly found friend. Straw was placed on the floor of the box and windows were cut in the sides. Something still didn't seem quite right. She'll be lonely in the box by herself. I started looking for pictures of chickens to keep my friend company. A lot of farm magazines were available, so several pictures of chickens were cut out and taped inside of the box.

I can't seem to remember how I decided to name my friend Hannah. I guess Hannah the hen just seemed appropriate.

After a couple of weeks of caring for Hannah, I thought it might be fun if I took her to school for a visit. The teacher approved the visit, so my mother helped me prepare Hannah's house and helped get her to school. The teacher and students all gathered around Hannah's box to see her before school started. About 10:30 that morning, Hannah began singing and nothing could quiet her. The teacher told me I needed to move Hannah to the entryway so my mother could come and get her. When I moved Hannah's box what a surprise I found. Hannah had laid an egg! That was the reason she's been singing. She hadn't laid any eggs since her injury, and now she had laid an egg, AND DURING SCHOOL! I knew then that Hannah was getting well.

Marilyn holding Hannah with her sister, Carolyn, and brother, Larry in 1958

After another week or so, mom though it might be time to remove the splints and see how Hannah walked. She seemed happy to have the splints removed. She hopped a short distance, but didn't try to put any weight on the injured leg. We decided to wait another week and let Hannah try to walk again. Much to my happiness and amazement Hannah tried to put some weight on her injured leg, barely touching her foot to the ground. I helped Hannah practice walking a little every day. When mom and I felt it was safe enough for Hannah to be with the other chickens we put her with them in the chicken house. Hannah now walked with a slight limp, but she blended in with the other chickens. I could always find her though, not because of her limp, but because anytime I would call, "Hannah, Hannah," she would sing out to me.

After a couple of years, mom decided to sell the chickens. A man and woman came one evening when it was almost dark and took all the chickens. It was after this I could no longer find Hannah, despite my calls to her. I decided she must have gone along with her chicken friends to a new home. I knew she wouldn't be lonely.

A lot of years have passed but I still think of Hannah, and once in a while, if I listen very closely, I still hear her singing out to me. I still miss her, but I know she's happy wherever she is.

What does God say about animals?

Animals are silent witness for GOD. Scripture states that God's Glory can be seen in all of His creation. If you read the scriptures and observe His animals, it is obvious. They are testimony of His power, His majesty, His design, and His love. You may not see it, but it is there to be seen. You may not hear their voices because they speak a different language, but they still speak and testify of Him.

They were given intelligence. That is evident by the fact that they can learn tasks. Isaiah 1:3 speaks of the intelligence of animals in stating that they know their owners and they know their homes. They can learn to communicate with, and learn to understand human language and behavior.

Can they not also feel pain, hunger, cold, hot, love, rejection, and fear as humans feel? It is not that animals are less than human. It is just simply that they are not human. God's Word tells us that He love creation, that He loves man, and that He loves animals.

The Valentine
By Mr. Leslie Groves of McPherson, Kansas

In September of 1938, my educational journey began. My twin brother Lowell and I would experience the first year of elementary school in Miss Bess Henley's first and second grade class along with 15 other classmates. Many of the children in that classroom we already knew from Sunday school at Bethany Church. Miss Henley was a very proper lady, always well-dressed and wearing her blonde hair pulled back into a bun. Her manner was a very kind, but she was firm on her discipline.

On that memorable first day, she put us at ease by asking us if we could write our names. She would let us print our names if we could. If we couldn't, she would print them very neatly on the blackboard. All of us could print our names on the blackboard, including a new, pretty little girl whom no one knew.

She went to the blackboard and wrote her name in beautiful cursive—Mary Lou Holgate. Mary Lou was the daughter of our school superintendent. From that moment on, we knew that she was very special. All of us in the room were in awe of her because she could write her name in cursive. That brief introduction would be the beginning of a childhood infatuation for me. It grew stronger as the days and months passed. The fact that she sat directly in front of me presented all sorts of opportunities for me to do special favors for her.

One day when I was especially enraptured by her, I got brave and wrote her a little love note. On it I wrote, "I love you." As I got out of my desk to walk by her desk to deliver it, it fell off her desk and landed on the floor. Miss Henley saw me drop the note on her desk and also saw it fall on the floor. "Leslie, would you please pick up the note and read it to the class," she said.

I picked it up, feeling my face get hot. I read it amidst the laughter and cheers from my classmates. "Now Leslie, would you take it upstairs to Mr. Holgate?" Suddenly I was shuddering with fear. My older brothers had suggested that if I ever needed to go up to his office I would see a very large paddle and an automatic whipping machine.

Slowly, I made it up the stairs to his office. When I opened the door, he welcomed me and said, "Well, Leslie, what can I do for you today?" I told him that Miss Henley sent me up with the note that I had written to Mary Lou. He unfolded the note and read it. He chuckled, "Mary Lou is my daughter, and I love her also." With a sigh of relief, I went down those steps feeling ten feet tall, ready to take on the world. When I got back to the classroom, the guys could hardly wait to see what Superintendent Holgate said or did. They were completely blown away when I told them what he said to me.

After Christmas, we got down to work, learning how to read and write and spell. We practiced our penmanship and worked on spelling words together. Because we sat next to each other, Mary Lou often practiced her spelling words with me—much to my delight. We read to each other and practiced out addition facts. When she practiced with someone else, I felt very sad.

Soon it was time to be thinking about Valentine's Day. As a class, we made a large valentine box covered with hearts made from construction paper with the names of our classmates written on them. Every heart I made had Mary Lou's name on it with little love notes written on them. I didn't know very much about Valentine's Day, but I soon found out we could write little love notes to those who were very special.

Everyone else was buying valentines with little candy suckers on them. I couldn't afford those, but I did see a really beautiful valentine in the grocery store. About that same time, the local seed store was paying school kids to go about the town harvesting seeds from the many lilac bushes in town. They would pay ten cents a pound. That beautiful valentine cast $1.50. I immediately thought my brothers and I could find many pounds of lilac seeds on our bushes and the ones in the neighborhood. We asked Mom if we could get those seeds to earn some money for valentines. She agreed that it was a good idea. We got busy, and before we knew it, we had a burlap bag that was full. We took the seeds to the store, hauling them on our little coaster wagon. When the seed store man weighed the bag, he gave us a crisp $5 bill. Wow! I had never seen that much money. When my brother and I split that, we each had enough to buy our valentines. I could buy the really beautiful one for Mary Lou. It had a large heart made of shimmery paper, and on the center was a beautiful Cupid covered with bright red cellophane. In gold letters was printed, "I love you, Valentine."

I put it in the envelope and hid it in my desk. All of the kids brought their special valentines and put them in the box. When all were done, Lowell and I took ours to the box, but I kept my very special one in my desk so I could give it to Mary Lou.

The week before the valentine party, we were making plans. I looked at my valentine and it was so beautiful. I could hardly wait for the day of the party to arrive. When it finally did, and the huge box of valentines was opened and all the love notes were passed out, I volunteered to help. Mary Lou got a large pile of little hearts on her desk. When all were passed out and the class was busy counting up the number of valentines they got, I slipped my valentine into Mary Lou's stack, then nonchalantly walked away, talking to my classmates about the love notes they got.

Every so often, I would walk by her desk to see if she had gotten to mine. When she did, she was amazed that it was so much larger than any of the others on her desk. She slowly opened it, and when she saw it was from me, her face brightened and she looked at me with this bright smile.

Then it felt like it was worth all the hard work picking the lilac seeds so I could buy it for her. I walked toward my desk when the teacher told us that we should put all the valentines in a big grocery bag. I was glad to give Mary Lou some help in putting all her cards in the bag. I put my card on the very top of the pile.

The class and Miss Henley had already walked out of the room. Mary Lou and I were the only ones left. She came over and gave me a big kiss on my right cheek. I wanted to tell the class of my good fortune. Mary Lou actually gave me a kiss! Yes! Yes! Yes!

My mom couldn't convince me to wash that cheek for days afterward.

I Love Thunderstorms

Even though you may know me as Les Groves, that was not always the case, for I had many aliases. Growing up in a family with seven brothers and sisters and a father who was a genuine tease, I sometimes answered to Pester, Windy, Pea Picker, etc. My mom was the only one in my family who addressed me by my given name unless she was correcting me for some transgression, then it was Leslie… Paul…Groves. You must understand that all of these aliases were terms of endearment, for we all loved each other. Well, so much for the nicknames. Everybody, and I mean everybody, knew I loved thunderstorms. I loved the loud claps of thunder and the dramatic flashes of lightning. Most of my family was sure that I would sooner or later be a statistic, struck by lightning. If I didn't get struck by lightning, I would more than likely get caught in a downpour, which happened quite frequently. In my mind, I thought that when it thundered God was expressing His displeasure with something we earthlings did that He didn't like. When there was a sharp bold of lightning, He was really upset. When it started to rain, He was telling us, "Its okay, I love you in spite of your misdeeds."

Back to the nicknames—I had one more, which came from my favorite comic strip, "Li'l Abner." I liked Li'l Abner because he had large bulging muscles, and I was a weakling with no visible muscles. Li'l Abner had a cute li'l girlfriend, named Daisy Mae. Now, at my young and tender age, I thought she was really a foxy babe; I wondered why Li'l Abner didn't just up and marry her! But what did I know about how the comic strips worked? The etymology of my more humorous nickname was "Skeleton McKlossett." Wherever he was, there was always a thunderstorm nearby, so I guess you can understand why I thought he was kind of like me. My family always admonished me, "Now Les, don't get caught in the rain." I guess I hadn't heard of the saying, "He doesn't have brains enough to come in out of the rain."

Let's fast forward to when I had grown up, kind of anyway, and I moved to Kansas on the advice of a college buddy. I had been to Kansas a year earlier, and my buddy suggested there were many of the cute "Daisy Maes." And wouldn't you know I found one who just right for me! So here, I am back in Kansas and I am here to marry my little lady. She beguiled me with her charms and her art. Yes, she was a real live artist with a compelling desire to recreate all of the beautiful things in nature.

Les Groves

This brother of "Ellen" was also a Li'l Abner fan, and the first time I got caught in the field and mopped up a thunderstorm, he nicknamed me "Lester McKlossett." I thought that term of endearment was more imaginative than any of the others I had.

Lest you are thinking, "He's a real dingbat," I need to share with you that I do have a serious side. So when Ellen and I had two adorable little fellows, we knew that job number one was to teach them about God's wonderful creation—including thunderstorms. One Sunday after church, we were having lunch at the old Sirloin Stockade in McPherson. We sat next to the windows where we were watching the clouds. A thunderstorm was building in the west, so we finished our lunch in a hurry. We jumped into our old 1950 Ford and raced home. The storm was fast approaching. I took my favorite writing tablet and carefully described the storm. It was then and there that "Music for a Sunday Afternoon" was born.

Ardith, Caroline, Arlene, Henry, and Wilbur in 1934

No Excuse for Things to Be Dirty
By Arlene Schuler Grinnell of Longmont, Colorado
Born 1929

The memories of the dust storms in the '30s that Ness County, Kansas had. First part written about 1985. Arlene was born February 14, 1929, her older brothers Wilbur, December 3, 1924, Henry, November 18, 1926, her younger sisters, Caroline, December 3, 1930, Ardith, November 22, 1932, brothers, Richard Dewey, June 25, 1935, David, March 20, 1937, sister, Donna Lou, May 7, 1939. So we all experienced the dust storms of the '30s.

I remember back in the '30s when we had the dust storm days. We had to use wet strips of old rags, some were made out of sheets, or whatever we happened to have at that time. Mother would have us use milk buckets for dishpans to fill with water. Remember we did not have dishwashers. We took the rags, dipped them in water, squeeze them out a little, took a table butter knife, and stuffed them around the window's frame to keep the dust down. One time it was so bad we all went to the cellar.

I think it was Caroline mother was telling me about; we just about lost her. The wind blew her right out of the folks' hands, not sure, if mother had her or daddy. The wind whipped her loose she was so light, so small and so young, she was always much smaller than the rest of us children. Probably had their hands held on to more than just one of the children, plus a kerosene lantern so we could see. It really could have been anyone of the children that was born during those times. But the first one was frightening. The children who were born in the '30s listed above. I wasn't too old, but did remember it was really a bad sky and was so dark that the clouds were rolling along the ground and seemed to pick up the dirt. I just knew we were all going to die. After we got to the storm cellar, I especially worried about the house falling on top of the storm cellar, and we all would be trapped for days, before someone could dig us out. But we all managed to get through those bad dust storm days. They did last for quite a few years, but not as bad as some the early days. That's when the president decided to have farmers begin planting trees and do what they could to keep the soil from blowing.

Yards had gravel since most could not have grass. Because short of rainfall. It was bad whenever the wind blew hard. Because most of the time we had to keep the windows shut and sealed. Especially where we had to seal the windows shut with wetting rags torn up and stuff in between the window frames to help catch the dust.

When we were young and growing up in the old farmhouse, I was still quite young. I remember in the wintertime we had an old cook stove to mostly heat the kitchen and

Richard, Donna, and David in 1941

do all our cooking on, winter and summer. That's what they call the Good Old Days. In the wintertime it was too cold to shower in the shower house, so when we took baths, it was in an old aluminum tub that was sitting in front of the oven door of the cook stove. Our water was heated in the stove reservoir, which held water for several uses. Would use it for washing dishes, but heated water in a teakettle for scalding the dishes. Mother was always sure that we got enough hot water to kill germs.

Back in those days, we didn't have a hot water heater or electric in the house. No gas either living on a farm, later mother got propane so she could have some gas things. When in a hurry mother used hot water out of the teakettle to get the potatoes cooking in a hurry. When you cooked on an old cook stove, sometimes it would take longer, in case the fire wasn't too hot. We also used the teakettle water to sterilize the cream separator. Whoever ended up washing it was the one that needed to walk to the house, get the teakettle with the boiling water, and take it to the separator room, which at that time was the same area as the washhouse.

I think back and wondered just how much walking we did. The barn was pretty far from our house. Then the washhouse was by the windmill. We didn't have separator room in the barn until 1944 when the new barn was built. Men made sure we had water close to the barn. Now I wonder how the separator got sterilized? I know I work away from home a lot to help earn money for food. In those days, we didn't have a lot.

Sometimes the crops were either hail out or we didn't get rain enough to get the crops going good. I remember only one-year mom and dad had to get help with our food supply. Things like flour, navy beans and probably a few other things I can't recall right now. Since daddy had a windmill and could raise good garden crops, we managed to put up plenty of string beans, corn that was cut off the ears. They grew lots of beets and when mother canned them, they were always pickled. Really had a wonderful flavor.

When daddy butchered in the early spring mother would can the beef in jars, seemed like the smaller the old pressure cooker was going a lot. We did not have locker plants early in our childhood life. If mother could afford to get a bushel of peaches, we canned them. Also, pears maybe those were some of the things the government helped pay for. I remember some neighbors would also help if they had more gardens than they could use. None of the farmers ever let any produce go to waste. Dad and mom raised their own cabbages. I have examples how they made their own sauerkrauts. When us children were young and we babysat, or helped to clean house for any of the neighbors that needed help, we received little money, that would go to help pay for food. Also, we all pitched in and would help shock feed for quite a few of the neighbors.

Besides that, we didn't have indoors bathrooms, so we used enamel pots called chamber pots at night only. The colors of them were white with a beautiful red trim. When we were young mother didn't want us going outside at nights. Those had to be emptied every day and cleaned. We had an outside

Arlene (Schuler) Grinnell using a sad iron

toilet called an outhouse. Since there was a child around, daddy put a big cement seat in for the bigger people and a smaller one for the little ones. In the beginning, we had Sears Roebuck catalogs to wipe with. We would crumby the sheets of paper several times to try and soften it up a little so our behinds wouldn't get sore. Never dream of using toilet tissue, which we could never afford to buy. One thing about it we got plenty of catalogs in the mail, so we never ran out of paper.

Daddy would use some kind of lime to keep the odor down and when it got full and needed to be moved to another spot, daddy was in charge of that. I remember several times he dug a big, deep hole and used the dirt from the one digging to fill up the rest of the old hole where we he had just moved the outhouse to a new spot. Daddy hooked onto it with a chain and tractor and pulled it over the new hole. Always lined it with lime so it would stay smelling nice for quite some time.

The outhouse was cleaned daily with Lysol to kill all of the germs. Mother taught us children to keep things as clean as we could because it did keep our illness rate down. She taught us that as long as we had soap, water, a pail, and cleaning rags, we couldn't come up with an excuse to have things dirty. What we used in the outhouse was a special broom.

around and finally allowed me to pick her up. In time, we became close buddies. She enjoyed sitting in the old tree swing with me while I serenaded her, as we swung back and forth. When things happened at school, I would confide in her. She would look at me intently, cock her head to one side; and I knew she understood.

I thought myself to be the luckiest girl in the world to have such a confidante. At last, I had something to call my own! I named her "Shirley."

Eventually she learned to race down the lane to greet me when she saw me coming home from school. I loved her dearly – and couldn't wait for her to jump into my arms, and make little chicken sounds of happiness.

But one tragic Sunday morning, returning from Sunday school, I discovered she was nowhere to be seen. I called and looked everywhere. Finally, I dashed into the house to ask if anyone knew where she could be.

My brother, a few years older than I, said that a coyote had caught her, but I smelled chicken cooking in the kitchen! And rightfully guessed that he wasn't telling the truth; when my Mom had sent him out to get a chicken for lunch, Shirley became his victim.

I've never forgotten how dear she was, nor of the void, she filled in my life. Needless to say, I still find it difficult to eat chicken.

Shirley
By Larue Lennen of Coolidge, Kansas
Born 1925

One of my saddest childhood memories occurred when I was eight years old. We lived in the country about a mile and a half from a small town.

I loved walking to school each day. I passed over a river where I sometimes saw wild animals and pretty birds. Occasionally, the temptation to go wading was overwhelming and I took off my shoes and splashed in the pool of water under the bridge. It was my secret. Yet, I sometimes grew lonely for something of my own.

Since we were very poor, we couldn't afford any pets or playthings, but we had chickens that I fed each evening after school.

One of the chickens began following me

When Children Could Experience Simple and Happy Childhood
By Betty Swendson of Newton, Kansas
Born 1927

Spending my childhood in the 30s and 40s was much different from the childhood of my children, grandchildren, and great-grandchildren.

Many of our toys were handmade. My brother made some our toys. He made a rubber band gun for me. It was made out of wood with a pinch clothes pin to hold a rubber band, which was made out of a strip from an old inner tube.

Push the clothespin down and away the band of rubber flew, which was fine unless one aimed it at a person, which is what I did. I released the band of rubber and it hit a lady in the face while she was driving by. She stopped the car and I ran away as fast as I could! My parents never knew what I did until much later.

My brother also made a wooden scooter out of an orange crate with rollers on the bottom. I had just as much fun and went just about as fast as my great-grandchild with his motorized scooter.

Money was scarce, so my brother and I made money by selling metal clothes hangers and pop bottles when we could find them.

A game, which we played with other children, was "Marbles for Keep." I had a bag of marbles with a "cat-eyed-shooter." The purpose of the game was to shoot other children's marbles out of a circle drawn in the dirt and then keep them. My father said that I could not keep the marbles. Of course, I really wanted to keep them.

Simple things in life gave me so much pleasure, such as trying to decide which penny candy was the best (it wasn't every day that I could spend a penny).

Chasing the iceman who brought ice in his horse drawn wagon was a treat, especially when he threw a piece of ice to us.

Children of all ages played together outside without special shoes, uniforms, or equipment. We played games such as Annie-over-pigtail, hopscotch, capture the flag, kick the can, jacks, run sheep run, work up, and punch the icebox.

We enjoyed our freedom. We could walk anywhere in town or country without being afraid someone would be following us. We had Saturday movies while sitting on benches in the middle of town, free ice cream on Easter Sunday and had time to use our imagination.

Other special memories come to mind, lying in the grass while looking at the clouds, making necklaces out of dandelion stems, catching lightening bugs, and putting my fingers in smoke rings made by my Dad while smoking his pipe.

My Dad was a teenager in 1914. He raced other young men with his horse and buggy, shot firecrackers at Christmas time and shot Roman Candles at each other.

May Day was a special time for my Mother. She and her friends made many, many May baskets to give away and a special parade was the main feature of the day.

I experienced a happy childhood at a time in our history when people seemed to be good neighbors to each other and a time when children could experience childhood without distractions after distractions.

Pretty Prairie Pigs Gone Wild
By Joel Voran of Leawood, Kansas
Born 1952

Back in the late 1960s, the booming metropolis of Pretty Prairie, Kansas had a main street a mile long, the Kansas largest night rodeo. However, the town did not have a swimming pool, nor were there any pools for miles around other than muddy farm ponds. Then my best friend's grandparents moved to town from their pig farm three miles north of town. They took their house with them, literally, by lifting their house off of its cinder block foundation and moving it on a trailer to town. This move left my friend and his family living in the remaining farmhouse that overlooked the hole that was left by the departed house. This hole was the perfect size for a swimming pool. It was then that my parents made, in my mind as a young teenager, their best decision ever. They decided to join three other families to build a swimming pool!

Now, the ambiance was lacking a bit—what with the relentless southern wind creating white caps on the pool. The hot south wind was occasionally interrupted by an east wind, resulting in a noxious pig odor wafting over the pool. This gave the swimmers yet another reason to use nose plugs. However, it was the perfect way to beat the summer heat,

Pretty Prairie Pig

that is, until one fateful August day several years later.

My best friend's parents had taken a short vacation, leaving my friend and me in charge of the farm operations. We took this responsibility very seriously and immediately headed to Hutchinson for some cool beverages. The next morning we were awakened at the crack of 10:30 by a knock at the door and a young, would-be swimmer yelling that the pool had turned brown. Having been out quite late the previous night, we failed to see the humor in what we thought was surely a practical joke. We had also failed to check on pig lots earlier that morning.

Now pigs may look dumb, but they are smarter than the average bear. Some of them had actually escaped from their pens and decided to head for a dip in the pool, as evidenced by their footprints on the sidewalk by the pool. As we approached the pool, our faces turned ashen white as we viewed the brown, muddy pool. How would we ever explain how we had let several prized pigs sink to the bottom of the pool? How would we ever get these 300-pound pigs off the bottom of the pool?

Then we saw something curious by the cement steps leading out of the shallow end of the pool. It was a trail of water left by the pigs after they found the steps and scampered out of the pool. My friend and I looked at each other, laughed, and put a sign on the pool reading: "Pool closed due to filter problem."

Now we pondered how we would ever get the pool clean. Then it dawned on us that the dirt would eventually settle to the bottom of the pool. Later that evening when the dirt had settled to the bottom of the pool, we vacuumed it up, threw a couple of buckets of chlorine into the pool, and the pool was as good as new.

The next morning when my friend's parents returned home, they asked, "How did everything go?" With a deadpan face, my friend replied, "Things went swimmingly well." Meanwhile, at the other end of the farm, I imagined that two clean and slightly sunburned pigs in dark glasses were regaling their brothers with stories of back flip dives and sipping piña coladas while floating lazily around the pool in an inner tube on a "pigs gone wild" type of day.

The South Lot
By Shirley Ummel of Harper, Kansas
Born 1940

The "South Lot," so called, simply because it was just south of the house I grew up in, in Dighton, Kansas, was un-kept, weedy, and overgrown. It was a poor kid's substitute for an amusement park, playground, camp and all the other places the rich kids of that era got to go to for summer vacations.

Right in the lot's center, lay a huge tree, uprooted in some long forgotten storm. Having not a leaf or a shred of bark left on it, this grand tree wore its nakedness proudly, knowing it had earned the right, just as an ancient weathered woman wears her wrinkles.

Some days, that naked tree was a lofty pirate ship, home to a bunch of neighborhood swashbuckling cutthroats. Other days, it was a covered wagon crossing a sea of grass. In winter months, it would become a dogsled crossing the artic. The youngest, weakest and newest had to be the dogs! So was it, in the unspoken laws of childhood.

The lot itself, on a snowy day was a clean canvas, exciting and ready for the art of snow angels and fox and geese games. There was an unlimited supply of ammunition to defend our snow forts from any imagined intruders.

Most of the year, it was a jungle of head-high weeds-mysterious and shady, where we tunneled through to make a maze. Trampled out hidden rooms were hideouts for the games of cowboys and Indians.

Mother always worried about snakes and trash and all the things that made the lot most inviting. Probably, trying my first cigarette was the worst thing that ever happened to me there.

In the summer, Mother always knew when we had been to the lot playing, by the strong aroma of wild garlic and onion wafting on our breath. We never could seem to resist serving these smelly, but tasty treats along with the vegetables swiped from her garden, with our playhouse meals.

If one of us felt really daring, we had a special treat of home canned fruit, filched from some parent's cellar. We got in trouble when the empty jar would be found hidden at the back of the dark storeroom shelves, but not nearly as much, as when we were caught throwing away a perfectly good canning jar.

No matter what the season, dusk was the time for everyone to vacate the lot for their own yards. My mother has been gone for many years now, but I can see her yet, standing in the porch door, lights glowing behind her, calling us to come in for supper. That dilapidated porch seemed only to be held to the old house by masses of trumpet vines, but when you crossed the doorway, you were safe from all the could-be dangers of the oncoming night.

I never really knew who owned the piece of ground. I claimed it as my domain, because it was closer to my house than anyone else's. Long ago, progress caught up with it. Someone came in and cut up the old tree and hauled it off, never knowing they were destroying a beautiful ship, a sturdy wagon, and a swift dogsled. The ground was graveled over to make a church parking lot. Even the old home place was eventually torn down to make room for a government office.

No amount of gravel, or bricks or mortar can cover the memories left behind of those carefree days. Especially, when I see an old building adorned in robes and crowns of cascading emerald, bright and orange trumpet flowers, or a group of kids playing just at dusk, making the most of the last few minutes of dwindling sunlight and of childhood.

Linnie Marlene Roe in 1940

A Blizzard and a Stolen Car
By L. Marlene Roe of Argonia, Kansas
Born 1935

At age ten years, I well remember the blizzard of 1945, my school days in the Lincoln County school in Summer County, Kansas, the old coal fired pot-bellied stove, the one room school with a long row of north windows, and the raging, vicious, wicked north wind.

We lived exactly one fourth of a mile from school. During a rare, late March snowstorm the teacher let school out early because of very heavy snow. A few families had a telephone; mine did not. I had no siblings so I started out alone, loaded down with heavy books and a lunch pail, against a strong wind in below freezing temperatures. Half way home, it got *much* worse. I could not see the house or trees or fence along the side of the road. It was a total white out! I stumbled and ran, scared beyond words, my heart pounding. I was running out of strength and out of breath. I thought, "I'll never make it; this is the end." Still I struggled on and on. Suddenly, up ahead, I saw a mailbox. We had one of those! The only one in over a half mile. My hopes rose. Yes, I made it to the box, turned right, went down the very long driveway to the house. It was the longest walk of my life! Mother was so surprised to see me and was I ever thrilled to see her. You bet! To this day, I dread Kansas winter and wind and have a special dislike for snow!

Now fast forward a few years later. I was all of thirteen, spending a lazy afternoon, in summer, in town with my Aunt Stella. Her husband, my Uncle Orville, owned a gas station on South Main Street. They lived four blocks west of the station. Often, my uncle walked to work or sometimes drove the pickup or family car. That afternoon, Aunt Stella had a sudden and delightful idea, "Let's go to the station, pick up the car, drive downtown, and buy some ice cream."

Well, we started out together and got to

the gas station, but there was no car in sight. Well, we went around a few blocks, looking for the car at the station and elsewhere. The car had simply vanished! We stopped and spent considerable time talking over this strange situation: was the car stolen? Would someone really steal it in broad daylight? Then we looked at each other in astonishment. How could it be? We were IN the car, thinking all that time it was the pickup! Well, we laughed until we cried, and Aunt Stella said, "Don't *ever* tell anyone what we did. They will be certain we are crazy!" So I promised, and I've kept my promise until now. Aunt Stella has been deceased many years. So, I'll confess to the whole world about the big, embarrassing day we committed "grand theft" of Aunt Stella's car.

Oh yes, you have never lived unless you have been part of a home phone party line. Although we were country folk, we did move a lot closer to town – one mile out. In my late teens, in the '50s, my dad bought five acres from the Tracys. Dad was a shade tree mechanic and a good one, too. He also bought and remodeled a school building, which made a very nice home. It had hard wood floors, which were a plus. The move gave us access to our first electricity and a phone line. Hook up was quick. Now our entertainment begins.

The Tracys came in threes, all brothers, and surrounded us: Melvin to the east, Gene to the south, and Ralph to the west. We were on the section corner, north. All the Tracys were farmers. In the winter, they were in the house a lot, especially in the evenings, and there were no televisions yet. And did they ever love to talk on the party line! Might we have a chance to use our phone? Seldom, as it was always busy.

I won't repeat what was said, but we did listen in a lot. Mother especially liked to listen in. She and I were politically minded and did we ever get an earful! It was nothing all that bad, but tempers did flare quite often. Later most of the Tracys left the farm and are now deceased. What do their descendants now believe and where do they stand on politics? Who knows? There is no party line entertainment available. How sad to see it go. I do wish I could bring it back once more.

The Poor Cousins
By Paula J. Etrick of Longmont, Colorado
Born 1938

We were the "poor cousins." That is why it surprised us when our "rich relatives" invited us to attend a mid-summer family reunion at their impressive home. Times were hard for everyone, and it was difficult to earn a living as hired help on a farm or ranch where we lived in South Central Kansas. Most of the people we knew were experiencing economic problems, but there was a giant chasm between the lifestyle of my family and the lifestyle of our "rich relatives." The facts of our economic situations were determined by the father of each family.

A farming accident left my father a cripple and unable to work, even if there had been steady employment. Not long after the accident, he disappeared and no one knew where he went or the details of his departure. He never returned.

My father's absence created a great hardship for my mother and my older brothers, who struggled to support our large family in those dismal times. My brothers were 13 and 14 years old, and when they applied for work, they were often overlooked if a full-grown man was available. My mother was not in good health and could only do limited types of work. My three sisters, ages nine, ten, and eleven, took care of the household and our mother when she was sick. Out of necessity, we learned to do without many things that other families managed to buy.

Our more fortunate kinfolks were called the "rich relatives" because the father of that family was a professional politician. He received a salary from the state, in addition to the profits from his family business. This man was my mother's brother and my uncle, but he never offered financial help to us because he disapproved of my parents' marriage. His philosophy was "you made your bed; now lie in it." My family believed we were an embarrassment to our more fortunate kinfolks, which explained our surprise at being invited to the family reunion at their home.

Children of misfortune often make the mistake of assuming they are somehow to blame for the adversity in their lives. My brothers never exhibited any of those emotions because they were too busy searching for work of any kind. My three sisters formed an inseparable group and found their support in each other. I was seven years old, the youngest child, and I believed my father disappeared because he was disappointed in me. In those days, in poverty-stricken families like mine, there was little time for attention to self-esteem. I nursed the idea that if I had been prettier or smarter, my life would have been better. I was an unhappy child who felt inferior to others and unloved.

At the family reunion, my uncle hired a photographer to take a group portrait of all the relatives. A flurry of activity took place as the other relatives changed into their "Sunday clothes" for the photograph. When my aunt discovered my family was not changing clothes, because we did not have "Sunday clothes," she hurriedly provided outfits for each of us.

The dress that I was allowed to wear belonged to my "rich cousin" who was my age. This red velvet dress was the prettiest dress I had ever seen, but it created another problem. You could not wear an elegant dress for a photograph when you had bare feet. I came to the reunion with bare feet because I had outgrown my shoes and we could not afford new ones. In the hot Kansas summer, it was easy for me to go barefoot until fall, when I would get shoes that must last through the school year. My aunt solved the problem with a pair of black patent Mary Jane slippers. They were so beautiful and so shiny that they reflected my face like a mirror.

The moment my feet slipped into those shoes, they became the most magical shoes in my life. I was no longer a poor little girl, but a princess. I whirled, danced, swayed from side-to-side, and admired myself in the full-length antique mirror. I modeled those shoes in as many poses as my young mind could imagine. This was truly my Cinderella moment. I looked as elegant and as pretty as my cousin. This transformation changed my appearance, but more important, it changed my self-image. I looked beyond the clothes and saw my own personality. I liked what I saw—I liked myself!

The photographic session was thrilling because I had discovered my self-esteem. All too soon, the photographer finished his work, and I had to relinquish the finery I was wearing. As I undressed, my cousin celebrated her good fortune by reminding me that, in the future, when I looked at the photograph, I would remember that I had worn her dress and her slippers. She wanted me to remember how much her father loved her and pampered her with fancy clothes.

My cousin may have intended to keep me in my "place of poverty" with her insensitive comments, but her words had lost their power over me. I had caught a glimpse of what I could be. That was the memory I embraced and carried with me. I came home a happy little girl.

A few weeks later, a package arrived which contained our copy of the family reunion portrait. I remembered my cousin's comments and, for an instant, a bittersweet feeling passed over me. Those negative feelings were quickly banished as I admired myself in the portrait. I was smiling on the front row. The portrait had captured my look of self-confidence—that exhilarating feeling of knowing I looked good and felt good about myself. My cousin took away the borrowed clothes, but she could never take away my newfound self-esteem. Each time I looked at the family portrait, I relived my elegant experience and how it transformed my life.

Summer turned into fall and fall turned into winter. One cold and bleak morning I walked to school with my two brothers, one on each side of me. We did not have gloves because we could not afford them. The temperature was so cold that both brothers plunged their hands deep into their coat pockets to stay warm. My coat did not have pockets and my hands were forced to endure the freezing cold.

My brothers must have noticed my problem at the same time. Without saying a word, each brother pulled his hand from the pocket that was closest to me, reached out, and enclosed my little hand with his larger hand. The three of us walked on, hand-in-hand. Each brother had sacrificed his own comfort to shield my hands from the cold. While my brothers warmed my hands, they also warmed my heart. They gave me the gift I had needed most—a gift that I have cherished for a lifetime. At last, I knew I was loved!

This memory was shared with me by a dear lady who overcame the burden of poverty and achieved many outstanding and unique accomplishments in her long and eventful life. When she shared her "treasured" photograph, which had been taken over 75 years ago, I saw a charming little girl who was very happy with herself.

The Wichita Forum
By Lois M. Theis of Nashville, Kansas
Born 1936

Some will remember that the southeast part of Wichita, Kansas in 1944 was home to a federal public housing project named, "Planeview." The sole purpose of the makeshift town within the city was to have an aircraft place workforce for Boeing, Cessna, Beech, and smaller aircraft-parts suppliers.

My father and mother both secured jobs that qualified our family for housing in Planeview. Consequently, our family migrated from Winfield to Wichita during the fall of 1944 after my oldest brother was drafted into the Army when he turned eighteen.

I was the youngest of the remaining children, and entered the third grade in a portable classroom among many others that satisfied an influx of children. MacArthur Grade School was just one of three elementary schools in the project. A sea of children flooded Planeview with over 1,000 attending my school alone.

We were among thousands of families that lived in four-family, two-story, white-wooden barracks erected in long series of courts of barracks, along a maze of streets. Single-story duplexes and triplexes were sought after, but were typically filled by first come-first served plant workers.

Every one of us children knew the whole country was at war. It was a rare window that did not have a star flag in the window that identified families with a member in uniform. Gold star flags told us that someone in the family had been killed fighting the enemy.

That first summer in Planeview all the young boys in our court, including my two brothers, created an obstacle course out of discarded boxes or rocks, anything imaginable. Fabricated guns and grenades were part of the war play as the boys crawled on their stomachs under and around obstacles to beat down the invisible enemy, (we girls watched and nursed them later). Fighting a war was an integral part of our lives.

We all shared the smell of coal smoke used to heat our barracks; and, would hurry to the huge cement bins along the streets to fill buckets when trucks dumped new coal. Each barrack had a coal bin on the back porch that served as playhouses during the summer months. Every unit had a clothesline where beating wind would dispatch underwear across the yards if the person doing the hanging wasn't diligent in securing each item with multiple clothespins. The black coal soot that filled the air also clung to those newly laundered white blouses, socks, towels and bed sheets.

Each housing unit had an icebox that meant the iceman would deliver ten or twenty pounds of ice depending on the amount the sign that Mom or Dad would hang in the kitchen window. Our iceman lived in the barrack across from our back door so it was handy to get him paid or get more ice.

The problem was that we often didn't have too much to eat in the icebox, or was regularly reminded by Mom not to eat certain items designated for an upcoming meal or Dad's black metal lunch bucket. A steaming pot of navy beans seasoned with margarine, salt, and pepper, or a rare strip of bacon, was a frequent meal.

Planeview had a doctor's office, drug store, post office, police station, small restaurant, beer joint, two grocery stores, a dime store, a movie theatre, and a bowling alley. Most inhabitants did not have cars in 1944 until the war was over, so walking was the usual means of getting to and from anywhere in Planeview.

Lois at the Planeview barracks in 1950-51

Bill McKnight in 1945

However, a bus service had a regular schedule to downtown Wichita that could take Mom, and older brother and me to the Wichita Forum.

The Wichita Forum was an exciting place because wrestling matches were held with big name wrestlers (big name to us) like Orville Brown. The lady next door with her boys and daughter would go with us on the bus to watch the wrestlers.

The two ladies (Must have been ladies night out!) got ringside seats and relegated us kids to the cheap seats in the balcony where we were free to scream, jump up and down, flail arms, without anyone objecting. Money was saved up for these infrequent night outs that allowed for a hot dog, popcorn, or cola. Mom and the neighbor lady were the most fun to watch, because we could see them so close to the wrestlers that one or both would pound the mat and scream something indescribable.

The Wichita Forum had a mystique about it – so big and echoing sounds of a multitude of people excited and having fun – far from the somber rows of barracks and their reason for being.

One event that Mom and I took in was a dance on the second level of the Forum. We went with a different neighbor lady and daughter. Unfortunately, the dance was not nearly as rowdy or as much fun as the wrestling matches. In retrospect, the occasion was probably a way to introduce young ladies on the proper way to dance.

We watched couples circling the floor in style to music ranging from a nice beat to square dancing. The outing was very tame and subdued when compared to an evening at the wrestling matches.

The only other fun event to look forward to during 1944 and 1945 was going to Saturday afternoon matinees that cost less than other times. We grew up on movies that always included short newsreels on the war happenings, or Greer Garson (famed movie actress) encouraging everyone to give to the March of Dimes to fight polio.

Midst the anxiety of war that everyone experienced, the Wichita Forum building stood in central Wichita as a semblance of normalcy for our family. For a few hours, our thoughts and feelings were off the reality that any day a telegram could come to our house that would say my big brother was wounded or worse, killed in action. The outcome for our family was a grateful return of the oldest son after his absence for two long years. Not all the families in Planeview shared a similar welcoming home a loved one at war's end.

You Should Have Been There
By Edna Irene Jacobs Butler of Greeley, Colorado
Born 1926

When my mother was in her early nineties, she often commented, "I just have one thing to say to those folks who are forever talking about the good old days: 'You should have been there!'"

My mother, Florence McDaniel Jacobs was born in 1892 on the land, which my grandfather, Vermillion Emery McDaniel had homesteaded in Rush County, in the early 1880s. She graduated from La Crosse High School with the other two members of her senior class and then went on to study for and to attain a teacher's degree.

One day when she was teaching in a one-room schoolhouse, with her twelve students seated in front of her watchful eye she glanced out of the window and beheld a tornado funnel moving through the sky.

Abruptly she announced, "Children, we are going to have a special recess; we are going to lie in the ditch alongside the road and play worm."

They lay very flat in the ditch to avoid any low swoops from the tornado. They wiggled and they squirmed. Eventually the funnel moved on to the east and finally dissolved into the sky.

When they went back into the warm schoolhouse, one little boy asked of my mother, "Teacher was you scared?" That's how the good old days went by.

New Outhouse
By Nell Moore of Aurora, Colorado
Born 1929

My father was a large man! We had an outhouse we all used!

One day we heard yelling and we all ran out to see what was wrong. Well, the outhouse was old and he was a large man!

Boom! The floor had given out and down he went! Good Lord! He went to the well to clean up and we all had a good laugh!

Mother would not let him near the house! Guess what? We got a new outhouse!

Blue Racer
By Richard D. Blackburn of Dodge City, Kansas
Born 1948

In the early 1950s when I was about five years old, my dad was a fishing nut. We fished every lake in Kansas, Missouri and some in Arkansas. Every year, when dad had a vacation, we went fishing. There was dad, mom and six of us kids.

One year, dad told us he would give us a penny for each worm we found. Mom was the counter for us. That year we found close to six thousand worms! Dad thought that was a lot of money so we settled for a penny for every two worms.

My oldest brother was crazy about snakes. One day, on the way to school he found a bull snake. He wrapped it around his neck and showed up at school that way. The principal brought him back home- with the snake.

We were at the lake looking for worms. I turned over this big rock and there was an unusual looking snake! I took off running to my big brother. He caught me and told me to stop and look at the snake. He called it a Blue Racer snake. It was chasing me! He stopped when I did. My brother took three steps forward; the snake turned and started the other way. My brother stopped. The snake stopped. My brother backed up three steps; the snake followed. We played with that snake in that way for more than half an hour. Then the snake decided he didn't want to play anymore and went on his way.

That was a beautiful snake but I never played with another snake!

Anything with a Roof on It
By Naomi Chestnut of Chanute, Kansas
Born 1933

The year 1936, we were on the move looking for work; my father was a cook but would take any job that would pay a wage. Jobs did not come easy and the depression was just starting to end.

Dad took a job working with the OWPA, he got a dollar a day and commodities once a month. We stood in line waiting for our "paper" that allowed us to have a new pair of high top brown shoes; at least one size too large, so they would wear for a year. We received two pair of union overalls, how I hated to wear them to school. There was no kindergarten only grades one through twelve. Neither of my parents ever enrolled me in school. I had one lead pencil and one big chief tablet and a reader. I was lucky I could learn fast, as it didn't take dad long to move on.

He was always looking for a better job. Needless to say, I finally had to get a transit report card as we moved as much as nine times in one school year.

We lived in anything with a roof on it, chicken houses, garages, porches, culverts under the road, attics or basements. We even shared a house with a family of eight people. I remember mom trying to get $2.50 for our half of the rent. Living with another family was nice. We had two rooms, kitchen, and bedroom. Mom and the other lady exchanged used coffee grounds, yeast starter; grease from the cooking of meat, life was good; we even got to listen to the battery radio one hour a day. Life was good at this time for a six year old, but slower than today, so was it really the good ole days, I wonder?

Intermission
By Julane Ediger of Hutchinson, Kansas
Born 1933

I was born in the 1930s and grew up in a small town with a movie theater called: *The Royal*, which seated four hundred people. I do believe I was born loving movies and I would go every night if I could talk my folks into it which I did a good deal of the time. You have to understand, this was a different time and era when it was safe, and my parents were good friends with the people who owned the theater.

In 1939 when I was six years old "Gone With the Wind" came out and of course I wanted to go; my non-going movie parents did not object to me going because of some of the movie subject matter as to them it was just another matinee I wanted to go see.

On a Sunday afternoon, my dad drove me to the theater, checked about the time the movie would be over so he could pick me up. So, off I trotted to see "Gone With the Wind" and it was going great until a big word came across the screen that said INTERMISSION, and the people were getting up and going out, and I followed suit but went even further and left the theater and walked home! By the way, I lived a whole two blocks from the theater. It was all because I had no idea what that word intermission meant! My dad explained it to me that it was a short break in the movie for people to go to the concession stand, go to the bathroom, or stretch their legs and then after twenty minutes the movie continued. My dad knew it wasn't time for me to be home yet so he drove me back to the theater, I went right in, got in my same seat, and saw the rest of the movie.

Julane (Smisor) Ediger in 1939

To this day, I still love "Gone with the Wind" and own it on DVD, and watch it every time it is shown on television. I would bet I am one of its youngest and oldest, as I am now eighty, fans!

My Mother
By Jean Peintner of Dodge City, Kansas

Beneath Mothers lady-like attitude, she was a fighter. I don't think she would have thought herself a fighter. In my youth, I wouldn't have either. There were times when I saw her cry, but in her eighty years of living, she had learned she could choose between being a "panty-waist," or a pioneer woman. She had lived through dust storms, rust in the wash water, grasshoppers, twenty-five cent a bushel wheat, and later, the death of a grown son and daughter. These things are what she would have said, "Give you character if you have faith in God." She was seasoned for her last two years.

One morning in November, she got out of bed early to get a drink of water and fell, breaking her hip. We took her by ambulance to a specialist in Great Bend; there a plate was put into her hip and she soon came back to Kinsley to be near my dad. She was determined to walk but her progress was slow. One evening I visited her in her hospital room and an aide came in, and said, "It is time for us to do our exercises." Mother said ok, but she wanted to do them by herself. She knew her leg would not become stronger if the young lady did it for her.

Her back was rounded with arthritis and osteoporosis. The pull on her muscles caused persistent pain and the electric hot pad seemed like part of her back. Her doctor prescribed pills that took some of the pain away but they also made her unsteady. She fell twice and was not hurt, but nine months later after the first broken leg, she fell and broke the other. That night I was going to see her I wondered what I would say. How would I comfort her? As I came into the room, she smiled and said, "I'm glad I'm not a centipede, I only have two legs to break." The next day she was transferred to Great Bend for her second operation.

She did not respond to treatment this time. Her heart became weak and three weeks later, she went into a semi-coma. My sister Wilma and I were in her room the day before she died. Wilma picked up a newspaper and said, "I wonder what Nixon did today." Watergate was top news then and mother's disgust for him and his cabinet had kept her mind occupied for the past nine months. Now she mumbled and half-opened her eyes. Wilma and I looked at each other. Our eyes filled with tears but we laughed. Mother thumbed her nose.

Snow Blizzard in March
By Margaret Surprise of Scott City, Kansas
Born 1921

As my birthdate is January 22, 1921 there wasn't too much in the twenties I remember, but the thirties were quite significant.

A snow blizzard in March was important. We got up to go to school, my brother and I. It was cold and wet outside so my brother didn't want to go to school. He complained with a bellyache so we didn't go. Before the day was over the snow started getting heavier. By noon, the rural mail carrier drove in and asked if he could stay awhile, as he couldn't see to drive! It turned out that he stayed two full days.

The snow blew and drifted over the fences and very high around the buildings. The cattle that were on pasture walked over the fence and strayed away. Many of them either froze to death or were never located.

A school bus near the Colorado line west of us stalled in a snowdrift. The bus had already picked up the children. There was no communication telephone, radio, etc. so part of the children froze to death. Most people came through safe.

The jackrabbits were very numerous. There were no phones but by word of mouth, the neighbors in the area arranged a certain day and time to all get together and form a very large circle to drive the rabbits to a pre-built fence to capture them. At the end of the drive, there would be thousands of rabbits. They were slain and hauled off, I don't know where, and used to make some kind of animal food.

A very bad drought left fields dry, nothing would grow without rain. When the wind blew, which was after the dirt would blow, it was heavy enough that it was darker than night. When we were at school and a black cloud formed, the teacher would tell us to go home and go fast before the storm reached us. There were many people lost several found dead and many got what they called dust pneumonia.

There were no phones or communications to pre warn anyone.

Usually Monday was washday. A fire was started in the big range stove. We burned shelled corncobs and scrap lumber for heat. We went to the windmill and carried pumped water in the buckets to the metal boiler on the range to heat.

Earlier we scrubbed the dirty clothes on a washboard. Later we had a washing machine with a stick lever, like a broomstick, to push back and forth to agitate the dirty clothes, then turned a wringer to get the soap water out and rinsed it through two tubs of clear water before hanging on an outside clothesline to dry. When the laundry was done, an all-day process, the clothes, which were dry, were brought in. Most things had to be ironed the next day, with three flat irons, which were heated on a burner of the coal oil stove. As one iron cooled, it had to be rotated with the other two. There was no electricity or fans, a large garden was planted each year, and everything was canned in glass jars.

Sunnyside Country Store
By Marie Fletcher of Leoti, Kansas
Born 1928

Rural country stores, as old-timers knew them, are a dying American institution. In fact, the homespun charm, crammed shelf practicality, has had a quiet passing. Sunnyside, northeast of the small town of Leoti, receded into the history of the western Kansas plains many years ago. It was a place where rural folks could get their mail and pick up a few items they could not grow, hunt, or make themselves.

It also was a meeting place. Men could pull chairs around the potbellied stove after they had bought their tins of Prince Albert tobacco, and chat. It was yesterday's trip to today's Coastal Mart or Presto to discuss farming, community new, and gossip. The only difference being they were surrounded by glass cases, barrels and bushel baskets containing potatoes, dry beans, and other items necessary to farm living. A big roll of paper hung handy to wrap purchases.

A gallon of kerosene cost five cents. Flour came in printed cloth bags that later became dresses, blouses, and skirts. The King Edward and Roi-Tan cigar boxes that left the store collected papers and small treasures in area farm homes.

Most of the community brought their milk, cream, and eggs to Sunnyside. Twice a week, this produce went on to Leoti by horse and wagon.

In 1888, some local residents decided it was time for some recreation. The first Harvest Home Picnic occurred at the school, north of the Joe Burr home in the fall of that year. In 1909, the event moved to Sunnyside where Ransom Newton, "Newt," Norton had established a country store and post office. The picnic was organized and named "The Old Settler's Picnic of Sunnyside." John White was elected the first president. Thus started the making of memories at Sunnyside. There were horse races, including riding and racing Roman style, in which the rider planted a foot firmly on each back of two horses and raced with two other contestants doing the same thing. They also had greased pole climbing, ball games, a program of recitations, music, and long tables groaning under their burden of delicious food.

Old Settler's Picnic had some outstanding orators. Tom McNeal of Capper's Weekly spoke at one gathering. Another time, a surviving member of the German family massacre that happened near Russell Springs gave a heartrending account of that tragedy.

Sunnyside had a topnotch baseball team. They won many games. One of their rivals was the community of Dinas in northwest Wichita County.

After a day of events, including a pretty baby contest, the music, provided by local residents, began and the crowd took over the dance platform and kept it filled as evening waltzed into night.

The old Sunnyside General Store

Newton Norton came to Wichita County from Kentucky in 1886. The closest town was Leoti and it took a full day by wagon and team to get there and back. Newt decided to set up a general store at Sunnyside. He obtained a grant from the government to buy 160 acres from Herbert Seeley of

Nebraska for $150.

Over the years, until the store closed around 1930, there were several operators. Through the years, there were many changes. Transportation evolved from horse and wagon to cars, and a gas pump became part of the scene.

Nature has a way of reclaiming its own, and that happened at Sunnyside. The weathered building now stands on shaky legs. The cement platform once filled with cream cans is nearly screened from view by volunteer locust trees. The sounds of laughter and music have drifted away. Memories soon will be all we have of a special time and a special place- Sunnyside.

Who Threw That Eraser?
By Rev. Allen Smith of Bloom, Kansas
Born 1952

My story begins February 18, 1952 when I was born east of Mulvane, Kansas, about four miles. I was born eleventh of the twelve children my younger brother was born exactly two years to the day after me on February 18, 1954

We lived in an old converted garage/house for the first four years of my life. Then we moved south and east of Mulvane about eight miles into a three-bedroom house, which was much larger than the house we had moved out of. The farm had ninety-six acres of mostly trees and we farmed with horses, the land that wasn't grown up in trees.

When we moved there were only six of us children left at home. The rest had married and started their own lives other places, mostly in Wichita, Kansas. Us children left home was one girl and five boys, the sister being the oldest. My sister and one brother went to high school in town in Mulvane.

One and a half miles from our house was a one room school house where they taught grades one through eight with one teacher, her name was Miss Brewer, she was probably in her early sixties in age, she was also a spinster, she had never been married.

After one year of living at the house, we had moved to, the county school was having trouble finding enough students to be allowed to stay open.

The head of the school board came out to visit my father and mother and ask if I could start school that fall in the first grade even though I was five years old and wouldn't be six until past the middle of February.

After some discussion, my father and mother agreed to allow me to start in the first grade that fall and the school didn't have to consolidate and bus students in to town.

Some of the students lived in the Mulvane school district and some lived in the Udall school district.

Five years later a family of eight moved away and we had to consolidate any way. But during that time, I graduated to the third grade in the next three years.

At that time my little brother Leonard who was born on my birthday two years after me, started the first grade, so there were three years between us in school and only two years between us in years.

The rule at our home was, if you get in trouble at school we were in trouble at home (imagine that.)

One day my little brother who was in the first grade threw an eraser at someone else in the class and they ducked and the teacher who was writing on the blackboard with her back to the class, wouldn't you know, got hit by the eraser my brother had thrown.

She immediately spun around and not knowing that the eraser wasn't meant for her, and yelled, "Who threw that eraser?"

For just a moment, there was absolute silence. But at the second demand, "who threw that eraser!" One of the older kids gave up my little brother.

In the one room classroom in front of the student's desks was a bench where unruly kids sat and then just about six foot in front of that bench was the teacher's desk with scroll maps on the wall behind the teacher's desk.

The teacher yelled "Leonard Smith come up here right now."

Leonard got up and slowly walked to the front of the class where the teacher was waiting and the longer it took the madder she got. Finally, my little brother got to the front of the classroom, and by this time, she was really angry.

This spinster schoolteacher, who had never been married, grabbed my little brother under the arms, one hand under each side of him, and stood him on the seat of the bench in front of the class, pulled down his pants expecting him to have under pants on but guess what! None of us kids wore underwear.

She had a paddle about 18 inches long and about three inches wide with a handle cut in one end in one hand and my little brother under the other arm, and when she looked down, he didn't have any underwear.

She dropped him her face turned red, she walked over and put the paddle where she normally kept it, walked over sat down behind her desk, her face still bright red and calmly told my little brother to pull up his pants and go back and sit down.

Our parents never found out about this until some years later.

I don't think this incident had anything to do with it, but at the end of that school year, she resigned and went to work in Belle Plain, Kansas. And for the last year of school there, at that one-room schoolhouse we had a teacher named Mrs. Ayers.

Gold Lapel Crosses
By Shirley Friesen Knackstedt of Inman, Kansas
Born 1936

April 19, 1944 started out like a normal spring day. I was seven years old walking to school with our dinner pails. I was the youngest of three sisters and had a mile and a half walk to our school.

Hayes Center was located in the center of Hayes Township in McPherson County. A couple of hours after we arrived at school a Kansas spring thunder storm decided to

Verla, Shirley, and Jeanne

Jeanne, Shirley, and Verla

turn the day into a very dark uncomfortable feeling.

The teacher decided we needed more light so she took lamps down and set them on the teacher's desk to be lit.

She, with the help of the older boys, pumped the lamp full and then opened the valve, when she struck the match, the valve dropped out and landed on the teacher's desk. The fire followed the stream of gas and hit me on my chest. I was in flames immediately. All the kids and teacher ran out of the school, they didn't realize I was still standing by the desk. My sister came looking for me, and when she saw me she hollered, "Run Shirley, come here to the door!" When I got to the front door two of the older boys rolled me in the mud to put the flames out. The other kids formed a bucket brigade and they did put out the fire.

I was taken to the hospital by my aunt and uncle who lived close to the school. The roads were so muddy they had a hard time getting to the school. The only car they had was a Chevy

Coupe with one seat. Two of the boys' rode in the trunk so there would be someone to push if we got stuck.

I remained in the hospital for four weeks. The one thing that saved my life was my hair was covered.

My mother and we three girls were to be the program at a neighboring school for their PTA, so mom put our hair up in curlers and had scarves to hold the curlers in.

The doctor said if my hair would have caught on fire I wouldn't have made it.

When I ran to get out of the school, the flames stayed out of my face. I did get third degree burns on my upper arms and neck. The ends of my ear lobes burned off where the scarf didn't cover them.

The McPherson County School Superintendent visited me in the hospital and said I didn't have to take the end of the year county exam, which I thought was just great.

My parents and grandparents awarded the boys who rolled me in the mud with gold lapel crosses.

Jobs Teens Probably Should Not Have
By Larry Schlotfeldt of Bastrop, Texas
Born 1944

When I turned 13, I got a part-time job at Tribune Grain, a small grain elevator jointly owned by my stepfather and my uncle. The manager, a Swede named Gunnar Wicklund, taught me about the shipping and handling or various grains. He also taught me to make coffee strong enough to stand-alone. Gunner and I sucked the coffee through sugar cubes, me from my cup and Gunner from his saucer.

The job was dirty as I loaded railway grain cars and swept out the grain bins. In the center of the grain elevator where the trucks drove through and emptied into the floor, was a narrow shaft leading upward through the dark to the top of the elevator. In the shaft was a small lift with a hemp rope running through the center of the floor. The lift was weighted so that it would go neither up nor down with the weight of a man on board. I was light, so I had to add a few pounds of ballast in order to maintain equilibrium on the lift. There were small blocks of iron for that purpose. At the top of the elevator was a mechanical grain cleaner. It was a room full of pulleys and shaking platforms driven by large electric motors. Inside each platform tray was a sieve, which would shake the grain and allow the smaller, purple weed seed to fall into a container. I had to scoop the weed seed into a gunnysack until it was half-full, remove the weight on the lift to descend, and then dump the weed seed down and old well. That worked fine as long as I followed the rules. But, being a teenager I thought I could speed up the job. First of all, I loaded the gunnysack full instead of half-full. Also, why should I take off the extra weight to compensate for the bag of weed seed? I could simply hold the center rope tighter with my gloved hands. Unfortunately, I had an overly optimistic view of my own strength and capability. I loaded the 120-pound bag onto the lift and stepped aboard. I had trouble pulling the release pins and the bag obstructed the brake lever. As I pulled the locking pins, the lift, now a full 170 pounds heavier than its point of balance, took off like a rocket down the shaft. The ride was literally hair raising and my stomach felt like it was coming up through my throat. For dear life, I held onto the rope with both hands, acutely aware of the smoke and burning horsehide gloves three inches from my eyes. With a crash, the lift hit the springs at the bottom of the shaft, bounced a few times into the air and then settled in a cloud of dust and total silence. My gloves were still smoking and I was vaguely aware that my knees were knocking together.

Another time I boarded up the sides of boxcars and then filled them with wheat from the elevator. The job was to fill, seal, and move the cars down the siding during harvest. A train would come by and take them east in the morning. It was hard, tedious work. The real fun was taking the loaded boxcar down the end of the siding where a clamp and buffer (bumper) stop kept the cars from entering the main Missouri Pacific rail line. I used a lever to get the boxcar moving, then would run after the boxcar, climb up the ladder and grab the brake wheel to stop the car gently at the end of the siding. It worked out great with empty boxcars; however, one loaded with grain just did not want to stop. It was a harrowing ride with a crashing into the next boxcar and almost jumping the track. (Or worse yet, being pushed out onto the main track.) My knees were shaking again after that experience. Even so, it was great fun to run across the top of a series of boxcars that I had loaded.

It seemed I always had a job. At age eight, I washed bottles in the local drugstore. When I was ten, I would carry out at the local IGA grocery store. The neatest job was running the projectors at the local theater. As a teenager, my family owned and operated the local movie theater. During the summer, after the last movie, we would head eight miles north to change the irrigation water. My stepbrother Billy and I ran the projectors for five dollars per night. Russell Engel taught us the complicated process of running the old 20s vintage simplex E7 projectors that are now in the Greeley county museum. (They had actually been converted from silent movies.) My sister Sherry ran the popcorn kiosk and my stepfather managed the theater. One night it caught on fire by the screen and carried acrid smoke throughout the building. I remember hearing that we needed to clear the heavy smoke from the building. Like any dumb self-confidant teen, I said that I could easily hold my breath and make the run through the lower level and up the stairs, unlock the projection booth, open the window and climb out on the marquee without taking another breath. And, I did. What was my stepfather thinking to allow me to run through the toxic, smoke-filled building?

Rain
By Dortha Schroeder of Derby, Kansas
Born 1925

Dirt storms were severe in Hugoton, Kansas. Clouds of dirt rolled in from one direction one day and winds turn and blow the sand from the opposite direction the next day. The sand would pile up around the house like snow drifts. My mom would tape around the windows and hang wet sheets over them to keep the dirt out.

If rain clouds ever appeared, we three sisters would stay outside, and smell the rain clouds and sing:

"Rain, when you going to rain again. Rain, make the rivers deep again. Shower your blessings on me. The sheep are in the meadow, the cows in the corn. They know that something is wrong. Old Mother Earth can never give birth, when you are away so long."

We would stay outside to feel the moisture and smell the beautiful fragrance of the rain.

The Dugout
By Marie S. Clemence of Valley Center, Kansas
Born 1928

The year was 1918. Oliver Brockett had brought his wife, Waty, and their three small children, Lloyd, Irene, and Rose Ann from the Missouri Ozarks to Syracuse, Kansas in order to get work. His uncle had a business there but I don't know what it was.

I don't know if there was not a house for rent, or if finances was a problem; whatever the problem Oliver's little family moved into a placed called a "dug-out."

How would Waty describe the look of her new home to her uncle, aunts, and her younger siblings? Their parents had died years ago of pneumonia in the Arkansas Ozarks.

Her home was a hole in the ground, but not like any cellar in their part of the country. Not the one that looked something like an igloo with its round shape; not like the two

Oliver and Waty Brockett

Oliver, Waty, and Rose Ann in 1920

wood door lying side by side on the ground; not like the tall door standing against a right angle above a hole; or anything they had seen.

This was invented by Scandinavians who came to parts of the United States where trees were not plentiful so log cabins were out of the question.

They dug into the slope of a hillside deep enough for adults to walk inside. They formed berms that were wide enough, probably like in my parent's cellar under the house, for several rows of quart-sized jars of food, next to all walls, except for the steps to exit, the width of their berms is only my guess, and they probably varied.

The door and windows were all on one side of the dugout. The roof could be made of logs, maybe with sod or turf on top, and oiled paper was used to cover the windows. At least light could reach inside.

The advantage of these dwellings was that they were warm in winter and cool in summer.

Waty like her mother, Rose, was both industrious and artistic so she probably made the most of materials available to make the place as comfortable and attractive as she could.

Sometime after the family moved into the dugout, Oliver and the children become victims of the flu in the epidemic of 1918.

Waty was exhausted from caring for her family. Finally, she felt her family was well enough she could now go to bed and get some rest. So this is what she did! She never awoke! Waty died in January of 1919 at age twenty-two. She was laid to rest in Syracuse, Kansas.

Oliver allowed his brother Edd and wife Blanche who had no children to raise his children.

Years later Irene Brockett Stowe told her mother's sister, Eva Donaldson Steenborg, that the only thing she remembered about that time was being held by someone so she could look down into a box to see a lady whom she knew as mother.

In the year 2013, some people, including doctors discussed the flu epidemic of 1918, and expressed the belief that those who died the way Waty did had died from internal hemorrhage.

I once heard or read about a dugout in the Syracuse area that was available for overnight rent, just as any tourist cabin.

I wanted to see the place, but wasn't able to at that time. I wanted pictures! Later, I tried to locate the place but those I asked didn't know about it.

I also heard some years later, about a military veteran living in a dugout that was described to be bigger than most know about; but I don't remember when or where that was.

My husband Dale, and four-year-old Sherry and I came to Kansas in 1951 to find work. Dale served in the Navy in WWII, and took advantage of the GI. Bill to become a teacher. In Arkansas, they were paid nine months of the year. Years later, he retired from Boeing.

I was born and lived in the Arkansas Ozarks for twenty-three years. I've lived in Kansas sixty-two years so far! Kansas has been good to us. Dale died July 15, 2009. We have a son Stan and daughter Sonja. Eva was my mother; Waty was my aunt. Eva was eight years younger than Waty, the oldest of five siblings.

Dodge City
By Jim "Pete" Carmichael of Dodge City, Kansas
Born 1939

In 1876 when my great grandpa homesteaded our land north of Dodge City, Kansas, the deed stated (I quote), "An Mr. Carmichael what do you give for this ¼ section of land?"

He states, "I give $8.00 and my good name sir." Grover Cleveland signed it. (I have this deed).

My grandfather, born in 1887, told me

Carmichael Homestead in 1910

many stories about the Indians being run off, and the white people shot all the buffalo. He said, "Of all of his young days, he only counted about twenty to thirty left and a few wolves and a few antelope and jackrabbits. No deer."

My great grandpa worked in Dodge City along with Wyatt Earp and Bat Masterson and was a great friend of Colonel Dodge at Fort Dodge. We have the wedding gift that Colonel Dodge gave my great grandpa (on his wedding).

I've spent almost seventy-five years within a ten-mile radius of where I live now here in Dodge City, Kansas.

I was born to a farm family and the oldest of six kids.

I was on a tractor plowing up the earth with a steel wheel tractor 22-36 International at the age of 8 years old.

I and my brother milked by hand four to six cows before we went to school in the morning, and then again in the evening and also took care of the chickens, turkeys and hogs.

We bathed in a round washtub and heated water on the kerosene stove. We did have electric in the house and cold running water.

I guess we had a modern home in the 40s. An old icebox sat there in the kitchen and the iceman would come about once a week and put in a new block of ice.

Down in the basement sat an old Maytag washing machine with a gas motor and the exhaust pipe running out the basement window.

In the winter, we would sit down the basement and pick chickens and turkeys and dress them out and that the way we would pay our doctor bill with vegetables out of the garden, and chickens and turkeys, churned butter and made cheese.

We also made our own soap out of lard, ashes, and lye and we shaved it with a paring knife after it cooled and the lye in the soap would make your hands raw and red.

Our first telephone just had a ringer on it and an eight party line. Our call was two shorts and a long. Later in the 1940s, we went to a rotary dial and I remember our number to this day 55N14.

We rode the school bus to town as we lived about five miles out in the country and our treat was to get home before 4:30 and we would all sit around the battery powered radio and listen to the Cisco Kid, Poncho and sometimes even Tom Mix, and the Lone Ranger and Tonto.

There were no TVs, I was fifteen years old before I seen a black and white TV and it was all snowy.

In the late '40s in the summer, we went to the drive in theater about four times a year that was great entertainment.

The 1928 International Tractor that Pete started farming with at eight-years-old

My greatest fear was during WWII, I was about five, or six years old in 1944-1945 and we lived two miles from the Army Air Base that trained pilots on B-26s.

They would fly real low over our house when they landed and we could see the pilot and count the rivets on the planes.

They crashed a lot of those big planes not far from our house.

I remember when dad said come on boys lets go. We all jumped in the old Model A truck and drove north on 14th Street about five miles and on the Ford County and Hodgeman County line a plane went down.

The nose was in the ground and burning and next to the site; there were two heads of the pilots burning in their skullcaps. I will never forget that day and I had trouble sleeping at night for a long time, and I can take you right to the spot today.

During those WWII days, we got ration cards and tokens for food, gas, tires and about everything. You couldn't get tires for the old car and truck you just patched and patched old tires.

We saved tin foil off cigarette papers and took it to school and the teachers turned the foil into the government to make bullets out of it.

We didn't take too many because dad and mom rolled their own cigarettes and called the ones in the package tailor maids.

There was no money back in those days. In the summer, we would walk the ditches along the highway five miles to town, gather pop bottles, and get three cents apiece for them. We could get about thirty cents in a good day.

Our recreation was to hunt and trap animals, especially in the winter months.

I stocked feed and put up hay for fifty cents an hour up until I went into the Navy at the age of seventeen.

I did work at the stockyards on Wednesdays for ninety cents an hour. It was hard work and being poor never hurt anybody.

In the fourth grade, my dog buster got me sent home from school. In the morning, before I caught the bus to go to school Buster cornered a skunk in the outhouse and I got a stick with barbed wire and fished him out for Buster.

My school desk was right by the steam radiator and yes, you can guess what happened.

Then there was the time I was teaching my cousin Melvin how to trap rabbits. A few days later, he caught a rat in the trap and got bit and the rat got away. The next two months he had to take rabies shots in the belly every day and caught hell over that one.

Dust and Horse Drawn Jalopy
By Joyce A. McMannis of Hutchinson, Kansas
Born 1928

My family moved from Burrton Kansas in August 1930 to a farm 19 miles southwest of Dodge City, Kansas. It didn't have electricity, gas, water, or bathroom. The outhouse was about 25 to 50 feet from the house. We didn't have a family doctor. We used aspirin, cough syrup, and iodine. Once when Daddy was building a new garage door, I stepped on a nail that almost went clear through my foot. Mom put a bread and milk poultice on it so it would not get infected.

During my young years, I remember it was really hard times. Daddy and Mom kept us fed. Our school lunches were packed in a half-gallon Karo syrup bucket. Our sandwiches sometimes were two slices of bread with syrup. They got awful sticky and soggy; we had some lunchmeat and cheese. We also had ration stamps. The stamps covered things that were rationed during the war. Some of the rationed items that I remembered were sugar, coffee, flour, tires, gas, and propane. All of these items were hard to get.

Daddy would get up around 6:00 in the morning. In the winter, he would light the wood-burning stove in the living room, go to the barn and milk four to six cows, and feed the cows and pigs. By that time, Mom would have breakfast ready. Then they had to get my two older brothers, me, and my younger sister up. My brothers were harder to get up than me and my sister. She would holler up stairs and tell them to get up, and say, "It's Monday morning, and tomorrow is Tuesday, and the next day is Wednesday, and here it is the week is half over and you boys are not out of bed yet!"

After we had breakfast and ready for school, we rode a horse to school with my oldest brother in the front, me in the middle, and my other brother behind. We rode bareback. We went to a little one-room school three miles from our house. When I was in the eighth grade, I was the only one in that grade. That year the teacher broke her ankle, I taught school until she could come back, about two weeks.

We made the 19-mile trip to Dodge City for groceries and supplies that we got with ration stamps, commodities, and by selling cream and eggs. We had a big wooden icebox on the front porch. The last stop on the way home was to pick up a 100-pound block of ice. We put in the back of the truck and covered it with gunnysacks to keep the sun off of it. By the time we got home, we only had about 75 pounds of ice. It would last about a week. We also stopped at a root beer stand and got an ice-cold root beer. I was about four years old. We found out later the girl that brought us our root beer was The Moll in the Dalton Gang.

Laundry day was always on Monday, we had a Maytag washer with a hand turned wringer and a Briggs and Stratton motor. It was kept on the little back porch along with the cream separator. The washing machine was brought in to the kitchen in the middle of the floor with two rinse tubs. Water was brought in from the windmill and then heated on the kerosene kitchen stove. When Daddy started the motor, it sounded like a motorcycle in the house. Everything was dried on the clothesline; in the wintertime, it would freeze dry. Wash day took all day and was real noisy. Mom always put on a pot of beans so she didn't have to stop and cook supper.

Mom made our school dresses out of chicken feed sacks; they were a printed cotton material. Mom would trim them with rickrack. We had one dress that was bought for church. We had very few toys; we entertained ourselves with imaginary toys. Our playhouse was made out of old boxes and empty cans. Daddy made wooden toys from sewing thread spools. He could make anything out of nothing. He made a little tractor out of spools and little blocks of wood. The unique thing about that tractor was he took the inside works from an old alarm clock and put it on the tractor, wound it up, and it rolled across the linoleum floor. That was the first wind-up toy.

I can remember sometime after I started to school, Daddy made what we called a cart. It was pulled by a horse. It was made from an old car body. He cut it off in front of the windshield and put an axle under the front seat and cut it off between the front and back seat. He cut the roof off and the top half of the front doors. He then put shafts on the front to hitch the horse to. The reins came through the space in the dashboard where the speedometer was. So we had a ride with upholstered seats and rubber tires. I don't remember how Daddy made that cart, but I do remember riding to school in it.

Now going back to 1935 on April 14th about 2:00 in the afternoon, I was seven years old and my sister was five. We were in the yard playing in a dust drift. The drought was still on and it was really dry. My sister looked up from playing and pointed to the north and said, "Look!" I looked up and I saw a big black cloud rolling right toward us. We saw later in the newspaper it was 1,000 feet high. I, being only seven years old, didn't know what it was. My first action was to get me and my sister in the house and tell Mom. I grabbed her hand and ran as fast as I could.

When we got in the house I told Mom there was a storm coming, she said, "I don't see anything." The sun was shining. I said, "Look out of the kitchen window," and at that time it hit. Everything went from sunshine to pitch black instantly. It was so dark we couldn't see the outline of the windows. That was something I could never forget. Mom grabbed our hands and told us not to move. We could tell Mom was scared; she kept saying, "I don't know what to do," and "I wonder where Daddy and the boys are?" They had left in the truck to find a cow that got out. I don't know how long we waited to see; some say it lasted a couple hours.

After it lightened up some, Mom lit a kerosene lamp. I think Daddy and the boys got home after dark. Daddy told us what happened while they were out. As soon as the cloud hit them, the truck stopped, it wouldn't start, and the lights on the truck went out. Daddy said the reason everything quit was because of the dust particles in the air was causing friction electricity. They stayed in the truck until they saw a dim light in the distant. While they were in the truck, they felt disoriented. After they saw the light, they walked toward it; a farmer had gotten to his barn and lit a lantern. After dust settled some, Daddy could start the truck and come home. Everything was covered with dust. There were drifts of dust that covered some of the farm machinery. Mom and Daddy covered the windows with wet sheets. The dust was still blowing some. The dust was so thick in the house we used a scoop shovel to pick it up. The drought was still on and no rain in sight. Some people who were caught in the cloud got lost and some died. People in that area were getting sick. It was called dust pneumonia.

Some moved west, some as far as California. We were lucky we stuck it out; we didn't get sick. We planted a garden and carried water to it. It grew until the grasshoppers came and ate most of it. Sometime later, we were overrun with jackrabbits. They came in groves and ate any little blade of grass they could find. The farmers got together, carried clubs, and walked herding them in a circle. When they got close enough, they clubbed them to death. I can remember seeing mounds of dead rabbits. We could not eat jackrabbits because they were tough and we were afraid of disease. We had very few cottontails.

Every farm had one or two dogs. We had a rat terrier and a mixed breed of hound. In the summertime, the hound would go to the neighbors, about two miles away, and stay a few days. It would then come home and stay a few days, and then go back to the neighbors. This made it convenient for us kids to write a note for the neighbors, tie it to the dog, and in a few days, we got the answer. We would then write another note. In a few days, we would get the answer to that note back. That was our communication with the neighbors.

Our other pet was a pig. It was the runt out of a litter of about eight or nine piglets. Daddy was afraid it would not get big enough to eat, so he brought it in the house, and behind the living room stove, put it in a washtub with a blanket. Mom fed it with a baby bottle. That little pig was cute; it was reddish brown with little black spots all over it. Daddy called him Pork and Beans. Well it grew up and Daddy put him in the yard. However, he didn't stay there. He would come in the house any time he wanted to. He never got full-size. He also got mean, not to the family, but visitors beware. When they got out of their car, he would charge right toward them.

Our landlord, Old George, was a pretty good old guy. He came over and Daddy got him in the house before Pork and Beans seen him. He was sitting in the rocking chair on the front porch. My uncle came over got out of his car. When the pig charged him, he ran. Now Daddy was the only one who could stop him, and the only way to do that was to snap him with a bullwhip. Daddy grabbed the whip, which he kept handy, and ran after the pig. So there went my uncle with the pig right behind him and Daddy with the whip right behind the pig! They ran around the house, and every time they went by the front porch Old George would rock and say, "Well whadda ya know 'bout that?" Finally, Daddy got close enough to snap him. The pig stopped instantly. Of course, I and my sister just couldn't stop laughing!

We took a vacation every summer. He would tell us, "We are going back east." Back east was Burrton, Halstead, and Wichita. That was where my Grandmas lived. It took a while to realize that there was more to back east than that. The winters were long and cold. We didn't get a lot of snow, but because of the wind, if it snowed a few inches it would drift in deep drifts. I remember one snowstorm where the snow drifted so high we could walk into the hayloft door of the barn. I don't remember much about the winters. There are so many memories. After the drought the rains came, we had some good wheat crops. Life has been good. The good old days were in the '50s and '60s, and the '30s and '40s are what memories are made of!

Weeds Not Accepted
By Jack Wolfe of Chatham, Illinois
Born 1945

This memory is from a farm four miles north of Conway Springs, Kansas in the mid to late 1950s. It was a hot August day on a dusty country road two miles north of Kansas HWY 49 when the hot 100 plus wind blew against my face. I was riding in our red and white Ford pickup with the windows down, its rusted and much-used half-ton bed shouting, "Farm truck." My father was driving and I was in the fifth or sixth grade. The wheat crop had been harvested, the fields plowed (with moldboards), and the clods broken up and the ground made level with what we called a spring tooth. This working of the ground was to get rid of the weeds, especially. In a few weeks, a new winter wheat crop would be planted—with no weeds accepted!

My father, Ed Wolfe, had a strong German heritage and the work ethic to go with it. He pulled to a stop to observe the condition of the field that he farmed. Some very big weeds had survived the previous week's efforts to eradicate them. There were maybe 20-30 from an eye's view of the 80 acres before us.

My father promptly exited the pickup and started walking and pulling those big, stubborn weeds one by one—some with great effort. Dad was stubborn, too, and did not stop his "walk" until all weeds lie defeated across the landscape. Dad returned perspiring and thirsty, but he would not be defeated!

On that day, I learned my Father's determination to provide for his family and how deep a parent's love can go. For, you see, Dad worked hard so that my brother, John, and I received good educations so that we had a choice to farm or not. We both went into professions other than farming. Our dad and mother remained on the farm, however, all of their 56 years of marriage until Dad passed away.

Life at the House on the Corner
By Linda Gering of Hutchinson, Kansas
Born 1952

My name is Linda Gering. My maiden name is Linda Swafford. I was born on August 20, 1952 in the St. Elizabeth Hospital. I was the ninth child of my parents and the fifth girl. We lived at 327 East 1st Street, a two-story home on a corner. There was five bedrooms, a dining room, and a living room. There was three to each bed. In the winter, that sure was nice!

On Saturday morning, we would do laundry. Our washing machine had a wringer and two rinse tubs. Then we'd hang the clothes up on a clothesline. On Sunday night, we would splash water on them. After that, we'd roll them up in a ball. Monday morning, after we got to school, my older sister would start on the ironing.

On Saturday nights, we all had to take a bath. There was no shower. There was two to a bath. Every second bath we got clean water. We would sometimes have a Pepsi. We could either drink it all that night or sip

The house that Linda grew up in

on it during the week. My parents would get dressed up. Dad would put on his suit. They loved to dance. The roller rink would host a sock hop dance once a month on the 30th. At the South Hutch IGA store, they would have a twist contest in the parking lot. There was a place on the corner of South Main and West B called Crystal Ballroom. People would take their liquor in the club and buy their sit-up. Back then, if you were stopped by a cop, he would pull you over and take you home. If he saw you out again, you went to jail.

I was the very first woman in the state of Kansas to work in a cemetery. I would help sit up funerals. Hutch News did a full page on me back in 1963.

I hated the party line thing. You never knew who was listening in on your conversation while you talked. Sometime in the fall or spring, a radio station would bury a couple thousand dollars and give clues out via the radio as to its whereabouts. Eventually someone would dig it up.

I don't ever remember locking up cars or our home before bed. You would have your windows open as well. The whole night you slept. This was back in the late '60s, early '70s.

Future Farmers of America
By Vernon Pauls of North Newton, Kansas
Born 1930

I attended Inman High School from 1944-1948. I was a farm boy, so consequently I enrolled in vocational agriculture classes and was a member of FFA (Future Farmers of America), a school club for those interested in vocational agriculture.

It was assumed that every FFA member would participate in the annual "Pest Eradication Contest." For this contest, all the FFA members were divided into two teams. The idea was that the FFA members would help farmers by helping to get rid of pests that destroyed crops and stored grains. The team that won the contest by destroying the most pests would be hosted by the losing team in a "Bean Feed."

The score was kept as follows: All sparrow heads would score five points. All mouse-tails would score five points. Each starling head would be ten points. Each pair of cottontail rabbit ears would be ten points. Each pair of coyote ears would be 30 points. Each possum tail would be ten points. Each rat-tail would be ten points.

It was customary in the 1940s that farmers would bind their oat crop in bundles with a binder, stack it in round stacks, and thresh it in the winter during slack time with a threshing machine. Thus, when the threshing day came, the best place for a FFA contestant to be was near a threshing scene. The mice had collected around the oat stacks and, as layer after layer was threshed, out rushed the mice. It was possible to encounter and "harvest" over 100 mice and rats on such a day.

Another "party event" for FFA members was a sparrow or starling roundup. Several members would ask a farmer for permission, and on a given winter night, would enter his barn and descend on the sparrows and starlings that sought shelter there. They would be occupying the eves and the haying equipment tracks in the haymow. The boys would use portable spotlights to find their prey. All had a great time.

All this took place before PETA became active. Sparrows and starlings were known to be carriers of diseases that affected poultry.

The Old Rock House
By Shirley Kempke of Ellsworth, Kansas
Born 1935

Located on Highway 40, there is a rock house about two miles east of Carneiro, Kansas. Many years ago before my family lived in this house, it was a stagecoach stop.

The old Rock House

Many people have memories of this house, but I lived there. I was born here in August of 1935 and lived with my parents and older brother and sister. My younger brother was born here, too. To look at this house it is hard to imagine that it had three floors. In the basement were the kitchen and a room where we kept the wringer washing machine, cream separator, and jars of food that Mom had canned from our garden. In the kitchen was a wood cook stove and washstand where we kept a wash pan for washing our hands and a pail of water and soap along with the kitchen table. The bedrooms and living room made up the top floors.

Once after returning from town, we headed downstairs to the kitchen. Mom shushed us, "Shhhh, I think I hear a snake." We waited for her on the steps as she checked it out. Sure enough, wrapped around the leg of the washstand was a rattlesnake. Mom went past us up the stairs, came back with the garden hoe, and killed it. This was not the first time she killed a snake in the house and it wouldn't be the last time, either. Once a bull snake slithered between the window and the sash, and once again, Mom took care of it. It seemed like Mom was always killing snakes.

It was dry in the Dirty Thirties. Mom would wet sacks and put them along the windows to help keep the dust out of the house. We had guineas running around the yard to help control the grasshoppers and insects. One particular day, Mom was busy and saw me hurry past the window with a big stick headed towards the nests of guineas' eggs. She wasn't sure what I was up to, so she followed me, and it was a good thing she did. In the nest of eggs was a snake. I was going to take care of that snake before it could eat any of those eggs.

Mom killed it before I had the chance to stir it up and make matters worse. Needless to say, we had plenty of guineas running around the yard that summer.

Many people were poor back then and found themselves headed west walking along Highway 40. Often people passing by would stop and ask Mom for something to eat or drink. Mom always had at least a bread and butter sandwich and a cool drink from the well for them, even though we didn't have much ourselves.

At the start of World War II, my dog Bouncer didn't walk or run, he bounced like a ball everywhere we went, and I would sit on a rock bank not far from the house so we could watch the cars and trucks pass by on the highway. Many army trucks and jeeps passed by us, too. I would wave to them and they would wave right back at the little girl and her bouncing dog.

In March of 1942, my little brother was born and that May we moved away. Although many years have passed since I lived in that old rock house, driving past it brings back all those wonderful memories of my time there with my family.

Outhouses and Wringer Washers
By Marlene L. Goertz of Farmington, New Mexico
Born 1931

I remember the outhouse that we had at our school. One day the boys decided to wrap string or wire around the toilet while the girls were inside. We couldn't open the door! I was in the first grade and I remember I cried and wondered if we were ever going to get out.

I grew up in a two-bedroom house without running water and electricity. We heated with a wood stove and there was no heat inside the bedrooms. The chamber pot in the bedroom froze at night. It got that cold!

We were on the same party line with 15 other families. Our ring was one long and one short. Listening in on our phone line was very common, as everyone knew each other's ring. The phone was for adults, not the kids. The more receivers went up, the harder it was to bear. Rotary phones were great in the '60s. We had a black one and later colored phones came out. We had to pay $5.00 for a colored phone; ours was beige.

Bathing was a once per week ordeal. It always happened on every Saturday evening. We heated the water on the wood stove and poured the hot water in a metal tub, which was placed in the dining room in front of the heating stove during the winter cold months. In the summer, baths were taken in the tub in the bathroom. In the summer, Mom would sit in the stock tank to cool off. One evening as Mom was cooling off when a neighbor drove into the yard. I was told to head him off before he reached the tank. I did!

We had a wringer washer when I grew up. We heated the water in a metal kettle with a wood fire underneath the kettle. Kids weren't allowed to use the wringer, as we could get our hands and hair caught. There was no dryer, and so the clothesline came next. I did the hanging of the clothes on the line. In the zero degree weather, the clothes would freeze in the basket before they were all hung up. My hands got so cold I had to warm them up before I finished. Clothes would freeze dry. My fingers got so cold they wouldn't bend!

When I was in the seventh grade, we had a teacher named Marjorie. She was my best teacher I ever had. She would play with us at recess. She was kind and loving in every way. She married my cousin. We had a one-room schoolhouse and the teacher taught all eight grades. There was never more than ten kids. I was alone in my grade most of the time. The school still stands and is not used anymore, as we consolidated. School is now in town and kids are being bused to school.

Growing up in the Newton, Kansas area, I remember the snowstorms we had. Our road ran north and south, and one week we didn't have any mail. The mail wagon couldn't get thought the drifts. The snow would harden and one could walk on top of the drifts. Eventually, the grader came and opened the road. My dad took the team and wagon and took us to school. The horses were knee deep in snow. We had wind and more wind. The snow would come through the windowsill. Rags were packed in the windows to make them seal tight. In 1937 or 1938 in February, Oklahoma had a dust storm. Mom had diapers on the clothesline and they were red from the dust.

I had an Aunt Lena who was very special to me. She was a person you could really talk to. She always had time for me and understood.

Our clothes were always handmade. When I graduated from the eighth grade, I got to buy a dress from the store. It was on sale. The dress was gold with a green bead for trim. I had red hair, and I thought the gold dress looked awful on me. The dress didn't go with my hair at all, but the price was right.

I lived in the Newton, Kansas and Hillsboro, Kansas area for 32 years before moving to New Mexico. I have the Newton, Kansan and it has been in our family for over a hundred years. My parents were never without the Newton, Kansan paper.

My "Boyfriend" Johnny
By Karen Poynter of Augusta, Kansas
Born 1940

I was born in 1940. I lived on the farm with my parents along with one brother and three sisters. We lived about 15 miles from a town of any size. My parents worked hard to make a living and they were quite frugal in order to support the family. So we only made trips to town to go to church and to buy groceries. Many times when mother went to town for groceries us children stayed home to do chores. All of us had chores to do such as feeding the pigs and chickens and helping to milk the cows.

I started school three months before my 6th birthday. It was a one-room schoolhouse and there was only about five or six students. We almost always walked to school, which was at least a mile from our home. I didn't know any boys my age until I started school. So my memory was of our neighbor's boy, Johnny. He was maybe a little older than me, but not much. I don't know if he knew it or not, but I thought he was my boyfriend. Several months into the summer, after 1st grade, I was missing Johnny. I asked mother if we could go visit Johnny and his parents. She told me no because she said they were not at home. I thought she just told me that so she wouldn't have to take me.

That afternoon I decided to walk down to see Johnny. I didn't tell anyone I was going and started out. I didn't wear any shoes. When I got about ¾ of a mile south of our house, I decided to take a shortcut through a cornfield. The corn was over my head and it didn't take me long to figure out that I was turned around and didn't know which way to go. I finally figured out to try to figure out which way I came in and go back. I came out of the field near to where I had gone in. I don't know how long I had been gone but mother missed me and came looking for me. When she found me I was hot, tired, scared, crying, and my feet were full of stickers. I don't remember if mother spanked me or loved me.

Needless to say, I never left on my own to go see Johnny again. We went to school together for several more years. After that, Johnny changed schools and I don't remember ever seeing him again. I never had a boyfriend after that until I started high school.

My Bus Family
By Lottie Harder of Buhler, Kansas

In the country around small towns, students living on farms found it difficult to get to and from schools. So in the late 1930s the Buhler School District provided bus service. The first such bus was owned and operated by Allen Teter. In 1944, he sold his two buses to Mr. J.J. Unruh. In 1956, the school district bought the buses. There were six by that time. I began driving a school bus in October 1973. Before that I had been a babysitter, a clerk, a carhop (in younger years), a payroll clerk, and a caregiver for the elderly (which I truly enjoyed), but bus driving is the best.

Some of the best things were getting to see the Kansas sunrise, watching, deer jumping fences, seeing skunks out for a walk, watching wild turkeys strut their wings, and see geese swimming. But the very best thing is my bus family. One special memory is of a kindergarten girl on her first day of school. She was frightened and was crying. Talking didn't help, so I went with her to class. As she calmed down another student asked if I was her grandma. She proudly answered, "No, she is my bus driver." These families have given me happiness and also many gifts of buses. I have over 300 models, puzzles, cups, shirts, etc. A collection I'm very proud of.

The Infamous Bonnie and Clyde
By Vera Jean Swafford of Dodge City, Kansas
Born 1927

This event took place in Dodge City, Kansas in the year of 1931 or 1932. I was only 4 years old. My family had moved to Dodge City from Oklahoma. This was the Great Depression days. You had to go where the jobs were. A few of my dad's friends also moved to Dodge City at that time to find work.

One day, a long-time friend of my dad, who was also from Oklahoma, called him on the phone where he was working and ask if he could borrow his car and also my dad's dress hat for the evening. He told my dad that he had a date with a very good-looking girl that he really wanted to impress. My dad told him to come down to the shop where he was working and get the car and he could go to our house and pick up the hat. This man drove to our house in my dad's car with this very "sexy" young lady in the car. He went into our house to get the hat that my dad said he could borrow. The sexy young lady stayed in the car. My brother and I were playing out in the yard. My brother ran over to the car and stepped on the running board and spoke to the "sexy" young lady in the car. She was smoking a cigarette. She had on a hat that almost covered one eye and she wore very heavy makeup. The young lady told my brother to get off the car and she called him a not very nice name. Needless to say, we two kids were impressed. She was a very different person than we had ever known.

Needless to say, my dad was really mad when his friend did not return our car. The first thing he did was to call and report the theft of his car to the Dodge City sheriff or marshal. I think it was Ham Bell. He had to walk to work the next morning. He also took his gun to work that morning. He was crossing the street at the corner of what is now Central Avenue and Gunsmoke Street. Imagine his surprise when he saw his car going around the corner. There was a strange man driving it. The man had some other men in the car with him. As the car slowed to turn the corner onto Gunsmoke, my dad stepped on to the running board of the car and demanded that the driver pull the car over to the curb. Since my dad had a gun, the man pulled the car to the curb and the men all got out of the car and walked away. My dad then drove to the sheriff's office to tell the sheriff he had his car back. The sheriff said to my dad, "Do you know who you just took that car from?" Of course, he didn't know. The sheriff told him the men were the gang that travelled with Bonnie and Clyde. Bonnie was the sexy girl that had gone out with my dad's friend and when his friend got drunk, Bonnie dumped the friend and took the car from him. The sheriff told my dad that Bonnie and some of the gang members were hiding out here in Dodge City but Clyde was not here in Dodge City. The sheriff thought Clyde was somewhere in Oklahoma also laying low so the law couldn't find him. I never understood why the law enforcement didn't arrest Bonnie and the gang members that were here in Dodge with her.

We Learned A Lot Growing Up During the '30s
By Loren and Arlene Schamaun of Great Bend, Kansas
Born 1931 and 1932

Growing up in the 1930s brings back a lot of memories. I grew up in Bazine, in the big rock house on the edge of Main Street. We had no electricity or running water until in the 1940s, so that meant going to the outhouse. It wasn't too bad in the summer, but oh, my in the winter, we knew how many steps from the back door of our house to the outhouse. At that time there was not too much money, so we didn't have toilet paper, we used newspaper and the Sears Roebuck catalog; it was not as soft as the tissue. Those were the good ole times. The chamber pot was put in the hallway in case it was needed, and then in the morning cleaned and ready for the night.

We had a radio that we would gather around and listen to *Fibber McGee and Molly*, *Amos and Andy*, and the *Grand Ole Opry*, how we looked forward to when we could listen to our programs. I also remember when President Roosevelt came on and told us we were in war. Pearl Harbor had been bombed, we were in war. I had three cousins on the ships that were bombed, what a sad time.

Saturday was always bath time; we carried water from the windmill and put it in a big kettle on the stove in the washhouse. In the afternoon when the water was hot, we would start our baths in a round galvanized tub; first one always got the cleanest water. The washhouse was a little ways from the house and was not heated, so it didn't take long for a bath. Don't know for sure what kind of soap we used, but guess we got clean!

The wringer washer was also located in the washhouse, so the water had to be heated in the kettle. There were two tubs, one with bluing to rinse the clothes after they were washed then put thru the wringer to remove water, then in a big basket, then hung out on the line to dry. The clothes were all hung certain ways to make them air dry faster. After they were dry they were brought in, folded, and put away. Many times putting sheets, towels and others thru the wringer we would get our fingers stuck in the wringer, ouch, kinda hurt. Doing the laundry now takes little or no effort.

My mother always made our clothes when she would buy fabrics. She would look at a pattern then be able to cut the same pattern on newspaper to use. She was a very talented seamstress. She made pillowcases, sheets, and tea towels with the sacks that flour was in. We always had something to wear.

My mother always did a lot of canning, all kinds of fruits, vegetables, and meats. When winter came our cellar was all stocked with food. It seemed like when it got cold back in the '30s in October it stayed cold until April. The wind and blowing snow made it hard to get around. Our house was heated with a wood stove, also used for cooking and baking. My job was to bring the wood to the porch so it would be handy. I had a wagon and used it to do the wood job.

The dust storms of the '30s were very bad. My dad tied a rope to the barn so he could get there to do the chores. My mother hung wet towels in the windows to keep the dust out, but it still came in. We had to cover things to keep dust off. I don't know how we managed, but someone was watching over us. There were always farm chores to do, we had to help milk cows and feed chickens and pigs; we did this before school, then we ate breakfast, and off to school. We always had to walk to school rain, snow, whatever. We also had chores to do after school; we never got bored.

Growing up in the '30s was hard, but also taught us a lot of things that many of the kids now days haven't learned. Things today are all technical. The hard work; doing without things didn't hurt us and makes us appreciate what we have now.

Losing My Brother
By Robert A. Strong of Dighton, Kansas
Born 1930

At 84, I can remember many things, but my brother's death is one I remember best. I was in the kitchen and my mother was going to the door to see what the commotion was outside and who was coming up the walk. It was the message that my brother was missing in action; he had been lost at sea. My dad (also in the Navy) and brother met in the south pacific two times. My brother had come through the Panama Canal on his way to New York for repairs to the ship. Before repairs were complete they were sent out to sea, as a result the ship's smoke staff blew off and the ship went down and my brother was lost at sea.

Summer Visits With My Aunt and Uncle
By Juanita Grantz of Bel Aire, Kansas
Born 1946

When we were growing up, my brother and I stayed two or three weeks each summer with our Aunt Thelma and Uncle Bill on their farm. There was always lots to do on the farm and we were expected to help with the chores while we were there. I especially liked feeding the chickens and gathering the eggs. We were expected to get up early, and once the roosters started crowing, it was difficult to sleep anyway. We usually had to go to the fields and pick whatever crops that needed picking. My Aunt, Uncle, and older cousins milked the cows, but we had to help with the cleaning of the milk buckets and separator. Whenever we were there if anyone was sick, my Aunt would make all the kids line up and take a dose of castor oil. I did not like castor oil then and I still don't like it, but my Aunt felt that taking castor oil was a good preventative measure to keep you from getting sick.

On Mondays, my Aunt always washed clothes. She had two round tubs she used, one for washing the clothes with a scrub board and the other one she used for rinsing out the soap. Then she would run the clothes through a wringer washer and hang the clothes on lines for drying. On Tuesdays, she always ironed the clothes. On Friday nights, the whole town gathered at the high school for various activities. There was a potluck meal for everyone who came. The young people played basketball or listened to music. Senior citizens often played dominoes and there were also many who played board games or cards. The younger children often played outside when the weather permitted it. My Aunt and Uncle did not have indoor plumbing 'til I was in high school, and thus we had to go to the outhouse when we had bathroom needs. I did not like going there at night because they had a mean goose that often chased me on the way to and from the outhouse.

My birthday was in the summer and I spent many of them at my Aunt and Uncle's home. I don't remember getting any presents but my Aunt would bake me whatever kind of birthday cake that I wanted. My Aunt Thelma was a super good cook. She made the best chicken and noodles and homemade bread. Her blackberry cobbler was the best I have ever tasted. Every Sunday she hosted a big dinner. Friends, neighbors, and family were always welcome. On Saturday, she would bake pies and homemade bread for those Sunday dinners and those dinners were well attended. It seemed that half the town showed up to partake of her endeavors.

The town they lived closest to was Kendrick, Oklahoma. There was a sign posted as you entered Kendrick that stated the population was 200. I think they must have counted the dogs and cats too because it never seemed like there were that many people. Kendrick, Oklahoma is where my mother and her family were raised. When I was growing up, I loved to visit there, because it seemed like Heaven.

Juanita's Aunt Thelma and Uncle Bill with her cousins Carmen Alice and Sonny Boy

Brothers Are to Protect Sisters, Not Scare Them to Death
By Earleta Selm of Attica, Kansas
Born 1935

We lived on the edge of a small prairie town that dated back to 1886. By we, I mean dad, mom, brother, sis, and finally me. By the time I arrived it was the mid-1930s. The town had two churches, one school (eight grades) a two-story red brick, two general stores, the telephone office, the post office, oh yes and the old hotel. I guess you could say the main business was the elevator-feed business, which dad managed. There were also the stockyards at the railroad.

I will never forget the herds of cattle driven into town by men on horseback to be shipped out by rail. They always entered town from the south going by the school. Us kids would run for the schoolyard fence to watch them go by. The teachers would come charging out and make us move back from the fence to the side of the building, which they thought was safer. Something special to have witnessed as I look back into the past.

As little kids we attended bible school at both churches (Presbyterian and Assembly of God). I think this was to get us out of mother's hair, not that we were that bad. I remember one summer at the Assembly of God bible school the most. We always had a little program the last night of school, and this year still lingers in my mind. The church was filled and the lights were turned out. Each of us kids had a little lighted candle and we marched in down the center aisle to the stage singing, "Brighten the Corner Where You Are." At that age it was really something. We attended the Presbyterian Church and were on the cradle role list.

The red brick school was something, two classrooms and all eight grades. The best part was the playground. It had an old merry-go-round that was great. They don't make them like that anymore. It also had two separate outhouses. It's amazing how bad my bladder control got with the arrival of spring weather and any excuse to get outside.

Another great thing about the school had nothing to do with learning. There was a man who showed movies in the upstairs once a month. The price of admission was whatever you could afford. We saw some great movies there, having a lot of fun. At least I thought so at the time. One I remember most was about the Wolfman. That night when us three kids were walking home to the hill, there was snow on the ground, the stars were shining, and the moon was out, I don't remember if it was a full moon or not. Anyway, dear brother ran off leaving us girls behind. Now the path we had to take was through some trees and we had to cross a wire fence that bordered the schoolyard, then up to the road to the driveway that lead up the hill to home. Well, as I said, brother ran off and left sis and I before we got to the trees and you guessed it, he hid in the trees and jumped out behind us and like to have scared me to death. Don't think I ever crossed that wire fence so easy as I did that night. It goes without saying that dad and mom were told of his prank when we arrived home out of breath. Dad gave brother the understanding that he was to protect his sisters, not scare them to death.

The smoke belching, coal burning, fire starting trains. Yes, I said fire starting, as the engine chugged through the countryside, fire red embers would fly out of the smoke stack, and if things were dry where they dropped, a fire was a sure thing. Setting right of ways and more often than not the wheat field next to it would go up in flames. The smoke would be spotted and a line ring would go out from the telephone office calling all able body men to join the fight and stop the fire. Using shovels, rakes, wet gunnysacks, and most important guts, faith, and determination. As bad as this often was the train was very important, picking up boxcars of wheat, barley, and oats, and sometimes stock cars of cattle. Yes even picking up bales of wool from the local farms that ran sheep as well as cattle. The trains left cars of stock and poultry feed for the local co-op to sell. The trains were an important must have back then. So many things we accept now days without a second thought were vital to our lives back then.

We're Still Rural
By Charlotte Ringer of Medicine Lodge, Kansas
Born 1935

Armistice Day, November 11, 1935, a chubby 9# baby entered this world. Charlotte Ann was the daughter of Carl E. and Mae (Ohnemiller) Becker. Grandfather George V. Becker was visiting that day. When Dr. A.H. and wife/nurse Helen Bierman drove in the yard ½ E and 2 ½ S of Schulte, my grandfather asked, "What's going on?" When dad told him, we were having a baby he took out of the yard pronto since he'd been thru it 8 times, guess he didn't want anymore! I wonder how many babies Dr. Al delivered over the years. He was such a colorful character. There should and should have a book written about him!

Thus, started my "rural" journey of life in Kansas. Memories of living at home are great, funny, and sad. We, my sister, Gladys, and brother, Charles, had a great time growing up. We were poor (it was depression time) but the folks didn't let us know. We were a happy 4-H family. In fact, my husband, Ronnie Ringer, and I met at 4-H camp in Rock Springs. My dad was quite a prankster. We loved to hear all of his shenanigans when he was in school at Goddard, especially around Halloween! Sitting the principal's car on his front porch or moving outhouses just back of the "hole" were just a few. But, our most memorable Halloween was when the neighborhood boys slipped into the milk house to sink pails, etc. inside the water tank. Dad had them figured out and he had removed the pulsars. We watched for them. When they had done their fun deed, they were slipping over the fence just as dad flipped on the yard light. You should have seen them scramble, right in the manure around the stock tank!

I just barely remember dad being the warden in World War II, checking to see if all the neighborhood was dark during an air raid test. Some of our neighbors spoke German in their homes, but never in public. It was a scary time. It was fun listening to the stories of all the bootleggers in the area and how they operated. One incident dad told us about happened at Grandpa Becker's farm. The bootlegger's car broke down close to their place. He came in and asked for help even though he didn't know grandpa's feelings toward bootlegging. As it turned out grandpa, who was not a drinker, hid his car in the barn and they got it fixed so he could be on his way. Grandpa said he was only trying to provide for his family. Times did get better.

Remember when the folks bought their 1948 Plymouth. We had been driving a green 1938 Plymouth. Charles and I made the prettiest designs with the cigarette lighter on the upholstery. That was one time we both got a lickin'. The other was when I threw a brick at Charles (thank God I missed). Dad disciplined mostly with his voice!

St. Peter's Church and School at Schulte were quite memorable. The many times I was a flower girl for graduations, communions, and special occasions mom always made my dresses. She was a one of a kind! I still have most of them. One of the most fun times in grade school was when Fr. George Schmidt got out boxing gloves and we all formed a circle to watch Mike and Lou Girrens "duke it out" during recess. We played anti over the coal shed, which had three stalls on each side for outside facilities!

No such things as school busses back then. Many times if the folks were late picking us up we walked to Faker's Grocery Store and played a lot with Myrna upstairs. The south door upstairs opened and wow there was sugar, tires, nylons and all kinds of stuff that was rationed during World War II. Not everyone used their ration tickets or tokens for legal items! Sr. Norberta always put "monkey blood" on scrapes from playing at recess (mercurochrome). Mom traded eggs for piano lessons for Charles and I. We took them over the lunch hour once a week!

When I was in high school at Sacred Heart Academy I drove a 1939 black Ford coup. The day before Thanksgiving of 1952, Kansas had a doozy of a snowstorm. My rider, Georgiann Hemmen, and I made it to Cessna Prospect Plant. Her brother, Paul, took the back roads and rescued us. He towed the car to their place, as I wasn't sure about the anti-freeze. About 18 others got stranded at their place. Most had grocers on their way home. We ate like kings. Theresa had beds for all the women and children and the guys stayed up and played cards. Most got out the next morning, except me. My folks were so snowed in they wouldn't let me try to get home. Thus I spent Thanksgiving plus one day. We had a wonderful time! Still have the butterfly potholder we made. Now, that's country hospitality!

We all belonged to Schulte 4-H. Have a Wichita Eagle article and picture of us unloading our Holsteins for the show at the old Wichita Forum, now Century II area. 4-H was a big part of our lives. In 1953 at Rock Springs Ranch Ronnie and I met while learning the "Beer Barrell Polka." We never quite got that down pat, but we sure learned to intermission! Although we only lived five miles apart on Maize Road we had never met. He went west to Goddard school and I went east to SHA. We were married at age 18 and 19. They said it would never last. We fooled them. Come October we will be married 60 years. We've had a wonderful life with many careers. Need to write it down someday for our two sons, Roger and Rodney. After all these years, we're "still rural." Leaving Sedgwick County in 2006, we now run the Bunkhouse Bed & Breakfast at Wildfire Ranch in the beautiful Gypsum Hills in Barber County. Having guests from all over the world is keeping us young.

The Cow Milker
By Marilyn Small of Cimarron, Kansas
Born 1950

My earliest "good old days" memories start out with my family living on a farm northwest of Hanston in a house that we called the "wrecky house." I was the fourth of nine children, and this house had no paint on it, no electricity, no running water, and no basement. We lit our house with coal-oil lamps and heated our water, which we got from a windmill, on a gas stove. On Saturday nights, we took our weekly baths in a round tin tub, which was about four feet in diameter, all in the same water, with a little hot water added for each kid so that it was warm.

We went to the bathroom in a "two hole" outhouse and I remember going into the dark cellar during tornado scares. An "outhouse" memory that I have is when I was playing with my doll. We were going to church in the outhouse and she was being bad and wouldn't stop crying so I spanked her and threw her down the toilet hole! Since she was my only doll and toys were hard to come by for us, she had to be retrieved! My mother held my older sister by the ankles and put her through the hole to get my doll for me. My sister, to this day, is not happy with me for that one. I also recall, at Christmas time, going out and cutting a limb off of our evergreen tree for our Christmas tree. We then decorated it with paper cut outs that we made and colored. It was such a good time and our tree was gorgeous!

The Blizzard of 1957 was a vague memory to me. I was six years old, and remember being inside for what seemed like forever. I also remember that my parents were very worried about our livestock. After we could finally "get out," we discovered most of our cows and calves all around the house in about a four-foot space between the house and ten foot high snowdrifts. I also remember the neighbors coming to our place to help us dig out cars, driveways, and the outhouse! When they finally got to it, we had a 10-foot high tunnel that we had to walk through to get to the bathroom. It was awesome, but only for a few days. We learned to "hold it" for a long time, rather than trek through the freezing tunnel!

When I was seven years old, we moved to a "new" farmhouse. It had two bedrooms, a living room, a kitchen, and a bathroom. It also had running water and electricity! We thought we were in heaven! Four of us slept in one bedroom, three were in the other bedroom, and my mom and dad slept in the living room. My oldest sister had left home to become a nun before my youngest brother was born. My mother always cut house plans from the newspaper and dreamed of a new big house for us, but this would be her home for the rest of her life.

Marilyn's family ready for Sunday church

I had no idea what electricity was when we moved there. Lights came on by pushing a switch - it was like a miracle to me! I had one scary incident with electricity, when I tried to figure out what an outlet was by poking tweezers in one. As I asked my mom, "What will happen when I put this in here?" she screamed "No," and I hit the wall on the other side of the room! The tweezers was melted into a ball of metal, and I was a bit stunned for a while but was okay. The outlet never worked again!

On this farm, our family was pretty much self-sustained. We planted a huge garden and harvested, canned, and froze tons of vegetables. I recall helping my mother till the garden with a spade shovel. For hours, we would turn over the soil with a spade until it was ready for raking and planting. I still prepare my garden with a spade! Old school! We butchered and processed all of our own meat. We would cut, trim, and packaged enough meat to fill two freezers. We raised baby chicks and butchered about 100 chickens every summer. We milked two or three cows each day for our milk, cream, and butter.

Our main source of income was buying and selling livestock. In the fall, my father would buy several hundreds of yearling cattle and fatten them up to sell in the spring. This life-style employed all of us. For some reason, I ended up being the cow milker. I milked, by hand, every day. If we needed cream, then I put together the separator, which was a machine that separated the cream from the milk. We always drank whole milk, so the separated milk was fed to livestock. Our whole milk always had to be pasteurized so I would get the milk put into the pasteurizer and then bottled. Washing and cleaning the separator and pasteurizer was also my job because I was the "milker."

Five of the nine children in Marilyn's family in 1960

My brothers usually helped my dad with feeding the cattle, but every once in a while I would fill in. I remember getting into a lot of trouble one time. We had filled three bunks with silage and were on the fourth when a chicken got into the first bunk. If a chicken pooped in the feed, the cattle wouldn't eat there, so I quickly jumped into action. I picked up a rock and threw it as hard as I could at the chicken. I hit the chicken right in the head and killed it! My dad was not very pleased with me, as I had eliminated a possible meal for the family!

Another cattle feeding memory is one that could have been a horrible tragedy. It happened when my brothers, my younger sister (who was nine or ten years old), and I were taking grain out to the pasture to feed the "fat cattle." These were steers that we were fattening up to be butchered later on. We had a bucket that we used for grain, hanging on the post by the gate. We were in a hurry, so I opened the gate and my sister, who was standing on the running board of the pickup, was supposed to grab the bucket as my brother drove through. Well she didn't get it all of the way off the post and she was thrown to the ground and her hand was run over by the pickup! The ground there by the gate was soft and sandy so her tiny hand wasn't hurt badly, but she had tire tread marks on it for about a week! We still die laughing when this story is told even though it could have been quite tragic.

Other cattle memories are those of the days when we had to move cattle or load them for sale day. Moving cattle was quite a process since we did not own horses to ride for guiding the cattle. We moved them from close to town on my grandma's land to our place, which was about seven miles. My dad would drive a "lead" pickup for the cattle to follow and my mom would follow behind them in another vehicle. Us kids would run along the sides to keep the cattle on the road and stop them from going into fields where there were no fences. I never looked forward to those days because it never failed, some calves would get into the fields on the side, and then the chase was on to try and get them back. My dad would be very upset with us kids and we knew the "butt chewings" were coming when we finally made it home!

The chore of loading livestock for sale was even worse it seemed, especially if they were hogs that we were loading. We had to sort the big ones out into the loading pen and then get them up the loading shoot to the truck. Hogs were horrible; they would run directly over you! I remember all of us getting up early on sale day to find the best "club" to use on

Marilyn sorting the cattle for the sale

the impossible hogs. Also, we would all be standing in line to go to the bathroom before we started because our nervous stomachs were working overtime!

Our entertainment on the farm was mainly playing sports, since we never owned a television. Baseball was our favorite and the whole family played on Sundays since that was a day of church, fun, and rest. We used landmarks for our game pieces. By the ditch was home plate, first base was across the driveway, second was in the nice grass, third was by the plowed field, and the chicken house was the "home run wall." If you could hit it over the chicken house, you were a slugger! Our basketball goal was on the chicken house, but we didn't play basketball very much because you couldn't dribble the ball very well on the uneven ground. Football was also difficult because of the hard ground, so baseball it was and we played for hours! My dad's favorite team was the St. Louis Cardinals and he never missed listening to each game on the radio. Sometimes he would have to listen to the game on the pickup radio because it would come in clearer than it did in the house. Us kids learned to know every baseball player on St. Louis's team and when we played we would each be the name of one of the Cardinals' players, Curt Flood, Lou Brock, Dal Maxvill, Tim McCarver, Bill White, Ken Boyer, Bob Gibson, Julian Javier, they were the best and we felt like we were too!

I learned to drive by using the "landmarks" on our farm also. My dad put a telephone pole on the ground between the old Model A Ford and the truck so I could practice parallel parking. I practiced driving in the pasture on the path of tracks that led to the feed bunks. At age 14, I got my license and drove 25 miles to school every day. Many flat tires, stuck in the mud, hood flying open, sliding in the ditch, and "tickets" followed, but what a great experience!

Today, I am a mother of four grown children and have five grandchildren. Through the years of raising my children I tried hard to teach them "how to work," but nothing compares to the work ethic that one can learn on a farm. As a child, I never thought I was poor. I never realized how really poor we were until I was older and found out that other children didn't live like we did. I credit my parents for this. They gave us everything we needed to feel rich. They gave us the best work ethic one could hope for and they gave us a family love unmeasured! I dream of going back to those "good old days" sometimes, but you can't live in the past. The memories are wonderful though and I thank God that I have them. The next phase of my life would be the story of my adulthood and oh, what a story!

Now I Know How the Pioneers Felt
By Susan Edmonston of Protection, Kansas
Born 1946

Ah, the good old days. I can remember them well, even though I have trouble remembering today where I put my purse and keys last night. I'm almost 68, and have lived in the small town of Protection, Kansas most of my lifetime. Our high school had 100 students in it when I and 23 other classmates graduated from PHS in 1964. At that time, my sister Sally was a junior and sister Nancy was a freshman. We three helped our parents, Orin and Judy Strobel, put out the weekly newspaper, *The Protection Post*.

Some reflections from me as a young child include the little four-room house we lived in across from the post office in 1950-1951 and the block of ice our parents put in the small icebox in the kitchen. I remember trying to smoke a cigarette that my mother left nearby as she was putting metal type in forms so newspaper pages could be run on the big printing presses in our shop. I think I turned green so Mother gave me some money to walk a block to the grocery store to buy a pop. A large candy bar only cost a nickel, as did a bottle of pop. That experience caused me to never try smoking again, even though a large number of teenagers and adults did. And another thing, Mother would tell me to go to the grocery store and pick up a pack of Raleigh cigarettes. The clerk never thought a thing when the pack was handed to me and 25 cents was written down on Mom's account. And we could collect the glass pop bottles that people just threw along the highways, turn them in to the grocery store and get some money back. We did not know we were littering then "recycling."

Old newspapers were saved in our family's garage and my folks would bundle those up and take them to Dodge City to get money for them. We didn't go to Dodge City a lot in the 1950s. Usually it was at the beginning of a school year to buy new clothes at Montgomery Ward. I marveled that our cash was placed in a container at the counter and then traveled up to a room upstairs where change was made and returned to the counter for us. Most of the time our family just ordered out of the Sears or Penney's catalogs that came to the post office in the spring and fall. Dad was a substitute mail carrier and I got to go along and place those heavy catalogs in the rural mailboxes. Protection at that time had a car agency, hotel, department store, shoe cobbler, seven grocery stores, four or more filling stations, several cafes, an appliance store, jewelry store, and people shopped "at home."

Walking around the block on homemade stilts was actually four blocks of staying upright and I could do it! Activities were roller-skating all over town and using empty appliance boxes for playhouses and stagecoaches. Walking the railroad tracks that went by our newspaper office to a pasture east of town and "ice skating" in our new boots from Christmas on the frozen water in the creek there, my sisters and me got in trouble for that!

I remember riding my bike all over town alone or with friends at all hours of the day and night - and one day proudly not using the handlebars to guide the bike, which resulted in the bike wheel crashing into our family's dog who ran alongside the bike and with me sprawled on the ground. My left arm wobbled as I put weight on it to get up off the ground. I was only a few yards from the newspaper building when the crash occurred. I walked inside, found Mom at the Intertype and told her I thought my arm was broken. She carried me (I was a 4th grader) a block and a half to the doctor's office. Dr. Glenn ended up doing surgery on my arm at the new Comanche County Hospital 14 miles from Protection; it was broken at the elbow joint. Back then to put a patient asleep for surgery, ether was used and that was an experience I will never forget. I stayed in the hospital a whole week and my Vacation Bible School class gave me a "Sunshine Box" and I could open up one gift each day. I remembered getting a box of four different colors of clay dough to make objects. Nowadays, perhaps that would be therapy to exercise the muscles in a broken arm. My arm was in a cast all summer and my biggest disappointment was not being able to go swimming in the town's pool a block north of the newspaper office. Maybe that is why I became such a bookworm. I used the town library a lot, checking out and reading the whole collection of Nancy Drew, Hardy Boy, and Bobbsey Twins books.

Our family moved in 1955 to a brand new house at the edge of town. It had 5 rooms. At that time, Dad drove a Hudson with a water cooler in the side window. We thought that was great! Our town had dirt streets and Dad wrote editorials and argued for curb and guttering to improve Protection. Sixty years later, many of our town's streets are still unpaved.

Protection had so many memorable events in my growing up years. Our town was used nationally in 1957 to publicize the importance of becoming 100% protected from Polio. It was a big deal when Red Foley and Miss Kansas and other celebrities came to town. There was a big parade. I found a $20 bill that had been trampled on, on the sidewalk in front of our newspaper office. That was a lot of money back then.

Other joys I had in the 1950s were reading and collecting comic books bought at the local drugstore, playing with Katy Keene paper dolls or jacks or "pick-up sticks", attending the movie show in town, earning money as a typesetter for *The Post*, going for eight years to the ball field near the city park for softball practice twice a week, being in Kayettes and doing all kinds of service projects to earn points, wearing a band uniform and marching down Main Street from the school to the football field and performing half-time formations. I also had to fill out a time card every week to show my band instructor how much I played my horn at home every day.

Both sets of grandparents lived 300 miles from Protection, so it was not often I was around them, maybe just Christmas or an occasional weekend. They lived in Hiawatha, Kansas and Falls City, Nebraska. But both grandmothers always sent me a dollar bill on my birthday. I spent time writing letters to them and friends all the time. The phone was seldom used for long distance calls. It cost too much, or so we thought at that time.

During high school, I dated lots of boys on the weekends, mainly going to movie theaters. They treated me like a lady. Girls wore dresses or sweaters and skirts. And I dressed up and wore high heels walking to classes at the University of Kansas in the '60s. I thought it cost too much to ride the bus on campus. And I continued to "dress up" as an elementary school teacher until pantsuits became popular in 1975.

In the 1970s, when I gave birth to four daughters in eight years, I stored the bills received in their baby books. In 1973, office calls to the doctor were $4; it cost $350 for delivery and a five-day stay in hospital.

I also returned to my love of reading and subscribed to Readers Digest Condensed Books and spent hours curled up with a book. I also did a lot of sewing and never regretted the four years of home economics I had in high school.

Gone from the scene now in Protection are the fruit orchards that were popular here in the 1950s-1970s. Nevan and Faye Riner had a peach orchard north of town and Joe and Viola Schumacher had an apple orchard south of Protection. Both were open to the public to come pick and purchase.

Times have changed and I am learning to adjust with them as the digital age is here. Now I know how the pioneers felt when electricity and water were made available, as well as inventions and improvements in machinery, telephones, automobiles, airplanes, appliances, and medicine.

Perks of Being a Stone Boy
By Gregg A. Stone of Burrton, Kansas
Born 1956

My name is Gregg Stone. I grew up in a little town called Burrton, Kansas. It was the late 1950s and 1960s. Growing up in Burrton was definitely a Mayberry experience. I lived on a small farm just outside of town. We had the usual menagerie of animals, horses, cows, pigs, sheep, chickens, and dogs. Everything a young boy could wish for.

My father and grandfather taught me the ways of hunting, fishing, and building a fence.

For me, the perfect summer day would be riding horses in the cool of the morning, an afternoon of swimming at the pool, and a double-header of Little League baseball in the evening.

But growing up a Stone boy had its extra perk. My father, B.E. Stone was a cousin of Milburn Stone, who was Doc Adams of *Gunsmoke*. Milburn, who was born and raised in Burrton, often would come back to Burrton to visit family. He was a warm and generous man who always brought me a gift. The ones I still have are treasured heirlooms.

Once on our family's annual trip to the mountains at Manitou Springs, Colorado, it coincided with the Pikes Peak or Bust Rodeo in Colorado Springs. Milburn and Ken Curtis, who played Festus Hagan on *Gunsmoke*, were the specialty act at the rodeo. They both sang with the Sons of the Pioneers. They were both treated like royalty, as *Gunsmoke* was the

Gregg Stone with Milburn Stone riding Flash

highest rated TV show for several years. My father took me to the Broadmoor Hotel where they were both staying. Milburn opened the door to welcome us in, and I could see Festus sitting on the couch in full *Gunsmoke* costume. They were getting ready to perform at that day's rodeo. Festus looked at me and said, "You ol' scudder, you're uglier 'an a ape!" I asked Dad, "Did you hear him?" My dad said, "Yes, son, I heard him. He said you were uglier than an ape." We all had a big laugh at that one.

That's just one of the many wonderful memories I have of being related to Milburn Stone. Because of Mil, I was able to meet Dennis Weaver (Chester Goode), Amanda Blake (Miss Kitty), Ken Curtis (Festus Hagan), and rodeo stars Larry Mahan and Don Gay. I honestly don't think a young boy could have asked for anything more or had a better childhood.

J. F. K.'s Death
By Brian T. Lohrenz of Wellington, Kansas
Born 1961

I was raised on a farm in western Kansas, Rush County, Alexander, and a small town, La Crosse, in school. My brother, sister, and I were playing outside on the farm and my parents came running out, "John F. Kennedy's been shot!" The rest of the year remains a blur. We were so young.

Wilbur Yingst
By Michael Hathaway of St. John, Kansas
Born 1961

Every now and then, when old-timers gather to drink coffee and reminisce, someone will mention a name with a twinkle in his eye. All the other old-timers standing around will smile real big and shake their heads. Then the stories come.

Wilbur was a bootlegger who lived in Stafford and operated here in the county. One old-timer recalls her teen-age days, following Wilbur around Stafford with a bunch of friends, hoping to find one of his bootleg stashes. They did find a bottle of booze one time in the crook of a tree where they saw Wilbur toss it while walking, without missing a step.

The most often-told story takes place in the late 1940s in St. John, the county seat of Stafford County. Wilbur ended up there now and then in the jail on the top floor of the county courthouse.

Wilbur was a genius at anything mechanical, had an innate sense of how things worked. He could unlock any lock. At night, after Sheriff Jim Corn left for the evening, Wilbur would unlock his jail cell and wander around the top floor of the courthouse all night. By daylight, he would be back in his cell as if nothing happened, the sheriff none the wiser.

When county citizens brought money in to pay taxes or other expenses, Sheriff Corn put the money in the top drawer of his desk, which he kept locked. One of Wilbur's favorite pranks was to unlock that drawer, take the money, and hide it somewhere else on the top floor of the courthouse, causing Sheriff Corn all manner of consternation.

As everything does, Wilbur's legendary night meanderings on the top floor of the Stafford County Courthouse came to an end. One of his fellow inmates was bound for Lansing. This inmate resented Wilbur for not unlocking his cell to allow him to escape the night before he was transported to Lansing and reported Wilbur's nighttime activities to Sheriff Corn.

A Great Teacher
By Mickie Gillette of Valley Center, Kansas
Born 1935

My best memories are of my grade school teacher who taught me for eight grades in a one-room schoolhouse. It is amazing to me that she could teach eight grades with as many as 50 students! It was "Valley Pride in South Hutchinson, Kansas.

We had lower grades (first through fourth) and upper grades (fifth through eighth) but sitting next to each other allowed us to participate in the next grades curriculum at times.

My teacher (Edna Anderson) was a single, middle-aged lady who wore tie shoes with chunk heels and always a dress. Yet she managed to umpire our softball games and I can still see her running up and down the basketball court (outdoors) with a whistle in her mouth.

We had spelling contest and tract meets with the other one-teacher schools in the area. We received gold medals and ribbons if we won. I still have mine.

Our teacher let us have Halloween parties. We dressed in costumes and she picked out the three best. Then we did games and treats.

Then came Christmas and we made a stage and put on a play for our parents. Also, we had singing and a rhythm band. We worked on this for a couple of weeks at least!

Next was Valentine's Day and we got to have parties again. The fourth and eighth grades made Valentine boxes and we all put in what we wanted and then got to open them at the party.

In the spring, we had the track meets and also played games at noon and recess. "Capture the Flag" was the one that was exciting to me. Teacher was there also.

One year, I remember teacher hooking a sleigh to her car and pulling us in the snow. I'm sure that would not be allowed today!

I was always wanting to get to school early as teacher let us ring the bell for school (we took turns).

One eighth grade student got to be the librarian each year. I got to be the one when I was in eighth grade. There were five people in my class.

We did not have hot lunches, so teacher ate her lunch with the students and played dominoes. Also, we had outside toilets and had to hold up our hand to go out!

When my children and grandchildren started school, I realized what a difference it is now. I think we had much more fun in school and always wanted to get to school as soon as possible. Not so, today.

My one regret is that I didn't go back to see my teacher after I went on to high school and got married. I wish I had told her how wonderful she really was.

My Parade Bride
By Jack Adams of Deerfield, Kansas
Born 1925

My story begins 88 years ago. At the time, I had been discharged from the U. S. Merchant Marine and was at home in Rocky Ford, Colorado.

I was setting at the counter of the local town confectionary visiting with a young friend. He had been telling me about a new, pretty, young girl who just moved to town and started junior class in high school.

While we were there talking, she and several other schoolmates came out of the back meeting room on the way back to school.

I and my friend looked her over closely and I spontaneously said to him, "I am going to marry her!"

During that summer after school was out, a Rocky Ford business held a parade for advertising and the lady (Pat) was chosen Queen of the parade.

As Queen she was to ride in a parade, full length and back of Main Street on my dad's old 1947 Chevy truck and I was the driver of the truck.

After spending the time it took to complete the trip, Pat said to me, "I am tired of this!"

I said, "OK, let's go get married." Without thinking, she immediately said OK.

We immediately got into my special Pontiac Silver Streak car. That was the only one like it in the country at the time and drove to Syracuse, Kansas and got there in time to be married by the local Justice of Peace and race back to Rocky Ford before dark so that our parents would not know about the wedding.

We were successful keeping it in the dark while I made my way back to Army base in Texas in time to check into the barracks in time not to be caught AWOL. Lucky day.

Pat (my new wife) was to receive half my Army paycheck at my uncle's rural mailbox in order to keep the secret, but I soon realized our local, rural mailman would tell my father about the check as soon as he realized what was happening. Therefore, I decided at last to tell my parents what happened. My folks thought it was OK. Lucky day. Pat stayed at her parents while I was back at Texas Army base.

After completing basic training in Texas and being assigned duty in the Pentagon, Washington, D. C., my new wife Pat and I drove my grand Silver Streak Pontiac car to Washington, D. C. and began duties there.

After a few months in D. C., working with three other men (all of us sworn to secrecy) worked on a secrets report, which had been divided into four parts and was not allowed to see the other men's parts, I was discharged from service and sent home to Rocky Ford, Colorado to begin the rest of my life.

I took my prized Silver Streak Pontiac car, gave a ride home to four other discharged men to their homes in Kansas. And then went on home in Colorado to begin new life with wife Pat and beginning my family of two boys and three girls.

Things have continued until I am now 88 years old. Good life.

Okey Elliott

Obeeville
By Carol Redd of Buhler, Kansas
Born 1937

There was once a place called Obeeville, Kansas. It was centered around the Obee School located at Obee Road and Highway 50, now known as East 4th Avenue, two miles east of Hutchinson city limits. Albert and Maude Elliott built a small grocery store on the northeast corner in the early 1920s named Obee Grocery & Market. Mr. D. J. Ward operated the business for many years. Then it was purchased by Ray and Elise Cannon. It was a bit like today's convenience stores because they not only sold food but also gasoline, oil, and kerosene. Several homes did not have electricity and needed kerosene for their lamps. (Bread, wrapped in wax paper, was 10 cents a loaf.) Just a few feet behind the store there was a blacksmith shop operated by Fred Evans. Neither building remains today.

Then in 1947, the Sproule family built the "Iris Drive-In" theater on the southeast corner of the intersection. They hired local young kids for 50 cents an hour to sell popcorn, tickets, sodas, etc. The older boys directed traffic after the movie ended. They had flashlights with red caps to help customers leave safely. Remember, these cars were going onto U. S. Highway 50.

Along came television! A tower was built on Buhler Road and E. 4th Street and on July 1, 1953, KTVH, Channel 12 began broadcasting television. This really made quite a negative impact on the movie business.

Those of us that lived in this community attended the three-room Obee School. There were two or three grades in each classroom. There was a music room with a raised stage, which had a large roll-up curtain in front. This canvas curtain was covered with advertisements. We did not have music lessons, but all eight classes would get together monthly and sing. Mrs. Fountain formed the first band with about 12 students in 1950.

Our homes had no natural gas for heat and many heated and cooked with wood and coal. Telephones were wooden and hanging on the walls. They were shared with neighbors on what was called "party lines." Nothing was private because everyone could hear any conversation by simply picking up the receiver. We had certain rings, and could hear others (example: #14K14 had one long ring and four short).

Washday was a full day of work. Heat water on the stove and carry to the wringer washer. Then carry and fill rinse tubs with cold water. After a load finished, the clothes had to be pinned to a clothesline to dry. After the final load was done, the water all had to be emptied. Since there was no such thing as "perm a press," many of the articles would need ironing, usually left for the next day.

Obeeville

The Stool at the Sink
By Diana Dry of Wellington, Kansas
Born 1942

I remember when I was a kid there was no jobs. So my dad and his family, sisters, and brother went to California to work in the shipyards because the war was going on. My mother and I went out after my dad had made some money for us to come. We rode out on the train with soldiers headed to war. I remember my dad said they fed me horsemeat and they had stamps for gas. My sister was born in California. We came back to Kansas after the war was over.

My dad work for the W. P. A. planting trees. Money was hard to come by. He did what he could to put food on the table.

The years passed and I have three sisters and two brothers. We live in the country. Went to a one-room school. One teacher taught eight grades. I remember a boy always acting up. The teacher would whack his hands with a yardstick. He would have to sit in the corner with a pointed hat on. He still acted up. We had outside toilets called "privy."

We got our first T.V. It was black and white. My dad was the only one to operate it when he got home from work. We walk home from school three miles.

We did washing on a wringer washer and hung clothes on a line. We iron our clothes, burn wood to keep warm.

I remember my two brothers. My oldest told the younger brother to open the umbrella, jump off the roof of the house. He always use his little brother as a ginny pig. It didn't work.

You never wanted to get sick because my mother would get out the castor oil that was nasty. Some of the kids had to be held and nose pitch off so they swallowed it.

I remember when a tornado came through my dad tie a rope to the cellar and the house. So all of us were to hang on. So we didn't blow away. My little sister flopped in the wind. I grabbed hold of her. We all made it to the cellar til the storm was over. I remember we moved to town where we saw our first in side bathroom. We never saw a stool before and sink and tub. We ask our dad what the stool was for. He said to wash your feet in. We were told later what it was when we ask where the privy was.

I got a job doing dishes in a restaurant with my best friend and her parents ran it. That's where I got my first kiss from her brother who was cooking. My best friend and I went to a sock hop and I didn't like the things going on so never went to another.

We got our first phone, which weigh 16 pounds. Black rotary. My middle sister got that for her 16th birthday from my dad.

We had bad times but we had good times. Makes you wonder how we all survived. I guess we were all tougher back then.

I even pick cotton with my parents in Texas. After a week, I made $1.00. I was six going on seven years old. My sister rode on the cotton sack that my mother pulled behind her.

The Plight of the Wheat Farmer
By Don Graber of Hutchinson, Kansas
Born 1934

Farming is an occupation that has many privileges as well as risks. I grew up on a farm and from the time that I could remember was outside with my dad, riding on the tractor, going after the cows for milking, etc. My dad raised wheat, cattle, pigs, and chickens.

When I was about four years old, it was near wheat harvest time. Dad and I went to check the ripening of the wheat, and he said, "It looks like we can try to harvest tomorrow." He pulled out the old combine so he could check things over to make sure it would be ready to go. That night, a dark cloud rolled in and we had a terrible hailstorm. On the north side of the house was more than a foot of hail that had rolled off the roof of the house.

The next morning we went out to check how the wheat had fared. There was not a single stalk of wheat standing. In fact, the ground was bare, nothing. Dad said, "I guess our harvesting is done." He pushed the combine back in its place and had to wait until the next year in the hopes of a crop. So is the experience of a wheat farmer!

A number of years later and at a different farm, the wheat had been planted in the fall. This was done in about October, usually. By December it had grown and covered the ground with its rich, dark green foliage. In January, the Canadian geese made their way down to Kansas to avoid the severe cold up north. While here, they got hungry and looked for something to eat. Our nice green wheat field looked very attractive, and they invited themselves to feed on our wheat. There were thousands of them that came swooping down on our field for their dinner. It didn't take long for us to notice that the green was disappearing. My mom was concerned that they would ruin the wheat crop, and she would run out to the field with a broom to chase them away. The geese would all take off, but in a little while they would be back.

By the time the geese left for Canada, the ground was bare and no green was showing. My mom thought for sure that the crop was completely destroyed. However, the roots of the plants were still there, and when spring came the wheat began to grow. It matured and was some of the best crops we raised. And so is the plight of the farmer. He is at the mercy of a lot of different things!

The Day I Saved My Sister's Life
By Jane Keel Sapone of Wanchese, North Carolina
Born 1930

Doloris Lipprand Ungles and Marie Jane Lipprand Keel Sapone in 1932

Growing up on a farm in Russell County, Kansas during the 1930s provided a number of interesting incidents in my life, including having been kicked in the face by one of our work horses, being chased across the pasture by a heifer with horns as she protected her first newborn calf, and even talking my sister into running away from home.

The most memorable event was the day I saved my sister, Doloris' life. It was a balmy summer day with fluffy white clouds floating in the pretty blue sky. Being only four and two years of age, we were too young to help with household chores, so Mama sent us out to play. We had no toys, so what did we do? We got some old zinc fruit jar lids and headed down to the stock tank to make mud pies, even though we had been told never to play there.

The tank was made of cement by our father. It was about eight or ten feet in diameter and perhaps two and a half feet deep with walls six or eight inches wide. There was barbed-wire fence across the center to separate the pasture from the yard. The water was really low that day, so it was quite a stretch to reach down for it. Sister and I proceeded to make our mud pies and successfully reached the water a time or two. About the third time, Sister reached down for water she toppled in headfirst!

I don't know how I knew the meaning of death or being drownded (that's how we pronounced it back then), unless it was from having seen a chicken drowned after having fallen into the tank. Fear gripped my entire being, so I began running up that gently inclined hill toward the house and yelling all the way, "Mama, ditty bodie in da tank!" This was baby talk for, "Sissy fall in the tank!" Fortunately, Mama had all the windows open to help cool the house. There was no electricity back then for fans or air conditioning. Mama came running, with me following closely behind. She jumped into the tank, shoes, and all. Remember, this was the Depression and one did not mistreat their shoes. She lifted Doloris onto the tank's edge, face down. Water came pouring from Doloris' mouth. She finally regained consciousness. What a relief! Mama said that Sister had a huge blue lump on her forehead so she felt Doloris was knocked unconscious when she hit the bottom of the tank, which more than likely kept her from drowning.

People say that I surely couldn't have remembered such an incident at such a tender age, but I remember all too well the feeling of the rush of adrenaline through my entire body, the tight knot of fear in my stomach, and the heavy leaden weight of my short chubby legs while running up that hill.

I don't take full credit for saving Sister's life. God had to have had a hand in it, too. I'm so thankful that all turned out well for our family on that fateful day. Sister and I have been the best of friends all of our lives. A terrible tragedy was turned aside that day due to God and me.

Doloris Lipprand and Marie Jane Lipprand

Store String
By Lois Schroeder of Buhler, Kansas
Born 1934

During the 1920s and 1930s when I was born, disposable diapers were unheard of. The diapers were made from cotton flour sacks. My mom baked all of our breads, cakes, etc. and cooked using flour, therefore flour was purchased in large quantities. Flour came in 50-pound, cotton sacks. These sacks were laundered and used for many things, tea towels, and diapers to name a few. As soon as a mother knew she was expecting a baby, she started sewing diapers from these sacks and as well as homemade baby clothes. The flour sacks were loosely stitched with a thick, cotton string, which, if done right, unraveled easily after the flour sack was empty. The cotton string was saved; the ends were tied into a continuous string and rolled up into a ball. This was called "store string." It had many uses around the house. Children used it to make button yo-yos and attached the string to the toys to pull around the house. Packages were tied with "store string," just a few examples. The flour sacks were hemmed and folded as a diaper. They were not very absorbent. Mom bought thin rubber pants to pull over the diaper to keep it from soaking through. In the summer, this was very hot for the baby and often the baby had diaper rash because the air couldn't circulate through the diaper. The diapers were placed in a kettle or bucket and covered with water to soak and made ready for the laundry day. There was no electricity or running water so, on washday, water was carried in buckets from the well, where the windmill pumped the water out of the ground, and poured into a rendering kettle located in the washhouse. A fire was built under the rendering kettle and water was heated to very hot for the laundry. We had a gas-driven washing machine. The laundry soap was usually homemade lye soap that mother had made for that purpose. She loaded the washing machine with hot water, then shaved some soap off of the lye soap block into the water to dissolve and make soap suds for the dirty clothes. After the wash was swished around in the washing machine and declared clean, it was sent through a hand-cranked wringer into a tub filled with clean water to rinse the soap residue from the wash.

Then it was wrung out once more into a wash basket, usually a lined, wicker-type basket, and ready for the drying process on the wash-line out in the yard. The wash dried beautifully in the breeze. The breeze helped to soften the fabric. It smelled so clean and crisp, BUT in the winter, it was a problem because the wash froze to the wash-line. Mother strung lines throughout the house, where the wash was hung to dry. The children thought it was neat to run in and out of the clothes as they were drying. Mom didn't always appreciate our fun.

Baby clothes were sewn for the new baby. Store-bought clothes were too expensive. The chicken feed came in coarser cotton sacks with different designs stamped on them. Mom sewed dresses and shirts out of these sacks for children of all ages. The white feed sacks were used for underwear.

Toys were made from old socks and yarn. Dad made wooden toys out of old lumber or wood he cut from trees. These were very durable and fun toys to play with.

Terrence Keenan and Dennis Keenan in 1956

Early Spring Blizzard 1957
By Terrence Keenan of Ness City, Kansas
Born 1945

The day was Friday. Spring was a week old. I was awake before dawn. A school day and chores awaited. After milking the cows, taking care of the horse, the pigs were next. They really chomped down on the skim milk and ground maize.

I lived on a farm in northern Stafford County. Great Bend was 12 miles to the north. I was 12 and in the sixth grade at St. Francis Xavier school in Seward, a nearby town. A younger brother, Dennis, was in the fifth grade. He always chose to sleep in. My parents, Pat and Mabel Keenan, along with my brother were at the breakfast table listening to the weather on KVGB Radio in Great Bend. They were warning of early spring storm brewing. The day was Friday, March 30, 1957. The rest of this warm spring day went uneventful, until later that evening. The warm air turned cold, with a strong northerly wind. First, it rained, and then came the sleet and snow.

The electricity went off. The phone lines were dead. Trees were popping. Limbs were everywhere on the ground. The weather got worse. The blizzard raged for three days. But we were fortunate to have a floor furnace supplied by natural gas. Not many farms had natural gas. Since we had producing oil well on the property, a natural gas line ran by the farm. Part of the agreement with the oil company was natural gas at a flat rate. We had fresh water from the windmill, fresh milk, and eggs. Mom baked bread, made her own butter, cheese, and ice cream. Since we separated the milk, there was plenty of cream. Our large freezer was stocked with beef, chicken, and pork. We were in good shape. Finally, the storm ended on Monday.

On Tuesday, the day was clear and we could finally see all of the snow. The roads were impassable. My dad asked me to saddle Red, our bay Morgan, and ride into Seward for the mail and any news about the electricity. The ride into town was amazing. Red went right thru the drifts without a problem. I arrived in town, went to the Post Office to pick up the mail. Along the way, I noticed all of the power and telephone poles were down and lines laid on the ground. At the Post Office I found out power would be a long time coming. Hopefully, they would get the town in power in two weeks.

Our farm was another matter. We were on the end of a "J," meaning that we would be last. Our power came from the REA in Great Bend. I returned home with the mail and the news. After two weeks, power was restored in Seward, and school came along with it. We were still without power at the farm. Finally, in May, six weeks later the power came on. That was a day to rejoice.

During the six weeks, my folks and brother played 10-point pitch to a kerosene lamp. My brother and I played endless hours of checkers. My dad provided some music with his violin. He also finished reading the Bible. My mom worked crossword puzzles and finished her hand sewing. There was an east-west road just south of our farm with a shelterbelt on the south side. Finally, in May, the snowplow got thru. When I think back to that time. We did not have the Internet, I-pads, or TV, even radio due to no power. We had everything. We were warm, had plenty to eat and drink. And the best thing of all, the best company in the world, my parents, and my brother.

Patrick Keenan and Mabel Keenan in 1957

The Dog Poop Game
By Judy Farris of Garden City, Kansas

When I was a kid growing up in Hutchinson, Kansas until the age of 13, then we moved to Garden City, Kansas.

We had a party line phone service, where the phone number was shared by several others. I think our ring was one long and two short rings. A lot of times, you could hear the others listening in on your calls.

When we finally got our own number, we were teenagers. We were allowed to only talk for three minutes (set an egg timer) because my dad said it was a business line.

My mother had a wringer washer, seem like clothes were cleaner back then. She had to be careful when she bent over to run the clothes thru the ringer so she wouldn't get herself caught in the ringer.

My mother always made our clothes, she was an excellent seamstress. Once my sister was griping because we had homemade clothes. My dad said, "Well then build your own." (Ha, ha)

I attended school in the first grade. There were six rows of desks. One row was for the first graders, next was second graders, etc. I don't know how the teacher taught all six grades at the same time. She had a good hand; some of the boys would get an eraser throwed at them for acting up.

Back then, it seemed like we always had blizzards. We would play in the snow; pull each other on hoods of cars, which was used for sleds. We always played "King of the Mountain." The snowdrifts were always piled up very high.

In the summertime, all kids played outside. We climbed trees, had a rope like Tarzan, swinging over and landing on a dirt pile.

Our most main and fun game was putting dog poop on a stick and chasing others. We sure learned how to run fast and sway to keep from getting it on us.

We grew up watching Elvis. After school, we (and the neighbors) would lay on my parents' bed to watch TV in their room and just scream when he sang a song. He is still very popular today in my house.

I had a Panasonic record player and always played the same old record over and over. The Monkeys and the Beatles, along with Elvis, was my favorites.

We walked three miles to town just to get a coke and go to Woolsworth Store. Some businesses had elevators and doormen back then. I remember going to the Wiley building and taking the elevator up and down to different floors. The doorman never said anything. I remember him wearing a tan suit. He always opened the elevator door for us.

Everyone laughs now when I still say "ice box," they all look at me like what it that!

We had Myers Milk & Ice Cream truck come by weekly. We always ate ice cream when the Newlywed Game came on.

I always like when my folks tell us about their "good ole days." Once someone gave them sandwiches from some occasion. Was told to share it with another family. Well, they did, but they took the meat and left the other family the bread. This was back in the Dirty Thirties during Depression.

When I was 16 got a car. My brother-in-law was showing me and my sister how to check the oil and water in our batteries. Well, stupid me read, "Add 1 QT." I said, "Oh my gosh, it says to add one quick." I thought he was gonna roll forever laughing. Then my sister was going to stick her finger in the battery to see when the water was. He pulled hand back laughing and said, "You don't do that."

We spent the night once with our grandma. We got our socks dirty while playing outside and didn't say anything until the next morning when we were getting ready for school. "Too late to wash them now," Grandma said. She dug thru an old trunk and pulled out her son-in-law's knee-high, green, Army socks. I had to wear them to school with brown shoes. Back in them days, the girls wore dresses to school.

I waited tables for 90 cents an hour. Tips were very good back then. When we had a party to work, the tip percentage was six percent.

Runaway Horse
By Cecile M. Thomison Shoemaker of
Wichita, Kansas
Born 1930

I grew up in the 1930s in Wichita, Kansas on Mathewson Street off of E. Central Avenue. We had no fans and burned coal in the stove. There were six of us kids, two boys, and four girls. We didn't realize we were poor and enjoyed life. There were many incidents I remember. Some funny, some exciting, and some sad.

Us kids all did chores. One was emptying the pan under the icebox that caught the water when the ice melted. If it ran over then one of us had to mop the kitchen floor. Us girls did the dishes before we left for school. I was in a hurry one morning and forgot to take off my every day dress. I put on my school dress over it, but when I got to school, everyone started laughing at me. I looked down and my every day dress was hanging a foot below my school dress. I was embarrassed. The teacher sent me in the coat closet and I changed. There was always a lot of ironing to be done. My older sister, Dean, was blind in one eye so missed spots and wrinkles and my younger sister, Elda, was too small. When I was 11, I was ironing a bushel or more of sprinkled clothes. I did learn to iron very well.

Bus fare was five cents to ride to downtown Wichita. We hardly ever took the bus and walked to school, to church, to the park and anywhere we wanted to go. In the summer we would pack a lunch and put my younger brother, Charley, (born after my sister, Catherine, passed away) in the wagon and walk to Riverside Park, a mile or so. Go look at the animals in cages, play, and eat lunch. We also went some evenings to the park and seen free movies.

My uncle had horses. One day he came over with a horse and told my dad it was tame and us girls could ride it. My sister and I got on the horse for a ride to the end of the block. My uncle said when we got back to pull on the reins and the horse would stop. I pulled on the reins and the horse took off on a gallop right down Central Avenue. I was up around the horse's neck and sis back by the tail. My dad got on the front of a car and stopped the horse a few blocks down at Bonds Bakery. I never wanted to get on a horse again, it scared me so bad. Of course, anyone on the streets were all laughing.

My brother, Cy, a year younger then me was ornery and always doing crazy things. He went to Boy Scout camp for a week. When he came home, he told mom he brought her a pet. He brought in a gunnysack and opened it and a skunk ran out. What an awful smell. I think he got a lickin' over that. One day he told my younger brother they were playing cowboys and Indians. He dug a large hole in the back yard and buried my brother up to his neck. My brother started yelling and mom came out and ended that in a hurry. There were empty lots of ground across the street on Central. The Barnum & Bailey Circus would come every year. My brothers would get jobs feeding and watering the elephants. All the side shows were 10 cents. They would find quite a few dimes people lost in the sawdust. Also, the Army camped there three days once. They left orange flags that marked their area. Mom sent the boys over to get the flags and made them shirts out of the flags.

In 1935, when I was five years old, my sister Catherine was born. She was beautiful with dark brown hair and brown eyes. One morning, in 1936, mom was doing the wash on the wringer washing machine in the kitchen. We were all at the breakfast table and Catherine was in her high chair. All of a sudden, she twisted around and stuck her hand in the wringer. It drew her arm in before mom could hit the release on top of the machine. My uncle was there and him and mom took her to the county hospital. The doctor said she would be ok as her tissue was soft and the bones hadn't developed. They put her in a ward with six or seven babies. One had scarlet fever. My sister was weak and caught the disease. She passes away a week later. It was so sad.

Our family started attending church after her death.

A Day in the Life of a Boy
By Clement A. Smith of Haysville, Kansas
Born 1924

I grew up on a farm outside Dearing, Kansas. It was a two-bedroom house with no electricity or running water on about one and a half acres. We would carry water from the well each day. Dad built in a porch where my brother and I slept, and my two sisters slept in the bedroom.

We had two cows and two hogs. We had chickens that provided eggs and eventually ended up on the table for dinner. We would

Clement, Jean, Charles, and Margaret in 1935

feed and milk the cows and feed the chickens and hogs each morning and night.

We also had a large garden that provided the vegetables. All four of us worked in the garden, planting, weeding, watering, and picking, because Dad worked at a refinery during the day.

We would get up early to do our chores before school, and then walk the one and a half miles to school. Once in a while, our teacher would stop and pick up as many of us as would fit in the car. The rest would have to walk all the way. We went to a one-room country schoolhouse. It held all grades through the eighth. We sat in chairs at desks by age groups. We would take sandwiches and milk for lunch. At recess, we would run and play games. Once I got in a fight with a boy and the next thing I knew, my sister, Margaret was pulling him off of me. I was about six or seven, and our mother had died when I was only five. Margaret helped take care of me. She was a good big sister.

After school, we would walk home and do our chores. On hot days after we worked in the garden, my brother and I would run down to the river, strip down, and go swimming. We would climb out after, get dressed, and run home.

Usually we boys helped with the outside chores while Margaret helped our stepmother cook the evening meal. When we were a bit older, we all took turns, with two of us cooking and the other two cleaning up. I learned to be a pretty good cook.

After dinner was cleared, we would play card games or checkers. If there were batteries, we would listen to the radio. Later, they built a new house with electricity and running water.

We would bring in water, heat it on the stove, and take a bath in the washtub once each week. We all learned to iron and wash our clothes and even darn socks and sew buttons.

When winter came and it was cold and snowy, we boys would help Dad cut and split wood and carry it inside to the wood stove that heated the whole house. We would sleep in our socks under a lot of blankets. We boys would do the outside chores while the girls helped inside and then we walked to school in the snow.

We boys learned how to embroider and help our grandmother make quilt squares to help keep us warm. That came in handy for me to make a bit of money selling dresser scarves and doilies I had embroidered.

Life was really different in those days. It was very hard at times, but we made it through. All of it helped make me the man I am today at almost 90 years old.

Written as told by Clement by his daughter, Carol.

My Brothers and I Rode a Horse to School Every Morning
By Norma Caldwell of Ingalls, Kansas

During the 1940s, my father still kept a few horses. He owned a team of workhorses, which I recall being used briefly to pull a wagon as grain was being harvested and thrown into the wagon. He always kept a couple of riding horses for use with livestock and also for use as transportation to and from school. As children we often rode the horses for enjoyment, racing with each other, going for the mail a half mile down the road, or just riding. At the age of eight or nine, I was riding a gentle horse, but I was not very brave and did not like riding a spirited horse. Many times, we rode bareback and had to bring the horse alongside a fence or barrel in order to mount. Other time we would just help each other get on. We also rode calves, which gave a real challenge for us to stay on their backs without a bridle. I got quite good at staying on their backs as long as they stayed out from under the trees. I very much enjoyed playing with my brothers and especially Earl.

My two older brothers were already in school, which was located approximately three miles from our home. They were riding a horse to school when I began first grade. When the time came for me to enter first grade, I was also put on the horse.

The name of our horse was Doc. He was white with brown spots. He carried a scar on his neck from a rattlesnake bite, which he survived. He was a very gentle horse and very good for children to learn to ride.

The memories and events of happenings in the saddle are precious to me. One day while riding a horse to school on a wintry day, the snow was about 18 inches deep and had crusted over. The crust was strong enough to hold us and even hold the horse until all three of us got on. We were heading up the road to school and Doc was doing just fine on the crusted snow. Suddenly his rear hooves broke through the top crust of snow. This frightened the horse as well as us. As the horse was struggling to get his footing back up on the snow, my brother slid off the rear end of the horse, landing in the snow. This was a very difficult trip for the horse as he kept breaking through the snow. He was faithful and he continued on with a heavy load on his back.

On another occasion, my two brothers and I were coming home from school. We had taken another route and were about a mile from home when suddenly the cinch belt, which kept the saddle in place, slipped to the side, dumping all three of us to the ground. Apparently, my brothers had failed to fasten the cinch belt securely. I was quite young, being probably in the first or second grade. The boys tightened the cinch belt and got back on the horse, but I refused, so I had to walk home alone. Needless to say, I cried all the way.

Another incident happened during and after school thunderstorm. The clouds were black and ominous. Suddenly we were engulfed by a severe thunder and lightning storm. We had no place to stop and wait for the storm to pass, so we kept on riding. Suddenly our father appeared on another horse and helped escort us home. I rode with my father and my brothers kept riding on their horse. I can remember the thunder booming loudly and the lightning flashing. I sensed fear in my father each time the lightning would strike which of course frightened me as well. We dashed for home as fast as we could and arrived there without incident, although quite wet.

When my sister Josie started school, she was put on the horse too. That meant four of us on one horse. The horse said no and bucked us off. I think that was when we quit riding a horse to school.

While at school, our horses were kept in an old, red barn. We fed them hay during the day and the boys also watered the horses.

Horses were not only used for transportation and recreation but for other activities on the farm. The era of using horses has left many memories of days gone by, but we are constantly making new memories for the generations that are yet to come. May we live to make these memories pleasant to those generations.

The Galvanized Tub
By Darlene McMillion of Stafford, Kansas
Born 1936

A galvanized tub was usually given to a newly married couple as a wedding gift, and if they were lucky, they might even get two tubs. A galvanized washtub was one of the most versatile objects on the farm, so every family needed at least one. I really don't know how Mom and Dad got their tubs. Perhaps they were gifts or maybe they were purchased later as the need arose. If I recall correctly, we had two or three on our farm. Our tubs never stayed in their place for long, wherever that place might be, as they had a use almost every day.

On Monday, Mom took a tub or two down from the wash house wall or off the old picnic table and scrubbed them until they were clean. She filled one with clear water and one with bleach water, which she used for "rinching" (Mom's word). If she wanted some clothes to be even whiter, she might add a bit of "bluing" to a bucket of water and dunk them into it before the final rinsing. Every homemaker wanted to have the whitest wash in the country hanging on her outside clothesline, so this blue liquid, which could be purchased at the country store, was the magic potion that "took the yellow out" of the clothing.

All during the wash day morning, loads of clothes were washed, dunked in and out of the tubs of cool rinse water, passed through the wash machine ringer, then hung on the line to dry. When all the washing was done, one of the tubs was turned into a "mop tub" and was used to clean the floor in the washhouse. The leftover water was perfect for the job. After the washing was done, the tubs was again rinsed out and turned upside down or hung up to drain.

On Tuesday, the galvanized tub might be forgotten while we ironed all the clothes, unless Dad decided to go fishing in the nearby pond. If that was the case, a tub of cold spring water was the perfect place to keep his fish until Mom was ready to clean them.

The 'ole tubs were taken down again when we needed large containers to hold our garden vegetables. I remember sitting in the shade around a tub, snapping and snapping and snapping all the green beans that had been we had gathered early that morning.

During the canning season, we carried loads and loads of fruit jars up from the cellar,

A galvanized washtub

checked them for nicks, and then washed them in a tub out on the lawn. Sometimes if the old, black kettle wasn't handy, a washtub was filled with scalding water and used for skinning beets or tomatoes. In the fall, we filled the tubs with water and dunked peaches and apples before pealing them.

When the bees swarmed on a hot day in June, Dad got on all his paraphernalia and robbed their hives. He placed all the honeycomb in tubs and brought them to the house where we extracted the honey.

On hot summer days, we often filled a tub with water and let it sit out in the sun until we were ready for our evening baths. The "solar heated" water was perfect. I have a picture of my baby sister playing in a tub of warm water, which was sitting in the yard. Dad and the boys often took their baths out in the yard, using a tub of warm water, heated by the sun.

In late November or early December, when it was time to kill hogs, we cleaned all our washtubs and filled them with different cuts of meat. We ground the smaller pieces of meat into sausage, which we mixed with our hands in the tubs.

There were many, many uses for the galvanized washtub. If one was cared for properly, it could be used many years as a household utensil and after that be taken to the barn or chicken house to be used as a feed or water container for the animals. After several years of use at the barn, it might finally be abandoned and dumped on a rock pile in a deep gully somewhere on the backside of the farm. Then, one day many years later, some antique collector might discover it sitting idly alone atop the trash pile and be delighted with his discovery; whereupon he might recover it, take it home, polish and paint it, fill it with flowers, then put it in a prominent place in the house or yard to be admired and exclaimed over by every visitor.

Yes, a galvanized tub was a valuable object in days gone by. Some of them probably lasted 100 years before being completely abandoned. Even though they have been replaced with various stainless steel or aluminum pots and pans, the 'ole tubs have not been forgotten. Today, if you look closely, you might even find some reproduced ones for sale, sitting on a shelf or in the floor of a modern farm store. Whether the new ones are better or not—only time will tell.

Goosecumbers
By Jana Sibley Finkbiner of Wichita, Kansas
Born 1944

My sister and I were idly strolling through the aisles of the Wichita flower show. Although we both enjoyed gardening, we tended to rely on the dependable, undemanding geraniums, marigolds, and zinnias that could withstand Kansas's hot winds and dry summers. So we admired the exotic blooms that demanded careful attention and lavish watering, while realizing we weren't willing to make that kind of horticultural commitment.

The dried flower arrangements caught my eye. I admired the imaginative combinations of materials—weeds, many of them—that made up the wreaths and other displays, and tried to identify some of the flowers and grasses. Those were dried water lily pods, and there were some lovely filigreed sweetgum pendants, and…

"Peggy, see what they've used here!"

She turned toward me and then looked beyond at the dried arrangement. Her eyes brightened and we stared at each other.

"Goosecumbers!"

In 1949, when Peggy was nearly four and I was not yet six, our little family moved to southwest Kansas. We had always lived in the western half of the state, but this move took us into the far corner, to Feterita. We were nearer Oklahoma and Colorado than to most of the Kansas towns we had known, and only 30 miles of Oklahoma panhandle separated us from west Texas. People still talked about range wars and told tales of county seats being moved overnight when one town's ruffians stole the county charter from another town's solid citizens. Our nearest town was Hugoton, regionally famous as the center of the greatest natural gas field in the world.

Feterita wasn't a town; with only two houses and the grain elevator Daddy managed, it didn't even qualify as a settlement. If you've ever driven across Kansas you've surely noticed these lone elevators—prairie skyscrapers, we like to call them. These days most of them don't have housing nearby. But our Feteria house, along with the chicken coop and a few other little sheds, sat somewhat east of the elevator, next to the windmill. The yard was packed dirt, but it was fenced and there were huge cottonwood trees nearby. West of us, on the other side of the highway, was Mr. and Mrs. Fiddler's home. Their two girls were near our ages.

We all played outdoors during the short springs and shorter falls and during the hot summers. We played house and graded narrow roads to our little farms and played with the kittens and chicks and with Lady, a beautiful little fox terrier who had large hairy boyfriends and frequent litters of large furry puppies. Sometimes Daddy would take us on the lift to the top of the elevator, where we could see the far horizon, flat in every direction, the highway and railroad tracks disappearing into a shimmering haze.

We went barefoot, and were nearly always grimy from the grassless yard, the blowing dust and stinging sand, and from the games we played. The bottoms of our feet were hardened and tough. But toughened feet were no match for cockleburs and sandburs and, especially, devil's claws. These were split dried pods about three inches long, with each side of the split ending in a curling, woody, five-inch spike. They looked like weird, otherworld insects, and seemed to reach out and grab us around the ankles as we ran through the arid landscape surrounding our home.

The Fiddler girls told us these dried pods were called "goosecumbers." It seemed a strange name for the wicked things, but goosecumbers they were. It was several years before I realized other people called them "devil's claws," which was certainly a more appropriate name. Even Mother and Daddy came to refer to them as goosecumbers, while wondering out loud where in the world the Fiddler girls came up with that strange word.

In the late winter of 1953 we left Feterita. We had acquired a baby sister while we were there, and another baby was on the way. Our new home was nearer the center of the state. After a few years, and a few more sisters, we moved again to southwest Kansas, although not as far west as Feterita had been. Then Daddy's work took us to a small town 50 miles south of Kansas City. From then on, my heart belonged to the green hills and trees, and to the lakes and rivers of eastern Kansas, and I have lived in the eastern half of the state ever since. I like my comfort, and the harsher west holds little temptation for me.

Jana Sibley Finkbiner in about 1951

But the dried arrangement at that flower show, with those cleverly positioned curling pods, brought a rush of memories, while I thought, "I'd like some of those to put in an arrangement of my own." However, subsequent trips through western Kansas—usually en route to a Colorado vacation— showed me a cleaned-up country. The sagebrush and milkweed and yucca—and the goosecumbers—were no longer crowding onto the highways. So I did without my dried pods until last year, when Bob and I stopped to read a historical marker. At the base of the sign, there they were, two of them, poking their tails into the sand, the woody tentacles reaching for me. My husband, a farm-raised boy who knows a noxious weed and pest when he sees one, thought I was crazy for hauling those oddities home. But I wanted them for my rock garden. And they were perfect, one hooked into a porous rock and the other curling around a cactus. My goosecumbers!

This past spring an odd little plant appeared in the rock garden. This isn't unusual in our gardens, as Bob's policy is to let strange things grow until he determines what they are and whether they will be allowed to stay. This looked like a squash or pumpkin plant, and eventually grew much larger and put forth some pale pink flowers. But finally it began bearing some sort of fruit—a gourd, I thought. As I looked closer, the gourd looked strange and yet familiar. Its shape resembled a crookneck squash, except the small end has a definite curl to it.

I hurried into the house, "Bob, I think I know what that funny plant is. It's a goosecumber!"

Bob had never known the Fiddler girls, but he knew what I meant. "Do you think so? We'd better pull it out, then."

"Don't you dare! Those things are hard to find—they're collectibles! I'm going to use them in dried flower arrangements!"

As the strange plant continued to grow and add more and more little gourds, we kept changing our minds. Bob decided it couldn't be a goosecumber plant, and I had my doubts. After all, it did look squash like, and squash don't turn into hard little pods; they just get squishy and rotten as they get old. I decided it was just an ordinary wild gourd that would decompose in the fall.

Late summer was drawing near when I looked closely at the plant again. It was getting larger and spreading, and I thought, "We really should pull this thing out before the neighbors complain." Then I saw it, partially hidden by soil and shriveled leaves. A gourd had split and dried, and formed its long pointed claws; a goosecumber was skulking next to my tame green lawn.

Peggy drove by to see the notorious plant. As we admired the sprawling thing, a sudden thought came to me. I looked at the slightly fuzzy green gourds, with their fat little bottoms tapering and curling. "They look like a cross between a goose…"

"…and a cucumber!" she cried.

I have no idea where the Fiddler girls are today. Would they be pleased to know it took us 50 years to figure them out?

The Gizzard Gold Ring
By Roy F. Parker of Derby, Kansas
Born 1944

For sure, "Those were the good old days," the days when you were away from everything busy, evil, dangerous, frustrating, or loud. I had no responsibilities except for the chores that were given to me by my dad or mom. I would spend hours on the old pedal-powered grinding wheel where I would grind bolts until the outsides of the stone wheel were rounded off. My time was usually spent in the sand pile where roads were created with Tonka trucks and earthmovers. These roads would cross over lakes and rivers and valleys, go

Roy F. Parker

Roy Parker

into the sides of great hills then back down to the starting place and then rebuilt again. There was a field to the east of our house where I would fly my homemade kite with the long tail. Beyond that field was the Cowskin Creek where I would spend endless hours catching bullheads and carp. I used a cane pole and a ball of string found in my dad's garage and a hook. There was a natural spring, which came out of the ground near that creek, and I left my dad's spade shovel nearby to dig my worms.

For a short time, we used the outhouse, which was located west of our garage. It was a two-holer and my dad used to say that it was a sign of prosperity. At night, it was spooky to go to the outhouse. There was a pathway leading to that old, gray silhouette standing there waiting to be used. As we approached and opened the spring-loaded door, we would feel the top of that surface to see if there were any snakes there just waiting for us. We did our business quickly and ran back to the house. Before long, we got inside plumbing into that old house. My uncle was a finish carpenter so he fixed things to look like a fancy room with a porcelain stool that flushed everything away. It was equipped with a tub, where my sister and I would take baths together. We were still in the tub one night when her jealousy over my long eyelashes got the best of her and she tried to cut them with pinking shears and then got me on the stool and threatened to flush me away. My screams brought my parents to my rescue.

Our telephone number was 5-0-8 and we were on a party line with about three other families. We had to use the crank on the side of the wooden phone to call our operator, Meb, in a nearby town. In one of those families, the mother would listen to all of our calls. We could hear her breathing. The ring at our phone was long-short-long and usually it was something pretty serious to get a call. My grandfather lived with us and was always falling. Once he pulled down our towel rack and bumped his head on the sink. When he wasn't falling, he would be chewing a piece of plug tobacco and wolling it around in his mouth. When it was time to spit, he would go to the "east door" of that old white house and let her fly. If it was windy it would get all over the east side of our house and my dad had to occasionally go out with a bucket of soapy water and a scrub brush to clean it up for my mom's sake.

My mother was a wonderful cook. She grew up in an era where they ate brains and eggs—I never was that brave. Some of my favorite breakfasts were fried mush, eggs in a nest, milk toast, hot coco, French toast, and homemade waffles. Since we raised our own beef, we had lots of great meat dishes… steaks, ribs, roasts, and a lot of ground beef. She also prepared liver and baked heart, which I loved. All of our meals were around the table. Our doctor was "Old Doc Beale," who lived and worked in a town 15 miles away. He would simply recommend a mustard plaster for congestion and a squirt of castor oil for constipation.

My father loved animals and you could tell it by the one that roamed around our place—a dozen hogs, 20 sheep with a ram that would try to butt me. He had a dozen milking cows named "Helen" and he milked them by hand. He would take his one-legged stool in one hand and a three-gallon bucket in the other and set at "Helen's" right side. As he milked, my job was to feed these old cows some grain and molasses. I ate molasses by the hand full and my cheek looked like the milk man's cheek. He spit stuff out and I didn't. He could take a 10-gallon can of milk in one hand and one in the other and with one swift movement lift them into the back of his truck. When I fed dad's cows I would listen to the great, old radio programs like "Our Miss Brooks," "Amos and Andy," "The Lone Ranger," and "The Shadow." We had chickens, two horses named "Babe," and guinea hens that were our best watch dogs. At times, we had calves to feed by hand and, when they got big enough, the boys from our neighborhood would come and we would have a rodeo, which didn't please my dad. He didn't want us to rope and ride his calves.

It took a lot of chickens to feed all of our hired help. We ate a lot of fried chicken. My mom would use those old, cast iron skillets three times a day. I've even seen her popcorn in them. There was just something special about her fried chicken cooked in lard. We had a ton a chickens. One house was full of "fryers" or young roosters. The hens were kept in a separate building along with the "layers." My chores were to keep all of them fed and watered and gather the eggs daily. To make this more appealing my dad bought me a galvanized bucket and painted my name on the side of it. This bucket was to gather the eggs. Once I went out to gather eggs and this old hen wouldn't move for me. She just sat there and tried to pick my hand every time I reached out. So I slowly slipped my hand under her and there was a black snake coiled up staying warm. Once, late at night, I had forgotten to water the chickens and my dad sent me out in the dark to water them. I used the yard light to do this, but my sister turned the light off while I was a long way away from the house and I started screaming, to her great joy. On a given day, my mom would say, "Now go out there and get me a dozen of those fryers…the biggest ones you can find and take their heads off." I had a special #9 wire with a hook on the end of it. I could swing that hook out and snatch a young rooster in a flash. My goal was to have all 12 of them dancing without their heads at one time. This part seemed comical to me, as they set off headless across the yard flopping. Next, we had to dunk them in boiling water, peel off the feathers, pin feathers, and wash them. My mom would sit on the front step and cut these fryers in perfect pieces and start frying for the men at lunch time. One time we found a little, gold ring in a gizzard and thought that this was the greatest find. All of our laundry was hung on clothes lines to dry and had to be in before dark.

One day I made the announcement that I was running away from home. My parents didn't even bat an eye. My mom prepared a picnic lunch for me and packed it into a bandana and my dad brought in a straight stick from outside and tied the bandana to the end of it and told me how to dress. They told me that it would soon be cold out there near the Cowskin Creek. They thought I needed a hat to shield my eyes against the sun. They told me to carry this jar of water because I would soon get thirsty. They kissed me good bye and sent me out. By now, I wasn't really sure, but I was committed. I got as far as one of our grain bins and ate my PB&J and drank my water. Now what? I stayed gone for about 30 minutes and came home, ready to do my chores.

When I was six my parents dressed me up and put me on this big, yellow bus and sent me off to this thing called school. Some girl chased me on the playground every day. When I told the people on the ends of the jump rope "faster," I really didn't mean that fast. I was perfectly content to stay in the sand pile at home and play with my sister. Once, my sister and I filled our pockets with baby mice and my mom found them all crunched up in the laundry. We could make mud pies, wade in the mud puddles, and collect buckets of tadpoles and tomato cans full of fish worms. We could hand-pump water out of my grandmother's well and stand on our heads to entertain her. But they told me I had to go to school. I was the first one on the bus in the morning and the last one off in the evening. One of my school mates was my neighbor, Mack, who showed up at my door one day and told me that his parents had given him permission to dig a swimming pool and if I wanted to swim in it, I had to come and help dig. We still don't have that pool dug. When I was in the third grade, the boys came up with a great prank. One at a time we boys would go up to sharpen our pencil and ask the teacher if we could go to the bathroom. What fun…and before long we were all in

Roy with his catch

there, telling jokes and congratulating each other. Our teacher came in to our bathroom and Jack said, "You can't come in here." Very casually, she said, "I think it is time to come back to class now." We all trailed into the room where she had us form a line. One at a time, we came to the front of the class room with all of the girls and took our swats with a tetherball paddle. I was the last one so I got an extra one. In the sixth grade, one of my classmates shot a hole in the bathroom window with something new called a spoke gun. We all carried a yo-yo or a bag of marbles.

As school progressed, I got into sports at school and my father felt I had betrayed him. There were school dances and school parties and there were these new things called GIRLS! Maybe school wasn't too bad after all. I think it was at a New Year's party when I was forced to kiss the girl nearest to me. I had to do it.

Living on the farm was a good life. There were times when I really wanted to be dancing or swimming but there was so much plowing to do that this was impossible. My dad said that we wouldn't be going to California and Seattle if I didn't get the plowing done. It became the incentive to get the plowing done. Today I review all what we did when on the farm and think that it was a very good life. Yes, those were the good old days.

Old Derby and a New Church
By Milton B. Moore, Sr. of Derby, Kansas
Born 1921

In the year of 1871, Mr. Garrett and his family came to what is now called Derby. They stopped on Spring Creek and built a sod house and dugout on the creek. Later, in 1880, the city of Derby was platted and named El Paso after a town in Illinois named El Paso. The Santa Fe Railroad changed the name to Derby due to mail mix-ups and problems. The Derby name was officially changed from El Paso to Derby in 1956. In 1890, the population of Derby was 236. In 1950, the population was 432. In 2010, the population of Derby was 22,158. Derby's first city manager was elected in 1981. The town hall was built in the 1880s and the first senior center was built in 1970. The fire department was organized in 1953. The first police chief was elected in 1955. The first school district was organized in 1872.

The first time I ever saw Derby was in 1933. My dad had a job in Douglas, and we were on our way there. I was only twelve years old. We left Wichita on Kansas Highway 15, which was Oliver and went south to 63rd Street on Sand Road, turned east on 63rd to Buckner, then south into Derby. As we came into town, on the east side of the street was a brick Presbyterian Church with a cluster of bells in the tower. These bells rang every Sunday morning and could be heard all over town.

Just south of the church was a small gas station with two pumps with a sand driveway. South of it was a long two story hotel that needed a paint job bad. It had a long porch the length of the hotel. Across the street from the church was a feed store with farm supplies, etc.

South of it was the Farmers and Merchants State Bank. Philo Butterfield was the banker. The bank has a story. It was robbed one time. Everyone was made to lie on the floor. The robbers, two of them, took the money and Mr. Butterfield and drove west to Hydraulic Street, where they put Mr. Butterfield out and sped away. He wrote the license plate number down on the sleeve of his shirt.

South of the bank was the two-story town hall building and south of it was a small café. This is where we stopped to get a drink. The walls were covered with matchbook covers. South of it was the street that crossed the Big Arkansas River for about a mile and dead-ended to a north-south road. At this location was a little red schoolhouse, which still stands there. North and west of this were peach and apple orchards.

In Derby east of Kansas Highway 15 about a half mile on the Rose Hill Road was the school, which now houses the historical museum. It is very interesting to go through. It was formed by Deral Butterfield. The school gymnasium in those days was used for pie suppers, cakewalks, square dances, and amateur contests. Many people came from all around to these events.

In 1941, things began to change. Gas prices jumped from five cents a gallon to ten cents a gallon, milk went up from five cents a quart and Beech Aircraft, Cessna and Boeing began to grow. My job at Beech Craft was a good one. I started at forty cents an hour. I went to serve my country in 1944 and spent my time in the Infantry 41st Division. I came back to work for Boeing. We bought a three-bedroom brick house built by Jack Hunt on El Paso Street for $4800.00 in 1954.

One evening some men came by from Sharon Baptist Church and asked me if we would help start a church. We agreed. We acquired the town hall for the church, all met, and went to work. We tore paper off the walls, built a fire escape up the south side to a window out of 2x12 lumber, cleaned, and painted. We carried a donated upright piano up the stairs where the seating was to be. John White was pastor and Agnes Barton was the music director. This building is now in cow town with the fire escape still on it. Names I remember are Schrichfield, John Barton, Audry Altom, and Mr. Bell. In cow town, you can still hear "Amazing Grace" being sung in that old building. Most of the people who helped start the church have passed on, but the church, Pleasantview Baptist still remains and has a wonderful pastor, Don Mayberry and some wonderful Christian people.

Small Town Happening
By Merrill R. Deck of Muldrow, Oklahoma
Born 1934

The following story is an event that happened in 1950. The story is true and only the names will be withheld. The two towns that are involved are Protection and Bucklin. We were sophomores in high school at the time. As you read this story, it is important to understand that, at this time in history in our locale, one of the greatest sins a young person could indulge in was the partaking of an alcoholic beverage. It is also important to note that most "town students" did not own their own vehicles. We got to use the family car when the folks were not using it and/or when older siblings were not using it. Thus, the losing the right of usage for us for a month was a monumental setback to our social lives.

Setting the Stage
One Saturday night, four of us decided to go to one of the famous "Saturday Night Dances" held in various towns in the area. The information that we had was that the dance was to be held at Bucklin. We obtained a six-pack of liquid refreshments, and the four of us headed to Bucklin in one of the boys' parent's car. When we arrived in Bucklin, we drug main for a while. In the process, we finished some of the beverages, crushed the cans, and discarded the empty cans out the window. We then proceeded to go into the corner drug store where one of the local Bucklin girls was working. We learned that the Saturday night dance that had been scheduled for Bucklin had been changed to Greensburg. We then proceeded to go to Greensburg to the dance and then on back home.

Approximately four days later, the parents who owned the car received a summons from the court in Bucklin. The summons specified that the car owner, the four boys, and the other parents were to appear in court on a specified date. The summons notice thus made it necessary for us to tell our parents of the consuming of the liquid refreshments, plus the discarding of the cans along Main Street. Naturally, many tears and lectures occurred.

Courtroom Scene
On the specified date, we boys, along with our parents, did appear in court in Bucklin. As I recall, the court was held upstairs of one of the buildings in town. The judge called for the four occupants of the car to go up front and stand and face their parents and a few others in the room. The judge then read the charge to us and asked us to plead guilty or innocent to the charge. The charge was the act of urinating on a public street. One can only imagine the facial expressions of all those present in the courtroom. I am sure the most shocked were the four of us.

The Scene of the Crime
When we had gone out of the drugstore, the other three occupants said they had to urinate before getting into the car to head to Greensburg. I told them that there was a woman and child in a pick-up parked beside us, and they replied something like, "Aw, so what?" I did not feel the need to go so I did not urinate. We then got into the car and went on to the dance in Greensburg. The woman, upon witnessing the deed, had proceeded to get the license tag number and get in touch with the night marshal.

Answering the Plea Charge
I was the third boy in line when the

charge was read to us. The first two answered guilty, and I answered not guilty. The last boy answered guilty. The judge then asked if it was correct that I was innocent. The others verified my answer. The judge's reply was words to the effect that the evidence showed that one was innocent. In other words, there were just three moist spots at the site. Again, one can only visualize the expressions on the faces.

Final Result

As I recall, the final outcome was that the three guilty parties had to pay a one-dollar fine and two dollars for court charges. The ironical and comical thing about the whole affair was that we would never have had to confess to our parents that we had been drinking the beverages and throwing the cans out of the window. If the summons had stated the charge, it probably would have saved a lot of parents' tears and the resulting lectures.

Aside

The most amusing thing about the complete affair was to have seen the looks on everyone's faces when the judge mentioned the bit about "checking the evidence and seeing three small puddles." There was no indecent exposure involved, as the guilty parties did their deeds on the side of our car away from the occupied vehicle.

The Three Generation Excursion
By Bernice Steinmetz of Colorado Springs, Colorado
Born 1931

The three generation excursion was a trip that my children, Lennie, Randy, and Genie and their cousins, Debbie, Steve, and Brenda remember and laugh about. Their ages now range from 48 to 62. Think about it, nine people in a four-door car with no seat belts. It can't be done in this day and age. It would be illegal. But it is still a very pleasant memory.

In the fall of 1966, Mom and Daddy came to visit us in Holcomb, Kansas, which was not unusual. They came to visit often. This time, however, was different for a couple of reasons; they had purchased a new Buick, Mom's favorite brand of car. It was a 1966 white, four-door Electra, a real beauty. Mom and I were visiting at some point and she suggested a trip to central Kansas to visit family during the summer of 1967. Even this was not unusual since Mom and Daddy were very good about keeping in touch with their siblings and families as we (Nadine, Robert, and I) were growing up. They were always busy on the farm but never too busy for family. The difference about this trip would be three generations in one vehicle. It was exciting to think about, so I talked it over with Leo, Lennie, Randy, and Genie. They got excited about it, too. Mom talked to Betty. She, too, liked the idea. It was a go.

Serious planning started. We decided the best time would be in mid-July 1967. The Steinmetz kids and Debbie, as well as Betty, a teacher would be on summer break from school. Letters went out to each family we planned to visit about the best dates to be in their homes. All responded, looking forward to our visit. Farming was the livelihood of each family, so Daddy, Leo, and Robert would stay at home and farm, and the women and children would vacation.

On a Sunday morning in July, Mom drove to Las Animas and picked up Betty, Debbie, Steve, and Brenda. They arrived at the Steinmetz farm mid-afternoon. After a good night of rest, it was time to load and board the Electra. Before that took place, this was the picture: a big car with bench seats and no seatbelts; three women and six kids; and clothes and snacks for the week. Seating arrangements were agreed on. Mom would be the driver, so she always sat in the same place, behind the wheel. Betty and I took turns, front or back, with four kids in the back seat and one in the front. Brenda always sat on someone's lap. It was good we were on the thin side! Leo was a good loader, so he volunteered to put our stuff in the trunk. So with all that done, we were on the road to central Kansas.

After traveling a couple of hours, we stopped near Hanston, Kansas at a picnic table for lunch. I had fried extra chicken for our Sunday dinner to take along on Monday (notice I said fried chicken). After our meal break, we got back in the car and continued on our journey. Some of the kids slept.

At no time do I remember any of the kids asking, "Are we there yet?" I do remember Brenda asking me, "What time is it, Aunt

Bernice?" For a two and a half year old, she spoke very plainly. Time to a child this age is not relevant, so I would look at my wrist and say, "A freckle past a hair." That seemed to satisfy her. She asked the question many times and got the same answer.

We reached our destination in late afternoon, at Uncle Ed and Aunt Helen's place. We were all ready to get out of the car by then. After warm greetings, Helen had a nice meal ready, hamburgers, hot dogs, and all the trimmings. We ate in their lovely backyard in Great Bend, Kansas. Later, the kids played and the adults visited until bedtime. It was quite a group, nine of us, but there was room for all. We always had a close bond with Uncle Ed and Aunt Helen.

Tuesday morning, all were up and around. We had a hearty breakfast and were ready to board the Electra. That day, we visited Mom's mom, Grandma (Krug) Eichman. Grandma was about 80 at the time and in relatively good health. She had prepared a fried chicken meal with all the trimmings. Uncle Jule, Mom's oldest brother and Aunt Pauline, who lived in the country, joined us for dinner. After the meal, the adults visited and the kids played outside. This form of entertainment seemed to be good. There was no sightseeing.

Being in central Kansas in July was totally different than eastern Colorado or western Kansas. It was hot and humid. People didn't have air conditioning in their homes like we do in this day and age. Grandma had fans going at all times. The Electra had an air conditioner but Mom did not turn it on. So with plastic seat covers and high humidity there were times when we stuck together like glue. I don't remember anyone complaining though.

Wednesday morning, all were up and about and in good spirits. The kids were very good. It seems without being told, the Steinmetz kids made it their responsibility to look after one of the Grasmick kids. Whatever it was, it worked for a pleasant excursion.

On this day, we travelled to Russell, Kansas to visit Aunt Christine, Dad's oldest sister. This was the town Bob Dole, who in

Bernice Steinmetz's family

recent years was a presidential candidate but lost, came from. Aunt Christine still lived in the country. It was good to see her. We arrived near lunch time, and she was ready for all of us. At one point, we had told the kids not to say they had had fried chicken before if it was served again. Guess what Aunt Christine served? That's right, fried chicken. But she had butchered them the day before. They were fresh and the best. She served them along with mashed potatoes, gravy, and green beans from her garden – a five star meal.

Aunt Christine was in her 60s and had been a widow for several years. She was always interested in what was going on in our lives. She would sit down at some point, look us in the eye, and really communicate. What a blessing she was!

Later we loaded up and headed to Paradise, Kansas to spend time with our friends the Shorters. They had moved from Holcomb to this area a couple of years before. Clyde worked for a big cattle ranch, and Betty was a registered nurse in Russell. They had two sons about our kids' ages. The area they lived in was truly a paradise. It was in Russell County, the same county as Aunt Christine. When we neared their place, it was beautiful: rolling green hills, ponds full of water, and cattle grazing in the distance. The house they lived in was a two story old house that could have been in the Old West and probably was.

They greeted us warmly. They had never met Mom, Betty, or her kids. It was suppertime when we got there. I don't remember what we ate, but they had the gift of hospitality and whatever they served must have been good. After supper, the kids played outside until dark and the adults visited. I remember it as a very peaceful time and place under the starry skies. We spent the night here. What special friends to lodge nine extra people!

Thursday was a travelling day. We were all up and about and ready to go after breakfast. We said our farewells and were on the road west. We got back to Holcomb in late afternoon. We were glad to see Leo, who greeted us warmly. He had everything in order and a meal ready for us. The Grasmicks spent the night and headed home after breakfast on Friday.

After pondering that excursion, 46 years later there were many thoughts that came to my mind, things I really never thought of before. Daddy, Leo, and Robert were good examples of husbands and fathers by allowing their families to leave for a few days as they tended the farms. Kansas has so many natural beauties: sunrises, sunsets, starry skies, and wonderful people. This is from the New Testament about families, from Ephesians 3:14-19 (KJV): "For this cause I bow my knees unto the Father of our Lord Jesus Christ of whom the whole family in heaven and earth is named, that He would grant you according to the riches of this glory to be strengthened with His Spirit in the inner man; that Christ may dwell in your hearts by faith; that ye, being rooted and grounded in love, may be able to comprehend with all saints what is the breadth and length and depth and height; and to know the love of Christ, which passeth knowledge, that ye might be filled with all the fullness of God." We are a blessed family because of Daddy and Mom, Conrad and Elizabeth Grasmick. This act of taking her family on a four day excursion set an example. She was a Proverbs 31 woman. I am so thankful I am part of this family, and may this legacy live on because families are forever.

I'm Proud of My Family
By Gerold R. "Jerry" Falls of Wellington, Kansas
Born 1952

My family is from southern Kansas and northern Oklahoma. I was born in Enid, Oklahoma in August 1952. My mom and dad met in Wellington, Kansas in high school, I think. Mom was 18 years old when I was born. My family was "countrified." Grandpa Stonehocker and Grandma Stonehocker lived just west of Enid, Oklahoma, about one mile west of Drummond. After Oklahoma, my family moved to Perth, Kansas.

I remember Grandma. She had gray hair put up in a bun, and she was short and heavy. Hence, she was lovingly known as Big Fat Grandma. The kitchen in her two or three room house always smelled of fresh baked bread. Grandma made about 16 loaves of bread each day. All the families nearby got her bread. She also baked and cooked on a cast iron cook stove. It was large. I don't know or can't remember much more than that, but I do remember the smell of homemade bread in Grandma Stonehocker's kitchen.

The holidays were always large family get-

Jerry with his dad, Robert "Bob" Falls and his great uncle, Merion Brown

Grandma and Grandpa Stonehocker with Jerry's sister, Sharon Kay Falls

togethers. On Thanksgiving, the men grouped up in the living room to catch up on the farm news and just shoot the bull. After the noontime meal, the men went hunting. I don't know how old I was my first get to go with my granddad, my dad, and many uncles and cousins. I got to go once.

The summer time I remember all my uncles, cousins, my dad, and a few close family friends butchered steers, hogs, and chickens. The hens were the women's job.

My dad, Robert J. "Bob" Falls was and is a farmer and in my opinion, the best. Dad worked hard to give us a good life for the times in the '50s. Grandpa and Grandma Stonehocker had a pump in the kitchen by the sink for water from the well. Plain and simple, nothing fancy.

Uncle Joe and Aunt Margie Stonehocker lived about a mile west. I think I was four or five years old, but I do know they raised 16 kids in a four-room house, two bedrooms and a living room and a kitchen. They had wood burning stoves for heat and drank their milk by the gallon from their milk cow. The boys had a room and the girls had a room. When my cousins, J.B. and David got older they made a room out of a butler building (a small grainery) for more privacy and room. I do know they lived on 80 acres, covered with black jack oak trees, which they cleared for firewood. Uncle Joe had two wooden legs. When it rained, he squeaked when he walked.

I got my first whipping in school in the first grade in the two-room schoolhouse in Perth, Kansas. I got swatted with a ping-pong paddle. Yep, it hurt! The teachers were Mr. and Mrs. Haymer. The principal taught grades seven through twelve. I was in his wife's class for grades one through six.

I'm 61 years old now, a lot weaker, can't say smarter, but I live pretty much like my forefathers and mothers did in the fifties, simple and easy. I know I'm healthier for the way I live. I'm proud of my family. I understand the hard times they went through, and I try to experience life, as close as I can, to the way they lived.

School Days and 4-H Fun
By Clara Cottle Ginn of Caldwell, Kansas
Born 1937

My family was bred, raised, and lived in Sumner County, Kansas. Sumner County is located on the Kansas-Oklahoma border in the middle of the state. My parents and I lived in Sumner County throughout our whole lives, and even though they have passed on, I still live here.

I started school when I was five at a one-room school called Attebury, which was three miles west of Rome. There was only one teacher, and she taught all eight elementary grades. We lived one fourth of a mile from school and walked. I was the only one in the

Grandma and Grandpa Mosby in 1955

first grade and enjoyed playing at an inside sand pile at recess. We did not have electricity or inside plumbing so went to one of the two outhouses behind the school. Each student had a tin cup they drank from after dipping into the water bucket that was filled with fresh water every morning.

My most embarrassing moment happened in the first grade, when I held my hand up with two fingers to show that I needed to go to the bathroom. My teacher ignored me. I got up anyway and headed for the outside privy. I did not make it out the door before Montezuma's Revenge took over, and I left a trail all the way to the door. I ran home, and my mother cleaned me up and made me go back to school. When I walked in the door, my trail had been covered with ashes from the stove and was in little piles staring me in the face. I will never forget that. I'm not sure who cleaned it up, but it was probably my mother and not the teacher. I wonder why that teacher was not my favorite.

Our mothers packed our lunches, and we placed them on a bench at the back of the room and hung our coats on hooks above the bench. We sometimes ate at our desks, but one of my favorite things was in the spring on Fridays, the teacher would bring a large blanket and we would eat outside, trading what we had in our lunchboxes with one another. One girl often had a tangerine, and I felt really lucky to be able to trade something with her and get that tangerine. We had egg sandwiches, wiener sandwiches, or whatever our moms had left from supper the night before. Sometimes we had pickles and maybe a cookie or home canned fruit in our lunches but seldom had any fresh fruit.

We played all sorts of games; Annie Over, kick ball, and blind man's bluff, had races, played ball, etc. It was a happy time.

The teacher was responsible for making the fire every morning when it was cold in an old wood stove in the middle of the room. She was also the janitor. If we could stay after school on Fridays, we sometimes got to pound the erasers on a rock to remove the chalk so they would be ready to use the next week and maybe carry out the ashes from the stove. School started after Labor Day and was usually out around the middle of April.

When I completed the fourth grade, we moved two miles east when the Attebury School closed. Our dad was on the local school board, and the consolidated district bought another large schoolhouse and used the one already at Rome, dug a basement and put the two school buildings on top of the basement. They added restrooms and we had a new school. A few years later, they put in a kitchen and began a hot lunch program, and the students did not have to carry their lunches and got a hot meal at noon.

When school started that fall, I was in the fifth grade and got to go to the "big" room. My sister was two years ahead of me and my brother three years behind me. Sitting and listening to the older kids classes provided us with an education ahead of our years. Of course, the older girls always shared their knowledge about the birds and bees with the younger ones, so that is when my sex education began.

Mrs. Harris was my teacher for three years and will always be remembered as my favorite. She was a stern but gentle person who listened to me and gave good advice. Upon her death, scrapbooks were discovered full of clippings and pictures of each of her students from the time they graduated the eighth grade through adulthood, marriage, and childbearing. She taught there for many years, so she influenced many kids.

We always had community meetings once a month and someone would be in charge of a program. It was usually a potluck meal in the evening. People of the community and sometimes students provided the entertainment with plays, piano solos, songs, etc. Usually they would have a school Christmas program. One year, Mrs. Harris let me take the decorated Christmas tree home after the Christmas program, and that was the first Christmas tree we ever had in our home. We drew names for Christmas and Valentine's Day and tried to keep it a secret who we were giving to until the time of gift unwrapping. We would make individual Valentine boxes and decorate them up, and the other kids would put their Valentines in the individual boxes. After the party at the end of the day, we took our Valentines home to look at and hoped we got a special one from someone who we had a crush on.

In the spring of the year, each rural school would have a softball team and practice for track meets. We would go to the different schools to compete. It was always a special time, as we would usually spend the day with a picnic lunch, and the parents would come to see their kids perform. They would give out ribbons for the winners in the track meets and a trophy for the team that came out on top.

There was an eighth grade county graduation in Wellington where all the eighth graders from the rural areas would graduate at one time. Usually it meant a new dress and it was a day to look forward to. Then in the fall, we would begin our freshman year at the school that was in the designated district where we lived.

When we went to high school, the folks would give us money to buy our lunch. We had an allowance of fifty cents per day, but with that fifty cents we could buy a hamburger and drink and still have enough left for a candy bar. There was a drive in that we went to my senior year, but before that we would walk up town and go to the Cat'n'Lantern, which was the local teen hangout. The guys would frequent the pool hall, but of course girls did not go there.

4-H was a big thing when I was a kid growing up. It was about the only outside activity that farm kids participated in. The projects were things that we had grown up with, like cooking, sewing, canning, and livestock. My favorite project was my sheep. There would be a project tour in the spring when everyone in my club would go to each other's place and view what projects we were taking. Then in August, we would have the 4-H and county fairs where we would show our finished projects in competition. One year, there were four girls who had a breeding ewe project, and we were in several classes together. We got to the place where we thought the judge was remembering the girl rather than paying much attention to the animal, so we would exchange our sheep and show one another's sheep just to throw the judge. We had a lot of fun, and of course our parents realized what we were doing and went along with us. That was one confused judge, but we had a lot of fun. If we had a top-rated project, we could take it to the state fair at Hutchinson. I took my breeding ewe one year and stayed at the 4-H encampment for a whole week while showing and taking care of my sheep. It was a new and eye-opening experience for this country gal.

We went to county 4-H camp at Camp Wentz in Oklahoma, and the older kids also got to attend music camp at Rock Springs Ranch south of Junction City. Another fun activity was when our club would get together along with our parents and go sheep dipping. Everyone would share in the packed lunches at noon, and of course we were all covered with sheep dip and did not smell too good. We worked hard, earned some money, and had a lot of fun.

Parental involvement was the key to the success of 4-H, both then and now. The Sumner County Fair was first held in Caldwell in 1926 and has been held every year there other than during World War II when the War Department requested that it be discontinued during the war. Some of the kids and even their kids and grandkids who were in the 4-H when I was growing up are involved as department superintendents at the present time, so it has become a legacy that has been passed from one generation to the next.

We had several pets while I was growing up but one stands out in my memory. My dad came home with a black and white female puppy stuck in the bib of his overalls for us kids, and we were thrilled. We named her Fanny. When Fanny was about half-grown, she chased the mail carrier when he delivered our mail and of course got run over. We nursed her back to health, but she never gave up her hatred for the mail carrier and chased him on a daily schedule and got run over multiple times. You have heard about cats having nine lives; I know Fanny possessed at least that many. She finally died of old age a few years after I got married and left home, so she had to have been at least 15 years old.

Dad caught a baby rabbit and brought it in from the field one time. We made a box for Charlie in the house and had fun every morning chasing down Charlie, as he would get out of the box and hide somewhere. We fed him from a small doll bottle and had him longer than most of the rabbit pets. Charlie died when he was about half-grown, and all the neighbor kids came over and we had a funeral for him. We dug a grave and padded up a shoebox to put him in. We picked some flowers and made a cross for a marker. I don't think any of us had been to a funeral before but we did what we thought needed to be done. I think I could point out the exact place where Charlie was buried. I doubt if any other rabbit has been thought about for the 65 plus years that Charlie has been remembered.

I have enjoyed writing down some of my memories and hope you enjoy reading them. Thanks!

Frank Is At It Again!
By Phyllis Yockey of Grove, Oklahoma
Born 1946

I lived in a small agricultural town in southwest Kansas with a brilliant father. I look back on the memories I have from back in the 1950s. I had a father who had a brilliant mind and was extremely adept at making and inventing different things. I remember he always had a "blueprint" before he retired to his garage to make it his way with the latest thoughts drawn out on paper and knowing he could build it.

He made a homemade motorcycle. I still can see him going up and down the gravel streets of Mullinville, Kansas on it as it went down the road. I remember later seeing my sister riding it in the small park down the street, jumping, and air born off the small hill in the park.

My father made a three-wheel "hoopie," as it was called. My brother delivered many a newspaper on it. Only in a small town of 400 people or less could everyone in town see his

Phyllis Yockey riding Frank's homemade mower

young son or daughters sitting on this machine and driving all over the streets and not worry about them getting run over by someone or arresting them for driving underage.

My father had an amazing ability to work on cars and make them run again. He owned a yellow and black Pontiac that he would "soup up" when he wanted to see how fast he could make it run. There would be numerous drag races to see who had the better vehicle, and the Pontiac always won. I understand that he even agreed to race a horse in a quarter mile. The horse got the drop on my father starting out but by the end of the quarter, he was flying past the horse.

He worked on countless vehicles and fixed them for the lowest prices in the nation. He just wanted to fix them so someone would have their vehicle back and running again until the next needed service.

He became an inventor in the mid-1950s by patenting a pill dispenser that would dispense pills one at a time by a top on the bottle rotating to drop the pill. It was a very unique device, but there was no money to promote the patented invention, and it never made him the fortune he hoped for.

My father worked for a company that made bins to hold cattle feed with an auger. He made several of these feed bins and augers built his way with much thought of how to make them work great. These were used for many years in the Mullinville area and surrounding southwest Kansas. Also, he built a much needed irrigation system that was seen in use in the area for years.

I remember one particular interest my

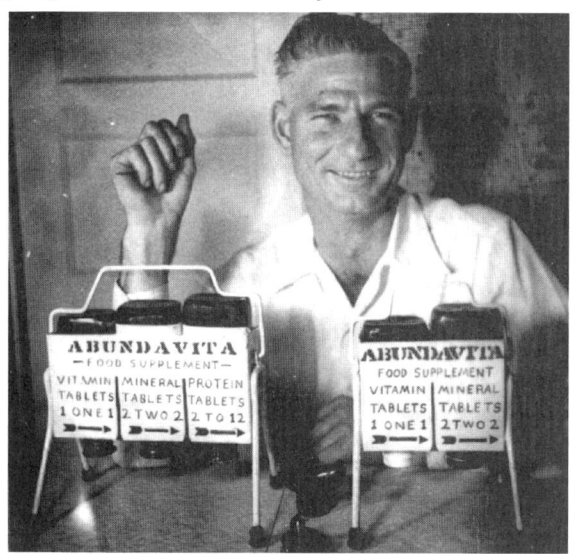

Frank's patented pill dispenser

father had was in flying. I remember seeing the hand-drawn blueprint on the kitchen table that he made of wings that would attach to his body that would allow him to fly like a bird does. He was willing to believe his wings could hold him to fly. He climbed a microtower south of town to test his invention. It had no motor on it, however. My brother managed to talk him back down off the tower without testing his wings. Thank God! I think there was too much gravity in the air for his invention to hold him. So then, I started seeing blueprints for a helicopter! The helicopter was never built, but I feel that it would have worked if he had actually built it.

Whoever thought things couldn't be exciting in a small farming community? With my dad's inventions running around town or his love of speed, he had the town people shaking their heads and saying, "That is just Frank at it again." He definitely lived more than the normal cat's nine lives!

A Wonderful Country Life
By Erlene R. Unruh of Goessel, Kansas
Born 1929

I recall some of my memories about growing up here in rural central Kansas. It was a good life for my three sisters and me. I was usually the ringleader for the adventures my two younger sisters and I had. I could almost always come up with some brainstorm about what to do for entertainment back then when we had no TV, video games, and technical apps.

For instance one winter evening, I thought it would be fun if the three of us could make ourselves a hideout. So we took three wooden chairs and placed them so their straight backs made a small square room with an opening for a door. Then we spread a large blanket over it, and we had a neat tent. But it was dark in there. So, my bright idea was to bring in a kerosene lamp and set it in the middle. We sat around it in a circle feeling cozy and safe. Then I had another brilliant idea. I ran downstairs to the kitchen and got two wieners, some crackers, and some hairpins. We sliced the wieners into thin, round slices, flattened the hairpins to use as wiener sticks, and roasted them over the flame of the kerosene lamp. What fun to have our own private picnic in our own little tent! It never dawned on us that we could have burned the house down. I don't remember if we ever told our folks about it.

Those were the days of the good old outhouse. Oh yes, after dark my younger sisters and I tried to cajole each other into going with each other to the outhouse. Just in case we needed help to scare away the skunks we were sure were lurking behind every shrub.

But the outhouse experience that sticks in my memory happened on a summer Sunday morning. It was Children's Day. I was so excited about my pretty new white sandals as I put them on to dress for church. Then, my older sister began to pester and tease me. Since I could run like the wind, I thought I could get away and find a place to hide. The outhouse! Perfect. The outhouse had a platform of boards with a hole cut out for a seat. And the side had a nice half-moon window. I waited for quite a while. When I didn't hear anything, I thought maybe she had given up. I stepped on the platform to peek out the half-moon to see if I could see her. Just then, a stick came poking in at me. In my surprise, I backed up and stepped into the hole! Needless to say, I didn't wear my new sandals to church that morning.

Another thing we spent a lot of time entertaining ourselves with was making play houses under the trees and baking mud pies and mud cakes. Our cooperative mother let us have a teaspoon of vanilla to put in a bottle of water and a tablespoon of cocoa to put into the sifted dirt that was our flour. That added a great smell of realism to our baking. One day, we were going to make a very special three-tiered layer cake. To add a bit more realism, I had the idea to get an egg from the hen house and stir it into the mud. Now we felt we were really "cooking." We decorated it beautifully with many multicolored flower petals. We stood back to admire our masterpiece. Can you imagine our dismay when later in the day we saw our cat gulping down our beautiful cake? She must have smelled the "realism" of the egg.

Another memory that comes to mind is the Saturday night bath. One of our farm chores was to carry in the wood and kindling to build a fire in our large wood burning stove. When it was warm and glowing, Mom set up a large galvanized tub beside it. Then she filled it with the warmed water, which we had also hauled in from the well outside. Then, one by one, we luxuriated in our wonderful bathtub.

I was usually a good little girl. But if I'm honest, I have to admit I also had a bit of a naughty streak. My younger sisters and I usually stuck together and thought of things to do with each other. But this one is mine alone. We had an older sister, a wonderful person, but she kind of kept herself aloof from us, because we must have seemed like pesky brats to her. She had her own room, and we didn't really get to know her well until we were older. Like me, she was an avid reader, and she had a book I was just dying to read. But she wouldn't let me use it. For some reason, she had the idea I might not take good care of it. I wonder why? Anyway, what could I do but sneak into her room and get it out? Then sneak to my favorite perch way up in the big cottonwood tree and spend happy hours reading.

Then came my mother's call, "Children, come quickly. We need to run into town to pick up a few groceries." Well, there was no way I could come down from that tree carrying my sister's book! So I tucked it into a little niche in the tree and hurried down to the car. I planned to get it later, after we came back. Only later, something else got my attention, and I promptly forgot about it. That night we had a huge thunderstorm. On my, what now? The next morning, I faced one of the biggest crises of my young life. I knew I had to go to my sister and confess, but how could I find the courage to do that? After much earnest prayer, I took the wet and tattered book and told her what I had done and how sorry I was. She was deeply disappointed, of course. But that dear, loving sister forgave me! I think that incident was the beginning of a strong life-long bond between us. It was also a hard lesson learned for me.

Well, there are a lot of other memories from those long ago days. I wonder how we could ever have had time for TV and video games in our busy schedules. We had a lot of chores to do; that was a normal, expected part of growing up. We fed chickens, gathered eggs, hoed weeds in the garden, got the cows in from the pasture at milking time, picked and shelled peas and corn, did dishes, hung laundry on the outside clothesline, etc. It was a wonderful life, growing up in the country with my family. I have always loved nature and the out of doors is still one of the biggest joys in my life.

A Letter from a Pioneer Woman
By Galen Rapp of Topeka, Kansas
Born 1935

This letter was written by Mrs. M.C. Wright, mother of Will Spaniol. Mrs. Wright resided in Plevna, Reno County, Kansas. Her son, Will Spaniol was the husband of Matilda Spaniol Rapp. Aunt Till was the sister of my father, Water E. Rapp. The letter was written in December of 1948 in response to my request for information about pioneer life. This was for an assignment for Mennonite District #113 Grade School in Reno County. This school was located on the same quarter of land as the original George Gottlieb Rapp farmstead. This quarter section of land was inherited by my grandmother, Mary Kathryn Wurst. My home was one mile west and one mile south of the school.

Plevna, Kansas
December 2, 1948

Dear Galen:

In answer to your letter, I will try and give you some on experiences in early days and of the rest of pioneers in the year of 1883 and later. We arrived in Sterling, Rice County on January 20, 1883 on the Santa Fe train. My cousin and I took the train, for my husband was with our stock (livestock) and furniture.

Geo G. Rapp with his spouse, children, cousins, and parents

Mary K. (Wurst) Rapp and children

Sterling was a small place. There were just a few buildings. We started to Huntsville, Reno County, about 20 miles south and west of Sterling in a wagon and about half way out we stopped to warm as I had two small children. There we saw what Kansas really was, for in their home in the kitchen one-third was a pile of corn stocks and firing all the time. The people were real nice to us. Their name was Stiggens.

Next, we came to a place in Huntsville belonging to a family by the name of Shores. They were also very nice but their house was small, and there were seven and me and the children. This made a large family so the children and I slept on the floor. As soon as our car (railcar) was unloaded, we moved to ourselves.

We bought our land in June, 160 acres from the railroad for $600.00. We paid cash so they let us have it for one-third less. Now about the land, it was all prairie and no trees. The farm machinery was very simple, just a plow and cultivator was about all anyone had for some years. The land had to be broken and lay idle to the next year before it could be put into crops. Our country had no public roads. We just drove in any direction across anywhere. However, later when settlers came, they fenced their land. Electricity was unknown; all farming was done by horses and mules for years and then binders and later headers. Our worst fears were prairie fires for so much prairie. We staked our cows on ropes but those with a lot of cattle had to herd them until later when people built fences.

Now for daily living in homes: we didn't have much to do with, but everybody was or seemed happy and content. More so than now. We baked our own bread and all we wanted. Things was cheap. We bought coffee for ten pounds for a dollar. It was good and we ground it ourselves. We didn't go to town very often for we made our butter and we had our gardens. In our homes, we didn't have carpets on our floors for several years, nor did we have mattresses. We had good beds but only those filled with straw or corn shucks. We had no washing machine, only those run by hand. But we were happy and content.

We lived in Kansas for ten years before I went to Hutchinson, the county seat of Reno County. It was not much of a town. Streetcars were drawn by old mules and the streetlights was some kind that had to be lighted every night and turned out every morning. We only saw boardwalks. We had a Methodist church across from our place and it was full every Sunday. People came and some walked three to four miles and some came in wagons.

I don't know if you can read this for my eyesight is so poor and I wonder what you wanted from me. So you will excuse me for my poor scribbling. Maybe when you get to be as old as I am you will really know how hard it is when your eyesight is poor. You can use this or destroy it.

I came from Denmark in 1877. I crossed three seas, the Baltic, the North Sea, and the Atlantic Sea. I have traveled. I have been visiting in California for two months and in New York for four months and other places and now live in Plevna, Kansas. I have never attended school in America, but where there is a will there is a way.

This letter was written by Mrs. Maria C. Wright on December 2, 1948.

Comments by Galen Rapp, May 2003: Maria C. Wright was 16 years old when she left

Geo F. Rapp and Family

Denmark. I don't know where she spent the seven years before she came to Kansas. I assume her first husband's name was Spaniol, and after his passing, she married a Wright.

A Solid Foundation for Life
By Peter J. Neufeld of Hutchinson, Kansas
Born 1929

I was born in a farmhouse located three miles east and one and a half south of Inman, Kansas. The day was a cold February 27 of the year 1929. It was common practice to call the doctor a long time before the birth, because they wanted to be sure that he was there for the birth. I was the second one in the family of Jacob B. and Katherine Pauls Neufeld. My brother, Walt was born 15 months earlier. Three sisters and three more brothers were to be born later, for a total of eight children in our family. My parents have never told me about my birth and early childhood, and I never asked. According to one picture, I was fat and plain looking, with hair combed straight down all around. In those days, babies were considered unhealthy unless they were fat.

We were not rich; in fact, we were poor. I was born in the Great Depression of the '20s and early '30s. Many people went broke and lost their farms to the Dust Bowl. My parents, thanks to some help from their parents, were able to hang onto their farm.

The house I was born in was then already an old house. On one end of the house, it was two stories with a couple of bedrooms upstairs as I remember it. We had a good sized living room and a kitchen. The living room had a table in it and was used as a dining room. Then we also had a "Grota schtov" or a great room, which was always closed during the week. We were ordered not to go in there. It was reserved for Sunday visitors. At some point in my youth, we bought a piano, which was placed in that visitor's room. The piano was used for lessons for my brother, Walt and on special occasions such as Christmas, when Mom insisted that we all gather around the piano and sing Christmas carols.

Our house had no air conditioning and no fans, because we had no electricity. Summers were awfully hot. One way to cool off was to

The Neufeld family on a picnic in Coronado Heights

lie down on the living room linoleum floor. It was somewhat cooler. At night, the air usually cooled off and since the house had big windows, the summer breeze blew through the house. We had a row of shade trees south of the house, which also helped cool the house during the day.

We also had no electric lights. I remember that in the evening, we all gathered around the kerosene lamp on the living room table. Sometimes we had to do our studies. But sometimes we played games on that table. It seemed to be Mom's job to trim the wick of the lamp and clean the glass cylinder. She did this by blowing in it to dampen it, and then she wiped it with a cloth.

We, of course, had no refrigerator and no freezer. Mom's butter was kept cool in the cellar during the summer. That is also, where we stored the hams and bacon from butchering our hogs. They were smoked and salted down by Dad after butchering, and so they were kept from rotting. Our stove in the kitchen was a kerosene stove and I guess earlier had been a woodstove. The heating stove in the living room was also a kerosene stove. Our bedrooms were very cold in the winter, because there was no heat in them. In the morning, we kids all grabbed our clothes and ran downstairs and all crowded around the heater and dressed there.

Later in my teen years, we did get an ice box. The ice man came around every few days and brought us a big fifty pound chunk of ice. We used to like it when he came, because the ice looked and felt so good on a hot summer day. My dad kept some pop in the ice box for his gas customers. Dad had a repair garage on the farm and also sold gas. If a customer bought a fifty-five gallon barrel of gas, he got a free bottle of pop. Sometimes Dad sent me in for the pop. I had to open it with an opener on the ice box, and then bring it out to the customer. It was so tempting to take a swig from that bottle, and I suppose that I did so on occasion.

Once in a long while, perhaps once a week, all of us kids were permitted to have half a bottle or even a whole bottle of pop. It was so hard to decide what flavor I wanted that bottle to be. The reason I talk about bottles is that we had no pop cans or any plastic bottles in those days. Pop came only in glass bottles and it was good.

We had no running water in the house. But we did have a pump out in the yard by the windmill. The windmill was a tall tower over 30 feet high with a wheel on top. When the wind blew, which it usually did in Kansas, the wheel turned and pumped water for the cattle and horses. The water ran in a long pipe from the windmill to the stock tank. When it was hot, the stock tank became our swimming pool. When we were young, we always had to ask Mom if we could swim in the tank. Some little children had drowned in the tank because they went in when their parents were not watching. So we always had to ask Mom if we could swim in the tank. When Mom said yes, we stripped off our clothing down to the bare skin and jumped in. When there were neighbor girls around, we had to keep our pants on, since we did not have swimming suits. Water had to be carried from this pump to the house in a three gallon pail. There was a dipper in the pail, and all of us drank out of the same dipper. The water was sure good when it had just been brought in fresh from the pump.

Later on, we built a summer kitchen onto the house and a small pump room. This summer kitchen had a cement floor and seemed cooler in the summer. So we often ate in the summer kitchen in the summer. I always enjoyed this. It was so different and food always tasted better there. In the summer kitchen was a large steel kettle with a fireplace underneath it. This was used to heat water for Mom's laundry and to scald hogs on butchering day.

We had no bathroom in the house. We had an outhouse about a hundred feet in back of our house. In those days, the *Sears* and *Montgomery Ward Catalogs* were sent out free to all families. We ordered out of them very often, because we simply did not get to Hutchinson where the stores were very often. These catalogs came in handy. When they were out of date, they went to the outhouse. All my growing up years, I wiped with this slick catalog paper and so did everybody else that I knew. At night when it was dark, we took a flashlight with us, but even then, it was scary. The little kids always asked Mom to go with them. In winter days, we kept a "nacht ama" or night pail in the house that everyone in the family used instead of going to the outhouse. By morning, that pail had an awful smell to it. It was often my job to take the thing out and dump it.

Peter J. Neufeld in 1947

We siblings did have a lot of fun playing together. We made many of our own toys. I once made a nice, large barn, which I used to play farmer and cowboy. My dad did play basketball with us at times. Once I remember he took me fishing to the sinkhole a mile and a half from our home. It was a lake that kept sinking and getting deeper because of core drilling for oil. I caught a large carp fish and that was a thrill. We lived near a large drainage ditch. When it rained and the water was up, our dad took us swimming. The water was muddy, but we didn't care. Dad said we had to learn to swim so that we wouldn't accidentally drown someday.

Very often in April or May, our pasture flooded because of the heavy rains. Fish came into the pasture through the culvert. Then we put screens across the culvert so they could not get back out. Then as the water got shallow, we could see fish swimming with their backs showing. We took a washtub with the bottom out of it. We ran after the fish and threw the tub over them to catch them. When the water in the ditches got low, we went in and caught hundreds of fish with our hands. With both hands, we would push the fish down into the mud and grab it. This was more fun but a bit scary since there were also snakes in the water.

We had a lot of snakes on the farm. I never did like them. One day I stepped on one in the grass with my bare feet and this scared me. We had garter snakes, water snakes, and some large bull snakes. None of them were poisonous.

One year when we had a lot of flooding, we decided we needed a boat. We could not afford to buy one, so we decided to build one out of used sheet metal and wood. We took it out into the pasture water and had more fun with it. There was only one problem; it leaked and we had to bail water.

As I grew older and saw what the flood did to our crops, I became very unhappy and discouraged about the flooding on our land. Our driveway was often under water, and we either had to stay home or walk. Sometimes like when we were going to church, Dad would start up our Model L Case tractor and pull the cars through the water. Sometimes the road to the highway one and a half miles away was also muddy and flooded. So Dad pulled us all the way to the highway.

We could not always play. Very often, when we got bored, we would start fighting. Then Mom would give each of us a hoe and order us to hoe weeds and stickers. We always had a lot of weeds and all kinds of stickers on the yard. There was never an end to them. I think I must have hoed millions of weeds as a child. This was one way for mom to keep us boys in line.

My grandparents all came from Russia in 1874 as children. When they came, they spoke low German in the home and high German in church. The reason being they were actually of German descent. I learned to speak English in grade school. Their primary reason for migrating to America was for religious freedom. Russia was forcing their young men into the military. They were religious objectors to the military.

I have good memories of my childhood and some not so good. We siblings played together and fought together. The good experiences and the difficult, I believe, served to provide a solid foundation for my adult life.

Oh, the Changes I Have Seen!
By Carol S. Blankenship of Pratt, Kansas
Born 1948

Sixty-five years ago, I was born in Anthony, Kansas, as they had the only hospital then. My daddy was ill, and my mother had taken him and put him in the hospital that morning. She then went back home and milked 16 cows, put the milk away, and then told my 20-year-old brother that she needed him to take her to the hospital, and I was born. I was the last of five children. I was raised in Sun City, Kansas. I lived in a two-room house with my parents, three of four other siblings, and my maternal grandmother.

Our farmland was south of town and even today has The White Sand School House on it and a cistern in front that we cranked our

White Sand School

water up with to water the horses. We had no running water in our house. We got our water from a pitcher pump outside the kitchen door. We had no bathroom either, as we had an outhouse that we had to get to by going through the chicken lot. This was home to a mean rooster that would flog us. Of course, it didn't help matters that I teased him. We had a wood cook stove for heat as well as cooking.

Laundry day was interesting, as we had to pump and carry water to a big kettle hanging over a fire to get it hot and carry it from there to the washer. Then we had to wring out the clothes and put them in another tub of water to rinse them. Then we would hang them on the line to dry. Summer wasn't bad but in the winter, most of the clothes would freeze dry, and then we had to finish drying them around the stove in the house.

We did not have air conditioning for keeping cool. We just splashed cool water on us or wet a cloth for around our necks. We didn't have a phone until several years later. We had to go to the phone office uptown to use the telephone switchboard, and someone would come and get us if there was a phone call for us. Later then, we had a party line. Our phone ring was two long rings and two short rings. Several other ladies in town would also pick up and listen in and in some instances would even make comments during our calls. I still have the black rotary dial phone with my parents' number on it.

If you have ever heard of the McLain Rodeo, my daddy helped with that. He was the chute boss. That was a really big rodeo at the time, and a lot of people attended. The rodeo is even discussed in a video made by Dr. Jim Hoy at Emporia State College for a class that he teaches. When he was a lad of eight years, my dad also saw the Indian Geronimo who had been captured and was being held in a wooden cage on what was known as the 101 Ranch. Dad also was the foreman who oversaw the cobblestone streets in Pratt, Kansas and helped dig the brood ponds for the Kansas Fish Hatchery with a horse and Fresno. Then he farmed and raised cattle, and we lived in Sun City. We had to get our cattle off of what was known as the Harmon Land before 7:00am being that is the gyp mine, and they would start dynamiting for the gypsum.

When I was seven years old, I would herd the cattle along the road all day. I had a water jug, a sack lunch, a book, and my trusted paint mare. The mail lady would go by and honk or sometimes stop, but the cattle were mine to tend while my daddy farmed with an Allis Chalmers tractor with a push in crank to start it. When I heard two long honks and two short ones on the pickup horn, I would head the cattle back to the pasture, and he would help me get them in. Then we would go to the other pasture by the barn and get the milk cows gathered in.

One day it took me longer to bring in the milk cows, and Daddy wanted to know why. I told him since my brother wasn't with me to help it took longer. He asked me why I hadn't ridden the jersey cow in. Riding the cows was something we were not supposed to do. He said he knew I had been riding her by looking at the seat of my pants. Oops, I was caught. I didn't think he knew.

Daddy raised and broke horses to ride when he wasn't in the field and as I got older, I helped him with them, being the first one to get in the saddle when the time was right. I never was thrown off.

Morning milking in the summer produced

Carol Blankenship

a rattlesnake almost daily under the feed tub. I would keep the cow back until my mother would jerk up the tub and kill the snake, throw him aside, and then start milking the cows. I always had my cup ready for her to fill with my milk straight from the cow. We always had about three or more of the "farmers match boxes" each summer full of the rattlers that were cut off. We would have fun with the city folk, telling them the auto gates were there to shake the snakes off the bottom of the vehicles, because farmers would get upset if you stole their snakes.

Daddy always planted a very large garden and Mother canned enough and stored her canning in the storm cellar along with a lot of potatoes, onions, etc. to last us through the winter. We picked fruit and berries to can or for jelly or pies. Daddy always made the best plum leather from wild sand plums. We had our own chickens for eggs and eating, steers and pigs for butchering, and cows for milk, cream, and butter. We made our butter in a churn and then pressed it into butter molds. Mother turned the cream into the best whipped cream for my whipped cream sandwiches, which I thought was better than any cake. My parents usually only bought flour, sugar, and that sort of stuff as we had everything else. Relatives from Oklahoma would bring us assorted melons and peanuts they raised.

Sun City was a thriving little town with three grocery stores, a hardware store, a post office, two gas stations, a mechanics shop, a blacksmith shop, a café, a school with kindergarten for two weeks in September and then 1st through 12th grades (my favorite teacher was Mrs. Julia Knowles – I loved the way she read stories to us), a pool hall, an outdoor movie screen (in the summer on Saturday nights, everyone in town that wanted to could bring a blanket and popcorn and sit outside to watch a movie), and of course the famous "Buster's."

Buster and Alma Hathaway were great people. He was wounded in the service and had a wooden leg. He had to have a special car to drive and every few years he would trade it in for a new one. When he would get his new one, he would come to school at the end of the day and deliver all of us kids home so we could "ride in his car." I was friends with their niece and spent many hours at Buster's playing dolls in the back room. Or

Carol on one of the family horses

we would sit on Alma's lap in her big rocker, and she would read to us. I would get to go up to Buster's three times a week to get an ice cream cone, which was five cents a dip. Alma's parents, and later her sister owned one of the grocery stores. At one of the grocery stores, they would cut bologna or cheese slices which they then wrapped in paper to be taken home. They also sold sewing material and items there.

My parents and relatives always helped with the Peace Treaty Pageant. Daddy harnessed the horse and mule teams, and he and his brothers drove the wagons in the parades in the pageant events. Mother helped with the cooking and helped feed everyone. One time they were a wagon driver short, so my dad asked Mom to drive a team of mules in the parade. Something spooked the mules, and they decided to run. She quickly got them back in control, but being a kid I thought the fast ride was great and wanted her to do it again.

Many of our clothes were hand me downs. My mother would move the pocket down to the bottom on my brothers' shirts and cut the cuff off and make a jacket for me with roll up sleeves. We usually went barefoot in the summer and would get a new pair of shoes for school. Envelopes were carefully taken apart and turned inside out so they could be used again. Many times, we could still see the previous address on what was now the inside of the envelope. Stamps were two cents. Glue was made with flour and water. Nothing from our table was thrown away. It was either fed to the cats, dogs, chickens, pigs, or whatever needed to be fed.

There was a four room house that was going to be torn down or moved to put the road in. My daddy purchased it and moved it on big logs in front of the two rooms we were living in. He attached them by building three more rooms in between them. We could have a bedroom. Several years later, he added two more bedrooms, a walk-in closet and a bathroom, and we had a sink, a toilet, a bathtub, and running water in our house for the first time. We had a propane stove and tank put in, so all the wood my brother and I had to cut and carry in every evening for our mother to use during the day to cook with or heat with was ending. I missed the big wood heating stove though, because before, when anyone would get sick, my mother would throw a pinch of sulfur on the hot stove to kill the germs in the air. It was always a pretty sparkling blue when it would burn.

Daddy was the town mayor and a school board member for many years. We were always told that if we ever got in trouble or used the fact that he was on the school board to try to get by with anything, we would get a spanking when we got home. I always believed him so for the most part did what I was told. He gave three of us our school diplomas when we graduated.

About a year ago, our youngest grandson was asking about "things in the olden days." We were discussing butter, so I thought this was a golden opportunity to go through our house and show him some of the things we have from our parents and explain to him how they were used. So we gave him explanations for how to use the churn, butter molds, coal oil lamps, and rotary telephones. He could not believe we could exist without cell phones. We told him we had to know our math or use paper and pencil to figure it, as we didn't have calculators or computers. There were no video games, and he wanted to know what we did for fun. I told him we played outside with friends or pets, played ball, jumped rope, and things of that sort. He was astonished that we could even exist without a Wii. And so the story goes!

A Valued Education
By Sister Teresita Huse of Great Bend, Kansas
Born 1918

Frank and Clara Huse and Leo, their two-year old son, were happy to welcome Marcella, the second child into their home in Kingman, on July 23, 1918. They lived in a very nice area with friendly families and children on a dead-end street just two blocks south of St. Patrick Catholic Church.

Years passed quickly and it was time for Leo to go to school. However, a Catholic education for the children was a priority for the parents. Sadly, there was no Catholic School in Kingman. So in early September 1923, with their three children (Cletus, a baby had joined the household) the parents drove 20 miles west of Kingman to Willowdale. Fortunately, Grandma Huse lived just a block north of St. Peter's Catholic School. The Dominican Sisters from Great Bend, Kansas, well known for their excellent teaching, were the teachers. The family was well acquainted with the Sisters because Frank's sister, Sister Regina, had entered the Dominican Sisters' Convent a number of years earlier.

Can you imagine a little first grade boy living with Grandma from Monday morning to Friday and at 4:00 o'clock jumping into the car with his little suitcase and headed "home" for the weekend! Two years later Marcella joined the weekly travelers. Leo did this for eight years! Cletus, the third child died at age 5 and Sylvester, the youngest, was a passenger for one year. In 1930, the year the Catholic School in Kingman was built, the family moved to Wichita. The children enrolled in the school of the Cathedral of the Immaculate Conception Parish.

Sister Teresita Huse (Marcella), a Dominican Sister of Peace in Great Bend, recalls the six years she spent with Grandma, only twice because of the weather. The parents were not able to pick up the children on a Friday afternoon! What a record of dedication!

Another grateful memory of Sister's is every noon the children enjoyed a "warm" lunch with Grandma while the other children carried theirs in a little tin bucket.

The Sisters were most grateful for the service the Huse family provided them. When shoes needed to be repaired, a Sister would ask Marcella to come to the house. On Friday at 4:00, she would pick up the shoes and take them to the cobbler in Kingman. Eventually, she learned that the largest package always held the one Sister's size 12 shoes. Of course, when the shoes were returned a week later to the Sisters, Marcella always received a "generous surprise thanks."

My Graduation Gifts
By Maxine Kirkpatrick of Kingman, Kansas
Born 1928

As a member of the "Greatest Generation," I have experienced some of the most memorable events in American history. An old country doctor from the tiny town of Belmont, Kansas delivered me at home on April 17, 1928. His motto was, "My Ford is always ready," his Ford likely being a shiny black Model T.

The Great Depression is firmly embedded in my memory. We were like most other families, dirt poor. Every penny counted. Nothing was wasted. In the summertime, big gardens were planted and what wasn't eaten then was canned for our winter sustenance. My dad worked at odd jobs when they were available, and my mother took in laundry and worked at the local telephone switchboard. Washing clothes was hard work with no electricity. A washboard and also a manual washer were used.

Franklin D. Roosevelt was the first president I remember and when his administration implemented the Work Progress Administration (WPA), my dad was employed planting shelterbelts and building roads and bridges. Our family was then entitled to edible commodities and what a treat when we received fresh fruit on occasion! The flour, sugar, and other staples came in colorful cloth bags, and my mother used that fabric to sew clothing for herself, my sister, and me.

The "dirty thirties" were aptly named. The dust obscured the sun most days. Most of the houses in our little town were old and not insulated and the window and doorframes were poorly crafted, so the dust sifted in. Wet towels and rags were stuffed into cracks around the windows to absorb as much of the dirt as possible.

My parents were musical, my dad playing the violin, and my mother playing the piano. Houses dances were part of the entertainment during the depression and my parents were busy on weekends playing for those dances. People rolled back the rugs in their homes and invited all the neighbors to come. We children played together and then wound up going to sleep in the hosts' bedroom on top of the guests' coats until the dance ended. Everyone had to go to work the next day, so the evening usually ended about 11:00. On certain nights, we listened to our favorite radio shows such as *Amos 'n Andy*, *Fibber McGee and Molly*, and *Jack Benny*.

We survived the depression and the dust-bowl days. From tiny Belmont, we moved to the county seat, Kingman, a town of approximately 3,900 people, where I entered the 6th grade. Being a larger school, it was very scary for me. My parents continued their music and made extra money playing for dances in Kingman and surrounding towns. My mother later formed Kingman's one and only, all-girl dance band called Zora's Offbeats.

On December 7, 1941, I was a freshman in high school, and when I heard the radio announcement that Pearl Harbor had been attacked; I was devastated. My high school years during World War II were the most patriotic years in America that I can ever remember. Some of my friends enlisted in branches of the armed forces and some never came home. All of us lived with rationing and made other small sacrifices, but there were no complaints. We all wrote letters to our servicemen and women, sending funny clippings, cartoons, and everything we could think of to keep up their morale.

I graduated from high school in May of 1945 and since V-E Day was announced on May 5th and Japan surrendered in August of 1945, those were the most wonderful graduation gifts any person could have received. Memories of all of these events are very special, as they played an important part of my life.

Helping Out Those Passing Through
By Carla Rains of Wellington, Kansas
Born 1944

Back then, people that traveled through the countryside were called bums. Perhaps transients or misplaced persons are kinder. However, without being disrespectful it simply meant they "bummed" food or housing as they crossed to wherever they wanted to go. Traveling across the part of Kansas where I grew up meant you were on a "blacktop," two-lane road. Approximately 50 miles from Wichita (a big town), or 15 miles to the Sumner County Seat of Wellington, probably 8,000 people, or 15 miles to the town of Caldwell, 2,000 people that housed our high school, or approximately 5 miles to the country church town of Corbin, which also offered a grocery store, filling station, post office, restaurant, and maybe 35 people.

The reason I gave all this information is because the afore mentioned transients probably wouldn't be transgressing to any of these towns except for some who were either coming from or going to Wichita. The bums were probably categorized into, could my daddy help them, or they better just keep on keeping on.

Daddy had a big heart and a Christian attitude to be kind. There were actually several that came through coming or going to wherever that returned to our place. Usually, Daddy would let them save pride by letting them hoe in the garden or use the weed whip for a meal or to sleep in the barn. Now I don't know why some were not welcome. Maybe they were cocky or caught trying to take something, I don't know. For whatever reason, something would trigger a result that Daddy would tell Face, our dog, to just keep them walking, away from the house and on down the road. Face was named from the comic strip "Dick Tracy." He was an ugly puppy, but an amazing dog that knew to "sickum," when to bark alarm, and even saved my Daddy's life, but that is another story.

Back to the bums, one man that came every year always carried a huge case. I was smaller so, maybe it wasn't a cello case maybe it was just a violin case. He only stayed one night in the barn and usually worked with the weed whip. We always wondered what was in the case. An instrument or just what he found to carry his belongings in. He was tall and slender with blonde hair. Always wore a sort of English Duffy style hat or was that a Fedora?

All the bums seemed to be around my Daddy's age. Some told Daddy they were going to find work or had a job promised somewhere. Others were going back home to family or parents. They were just people down on their luck or going home without a car. I never feared or gave them too much thought. Except I do remember one man came after mother had gone, probably to Corbin. I saw him or heard Face barking. Anyway, he must have been at our place before, because he just sat on the back porch and waited for mother or Daddy to come home. Like I say, I don't remember being afraid of them, but for some reason I hid in the back of the closet 'til mother found me. I don't know how she knew where I was. I do remember being relieved that it was mother that came in the house and found me in the bedroom closet. For this generation leaving someone approximately 10 at home with all the windows and doors open sounds terribly irresponsible, those were different times and people were different. Thus said however, now I wonder why I hid instead of going out and visiting with him!

Those were the bums; the transients were the ones whose car always broke down at our house. Or those whom 7 or 8 people were crammed into a vehicle with slick tires and an overheated water pump. Many, many ran out of gas and offered or asked for some gas from our gas tank. The gas tank was gray and the diesel tank was red. It was up on stilts with a nozzle that seemed to say: "Take some; this farmer won't miss any if he doesn't see you."

More than once people would drive in and honk. Once in the middle of the night I awoke to notice someone turning around without lights on in the driveway. I went down and told the folks. The people had stopped at the tank. Daddy stepped out the back door and shot off the shotgun. Then he walked down to the tank. They scrambled all over themselves with excuses and offering to pay. Don't remember how that worked out with the dark night. It is a wonder they didn't just take off and let the fuel drain onto the ground. That did happen another time; we come home to find that the tank was drained, but that was after we tried to put a lock on it. So instead of a tank for gas and one for Diesel we just kept the Diesel and did paint on the tank "Diesel." People still ask if they could have some, those that didn't ask probably ruined their vehicle.

Daddy hauled people to Wichita and Enid with hard luck stories. We were a long way from town, what else could he do. It seemed especially desperate if the weather was bad. Back then, every time the wind blew, we lost electricity. That also meant we didn't have water. So extra people we didn't know were easier taken somewhere else. Actually, the bums probably had a secret code or marker that led to the house just at the rise in the road between here and there. The code shared that we served country-raised chickens and fattened calf or hog cooked up country style with all the trimmings. What a deal.

Now we were ready to hang the pictures we had cut out of old seed catalogs and to hang our stockings, hoping Santa would be as pleased as we were with our artistic endeavors. After all, we had been making plans for this long before the dead, drought-deformed, shrub had lost its last fight for life. We had walked the mile and a half, with Daddy's saw in hand, and the blowing dust stinging our eyes, to drag it home. Now it stood in a bucket of sand and transformed into this wonderful Christmas tree. Sure enough! Christmas morning we found our stockings filled with a "once a year" orange, nuts, and candies. I don't remember what little gifts were there but there was always something. After the Christmas story of Jesus' birth, we felt we were the most blest kids in Stevens County, Kansas and truly, we were!

The Christmas Tree
By LaVern Gregg Thomas of Liberal, Kansas
Born 1924

My older brother, Elmer, and I stepped back to admire our handiwork. It was beautiful beyond description. We had worked hard. Green and red Crayolas were worn down to nothing as we followed the lines in our Big Chief tablet, and carefully cut them apart and glued the ends together with the glue mother made for us out of flour and water. We interlaced the rings together to make long chains. Now they were carefully wound around our tree. Not only did it have the beautiful chains, but we also had used Mother's needle and thread to string together kernels of popped corn to go with them.

LaVern and Elmer Gregg in 1930

Butchering Day
By Galen Rudiger of Newton, Kansas
Born 1926

At our home, the day started very early. First, we did our regular chores. We milked our six cows by hand and fed the cattle and chickens. We had a large cast-iron kettle, 36" diameter that we filled with water. We heated it up with an outside wood fire. The water was used to scald the two pigs that were killed by gunshot. The first pig weighed 750 pounds and the other was smaller at 350 pounds. To test if the water was hot enough we would dip a finger into the water three times. If you could only dip it two times, it was too hot, also one small shovel of wood ashes were added to the hot water for a better scald.

The hot water was placed in a scalding trough then the pig was placed in the hot water for several minutes. It was then removed from the trough and scraped to remove the hair. Next, the pig was hung by the hind feet by a piece of wood that looked like a boomerang stick, but very strong. It was from an Osage orange tree that grew in just the right shape and was used year after year.

Next, the pig was gutted. The ladies' job was to clean the guts and cut them to length, wash them, and then turn them inside out. Then they scraped them with a dull knife so that the only part left was a transparent casing to be used later when stuffing sausage. Only some parts of the hog were ground for this. These hogs were very fat. The fatty parts were cut into strips approximately 1-½ inches wide with the skin still on. The skin was then removed with a sharp knife. The fatty strips were ground up then placed in the same kettle (after it was washed) that was used to heat the water. Once the ground fat was in the kettle and the fire restarted, one person was needed to constantly stir with a long paddle. Some of the fat would turn to liquid and the rest was called "cracklings." This liquid fat was placed in a 20-gallon stone crock to be used for baking.

To preserve the hams and shoulders and other parts, a large barrel of salt water was prepared. To test for proper saltiness, a raw egg was put into the salty water. If the egg would float, the brine was ready for the meat to be placed in it.

After several weeks, the meat was placed in the smokehouse. The smokehouse was a small building that resembled an outhouse. Hot coals were taken from stoves in the house and placed in medal containers. The hot coals were covered with sawdust (Osage Orange) to smoke and dry the meat. Sausage and all the meat to be cured was hung there. The meat was smoked for days. Sometimes dad and I would check the meat; it was nice and brown. Dad would take his pocketknife and cut some off. We would eat it raw and it was very tasty. The large hams and shoulders were cut into smaller pieces and taken to McPherson and we rented space in cold storage (a lock box in zero temperatures). Each week we brought home what was needed. We did not have electricity at that time.

It wasn't all hard work on butchering day. Soon someone would take the pig's tail and place it on a metal hook and casually walk by someone and hang the tail on their backside. Soon comments like "I was just wondering if I had a pig's tail hanging on me if I could squeal like a pig," or "Maybe then I could grunt like one." When the tail was discovered, it was an occasion for a big laugh. It didn't take long and the tail would be on someone else's backside.

Very little of the hog was wasted, only the squeal. The feet, head, ears, and most of the pig's skin was used. The feet, we pickled. The liver, some skin, and other parts were ground and boiled, and then put into some large casings and called liver sausage. This was then placed in the smokehouse for flavor. We preserved it in cold storage. The head meat and ears and some of the skin was boiled and ground up and we called it headcheese. We cut the skull open and removed the brains. Our evening meal was the brains mixed with some sausage and lots of onions and fried together. This was served on toast.

There were six or seven neighbors that came to help. Next week this was repeated at other neighbor's houses 'til all were served. Special food was prepared for these occasions. My mother made a special blueberry pie. The crust was flaky, just blueberry juice with tapioca and a thick layer of real whipped cream. That was oh-so-good.

There Was Never a Dull Moment
By Leah Sellers of Florence, Kansas
Born 1944

Growing up in a large family in the small town of Eureka, Kansas was never dull. There were twelve girls, four boys, and one set of parents in our family. I was born in 1944 and was next to the youngest child. Because the first five children were all girls, dad decided to give them male nicknames since he had no sons at that time. Thus, some of my sisters became known as Tom, Henry, and George.

My dad, Wilber Soule, was a handy man; he did repair work for others and had a trash pick-up route. He and my mother, Sarah, ran a hatchery in Eureka at one time as well. Mom was an excellent cook and some of our family's favorite baked goods included her doughnuts and angel food and sponge cakes. She did a lot of canning as well, which the family enjoyed all winter long. It was not unusual for Dad to stop at the grocery store and come home with a bushel or two of very ripe peaches, apples, etc., which had to be canned on the spot. We always raised our own chickens to dress and take to the local locker plant where we rented space. Town residents were even permitted to keep livestock at that time so we raised a beef to have butchered and frozen as well.

We had several lots in town that provided space for a huge garden. It took days to dig the potatoes and carry them to the basement. Dad required us to place them on the drying racks according to size. Any of the spuds that we had accidentally stuck with the potato fork were peeled and cooked at the next meal.

All of us kids had chores that included setting the big round oak table, washing and drying dishes, which almost always ended with a dishtowel flipping at one another, and sweeping floors. As we got older, other jobs included helping with paper routes, cleaning local offices, and babysitting.

Monday's were always washdays in our home. We knew to strip the sheets from our beds and bring all the dirty clothes downstairs so Mom could do laundry. Her wringer washer and two rinse tubs, one with plain water and the other with bluing added to it, did mountains of laundry for our large family. Our shirts, dresses, and even pillowslips were starched stiff. The clothes were hung outside on the clotheslines in nice weather or inside on rainy and cold days on makeshift lines near the stove. The blue jeans and Dad's overalls were hung and metal "stretchers" were placed into the legs so there would be a neat crease down the front and back. Mom ironed all day on Tuesday and when we kids got home from school, our separate stacks of clothes were ready for us to take and put away. Of course, as we got older, we helped Mom with the laundry too. Thank God for permanent press! Mom sewed all the dresses, skirts, and blouses for us girls as well as shirts for the boys.

Clothes were handed down from one child to the next youngest as were shoes. Dad had the tools to half-sole and add new heels to our shoes to make them last even longer. We went barefoot in the summertime so we always had someone with a stubbed toe or a wound from stepping on a nail. When one of us got the measles or flu, it ran its gamut through the family. What one of us couldn't think up, the others did and as a result, we had many injuries from our various stunts. To this day, I can still remember the doctor's phone number, 40.

School was important in our family. All assignments were done before playtime. We had to bring our report cards home to be seen and signed by our parents. We did manage to find plenty of time for fun though. Our house was always a gathering place for neighborhood kids to come and play. We had many baseball and basketball games and played other games like hide and go seek, red rover, New York and Boston, and Annie, Annie over, and caught fireflies in the summertime to make ourselves "diamond rings."

We didn't travel far but occasionally went to see relatives near El Dorado and Emporia. On these trips, we would ride on the back of Dad's truck once the sideboards were removed. As people passed us, we could tell that they were trying to count us kids so we'd wave to them real big.

With such a large family to look after there was always excitement to be found. One calamity occurred when the folks were getting everyone ready to go someplace not too far from home and when they got there, realized that they didn't have the baby. Mom thought one of the older girls had gotten the baby. A quick trip back home found the little fellow in the crib, probably enjoying the peace and quiet.

Family has always been important to us. We have always been proud of the fact that my ten times great grandfather, George Soule, signed the Mayflower Compact and journeyed to America with the Pilgrims. Our family has had lots of gatherings to celebrate birthdays and holidays over the years. In 1964, we began having a family reunion at Christmastime. As the family grew, we changed the reunions to the second Sunday in June and always met at an old rural schoolhouse where we could visit, play, and make all the noise we wanted. In June 2014, our family will celebrate our 50th reunion. Growing up in a family with 16 children, we might not have had all the luxuries that others enjoyed, but we did learn many valuable lessons. We all learned responsibility, how to work, to appreciate what we had, and most of all, how to have fun.

Main Street Saturdays
By Helen Sindelar of Medford, Oklahoma
Born 1928

I have many memories of South Kansas, Caldwell, Kansas. We lived 12 miles south of Caldwell on Highway 81 in Oklahoma. My grandparents, Joseph and Threasa Selmat, left Czechoslovakia because they wanted freedom of religious. They arrived to Caldwell by train from New York and were welcomed by a flood. There was water everywhere around the railroad tracks. Threasa had two sisters,

Anna Skorepa that lived in Caldwell and Barbara Albert of Bluff City. They stayed with them 'til jobs were found. The Selmat's settled west of Caldwell. Joseph, my grandfather, found work at the Blackstone grain elevator, which he walked to each day. My father, Charles Selmat, was born March 23, 1902 west of Caldwell. Later the family moved west of Renfrow, Oklahoma. That's how my family came to settle in this area.

Mary's parents, Charles and Emma Selmat with Helen (Selmat) Sindelar

As a child I remember every Saturday my parents and I went to Caldwell before noon. You had to get there early to get a parking spot on Main Street. It was very busy. Sometimes you had to wait to get a parking spot or even double park. I remember once that a mother left two children in her car (double-parked) while she did her shopping. Her son, a little guy, saw a parking place. He wanted to help, but was too little to reach the peddles. So he started the car not realizing it was in reverse gear. He hit many cars parked behind him. You could hear the bang of hitting cars all over town. Everyone was looking at what happened. Little boy really caught it from his mother. But he meant well.

Caldwell had a big crowd every Saturday. Everyone went to Caldwell. Men went to the sale barn or pool hall. The men wore white shirts and striped overalls, even the young boys. Women all dressed up in their best hats, gloves, and favorite dress. No women wore slacks, always a dress. The women would meet in circles on the streets, visit, or sit on a long bench in front of Detrick's Grocery Store. The women would purchase groceries early in the day, and then put their name on their bags of grocery and would leave their groceries at Detrick's 'til it was time to go home. Children got together and walked the streets or went to the movie theatre. It cost $0.11 admission. At that time, $0.11 bought more. But I didn't get to go that much because I had to save my money. The theatre showed cartoons, Shirley Temple movies, Westerns, Henry Aldrich Family, Clark Gabriel, Veronica Lake, Mickey Rooney and many other old movies.

Farmers would bring their produce to town, eggs and cream and even poultry in cages to sell to have money for groceries. Selling their produce also bought gas for their vehicles. The creamery was located ½ a block west of Detrick's store. A grocery list consisted of bologna, salt, pepper, sugar, flour, coffee, and oatmeal. Farmers raised vegetables, meats, eggs, milk, and they baked bread and pastries. Vegetables they canned. They made their own sauerkraut in a large crock. They stored potatoes and onion in their cellar.

Most embarrassing thing that happened to me, a bunch of ladies were talking in a circle on the street and a bird flew over me and his droppings fell on my head dripping down my forehead and to make matters worst the bird must have eaten mulberries. After an enjoyable Saturday at Caldwell, we would go home to do our chores of milking the cows and eat supper then go to a dance either at ZCBJ or Sokol Halls (west of Caldwell),

After the women cooked the big meal, the men were suppose to wash dishes in 1940

which there was a dance every weekend.

As a teenager I worked Saturday afternoons at Marie Olson's dress shop, located on the north end of town on the west side of the street where KanOkla is now located, across from Impact Bank. I remember when Detrick's Grocery store burned. We came the next day after it happened and they were selling groceries cheap that was salvaged. I remember how we all missed Detrick's. We all looked forward to Czech days. There was a carnival, large parade, fair with exhibits, Czech foods of sauerkraut, Kolaches, and kabashes.

We went to attend music entertainment. My cousin, Charley Truhlar's band played at Drury, Kansas. I met my future husband, Frankie G. Sindelar, there. At that time, there were two dance halls at Drury near the old mill and wooded area. On our first date, we attended the Caldwell Czech Days. We drank a bottle of Grape pop, then rode the Ferris Wheel ride and got so sick that we had to sit on the street curb for a while before we could get to his car. To this day, I never drank another grape pop. We married a year later. Our daughter was born on May 4, 1954. As a family, we would go to the Bi-State Drive Inn near Caldwell a lot. Middle of the week in the summer they had a free movie, which brought in a large crowd. We would make our own snacks, never bought anything from the concession stand. My husband popped a grocery sack full of popcorn, filled a thermos full of pop, and six candy bars for our snacks. You could buy candy bars for a nickel each or 6 for a quarter. We would go home full and happy. My husband is deceased now, but I still live on the same farm I grew up on and I still bank and doctor in Caldwell, Kansas. Some things never change.

Pumping Water for Chores
By Mary Hershberger of Hesston, Kansas
Born 1939

We didn't listen to the radio very much because it ran off of a battery. Think we listened to *Amos and Andy* sometimes. We had a crank phone that was on the wall. You would crank a long or short ring to call the person on your line. We didn't make many calls. One family that was on our party line would get calls late at night from someone and it would ring several times. Sometime we was in bed.

We went to one-room schools, with all eight grades and one teacher. To go to the toilet, you had to go outside to the toilet. There was one for the girls and one for the boys. They were cold in the winter and hot in the summer. We walked two miles or more, to and from school. Sometimes we would walk with some neighbor girls. One time we got several inches of snow, so our dad put the three of us girls on a horse and he walked, leading it until we got to school, and he left us there and he rode the horse home.

We had to pump and carry buckets of water to the house for drinking and doing the dishes. We had to heat the water on the cook stove for the washing machine and pumped several gallons for the rinse tubs. To wash the clothes in the washing machine, you would move the handle at the front of the machine from left to right, to swish the clothes back and forth in the soapy water. When you was through washing them, you picked the clothes out of the water and ran them through the ringer at the back of the machine. Someone had to crank the handle on the ringer to ring the clothes out.

When you was putting clothes up to go through the ringer you didn't want to get your fingers in the ringer. From there they went into the first rinse tub. After lifting them up and down in the water a few times, you put the clothes through the ringer into the next rinse tub. After rinsing them, you ran them through the ringer and put them in the basket and took out and hung on a clothesline with clothespins.

When we was through washing the clothes, we drained the water in buckets and carried it out and dumped it. When the clothes were dry, we took them off the line and folded them and put them in a basket and took them into the house. The clothes we ironed we would take our hand and put it in a bowl of water, then sprinkle the clothes and roll them up for a few minutes, then iron them. The iron was one we heated on the back of the cook stove, when it got cool, we would take it to the back of the cook stove and unhook the handle and hook it on another iron that was hot, and use it 'til it cooled. In the winter when you hung the clothes out, they would freeze and so would your hands.

The little town that the folks went to get

groceries in the summer, would show a movie on a screen hung on the outside wall of the drug store. We would sit on a blanket on the street and watch it. Mom bought flour in print sacks. She used the material from the sacks and made us dresses from the material.

I remember one snowstorm, we had several inches of snow, and it was slick out. Our home set on a small slope of a hill, and us girls would go up by the chicken house and slide down 'til the garden fence or the outhouse stopped us. Daddy slipped out by the barn and spilled some of the milk in the bucket. Mom went out to feed the chickens and gather the eggs and slipped and broke some eggs. I always worried about snakes in the outhouse. I remember seeing one in the chicken house in a nest.

Mom and the three of us girls would Old Maid and Canasta, some evenings. Our little sister slept with me, and one night after we had played Old Maid, she talked in her sleep and said, "Poor Granny Smiles." After that mom told us, we wouldn't play it so late. At one house we lived in, there was bedrooms upstairs. In the winter, us girls would sleep in the room that the chimney was in. It wouldn't be as cold as the ones without one. In the summer, my little sister and I slept in the room that the stairs came up and my twin sister slept in the one over the living room. One night, daddy was in the living room reading a mystery, and the wood rocking chair in my sisters' room got knocked over on the bare wood floor, and daddy yelled up, "What's going on up there?" We said nothing and all chuckled.

Mom always planted a big garden. After it came up, she would hook the horse to the small garden cultivator and she guided it while one of us girls would lead the horse between the rows. I always worried the horse would step on me. Mom always canned food from the garden and put it in the cellar.

Saturday night was bath night. We pumped several buckets of water and carried them in and put some on the cook stove to heat and some in the tub. When baths were over you had to carry the water out. We heated water to wash our hair. I remember we had a friend over and we washed our hair. When she washed hers, she said she was used to washing hers in cold water.

With three girls to wash dishes each day, we each washed after one meal and dried dishes at one meal. Our little sister would sometimes try to get out of it. I remember one time I took the empty dishpans out to hang on the wall. As I came out of the kitchen door some guys came around the corner of the house, and it scared me, so I rattled the pans together. It was a good thing I didn't have water in them. They wanted to get permission to hunt on the place.

When we was littler, we lived close to dad's parents. When we went to the grocery store with grandpa, mom told us not to be asking grandpa for candy. We didn't, we would say a certain candy looked pretty. He knew what we meant.

I Held on For Dear Life
By J. R. Jenista of Caldwell, Kansas
Born 1930

When a toddler; watching my father working on his tractor or family car, I always admired the cupola on top of the horse barn. I thought that one day, I want to climb on the roof to the cupola and look over the countryside.

I guess I was around 12 years old when the proper day arrived, a nice quiet day, and no wind. My parents were in the house and thinking I was in the enclosed back yard. It was time they wandered where I was. I was on top of the barn!

Part of the cattle fence butted up against a low part of the barn roof. I climbed up the fence, stood on the fence post and while grabbing edge of roof, I walked to the top of the barn, approximately 30 feet up.

On top of roof, had to scoot along, getting to cupola, had to stand up and guide myself alongside of cupola by grabbing cupola roof. I held on for dear life and looking over the countryside, later on, my parents came out looking all around wondering where I was. Then, Susie (Mom) yelled, "J. R., where are you?" No Answer, again, "J. R. where are you?" I had to answer, "Susie, I'm up here," waving my free arm. Parents looked up and I bet the horror they endured was terrible. Then Susie yelled, "J.R., come down the way you went up."

I eased on down, scooting along top of

roof, then grabbed edge of roof going down backwards. That was the scary part. It was so much easier going up.

Got on down, stepped on fence and down to ground. Walked over to parents. Susie grabbed me and squeezed me so tight against her body I could hardly breathe. Susie said, "J. R., don't ever do that again!"

We all walked to the house, and not a word was said about what I did.

Hammy Gave up Vaulting
By David G. Davis of Pratt, Kansas
Born 1927

My folks lived in 2-story house at end of south, the only house in south part of town; we raised pigs, cows (milk), and 4 acres of garden. Mom and Dad canned everything. We lived in a 2-story house on south end of 10th Street, only house there, and was 12 blocks to walk to school.

I was 10 years old and helped Dad build a two holler. It was cold in wintertime. I had to milk the two cows we had and slop or feed the five pigs. We raised chickens. For a long time, Mom washed our clothes in two tubs and hung them out to dry.

Me and my friend, Ralph Delwiler, built a pole-vaulting field in back of his house. We didn't get along with, Hammy, they called him, but we busted the pole we vaulted with and let him go, as it was broken in the middle. He never wanted to vault again.

My dad gave me a nickel to go to the show. It took a dime. I did not have enough money, but my dad told me to go to the Barkers, next door to movie store and borrow 4 cents to get in. We didn't have much money. I walked eight blocks to school every day and did pass all grades, (not good), but passed.

I got a job on the railroad when I was 18, worked there until I was 65, and retired.

I need help with this, because I was never smart. My friend went to college and got a good job with an oil company in Houston, Texas. Both of us are still alive, (86 years old).

Can recall some of the good times and most of the poor. I wish I could tell all (I did marry the best-looking girl in our class and still married today (86). I wish I could tell this better, but I don't incline this way, I guess.

Syracuse, Hamilton County, Kansas Medicine Shows
By Pauline Fecht of Syracuse, Kansas
Born 1931

1938 August 15, 16, 17—"Went to a Medicine Show."
1938 August 23, 36, 27—"Went to a Medicine Show."

These words were inscribed in my aunt's diaries that had been kept by her from 1938 to 2003.

As a young girl, I was able to attend these Medicine Shows with my parents. They would come in the summer when it was warm. They would choose an empty lot on Main Street to set up their Truck stage. There weren't any chairs to sit on, as I recall. We sat on the grass and watched their shows. The people in the Medicine Shows came to town with a truck with the back consisting of a closed truck with two doors at the back that opened, and there was the stage.

Many a singer, juggler, dancer, poet, and whomever would perform for a program. During intermission time, the performers would walk around the audience selling a tonic that was a Cure-all for all ailments to the body. It was very expensive. My parents were unable to buy any of the Medicine Shows Tonic, "known as the Cure-all for everything related to the well-being of our bodies," as they didn't have that kind of money for this expensive bottle of tonic.

During one of the performances, I was sitting on the ground with one leg wrapped around my neck. The owner of the Medicine Show saw me doing this. He immediately wanted my parents to come and join the show and for me to perform this act. My parents would not have anything like that to take place. Yet, I remember the incident very clearly.

The August 27, 1938 Medicine Show may have been the last one performed in Syracuse, Hamilton County, Kansas, as there is never mention of my aunt going to a Medicine Show again in her daily writings.

When a Medicine Show came to town, our family was there. I don't think we ever missed a Medicine Show when performed in our hometown.

I loved the Medicine Shows. They were grand entertainment for our community in the

1930s, for this very young girl and others.

Sitting out under the stars in the cool of the evening and being entertained royally was a precious moment to treasure by the MEDICINE SHOWS that came to Hamilton County, Ks. in the 1930s.

I Still Miss Grandpa
By Bob Metzler of Hutchinson, Kansas
Born 1936

My grandfather, William H. Stewart was born in Belfast, Ireland in 1866. He was six years old when he came to the United States. He married Belle Fordice and had 18 children. Later on, when he lived with us, Grandpa took me to town to the Pow Wow when I was five years old. He set me up on a pony in front of the bank at 2nd and Main.

He helped my mother keep us kids in line. One day, he got tired of listening to my sister and hung her up by her dress on a nail. Another time, he let me sample his beer and rolled me under his bed when I got tipsy. When my mother found out what had happened, she was really mad at him.

He worked at one of the Hutchinson salt companies as a dockworker. While working on December 17, 1941 he was hit and killed by a troop train that was passing through Hutchinson. He is buried in Marquette, Kansas.

I am now 77 years old, and I still miss him. He was a good grandpa. These are some of the things that were highlights of my growing up years.

Childhood Memories, While Growing Up
By Eleanor Smith of Ulysses, Kansas
Born 1936

I grew up in Hamilton County, in Southwest Kansas, in a big two-story house no heat, no electricity, and no running water. We all survived.

We had an outhouse. In the summer, we always had to watch out for snakes. We had to be careful when we gathered eggs, because snakes would get into the chicken's nest.

We had a grove of trees that grew in a circle. We girls made a playhouse there. We had wooden crates for our stove, icebox, table, and chairs. We cooked a lot of mud pies.

In the summer, we cleaned out the cow tank so we could swim in that.

We always had a huge garden. We had a watermelon and cantaloupe spot a ways from the house. The kids from town used to come out late at night to steal them. My dad would get out the shotgun and fire it a couple of times. He didn't do it very often, because there were two rows of barbed wire and he didn't want anybody to get hurt.

In the winter we played checkers or dominos and listened to the radio; battery operated.

We had a lot of chores to do, fed the chickens, gathered eggs, slopped the hogs, fed the cows, and milked them.

We went to a country school. It was a one-room school; all grades. Mom took us to school and if the weather was nice, we walked

Bob Metzler with Grandpa Stewart

home. Sometimes in the winter, we went by horse and wagon.

As far as medicine went, what I remember is Carter's little liver pills and if you had a sore throat, they greased you up with hot salve and it sure did burn, but it worked.

I remember a story my grandmother told us. She was in the outhouse and discovered a snake in there. She said the only thing that moved was her bowels.

We listened to Fibber McGee & Molly and the Thin Man on the radio. My grandmother was always listening in on the party line.

We had a wind-up record player that played cylinder records. It was the only one I ever saw.

We had a wringer washer that sat on the back porch. We had to carry water from the well to do laundry.

I remember going to the movies on Saturday afternoons. They were 5 cents, then 12 cents.

We wore homemade clothes. Our dresses were made out of sugar sacks.

We were snowed in for three weeks one time. That was the worst blizzard I remember.

We had a family that lived there that all played musical instruments. They would get together at somebody's house and have a dance. There was also a big concrete slab along the river, where in the summer they would have the dance there.

I also remember getting so much rain it would wash the roads out. Somebody would walk in front of the car to make sure there were no drop-offs, as it would take big chunks out of the road.

Fix the Plumbing?
By Helen Green of Costa Mesa, California
Born 1931

Oh the memories of that old outhouse. And the realization that we have come a long way in this modern world we now live in. That old outhouse I remember well. I grew up on a farm where in the beginning; there was no running water to be had (we did have a windmill) and no electricity for lighting. And yes, there was the two-hole outhouse. I could never figure out why it was equipped with two holes, but when the weather permitted, that's where we went. The winter months presented a real challenge when the snow was blowing and drifting over our path to the outhouse. Our mother would come to our rescue by providing a chamber pot inside our house out of the storm. In the summer, we just knew there were snakes down in there ready to nip at our bottoms. Don't remember having modern day toilet tissue. I think we used the flimsy paper from the old Sears Roebuck catalog. Fix the plumbing? No problem, we just moved the old outhouse to a newly dug hole and started all over again, not once did we have to call a plumber.

That Litter Born Was Me
By Pat Williamson of Lyons, Kansas
Born 1930

I am a resident of Rice County and have been for 83 years. I was born on a farm bought from the railroad and homesteaded in 1864 by my great-grandfather. At the time of my birth, my siblings, then 6, 8, and 10 years old were told they could stay home from school that day. Why? Then they heard noises from downstairs and decided dad had a new litter of piglets and had brought them inside to keep warm in the kitchen oven. That litter was me being born on March 7, 1930. Some memories: our schoolhouse was one room, all grades, and heated by a big coal stove in the middle of the room. One teacher taught all 8 grades. Since my big brothers and sister went to school the teacher let me go also (I was 5 years). They called me a kindergartener. My kindergarten days were cut short for I got pneumonia and missed the second half of that year.

One experience at going to school, we had a pony and when there was lots of snow, my brother led the pony, and the neighbors and I would take turns sliding off the rear of the pony. Of course, we got wet, so when I arrived at school the teacher would make me take of my long cotton stockings and hang them by the stove to dry. That embarrassed me terribly. A few of the games we played at school were anti over, softball (workup), jacks, and hide and seek. Probably others I have forgotten. There are so many memories of farm life I cannot begin to write about them all. So will close with this.

Halloween Memories
By Geri Shafer of Hutchinson, Kansas
Born 1932

I have some dear memories of Halloween when I was a girl. It was a safe time when we kids could go trick or treating on Halloween as soon as it was dark. We went in our homemade costumes. We went trick or treating by going from house to house not very far from home. Our trick or treat bags were any kind of a large sacks or even old pillowcases.

The best part was coming home out of breath from all the running and fun to show our parents what we had. I loved the popcorn balls and caramel apples and the candy of all different kinds. I liked the black jellybeans that were spicy. In grade school, the room mothers would bring us treats on Halloween afternoons.

Terror in the Outhouse
By Marjorie Terrell of Hutchinson, Kansas
Born 1944

As I look back on my childhood, I must admit that I have some rather fond, and a few scary, memories of the old outhouse. It could be quite smelly and was not at all sanitary, but it could be a wonderful alternative to dishwashing or other less than interesting chores.

Our outhouse was a rather unusual one, as it had three seat holes. It always reminded me of the tale of *The Three Bears*. There was a big hole, one a bit smaller, and one that was child-sized. Rather than a moon cut on the door there was a star on either side, and at night if you dared linger, you could gaze at the stars through the stars.

There was usually a box full of old newspapers and magazines stashed in one corner for the same use we now use toilet tissue. There was nothing more aggravating than to pick up one of those magazines and start a story, and then find someone had used the next few pages. The story was ruined, and it left me wondering what had happened between the beginning and the end.

I remember one particularly terrifying experience when I was maybe nine or ten years old. One afternoon after lunch, I headed for the outhouse, probably to escape doing the lunch dishes. I planned to finish a story in a magazine. I had shifted it to the bottom of the magazine pile earlier. As I reached for the magazine, I caught a movement out of the corner of my eye. There curled up in the corner beside the box was what to my childish mind seemed to be a very large, black snake.

I exited that outhouse on the run, and when I reached the house, I could hardly get the words out of my mouth to tell my mom what I had found. She quickly found a garden hoe and killed the snake. But believe me I was much more careful from then on. For many years thereafter, I checked the corners carefully for snakes or any other critter that might take refuge there.

Most of the outhouses are gone from the landscape now, except for at campgrounds and such, but they had a certain nostalgic quality that was uniquely their own.

Washcloth Slippers
By Garee Geist of Scott City, Kansas
Born 1953

My husband, Don, is the product of a large family who was born and raised on the flat plains of Western Kansas in Scott City. He was thirteenth of seventeen children, all of whom worked hard, played hard, and loved each other.

The family of nine boys and eight girls had no gender issues. In those days, it was all pretty much cut and dried: the girls helped their mother with household tasks, meals, and caring for younger siblings while the boys helped feed the pigs, care for the horses and other livestock, and learned the hot-tar business with their dad. One can only imagine the stories, the laughs the shared legacy when the Geist-Wade families joined for their reunions every few years.

L. C. 'Hap' Geist was a roofer by trade who could be found many afternoons cuttin' business deals around the domino table at the local tavern, not above doing a little trading 'under the table' if his luck was holding. He was strong as an ox and shrewd, but had a tender heart, calling his granddaughters 'doll baby'. As if there weren't enough children living at home, the Geist house was frequently home to extended family members as well.

Grandpa was no push over—having raised 17 children, there wasn't much he hadn't seen, few stories he hadn't heard—but he had a heart of gold. Long before the phrase 'pay it forward' was coined, Grandpa Hap got it. When a fellow human being was enduring tough times and there was something Grandpa could do to help, it was done. Because he knew it was just a matter of time—a bad roofing season, a vehicle breakdown—when he might be down on his luck, and the one in need of help. My husband never ceased to be grateful to the small-town grocers who allowed his dad to charge groceries during the lean part of the year. It's just how things were done in that day. People looked out for one another, and cared for their fellow human being.

It must have been on one of those long, hard winters with little work and less money coming in that the story of *WASHCLOTH SLIPPERS* came to pass. It never fails to touch people's hearts when I read it at Christmas time, adding some background Christmas melody.

Washcloth Slippers

Wash cloth slippers, wrapped in Christmas paper, the only gifts under the tree that year.
Times were hard, and money was always scarce, so to even a child, certain things were abundantly clear.
Little did I know or fully understand the width and depth of my parents love.
When a package beneath the tree for all my brothers, sisters and me, meant selling the tires off Dad's pick-up truck.
Thirty-four washcloths paired in color pink, blue, yellow and green, soon became slippers wrapped and placed beneath the Christmas tree.
How is it that a gift offered from a place of poverty, so enriches the soul, and meets a heart-felt need?
Oh, it might not seem like much in view of all we have today, but just recalling the story brings my eyes to tears.
When washcloth slippers, wrapped in Christmas paper were the only gifts under the tree that year.
(To Dawn, Jill & L. Jay from the treasured memories of their dad, Donnie Geist. 2006)

My Guardian Angel
By Wilma Steadman of Great Bend, Kansas
Born 1928

This true story happened probably in the early '40s or late '30s. I was still very young, living on a farm with my parents and eight brothers and sisters. On the farm, we had a large dam filled with water. One summer we always raised ducks. It was my job to take care of the ducks: feed them, lock them up at night, etc. One afternoon I asked my mother if I could take the ducks down to the dam and watch them swim. They were still quite small. My mother said, "No," it looked as if it might rain as she noticed the sky. My parents left shortly for a trip to town for groceries. One of my sisters was to babysit for us younger children. While my parents were gone, I decided to walk the ducks down to the dam. While watching the ducks enjoy the water, the sky got dark and we had a big cloudburst, rain from the fields and pasture all gushed to the dam. I got scared, I took buckets to carry the ducks home, as I was running in the rain, and water was traveling so swift, I could not tell which was part of the dam or land. I lost my

Wilma Steadman on the farm in the 1940s

balance and fell; the swift water drifted me faster toward the deeper part of the dam. Then everything went black and I was drowning. The next thing I knew I was at the edge of the dam on the land coughing up water and wet. I did not know how I got out of the water. To this day, I believe my guardian angels and help from the Good Lord brought me out of the water. There was no one else around who could have saved my life from drowning.

In Russell County on the Farm
By Doloris Ungles of Ulysses, Kansas
Born 1932

Growing up in Kansas with the winds, drought, dust, and cyclones wasn't for the faint of heart. I was born to Fred and Lydia Lipprand, No. 2 of six children in 1932.

We went to a one-room schoolhouse, no electricity, no running water and an outhouse. Our teacher taught all subjects for all 8 grades. She boarded with a neighbor and we all walked about a mile to school. Before and after school, we had chores to do at home and at school. We learned to milk cows by hand at about 6 years of age. It was fun when weather was nice, but it was no fun when it was dark out and blizzarding. Dad would light the kerosene lantern, as it meant to be out there by 6 A.M. So, we had to pack lunch pails and be at school by 8:30 A.M. oh yes, and eat breakfast too! It was hurry and hard to do. If we was late, we had to stay in 15 minutes and that meant chores would be late and Dad would be very unhappy with us.

At school, we all had chores, clean blackboards and the erasers. We did have tablets and pencils, but we used the blackboards a lot. There was about 12 of them, as the school was built way before our time when students didn't have tablets and pencils and all the work was done on the blackboards. Our school was District-55 Trap School. We all had a number and name for the school. Tablets were, 10 cents for small ones and 25 cents for larger ones, but farmers had no money for such things.

We'd take the cream and eggs to town on Saturday night and trade them for groceries and school supplies or shoes. Bankers Mercantile would give tokens, as even money was in short supply. Mom did not like the token exchange, as it was only good at Bankers and they had good merchandise, but it was higher than we could buy at another store there in Russell. We would maybe take in a movie, as it was usually free and shown on the side of a building in the summer time on special occasions.

Then we got the Mecca and Dream Theatres in town and if you got a 100 in spelling, you got a free pass.

If it was bad out Dad would come get us at school with horse and lumber wagon and he'd put hay in the wagon so we didn't get quite so cold coming home.

One afternoon late, we helped Dad to feed the cows as he brought them from the lower pasture up close to the barn for winter and he'd throw the bundles over the fence and we'd scatter them along the pasture. It was a cold winter day, and this cow chased me. I had on a very dark winter coat and maybe she thought I was a coyote, anyhow she horned me and got me down on the ground and rolled me. I was scared to death! Dad came with the pitchfork and got her off me. He put her in the barn and dehorned her and sold her to a man in town. He came with a big truck and took her away. We didn't have a phone, so I guess Dad went to the community sale building and found a buyer. I never learned the fate of the animal, but I was O.K.

Christmas Celebrations
By Esther L. Schroeder of Buhler, Kansas
Born 1922

How we enjoyed our Christmas celebrations with our many cousins! In those days, we had big families living on farms in south central Kansas. Since we had a big house, I remember our family hosting Christmas for Mother's side on the 25th and Father's side of the 26th. This was done from 1935 until 1943, during my sister's and my teenage years. We helped Mother with all this work while Father had my brothers doing the farm chores.

The activities included baseball or football for the bigger boys and uncles, weather permitting. The younger boys had

*Cousins getting together
Eight mothers with their babies in 1955*

their homemade wooden guns with pincher clothespins holding onto the rubber bands, which were made from ruined car inner tubes. They used these to play cops and robbers in the big barn, or they played in the hayloft, making tunnels or swinging on the ropes. The younger girls had their dolls, while the teenage girls gossiped or listened to our uncles' and aunts' stories. All conversation was in the Low German dialect, but the singing and Bible verses recited were in German.

Now I'll tell about the feasting. Every family brought an abundance of their favorite foods, which were eaten family style sitting at tables. We had never heard of eating buffet style or using disposables. Disposables were not available or cost too much to buy. Quite a number of the dishes came from cereal boxes. When buying a box of oatmeal, we'd find a pretty dish or cup and saucer, etc. in it.

The meal had to be eaten in shifts. After the first group was finished, the used dishes were cleared off. There was no leftover food on the plates. Everybody ate what they had taken and wiped their plates with bread, which was also eaten.

The dishes were washed in the dishpan and dried by hand. Then the table was reset for the next shift. The wet tea towels were hung on a line or two indoors to allow them to dry and be used after the next dish washing. The babies' wet diapers were also hung up to dry to be used again. Since the towels and diapers looked so much alike, we had to be careful to grab the right cloth to dry the next shift of dishes!

And that's the way it was in the good old days!

Memory of a Philosophical Kansas Brother
By Robert C. Dick, Ph.D. of Sedona, Arizona
Born 1938

Many "hometown memories from the good old days" are humorous and often are drawn from childhood experiences. This one lacks humor, and only indirectly relates to the "good old days," but nonetheless, is an unforgettable experience from an unanticipated return to my hometown, Hutchinson, some six years after I moved from Kansas as a young man.

First, some context involving the earlier years in Kansas: when I was ten years old, my half-brother, Freddie Markham, was born in the family. He had cerebral palsy (he was spastic, a source of cruel and ignorant jokes throughout the country during those times). He was never able to walk, and his speech was strained and unintelligible to all but the few of us who spent larger amounts of time with him.

Yet, he was highly intelligent, and we enjoyed having him with us. Whenever my Jr. League baseball team played, Freddie was there. Whenever I was in a school play, Freddie was there. My mother and stepfather took him to every event I was involved in, and he participated vicariously. Freddie was always my biggest fan, and the people attending invariably reached out to accommodate him with seating and in any other manner they could---we regarded that as Kansas hospitality.

Mother arranged for him to go to a special class in school, and my aunt took him to class regularly. She took notes for him and made sure he could participate in every way possible. In short, Freddie was always openly involved--out where the action is and never in the shadows.

My unexpected return to Hutchinson in 1965: In the spring of that year, I was coaching Stanford University's intercollegiate debating program while completing my doctorate. When the varsity team and I were at the National Tournament at Indiana University, I was a passenger in a car that was in a tragic accident. For six weeks, I was in a coma at the IU Hospital. They had to remove my spleen and one of my kidneys; my mandible was broken and several teeth were knocked out; my right side was semi-paralyzed and I had sustained some brain damage. The prognosis was, questionable at best.

Upon regaining consciousness, it was determined that I should be transferred by plane to Grace Hospital in Hutchinson, so I could be visited by family and hometown friends. That was to be an interim stay so I could learn to walk and talk again, beginning the pursuit of reentering a more active life.

During that period, members of my family stood by and gave me encouragement. Whenever possible, Freddie was there. One day they brought him to my room in his wheelchair and left him so we could talk uninterruptedly. It was on that occasion that my most powerful memory sometimes focuses. I was helplessly staring off into space-maybe partially because my glasses perished in the accident, and I had not yet been retested for new ones.

We sat silently for a while. It was evident to him that I was a broken person with much doubt about what might become of my life. Admittedly, I was feeling sorry for myself. In his stressed voice, he whispered, "It must be terrible for you. You once walked…talked frequently…and had an energetic life. I've never done any of those things, so I don't know what it's like to lose them."

I thought, "What selflessness, what love, what compassion." With all his incurable afflictions, he is worried about me.

From those Kansas roots, my mother had grown a beautiful person. Freddie had unmatchable class. After that encounter, I pushed down the road to recovery and never looked back.

In Life, Everything Changes
By Clara B. Thompson of Mulvane, Kansas
Born 1929

The roads were once trails but were becoming highways and hard surface. Concrete was put on them. One named Highway 81 went across Kansas. They were no longer muddy when it rained. Building the roads put a lot of people to work. Farmers were hired when work was in their area. People went to watch the building occur. My sister, who was one and a half years old, stepped on the cement and her foot sank in. As she was pulled back, her shoe was left there. How many cars have driven on that shoe is unknown.

The Orphan Train came through Kansas. Mainly orphans from New York were offered for adoption. There had been a great flu epidemic, and many adults died and the children were homeless. I knew several children who were adopted. There were nine children in our family, so there were no adoptions by my parents.

My parents were farmers, and all farmers grew and canned a lot of food. We would can more than we needed. Some was taken to the church and then taken to the hospital, as that was the main source of food for the patients.

Everyone had a manual water pump and pumped water and carried it to where it could be used for cleaning, cooking, drinking, and other uses.

It was a marvelous thing when electricity came. It was wonderful to get a washing machine with a motor on it. It had a wringer to take water out of the material being washed. We turned a handle and it rolled through. Next was a radio and we could hear things about the world. A lot of good things came about with electricity.

We had a lot of animals: chickens, turkeys, pigs, horses, cattle, sheep, and guineas. When a mother sheep had twins or triplets, sometimes she would put one outside. It was usually my job to bottle-feed the unwanted one.

Everyone had chores, from carrying wood to the house for fire in the stoves for cooking and heat to gathering eggs, feeding stock, milking, and all the things farmers do.

Everything changes. It seems a different world today than when I was younger. Changes are mostly for the better for everyone. As we grew up and married, we all experienced running water and inside plumbing, the great and wonderful changes of our lives.

My Grandparents Taught Me Well
By Janice Merrill of Argonia, Kanas
Born 1944

I was born in 1944. When I was two, my mother passed away. At that point, my grandparents took us three children to raise. My older brother was six, I was two, and my younger brother was six months old. We were raised on a sixty-acre farm thirty miles east of Emporia, Kansas beside a town called Waverly. My grandparents received $150.00 all together from Social Security. If we had not had chickens for eggs and a cow for milk and a huge garden, we would have starved.

We had no running water, no inside bathroom, and no heat in the house except for a wood stove. We also burned a lot of coal. When I would wake up on snowy morning, there would be snow on the inside of my windowsill. We took flat irons that had been heated and wrapped them in paper to keep our feet warm in bed. We were so poor that people would give us their old clothes.

My first year of school, we walked over a mile to the school. It was called Ivondale. The second year, we were bussed to Waverly.

My grandpa taught me how to garden, and I still have a garden today. My grandma taught me how to can things from the garden and how to make pies and bread, and I still do those things today. We were blessed to have a lot of fruit trees: apples, plums, and peaches.

We sold honey and popcorn by the gallon jars. I would crack black walnuts and sell them for one dollar and twenty-five cents. We took our eggs and cream to town and sold them to buy staples. Hamburger and lunchmeat was four pounds for a dollar on the weekend.

It seemed like every time we started to go somewhere either the car wouldn't start or it had a flat tire.

We got electricity in 1951. That was great, because doing homework by oil lamps was hard.

We played a lot of table games like checkers. I still love to play games and have passed that love down in the family.

My grandmother passed away when I was 13, and it was then up to me to do all the household things. Thank God, for all the things my grandmother had taught me, as we made bread to last a week and canned one hundred jars of green beans a season.

The funniest thing that ever happened to me was while my grandparents were away I tried to make doughnuts. I had them cut out and on cookie sheets all over the kitchen. Well, they did not rise. So, because I knew I would be in trouble for the waste, I took them outside and buried them in the ground. A few days later, my grandpa found them coming out of the ground after the sun had warmed them. I don't remember what the punishment was, so I guess it wasn't too bad.

Pie Suppers and Blackberry Picking
By Cleta Cornett of Clearwater, Kansas

April Fools' Day

One April Fools' Day, which was April 1st in a one-room country school, we decided to go to this cave, which was two or three miles from school. Most of us from the fourth grade on up planned to meet at the bottom of the hill when the bell rang to take up school. We took our lunch, as we planned to be gone all day.

We didn't go very far into the cave, as no one had a flashlight and it was plenty dark. There were also puddles of water. We got back about the time for school to be out, and we didn't get in trouble. It was an exciting day out. We figured the teacher enjoyed the day as much as we did.

Pie Suppers

In grade school, we always had pie suppers for the Christmas program. The girls each decorated a box to put the pies in. Some boxes were real pretty. The pies were auctioned off to the highest bidder. I wasn't thrilled with the pie suppers; I was always concerned about who would get my pie, as we had to eat it there together. My mom would make real good apple pies. The schoolhouse was always full of people, and it was considered a big occasion.

Blackberry Picking

I have fond memories of going blackberry picking. My brothers and I, and at times my mom, would leave the house by 7:00am. We would get five or six gallon buckets full by noon. We were always on the lookout for snakes, and the ticks and chiggers made us very uncomfortable. There was this spring of water in the pasture. We were always eager to get to it for a fresh drink of water. My sister would have lunch ready when we got home, which was a most welcome blessing.

The job wasn't finished when we got home, as we had to wash the berries and wash the jars for canning. If it was a good crop of berries, my mom would can 100 quarts.

Swimming

We lived on the bank of Spavinaw Creek. The water was clear and cold. Sunday afternoons it was interesting to go to the creek and visit with those swimming in the creek.

I had a wonderful home life growing up in Oklahoma with my dad, my mom, a sister, and four brothers. I went to a one-room school in Oklahoma through the eighth grade. Walking two miles to school carrying our lunch boxes was interesting. We learned to play basketball on a gravel court. I continued to play basketball in high school. It was an honor to become a star player.

Pearl Harbor Days
By Adolph Kuhn of Oceanside, California
Born 1921

I was born September 5, 1921 in La Crosse, Kansas. I was the 9th child of 12. After mom's last child, she told dad, "Eeny, meenie, miney, and I want no mo." I enlisted in the US Navy May 26, 1940 for six years. Boot camp was at Great Lakes, Illinois, and then three months in Pensacola, Florida at a Navy destroyer base. In San Diego, California, I boarded the U.S.S. Boise and sailed to Pearl Harbor 11 months before the Rising Sun's infamy day. There are approximately 300 survivors still alive, all in our 90s. I had 19 close calls that day. I was the tallest sailor in the Navy. I went two and a half years with undersized shoes, the Navy stocked size 12, I wore 13s in the 8th grade, and today I wear 15s.

I wrote four books about my Pearl Harbor 36-month duty and gave $19,000 to various Veteran organizations. At Pearl I was dog paddling in the channel, clinging to arms, legs,

Adolph and two survivors

Adolph Kuhn at age 92

and body parts, while all covered in oil from our bombed ships. The harbor was covered with floating sailors white hats with stencils of "Henderson," "Smith," "Galloway," but no "Kuhn" I thank God and my guardian angel daily in prayer. I saw a sailor beheaded by Japanese bullets, the pilot flying so low his wheels were scraping our palm trees and exposing his gold tooth in a grin while spraying hot bullets around my feet. Yes 19 close calls.

I participated in the Kansas depression days, jackrabbit dives, dustbowl days 1935, and the grasshopper invasion eating all the clothes on moms clothesline and much much more. Wringer washer, brother had his arm squeezed. No broken bones though. Rumble seat rides at Pearl as Japanese bullets pelted all around. One room school, eight students total. Blizzards. There were many snakes, 13 in one day on our farm. Dad popped their heads like cracking a whip. Swimming holes in Buffalo, holes in our pasture. First love. Esther Urban and I still correspond eight decades later. Wall mounted telephone with hand crank and two large batteries. Farm chores: slop hogs, milk cows, separate milk, and cream, churn butter. Games: marbles, hide and seek, horseshoes, tag, surrounding jack knife toss, baseball, Annie Annie over, merry go round, stilt walking, snowball fights, sword fights with long icicles, boxing tree climbing, and many more. In Kansas, our family was known as the Volga Germans. My grandpa Kuhn brought my dad and aunt from the Volga River area in Russia to America and Kansas made them feel more at home, climate wise.

Lost Our Dad to a Lightning Strike
By Stanley J. Smith of Garden Plain, Kansas
Born 1929

I'm age 84 now. This remembrance goes back to September 3, 1940, the first day of school at Hillsdale, a one-room schoolhouse with about 17 students, located east of Duquoin, Kansas.

Soon after the students had settled down after lunch break, a large bolt of lightning flashed in the west, coming down at about 45 degrees. We were all startled, then, went on about our studies. About an hour later, a couple of men came to the schoolhouse door and talked to Mrs. Yoder, our teacher. She called for us Smith kids to come to the door and said, "You kids are going to have to be real brave, then informed us that our father had been killed by lightning. Sharon was 12, I was 11, and Kathleen was 8. My dad had been plowing with three horses, Danny, Prince, and another horse that he was breaking to work. Our dad, Troley Smith, was 42.

Years later, an acquaintance informed me that Dad's bones had all been broken and that the horses went straight down, rather than toppling over, so their bones were apparently shattered also. We had been spared that information at the time.

My world changed, of course—that sort of thing happened to other families, not ours. I'm sure that night was somber as Cleo, my mother, and her three children coped with what had happened. We didn't have electricity, a radio, or phone, but that wasn't too unusual for that time.

We went on running our 80-acre farm—Mom may have managed it better than Dad did business wise. Mom said later, that our only real money came from selling our chicken eggs and cream. Today (year 2014) most people spend more on their cat than our total income was back in 1940.

Later that year, just before Christmas, Mom needed an operation to remove a tumor. Our farm was near Duquoin, and Mom drove 15 miles to Anthony in our 1931 Chevy with me going along. It had snowed quite a bit, and had drifted. Mom had taught me to drive, and after arriving at the Galoway Hospital, had me drive back home. She said to get help from a neighbor if I had trouble. While driving by the home of Forrest King, I almost ran into a snowdrift while glancing over to see if he might see his 11-year-old classmate driving by, got home OK.

We had some pork that needed to be ground into sausage, so Sharon and I undertook that project. For years, we would laugh at how course that sausage was, but I guess we ate it. Seems we managed to get along OK, and kept the coal stove going. I don't remember about cooking, but Sharon probably did that. We wrapped up a hot brick for the foot of the bed if anybody had cold feet.

Mom was back in a couple of weeks, and we were happy to see her!

Mom did get a radio so we could keep up on the news and listen to Fibber McGee and Molly, etc. She also made lye soap after butchering and our dishwater was fed to the hogs after being mixed with grain and scraps.

Earlier, Mom and Dad had bought a new washing machine. A neighbor, Henry, came over to see it, and said, "It's not worth a damn." Mom said he was right. I remember it being a wooden tub on legs, with a wooden lever. Heating water in a tub and using a "stomper" was the way I remember Mom washing the clothes, using her lye soap, of course.

Also, as I was growing up, I got into the habit of swiping a few matches as I walked through the kitchen. Dad was talking to me about something one time, and I was nervously running my fingernail over a match head in my pocket. It ignited and I tried to contain it in my pocket, but it was hot and I had to throw it on the ground. I could tell that Dad was surprised at all the expressions on my face, but as I recall, he let it go—probably figured I had my punishment.

Another time, I went on a wagon ride with several other boys. A used cigar was spotted along the road, so I decided to try and smoke it. It wouldn't light and someone said that wrapping it in paper would keep it lit. I did, and did I ever get sick. I lost my undershirt, but made it home.

In 1943, we auctioned off our belongings. As I remember, my Red Ryder BB gun got just what we paid for it--$3.50. We then moved to Topeka. Leaving that farm was hard for me. All that's left of it now is the land, in my mind it's still "home." With a tear in my eye—Stan Smith

Catching Chickens and Gathering Eggs
By Kenneth Lipprand of Topeka, Kansas
Born 1948

It was a cold, snowy day near Bunker Hill, Kansas. The date was February 24, 1948. My husband was about to be born. The doctor had spent the night because of the blizzard. My mother-in-law was anxiously waiting for the birth of her sixth child. His five siblings were also anxious to see the new baby. My father-in-law was also waiting, Fred had helped her with her other births, so he was probably happy the doctor was present.

A healthy baby boy was born. They named him Kenneth. He had coal black hair and dark eyes. His two older sisters, Jane and Doloris, helped their mom with Kenneth. Lydia said they would argue over who got to give him a bath. The family lived on land that had been purchased by his grandfather, Richard, many years before. He brought his 18-year-old bride there. They built a house and started farming. Their two sons, Clarence and Fred, also built houses, raised their families, farmed the land, and helped one another at harvest time. They had cattle, horses, and chickens, so there were many chores to be done. Kenneth likewise was taught to help out.

One of the stories he loved to tell was the time he was playing in the barn. Fred had traps there as he trapped animals for their furs. A chicken came in so Kenneth decided to catch it in a trap. When Fred came home he asked, "Who did this; it could not have been Kenneth, he is too little." My husband did not confess 'til years later at an anniversary party where we all got up and said a few words. He said, "Dad, remember that chicken caught in the trap?"

I moved to Kansas 48 years ago. Kenneth and I married in 1968. One of my experiences on a farm was gathering eggs; I was a city girl and I had no idea how many eggs they laid. I gathered eight eggs; I was so excited. Ken's cousin, Donna, laughed and said they usually only laid one egg a day, so many hens had sat on that nest. That story got told a lot!

I have enjoyed raising our children and grandchildren in a nice environment. Kansas's people are hardworking people. Some farms have the 3rd generation living on them.

"Black Sunday" Ended the Baseball Game
By Chester I. Bare, Jr. of Raytown Missouri
Born 1925

I grew up on a farm in Clark County, Kansas. I remember the dust storms of the 1930's. My father made a baseball field in our pasture about 3 or 4 hundred feet south of our house for neighborhood teams to compete against one another. One beautiful Sunday afternoon while the game was being played, my older sister and I were out there playing and we decided it would be a good opportunity to make a little money. We went out and picked some mulberries from the trees my grandmother had planted out by our clothesline and tried to sell them. We thought if we got a big pan of them, each pan ought to be worth a nickel. A few people helped accommodate us. We were having a good time during the baseball game, when all of a sudden we happened to look up to the north and saw a huge black cloud that was just rolling in. The baseball game was stopped right there, and some of the people jumped into their cars and started home. The rest of us ran for our house, but we did not make it before the dust storm hit. It became so dark from the dust in our house we turned on the Carbide lights. The dining-family room was about 20 feet long and you could just barely see from one end of the room to the other. My mother took wet pillowcases and sheets and stuffed and tacked them around the windows and doors. When we went to bed at night we took a wet handkerchief or washcloth and placed over our noses to keep the dust out of our lungs, but there wasn't any way to keep the dust out of our house. That Sunday was April 14, 1935, and later became known as "Black Sunday."

Another time my mother drove my siblings and I to a 4-H Club meeting in a one room school house about 2 ½ miles from our house. A dust storm hit during the meeting, and coming home my brother and I sat on the front fenders of the car holding on to the headlights as my mother drove, to help keep her from running into the ditches on each side of the dirt road as we slowly crept home.

All the cars used to have running boards and when the starter didn't work, they had to be cranked by hand. Sometimes this resulted in a broken arm when the engine backfired and the crank reversed itself. One time this happened to my friend, Theodore Thielen, who was the only boy in my class of 4 students in the one-room schoolhouse we attended through the 8th grade. Sometime in the 1930's when cars were built higher off the road, I remember that I could hardly believe it to be true when someone told me that a new car model was coming out that didn't have running boards. When I saw the car, it actually had mini-running boards that were covered up by the car door when it was shut, and I thought that was really a great improvement in design.

We drove an old Model-A Ford to high school that was about 5 miles from our farmhouse. We picked up a neighbor girl, Edna Fitzwater, on the way. About four miles of our route on Highway 160, were paved with asphalt. One morning my sister Marguerite, was driving and about a mile from the school. As we came down a hill to go over Bluff Creek, the back wheel came off the car and came rolling down in front of us and on into a field. We looked out the back window of the car and saw sparks coming down the hill as the back left end of the car slid down the hill. I had never been late or tardy in school, so when Lane Meyers, a townsman, came by, he picked Edna and I up and rushed us on to the school. He then sent help out from town to pick up the car and my sister and brother. I went 4 years of high school without being tardy or absent.

The Model-A Ford we drove to school had the gas tank over the engine with the gas spout in front of the windshield. It had enough holes in the car body that you could get down on the front floorboard below the steering wheel and keep a hand upon the steering wheel and see a little bit to guide. One time I drove down the main street of Protection doing this, so it would appear the car was going down the street with no driver. I didn't hit any other cars or any people, and didn't get picked by the town marshal.

All the tractors used to have lug wheels, but we got an Oliver rubber-tired tractor in 1936. It got stuck in a wet spot in the field once and had to be pulled out by a lug-wheeled tractor.

I was in the 8th grade when I had my first milkshake at the drugstore in Ashland, Kansas. My cousin, Glenn Booth, took me to the drugstore for one after I begged my mother for a quarter, because he thought it was the best thing he had ever tasted. I agreed! An uncle took me to the drugstore in Protection, Kansas, and bought me my first coke when I was in high school. I remember that I didn't like the taste of it very well at that time.

In high school, I had to help milk 15 to 20 cows each morning and night during the winter. After milking, we turned the separator by hand to separate the cream from the milk. We fed the skim milk to the hogs and used the cream to turn into butter and to put into cream cans, which we took to the train depot every few days to be shipped off. This provided much of our income for the winter. We also took eggs to the local grocery store and they were applied against the grocery bill.

During the summer we did our weekly grocery shopping on Saturday night and everyone tried to get early enough to get a good parking place on Main Street, so you could sit in the car and visit with your neighbors and friends as they came walking by. During the winter, we did our shopping on Saturday afternoons. I used to be thrilled when I got to go to the afternoon movie matinee to see a western movie. It cost a dime and my favorite actor was the singing cowboy, Gene Autry. During the winter evenings, we often hurried to get our chores done so we could listen to evening radio programs. One of our favorite programs was "Amos and Andy."

When I was about 4 years old, I didn't talk very plainly and went by the name of "Junior." My family went to the Kansas State Fair in Hutchison, Kansas that fall. While seeing the sites, I became separated from the family group. After being picked up by the Fair's police, they asked me my name and where I was from. I told them my name was "Junior," and that I was from Protection. They understood me to say I was from Texas, as I was saying "Tection" for Protection. After announcing over loud speakers, they had picked up a lost boy by the name of "Junior" from Texas. I was reunited with my family.

Kathy's dad, Ollie Erker on left fixing a tire

First Televisions in Garden Plain
By Kathy Ast of Garden Plain, Kansas
Born 1943

I grew up in Garden Plain, Kansas. You could probably say today that my dad, Ollie Erker was an entrepreneur. However, we called him a "jack-of-all-trades." I remember my dad being a mechanic, body fender man, plumber, carpenter, electrician, car salesman, landlord, TV repairman, appliance-store owner, and ditch digger. He seemed to be talented in many things.

The area I would like to touch upon has to do with my memories of getting our first television. When I was about eight years old, we took a trip to California where my uncle was living at the time. We children knew our uncle had a television set and we eagerly looked forward to seeing the amazing television set. It seems we had only just walked in the door when my uncle asked my brothers and me what we would like to watch. Of course, we had no idea what we would like since we had no concept of a TV. I sort of remember saying, "anything." That "anything" turned out to be a very blurry image of a man on a little box accompanied by a lot of static. I don't recall the whole television thing being much of an experience at that time, but it must have been a real impressive thing to my dad.

Not long after that, I remember getting our very own television. I'm pretty sure it was the very first television in Garden Plain. Not only did my dad purchase a television for us, he also set up his own TV shop where he sold Zenith and Hoffman TVs. I distinctly remember the Hoffman brand having a very green-looking screen. Dad had a very impressive display of console TVs setting around four sides of a square building that he built for that purpose. Customers came from all around the area to purchase a television from my dad.

My own personal experiences with early TV are many. I especially remember that when World Series time came around, my mom and dad would invite my class (about eighth grade) to come to our house to watch the Yankees and the Dodgers play baseball in the World Series. This would include the whole class and we would actually get the afternoon off from school to watch every day until the series was complete. I always felt very proud to have everybody come to our house, since ours was then one of the few homes that had a television set.

About this time, my dad also became a television repairman. On many evenings, we would be without dad because he was out making "house calls" to repair someone's TV. I remember him carrying his TV box to make his calls. It contained a variety of large

New 1949 Kaisers, all decked out for a parade

and small tubes that would be just the right one to make the TV work again. If the large tube, the screen itself, was the problem, it became a bigger expense with the whole large tube needing to be replaced. Sometimes if I knew the people who had a TV outage, dad would allow me to go along to watch or play. It seems many of these calls were made on our way to visit relatives or to go on other errands, because many times these calls were miles away.

The Small Towns Dried Up
By John "J. W." Minor of Ashland, Kansas
Born 1922

I am 91, soon to be 92, and I'm living in Ashland, which is about 20 miles from Oklahoma. The Cimarron River runs between here and Oklahoma. We are approximately 150 miles from Colorado.

I've lived on a farm most of my life. First, I lived in the Lexington community. I don't think it was ever incorporated, but it had all kinds of businesses. It was a shopping community. They were hoping the railroad would come there, but it didn't. When the railroad did come through, it was so far away south that most all of the businesses moved to the railroad track.

The tracks went through Sitka, Ashland, and Acres and terminated in Englewood. Ashland became incorporated in 1884, I think. It was approximately in the center of the county, so it became the county seat. Most of the towns were approximately seven to nine miles apart. Buggies or wagons could get to town in approximately an hour when they lived half way between towns.

We lived on the main trail for Dodge City from Oklahoma and the Texas cattle trails to early shipping areas. With the coming of the automobile, the small towns dried up. Sitka is nothing now except a grain elevator, which is owned by a private rancher. The railroad is no longer there. Even the rails and ties are gone. Acres is absolutely nothing now. Englewood has several residences and one service station with a few groceries. Ashland is about half what it once was. It has one grocery store and one drug store. It once had three grocery stores and two drug stores. There are other businesses in town.

Highway 160 is the most scenic highway in Kansas. It runs all the way along the southern part of the state. One of the interesting places is the Big Basin. It is a sinkhole that is over a mile wide. It is all flat and when it sank, it went down 50 to 60 feet. The highway goes down across it now. Another interesting sight is St. Jacob's Well. The water comes clear up to the surface and the cattle can drink from it. Meade City also has some interesting things. To see Meade City, go west from just north of the Big Basin.

I went to two different rural grade schools because we moved. I went through the eighth grade in town. Then we moved out of the county, and I went to high school in a small town, which has nothing but a grain elevator and a church. There are a few residences in the community. While I was going to high school there, I played hooky from school and rode a bicycle to Wichita. It was 150 miles and took a little over ten hours.

We had a blizzard in April of 1937 or 1938. There were flakes falling when I got on the school bus. By noon, it was so severe that the electricity went off. We had to find places in the community where they could create heat. It was a Thursday. We finally got to go home on Saturday when they got the roads opened.

A Childhood to Treasure
By Frances Johnson of Harper, Kansas
Born 1930

I had an unusual childhood. My father, Lem Laird was a collecting naturalist, a man for all seasons, an animal dealer, and a wonderful father. He taught me many things that most people could not imagine. He was interested in children and wanted to teach them all elements of nature. My mother, Stella Morse married Lem in 1927, and she went along with him in every way. Needless to say, that was quite a change in lifestyle for her! I have chosen to write about his years of catching and selling animals.

We walked miles along the railroad tracks and roads, collecting ornate box turtles. They later became the state turtle of Kansas. The neighborhood children would bring their finds to him and collect a nickel a piece for each turtle. This as well as snakes would provide them with spending money.

We walked along the banks of the Chikaskia River, picking up snakes and putting them in gunnysacks. It was mainly the boys who were brave enough to do this. A large bull snake would bring 25 cents, which was quite a sum of money back in those days. We kept the snakes in the silo until we had orders for shipping. One of my first memories is of sitting in the silo in my high chair, watching my parents feed eggs to the snakes.

A family affair, along with a few neighbors, was catching prairie dogs. These were kept in our animal pens until being shipped to other animal dealers and animal farms. We filled a large water tank from our pond and with a hose; we put the water in the prairie dog hole. We caught them as they came out in an adjoining hole. They were put in our animal pens to dry and then loaded in cranberry boxes that Lem had completed with lids. We took them to the railway express agency in Harper. I have some railway express shipping documents that state, "Two baskets of terrapins." They were shipped to various locations. Some helpers were Harold, Dwight, and Genevieve Honn and Russell and Max Fox.

We were fortunate enough to visit the farm of Otto Martin Locke in New Braunfels, Texas in 1967. We got to see some of our prairie dogs in captivity.

One of the most fascinating adventures was catching kangaroo rats in the sand hills of Oklahoma. My mother would pack a lunch basket and Helen, my sister and I would jump in the Model T, along with my parents. We would take off for a long, fun filled day in the sand hills. We had to watch out for rattlesnakes, who travel in pairs. Sure enough, if we saw one, there would be another close by.

One year, my sister and I caught enough rats to buy a red bicycle from Otasco, which still hangs in the brooder house at the Laird farm. As I recall, we were paid $2.00 apiece, so that was quite a haul for one day's work!

One of the highlights of my life was taking Lorene Squire to some sand hills close to the Chikaskia River Bridge, where we caught a few rats. Lorene was a photographer for *Life Magazine* and had many of her photos published. She spent hours at the Laird farm, taking pictures of our wildlife. One of my favorite photos is of a kangaroo rat in a teacup. Lorene lost her life in a vehicle accident when I was seven years old. I was heartbroken. She was the daughter of Lillie and Harry Squire and lived on East Main. This is now the Larry Moore residence. She a brother, Harris. He married Dorothy Clark, who had two sisters, Margie and Virginia.

Many other animals were involved, but these are the ones I remember the most. I am an animal and bird lover to this day, inspired by my father. I treasure and remember my childhood like it was yesterday.

Memories I Will Never Forget
By Douglas R. Van Horn of Newton, Kansas
Born 1936

I am 77 years old. We had a good wheat crop on our farm. The binder team of horses had made one round around the field. The binder makes bundles to be made and the shocks to harvest later. The binder had stopped at the corner to rest the horses. My uncle got off maybe to talk to someone. I don't know if a rabbit spooked the horses, all at once they turned and ran fast across the field. Bundles were flying out and over on to the ground. They never stopped until the other side; it was scary, but funny.

I was probably 10 or 11 and my cousin was 14 or 15. In the same field, we were standing on the road by the field. He saw a skunk go into a hole in the ditch. He decided to smoke him out; the fire went into the wheat field and burned about two acres. The skunk stayed there.

I was probably 12 or 13; my uncle and I were on the tractor plowing the field. The sky was getting darker and darker fast, a bad storm was coming. He turned the tractor around and headed for the house. We made it to the barnyard, he shut off the tractor, and we jumped off while it was rolling, about 30 feet from the barn. We ran to get to the cellar door. I looked back and the barn was on the ground. It didn't hit the tractor; we couldn't hear the barn come down. The house wasn't hit.

My uncle and I were helping an elderly farmer and his wife. I was probably 15 or 16. Each of us were on a tractor. There was a 15' drop at the end of the field, a creek with about one foot of water in it. As the farmer started to turn the tractor, he couldn't pull the rope to release the plow. The tractor started to slide. He jumped off and the tractor went over, landing upside down in the creek bed.

I was probably 10 or 11 out walking across the pasture. I looked back and a young Holstein bull was running fast towards me. I ran and made it to a tree. He finally tired of pawing the ground and left. I did too and fast.

I was about 19, working in a factory after work about four working buddies and I would pile into a car and drive 10 miles to hang drywall in some apartments being built. As we were driving down Main Street, we passed a church. A hurst was parked in front. The driver came running out waving for us to stop. He asked if we could carry the casket and deceased into church. He didn't have any help. We carried it in, he thanked us, and we went to our drywall job for two or three hours.

Tornado Watching
By Marita McBride of South Hutchinson, Kansas
Born 1936

I grew up on an 80-acre farm. My dad grew wheat. I had one brother and two sisters. I was the oldest. We had an outhouse. We had an old catalog in there for toilet paper. It had two holes and it was really cold in the winter. We had a party line phone. The people on the line would listen in. We had different rings for the people on the line. Talking about spankings at school, we had a teacher that used a 12-inch ruler and she made you stick out your hand and she would smack the person on the hand with the ruler. I thought that was cruel.

We had a big round washtub and in the winter, we took a bath in that tub right next to the front of the wood-heating stove. One side of the tub got pretty hot. We all took a bath in the same water. We had a wringer washer. It was a Maytag. It had a motor on it. Mom would heat the water in a boiler on the stove for the washer. We also had two rinse tubs; one had bluing and the other clear water. We hung the clothes on the clothesline outside. Mom did the white clothes first, then the colored. She made her own soap out of lye.

I had an uncle that took us to the movies with his kids. My aunt would popcorn and we could take it in the movies with us. On Christmas Eve, my dad would go to town and get a tree and one gift for each of us kids. He got candy and put it in cans and soldered them shut. We also got fruit for Christmas. We always had something to eat. We had a big garden with vegetables. Our mom canned green beans, at least 100 quarts, also tomatoes. We helped dad plant corn with one of those planters you dropped the seed in after you stuck the planter in the dirt.

I had an aunt that made a lot of dresses for us girls. She made them out of feed sacks and trimmed them to make them pretty. The toys on the farm were what we could find. When making mud pies I would take hail screen and a red brick and run that brick over the screen to make frosting for the mud pies. I let the pies dry in the sun. I dug in the dirt and made rivers and used sticks for a bridge. My dad fixed a pulley from one building to another and put a rope so we could hang on and ride from one building to another. Another thing we did was play in the truck full of wheat. We chewed on the wheat to make gum. When we got tired of it, we spit it out. In the later '50s, there was a flood and the water came up in the creek and close to our home. We had a tornado move our grain bin and we watched out the cellar door. Scary.

My sister and I got the big empty round water tank out and sit it on its side and I got in it and also our cousin. We walked in it to make it go and my sister was on the top walking. We got it going too fast and she fell off. It knocked the breath out of her. We never did that again. The family would go to town on Saturday and park in front of Smith's fruit market. Dad would go in and get bananas and we sat in the car and ate bananas and watched the people go by. We just threw the peels out the window.

The Special Gift of Christmas
By Judy Konrade of Offerle, Kansas
Born 1951

I am not positive of the year but I think it was in the fifties; we had a terrible snowstorm. We had a shelterbelt northeast of our house and the snow piled up from the top of the trees all the way out into the field. We would snow sled down that hill until we were totally exhausted. Not only did that snow bank serve as a wonderful fun past time for us but it also served as a freezer for my brother's jackrabbits that he shot and sold to the Jimmy Tieben's mink farm in Dodge City, Kansas. Many nights my brother Ves and I would go rabbit hunting with a spotlight. Of course, all I got to do was hold the light but it was a fun adventure.

I come from a family of 11 children. I am sure we were considered a poor family and looking back, I guess we were, but we always had clothes to wear and food to eat. I remember my mother, Ivra (Tieben) Heiland, going outside almost every morning to catch a chicken, kill it, clean it, and cook it for lunch. We lived on fried chicken and to this day, it is still one of my favorite meals. She made the best fried chicken in the world and I miss her and our dad every day. The meal always consisted of fried chicken, mashed potatoes, gravy, corn, and cucumbers with vinegar and onions. It does not get any better than that!

Of course along with raising chickens came roosters. Every time I would go out to play one of them would chase me right back to the house. My ornery brother, Ves, thought that was so funny watching me run so he started shooting at my heals with a BB gun so he could watch me run some more. It didn't take long before that got stopped.

Our mother's mother, three aunts, and an uncle lived across the road from us. They had the tradition of celebrating the feast of St. Nicholas. One of them would dress up in all white sheets from head to toe and come knocking on the door. When St. Nick was let in, he always threw peanuts on the floor. We always had to pray and sing *Silent Night* and then he left. I specifically remember two very special Christmases. Santa came to visit our house in person and he gave me my very first doll. Later, I found out that my brother, Jerry, bought the doll himself just for me. My parents would not have been able to afford it. Another brother, Bernard, bought my sister Mary and I our first bicycle for Christmas. When we woke up Christmas morning there sat a new bicycle. One handle bar had a brown paper sack on it with the name Judy and the other handle bar had a paper sack on it that said Mary. We were to share. Well, Mary learned to ride it right away but I was a little younger and I just couldn't get the hang of using those breaks. So I would come barreling in the driveway (we had a very long driveway) and jump off the bike and run with it until I could stop. No matter, that bike was so awesome!

I still remember one Easter when I got up in the middle of the night to see if the Easter Bunny had come and put goodies in my grape basket. I still have that basket today. Anyway, my brother Bernard bought a real live rabbit and put it in my nest. He stayed up all night until I got up so he could watch and make sure that rabbit didn't jump out. Imagine the shock of reaching in my basket to find nothing but fur that moved. Needless to say I woke up the entire household.

We lived in a three-room house with no bathroom. Mom and Dad would heat water on the stove, put it in a washtub and we would take turns taking baths. When the water got too cold dad would change it again. Back then we had Midnight Mass at Windthorst Catholic Church. The crib, the music, and the service were so special. We were always tired but you had to go to Midnight Mass or it just wasn't Christmas. Today our church at Windthorst is on the National History Register and still stands as beautiful as always. We come from a very strong German background with God as our strength. Faith was important then and it still is today. Looking back those were such special times. The simple life - our world needs to go back to some of that again, where faith and family are most important!

A Good Life in Liberal
By Jean L. Regier of Liberal, Kansas
Born 1935

In June 1953, I had just graduated from high school in Toledo, Iowa. I was on the way in a train to Liberal, Kansas to spend the summer working for my uncle, George Pitcher and his wife, Pearl. It was my first train ride. I was also welcomed by their son, George, Jr. I worked in the Oasis Motel in the morning as a maid and in the afternoon in Uncle George's architect office as a secretary. In the afternoon, I also learned to draft and draw plans to be built. Some of the drafts were for the Liberal Memorial Library, City Hall, the courthouse,

Jean and Vernon Regier in 1954

and the Saint Paul's United Methodist Church, as well as many homes here and the Catholic church in Ulysses, Kansas.

When they first moved back to Liberal from California, George had built the Oasis Motel out of four Army barracks. The Army base here was closed by then.

Back home in Toledo, I detasseled corn in the summer and tried to help my mother. My father had died of polio when I was nine years old. There were four of us children that Mom raised alone. In high school, I played on the basketball team. I was also in the school band and played the glockenspiel.

In Liberal, I worked hard and didn't have much time to meet friends, but I enjoyed the Light family, Aunt Pearl's family. I attended Rainbow with Barbara Light. It was a busy time. I really enjoyed life although I was very homesick, because it was my first time away from home.

One of the maids, Fern Judy was very helpful to me. She also worked at the Beech Aircraft Airplane Plant. She asked me to go with her to the picnic Beech was having for their employees. She had set me up with a blind date for the evening. That is when I met Vernon Regier for the first time. He spent the evening shooting me with watermelon seeds. Later that evening, Vernon's roommate, Jack Cundif and his girlfriend, Betty, the daughter of Fern, went to Garden City to the drive-in movie, as there wasn't one in Liberal.

I spent many busy days working and dating Vernon. At one time, he drove a water truck for the company that was widening Highway 54 from a two-lane to four lanes. One night, we even drew a heart with our initials in it in the fresh cement.

One morning, I was awakened by people moving around and thought it was early. I found out a bad dirt storm had moved into town. It was just black. I was scared as I had never seen or heard of the dirt storms.

In September, I didn't go back to Iowa to college. I was engaged to Vernon. We drove to Iowa to have Vernon meet my family at Christmas time and to set the date of July 18, 1954 to get married in my home church.

In April, I entered the Liberal Pancake Day Race. I practiced nightly. Vern would drive his car down the country roads following me. Someone thought he was harassing me and turned him into the police. It was funny.

My aunt, Pearl made pancakes for me to use in practicing. In the race, I would have to flip a pancake before and after the race. I put the pancakes she made in the refrigerator after I had used them for practice and dropped them on the highway. One evening, I realized my

Vernon and Jean Regier on their 50th wedding anniversary in 2004

pancakes were gone. Uncle George had gotten hungry and eaten them. That was funny, too. I came in fourth in the Pancake Race. I was also in the Miss Liberal Contest.

After Vernon and I got married, we bought a house at 615 North Pershing, right across from Mrs. Baker's home. Her house later became Baker Arts. We had two little girls, Laura and Brenda. They really enjoyed riding their stick horses across the street to visit Mrs. Baker and watching her dig weeds from her yard. She was a very friendly neighbor.

In the winter of 1955, we had a lot of snow. One evening, our friends, Nemo and Marilyn Freeman and their daughter, Dena had come for supper and to play canasta. When they decided to go home, they found they were snowed in, so we had guests for the night. The next morning, the snow was too deep to drive in so Vernon and Nemo walked to Ideal Groceries to get milk and groceries.

In 1957, we had a big snowstorm. There was so much snow that if we could get to the Blue Bonnets, we could walk to the roof in the drifts.

In 1978, we moved to 911 Maple Blvd, where I still live. Vernon worked for National Beef for 23 years. He has passed away. I worked for Walmart for 19 ½ years and now enjoy retirement. I am still selling Avon after 44 years, 45 years longer than anyone else in this part of the state.

Grandpa's Day
By Kyle Klenke of Alpharetta, Georgia
Born 1975

My son, Kyle wrote this at age nine for a school assignment. Grandpa is my dad, LeRoy Klenke. I am submitting this on his behalf.

This is a story about my grandpa as told to me. He was born on September 25, 1911 on a farm three and a half miles southeast of Spearville, Kansas. He was one of six children. His parents were Frank and Carrie Klenke. He lived on the farm for most of his life.

Grandfather heated his home with a stove. He used corn shucks to start the fire in the stove. They used coals to put in the stove, and the coals kept it burning. He also used cow chips instead of coal, which my grandpa had to go get.

In the days when my grandfather was a boy, he did not have indoor plumbing. He did get indoor plumbing in 1940. Grandfather couldn't run water in the bathtub as we do now. The family used a tub and filled it with water by buckets, and that is the same tub that they used to wash clothes in.

My grandfather had kerosene lanterns that were used for light. In 1937, they bought a 6-volt wind charger for electricity. It could only light one light bulb at a time. In 1945, electricity came to the farm so they could run more lights.

The radio was invented in 1919, when Grandfather was eight. His favorite shows were *Amos and Andy* and also *Fibber McGee and Molly*.

Ice blocks were brought around once a week. In the summer, they used 100 pounds of ice each week, because it was hot. Ice kept food from spoiling. Butter and milk were also kept in a hole that they had dug 12 feet deep in the ground. They pulled the butter and milk out with a rope at meal times. Meat was salt cured and stored in the cellar. They grew vegetables in the garden. Later, they got a kerosene refrigerator.

Grandfather had a telephone for as long as he could remember. They had a crank type phone. When it would ring ten short rings, everyone picked up the phone because it meant there was an emergency or there were peaches were in town to can.

My grandfather walked to school when it was warm. In the cold, Grandfather's dad took him in a horse and buggy. When Grandfather got up, he dressed behind the stove. Grandfather wore overalls to school. Before Grandfather went to school, he had to milk the cows. When it was dark out he brought a kerosene lantern so he could see to milk the cows. He also gathered the eggs two times a day.

Grandfather took his lunch to school in a syrup bucket. There was only one room in the school, so all the grades were in one room. For heat in school, they had a potbelly stove. Instead of a drinking fountain like we have now, they had a watering can.

At school, Grandfather played games. These were the games that Grandfather liked: marbles for keeps hide the button, spin the button on a string, and fox and geese in the winter.

At the end of every school year, the children went to the country to have a picnic. They all went in a buggy.

My grandfather played football and basketball in high school. He played halfback in football. The football helmets were soft, not like we have now, but they did have shoulder pads. Instead of going trick or treating, they would push over outhouses.

Grandfather saw a movie in town one time. The movie was about a man who busted rocks with a sledgehammer on another man's chest. When school was out, the boys went behind the shed, and one of the boys lay down and another boy tried to bust coal on him. It almost killed him.

On Saturdays, my grandfather had to clean out the hen house and in the fall, he put feed in the barn. Steam threshing engines threshed the wheat. It took a lot of men to work the machine, so everyone in the neighborhood helped. They went to every farm with the machine.

When Grandfather went to bed when it was cold, he brought hot bricks or rocks wrapped in towels to bed to keep him warm. He slept on cotton mattresses with blankets.

When Grandfather saw his first airplane, it was 1918 or 1919. When he saw the airplane, he was going after the cows and forgot to get the cows. Instead, he ran to tell his folks about seeing the airplane.

Grandfather got his first car in 1930, and it was a Roadster. Its colors were black with orange trim. The car had a rumble seat in the back. The car cost $400.00 when it was new. To get the money for the car, he shucked 15 acres of corn by hand.

Grandfather got married in 1944 to a schoolteacher named Lottie Linebaugh. Grandfather didn't have time to tell me more as we had to leave for home.

Dreaded Childhood Diseases
By Joann Danley of Pratt, Kansas
Born 1931

One of the things in my childhood that was different from today was having childhood diseases. The first one I had was whooping cough. I was just a baby, and I caught it from my brothers who were in school. I was fortunate to only have a light case, as many young children died from it. At least it provided immunity for me.

When I was three, I had the pneumonia that was prevalent during the Dust Bowl days. Many young children died from it during that time, but I probably had a mild case, as mine was upper lumbar. Even so, the doctor told my mother to get me right home. She couldn't even wait to get the prescriptions filled and had to call my dad at work and have him go get the medicine. I only remember that I had to stay in bed and have some ointment rubbed on my chest and a hot pad put on it every so often. How long I was in bed, I don't remember.

When I was about four years old, my brothers brought home chicken pox. The only thing I remember about having it was my itching stomach, and my mother put some kind of lotion on it one time.

When I was in kindergarten, the Health Department came to the school and vaccinated against small pox. I am sure permission from parents had to be given. It was a very dreaded disease in those days. I had the scar on my arm for a long time. Since that time, small pox has been completely eradicated, and they don't vaccinate for it any more. I was also vaccinated for diphtheria by the Health Department while I was in kindergarten. There was an epidemic of it in Alaska, I think, at the time.

I'm going to say that it was in the Fall of my kindergarten year that I got scarlet fever. Our house was quarantined. That meant a sign was nailed by the front door, and our house was considered off limits to everyone. Any time someone got a communicable disease, the Health Department came out and did that. The signs were different colors to show what the disease was. I think red was for scarlet fever, but there was green, white, and yellow, also.

My brothers went to stay with an uncle and aunt so they could stay in school. Our house had three rooms: a kitchen, bedroom, and the main room. The main room had a bed in it, and that is where my parents slept while my brothers were gone. I slept in the bedroom and had to stay there so I had no contact with my dad. I can remember he would put pennies under the door for me.

After the Christmas holiday, my brothers

both came down with scarlet fever. It was going around everywhere at that time. We were quarantined again. I had to stay home from school. They stayed in bed in the main room. My folks and I slept in the bedroom. My brother told me that Daddy would climb in the bedroom window to go to bed, because he wasn't to be in the rest of the house. Mom would hand his breakfast and supper to him on the back porch that had a small enclosure there. He worked for Darlingas and carried his lunch.

One of my brothers developed rheumatic fever from the scarlet fever and was very sick. Earlier we had lost a cousin to rheumatic fever, so that was a scary time. There were no antibiotics to treat it in those days. My brother was fortunate to be able to see a heart specialist in Wichita and finally recovered, but he lost a year of school.

After someone had scarlet fever, we had to fumigate the house. I don't remember that being done when I had scarlet fever, but I remember it being done this time. Mom had to do a major cleaning job on the house, and then special candles had to be burned during the night to kill the germs. We had to stay in the cabin camp that was across the street from where we lived. A cabin camp was like the early days of a motel. Mom washed what she could, but she put formaldehyde on the comforters. It made our eyes water and burned our noses. I can remember really complaining, but I finally went to sleep and survived.

I had measles right at the end of school when I was in second grade. I had to stay in a darkened room, because measles could cause blindness. I waited to have the mumps until right after I was a senior in high school. My little brother and I convalesced together. Many people in the senior class got them that year.

I was in the fifth grade when there was an epidemic of polio or infantile paralysis. It was a real dreaded disease. It could be mild or severe. It paralyzed parts of the body. The worst cases were when it affected the lungs, and many had to stay in an iron lung that breathed for them. They even delayed the start school that year because of it. It was a real blessing when Jonas Salk developed a vaccine for it. I had children at that time, and I remember taking them to the Municipal Building, where they were holding vaccination clinics. At first people got shots, but later they had the oral vaccine. The vaccine was put on a sugar cube.

We don't realize how blessed we are for the advances in medical technology that have been made over the years. Now babies are given vaccines for whooping cough, diphtheria, and tetanus and for measles. I don't know if they still give the polio vaccine. You don't hear about it occurring anymore. We also have antibiotics to combat some of the secondary infections caused by these diseases. Whooping cough has made a comeback, because parents have neglected to see that their children are vaccinated.

Eating the Heart Out of the Watermelon
By Marlene Shirley Neufeld of Buhler, Kansas
Born 1937

In 1926, two young adults met and fell in love and married. They moved into a home on an 80-acre farmstead and started their next chapter in their lives. The house on the farmstead had been in the family for some time. Then they thought about children, but it didn't happen right away. Eleven years later, mom had taken a ride on an airplane and thought she got sick from the ride. It was the beginning of having four children. The year I was born (1937) a loaf of bread was $0.09, a gallon of gas was $0.10, gallon of milk was $0.50, a new car cost $760.00, and a new house cost $4,100.00. As the children grew, there was a Saturday night ritual, taking baths. You can imagine heating water to put in a washtub for that. There were only a few

Marlene's house that was in the middle of the flood

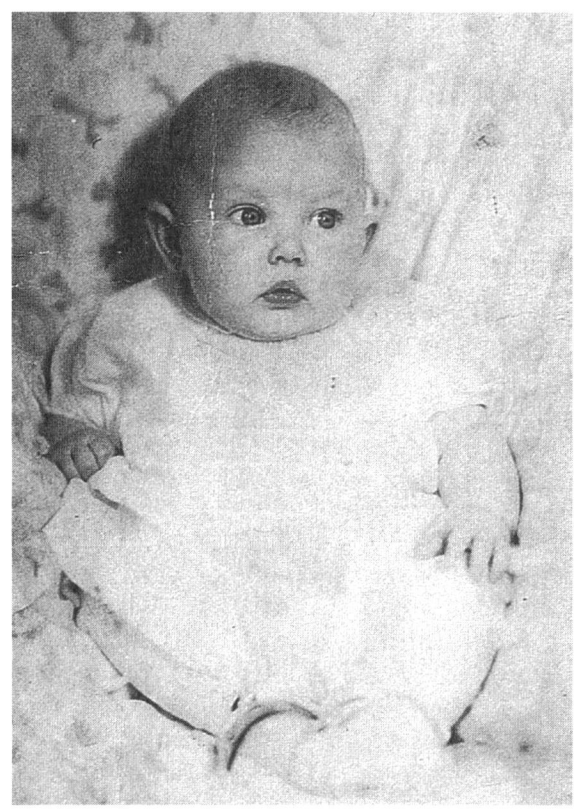
Marlene (Base) Neufeld in 1937

inches of water to bathe in. We took turns. I sure didn't want to be the last one. If I had to take turns now, I'd have second thoughts.

The party line phone was a hoot. We had one lady that listened to every conversation. My aunt's husband, before they were married, called her and asked her how their babies were and you can just see the look of shock that she probably had from what she just heard over the phone. My uncle and aunt were raising turkeys at the time. A person like her could write a book on the phone calls.

I don't know who hired the teacher we had in grade school but there were some doozers. The one old maid would spank our hand with a ruler for no reason. I don't think she even liked herself. There was a set of twins that were hired at the school we attended. One of them was supposed to introduce us to algebra, but I don't think they knew what two plus two was; that's why I took general math in high school. Also, I remember pin curling one of the twin's hair in school when I was in the 8th grade. The other school didn't hire them so we got them for the year; we got the rejected teachers.

My uncle had a car with a rumble seat. At the time, I thought it would be really cool to own one. There was a time we had a Maytag washer. We would have to heat the water and place it in the washer. We used lye soap, homemade soap. It is a good thing none of us had a skin condition; that stuff would eat you up alive. I remember having it out in the yard by the pitcher pump. It was an all-day affair. I don't remember what we did in the winter.

We had a creek that was close to our home. We liked to get in there and splash around, trouble is, I did not like the crawdads in there. When we were in high school, there was a group of guys that had a swimming hole they went to. Well the girls decided to go to that hole. The guy's clothes were on the bank of that hole. We girls decided to get the heck out of there.

My cousin and I told our moms that we needed a quarter each to help buy a watermelon that the teacher was going to get and treat the kids. Well that was a tall tale. My cousin and I bought the watermelon and broke it open when we were walking home from school. We ate the heart out of it. Boy was that good. We were walking home at that time. My aunt and

Marlene's parents, Jake and Mary Base in 1926

mom came to pick us up so we hid under the bridge.

My cousin (same cousin as before) was out on the country road and we picked some green wheat and were chewing on it. A gentleman drove by slow and we decided to spit the wheat out as the car passed. The man had his window open. Well, his white shirt happened to get in the way. He turned around and drove into the yard. He wanted to talk to my dad. My cousin and I hightailed it into the house and under the bed. I knew when I heard that screen door slam what was going to happen next. Dad came in and our house wasn't that big, so he figured out where we were. He told us in certain words to get out there and apologize to this man.

When I started to date we still had an outdoor outhouse and I had to go to the bathroom (outhouse), so I went east around the house so it wouldn't be so obvious, but the guy I was dating (my husband now) threw a rock and smacked the outhouse. Isn't that mean? When I was in high school, Elvis Presley came into the lives of the young people. Of course now days some of the entertainers are a lot worse than Elvis' gyrating. I have a Graceland in my basement. Man when I put an Elvis CD on, I'm young again and I start gyrating.

We lived three and a half miles from the closest town. We would go there on Saturday nights. It was a booming town at the time. The big oil boom was going on at the time. They would show movies, have dances, and would still be alive late at night. Now it is a ghost town. It is really sad how time changes things. I even have an article about how a town revived after the same thing happened to them. I was going to send it to their city office, but that is just dreaming on my part. Thank God for memories.

Stubborn, Curious, and On the Go
By June M. Henderson of Meade, Kansas
Born 1944

I will start the day I was supposed to be born, June 26, 1944, as my mother told me years later. My twin brother was stillborn that day, but Mom carried me until July 3 at four minutes before midnight. Mom and Dad were waiting to get a ride to Cook County Hospital, and Dad passed out. Mrs. Adams and her mom came over to help. I was born on the kitchen table, acting like I was a year old instead of just born. I crawled at seven months, walked at eight months, and started talking at six and a half months. I was stubborn, curious, and on the go. I was told this often.

When I was four years old, my big sister, Betty was who I went to for everything. My dad was blind and Mom worked. I had a little sister, Judy, who was Mom's eighth child. One day, I had Janet comb my long, dark hair and put it in banana curls. She did all right, but she put every piece of gum she chewed in it. That's when I had my first haircut.

I went to school at six and started first grade. When I told the teacher who I was she said, "Oh no, not another Henderson." There were eight of us.

I remember whenever I'd do something wrong at school, I had to hold my hands out and get three hard raps with the ruler on each hand.

When it was Christmas of 1950, I was all set to go to school. I had rheumatic fever. I couldn't move, and I couldn't lift my arms. I missed Christmas at school. I had to stay in bed so I missed a lot of school.

In those days, we all had to take a teaspoon of castor oil every morning. It was awful. Plus we had homemade medicines that Mom made.

Until we got an indoor toilet, we had to go out the back door to the outhouse no matter how cold it was. Or we would go in the chamber pot, but then we still had to take that to the outhouse. I never used the pot.

Our Saturday baths were in a round metal washtub. First Betty would take her bath, then Janette, then Al, David, Joyce, Don, and me, all in the same water. We had no running water in the house. We carried it inside in gallons. By the time it was my turn, I put enough dirt to get it really dirty. So our Saturday bath day stopped. Mom got many drums and let them fill with rain, and we had water hauled and put in the rail barrels for baths and washes.

We had to wear a dress in school. Since I had about three dresses, plus two pair of pants, four shirts, and one-piece cut-off long johns, I learned to use the wringer washer at six. I did this so I could wash and hang my clothes every night for school the next day. I still today in 2014 use my wringer more than my washer and dryer. I hang clothes so they are fresh.

Mom used to make our clothes and toys until she found out about the rummage sales in the church basement in Teadville.

When I was seven, we all would sit around the radio and listen to *The Shadow Knows*. When I was seven, my brother, Al brought our first black and white television home when he was in the Air Force. Televisions had come out the year before I turned seven. We couldn't afford a color TV.

One day Doody's Bar burned down. My brothers and sister and I took bottles of alcohol over to Santa Fe Race Track and sold them to whoever gave us a dollar a bottle. We got that easily.

My favorite pet was my brother's crow. It followed us all over. It stole Mom's money, purse, and keys. It was mistaken for a hawk and shot. Then I took over his baby skunk. I would hold snakes by the tail and then snap them.

I met Elvis two times. When I was eight, I met him up the hill from us. When I was 28, he gave my two-year-old daughter a $100.00 bill signed "Love you, Nina. From Elvis"

Cigarettes were 25 cents, gas was 25 cents a gallon, and soda was 5 cents. That was a lot of money then.

Many a time I'd go to the farmer's field and let the bull loose. Then we'd run to the tree and climb it because the bull would chase us. That's when I knew that bulls chase people with any color on, even red. It is movement that causes them to chase people.

In winter, we'd gather on the hill and go all the way over the frozen swamp. I think I was 11 when I was standing on my sled going down the hill and fell on the ice. I woke and my mom was a stranger come to take me home. I had hit my head really hard and woke in the hospital. I didn't know who all the people were, even though they were my brothers, sister, Mom and Dad. I don't know when I finally recognized them.

My best friend and I were walking home from school when we stopped and asked for some apples. The two old men were talking about killing a horse and sending it to the glue factory. So my friend and I decided to save the horse. I crawled out of the upstairs window, grabbed the tree limb (it's a wonder it didn't break), swung down to the ground, went to where that horse was, led it to some trees by the river, tied it, and went home. There was plenty of grass there. The next day, my friend, whose dad was the village cop, said I was going to get hung for being a horse thief. I had taken the wrong horse. The one I took was a $25,000.00 racehorse. At night, I went and got the horse and took it back to his yard. The next day, the people were saying how amazing that the horse opened his gate, went off somewhere, and then returned the next day, as if he went for a walk and decided to come back.

My parents were very religious. We were not allowed to go to dances or celebrate Halloween, but I would go anyway, especially trick or treating at the farmer's houses. I went more than once, changing my looks each time, because they would give me quarters. I'd get about eight quarters before I'd go get candy.

Then I'd mow people's yards. I'd make one dollar for a big yard and fifty cents for a small one. I'd make two dollars for cleaning houses. I'd get free milk or bread or cake or a cookie. I'd promise the milkman or bread man a kiss, and they'd give me stuff.

A company was building houses across Highway 83. They left full bottles of beer and soda and a lot of times good food. I'd go with my older brother and sister and get as much as we could. We would keep the soda and food but go to Old Man Nobs and sell him the beer.

Finally, we no longer had to carry water. Mom had them dig a well, and we had water in both houses. Mom had a shell of a big house built, upstairs and down. I was 12 at that time. I had to help put walls in the big house. We moved in. Mom rented the little house.

I'd go pick strawberries and find nests of baby mice. I'd bring them in my bedroom until they were big enough to run loose. Mom often wondered where the mice came from. She even spotted my white rat a friend had given me. It was on her bed. She wasn't afraid of anything.

We would go swimming in a big manmade lake. It was really just a pond.

My first real cute boyfriend, Duain, asked me to his birthday party, and of course, I had to take a little trouble maker, Judy. She saw me give Duain a birthday kiss and told Mom. I never was allowed to go to friend's houses. Janet and Judy were always causing me trouble.

We had a dumb phone. We had to dial by

spinning the numbers. I always got caught trying to call my friends.

When I was eight, I got to babysit. I watched a scary movie when the baby fell asleep, *It from Outer Space*. The dad came and tapped on the window and scared me. I never babysat for him again.

At school, I never did any schoolwork. When I quit, I taught myself to read and do arithmetic. One time, I got caught chewing gum. I wore it on my nose all day sitting in the chair. I finally quit school.

At eighteen, I left home. I married at nineteen, had seven children, 15 grandchildren, and four great-grandchildren. Now I live in Meade.

Being Stood Up
By Sister Irene Hartman of Larned, Kansas
Born 1921

Eva Bull, my mother, was born in the Peck/Clearwater, Kansas area in 1880. Emil Hartman, my dad, was born in 1875, not too far from Eva's home. After they became acquainted, dad had asked Eva on one occasion if she would like to go to a barn dance with him. A barn dance meant that some farmer had a large loft on his barn in which he stored hay for his animals. On the night of the dance, the hay was pushed aside so the dancers had plenty of room. Some people adept with fiddles provided the music. Folks put on their best attire for the dance, climbed the wooden steps to the dance area, and the fun began.

Mother said she would be honored to accompany my dad. I can only imagine her preparations: a sponge bath in a small basin, a bit of powder on her body, perhaps some perfume, her hair fixed by an older sister, black high button shoes, and then she donned her best black silk dress. She was ready for the evening. Her brothers teased her a bit about her looks, but she was satisfied, and thought Emil would approve, when he came with his horse and small buggy.

It was 6:30 pm, the time Emil had promised to pick her up. Eva waited for the sound of the horse's hoofs against the hard road. Emil did not appear. She checked the clock in the kitchen, 6:50 pm. Emil was not in sight, nor could she hear the horse coming down the road. It was 7:10 pm. Still no Emil. Neither of the two farmhouses had a telephone so there was no way there could be contact. It was 8:00 pm when Eva finally gave up and decided she was being stood up for the evening. She was disappointed, she was angry, and she was determined she never wanted to see that Emil Hartman again. Her brothers added to her chagrin by teasing her for setting her sights on Emil.

Off with the black dress, off with the high top shoes, she mussed up her hair, and went to bed saying, "I don't ever want to see Emil Hartman, never, never!" Sleep came at last and in the morning Eva went about her duties, acting as if nothing had ever happened, but her heart was hurting and she couldn't deny it. She told herself that Emil seemed to be such a nice guy, how could he let her down like this? Maybe he had found another young girl and taken her to the barn dance. Was he sick? She couldn't give him the benefit of that doubt.

For days, Eva stewed over being left behind. Finally, on the fifth day, Eva's father went to Clearwater to purchase some food for his family. In the country store, the buzz was all about "Poor Emil Hartman on the verge of blood poisoning after stepping on a rusty nail!" His

Agnes and Gerald Hartman with Sister Irene, a friend, and Clyde Hartman in 1926

The Emil and Eva Hartman family in 1937

parents were very worried they would lose their younger son. The story came out that on the night of the barn dance; Emil had gone to the barn to harness the horse and stepped on a rusty nail. He was treated by the country doctor and ordered to remain in bed until the danger was past.

Grandpa Bull hurried home to give the news to his daughter. She received it with relief, with tears of joy, and with a determination that one of her brothers takes her immediately to Emil's home so she could see her beloved. On the way, all her thoughts of "I never want to see him" vanished and she was more than ready to offer Emil all the love of her heart. Their marriage took place in the not too distant future and "they lived happily ever after," being blessed with 16 children. I am number 14 and the only remaining sibling of Emil and Eva Hartman.

Living on a small farm near Clonmel, Kansas in the 1920s there was no such thing as electricity. Hence, there were no refrigerators. But our family did purchase an icebox, which could hold 25 to 100 pounds of ice. I always looked forward to the arrival of the iceman who drove out from Wichita to deliver ice to farm homes. It seems he came about twice a week. To order ice, customers placed in a window facing the road, a square card marked large with 25, 50, 75, and 100. The amount wanted was placed on the upper side of the card and the iceman knew at once how much ice we needed that day. Although I did not experience "harvesting ice," I remember my dad telling that his family would take chunks of ice from frozen lakes and ponds and place these in an underground shelter, which was then covered with straw. I don't recall how this ice was used in the summer; perhaps it became a kind of refrigerator. In very hot weather, it was possible to run out of ice before the iceman came; then the milk would sour and some foods would spoil. As the ice melted, the water was collected in a large tub under the icebox. It was my job to make sure that basin didn't run over or I would have a mess to clean up.

It was common to have a meat man who also came out from Wichita and visited farm homes with his products. He had a small-refrigerated truck, which held "goodies," like wieners and lunchmeat. When he came, there was excitement in the Hartman home, as we usually butchered our own beef, pigs, and chickens, and sometimes yearned for something different like wieners or lunchmeat.

Another visitor from the big city was the Watkins man who came to sell meds like Sloan's Liniment or Metholatum or bottles of gargle or various salves. He also sold vanilla in a small bottle and it was declared to be the very best. Because we did not get to Wichita often, his visit was welcomed at our country home. I remember he was a great talker and could easily convince customers that his products were absolutely necessary. Sometimes Gypsies also came to visit and they took a look at our hen houses. They camped on our property and we found we had fewer chickens after they departed. In our part of the county, we were grateful that we were not bothered with traveling salesmen called "Tinker Men" who came with their pots and pans to entice us.

The Flood of '55
By Frances Elffner of Fowler, Kansas

Crooked Creek comes into Meade County and wanders around for about 60 miles before exiting and emptying into the Cimarron River. My great-grandfather, John Conrad was a Meade County Commissioner and purchased a piece of property near his "79 Ranch." My grandparents, Henry and Lucy (Conrad) Salmon were married in 1900, and he sold the property to them. There was a small house on it from when it was proved up by a homesteader, John W. Farley in 1890. My grandparents added a living room, bedroom, and second story to the house. They lived there until 1915, when they moved to town.

In 1940, Mom and Dad, Ira and Agnes (Golliher) Salmon married and moved into the home place. The house sits on the highest point between the creek and a draw. In 1946, the creek rose high enough to break over into the draw, and the house was surrounded by water. This was the first time that it had happened, and Henry Salmon would not believe it until Dad took him out to show him. Dad happened to be in town when the water filled the draw south of the house. When he came home and saw the situation, he drove to Frank Chipman's, about half a mile upstream, left his car there, walked up the draw, and swam across. That was also the first time water went over the bridge on Highway 23, and that became a warning system. Helen Merkle would call and tell us the water was over the bridge, and we knew we had about two hours before it would get to our house.

The water surrounded our house several times between 1946 and 1955. We had a pasture north of the creek. I saw my father swim out in the main creek many times to help cattle that were caught in the trees find their way across floodwaters. The trees were just tall enough that the cattle would get their heads caught in the Y where the branches spread out. Dad would swim out, twist their heads, and push them backwards so that they were free and send them on their way.

In May of 1955, we had a lot of rain and the creek was running most of the time. On the afternoon of May 19, six inches of rain plus large hail fell upstream from the farm. The storm seemed to follow the creek as it came on eastward. About eight o'clock that evening, Helen Merkle called and told us that the water was over the bridge, and it was higher than she had ever seen it. She also said that it wasn't a steady stream. It was damming up and breaking out as a wall of water. Richard Lee said the reason for this was that the floodwaters were not following the creek bed but coming across the low-lying fields. The fields had not been cleared, and there was a lot of trash that was causing the water to back up. He said that the floodwaters were a mile wide at their house, which was three miles east of our home.

When we got the call, Dad called Dick Bradley to see if he could come help get the machinery up to higher ground. Dick said he would be there as soon as possible. My parents gave me instructions to carry everything upstairs that I could handle, and they took off to prepare for the floodwaters. They only had about an hour and a half, but with Dick's help, they were able to get most of the machinery out of the flood area. There was wheat on the floor of the round top barn, and they shoveled it into the 1941 GMC truck. Dick said that was the fastest he ever shoveled grain. The watermarks went over the wheels, but the grain stayed dry.

Dick said, "We heard the branches on the cottonwood trees at the creek snapping like gunfire before the wall of water. That is how we knew it was time to get back to the house." They grabbed hands, with my mother, who couldn't swim, in the middle and headed for the house. They were about halfway there when a wall of water hit them hard enough that they lost their grip on each other, and Mother when down. Dick said, "When Agnes went down, I thought she was a goner." He managed to grab her, so she came up soaked and spitting floodwater. To the day he died, Dad credited Dick with saving her life.

Upon arriving at the house, they quickly rolled up a new 12x12 piece of carpet and picked up some other choice pieces of furniture and took them upstairs. They left my piano until last. Water was coming across the floor when they decided to try to do something with it. It was one of the heavy, upright pianos. Dick and Dad picked up one end, and Mother pushed a walnut chair under it. Then they picked up the other end, and she pushed a matching chair under that end. As they came up with the second end, the seat on the first chair cracked, but it held. My eight-year-old brother, David had slept through all the excitement but finally woke up when we all moved upstairs.

As was true with many of the older homes, our house was not bolted to the foundation, so they came up with an evacuation plan. If the house started moving, Dick was to grab me and head for the trees south of the house and Dad would follow with Mom and David. Later, they decided that the flood didn't move the house because of the weight of the second story and my piano.

The water eventually rose to four feet around the house but never got more than a foot deep inside. None of the doors gave and none of the windows broke, so we were very lucky. We stood in an upstairs door and watched the floodwater, hail chunks, and trash float by.

Morning came and the water had gone down to below the house. The floodwaters had gone over the top of our water well and sealed it. Dick and Dad had to remove trash and debris from all around it, but it was sound and not contaminated. We still had electricity. We started shoveling the mud out of the house, along with the wet furniture and an old carpet. Then we washed the house out with a hose and fresh water. There was a huge log lying at the corner of our yard. We were glad that it hadn't come on across and hit the house.

The first day was spent cleaning around the house and the second checking out the condition of the out buildings. One was missing and another was smashed in on the side. A couple of old Model A car bodies near the creek bank were gone and are probably still buried in the dirt along Crooked Creek some place. Two metal grain bins that were near the car bodies were last seen east of Fred Beckerman's house, which was a half mile east. A 55-gallon drum full of Skelly Tagalene tractor oil was found ¾ of a mile east of Fred's house a week later. The silt from the flood filled in our fishing hole that was north of the house. We had two pet dogs. My dog, Bingo died when trash trapped him between the top of a wheel and the bed of a truck, and the other must have gone downstream with the water. He came home about two weeks later, dirty, hungry, and full of fleas.

The afternoon of the first day, Dick put my brother on his shoulders and waded through chest-deep water to get out. Dave stayed at Dick's parents until our folks were able to get him. That afternoon, I walked into the old garage and for some reason looked up. There were balls of snakes on a ledge between the walls and the roof. I didn't spend much time in there, but Dad said not to worry, they were just trying to stay out of the water and would leave on their own.

My eighth grade graduation was supposed to have been the evening of the second day after the flood. They postponed it until the following afternoon, thinking that I would be able to be there. The morning of the third day, Dave Goloby and Duke Dewell came in with a small boat to get us. By the time they got us across the water, loaded their boat, and we went by Meade to get to Fowler, I was still too late for graduation. They were leaving the schoolhouse as we drove up. I missed graduation but had my first boat ride.

We spent nearly a month in town at Grandma Salmon's house as things dried out and tried to get back to normal. When we finally went home, we had peeling wallpaper and watermarks on the dining room table legs. There were six men helping when they took my piano down off of the chairs, and they nearly dropped it. That shows what adrenaline will do for you.

The cattle that Dad had in the pasture north of the creek became a problem. The night of the flood, something scared them, and Dad found them south of Montezuma. As summer went on, every time they heard lightning and thunder, they jumped the fence and took off. Dad eventually sold the whole herd.

Today, it is hard to believe that Crooked Creek could ever go on such a rampage. There is very little water to be found in it until you get south of Meade. Some said it was the hundred-year flood, but I don't know. I just know that we survived the Flood of '55 and that it left quite an impression on our family.

Babysitting for Payback
By Colleen Lemman-Tarman of Tribune, Kansas
Born 1936

I was born July 9, 1936, in Oberlin, Kansas. A couple of years later we moved to Oakland, California. Dad had several jobs and finally ended up working in a big Sears and Roebucks store. He loved the job. When I was about six or seven years old, I remember dad listening to President Roosevelt's speech on the radio about the bombing of Pearl Harbor and war being declared. Dad said he was going to enlist right away and mom started crying. Tables were being set up on the sidewalks of our street where men could enlist. Dad

Colleen's grandparents, Claude and Mamie Paddock

ended up in the Navy and was deployed to the Philippines.

At that time, I had one younger brother and two sisters. About two years later, dad's brother, his eight-month pregnant wife, and a four-year-old son were killed in a tornado in Oberlin. My grandpa owned a seed house and farmed there east of town, so my dad moved us back to Oberlin to help grandpa. We moved out to the farm and grandpa and grandma moved to town. The old farmhouse had no running water or electricity. We had to use an old spooky outhouse. My brother loved to scare me saying a snake might be in there! He also liked to chase me swinging a snake by its tail. After we got R.E.A. hooked up to the farm, I found a bull snake laying in the bottom of the wringer washer. I always blamed my brothers who said they didn't do it. A couple years ago, my sister confessed to that evil deed! By then I had two more brothers that teased me. Since being the oldest when I had to babysit at night it was payback for me to tell them ghost stories so they would go to bed and cover up their heads and finally go to sleep.

Dad had his problems too. Grandpa had two large gray draft horses called Mac and Joe that were used to pull the farm wagon. To me they looked as big as elephants-hooves or as big as dinner plates and dad had to harness them standing in the barn feedbox. Another problem was they had been in the tornado and thrown into a large pit in a draw in the pasture. So when hitched up to the wagon and storm clouds started forming, they would get excited and run off. Dad finally had to sell them to a slaughterhouse.

Living on the farm was a lot better than living in Oakland, California. I did not feel safe there with air raids, searchlights looking for enemy planes, learning to duck under our school desks if we had a real enemy attack. Also there were men in white, long robes carrying signs saying the "world was coming to an end" on such and such date.

I enjoyed schools in Oberlin. I started in the 4th grade and was told that there was a paddling machine in the principal's office. Later when I saw the principal paddling an ornery boy on the playground I made sure I did not misbehave! Is that what is wrong with the school system today? Later on I liked riding the school bus to school since I had

Colleen Tarman Paddock

Colleen Tarman Paddock and her brother, Forrest Paddock

a crush on the bus driver that was a senior. We lived in the rock and roll era and loved to dance. We had a record player in the upstairs hallway of the high school and rock and rolled during the noon hour.

Our telephone was the old wall phone and our ring was one long and two shorts. If we were very careful we could listen in on the party line when we heard someone else's ring. We could only do it when the folks weren't around. Dad bought an old red Chevy stick shift pickup. We all learned to drive. There was an ensilage silo built into the side of a hill and we learned to back up into it. We caved in the sides of that silo many a time!

Grandpa Paddock would sit out on his front porch smoking a big cigar, blowing smoke rings and telling stories. One time he was almost killed by an angry hog. It knocked him down in the corral and was trying to get to his stomach. He held his arms over his stomach since hogs attack there first. Grandma was only five foot tall, but she managed to beat the hog over the head with a scoop shovel and saved his life. Grandpa was in the hospital for quite a while getting his arms to heal up.

All of us kids had lots of fun on the farm. We played Tarzan in the big barn. There was a big rope tied to the rafters and we would swing from the hayloft down to the floor of the barn (never broke a bone). Then there was an old rusty combine out in the south pasture that we pretended it was a big sailing ship.

At times during a storm we could see tornados forming on the horizon. Dad taught us how to spot them forming and what clouds to look for that had a possibility to form one. One morning when we went out to do chores and headed for the chicken house, it was upside down! It was a big three-room chicken house and we never heard the tornado during the night. That was another incident that dad said God was protecting us. Dad took us to church every Sunday but mom wouldn't go. Maybe that was the only time she had to herself?

One night when I was dating my first husband, we had a blizzard and he called out to the farm that he was coming out. My dad said to tell him no. He came out anyway. The highway was clear, but when he drove into the turn off from the highway he plowed into a drift that covered his car. Dad had to get the tractor to dig him out because, "By God, he wasn't staying out here!"

The first time I had seen my boyfriend he was walking across the street on the way to the high school. He had just been discharged from the Army after the Korean War. I told my girlfriend that I was walking with, "That's the guy I'm going to marry." She asked me, "Who is he?" I told her, "I have no idea and I have no idea why I said it." I did marry him right after my high school graduation. He was a carpenter working in lumberyards and we were transferred to a lot of lumberyards in Colorado, Nebraska, and Kansas. He died 49 years later from lung cancer. I said I'd never marry again. I just wanted someone to have coffee with. Now I'm back on a farm because I married a coffee drinking farmer! By the way, my youngest brother called me several years later to tell me that our old red Chevy pickup caught on fire in the middle of a field on the farm and met a blazing, glorious death!

On the Home Front
By Barbara Engelhardt of Abilene, Kansas
Born 1928

We have a tendency to make fun of the things we fear the most. During World War II, Hitler was portrayed as a pompous fool with stringy hair flopping over one eye and a mustache trimmed so that it didn't extend past his nose. Tojo and Hirohito were caricatured with squinty eyes and buckteeth. The subterfuge didn't work. I can still remember how I felt, sitting in a darkened theater waiting for the main feature film. The newsreel would come on and suddenly across the screen would march Hitler's hordes, thousands of them, immaculately uniformed, in flawless formation. One arm would be raised in the Nazi salute and one foot high in the marching goose step. Row on row of enormous swastika flags fluttered. My heart would jump to my throat in fear. This was not fiction. This was real. Those terrible people existed. Germany and Japan, those aggressor nations, half a world apart, had to be stopped.

Nearly every able-bodied man was in the uniform of some branch of the service: Army, Navy, Air Force, Marines, and Merchant Marines. Many rushed to the recruiting offices; others were called by the draft board. The only ones exempt were those in essential jobs - doctors, farmers, those with crucial jobs in the war plants, or those who were physically unfit, designated 4F. On the streets of our little town of Kingman, Kansas, and throughout the nation, there was a unique phenomenon, a noticeable lack of men from a crucial age group.

When my dad bought the weekly newspaper there in August of 1941, the back room had a full complement of well-trained printers and linotype operators. Following December 7, they quickly disappeared into the service and Daddy struggled with the job of replacing them. For example, he sent my sister to be trained as a linotype operator, a dirty demanding job, unusual for a pretty high school girl. I helped up front, shagging ads or phoning for local news, or in back rolling papers to be mailed. Daddy followed the progress of the war closely, carefully studying maps of both theaters of operations.

The manpower shortage in Kingman was made worse by the fact that many people got up in the dark of night and drove to work in the airplane factories in Wichita. Rosie the Riveter came into being at that time. Women proved themselves capable and the world hasn't been the same since. Adequate tires and gasoline were available to such workers or to the farmers, but not to the rest of us. We did a lot of walking. Automobiles were treated tenderly. There would be no replacements, no new cars, no new tires, "for the duration."

Traveling outside the local area was infrequent and usually by train or bus. They were packed with uniformed men on leave, going home or returning to base. We considered ourselves lucky if we found enough room in an aisle to put down a suitcase and sit on it. Many times travel hours were spent standing in a crowded aisle. The atmosphere was exciting and talkative, with the men comparing experiences and the civilians wanting to hear. Men in military uniforms could be seen hitchhiking on every road. No patriotic citizen would pass up a young man in uniform. The war separated many young couples, married, or sweethearts, at the time in their lives when they should be building lives together. Instead, they were apart for years sometimes and always with the knowledge that losses were possible. Those faithful girls who stayed behind were as brave as their loved ones.

Ration books were important, not only for gasoline and tires, but for such things as sugar, butter, or meat. In place of butter, margarine came into use. It was pasty white and we had to color it yellow with a small capsule of dye provided. The women had to give up newly invented nylon hose. Not panty hose, just hose. We held them up with garter belts. Nylon was needed in making parachutes. We bought liquid make-up and painted our legs.

Daddy, whose gardening experiences were minimal, planted a "victory garden" which was never very successful, but at least we did our duty. I was never very sure at the time just why, but I diligently saved bacon grease, and every scrap of aluminum foil to be used in munitions. The walls of the post office and every other government building were plastered with recruitment posters or posters urging citizens to buy war bonds and to keep all military information secret. "Loose lips sink ships." It seemed rather remote to me that I, a teenager in a small Kansas town, could possibly be a danger to safety, but I complied with the admonition, of course.

We had no immediate family in the service. But my dear Aunt Myrna watched five of her six boys leave, most of them for front lines, one saved by the French underground. We rejoiced when they all came home. We young girls wrote many letters, usually on V-mail, tissue-thin paper, so they would be less bulky. They were letters filled with hometown chatter to young men of the community. We knew those letters meant a lot. It was a small contribution to the war effort for a teenage girl. I was young enough that my boyfriends were not in the war, but were high school boys chafing to get out of school and into action. My sister's boyfriend was in the service and I considered her loneliness quite romantic.

For the girls a little older than I, the supply of dating material was slim. One popular song of the time said it well: "They're either too young or too old. They're either too gray or too grassy green. The pickings are poor, and the crop is lean. What's good is in the army. What's left will never harm me. I'm finding it easy to stay good as gold. They're either too young or too old." 1941-1945

My Bucket List
By Joyce Murphey of Protection, Kansas
Born 1931

Somebody said, "You only live once, but if you REALLY live, once is all you need." One can learn a lot from challenges at nursing homes, even more unexpected ones. I have been spending my life for the last two years at Protection Valley Manor, the local nursing home. It has room for some 50 residents, who for one reason or another cannot take care of themselves on a daily basis. It could be called the "Loony Bin" for all but maybe three of the residents. Most of them seem mentally disabled as well as physically handicapped. While residents routinely play bingo and other indoor games, outdoor activities like bowling, walking, zoo trips, shopping, dinner out, and fishing might make their lives more meaningful.

In August of 2011 at the age of 80, I was diagnosed primarily as having had a stroke, which leads (still) to dizziness and falls. That resulted in my move to Protection Valley Manor. For instance, recently I fell in the bathroom and hit the door with my head, which resulted in the most glorious black eye ever, amusing observers for several weeks. On my normal claustrophobic pre-stroke and post-husband's death (02/01/99) days, I participated in fun entertainment along the line of "bucket lists." In past years, I tackled countless adventures like whitewater river rafting, including two weeks floating down the Colorado River through the Grand Canyon. I also floated once over the Arizona desert in a hot air balloon, and another parasailing over the western Caribbean with my daughter Shauna, as well as enjoying trail rides and cruises with her family. Since then I have been contemplating another item on my bucket list: zip lining. Unfortunately, Protection Valley Manor is far from canyons in Kansas or elsewhere, so I'm ready to try the nearest piece of likely real estate. That may be a short trip to Branson, with Shauna and family.

I admire all the staff members and the remarkable work they do. They help me in many ways, more than just being friends. My major problem is dealing with mental residents who come into our room uninvited to steal, snoop, and hurt us. For instance:

Entry Through Hall Door
1. Jennie came in one afternoon to steal items on the table (water jugs), climb into our beds, claiming that this was her room and this was her stuff.
2. On Nov. 13, I found Jennie in my roommate's bed with lunch crumbs after staffers shampooed the carpet and didn't shut the door. She was also determined to keep my roommate's bible. It took two staffers to put her in a wheelchair and take her away.
3. Shirley came in at 5:00 am and tried to back me into a dresser.
4. Shirley is a wee-hours wanderer who woke me up at 3:00 am by messing with my feet. She is very strong and I can't turn her wheelchair around. I had to keep hold of her feet until help came. She has been moved to Ashland.
5. I caught Billy pawing through my dresser drawer one afternoon. My roommate and I called for help, and staff came to take him away. I have heard nothing further, but he's

still here.

6. Billy entered our room on 1 1/20/ 13, but I was able to reach the "panic" button on the bed. Roommate Ella asked him what he wanted but didn't get an answer. Staff came and wheeled him away.

7. Jennie came in Nov. 24 to "ask one question." I couldn't understand what she wanted, so pushed the panic button. Staff came and wheeled her away.

8. Jennie came to the door Nov. 25 to say, "If I get a screwdriver and take your name off the door, then this will be my room." Staff heard her and took her to her own room next door.

9. Jennie came into the room at 5:00 am Dec. 7. I pushed the panic button to no avail, so Ella pushed her back into the hall and to her own room.

10. Ruby entered at 1:30 am on New Year's Eve, and headed for the TV. I yelled at her several times until she turned toward the door. I didn't think about the panic button, but two staffers came to see what I was hollering about.

Our hall door was cut in half at my request. That worked really well to keep unwanted pests out, but the fire marshal said it was unsafe. Nurse Penny said she had worked at Golden Acres Rest Home in Newton, where a door was cut in half for a blind resident. I have glaucoma - a progressive blindness - would that make my half door safe?

Entry through bathroom door:

11. Laurine came in repeatedly through the bathroom door. Her family moved her to another facility.

12. Juanita started to come in, and I tried to head her off. For my efforts, I was slugged on my jaw. Staffers came to take her away, and she was quickly moved to a private room at the other end of the hall. I reported the incident to staffers and administration. A state ombudsman interviewed me at some length after the slugging incident, and I have heard nothing further as of 11/13/13. I am aware that my temper is totally lost when these incidents occur.

The new screen door arrived 12/22/13. I am not sure how that is going to work, but the plan is put it on a room for two residents that has a private bath down the hall and move Ella and me into it. I hope that will settle my problems with those wandering residents who try to come in by the hall door and the bathroom door. Maybe this will soothe my complaints. As of 0l/06/14, we have been moved and settled in the new (to us) room down the hall, with a private bath and somewhat smaller closet. Ella is not impressed, but it seems great to me. The screen door will require some adjustment by staffers, but I'm sure we all can handle it.

A Formal Education
By Richard O. Stineman of Newton, Kansas
Born 1937

We finally got on the train! Returning to south-central Kansas after living in eastern Iowa for six years. Mom, my two brothers, ages one and a half, six, and me being the oldest at seven and a half. It was late summer of 1945. The war was over and the train was overflowing with soldiers and sailors celebrating going home, some for the first time in years. I felt like I could relate to their joy, as we were headed to my grandparents farm from the big city on the Mississippi. Dad had driven out earlier to accept a job but had been unable to find a house to rent; hence, we were going to live at the farm for what turned out to be almost a year. As the train came to a stop, ladies from a support group were tossing fresh fruit to the military guys through the open windows, but we were more enthused to see dad, grandpa, grandma, and my Uncle Gene, 10 years my senior and living at home to help grandpa with the farm work. I misjudged the height of the curb when jumping to the street, and crashed into the 1937 Terraplane, which was our ride home. It seemed everyone was laughing at my anxiety to get to the farm. It was now past dark, but the eight-mile ride was pure joy when all my questions about horses, cows, pigs, and chickens were answered with the assurance that they would all be there in the morning.

Indeed they were. I learned how to gather eggs from under setting hens, feed hogs, ride horses, milk cows, hunt jackrabbits, steer the old 1927 Oldsmobile that had been converted to a pick-up, climb the big straw stack, as well as fill and pump up the kerosene lamps, which was our lighting. I learned to distinguish between wood for the cooking stove and the heating stove. I could climb the wind charger tower next to the house and adjust the pitch of the blades. The dry cell batteries it charged provided power to the radio and if they still held a charge after Gabriel Heater's news was over, we could listen to Sgt. Preston of the Yukon, Matt Dillon, and maybe the *Lone Ranger*.

I learned, first hand, by experience, what a hot wire fence was; why it was not smart to ignore the old ram when crossing the sheep pen; why not to touch your tongue to the pump handle when it was below freezing; and that the mud at the shallow end of the pond was deeper than high top shoes.

A more formal education began when school started. Half a mile down the road stood the one-room building, which would house eight grades, fifteen students, and one teacher. We couldn't ride old Babe because the lean-to type shed could barely hold the ponies of the kids who lived farther from school. I learned there was a perimeter around the girls' outhouse that boys don't cross and vice-versa for the boys' outhouse. The real neat thing for me, being in the 2nd grade, was that I could learn from the recitations of the six grades above me. A humorous incident occurred when a nephew of the teacher offered to play his guitar and sing at our Christmas program. When it was time for him to perform, he asked where he could plug in his guitar. Alas, the school had no electricity.

Shortly after Christmas, we received a two-day snowstorm, which gifted us with nearly two feet of snow. Mom's brother and his family, including five of my cousins, lived half a mile east of the school, but that road was lined on both sides by double rows of hedge trees (Osage orange), which caught and held the snow to an even greater depth. With no telephones in the area yet, the older folks were concerned for their welfare, so dad and Uncle Gene harnessed up the team, Babe and Tony, and hitched them to the wagon we picked corn in. We all bundled up, climbed in and covered up with the old, heavy, and fur lined cowhide robes and set out for the schoolhouse corner. As we turned east into the deeper snow, the big wheels on the wagon provided barely enough clearance to keep the wagon box from plowing the snow. The horses pulled hard and when we got there and turned in at the gate, grandpa headed the team directly to the barn, opened the big doors, and drove them inside. We all ran to the house as dad and Uncle Gene unharnessed them, rubbed them down with burlap grain sacks, and got them a pan of oats. All was well inside and the warmth of the big heating stove was so very welcome. Laughing, hugging, and the joy that prevailed allowed for a reunion atmosphere as though it had been a year since last week.

Richard Stineman in the center with his cousins feeding a goat in 1945

Good Friday before Easter made me realize we would be moving to town soon and I began to think it might not be all bad. Some cousins from town school had a holiday on that day and we saw them drive by the school on their way to grandpa's farm. They would be playing and we had to go to school and we knew they would rub it in when we got home. A bit of solace surfaced, when at recess we saw them helping grandpa and Uncle Gene load corn shocks on the hay wagon. Uncle Gene had talked them into catching the baby mice nesting under the shocks, and touching them to the hot wire fence surrounding the field. I had already learned this lesson and knew it didn't hurt the mice, rather conveyed the "shock" to the person who was standing, providing the ground to the circuit. My cousin's reaction was much the same as the screams accompanied the mice heading into orbit. We were still laughing when the teacher rang the bell ending recess.

Another memorable experience was wheat harvest prior to the coming of combines. The wheat was swathed, bundled, and put on horse pulled hay wagons, by men with pitchforks. It was hauled to the location of a big thresh machine, powered by a big pulley belt from a stationary tractor. More men pitched the bundles into the threshing machine, which separated the grain from the straw. The grain was funneled into horse-pulled grain wagons while the straw was blown in a high arc to form a giant straw stack. I could ride on the wagons all day but the main attraction was riding the grain wagon to the elevator to sell the wheat. The elevator was in a small town nearby and anybody on the wagon got a free bottle of soda from the icebox next to the blacksmith shop. Grandma and mom and some neighbor ladies served lunch in the front yard to all the men who came to help. My job was to sweep the yard with a broom and help set up sawhorses and grain doors for a table. After they had all washed off at the pump by the back door of the house, bowl after bowl of vegetables and plate after plate of fried chicken, roast beef, and ham was consumed by hard workingmen in a very short time.

Picnics were a festive time. There were the watermelons cooling in the horse's water tank and multiple pies set out on the screened in porch. Making ice cream had become a science. Jack up one rear wheel of dad's old Ford, pull off the tire, and start the engine. Set the idle down to very slow and wire the freezer crank to a lug bolt. All that was left was to put it in low gear and wait.

Dad came home from work in town early one day and said there were tornados in the area. We had a storm cave just outside the back door, which was used primarily to store vegetables from the garden and hang hams in to be cured. Uncle Gene climbed the windmill tower, which stood between the garden and the storm cave and hollered to get to the cave. He could see a funnel cloud coming from the southwest. My six-year-old brother tried to get there but was being blown down along the garden fence by the strong winds. Uncle Gene grabbed him under one arm and with the other hand, pulled them along the fence to the cave. When we emerged a short time later, we found that the machine shed had lost its roof but no other damage was incurred. The next day, dad brought home a local newspaper showing a neighbor's barn had disappeared.

Our Pranks Growing Up
By Glenda Crone of Garden City, Kansas
Born 1946

I was born in 1946 in Garden City, Kansas. I grew up on a farm a few miles outside of the big metropolis of Deerfield, KS. The population was around 680. Our family consisted of my Father, Mother, brother, and sister. I was the "middle" child.

My Father was a wheat, beet, and corn farmer so I was a little farm girl. We also raised cattle, chickens, and at one time a few lambs.

During my growing up years we had many, many pets ranging from a pig named Roger Rosterdouster, to a pet chicken named Peaches, and two cows named Sheik and Sheba. My Father was going to take the cows to the sale and we cried and cried so those two cows remained at home as the "pets" in the corral. When I was only about 4 I was out by the irrigation ditch and saw the prettiest "worm" so I ran up to the house and told my Mom to come look at the pretty worm. Of course it was a snake.... She very calmly told me not to try to play with it.

My brother and I would go out to the corral, get up on the loading chute, and pretend we were giving the cows a lecture. What a grand time we had playing in the corral in the hay - moving bales around to build a fort and just feeling like we were "somewhere" else.

We had the typical farmstead with a granary, chicken coop, washhouse (because we had the old ringer washer and a shower there), brooder house, and a huge storage building we called the "round top." We couldn't have asked for a better childhood with so many places to play, create, hide, work etc.

So many experiences... we had a man-made lake on the farm to accommodate irrigation so where the water came out to the ditch we had a little swimming area we called the "frog pond" where we would swim. Several times when we brought our head up from under the water we were looking at a little snake swimming along with us. As we got a little older and braver my brother and I walked out on the plank on the big lake. My brother was being a typical boy and fell in so like a big sister should - I stood and yelled "swim Jim swim"... now I wasn't going to dive in after him but stay on the side line and cheer him on to swim. All this time our Mother was watching from the front door of our home keeping calm. We all survived.

My brother and I would play outside from dawn to dusk using every avenue of nature we could to entertain us. One spring we were having lots of wind and dust storms with masses of tumbleweeds catching everywhere... so...we built a fort out of the tumbleweeds and were jumping around praying to God thanking him for the tumbleweeds.

And then there was the blizzard of 1955. My Father and several menfolk from Deerfield had traveled to Kansas City to watch a basketball tournament when the blizzard hit. My Mother and we 3 kids were there at the farm alone. Of course no electricity, but we had well water and a gas cooking stove. Mother would have all of us sleep in bed together to keep warm. Three days of howling wind, snow, we couldn't even see out because all the windows were covered. We couldn't get the doors open because of the snow. Back than the phones weren't all that reliable either so we just waited it out. About noon the third day one of our Uncles came to check on us and thought we were all dead because we finally got the back door open and we had it wide open. Another neighbor came to check on us by horseback and didn't realize that he and his horse were standing on top of our car. We tied rags in the trees at the tops of the snowdrifts and when they finally melted they were 26 feet high.

Speaking of phones, we had a little soap opera going on in our neighborhood so when we would hear a certain ring we would quietly pick up the phone so we could listen in on the "oh sweetie" conversation between 2 folks that were having a rendezvous. Several times my Father would need to use the phone for farm business and would have to ask the folks that were chatting if he could use the phone for a few minutes. They usually complied with no hesitation.

We didn't have any indoor plumbing until I was in the 5th grade. We would take a bath in the double kitchen sink when we were small.

As we got a little bigger we would have to go out to the "wash house" and take a shower.... Brrrrrrrrr... it would take a while to warm up. Than run back to the house. So... of course we also had an outhouse. My brother and I would go together for moral support because we had an old rooster that liked to attack as we were trying to get there. That mean old son-of-a-gun would run at us and jump on our back. A little mischief took place a stick... 3 hole outhouse.... You use your imagination. We had to ride the bus to school and one bus driver would pull in our yard, pull right up to the area of the outhouse, and wait for us. I was so embarrassed every single day... was so glad when he was no longer the bus driver.

My sister was 5 years older so she was "grown up" and didn't do that much with her little brother and sister. One day my Mom was going to keep her home from school to finish some 4-H projects. She told me not to say anything in school. Well.... When I got to school I told some of the kids that we couldn't find my sister that morning. WOW....A flurry of activity followed. They had one of my Uncles come up to the school to ask me what was going on. I thought I was helping by explaining why she wasn't in school... that she was missing!

One year the school district decided we didn't get to ride the bus because we lived on the side of the road that was in another county... so we had to drive. Each day after school my brother and I would ask my sister if we could stop for a coke at the local drugstore. By no means was she going to be late getting home... such an obedient child... even on the last day of school she wouldn't stop. Now as my brother and I got to high school we drove our car needed a new muffler so as we would come to the top of the hill coming in to main street we would put the car in neutral, reeve up the motor, and the car would backfire all the way down the hill... The kids at the high school a few blocks away knew we were almost there.

A favorite past time of kids during our growing up years was "dragging main street"... driving up and down main. Well... that wasn't good enough for our little group of relatives and friends. We would get a huge branch, roll down the window, hold on to this branch, and drag in also up and down main. We thought that was hilarious. Because of our mischief some parents didn't want their kids to run around with us.

We never did anything illegal or damaging.... We just thought it was all funny. Back to tumble weeds.... The boys would have basketball practice after school and myself and three other female compadres would drive out in the country, get a couple tumbleweeds, and then put them on top of the boy's cars.... Hilarious to us again. School mischief

My cousin and I had study hall right before our English class and our English teacher had an open period. We snuck into her room, got the book she would be using for our class and put a piece of the fake puke (throw up) in the book. Next period we get to class, she tells us to get out our book, and all of a sudden she starts hitting her book saying... "someone has earped in my book" we had to keep a straight face to no one would know we did it (12 kids in the class). To this day no one knows that we did it. Needless to say she started locking her classroom when she would leave.

We took a tootsie roll... squeezed it to look like some poo-poo and laid it in the water fountain... the principal came and took a drink and just went along with the prank.

Someone was TPing the trees at our High School. Well I just happened to go with my Mother to an activity at the grade school that was next to the high school. I stayed in the car and noticed a car driving back and forth in front of our school very slowly. I saw them finally stop... my curiosity got to me so I ran around the side of the school and hid behind the trees. Low and behold a group of kids came running right to the same trip area to start putting on the toilet paper. I jumped out and said... what are you doing? They hurriedly let. The following school day I was able to go tell the principal who was doing it. they thought my cousin and I were doing it and wanted to throw us out of cheerleading....

In our dragging main sometimes a person would be driving that wasn't quite old enough. Our local sheriff would come after us and we would somehow be able to change drivers before we would stop. He would come up and ask what we were doing.... Than let us go. He never did get us in trouble.

Another entertainment we pursued was following a "couple in love" to their favorite parking spots and harass them. We would drive up beside them, stop the car, roll down the window, and say we were from the "Society for the prevention of Babies".... Can you imagine?

And then there was the time a whole big bunch of us decided to "sneak" in to the Drive-in Theater. We all got in the trunk but the driver of course. She drove up to the window, paid for her ticket and then drove on in to a back row. We open the trunk and all the rest of us got out. We thought we were so cool.

We had closed lunch period so one day when I was a senior 4 of our girls decided we were going to the little local Cafe on main street for lunch (about 3 blocks from the school). By the time we got back everyone in town knew what we had done. We just got a verbal reprimand. We were so courageous!

One more school prank... we had a new music teacher right of out college and from a local small town. When we were to play a song in band practice my cousin and I played the clarinet so we would play one note apart.... The band teacher would say, stop, stop... and have just the clarinets play... well of course we would play it right and sound wonderful we were awful... we would do this over and over again. He only stayed at our school one year.

I have many more stories but am running out of space. I loved growing up in a small town and attending a small school. No regrets at all.

A Hog's Life
By Jack Moser of Vilas, Colorado
Born 1927

I was born July 31, 1927 to Eva and John Moser. They are both deceased, so I can tell a few things that happened when I was growing up. As far back as I can remember was when I was six years old in 1933. My older brother, Keith, came down with scarlet fever so my parents isolated him by putting him in the parlor. My dad hooked the team to the wagon and took me with him to hand top some Milo. He gave me a hawk bill knife to use for the day. Boy did I feel important. We hand topped two rows through the field and doubt if I was much help but this was a good way for me to learn how to work. When we got to the end my dad said, "Will get some corn to feed the horses." So we went a small distance and hopped to the ground and started to cutting the tassels off the corn stalks. Pop informed me that that wasn't what we wanted and showed me how to snap the ears off the stalks. When we arrived home and put the team away, I went in the house for supper. Mom took one good look at me and after one look decided, I had scarlet fever so I was isolated in the parlor with my older brother. My dad told me in later years that while I was in isolation that I got stiff as a board, so the doctor decided I had diphtheria and doctored me for it. We finally got well enough to come out of isolation; of course, we had our chores to do like milking the cows and slop the hogs twice a day.

I remember the first dust storm that come in. I was standing on the front porch and looking east towards a north-south road about a quarter of a mile away. You could see this roller coming from the north and from the south came a fancy looking automobile, one of those Ford coups with the doors that opened to the front and had white wall tires with yellow wheels. It had to be a salesman because anyone I knew didn't have one that fancy or could afford one like it. The car was traveling at a good speed and I could see he was going to run into the roller. I often wondered what the driver of the car thought when he ran into the roller. About this time mom called and the whole family went in the cellar. The cellar was just off the back porch about 10 feet. My dad stayed on the steps under the outside door. The door had about a two-inch gap in it that you could look through at the house. My dad reported that he couldn't see a thing and didn't know if the house was still standing or not. Finally he reported the house was still standing and so it got light enough that we went back in to the house. This roller was in the afternoon sometime. I don't remember the exact time, but it was bright daylight. During a lot of dust storms later on mom would hang white sheets in the house to settle the dust so we wouldn't have to breathe it.

Through all those dust storms we boys had chores to do besides other work. In October we always butchered hogs. My dad wouldn't butcher anything less than 300 pounds. He wanted it for the lard. We had a drive-thru granary east of the house about 200 yards. We would hand carry water from the well house to the granary to scald the hogs so we could shave the hair off the hog. We had a 55-gallon barrel that we used to scald them in. We put the barrel on the bricks so we could build a fire under it then we carried water with three-gallon pails filled the barrel half full because when you lowered a hog into it any fuller would over flow it. Then we had another 55-gallon barrel for water so we could replenish what splashed out after dipping a hog in it. This was all done on a Friday after school and before chore time.

Saturday morning the first thing before chores was to light the wood that we pilled under the barrel the day before so it could start to heating the water. Chore time and breakfast. Breakfast consisted of eggs, ham or bacon, fried potatoes, gravy, cereal and biscuits and of course milk. Then it was to the granary and get ready to butcher. The hogs were in a pen fastened to the side of the granary. My dad would shoot and stick a hog I don't remember how we got it around to the east side, but he must have used a tractor or horse to drag it around. When the water was hot enough, we would pack it into the granary to scald the hog. My dad had fixed wire loops on the barrel and he would get on one side and me and my older brother would get on the other and carry the barrel into the block to scald the hog. We had a steel rod we put through the wire loops to lift the hog up and down. We had the hog hanging before we brought the water in then we lowered the hog into the water half way and then pulled him out and laid him down on a table, hooked the block and tackle on the other end raised him up and lowered the other half into the water. Then we laid him on the table and went to shaving/ scraping the hair

Students at Faye School in 1939

off. The table was made with two sawhorses and boards laid on top of them. After he was scrapped clean, my dad would gut the hog and then us boys would help him hang it in the top of the granary off to one side of the block and tackle. After we had dipped both halves in the barrel and laid the hog on the table, we would carry the barrel back and put it on the fire. We generally butchered four or five hogs this way, of course then it was chore time. The chores always got done if anything else did. The next day, Sunday, after chores we would start to carry the hogs to the cellar. They put a rectangle box in one corner and put down newspaper to stack the hams and shoulder. My dad would cut and trim the hogs and us boys would carry the trimmed hams, shoulders, and bacon to the cellar. Mom would be waiting with the salt cure and when we put down any meat into the box she would salt it down. We didn't know what pork chops was as my dad always made tenderloin or back straps. Us boys would take the pig's bladder and take it to an old air compressor and air it up and tie it closed so we would have us a football.

The next day was Monday so it was off to a one-room school to get our education. When we got home from school mom generally had a big cast iron pot going in the back yard rendering lard. They had what looked like an oar we would take it to stir the lard in the kettle and bring up some cracklens, known today as hog rinds. We always had to chop wood and carry water for the house. This was included in our evening chores. We had a reservoir on the end of the wood-burning cook stove and I don't know how much water it held, but I do know it seemed to go empty mighty fast. We chopped wood and sometimes if the moon was bright enough we would go out after supper and chop wood until about 10:00 pm. I'd come home from school and mom had burned about all I had chopped. We would have dust storms and then nice days but as long as we had chickens, hogs, and cows we never went hungry.

The one-room schoolhouse was called Faye School. It had one main room and two clothes rooms upstairs and a full basement with a big furnace in it. The teacher had a stack of papers in the coal bin for starting fires in the morning. We had a volleyball team and played other schools and towards the end of the school year, we had a county tournament at the high school in, Hugoton. Our school had two outhouses and a horse barn. One dirty and windy day us boys had a marble game going out on the south side of the barn. Pretty soon we thought maybe school should be in session, so we sent one of the younger boys in to see. He reported back that school was in session so we hurried in and took our seats. The teacher didn't say anything, as there were nine of us boys and only three girls.

Nuclear Was Always On Our Minds
By Earl Polk of Burrton, Kansas
Born 1945

Growing up in the 1950s in a small town in southern Reno County, Kansas was wonderful!

I was a war baby born in 1945. My little brother was a Baby Boomer born in 1949. When my little brother was about 4 or 5 years old, The Cold War was very important in the news and on radio.

One night while listening to a KU basketball game with my father, my little brother Jerry was playing with his toy cars on the living room rug. The sports announcer for KU on radio said, "Direct from the Phog Allen field house." My little brother jumped up, holding his head yelling, "Fall out! Fall out!"

Nuclear was always on our minds. In school, we even had a drill to get under our desk. Like that would have saved us!

My brother walked on in July 2012. I miss him every day.

Washday High Jinks
By Barbara Woodman of Wichita, Kansas
Born 1933

My mother was very particular about how we hung the laundry on the clothesline on washday. For instance, the tea towels had to be hung so that the design was on the right hand bottom corner, all the bath towels were to be hung with like-colored towels, and, of course, the underwear was to be hung on the line farthest from the roadway! Just to upset her, my sister and I would mix the clothes up by hanging the things just any which way. She would always make us do it over even though we were out in the country with very little traffic!

One year, for Christmas, my parents bought a bicycle for us four girls to share. My dad hid it in the barn under some loose hay. My sister next to me in age, and I were playing in the barn and found the bicycle. We asked if we could have it since we had found it but Dad said no! He put it somewhere and told us if we found it again before Christmas, we could have it. We never did find out where he put it the second time! Christmas came, and of course, there was a problem because everyone wanted to ride it. I don't remember for sure, but me being the youngest of the four of us I'm sure I was the last to get my turn!

Saturday Night
By Roger G. Fox of Larned, Kansas
Born 1926

In the '30s and '40s during the Dust Bowl and Depression years, Saturday night was the highlight of the week. We didn't go to town often; but that night was the time, you wanted to go to town.

Farmers would load up their cream and eggs and off you headed to town to trade for groceries. Besides that, you put on your white shirt and washed your car; you wanted to look your best.

In Larned, the streets were full of cars, double-parked etc. but you always had to do what they call "Drag the Gut" a few times. You could really have a great time and spend not much more than a hard earned dollar.

There were two picture shows going. All the clothing stores: Montgomery Wards, Penney's, and Palace Clothier were open. All the barber shops were open. There were six or more restaurants open and besides that there as a pool hall and at least two dances going on, one at the City Auditorium and Woodman Hall.

In the war years, we had a USO that was going strong. Soldiers from the Great Bend Air Base would come to Larned and before that Rozel had a CCC Camp and these men would come to Larned. They were looking for a good time and to meet girls. Many a Larned or local girl would end up marrying a soldier. Larned also had a Minor League Baseball team that was well known around the area. After the war, the boys all came back home to farm or go to college.

Then the whole picture changed. TV came into our homes and what a thrill that was. Pretty soon, Saturday night in Larned just kind of folded up and it seemed like everybody was content on staying at home watching Lawrence Welk.

Saturday night was always special to me, and I know it was too many others as well.

The Other Place
By Gene Hirst of Shell Knob, Missouri
Born 1926

When Dad was a two-quarter section farmer,
And I was a young lad,
This was the quarter we didn't live on,
We called it, "The Other Place"

Two thick rows of cedar trees,
Running East and West,
A feed patch in the center,
That grew huge cocklebur, sunflower, and ragweed.

When we stood there, it was deathly still,
And in the stillness on a mid-summer afternoon,
You could smell the special odor of cocklebur, sunflower, and ragweed,
Withering in the sun's overwhelming heat.

An old cream farmhouse,
Vacant most of the time,
Except for real poor folk,
With runny nose kids.

Weather beaten old barn,
With milking shed on the South,
Horse stalls in the middle,
Shelter on the North end.

Haymow above the horse stalls,
The place I feared to go,
As someone said that is where,
Mr. Parrot hung himself to death.

Sometimes we kept our milk cows at "The Other Place"
To graze in the meadow there.
I remember well the terror and the frenzy,
Of fighting the meadow fire.

Old Dan and Bill were pulling the grain wagon,
We filled milk pails and grease buckets,
To wet the burlap sacks,
So with this and pitchforks and shovels,
We fought fiercely to save the cedar trees.

I remember well—milking cows in the muddy barn,
Melted snow running down my neck,
Cow's frozen, cocklebur tails,
Against my tender, cold, red face.

Cats silently glaring,
Waiting for a drink of warm milk.

On a still night from our place about a mile away,
We could hear the lonesome wail,
Of a coyote pup, tied up,
At "The Other Place."

Now, if that other place,
Is like our other place,
I don't want to go there.

If you go by that quarter now,
You will see just a good piece of cultivated farm ground,
No cedar trees, no cocklebur,
No farmhouse or barn.

No sign at all of the sad, sad,
Almost eerie place we called,
"The Other Place"

Rita's home in 1955

Spitting Through the Half-moon Outline
By Loretta (Rita) Casper of Attica, Kansas
Born 1949

This is an awesome chance to yak about my life and times how, when, where etc., that I learned respect, humor, honesty, embarrassment, the Lord, and anything else to do with my life lessons.

Being born in '49 was a time that has so far thrown me into three generation gaps, like going to Grandparent's for Turkey Day and smelling that bird for fifty feet before the kitchen and watching Grandma take that huge roaster from the oven stuffed with bird, potatoes, onions, celery, and bread she had dried for weeks. There were pies, MP gravy, and homegrown veggies. Lord, people now a days would freak to experience that.

After all that food the elders usually played pitch, which was another training sequence for me as Grandpa was a very sore loser, seen him tear a deck of cards in half because he got set. Didn't take us kids long to disappear when that happened.

Eventually all that food moved people towards the outhouse, which had a half-moon carved in the door. My Mom could spit thru that outline and hit anyone who was in line outside. It was a two-holer but very few went in together, as privacy was utmost, plus everyone wanted to practice their spitting aim.

As far as health problems, some of my family spent weeks in a shoebox in the oven as the Dr. said too small and probably not live. They were scrappers. No one owned toothbrushes so small pieces of material with baking soda were used to scrub teeth.

Then everything changed in the '70s when I got pregnant and had the first grandchild. Lord, I tried to raise him like I was, but the times changed so much by the time his 40s rolled around, I'm still playing the fine lines of three generations. We are still learning from each other. So many times to tell about, feel like I could write about them forever.

Twins–Separate Birthdays
By Larry L. Gates of McPherson, Kansas
Born 1937

It was a cold, snowy day, December 9, 1937. The roads were closed so my Dad drove a tractor four miles from our farm to Delphos, KS to get a doctor.

The doctor delivered my brother, Gary, around 11pm. Then my Dad drove the doctor back to town only to go back after him because my Mother was still having problems.

Back in those days' people did not see a doctor that often and technologies were not as available as they are today to determine multiple births.

Anyway, the doctor delivered me around 2AM on December 10. So that is how my twin and I had different birth dates.

We started school when we were only five years old so we graduated from high school at age 17.

We joined the Navy together. If you joined the service before age 18, you got out the day before your 21st birthday, so Gary was released one day before I was.

Gary re-enlisted and made the Navy his career until he retired. My twin passed away in February 2007 and I miss him.

Gary and Larry in 1938

Snakes in the Attic
By Robert E. Barton of Garden City, Kansas
Born 1922

As a student in Florence Lawson's ninth grade class, I let my emotions run away with me when snakes began crawling out of the attic. It was springtime: time to shag fly balls and swing the bat. It was April; I should have been out taking a few swings with the bat and shagging fly balls. I just wasn't too fond of the subject of math.

There was 37 in the class and the room was quite large. The southwest corner of ceiling had an empty hole that puzzled me. Why was it there? Also, there was a hole at floor level. Were they to install a new one? I would look at the ceiling hole, and then at the teacher, and back at the ceiling hole. I was not absorbing any part of the lecture. That hole captivate me. My seat was front row and four rows directly east of the teacher. I had the best view of that hole and Mr. Snake.

I looked up into that corner and there was about 24 inches of live snake swinging back and forth. It seemed to be quite contented doing his or her thing. He or she was looking over those lush ankles. That snake was cold. That snake wanted to go down that black pipe, but it couldn't grab the pipe. His hindquarters were cold in that attic and he couldn't back up, as he had no reverse gear. While I'm watching the snake, the class is concentrating on mathematics. Without any hands, this serpent had a real problem.

I had lost control. I stood up and grabbed the math book and brought my reliable left arm back and let it fly over the head of Teacher Florence Lawson. Her periphery gave her a look at the book traveling through space above her head. She exploded. She thought that I had thrown it at her!

She turned and raised that large right arm, extended in my direction. She was hot—red hot. She said in firm words, "Don't you *ever* do that again!" I thought by killing the snake, it would rectify the issue, but it didn't help a bit. I felt like a heel rather than a hero. I'm sorry Miss Lawson. She must have been about 40 years old. I would have liked to have visited her several years after World War II, but I was too emotional following the war. I served in a machine company of an infantry unit. I served in N. AFR Sicily and Italy.

The Cowboy Who Galloped Into My Heart
By Liz Miller of Scott City, Kansas
Born 1948

She gunned the engine, accelerator pressed firmly to the floor. Giggles, squeals, and delight filled the hearts of the children: "Oh, my stomach!" "Wee! Do it again!" We had just raced up the hill and down, leaving a bit of our hearts at the bottom of the ravine. Excitement filled the cool, fragrant morning. We were going to the ranch. My friend and her small children had invited me to come along. It was a joyous group that had brought donuts for their brother, uncle, special friend. I was caught up in my own expectations of the day since I would be meeting this much loved rancher for the first time.

Bob had fed the cattle and I had come in to clean up. Coming out of his remodeled soddy, he was more than I had even imagined. His muscular chest, shirt unclad, and vigorous stance brought ripples of elation to my soul. Hadn't my roommate in college giggled with me as we listed our requirements for a husband? And hadn't we gleefully decided that a hairy chest was paramount? Oh, if she could only be here now to relish what I was seeing!

After sharing our pastries and making introductions, we decided to ride horses. My experience in riding was limited to the carousel horses at the state fair. As Bob lead me on his mighty palomino, my knees shook with expectancy. "Are you too cold?" he gently inquired. Dare I tell him the real reasons for my trembling? His touch on my leg had stirred such long awaited emotions. "Just a little nervous, that's all," I stalled.

Felling more confident, I grasped the reins, deciding I could certainly lead this stallion as I encircled the Quonset. Assured that I could handle more freedom, I lead this mighty war horse up the embankment leading to the spacious prairie. The grass seemed endless as I scanned the horizon. What if he decided to run off with me as he had done on other occasions with novices like me? Reluctantly, I reined him back to the barn. His forceful hoofs increased in speed as we came down the banked terrain. My inner fears awakened in frenzy as I frantically pulled back on the reins. I would never survive a renegade stallion. My decisions must be quick. Time was not on my side. The only sane thing I could think to do was to "jump ship!"

The clods of dirt brushed my face as I dropped to the hard sod, hearing the clamor of the hoof beats echoing in the distance. Dazed, I awaited the firm grip of Bob's hand as he lifted me to my weakened feet. I had fallen hard. However, I had fallen even harder for this caring, tender cowboy who had galloped his way into my heart!

Memories are Made of This
By Carroll M. Snell of Hutchinson, Kansas
Born 1931

I went back to our old hometown today and almost wished that I hadn't. I went down to our old neighborhood just to look around and it was not the same.

I remember old Skeeter Park where we used to play baseball all day in the summer. It is now the home of a Senior Center. The old dirt path we used to walk is but a memory. Remember the old footbridge over Cow Creek, the shortcut to school, and movies? Gone—no longer providing a place to fish, and no concrete supports to climb on. The old Plum Street Bridge has been replaced. Remember swimming under the old one? That's not allowed now.

Remember the old house where I lived, the one where we played "Annie Over," "Hide and Seek," and "Cowboys and Indians?" Gone now, with only memories of when children played outdoors. No more children on homemade scooters or roller skates, only memories of riding our bikes, walking to school, and many other things we did.

I went down Maple Street to the park under the old Missouri Pacific railroad tracks.

They were still there, but now owned by some other railroad. I went over to "Detter Field" where we watched many class C professional baseball games. I started remembering the old teams in the league: Salina Bluejays, Topeka Owls, Joplin Miners, Muskogee Reds, and our home team, the Hutchinson Pirates. I forget the others, but I remember seeing Mickey Mantle in (I believe) 1949. The next year, 1950, I watched him play right field for the Yankees against the Washington Senators.

I went down and passed the places where the old cafes existed—the Blue Grill, the Nifty Café, and other places. All gone, along with my dad's old shoe and gun repair shop. Then I wandered over to B and Main, the Old Weeks Drug, and Dillon's Store. They are now an antique store and Salvation Army building. When I went to A and Main, I found that the old Isham Furniture Store had burned down and been replaced by a water park. There is also a new bridge over Cow Creek.

Further north I traveled to find that the old Wolcott office building had been torn down and replaced by a park. Gone were the days of the old Boren's Sporting Goods, the Midland Hotel, and the Santa Fe Railroad Station. The station had been replaced by a new building further to the east.

I thought: how sad that all of this history is gone. No more nickel movies at the old Iris Theater. I thought of all the old class B western movies we saw there: Buck Jones, Charles Starrett, Hoot Gibson, Ken Maynard, and Tom Mix. How many bad men went down under their blazing guns before they rode off into the sunset?

In the words of the old Dean Martin song: "Memories are made of this."

The Way Things Were
By Jacka Penner of Burrton, Kansas
Born 1930

The outhouses were very cold in the winter. I always asked myself, "Do I *really* have to go?" before I went. On our party line, one lady was always on the phone. You would have to tell her that we needed to use the phone. One time when we were kids, we were laying on the floor listening to the radio when lightning struck! What a bang! We also went to a small town where they showed movies on the side of a barn. If the car did not start when we pushed it down the hill, we did not get to go to town!

We got spankings as a kid at school and at home, and I think that they need to start doing this now! We had a round metal tub for our Saturday night baths. I got to take my bath first since I was the only girl. My two brothers were next, and in the same water! My mom had a wringer washer with a motor on it. I would help her. When I got married, I got an electric wringer washer. I had five kids with my first love, my husband of 62 years.

I went with my dad to buy the feed for chickens and cows so that I could pick what kind and color of sack that I wanted for a dress. My mom made me feed sack dresses. When I had children of my own, I also made my girls dresses and wedding dresses. Mom made my wedding dress as well.

My favorite teacher once said, "You can be book smart, but you also need to have common sense!" I went to two different schools. They taught seventh grade one year, then eighth the next year. I went from the sixth to the eighth, then back to the seventh. We only had three students in my personal class. I moved to Burrton High School to a class with 28 kids in it. That was a change for me!

There were a lot of things to do back then, so nobody ever got bored. My farm chore was to feed the chickens and clean the chicken house. I could also go out to the swimming holes. One day in a muddy pond in the pasture, a friend got a crawdad in her swimming suit. I never went back after that! We would play until dark.

My folks bought a boxcar from the railroad and we lived in it. Others did the same. The schools and towns boomed; the same old cottonwood trees are still there except they are starting to cut them down!

One thing I noticed most around our state and the Sand Hills in Burrton and Hutchinson are the Cedar trees. People planted Wind Brook with Cedars in them instead of hedgerows. When I started driving a bus in 1969, there were no cedar trees in the Sand Hills. I watched them take over; now there are no more pastures left!

After 43 years of driving the bus, the countryside has changed a lot!

Party Line Phones in the 1930s
By Elfreda Fast of Hillsboro, Kansas
Born 1917

A cell phone at the farm five miles north of Ingalls, Kansas in the 1930s? Not then, but today, very likely. I feel very advantaged to have lived at that farm in the 1930s, and yet, to be living in this time of the explosion of knowledge and gadgetry. My generation was born before radios, television, Scotch tape, digital clocks, contact lenses, penicillin, polio vaccines, and drip-dry clothes. We never heard of DVD players, electric typewriters, computers, heart transplants, or yogurt.

We remember when life was simple, but oh so hard. We remember when we saw the first airplane flying overhead and watched it until it was only a speck in the sky. We remember when we couldn't go to the faucet and turn it on for a fresh glass of water; we went to the windmill where it pumped water into a barrel, and we dipped into it with a bucket and brought up cold, fresh water.

My father, Abe Penner, had been privileged to have only a few years of education, but he was eager to learn. We moved to Ingalls from Meade, Kansas in 1922 because the Ingalls school system was consolidated. Buses picked up the children and took them to Ingalls where there was a grade school for classes from one to six and a high school for classes seven through twelve. My father, with his limited education, was a member of the grade school board for many years. He read a lot and became very knowledgeable.

One thing the people of the community were wishing for was a telephone system. The farmers formed a telephone committee. Their first job was to persuade everyone to join in with work and finances. There were poles to purchase and put in place. The homes in that area were not close, so that meant many miles of poles and wire. The destination of the telephone line was the town of Ingalls where there was a telephone operator who could connect you with people in other areas—even long distance to relatives hundreds of miles away. Each farmer purchased his own telephone, which was operated by a hand crank. This is when life became very interesting.

The members of this telephone group were on a party line, with each family having

Abe Penner's home place

their own ring. Our ring was two long rings. My uncle's ring was two long rings and a short. Of course, the idea was that when it was your ring, you answered, but that didn't keep everyone on the party line from listening in. if you were calling family to come over to help you butcher a hog, that was okay, but if it was about your daughter's boyfriend coming from a distance, not everyone was supposed to know that. I was told that you could have an arrangement to talk general things, hang up, and 20 minutes later lift the receiver without making a call, and talk privately.

The telephone was a wonderful help in many ways. There were times when the weather was bad that people could find out if the school bus had made it or not. Also, whenever there was a fire, the operator was notified and she rang a long continuous ring to let everyone know about it. Even community activities were advertised in this manner.

That house where our first hand-cranked telephone hung on the wall is still there, although it has been remodeled and kept in shape. There is no longer a hand-cranked telephone on the wall, but you can believe me when I say that there are probably several cell phones around.

Bluff Creek School
By Mary Ann Rix of Wichita, Kansas
Born 1931

The old one-room school building perches on its fenced acre, looking lost, but not completely abandoned, as it now houses a family instead of school children. It no longer hears the laughter of children on the slide and swing-set or watches a softball game, but broods over the adjoining wheat field and misses the stables and cistern that once were in the schoolyard. It still views Bluff Creek, after which it was named. The road beside it leads to Anthony, Kansas, three miles east.

Three generations of my family graduated from the eighth grade from this country school, District 39, Harper County, Kansas.

Nora Hatfield, my grandmother, lived just a bit south, near a spring, and carried water for her teacher. In the winter, she would go early to start the stove and warm the building. She was 10 years old in 1882 when the school was organized, and she started school there.

Gladys Hatfield, my mother, started to school in 1906 and could walk to school from her home, where Anthony Airport is now located.

I started school there in 1943 when we moved to the family farm on Bluff Creek, one-quarter mile east. By this time, the original building had been replaced by a tan, stucco building, but it still had just one classroom. Stables were in the schoolyard to be used by students who rode their ponies to school. I rode my horse, Star Baby, to school occasionally.

Christmas programs were in the evening. A gasoline lantern hung from the ceiling to supply light for the occasion. The evening was complete with a pageant, music and a visit from Santa Claus.

The last day of school was celebrated with a covered dish dinner at noon followed by a softball game the whole family could participate in.

A countywide track meet was held in the spring for all the county schools. I excelled in the events, winning firsts in the 50-yard dash, 75-yard dash, and relay race and seconds in high jump and running broad jump. I was so far ahead in the 75-yard dash; I looked back to see where the other contestants were.

Mother resumed teaching during World War II and was my teacher for the eighth grade. We got along fine, but I was a good student and she took care not to show favoritism. If there was any doubt, my grades were lowered and other student's grades were raised. There were 13 students in the school that year including the three in my class, Bob Coon, Phyllis Whitney and myself.

The quality of education in these small schools must have been all right, as I was an honor student in high school, made Dean's honor roll in college and graduated from Kansas University with a BS in Pharmacy.

Kansas–The Outlaw's Hideaway
By Larry Popovich of Pratt, Kansas
Born 1948

In this day and age, we rarely think of the areas we live in as former hiding places for the outlaws of days gone by, but 150 years ago, the South Central area of Kansas was a refuge for the outlaws that roamed the Cherokee Strip and Badlands of Oklahoma.

By the late 1800s, the Federal Government established a regional Federal Marshall's office at Ft. Smith, Arkansas, near the Kansas-Oklahoma border. These Federal Marshalls made it mighty uncomfortable for the ne'er-do-wells who were operating out of the Oklahoma Badlands. As a result, many a shady character took an extended vacation to the sparsely populated area of South Central Kansas to avoid the authorities.

One of these outlaws known throughout Oklahoma was Zip Wyatt. Born as Nelson Ellsworth Wyatt in 1863 in Indiana, the Wyatt family moved to Mulhall, Oklahoma, which was near the provincial state capital of Guthrie. Zip and his brother, "Six Shooter Jack," began their lives as cattle herders, but advanced to robbing banks and stores in both Blaine and Kingfisher counties in 1893.

Zip got his name from his uncanny ability to escape from the law. Folks said that when he was caught, he could just "zip" away.

After wanted posters with large rewards for Zip and Jack went up all over the strip, Zip decided that Oklahoma was too hot for him. The next time we hear about Zip, he was laying low in Greensburg, Kansas.

Things were going fine until Zip decided to steal a horse and buggy from one of Greensburg's prominent citizens. A posse was formed, which chased Zip south, but they lost him at the Oklahoma state line near Alva.

In April 1895, Zip surfaced again with a gang that robbed the Rock Island train near Dover, Oklahoma. The Federal Marshalls got on Zip's trail once again, and ran him down at a farm not far from Dover.

A shootout ensued, in which Zip was critically wounded. He was taken to Enid, Oklahoma, and placed on a pool table in a local bar, where he was given medical attention. Zip lingered for five days, and became quite the town celebrity during that time, enjoying all the attention, free drinks, and fine food that he could consume. His condition took a turn for the worse, however, and he died of his wounds on April 2, 1895.

Like a meteor, Zip Wyatt flashed across the Oklahoma and Kansas frontiers, and like the meteor, he died out quickly. But Zip Wyatt has had a lasting legacy in American western folklore. The story of Zip Wyatt's life was loosely played out by John Wayne in the western movie classic, *Angel and the Bad Man*. The character that John Wayne played was an outlaw by the name of Quirt Evans – A moniker for the real Strip outlaw, Zip Wyatt.

The Rest is History
By Laura (Lorene Hunt) Hart of Denver, Colorado
Born 1934

1952 "Miss Flipper"
Laura (Lorene Hunt) Hart

Ok...I admit it! Yes, Milan asked me to go on what was supposed to be a romantic moonlight Hayride and I fell asleep! For some odd reason he never asked me out on any more dates, but the good news is, it somehow didn't affect our being "just friends" and we had a lot of fun singing together with the Swing Band! We tried to capture that "Memory" at this reunion, when we sang "Sentimental Journey," a song that Toby had been asking us to sing at the Reunions...forever!

As far as other memories, it seems I may (or may not) have done (almost) everything on the list, and remember "chickening out" on about the 15th step up the ladder of the water tower, spending summers working as a lifeguard and mopping floors at the pool! Loved being a cheerleader and being part of the fantastic chorus, and doing plays like "Our Town" and "Spirit of The Prairie!" and of course "Old Doc." I was honored to go to Girl's State as well and, yes, being crowned Miss Flipper was a great honor, and sooo much fun being part of that whole thing! Sidebar: Speaking of Pancake Day, during the reunion, it was fun hearing Steve Leete's guitar and voice rendition of the Pancake Day Song as well hearing Table Seven's rendition of The Whiffenpoo song, plus The Alma Mater, and God Bless America led by Gary Warden!

Anyway! Getting back to memories... actually I do recall, one time, a bunch of us were out at the ranch, heading for the Cimarron, when we ran into an electric fence which was supposed to keep the cattle from getting into the quick sand. But hey, it was also kind of blocking our way to the river! So, we were all just standing there kinda wondering...what it would feel like to touch an electric fence...right? Hey, supposedly, it doesn't really hurt a cow; it only "scares" them. So it can't be toooo bad...could it? ... Well, the ONE brilliant thing we did was, we all held hands before we touched it, and to this day we all have electrifying personalities... and are happy to be alive.

Now, as far as that Milan thing,....50 plus

years passed and all I knew about him was, he lived in Denver, and was an Architect! So, I was surprised and happy when my long lost "best friend buddy" e-mailed and said he was flying thru Dallas, had a stop over, and thought we might need to have a cup of coffee and catch up, which we did and had a great time. No, this time I did not fall asleep...and the rest is history. (In 2008, Milan and Lorene were united in marriage.)

Milan and (Laura) Lorene Hunt

Memories of the Planes and Crew Members
By Beulah Gleeson Ratzlaff of Plains, Kansas
Born 1934

My most memorable part of my early life in Seward County, Kansas was the airport that trained the crews for the B24s during World War II. This airport was designated as the largest training facility for the crews of B24s in the world at that time.

I don't really remember the war; I wasn't quite seven years old when the war started. My memories were of the planes and the crewmembers. Our house was one and three quarter miles north of the two main north and south runways, our house in the middle. So, the planes flew over on each side of the house, 24 hours a day, seven days a week, good and bad weather, summer, and winter the biggest part of the time.

The three houses south of us had to be moved because of the nearness to the airport. There were no houses left south of us. When the planes flew over, the dishes rattled in the cupboards. The beds vibrated, and we always heard the sound of the planes. Some planes gained altitude quicker than others, so it wasn't as noticeable, but the sound was still always there. We became used to them.

I stood out on the front porch of the house and watched the planes. I waved to the pilots and they waved back. I'm sure they smiled at the little blond girl waving at them, but maybe I helped to make their day a little brighter. I watched one day as the plane was coming near that both engines on the right side were not working (B24s had four engines, two on each wing). I could see the pilots working diligently trying to get them to start, which they did not too far from the house. There were many wrecks in the area and many were killed. Thankfully, we were not close to the wreck scenes and did not know any involved.

Each Sunday we would go to church at the Presbyterian Church in Liberal, Kansas that was five miles to town. After the service, my parents would invite a pilot and his wife or two enlisted men to go home with us for dinner and spend the afternoon with us. Daddy took them back to the base after supper. Several were invited more than once. Many a delightful afternoon was spent with these people, and my parents kept in touch with some of them for several years. We became particularly close to a few of the pilots, and when they flew over our house at night, either going up or down, they would dip the lights of the plane as they went over, lighting our yard like daylight so that we would know that it was them. We would sit out in the yard of an evening waiting to see if they were flying that night or not. It gave us a good feeling that we knew that person flying.

One time, Daddy and my brother went out in the morning and there were deep ruts in the field north of the barn. There seemed to be no explanation as to what caused them. Several years later when my brother was working for a large gas company he went to a meeting and met a man who had trained at Liberal Airbase.

In their conversation as to where we had lived the man told him that he was a pilot of a plane at night that misjudged where they were, set it down in our field, and saw the barn directly in front of them and were able to pull the plane up and over the barn, a disaster that did not materialize as it would have taken the barn and also the house if it had not been for the experience of the pilot.

I know that the war caused problems with people, but we accepted the fact. We bought stamps and when they equaled $18.75, we traded them in for a savings bond worth $25.00 in ten years. There was rationing of sugar, gas, and many items. Shoes were rationed; we got one pair a year. We sold scrap iron, and we spent time around the farm picking up small pieces of metal, including nails to sell to help the war effort. My father had to report to the draft board, but due to his age and the fact that he was a farmer kept him from going to war. My brother was not old enough to be drafted.

I will never forget the planes and crewmembers that were in my home.

Most of the Life and Legend of Arthur Green
By Arthur G. Green of Holcomb, Kansas
Born 1926

This is a memory about me and my family as I remember and what I was told from my parents. My folks started for Colorado, they were easterners, not knowing or heard of a mirage. But they got in Western Kansas area and thought they seen a body of water. They kept trying to go around it, but could not. When It got late in the evening, the lake disappeared. That is when they found out that it was a mirage. Because of that, they settled in Garden City, Kansas. Dad and Mom met, married, and four children were born in this town.

Then they decided to move to Missouri. That is where my brother and I were born, me being the youngest. They moved around and back to Kansas when I was about three years old. There was no electricity, phones, and no running water. We had outhouses with two large seats and one small one. Our pots were a gallon can in our bedroom, but they were only to pee in. The next day one of us took it out and emptied it. Mom had an old hand washing machine with a wringer on it. Many times, I had to help work it. We settled in a small town called Wilsey. In the summer on Saturday nights, we would go to town in the park. They would show silent movies. Us kids would all set on the ground and watch. It was free.

My first grade was a town school. Then we moved and I went to a one-room school. I was in three different one-room schools with one teacher teaching all eight grades. The second one I went to is still standing. Someone made a home of it. I don't think I had a special one that I liked. I liked sports, and we had a good softball team. We played a school called Parkerville, and we beat them 72 to 8, one of our biggest wins.

As far as my favorite pet, I had a dog named Jack. Dad brought him from Indiana. He was a shepherd. Then, someone gave Dad a small goat, and it ended up being mine too.

My folks were poor, so of course we did not have electricity back then. To keep our milk, cream, and butter cool, we hung it in a bucket in the well. Most all wells back then were hand dug, about 20 or 30 feet deep. Walls were laid up with rock sides. Well, once a year the rope would break, and down in the water went the bucket. So, me being the smallest, Dad put a rope around my arm, under my arms, and let me down in the well to get the bucket. One time he was letting me down, I yelled, "Dad! Pull me up! There is a snake down here!" Dad wanted to know what it looked like. I told him, and he said, "Oh, it is only a garter snake. He will not hurt you." You know, as long as I could see the snake I was fine, and I have never been afraid of one since.

Farm chores—oh man we each had our specific ones to do. When I got older, I had to gather eggs and carry in wood for the cook stove. We had several swimming holes, and most of them were in a creek. Once in a while, we would swim in a pond.

I guess a memory of a person would be my mom. You see, she died when I was only twelve years old. In the summer after dinner, she would get me on her lap and get her Bible and read me verses until I fell asleep. I never will forget them times.

Another thing I remember is that we

always had a large garden. Mom done a lot of canning. We had no freezers or any ice boxes, so when we dug the potatoes and other veggies, Dad would dig a trench two feet deep by two feet wide, line it with hay, then put potatoes in first, then sweet potatoes, then whatever came next. Then, he would cover them all over with burlap bags. After that, he would put another layer of hay. When Mom needed some, he would go dig them up, get what we needed, and then re-cover them up again. You know what? They kept good until they were all gone.

Back in the '30s was a dry time. There was not much rain. We had to haul water for the livestock. All the other kids were hoeing weeds in the cornfields. Dad came to me and asked if I thought could take the mules and water tank, go to the creek, fill the tank, and bring it back. I thought to myself, boy, Dad must think I am a man, for he would never trust me with his mules. I said, "Sure," and I made it.

I often wonder how Dad made a living and fed all the family on 160 acres, but he believed in working hard, and he could do about anything. He built his own sawmill, cut trees, sawed lumber, and sold it. Of course, us kids had to help. Here I am today 87 ½ years old doing what I can to make a living.

The First Meeting
By Jan Pinsince of Manhattan, Kansas
Born 1951

My parents both were born in Barber County, near Medicine Lodge, Kansas. My mom, Dorothy, entered the world on a warm day in the summer of 1921 and my dad, George, arrived on a cold day, the last day of 1919. He always said that he was "born on the last day of the last month of the last year of the teens"...and "the last letter of his last name was the last letter of the alphabet"...and his mom said that he was "always the last one in at night and the last one up in the morning."

They were both born in the country homes in which their families lived. Dorothy was the youngest of five children, and was the only girl. George had a younger sister; an older sister had died a few weeks after her

Dorothy and George Fritz in 1942

birth. They both, along with their siblings, attended one-room country schools in Barber County. My mom went to Mingona School and my dad attended Deerhead School. Sadly, both schools have been torn down...but the memories continue on. My dad had stories of how he and his sister rode a horse to his school. My mom remembered walking down the dirt road with her brothers to her school. She remembered being the only student in second grade and being moved up to third grade.

When my mom was four and my dad was five, they caught their first glimpse of each other. My dad's mother, Eliza Fritz, stopped by to pick up something from my mom's mother, Jessie Kimball. As the two women visited in the yard, my dad and his sister got out of the car to play with the four boys. My mom, who was told to stay inside, was curious about the additional children in the yard. She wandered out of the house very quietly, but before she had a chance to play, was told to get back in the house. She had the chicken pox and was still contagious. But she was outside long enough to see her "future husband" and for my dad to see his "future wife."

Following this meeting, their families endured the Depression and the devastating

"Dust Bowl" of the 1930s. My mom told stories of her mother covering the windows with sheets, trying to keep the horrible dust out of the house, while dealing with extremely hot temperatures during the day. But they survived.

My mom and dad entered Medicine Lodge High School together in 1934, and met once again. They eventually became high school sweethearts. After graduating in 1938, my dad went to Kansas State Agricultural College (now known as Kansas State University) and my mom went to Kansas State Teachers College (now known as Emporia State University). They married in the summer of 1942, shortly before my dad was drafted. World War II came and went, and their life together continued. They had children and had grandchildren. They were able to celebrate their 60th anniversary, and both lived to celebrate their 80th birthdays. Not everyone has that.

Their "first meeting" as small children started a relationship that continued to last a lifetime. That day gave them both a special "glimpse into the future." And I am glad that I was told the story of the first day they laid eyes on each other. Sometimes that "first meeting" in life is the "last meeting" a person needs to have. For them, it definitely was the "best meeting."

Wood Burning Stoves and Dust Storms
By Marcketta Peak of Hutchinson, Kansas
Born 1924

I was born January 24, 1924 at home in a two-room house on a farm six miles south of Alexander, Kansas during a snowstorm. Doctor Baker came from LaCrosse, which was about 20 miles away, to deliver all twelve pounds of me.

Now, you talk about poor folk—we definitely were. I started school at Sunny Side, a little one-room country schoolhouse that was a quarter mile from home. We carried our lunch in a little half gallon syrup bucket, and my drinking water was in a glass jug with a leather strap to carry it by. Most mornings Mom would visit the chicken house to catch, kill, clean, and fry chicken for breakfast. The cold leftovers were then taken to school for lunch. She also made biscuits every morning and I can still see the little dot of flour on the tip of her nose. She cooked on an old wood burning stove and baked all our bread. We'd fuss over who got the heel of the loaf and we'd spread sour cream out of the five-gallon cream can on top and cover it with brown sugar. If you haven't eaten that, you haven't lived! Nearly every day she would be taking fresh cinnamon rolls out of the oven as we got home from school. She never had a fancy mixer, but made the best cakes and pies you ever ate. She made angel food cakes from scratch and I can still see her beating the egg whites with her old wire whip. The yolks were then used for noodles. She also was the master of white cakes with seven minute icing covered with coconut. I don't know to this day how she knew when the oven was the right temperature, as there were no thermostats on the old stoves. She'd stick her hand in to check until it was "just right." She always had on an apron and most of them were covered with many patches. She even sewed patches on her tea towels when they got holes.

Mom's "modern convenience refrigerator" was an icebox, which Daddy created out of a water trough, which ran from the windmill to the cattle tank. He built a box around the pipe; put a lid on it, and Mom would put eggs, butter, milk, and even Jell-O in there to cool. Her first real fridge was a wooden box, which held 25 pounds of ice. We always had plenty of chicken, pork, beef, cream, butter, milk, and eggs, as did all farmers back then. We always enjoyed her red eye gravy which consisted of cream and lard drippings from the cured ham. Then, it was poured over her famous biscuits.

On Saturdays, Daddy would take eggs and cream to town to sell and we would look for the package of gum to share in the egg case when we got home. When I was junior in high school we didn't know if I would get a class ring, as they were $7.50 and that was a lot of money to us. I never knew where my folks got the money, but no one was ever more proud of a class ring than I was. I wore it all the time until my two kids were in high school. I was bowling and the ball slipped off my finger wrong and caused it to swell till the ring had to be cut off.

We had a windmill close to the house but the water wasn't good to drink. My older brother and I carried water in buckets from across the road. There was a well and we each pumped two buckets full and carried them uphill back to the house. I don't remember how much they held but they almost drug on the ground when I got them full. My brother and I went every afternoon and one day he stepped inside the house and slipped. Both buckets flew up and came down all over him. Of course, I laughed, but he wasn't too happy. We didn't have an indoor bathroom, just the old two-holer and a Sears catalog. We took baths in an old metal washtub and used a washboard to launder our clothes. In the winter, the clothes had to freeze dry, and I can still see Daddy's overalls standing alone. We made our own soap and at butchering time, we rendered the lard in a big black kettle in the yard.

My wardrobe consisted of two blouses and two skirts that my mom made out of old men's pants that someone had given us. Mom made my underwear out of flour sacks when I was in grade school, and for dress up, she made me black bloomers. How I hated those things! I never had a new coat until after I was married, as most of my things were hand-me-downs. What my family lacked in material things, my folks made up for with love. We never wondered if we were loved, we just knew.

I grew up in the dust bowl and could tell you many stories of Mom hanging wet sheets at the windows to keep the dirt out. The storms looked like rolling black clouds coming at you and lasted sometimes up to three to four days and literally covered everything, turning day into night in an instant. You couldn't see what color the floor, furniture, or anything was for the layers of dirt. Many cattle died from dust pneumonia. It would have been comical to see the wet rags with nose and mouth mud prints she tied around our faces so that we wouldn't breathe the dirt, that is, if it hadn't been so tragic. During one storm, my youngest brother wandered outside, unknown to Mom and Dad. If it hadn't been for the beam of his tiny flashlight, he would have probably died out there. But Daddy found him and got him back inside.

I must have been halfway intelligent, as I graduated Valedictorian of my class—but when you realize that there were only eight of us, it really wasn't much of an accomplishment. I had lots of freckles and used to cry because I wanted to be pretty, but I was ugly. It doesn't bother me anymore; what you see is what you get, and I plan on being around for a while yet!

Ode to Great Men and a Rewarding Childhood
By Russell O. Vail of White Lake, Michigan
Born 1941

I attended Bushton Grade School, Bushton, KS (population 500 in Rice County) from the 3rd to 8th grades, which school has since consolidated with the Claflin, KS school system.

There were many amazing and life impacting teachers and community people, but one stands out. Lawrence E. Timmons (who went by L.E. Timmons) was the eighth grade teacher, principal of the grade school, coach of all of the sports teams (basketball, baseball, and track), and Scout Master of Troop 175. L.E. Timmons, husband to Ruby and father of a daughter, Marlyn and son, Darrol, enjoyed huge successes at all of his endeavors. He put on an annual grade school graduation that would rival high schools, colleges, and universities. He had the touch to hire the right personnel to be assistants as coaches and top-rate devoted teachers, including a very good music department. Even in grade school, he seemed to have the ability to get the best out of each and every student. Some feared him, complained about being pushed too hard, but all respected and loved him.

Of all of his accomplishments, I would put his Scout Master position at or near the top. His son was a year older than me (which I now see as a stroke of luck for me) as we over-accomplished in the world of sports, and were as active as any troop in America in Scouting. We attended National Jamborees, Philmont Scout ranch in New Mexico, canoeing trips to Canada, yearly summer weeks at the near-by Camp Pawnee scout facility (where one could work on multiple merit badges and become members of the Order of the Arrow), weekend scouting camping trips near woods and creeks in our area, educational trips to expos, airshows, and exhibits.

From this little town in the middle of Kansas, about 75 (or more) members of Troop

1954 Philmont Scout Ranch Troop 175

175 became Eagle Scouts, with many also being awarded the God and Country Award. L.E., himself, was awarded the Silver Beaver Award (the highest adult Boy Scout Award). All of this memorabilia is presently buried in the basement of the Rice County Museum (the county seat), which is shamefully not prominently displayed to show this amazing story and history for the world to see and appreciate.

Some of my favorite memories of my childhood in Pulaski, VA. Revolve around "wash day." I remember helping my mom wring out clothes using the wringer washer and then hanging the clothes, sheets, and towels on the lines outside.

I especially remember how wonderful the sheets smelled after drying outside. They were simply delightful!

Another fond memory is of laying on the floor in front of the large floor model radio and listening to stories, like The Lone Ranger. Not many people had TV yet, but we totally enjoyed the radio. When we did get to watch TV, it was at my uncle's, who lived down the street. The first serial TV show we watched was "I Remember Mama"...a fun family show that was on Sundays, as I recall.

We had our milk delivered by the milkman on a regular basis. The glass bottles held the milk with cream on top, which we used to make whipped cream. Sometimes we used the milk bottles for games, such as drop the clothespin in the bottle. We were easily satisfied without electronics, playing outside, making up games with materials we had on hand, etc.

A favorite family activity was to pack a picnic basket using whatever food we had on hand...whether it was hard-boiled eggs, peanut butter crackers or something fancier. Then we would all pile in the car (4 siblings plus my parents) and go on a drive. The Blue Ridge Pkwy was a favorite area to drive. We especially liked the Mabry Mill area for our picnics.

Life was harder without the conveniences of automatic washers and dryers, only one car to a family, etc., but it was also simpler and in many ways less stressful. Kids could be kids... play outdoors until dark, and then you knew to be home. Everyone had the same rules.

Just a Sleigh Ride
By Shirley A. Schwarz of Derby, Kansas
Born 1940

When I was five years old in 1945, we lived in a tiny little town called Lost Springs, Kansas. There was a store, a restaurant, blacksmith shop, and a post office. If there was more, I don't remember them. I know that the town was more family than neighbors. All the adults watched over all the children and when there was some wrong by one of the kids, moms, and dads didn't side with the wrong-doer, but with the one who was done wrong.

My mom and dad ran the café for my grandmother, and at that café, so many wonderful things transpired. It was the meeting hall for the town. During the week, breakfast, lunch, and dinner was served and cooked up from scratch every day. My brothers did the dishes when they weren't at school. On Wednesday afternoons, the quilting ladies from the church met to quilt and gossip. On Thursdays after school, all the big kids came and hung out and played the pinball machine. Saturday nights it became a bar, and all the men form the oil fields came and drank beer and told big stories about the close calls they had experienced on the big rigs. Even though it was a bar on Saturday nights, I played in the old safe that was left over from when the building had been a bank till closing time, or sometimes I slept on a blanket that Momma put in there for that very reason. Daddy closed the place down at midnight, and he, Momma, and I would walk down the walk alongside the café to the rooms at the back of the building where we, along with my two big brothers, slept and lived when not at the café.

Just out of town, there was an old railroad bridge over a small creek. The hobos hung out there. They were a great bunch of what I, of course, considered old men. I, of course, did not go there, but my brothers did. Those men, many out of work and just traveling the country, taught my brothers and the other boys in town how to catch rabbits with their bare hands and how to cook them and many other different meals. They would also teach them how to season them from the things that grew in the fields and woods.

In the summer, all of us children were barefoot and out from dawn to dusk. I was five and I had a best friend named Kay Echols. We spent most of that last summer there on roller skates. My brothers, Weldon (who was 13), Larry (who was 11), and their friends decided to trap rabbits or squirrel, and I guess some muskrat, possums, and raccoons. Once they were running rabbits out from oil well pipes when they though they spied a rabbit. One boy would hold a gunny sack at one end and another would poke a rod with a can on the end into the pipe and run the rabbit into the sack. They had quite a surprise when that rabbit turned out to be a skunk! They had to strip off out behind the café, stand in a wash tub, and clean off with Momma's homemade tomato juice, then get doused with buckets of cold well water.

That last winter we were there it snowed often and all the older kids in town got to be pulled on a special sled that someone had built several years before. The sled was three inches thick, twelve inches wide and 16 feet long. On the front, there were runners on either side that were three feet long and were on a swivel. There were two runners on the back the same size, but were not on a swivel. There was a chain on the front that pulled the sled behind an old pickup truck that had been converted into a sort of all-terrain vehicle. One boy would sit on the front and each boy behind would wrap his legs around the one in front of him. To ride the sled, you had to be at least ten years old. Bing five and a girl, I didn't stand a chance, but it was a big dream of mine to get onto that old sled. My momma and daddy and I would sit in the darkened café and watch the truck pull the laughing kids around town. Often after the sleigh rides, they would come into the café to warm up with a cup of hot chocolate.

One evening, my brothers were bundling up for a sleigh ride and I was sitting on the edge of the bed watching them (and I suppose, pouting a bit.) It was early evening, right at dusk, and my big brothers were whispering to each other and casting looks my way. Weldon went out behind the café where the sled was loading. Larry said, "Come on, get your coat and leggings, gloves, and hat in a hurry." He stuffed me into my things, and out the door, he pulled me. The truck driver was in the cab of the truck and several boys were on the sled. With my older brother on the back, my younger brother piled me on the sled right behind big brother and then he got on and wrapped his legs around me and my big brother. All the kids on the sled knew I was there, but I guess they all agreed to sneak me on a ride. The truck took off and around the town we went. It was so exciting and I felt so grown up. When we stopped to have hot chocolate at the café, Larry whisked me away before any grown up saw me. It seems my Larry was supposed to stay home during the first ride to watch me. We then sauntered into the café like we had just gotten there.

I'm 74 years old now and I still feel that wonderful safe coziness tucked in between my brothers—my heroes. My whole life these brothers loved and protected me. The year after the sleigh ride we moved away to some other small town in Kansas. In fact, I went to 15 different schools growing up in Kansas. Every place was an adventure. I was happy with those two brothers and a daddy and momma who made every place a home.

Old Birds and Twin Calves
By Marion W. Nattier of Moundridge,
Kansas
Born 1923

I was born three and a half miles north of Hesston on the east side of the road. The second son of Sid and Mabel Nattier. According to my Dad, my arrival was on a rainy, muddy June day. He had to bring the doctor and Aunt Ella Cummings by wagon from Hesston.

I'm sure there was nothing like Planned Parenthood back then or I probably would have arrived at a different date. June 10th is the beginning of a very busy season for a wheat farmer.

My first recollection of life north of Hesston was being chased by a red and black rooster. That old bird would chase me and scare the be gabbers out of this kid. Mom got tired of rescuing me; she gave me a lathe and told me to give him a whack next time he bothered me. Well, I did just like Mom said, for once, and caught that old bird right on the head. He just flopped down and didn't move.

I took off for the house really letting it out, I killed the fighting rooster. Mom came out of the house and I told her I killed the fighting rooster. She said we better go see. By the time we got there, that old bird was staggering around like a drunken sailor. Believe me he was a much wiser and cautious bird after that.

Another incident I recall is of a preacher by the name of Dewey who came to our place. He came quite often because he was dating my Aunt Esther at that time. Anyway, that evening he stopped by and told me to tell my mother he would like to buy a chicken. I told Mom and she said that Rev. Dewey was just kidding or teasing and that he had no need of a chicken. Guess what? I didn't like to be teased, so I went to Rev. Dewey and told him he was lying about buying a chicken, just teasing me. He did want to buy a chicken, and I can remember Mom's lecture about calling someone a liar.

My first chores or work around the farm were gathering eggs. Now, the chicken eggs were not bad, but the ducks just scattered them wherever the urge hit. Oh boy, those geese were something else. When the goose left the nest, that old gander was on guard. Albert would try and get that old guys attention, then I would grab the eggs out of the nest and head for safety. I always made it but that old bird would sure make it interesting.

My new job was getting the cows in to be milked. We had a long lane going east then south ¼ mile to the pasture, on long walk on those hot summer days. The only exciting thing that ever happened was the old granny

Binders lined up in town

black and white cow gave birth to twin calves. I made it home in record time to tell Dad.

From getting the eggs, and getting the cows in to be milked, my next job was milking just as soon as I had enough squeeze. We had one gentle old cow that wasn't picky who milked her, so that's how I got my start in the milking business. We separated the cream from the milk, fed the skim milk to the calves and pigs, and the cream was sold to Uncle Bill Pfautz Cream and Poultry Store in Hesston. The eggs, ducks, geese, and old hens also went there.

I helped Mother pick the down from the ducks and geese for stuffing pillows. We made one feather tick for the bed. Down is those fuzzy breast feathers on the ducks and geese and is one mess to pick.

A Story to Tell
By Kenneth Howe of Dundee, Oregon
Born 1933

I was born in western Kansas, in Greeley County, one mile west of Tribune, during the Dust Bowl days. I added one to the county with the lowest population in the state. My father was fortunate to own one of two trucks in the county at the time, which enabled him to get extra work (and income) from Greeley County. He also owned a Twin City tractor and was sometimes hired to plow up the Kansas prairie on which to grow wheat; this acreage included a portion of the Santa Fe Trail. When

I was two, my parents moved back to Stafford County to live and farm property northeast of Stafford and owned by my mother's family; they felt fortunate to have a farm on which to live. The move was made because babies were dying of dust pneumonia, including a distant cousin of mine in Granada, Colorado. It was in Stafford that my younger brother was born.

My name is Kenneth and my wife is Ann. I am a retired pastor and we reside in Dundee, Oregon. My brother is Bob and our parents were N.J. "Bill" and Dora (Thole) Howe. I considered the farm northeast of Stafford my home until I graduated from Baylor University and Southwestern Seminary and married Ann, at which time we moved to Spokane, Washington to pastor our first church.

I have now reached my 80th birthday and it was in the fall of 2013 that I received a phone call from Brandon Harris of Office Products (a print shop) in Great Bend, Kansas, saying he thought the picture there may be a picture of me and if so he would like for me to claim it. At first, I was doubtful because he said the name of the second person on the picture was "Boffie" and I said I did not remember anyone with that name. When I stated that I have a brother named Bob the voice on the other end of the telephone said, "You know, maybe I am misreading it and it is 'Bobbie'." I responded by saying that when my brother was a small boy he was called "Bobbie." Brandon then surmised that the writing behind the studio photo read "Kenneth Howe, age 6 years and 5 months and Bobbie Howe, age 4 years." I added that I was 2 and one-half years older than Bob and that I was quite certain that, indeed, the photo was of the two of us.

I was inquisitive and had to ask, "How did you receive the photo?" His answer was, "One day, a person brought the picture in to our business saying they found it in the street directly in front of our store, therefore assuming it was meant to be inside the store." He went on to say that there was no person in the office who recognized having ever seen the photo; therefore they put the picture on display with a sign asking for identification. Approximately one month later an unidentified lady stated that she recognized the family name but did not know the two individuals on the photo. She then phoned Michael Hathaway, the curator of the Museum in Stafford, telling him of her experience, asking for his assistance, and requesting that he phone Office Products in Great Bend with information he could compile. Michael had my name, address, and phone number as the result of a previous purchase I had made, by telephone, during the time of the museum silent auction held in 2012. He telephoned the information to Office Products and they, in turn, telephoned me and then mailed to me the photo.

I now experience kind of a sentimental awe as I sit and look at this picture. It is a studio photo of Bob and myself with a cardboard frame along with extra cardboard backing, yet I can see the upper right hand corner is torn and there are numerous pock marks on the picture as the result of vehicles driving over the picture while it was laying there on the pebbled pavement. I try to imagine the life of a seventy-four year old picture and I ask myself "How did that photo travel the forty miles from Stafford to Great Bend and in who's hands was it held?" Then I ask myself how it might have gotten to its location on the street, "Was it lost, dropped, or was it disposed of and then fell from a garbage truck?" These questions continue to haunt me and will probably remain unanswered. Nevertheless, I am glad to have the photo and I believe it makes for a good story, which I have already had the privilege of sharing with many folks.

Outhouses and Old Threshing Machines
By Cecil Roger Thomas, Jr. of Garner, North Carolina
Born 1934

There are many things, which happened to me as a child I was born near Protection, KS on Sept. 2, 1934 and moved away from KS in May of 1954. There was an old steam engine in the shelterbelt between the house in which I was born and my grandparents' house about ¼ mile south of us. As kids, we would play in this old steam engine, shutting each other up in the "firebox!" At a later time, Daddy had an old threshing machine, which, while it was not usable, was excellent for us to play on as kids. One of us would climb into the "exhaust" which ejected the straw. Another of us would turn the wheel, which made the exhaust go out over the field. Another old piece of farm equipment that Daddy had was an old steel-wheeled tractor which had smooth wheels on the back, but which had holes into which bolts were placed to fasten "lugs" onto the wheels so it would have traction when it was being used for farming. It did not run either at the time I remember it.

There were a couple of times that I did something that was very dangerous. Daddy had taken an old icebox apart, preparing it for a junkyard sale in Wichita. The back of it had what could be called "runners" on it, and my twin brother and sister and I took this back up to the top of a hill in our backyard after a bad sleet storm. We put one knee on one back corner, one knee on the other back corner, held onto the two front corners with our hands, and slid down the hill on the sleet. At the bottom of the hill was a barbed-wire fence, and just before we got to the fence, we would raise one front corner and spin in circles! If we had "goofed" and missed raising the corner and hit the fence, we would have been cut "all to pieces!"

Another time, one of the guys in my PHS class and I went for a drive at night. He turned out the lights on a country road and drove in the dark. Fortunately, there was no other traffic!

Saturday night baths: there were five children and two adults. Because I was the middle-aged one, my bath came third. (We all used the same water!) I was taking a bath in the kitchen when some company came to look at some puppies we were giving away. My mother slid the bathtub under the kitchen table and pulled the tablecloth down so I could not be seen while the company was in the house! I do not remember how cold the water got during that time, but in the summertime, we did not have to worry about the water getting cold, as we had a tank on top of our out-of-doors shower, which was filled with water and heated by the summer sun! I remember when a neighbor came for a swim in our pond beside the road. He decided to dive into the pond with a straw hat on and he just about broke his neck!

This same neighbor, when he just learned to drive, decided he was going to see what would happen if he reversed his feet on the clutch and the brake (I think that meant that he had his left foot on the brake and right foot on the clutch, but I am not sure as this was when we didn't have automatic transmissions with no clutch.) He went through the backside of the garage! I also recall the time that my younger brother and sister (twins) and I decided we were going to try to "smoke" coffee. Because I was the oldest of the three, I got paddled, but the twins did not! In the fourth grade, after a rain, my class went out into the schoolyard to play. The boys (girls probably not) decided to wade in the puddles. When we returned to the classroom, the teacher (Mrs. Carey) felt our shoes to see who had wet ones. One other boy and I had returned to the classroom for overshoes, but only after our shoes were already wet. The teacher saw that we had overshoes on, but when she discovered that our shoes were wet under the overshoes, she paddled us anyhow! I do not recall whether I got a paddling when I got home or not.

Another time, I recall that when we had a drawing of names for our Christmas party, there were two of my classmates who had similar names. The middle name of both was Lee and the first two letters of the last name were the same. When the names were drawn, one of our classmates mistakenly thought that he/she had the girl's name when he/she actually had the boy's name. For this reason, when the party was held, the boy had no present and the girl had two presents! I do not recall how this situation was rectified, but it was.

Another time, I was going to ride our horse, King, to a neighbor's house. When we got to the mailbox, I got off for some reason and King went home (½ mile.) When I returned home walking, I fibbed to my parents and said that King had thrown me off! We had a rotary phone; each person had a certain ring and one family listened in on every call. One time, one of the ones on our line tried calling someone but when no one answered, he said, "Okay, folks, let's all hang up and try again!" Someone said that they heard, "click, click, click" all down the line!

Before we had REA (Rural Electrification Association) put in, we had an icebox. Daddy would go to town to buy a 100-pound block of ice for the icebox. This would be used to keep things in the icebox cool, but each Sunday we would take part of the ice and make homemade ice cream. Each of us kids would want to sit on the freezer while someone turned the crank. We did not get cold, as the days were hot and there was a cloth of some description on top of the ice in the freezer.

Our outhouse was a "one-holer" and was about 100 feet from the back door. For toilet "tissue," we used "Monkey Ward" catalogs, which we would read while we were "doing our business!" Since we could not afford ice skates, we put oil on blocks of wood and strapped them to our shoes; one time I fell on ice on a pond while using these "skates." I was unable to walk, but when I was left at home by myself, the next day and I needed to go to the outhouse. I had to drag my lower body along the ground for the entire distance. My parents thought that I was telling a lie when I told them about it after they got home. They probably could have seen the "tracks" I made in the sand but apparently, they did not.

I vaguely recall one of the girls getting her hair caught in the wringer washer; I do not know how they got her free from it, however.

In the second house we lived in, SE of Protection, Mama saw a snake stick his/her head out of the wall in the kitchen; she chopped its head off with a butcher knife! I have often wondered what happened to the snake's body. My brother and I had to do many chores on the farm; I do not recall what time we arose in the morning, but we had to dress, milk the cows, feed the chickens, eat breakfast, and be ready to get on the school bus when it came (7:30AM?).

We had a bowling alley in Protection but it was not the larger balls we have today. I often set pins for others who were bowling, as the pins were not automatically set by a machine. I had to get out of the way after setting the pins to keep from being hit by the next player. Also, we thoroughly enjoyed playing Monopoly on Saturday nights. I don't recall any other games we played but we did have a battery-powered radio (DC power) on which we listened to what I recall was the ten most popular songs (Hit Parade?) on each Saturday night.

When we got our first AC radio, it had to warm up when it was plugged into the electric outlet, and we thought that it was broken! There were no TVs in those days although I do recall one of the girls in my high school class having one but the reception was very poor. I do not recall even listening to a TV until I went to San Diego in 1954 with the Navy.

I "fell in love" with Phyllis Ford when I was in the seventh grade. Her mother was the operator on our telephone system and they had just recently moved to Protection from Dodge City. When they returned to Dodge, (she was in the ninth grade then), my "love" went with her (although she did not know it!) and I joined the PHS Glee Club when it went to Dodge just so I could see her again! I never got to hold her hand, date her, or kiss her at that time. My first date was when I was 17. I decided that I was going to ask a girl out for a movie (10-cent admission); I wrote a note to her, which I threw on her desk as we left the study hall. The note stated that if she would go with me, I would pick her up in our clean farm truck because we did not have a car at that time. She accepted, but rather than telling me in person, she told another girl in our class that she would go. That girl made fun of me because I was so shy; we never dated again but I do not know why.

I learned to drive on a 1928 Buick. The town of Protection had decided to buy a new hearse, so they sold the old one to my father who cut the back off of it and made a pick-up truck out of it! We had another pick-up at a later time. This was a 1937 Hudson Terraplane. We called it a "terrible pain" because it seemed that it always had something wrong with it! Just after WWII, Daddy bought a truck, which was supposed to have been sent to France, but because the war had ended, it was sold in the US. The speedometer showed kilometers per hour rather than miles per hour, so we had a lot of fun with that, as it appeared that we were going much faster than we actually were!

My Ancestors were Pioneers
By June M. Winslow of Hutchinson, Kansas
Born 1927

I was born on June 4, 1927 and that is why my name is June. I remember the "Dust Bowl Days" and the "Great Depression." When the dust storms were approaching, we would soak bed sheets in water and hang them at all our windows and doors to try and keep the dust out of our house. It would be so dark at noon that we would have to turn our lights on in the house. Sometimes we would be stranded in our house for 3 days at a time until the dust

Cassidy Hotel

storm was over. My dad would shovel a path on the sidewalk from our front door to the street, shoveling dirt instead of snow from a snowstorm.

My father worked at the Partridge Kansas Flour Mill for several years but it closed when the banks failed in 1929. My parents lost all their savings when the Partridge bank closed. My grandfather, J.W. Warnock, had just sold his farm, moved into Partridge, and lost all of his money too. My father, Earl Warnock, and my grandfather pooled what money they had left and opened a garage on Main Street just north of the Partridge Community Church. My father was a mechanic, so he repaired cars and trucks while Granddad sold gasoline. From the time I started grade school until I graduated from high school I remember helping my father at the garage. When very young, I carried tools for Dad and held the light for him when he was working on a car. Later I climbed up on car fenders to put gas in the cars when the gas tank was on top of the engine. While in high school, I ran the cash register and did the book work. Many times, I managed the gas station alone when Dad had to drive to Hutchinson (14 miles away) to get auto parts. In those early days, we were lucky if Dad made $1.00 a day at the garage. To supplement our income, my mother worked as City Clerk, City Librarian and wrote a column in a county newspaper called the Hutchinson Record.

To have enough to eat, we raised chickens and always planted a huge garden. I helped with the garden and canning of all the vegetables and fruits we raised. We had five different fruit trees in our yard: apple, apricot, pear, cherry, and persimmon. One year, we had a late freeze, which killed all the fruit trees.

We were very poor but we did not realize it because everybody else in our town was in the same boat. As the old saying goes..."we had to squeeze every penny." A rare treat was a five-cent ice cream cone about once a month.

Several of my ancestors settled in and around Partridge in the 1870s. My great grandfather, Robert Thomas Cassidy, built the first livery stable and the first hotel in Partridge in 1875. The first church service held in Partridge was in the "Cassidy Livery, Feed, and Sale stable." The service was led by Methodist minister Rev. Miller, who was visiting his son in Partridge.

My great grandmother, Elizabeth Cassidy, was the daughter of Dr. John McClain Harsha. Dr. Harsha moved to Hutchinson, KS in 1876, 2 years after Robert and his family arrived. Dr. Harsha was not only a doctor but a surveyor and soon became the Reno County surveyor. Many of the families that homesteaded in Reno County have his name on their documents. Elizabeth's brother, William C. Harsha, built the first grocery store in Partridge, but it was destroyed by a tornado in 1923. Another brother, John Paley Harsha, was mayor of Hutchinson, KS for 10 years (1897-1907). The Harsha Park and the Harsha Canal in Hutchinson are named after John Paley. Elizabeth's father donated some of the land for Eastside Cemetery and was one of the first to be buried there.

My great grandfather, Simeon Warnock, homesteaded on a farm north of Partridge in an area called Salt Creek in 1877. His wife, Charlotte, and their hired man came from Lacona, Iowa in a covered wagon with their six children ages 16 to a baby. Simeon had

Robert Thomas Cassidy and sons in front of the first Livery Feed and Stable in 1900

become quite ill just before the planned trip so had to come on a train. Simeon and Charlotte are also buried in the Eastside Cemetery in Hutchinson, KS. My grandfather (John William Warnock) was the only child to remain in the Partridge community after he married. Three of his brothers participated in the Oklahoma Land Rush and his one sister also moved to Oklahoma.

What I enjoyed most when growing up in Partridge were all the family reunions we used to have. With all the Warnock, Cassidy, and Harsha relatives living in the area, we would have 75 to 100 relatives attend our reunions. Almost every Sunday we would have a picnic or a dinner with some of my aunts, uncles, and cousins.

I graduated from Partridge High School in 1945, attended Hutchinson Community College, was married to Bob Winslow in 1948, and moved away from Partridge. My husband spent 33 years in the US Navy and we lived in Guam, Hawaii, the Philippines, San Francisco, San Diego, Jacksonville, and Washington, DC. When he retired from the Navy, we returned to Hutchinson, KS in 1978 and have lived here ever since. But I still claim Partridge as my hometown and have so many wonderful memories of growing up in this rural Kansas town. Every year we have a Partridge High School Reunion in October and I always attend so I can connect with my former classmates and friends. Partridge Community Church is still my hometown church and we still visit there occasionally. Growing up in a small town has many advantages, mainly the life-long friendships that we treasure.

Legends of Harper
By Jennifer Isenhower Beaver of Tampa, Florida
Born 1951

I love the '50s. I was born on the last day of 1951 and my first real memory is from October 1, 1954. That's the night my sister was born. My mom told me that she had her window open at the Joslin Hospital and there was a Harper High School football game going on at the field on Central. She could hear Mr. Briner announcing the game. Dr. Clark delivered Dana Jo, and then rushed off to see the game. The next day my dad took me to the hospital and walked me up to the window of the room where the tiny newborn babies were all bundled up.

"That's your new sister," my dad told me. Next, he walked me down the hall to see my mommy. She was sitting up in a bed, and daddy lifted me to sit beside her. She had a table with a tray and some peaches in a bowl. I wanted them, so I sat by my mommy and ate the peaches and wondered why she was having supper in bed in a place that smelled so funny. I looked in the rooms and liked the big jars full of wooden sticks, which would eventually be used to gag me when I visited the doctor, and the stethoscopes hanging on the walls, and the glass cupboards that held cotton balls & swabs and bottles of mystery medicine that the nurse would eventually use to choke me.

I remember being so happy to have my mommy & daddy, and Dr. Clark, and peaches in bed and a sister, although I wasn't really sure what a sister was. We lived in the house at 307 West 15th, and had wall furnaces, and a kitchen with a Hotpoint oven. There were little lights in blue, red, green, yellow and I could put my fingers on them, and they didn't burn. I loved it when my mom cooked bacon or fried steak and potatoes. The kitchen table was red and had shiny chrome legs. When the menu included Sloppy Joe's, I hated them and refused to eat. Once, my dad sat me down at that table until I ate my Sloppy Joe or until midnight. Midnight came first. After that, my mother must have lost the recipe. Sometimes I stubbed my toe on the chair legs and it made me really mad, so I'd go out to the redbud tree in the back yard, climb up, and sit where the branches forked. I stared at my toes and loved the smell of the grass that had just been mowed, and of the trash burning in the barrels up and down the alley behind our houses.

My dad was a fireman. In fact, he was the Fire Chief in Harper from the '50s until the '70s. The siren didn't blow very often, but when it did, I knew that he would drop whatever he was doing, grab his helmet, jump in his red Studebaker named "Henry J" and take off for wherever that sound was coming from. One night, the fire was so close to our house that we walked down that alley and saw the flames reaching high in the sky. We smelled the smoke and stood all night watching and it didn't matter that we might have to go to school the next day. We had heard and told all kinds of stories about that house and who lived in it, and convinced ourselves that it was haunted and that if we walked by too close the Gish Girls would come out and grab us.

When Daddy came home that next day, he was covered in soot and sweat. His beard was singed and it smelled really awful. The skin on his face was bright red and he collapsed and hung his head. He was crying. His Harper Volunteer Firefighters had tried to save the two sisters that were in the house that night, but it was too late.

I felt so sorry for Daddy and for the Gish Girls that had died. I found out later that my grandfather, Lem Laird, had done some work at the Gish house. The night of the fire, my Dad drove four miles to the farm where my grandfather lived to ask him where the sisters slept so they could locate them in the fire. My grandfather was the only person they knew that had ever been inside that house. It was a sad day for our family and a sad day in Harper.

Some of our stories got bigger as the years went by, and never more than at recess at Harper Grade School. We had a jungle gym and we'd climb and talk about haunted houses and the Gish Girls and just make stuff up to keep ourselves entertained. In our imagination, Harper had tornadoes, floods, and all sorts of danger, princes would ride in and save us, and we could be the Queens and Princesses and rule Harper. Our villain was Mrs. McGuilicutty, made up by my friend Connie Cochran. Mrs. McGuilicutty could chase us, hang us upside down, and throw us into big holes in the ground that we would have to dig ourselves, all the way to China. In the end, the bell would ring, and we'd go back to Kindergarten and watch the boys squirm to see if we'd tell on them for looking when we were hanging upside down on the jungle gym. My mother later told me she would have spanked me for that. And a lot of the damage Mrs. McGuilicutty inflicted on us was cured on weekend doctor calls to my next-door neighbor, who was Connie's grandmother. Mrs. Cochran fed us "pills" that we made out of white bread, all squeezed into balls, and let us do all the necessary surgeries with screwdrivers and spoons and thread. Connie and I still laugh about what great fun we had already had by the time we were 5 years old.

And then it was back to Mrs. Bauman's Kindergarten class, to face the threat of the Naughty Chair. Nobody wanted to get sent to the Naughty Chair. I was a good student and never got into any trouble unless a boy was involved. My mission at naptime was to squeeze my eyelids shut so tight my eyes would never open again, and that way I couldn't do anything that would get me put into that Chair. But one day I let my guard down. I opened my eyes and looked at Brad Yock, who was sprawled out on the rug beside me. He looked at me and I giggled. I went straight to the Naughty Chair. It wasn't so bad, and I've been laughing my way into taking risks ever since, and Brad Yock is still my friend.

I lived in Harper until the day I went off to college at the ripe old age of 17. Since then I've moved from Wichita to North Carolina to Maryland to Florida, but my roots are still in Harper. The aforementioned farm has been in the family for over 100 years and my mother still lives in that farmhouse—the one she was born in. That red chrome and formica table and chairs sits smack in the middle of my living room and still gets daily use. My sister and I are close, although we have lived halfway around the world from each other. She has travelled to China several times and doesn't have to dig her way there. Sometimes I make up a story about the two of us eventually living in an old haunted house together, scaring the neighborhood kids, and continuing the legend of the Gish Girls. Only we turn our legend around, and in the end, a Harper Volunteer Firefighter rushes in and saves us because we are Princesses, even though we're 100 years old.

A Time of Innocence
By Cyndee Huddleston of Larned, Kansas
Born 1948

I grew up in the 1950s in the small South Central Kansas town of Larned during a time of innocence. Both of my parents worked, so I stayed with my grandparents who lived next door. Grandma was a wonderful grandma. We played games, and many times, she let me win. We played Chinese checkers, dominoes, and a matching numbers game, which my grandma called "a game of books." It was a homemade game, which we made from old calendar sheets pasted to a thin piece of Cardboard. We made the paste by mixing flour and water. When it was dry, we cut the numbers into squares and we were ready to play. Grandma also played the piano, violin, and mandolin. Her favorite songs were, *Brighten the Corner Where You Are, In the Sweet By And By, In the Garden*, and *Amazing Grace*.

Grandma and I loved the outdoors. I also loved playing at the old stone quarry, which was across the alley. I climbed the walls and carved my initials in the sandstone. Many times, we sat in the backyard on an old stone bench that Grandpa made, listening to the turtledoves, and watching the goldfish in the hand-dug cement lily pond. Grandma's yard was full of beautiful flowers and lots of colorful butterflies. There were large orange poppies by Grandpa's shop, bright zinnias along the edge of the vegetable garden, and very tall hollyhocks along the fence line.

She grew a variety of vegetables and had several fruit trees. What our family didn't eat, Grandma canned and stored in the storm cellar. She also raised chickens. Her favorites were the Rhode Island Reds. We used an old oatmeal box for the chicken feed and a little basket for gathering eggs. Grandma was an amazing cook using the produce from the garden and eggs from her chickens. I loved her fried chicken and chicken and dumplings until one day I realized that we were eating the "pet" chickens. It took a while before I would eat chicken again. Usually on Sunday, she made her special meatloaf, stewed tomatoes, Jell-O salad, homemade bread, and peach cobbler.

We were poor but I didn't know it. Grandma was a wonderful homemaker; one of the ways she contributed to the family income was by cleaning houses and taking in laundry from some of the families in town. Sometimes I got to help get the clothes ready to iron by shaking water on them, rolling them up, and

Grandfather Charles Williamson's second hand store
Grandpa is on the left

placing them in a bag. It was my job getting the sprinkler ready by filling an old pop bottle with water. The sprinkler head had cork around the bottom and fit into the mouth of the pop bottle. One day I was running through the house, which I wasn't supposed to do. I ran through the kitchen where the ironing board was set up, knocking it over. The hot iron fell on me; I still have a scar on my arm as a reminder. My favorite room in Grandma's house was the kitchen. It was always warm from the sun and from Grandma's baking. In the northeast corner, she had a table covered with red and white checkered oilcloth. The table was full of the most beautiful African Violets of all colors; it was so easy for her to start a new plant with just a leaf. My favorite ones were the deep velvety purple ones.

Grandma had a special corner of the large living room for her sewing. She had a Singer Treadle Sewing Machine. I loved to sit and watch her move the lever with her feet. She made most of our clothes. She also like to embroider and crochet and made many of her doilies. The pineapple pattern must have been her favorite because she made a lot of them. She also taught me to chain stitch.

Grandma had a blue and white parakeet, which she named Billy. She would say "Billy is a pretty boy," and he repeated "Pretty boy," and bobbed his head up and down. Sometimes he would sit on my finger and sometimes he flew around the room. She taught me which weeds to pick for him to eat. I think foxtail was his favorite. One day when the front door was open, Billy flew outside; we never saw him again. It made Grandma really sad.

On cold days, it was so nice to sit by the wood burning stove in the living room. I got to help her carry in the wood and take out the ashes. There was a bucket and scoop sitting beside the stove and a cast iron kettle of water sitting on top. The bathroom was in the back of the house and not much heat reached it, so it was one place you did not want to linger.

Grandma had a large upright piano and a piano stool that had four claw feet, each clutching a glass ball. She kept her music on the top of the piano next to a bronze colored horse radio. For a long time I thought it only had horse news and played horse music, but then Grandpa was always teasing me.

Grandpa had his own corner in the living room. He had a big overstuffed soft green chair, a tall floor model radio, a floor lamp, and ashtray on a floor stand. He smoked pipes and cigars, which Grandma did not like. When he came home from work he sat in his big 'ol chair and read the Tiller and Toiler newspaper, then listened to the radio while he waited for supper. I loved to crawl up on the back of Grandpa's chair, straddle his neck, comb his hair, mess it up, and comb it again. One day he was sitting in his chair, cleaning his hunting rifle. He didn't realize it was loaded and shot a hole in the wall. I was scared and Grandma was mad. I loved it when Grandpa danced with me. He was six foot four inches and I was just a little girl, but he let me stand on his boots as he held my hands and we would go dancing across the floor. I also loved it when he carried me on his shoulders and I had to duck through the doorways.

Grandpa liked to hunt and sometimes he took me with him when he was hunting for jackrabbits and squirrels. He also liked to fish and grew his own cane poles in the backyard. When one wore out, he just cut another one. We lived near the Arkansas River and the Pawnee Creek, which made it convenient for him to fish often. Sometimes he brought home bullfrogs and one time an eel. It was hard to skin.

Grandpa owned a second-hand and antique furniture business. He had two large buildings at the south end of Main Street. The smaller of the two he used to repair and refinish the furniture. The larger one had an upstairs and both floors were full of furniture. Just inside the front entrance hung a large buffalo hide. Mom didn't like it much but I just loved it and always wanted to be lifted up so I could feel it. Some of the furniture Grandpa bought from estate sales and some from auction sales. Occasionally I got to go with him. He had a friend at the auction, a big 'ol man named Jake. I'm sure that Jake must have been joking with me when he told me he was going to hang me up on a nail on the wall. But just to be on the safe side I always stayed pretty close to Grandpa and hung on to his pant leg.

Grandpa's stores were less than a block from the Pawnee Creek. If business was slow he took his cane poles and fished off the bridge. From there he had a good view of the stores so he could see if customers were coming. One year we had a pretty good flood and the streets and gutters were full and overflowing. Grandpa let me go wading and play in the water. There was no plumbing in Grandpa's stores, but there were a couple of hand pumps outside between the buildings. Grandpa always kept a jug of water around to prime the pumps and I loved to do the pumping. I was too small to do much good, but

Cyndee's grandfather, Charles Williamson

he made me think I was doing a good job.

Across the street to the south and west of the stores was the sales barn where large auctions for cattle and horses were held every Friday. Once in a while Grandpa and I would walk over and watch all the activity. I'd climb up on the fence, hang over, and try to touch the horses. When I was a little older Grandma let me walk to Grandpa's stores by myself. It was about six blocks from home, but I had to cross a busy highway and the railroad tracks. Sometimes I took a different route and walked by a gas station that had a pop machine. If I had some money, I stopped and bought a five-cent Coke and a nickel candy bar.

I loved listening to stories about when my mom was growing up. One story Grandma told me was about surviving the dust storm in the 1930s. She said they hung wet sheets and wet towels over the doors and windows to help keep the dust out. They also held wet handkerchiefs over their mouth and nose just to breathe. They took a road trip and saw huge drifts of dust around farm houses up past the windowsills and the drifts along the highway looked like huge snow drifts. She said just shaking hands could be dangerous from the shock of static electricity.

My grandchildren also love to hear stories about their mom's childhood just like I liked hearing stories about mine. I told them about the time our family visited Uncle Alton's farm about 30 miles from Larned. Instead of saying that their mom and her brother got chased by a bull, the account was embellished just a bit...

Once upon a time long ago, and in a land far away, lived a handsome young prince and his younger sister—the fair and beautiful little princess. They spent long hours exploring their world, discovering hidden treasures, and bravely facing unknown dangers.

It was on a cool, crisp autumn afternoon that just such an adventure took place. The King and Queen of the realm took the young royals on a distant journey to visit the Duke and Duchess of an expansive estate. The young prince, proudly wearing his exquisite crimson cloak and the little princess with her long golden tresses flowing in the gentle breeze were eagerly exploring new and uncharted territory.

They had ventured a short distance when the young prince sensed danger approaching and said, "Hark! I perceive a large angry beast approaching with great speed!" The great horned beast had focused his attention on the elegant crimson cloak of the young prince. The young prince gently took the hand of the little princess and said, "Come, let us make haste to depart and escape this fury!"

They hurriedly made their way to the great fence that encircled the grounds of the Duke and Duchess. There the young prince leapt with much agility easily clearing the protruding barbs. Sensing the little princess was unable to ascend the massive structure, he quickly turned and assisted her through the lower railings, narrowly escaping the wrath of the great horned beast and heroically saving the precious life of the little princess.

Memories of the Past in Butler County Kansas
By Pat Curtis of Newton, Kansas
Born 1939

I grew up on a farm near Potwin, Kansas. One of my very first memories was the beginning of World War II. I was a very small child, but I remember my father's reaction when the Japanese bombed Pearl Harbor. I was too small to realize just how the war started, but I remember my father's reaction and what he was doing at the time it came over the radio. I remember my mother's sadness when my uncle was drafted and sent to Europe. I also remember when President Roosevelt died and my parent's reactions.

Living on the farm at that time, we had no electricity. We used kerosene burning lamps for the light at night.

We had wood burning stoves and we burned wood and coal for heat. Sometimes when the coal would burn, it would explode and blow the stove door open. That was scary to us children. I remember those cold winter mornings and jumping out of bed upstairs and heading for the stove downstairs to get warm and dress for school.

We had a wood burning cook stove. Eventually we graduated from a wood burning cook stove to a kerosene cook stove.

There was no indoor plumbing. We used and outdoor two hole toilet. My father used lime to kill the smell in summer. In winter, we used a chamber pot and it was taken out to the outdoor toilet and emptied as needed.

On wash day, my mother would go outside to the well and pump water by hand and fill a copper boiler and put it on the wood cook stove to heat it. She used a Maytag wringer washing machine and rinsed the laundry in two tubs. One tub was for whites and the other for colors. In the tubs for white items, she used a liquid called Bluing that was supposed to keep the white in things like sheets etc. In winter, we would sometimes hang the wash outside and it would freeze, but it would usually dry.

For a time we had no telephone. We did eventually get a large wooden phone that hung on the wall and it was a battery operated crank phone. I still remember the phone number. It was 14F242 and we had a party line. Our ring was a long ring, a short ring, and a long ring. Each party had a different ring. Whenever there was a phone call to someone on the party line, our phone would ring and anyone could pick up the receiver and listen to the conversation. We had two curious neighbors that would do that all the time. When it would storm, we could see electricity from the lightening jump across the two ringers on the phone.

Eventually we got a rotary phone and it didn't ring when others got a call. Some curious neighbors would randomly pick up their phone just to see if anyone was talking and they would eavesdrop if there was a conversation.

My father farmed with work horses. I remember raking hay with a horse myself. Oats were cut with a mowing machine and picked up with a machine called a binder that made bundles of oats. We would help our father shock those bundles. Then a neighbor that owned a thrashing machine along with neighboring farmers would come and thrash the grain out and we would have a large hay stack that fed the livestock.

When the thrashing machine came, in the yard, it would shake the house and it was so loud. It was run by steam. My mother and myself and neighboring women would come prepare a meal for the thrashing crew. Sometimes they were there for two or three days.

My father and brothers shucked corn by hand with a glove that had a hook on it that would cut the ears from the stalk.

After we got electricity, we had a radio and we listened to stories like *Amos and Andy*, *Guiding Light*, *The Squeaking Door*, *Portia Faces Life*, and of course the news. When I was in high school, we got our first black and white TV and that was a real treat.

We raised chickens and milked cows by hand. We would put the milk in a separator and it would separate the cream from the milk. If the milk wasn't separated, the cream would rise to the top when it sat in the refrigerator or icebox. My mother always claimed that when there was a storm and there was lightening it would cause the milk to spoil. If there was a setting hen when we gathered eggs, she would peck us when we tried to take her egg.

Food was stored in an icebox that required a block of ice to cool the food. Father would go to the ice house in town and used ice tongs to move the blocks of ice from the ice house to the car and into the icebox. There was a pan that had to be emptied when the ice melted or it would make a messy puddle. Eventually when we got electricity, we had an electric Kelvinator refrigerator. Kelvinator seemed to be the popular brand at that time.

Saturday night bath time was and adventure. Water had to be heated on the wood cook stove and poured into a round metal tub. The tub would set in the middle of the kitchen floor. We would all take a bath in the same tub and in the same water. We kids would bathe last. When we had our hair washed in the spring and summer our mother collected rain water and she washed our hair in rain water and rinsed it with vinegar water. That made our hair soft and shiny.

Being the only girl in a family of five children, there were no hand-me-downs for me. Chicken feed and flour was brought in flowered sacks. My mother would wash the sacks and my grandmother who lived across the drive would sew dresses for me to wear to school on her Treadle Singer sewing machine. I thought I was living high when I got those new dresses.

When my mother bought dish soap and oat cereal there would be tea towels in the soap boxes and bowls in the oatmeal. That is definitely a thing of the past.

There are many other memories, but it would take several pages to tell all those stories.

Christmas Made Special by One Woman for 70 Years
By Kathleen Risley of Caldwell, Kansas
Born 1946

Christmas and the family traditions that went with it were taken for granted by the Williams family year after year. If wasn't until the matriarch of that family passed away at the age of 89 that so many generations of that family truly appreciated what went into making every Christmas so special.

My mother was born in 1902 and lost her mother at age 8, so when she moved from Caldwell, Kansas, and had six children of her own, little did she know how big that family would grow and how many years she would make sure "a good time was had by all" each and every year.

First of all, she always cut her own tree from her own shelterbelt. She did that up into her eighties with a little axe. She used the same silver and china for seventy years, not minding if a piece or two got broken. She made sure every single person (including children age one and up) drank from stemmed crystal just so they would know how. A lot of punch was spilled and that was okay.

The same family punch bowl was used year after year with the exact same punch recipe. The same menu was repeated without exception. Sometimes a new member to the family would bring a new surprise dish, but the basic format never changed. No one ever ate the cranberry sauce, but the one year she didn't put it on, there were cries of outrage, and it was there the next year.

Every one of the fifty or more family members received gifts from this woman and

The Williams family

they were put in "age categories." So there would be perhaps a dozen gifts for the teenage girls exactly the same and wrapped alike so no young lady in that category felt slighted in any way.

The wrapping went on into the wee hours of Christmas morning with the last few barely getting a tiny bow when the exhaustion set in.

After the big fancy meal, that never allowed anything plastic or paper at the table, was completed and the gifts unwrapped, the entertainment began. My sister stepped to the piano and tinkled the ivory by ear until the whole house vibrated with the spirit of Christmas. The youngsters were eagerly waiting to present their talents, with tap dancing being the most popular talent. Ballet was tolerated also. My brother was always there beside her with his guitar and there were the Christmas carol request sessions. My father took the floor to culminate each show with his loud and off-key rendition of Jingle Bells.

Nothing changed year to year other than new generations of family being added and losses of others. The ritual became one of lasting memory to all who took part during those years from 1920 to 1989. The punch bowl still remains, the recipe is still used in various different homes and the family has separated into their respective branches now, but the memories will live on forever in the hears of those many generations that experienced the true Williams Family Christmas in Caldwell, Kansas.

When I decorate my mother and father's graves every Christmas, I do so in appreciation of what a true family Christmas meant to them.

The Williams Home

I hang the wreath on the family stone and tell them it was not forgotten. I never realized how much actual work went into such festive holidays until I began doing the same with my own three children, their spouses, and my eight grandchildren! Wow Mom! How did you do it for all those years and all those people? Thank you.

Hog Butchering In Depression Days
By Marie Regehr of North Newton, Kansas
Born 1924

"Get up. We're butchering the pig today," my father would call upstairs on a wintry morning in the early 1930s. When we heard those words we six children were awake immediately and scampered downstairs. We weren't going to miss out on any of the excitement of that day.

It was a typical butchering day on our farm in Kansas in the Depression years. Electricity had not yet come to rural areas. Farmers were worried about paying their mortgages and whether there would be enough money for taxes.

Even before daylight my Uncle Sol and Aunt Agnes, who lived down the road and a neighboring couple arrived to help. They wore layers of sweaters and jackets and carried extra buckets, dishpans, and butcher knives wrapped in newspaper.

My brothers would be allowed to be outside as my father shot the big pig he had been fattening. He would then stab it in the throat to let the blood run out. We girls watched as the pig was hoisted up by rope and block and tackle and lowered into a barrel of boiling water to soften the bristles of hair.

Next, the pig was lifted out of the water and the men would use round scrapers to scrape off the hair until all of the white skin could be seen. I can remember the rasping noise of three men scraping on different parts of the pig, including head and the legs.

The abdominal cavity was slit open from top to bottom. The heart and liver were cut out and saved. The slippery air-filled intestines were pulled out and allowed to fall into large dishpans. Next, came the smelly job of emptying the intestines by pushing out the

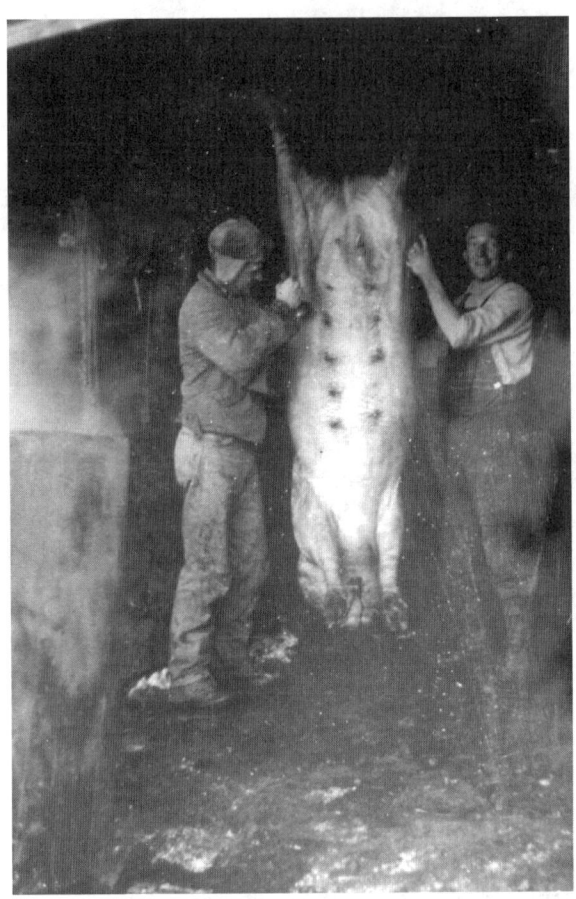
Two men scraping the butchered pig

contents.

The cleaning of the intestines, to be used as casings for two kinds of sausages, was given to the women. I would watch in amazement as Aunt Agnes, tall and robust, would find one end of the intestine, tie it shut with string, and push the end inside itself. With the rest of the casings inside a pitcher of warm water, she would have my mother pour water into the casing she was holding, which turned the casing inside out.

Then the casings were draped across a breadboard and scraped with a table knife. This removed any remaining membrane. If too much pressure were placed across the delicate casing, it would tear. The casings were then kneaded with dry, course bran. I was told this was a part of the cleansing process. After several rinses in water, they were considered clean and allowed to soak in salt water until filled later.

While this was going on the men were busy cutting up the hog carcass into smaller cuts of meat. Saws were needed for cutting through bones. Red meat was cut into strips, which were then fed into a meat grinder. Buckets full of this ground meat was placed in the middle of the large improvised table. My father would flavor this sausage meat by mixing a handful of salt and a half handful of pepper into the meat.

Next, the sausage meat was placed into a sausage press, which pushed the sausage into the casings the women had cleaned. The filled sausages were about one and one half inches thick and might be one or two yards long.

The second kind of sausage made was liver sausage, a kind of sausage you either loved or didn't like at all. It had cooked head meat in it, liver, and salt and pepper. Hams, bacon and the backbone were placed on the table to be allowed to cool off and to be salted the next day.

There was much jovial conversation on butchering day. My husband's family had a custom of having someone retrieve the cut off tail of the pig, and with a safety pin, pin it on the back of an unsuspecting person's jacket. This individual might walk around for a long time with this tail hanging behind him until the snickers of others alerted him to that possibility. He would then try to pin it on someone else who was busy cutting up meat.

Lard was a very important by-product of butchering in olden years. Farmers wanted their hogs fat so that they would have sufficient lard for use in baking and cooking. Housewives would be proud if they could report to their friends that they got fifteen gallons of lard from their pig. They had not yet heard of cholesterol or low-fat diets.

Lard was rendered by cutting the fatty white meat into strips and grinding them into course noodle-like particles, which were dumped into the black cast iron rendering kettle every household owned. A wood fire was stared under the kettle.

Stirring the contents of the kettle with a four-foot wooden paddle was necessary throughout the three hours that it needed to boil gently. If too much wood was placed under the kettle, and the fire was too hot, the lard would not be good.

After it was decided that the lard was done, it was poured through a sieve, which separated some brown meat particles (called cracklings) from the liquid hot lard. The lard was next poured into large dishpans until it cooled and started to become white in color. Then it was poured into stone crocks. When the lard had solidified, the crocks were taken into the basement to be stored.

Butchering day meant that there was much grease to contend with. My cousin remembers that her job as young girl was to tie a small rag around each doorknob that people would use during the butchering process so that the knobs would stay clean.

The last big job on butchering day was washing all of the greasy pans, knives, pails, grinding and stuffing machines, the butchering table, and the rendering kettle. By the time this was finished, it was starting to get dark.

Helpers were anxious to leave to do their evening chores. When they gathered the utensils they had brought they found that our mother had slipped some liver sausage and pork sausage into one of their containers. Amid "Thanks for helping," one was apt to hear, "You're welcome. Remember that next Tuesday we are butchering and we expect you to come help us."

After our helpers had left, our dad, tired but happy, would call us children to survey all the products from the butchering. "See," he said proudly, "we hope to make it another winter."

Early Phones, Old Lady, and the Train to Alva
By Larry Harsh of Flrgonia, Kansas
Born 1935

When I was a kid and we lived at the River Farm, our phone was a party line, meaning several farms were on the same line.

When people called us, they told the operator at the telephone office our number (ours was 6F43) and she in turn would, from the telephone in Argonia, ring up 3 long and 2 short rings on our party line and we would know it was for us.

One time Dad was in town early in the morning and needed to talk to Mom so he stopped at Grandpa Homer's to call home. He rang and rang to get the operator and finally Kate Reimer came on. Dad said, "Where in the world were you Kate?" She replied, "I'll have you know, Everly Harsh, there are certain things a woman might have to do this early in the morning."

Depot at Argonia

Whenever the church's got together to sing, Kate was always the first to jump and sing, and was usually a half note ahead of everyone else.

When Dad would call his sister in California, it was quite an ordeal. It might take 7 or 8 minutes to get through since there was no satellite in the early days to beam to.

The operator (Kate) would have to contact another operator in maybe New Mexico and she in turn Arizona and then finally San Diego. Dad could hear Kate arguing with the other operators in her own personal way to put her through or else!

Mrs. Redfern was an operator along with Kate Rimer. She had a son who lived in Alva, Oklahoma. At that time, Grandma Gordon was pastor of the Friends Church in Alva. Mom would call up Grandma and Grandpa to tell them that she, Everly, Joyce, and Larry would be down for church the following Sunday.

After connecting the two parties, the operator is not supposed to listen in on the conversation, but after Mom and Grandma hung up, Mrs. Redfern would call and ask if we were going to Alva anytime soon and if we were, could she maybe ride along to visit her son.

This irritated Mom because she knew Mrs. Redfern had been listening in on the conversation. Mrs. Redfern did always try to pay Dad for taking her along, but he always refused, until it got to be too many trips and then he took her dollar, which embarrassed Mom half to death. Don't remember her asking again after that.

The Redfern family were good people and hard workers in church and in the community.

I think the summer I made my first cattle drive to the north pasture when I was 5 or 6 was the summer I started getting into trouble.

Dad had gone to Wichita with a pickup load of hogs. Melvin and Pack were working in the field south of the house on the River Farm. I asked my Mom if I could ride Old Lady (my pony) out to the field. She said yes.

When I got out there, they weren't doing anything that interested me much, so I decided to ride over to Curly and Angie Wempen's farm, which my kids know as the Butler place. Curly and Angie were raising their grandkids, Glen and Don Rhodes, so my folks would let me play with them sometimes. Besides, Angie made the best cookies of anyone in the whole world.

I can't remember whether they were home or not, but back out on the road, I decided to ride to town to see Grandpa and Grandma Harsh. I rode north across Sand Creek, by June's Quarter, by Truman Pyles, over the railroad track, where the town or Post Office of Gurock once sat, by Ethel Berry's to Highway 160. I turned right and started across the three river bridges.

People passed going fairly slow and most waved at me. I waved back. This was kind of fun. When I was about to the little house west of town, Grandpa Homer called it the weaning house, I saw Dad coming home from Wichita.

I waved. He didn't wave back. He backed up his pickup into the ditch, got out, gave me a licking, loaded Old Lady in the pickup and we went home. I bawled all the way and my sister, Joyce, who was with Dad, seemed to enjoy every minute of it.

When we got home, Dad said to Mom, "Do you know where your son is?" Mom said, "Out in the field with Melvin and Pack." Then she saw Old Lady in the back of the truck.

Larry Harsh on "Old Lady" with his father, Everly riding "Ribbon"

Mom didn't give me another licking, but her stares made you want to go hide in the barn. That night I overheard Dad talking to Melvin and Pack out in the milk house and they were all laughing, so it turned out to be a pretty good day after all.

The first train trip I remember was to Alva, Oklahoma with Mom and Joyce when I was 6 or 7 years of age.

Art Swan was the Santa Fe agent in Argonia. When the train was due, Art would go outside the station, stand on the railroad track, and wave a white flag on a long pole slowly back and forth over his head. When the engineer saw the flag, he would toot his whistle and prepare to stop.

After stopping, the conductor got off, put a small stool down, and helped Mom up the steps. I didn't like that too much when he put his hand on Mom's arm. The conductor was black and had never seen a black man, but before we got to Alva, he had won Joyce and I over.

Looking out the window coming into Alva (which was 85 miles southwest of Argonia) we saw Grandpa Gordon leaning against his car waiting for us. He could hug tighter than anyone I ever knew. After fidgeting through church and visiting a couple of days, we boarded a train for home.

My Mom (Norma Fe) was a very nice looking woman and when the train got started, a man came up and started talking to her. He offered her coffee from his thermos and I don't remember if Mom accepted it or not but they talked all the way to Argonia. Joyce and I did not like this guy. I didn't want Dad to know about this, but that night I heard Mom telling Dad about what happened and they were laughing so everything was okay.

Boozer the Opossum Killer
By Jim E. Quillin of Caldwell, Kansas
Born 1940

I have had many remarkable dogs in my life, Boozer, Brutus, Missy, Blue Boy, Stubby, Jenny, and several others at various times. I have stories that I could tell about each of them as they all lived with my wife, four girls and I on a small farm South East of South Haven, Kansas. This will be a story about Boozer, a

Jim's great-grandfather's homestead

large German Sheppard.

I received Boozer my first year at Kansas State University, hence the name. Bob Boozer was a star basketball player in 1959. When my pickup left the farm, Boozer was with it. He learned very early that jumping out of the truck while moving was not good business. He would sit in the middle with a cap that Chet, my best friend, and I would provide him as we checked the grains and livestock. We would take along some beer or "cowboy whiskey" (peppermint schnapps), depending on the weather. When we returned home, Boozer was probably the best driver in the cab, but who cares out in the middle of nowhere.

I don't remember where the cute little pup with droopy ears that straightened, as he got older came from. He was very smart and a good cattle dog, although, a little too rough with the calves and cows. When I would sic him on an animal, he would sometimes grab them by the tail and bring them to the ground. We could leave him by and open gate and no living soul had better try to pass!

Boozer was a good watchdog, which was good because thieves and other scum of the cities would roam our area. Several people who drove in our yard would not get out of their cars. I remember a couple of lost German ladies who drove up to the house to ask for directions. The first thing heard was loud screams. I rushed from the barn to find both of them on the rider's side of the car screaming their heads off while Boozer was looking in the open window on the driver's side.

Boozer would follow me sometimes, as I would take the tractor to do some fieldwork. There were always rabbits and other varmints to chase and things to explore. He could easy whip a single coyote, but the coyotes were too smart. One coyote would come out in the

Boozer with Jim's first daughter, Jennifer in 1965

open and tease the dog into chasing it. Into a hedgerow or other cover he would go, where there were three more of his or her buddies waiting. Several times, I've had to jump off the tractor to run the attackers off with my trusty crescent wrench.

Our house had a small, screened porch on the back. This is where Boozer slept when the weather was nasty. He learned how to open and close the screen door. On the porch, we kept an open bag of dog food so he could just come in and help himself.

One night we were about to go to sleep, there was some barking on the porch which quickly stopped. Thinking no more about it, I went to sleep. The next night there was some barking again. I jumped up and turned the porch light on. On the porch floor laid an opossum doing what they do best: playing opossum. Seems as though the critter had learned where the dog food was. After a few sniffs, Boozer picked the animal up and carried him proudly out the door.

The next night it was the same scenario, but this time I followed Boozer carrying his prize off. He took the "dead" opossum out behind the propane tank. We had just buried a propane line to the house and the ground was still soft. The dog dug a hole with his paws and placed the opossum in the hole and covered him up.

The next night the opossum was back for another snack. This continued for a month or so. Finally, the dog got too rough, I guess, and the hungry opossum stopped his nightly raids. We used to joke about how many opossums that the dog thought he had buried out behind the propane tank.

Boozer was good with the little daughters, although I think he just tolerated them. He finally bit a little boy who came to a birthday party and so had to leave our family.

Thank Goodness, They Are Gone
By Marian Redford of Hutchinson, Kansas
Born 1926

The only thing good about the "good old days" is that they are gone.

I remember my mother wetting bath towels and placing them on windowsills to keep the dust out during the Dirty Thirties.

Forbidden Fun
By Patty L. Craven of Biloxi, Mississippi
Born 1937

When I was young, until I was age nine, we lived in the rural area in an old farmhouse that was made by putting two small houses together. It was our great-grandparents' homestead in Comanche County.

We went to a one-room schoolhouse, and when I was in fourth grade, my sister was in fifth grade. There were four children from another family in the school also. The teacher lived with our family of five. We had a merry-go-round and flagpole at the school. We made music with a rhythm band and a drum made from an oatmeal box. We walked across a small bridge and through a pasture to school.

If our mother wasn't home after school, we ran one and a half miles through another pasture to "visit" our Aunt Pauline and Uncle Ralph. Uncle Ralph always gave us peppermint candy that he kept in his pocket along with his tobacco. One evening our daddy made us walk home in front of the car to encourage us to quit doing it.

The creek under the small bridge was a fun place to play. The creek was shallow so we dug a hole and then jumped into it from the bridge.

The house upstairs was an unfinished, forbidden, and intriguing area, so we would sneak up when possible and rummage through boxes of stuff. I can't remember what any of it was. The only thing I remember finding was baby mice. Ugh!

Working in the Garden
By L. K. Adams of Anthony, Kansas
Born 1947

Down the fence line through the gate, we three kids raced to the garden. Of course, my brother, Chuck, won hands down. Being the oldest, he could run the fastest. When Dad got off work and after the supper meal was over and he had some time to rest, we all went to the garden. Mom came after she put the supper dishes to soak. The folks would work in the garden in the evenings. Our garden was big enough to feed five people and then some. Mom canned things from the garden for our meals during the winter months, all kinds of vegetables; tomatoes, green beans, lettuce, cabbage, squash, onions, green onions, radishes, rhubarb for pies, watermelons, and cantaloupes.

When we had a get together with my cousins, Sherry, Bobby, Marion, Chuck, Lois, and I would have a seed-spitting contest to see who could spit their seeds the furthest. The boys usually came in first.

In the garden, Dad would clear the biggest weeds with a weed whacker dubbed as an idiot stick. The weed whacker was an instrument with a wood handle and a waffled blade. It cut forward or backwards. It was sharp on both sides. Since it was dangerous, only Dad would use it.

We also had a push mower, the kind you powered yourself by pushing it. The blade would rotate as you pushed it. My brother and mom pushed it. My sister and I would pull the smaller weeds by hand, putting them in a bucket. The folks gave us some money for a bucket full of weeds, inspected by Mom.

Dad would then take the hand plow. It had a handlebar and a wheel in front, much like a bicycle only a steel wheel with a blade and a claw behind it. Dad would push the plow making long, straight rows. Each of us would put in some seeds. My sister helped me put my seeds in the rows. Mom would take the garden hoe and push the dirt over the seeds.

Then came the water. Day by day, we would watch to see as the plants came through the dirt.

Royce and the Combine
By Dr. Herb Frazier of Haviland, Kansas
Born 1939

My son, Royce, was born in San Antonio, and we lived in Kansas City and Wichita before we moved to Haviland, Kansas. When we moved to Haviland, a town of 600, he was 15 years old and a sophomore in high school. That year at high school, Royce heard the "farm boys" talking about working on the farm. One thing he learned is that the farmer will let you drive his tractor soon after you go to work for him, but you have to *earn* the right to drive a combine. This was the fall of the year 1967, and by the spring of 1968, Elmer Davis, one of the local successful farmers just outside of Haviland asked Royce if he would work for him. Of course, Royce wanted to work and make some money, so he said yes.

The spring of 1968, when school was out, Royce went to work for Elmer. Elmer had leased a brand new Gleaner combine from the local Chevrolet dealer, the Fankhauser Motor Company. The gleaner needed its header adjusted, so that job was eventually assigned to Royce. Elmer climbed under the combine with Royce and explained how the adjustments were made. Then Elmer climbed out from under the combine and went into his house. Sometime later, while Royce was still lying under the combine, Elmer came out and said, "When you get through with those adjustments take this out and cut the weeds in the front ditch." Royce was ecstatic. He had worked only a short time and Elmer was already going to let him drive the combine. Then Elmer hopped in his truck and drove to town.

Royce hurried and got the combine adjustments made and crawled out from under it and jumped up in to the cab. First, he had to know how everything worked. He tried the header and learned how to raise and lower it. After getting familiar with the machine, he proceeded to turn it around and headed down the driveway to the road. Upon encountering pickups and cars, he candidly raised and lowered the header to get past them. When he got to the ditch, he tried to get the combine on the most perfect angle to cut the weeds perfectly. Everything went well until he saw Elmer coming down the road, one half mile north, faster than he had ever seen him drive.

Elmer pulled up beside the combine, jumped out, and said, "What do you think you are doing?" Royce said, "You told me to take this and cut the weeds in the ditch when I got through adjusting the header." Elmer replied, "Didn't you see that idiot stick I laid against the tire of the combine?" Royce said, "No, I was lying under the combine looking up at the header." Elmer said, "Get down out of there and take this pickup back to the house." Elmer got in the combine and headed to the house. When he arrived at the driveway and saw the cars and pickups Royce had maneuvered around to get the combine to the road, he about 'lost it.' When Elmer finally got out of the combine and joined Royce in looking for the idiot stick, they found a curled piece of metal that was the result of it falling from the tire and being bent into a circle as the tire of the combine made the U-turn to head out of the driveway. Elmer said to Royce, "Don't you ever tell anyone about this!" I guess it is not the best use of a combine, to be cutting weeds – especially when it is brand new and *leased*.

As the years passed I taught in a school where Elmer's brother-in-law was principal. One day I told the secretary, Sharon Koehn, the combine story. I knew she would enjoy it, because she had been reared on a farm. She had a good laugh and then asked if I would tell the principal the combine story. Well, I said yes if he wanted to hear it. He did and so I told him, and then I realized I had told the story to Elmer's brother-in-law and Elmer had told Royce to never tell the story. I told Royce about this, and he said, "That's all right, I heard Elmer tell it himself." I did not know for years, until Elmer's wife told me, that she saw Royce in the front ditch on the combine and so she called Elmer in town on the CB to tell him what Royce was doing. That is why Elmer was coming around the corner a half of a mile north faster than Royce had ever seen him drive.

Also, years later, Royce became the Youth Superintendent of 70 churches. Part of his job was to travel from church to church to promote the youth program. Somehow, individuals in the churches had heard snatches of the combine story. At several churches, someone asked if he would tell the Combine Story. Royce would explain that he had come there for a reason. He would present the youth programs that he came to promote, he would then give a prayer of benediction, and if anyone wanted to stay after that and hear the combine story, they may. Invariably, everyone stayed.

The Shirley Temple Doll
By Virginia L. Ryan of Spearville, Kansas
Born 1930

Today on the news, I heard that Shirley Temple Black had passed away. What memories that has brought back. The first movie I saw was "The Poor Little Rich Girl." It was a long time before we went to another movie, but for Christmas, my uncle gave me a Shirley Temple doll. She had a beautiful yellow pleated dress with lace and a blue ribbon belt. Her blonde curls had a blue ribbon on each side and white shoes and socks with a sliver buckle on them. I was six years old and never was there a prouder girl. My mother helped keep my doll clean, and we stored her in the pasteboard box she came in when my sister and I weren't playing "big girl dolls." My mother had a lady glass doll that my sister played with when Shirley came out of her box.

The dust storms raged, and I started school, so playing didn't happen too often. The old house leaked dust, and Mother worked hard to keep things clean. When the rains began to come, all the windows and cracks leaked water. Instead of dust, we began to whip up water, thanking God to finally have rain.

Several months passed, and one day we decided to play dolls. When my mother opened the box, my doll had gotten wet and crumbled into pieces. Her beautiful dress had mold on the back and her curls were also full of mold. Those beautiful shoes were like melted except for the silver buckles. I don't have to tell anyone I cried for weeks. Mother washed the dress but it didn't fit my baby doll and was never pretty anymore. I kept the little silver buckles for a long time. I also watched in the catalogs and any magazine I could find to see if I could find another doll like mine.

As I raised my family and had five girls, they all had dolls, all sorts of them, but no Shirley Temple dolls. I wonder how many girls born in the 1930s had Shirley Temple dolls. I know none were as beautiful or loved more than mine. I'd still love to have her back.

Dusty Rumble Seats and Black Swimming Holes
By Pauline F. Hoopes of Anthony, Kansas
Born 1934

Pauline's parents and siblings in about 1937

My family had an outdoor two holer toilet on which my mother said I potty trained my sister who was two years younger than me. We had a chamber pot for night use.

My mother kept olive oil in the medicine cabinet for use on moles and warts.

My bother listened to *The Lone Ranger* after school. My sister and I hurried in the house to listen to *When a Girl Marries* on the radio.

We were on a party line on the phone. Our number was 223, which was four shorts when someone was calling us. It was five longs when someone needed help or emergency calling.

We didn't get spankings at school but we sure did when we got home from school. In other words, nowadays it would be abusive.

For our Saturday night baths, Mom and Dad had a long, galvanized tub. The baby got a bath first and then on up to the oldest child. Our folks set the tub by the stove to keep us warm. We used the same bath water all the way through.

We had a wringer washer. I always liked to try to help Mom. We wringered clothes from the washer and again from the rinsing.

We had a one-room school. There were eight grades in the one room.

My dad had a rumble seat car. We like to ride in it but it was sure dusty.

We had blizzards and snowstorms. The snow's banked height was higher than the snowplow. And of course, school was dismissed.

We had a fox terrier puppy. We called him Scrappy. He was "one of the family." He lived to be 18 years old.

When I took a drink of water to my dad in the field, I stepped right on top of a big black snake. It scared me so badly I have always been afraid of them.

My sister and I had the chickens to tend to. We scraped the dropping boards. We put the manure in baskets, and then we carried it to be sprinkled on the wheat field.

We had a swimming hole, which was on the neighbor's land. We would get in that water and come out black.

Our family would go to town and Mom would buy a pint container size of ice cream. The five of us would eat ice cream with little wooden spoons.

Our folks had a route man come around with an ice truck. The iceman would always give us three kids a little chunk of ice. We felt we were special.

Much more happened!

The Icebox Incident
By Laverne Griggs-Hiemstra of Garden City, Kansas
Born 1923

Yes, iceboxes bring to mind an incident I've never forgot. My husband and I were newlyweds. Apartments were hard to find after World War II. Through an acquaintance, we were able to rent this beautiful, sunny, and roomy upstairs apartment. We never dreamed its icebox would give us trouble. In the first place, we had no car but were on the car dealer's list, which was very necessary back then to buy a new car. This meant we had to carry our ice in a dishpan from the gas station three blocks away. Plus we had to carry it up a flight of stairs to get to our icebox.

One particular day when I arrived home, and as I started up our steps I felt drops coming from the ceiling. In haste, I ran upstairs to check our drain pan under the box, and sure enough, it was running over. It was running on to the lovely hardwood floor and through the cracks to collect on the plastered ceiling below. Our landlord was not the friendly type so I had to do *something* in a hurry before he arrived home from work.

I knew I had to make a hole from below into the ceiling to drain the water. I grabbed a bucket from our kitchen plus an ice pick. When I made the hole, the water just gushed out and filled my bucket. That was the end of the water situation, but what about the sagging ceiling. I kept hoping it would stay up. I put both hands flat against it and slowly pushed up. Lo and behold it stayed. The ice pick hole was not too noticeable. I cleaned up the water on the first floor, grabbed my bucket and ice pick, and hurried upstairs. Thank goodness, I never heard anything about my afternoon adventure!

Caught Listening on the Party Line!
By A. Aliene Bolton of Newton, Kansas
Born 1930

Growing up in the town of Hooser, Kansas in the Dirty Thirties and experiencing the poverty of Depression days was a character building childhood. Hooser was a cattle and prairie hay center fading fast into history with only seven houses remaining in existence and two of them empty.

The telephone was an oak fixture hanging on the wall, used mostly for emergencies. However, my mother and her sister, being on the same line, devised a method to visit without anyone hearing them. When the noon news on WIBW, Topeka signed off, they would each go to the telephone and say, "Hello, are you there?" They could catch up on family news without any of the other eight or so on the line being the wiser.

Living on a farm at the end of the half-mile lane with my husband and three sons in the late 1950s, we had a snowstorm that blocked not only our lane, but every other road. After a few days of isolation, I was needing some adult visiting! I lifted the receiver only to find it busy. Two neighbors who were brothers I knew well were talking. Yes, I knew better than to eavesdrop, but I thought maybe I could tell if they were about through if I listened briefly. One of them had been ice fishing that morning, and the telling of that story was more than I could resist. Yes, I forgot what I was doing and cackled out loud just before I "came to" and quickly hung up the receiver. I always wondered if they knew my laugh as well as I did their voices.

Don't Forget to turn on the Windmill
By Albert Hanlon of Jennings, Oklahoma

My dad, L. F. Hanlon, and I hired out as summer farm hands to the Chet Bare farm and livestock Operation near Protection, Kansas, in the late '40s and early '50s.

The work was hard with long hours and the wind blew every day. The farm hands all looked forward to a long shower in the late evenings. Water supply came from a windmill, which was pumped to an overhead tank located on a nearby building. One morning I forgot to turn on the windmill and that evening we were all forced to take a cold shower. I never made that mistake again!

We were treated like family sleeping upstairs and eating meals at the family table. The meals were prepared by Mrs. Bare and her teenage daughter, Ruby (Bare) Swanson. We worked 6 days a week and were off on Sundays. We were invited to attend rodeos, picnics, and stock shows with the family.

Robert Bare one of the older brothers was involved in the farming operation. He was a few years my senior, but he and I developed a close friendship on Saturday nights and Sundays that lasted 60 years or better. There was another older brother, Chat Bare that was away at medical school, who had a very successful medical career. There was another sister, Margarita who was married and away at college and was a well-educated person; she now resides at Washington State. Mrs. Bare was a very kind and gentleperson and a wonderful homemaker. Ruby married a college Professor and is located in Brookings, SD. Chet Bare was a big strong man a little rough around the edges but was a good employer.

My experiences with the family farm was very beneficial for me in later years in my agriculture career. The most important benefit for a teenage boy in a small town in Central Oklahoma was to know and love the Bare Family. This friendship has lasted a lifetime for I am now 84 years old and still reside in the small town in Central Oklahoma (Jennings).

The Blizzard of 1971 near Corbin, Kansas
By Suzie Yunker of Caldwell, Kansas
Born 1949

What a storm that was. It was February 21, 1971 and the worst blizzard ever (or so I thought at the time) hit our farm in South Central Kansas near the little town of Corbin.

What was especially bad about this particular blizzard was that it came the week of my wedding. I came from a large family and we had all come home the week before my wedding to make plans and get things done. I was to have a lovely church wedding in the small Methodist Church in Corbin. There wasn't much in the town of Corbin in those days. Besides the old white church, there was a little grocery story, my Dad's gas station, two big elevators and a hardware store, oh and a little cafe called "Margie's". Great home cooked food. Our big old white farmhouse was two miles north of Corbin.

Well when we all woke up on the blizzard-like morning and saw that snow had piled so high that it covered up our mailbox, my younger brothers and sisters were ecstatic.

Suzie Rice Yunker's wedding day in 1971

Suzie Rice Yunker

It had snowed closed to 12 inches and with huge drifts across all roads. The kids put on all their snow clothes and played in the drifts. No one was getting out of the driveway and all transportation was shut down. We were stranded, all thirteen of us!

Well, my mom had some stuff in the freezer (beef) so we could eat for a few days. By day three, we were mainly down to just potatoes and Mom was getting nervous. Later that morning we saw in the distance our robust neighbor headed across our wheat fields on a tractor and sled. He fetched my Dad and took him in to Corbin and they loaded up on supplies. He brought him back and we were all so happy to have food again. I know my mom was relieved.

All I could worry about was my wedding and were we going to have it or not. By the fourth day, the roads were finally cleared and we were able to have a rehearsal dinner at Margie's Cafe in Corbin that Friday evening. My beautiful candlelight wedding went on as scheduled in the little church in Corbin on that Saturday night, February 26th in the cold and snow.

We all laughed for many years at the memories made during that blizzard of '71. I still haven't seen another one like it and that was over 40 years ago. We didn't starve and we didn't kill each other. We had heat and electricity and food. We survived that wintry blast without even realizing the full impact of it for years to come.

My Husband, the Milkman
By Helen Normandin of Hutchinson, Kansas
Born 1938

Milkman stories were a source of amusement as well as aggravation at our house. My husband was a residential milk deliveryman, known as the milkman. We would both get up very early, and I had breakfast ready. He never got tired of pancakes or French toast. Usually he was starting out on his route by 5:30 a.m., having loaded the truck the previous afternoon.

There was rich 4% milk, which most people asked for in those days before all the concern about too much fat in the diet. There were many products for sale on the milk truck, including eggs, cottage cheese, orange juice, ice cream, and many others. Milkmen were a bit like the old time peddler, as they even sold items such as hand lotion. Rose Milk was a very good lotion.

The milk was delivered in glass milk jars that the customer would turn in to be picked up by the milkman and washed by the bottle washer at the dairy. Some people were happy with outside the door delivery. However, my husband remembered one outdoor delivery customer who ordered a five-pound block of cheese. After he left, a dog found the cheese and chewed about half of it. Many customers wanted the milk brought inside or even put in the refrigerator. Some customers had left for work by the time he got there so he had keys to their homes. Trust was very important. One memorable elderly lady customer was quite comfortable coming to the door very early in the morning with nothing on top and only underwear on the bottom.

One of the problems with delivering milk is the danger of having to stop suddenly. That could be a disaster. All the carefully loaded items for sale would be flying out of their place, and it could be a nasty mess. Broken milk bottles with milk running out, mixed with broken eggs, plus all the other items would greet him when he opened the door to check. There would need to be a major cleanup. In addition, he didn't have the products to deliver to his customers that hadn't been served yet. Thankfully, that didn't happen often.

Weather created problems for a milkman and especially on his country route. If there was a lot of snow on the road, it was hard to get through. Icy conditions resulted in possible dangerous falls and difficulty controlling the truck. Heavy rains could result in getting stuck on rural roads and driveways.

At the end of the month, there were other challenges for the milkman. He was to figure all the customer statements and deliver them to the customer. Some customers were very prompt, but others would give all kinds of excuses for not paying but they still wanted delivery. A big problem was the dairy had a policy of charging the deliveryman half of what was left unpaid. Usually, he would try to work with them to get it paid, but there were those times that didn't happen. Not only had he delivered the product to the customer, but he also had to pay for a large portion of it. It would be deducted from his paycheck. Also, there was no commission on unpaid bills.

There were the milkman jokes some people couldn't resist. That included our pastor. I had given birth to our second son, and our pastor came for a visit. He made a comment I never forgot. After admiring our new son his comment was, "Why, he looks just like the milkman." We didn't know him all that well, and he seemed so serious at the pulpit. We learned he did have a sense of humor.

On the plus side of being a milkman, my husband enjoyed all the nice people he met. Working on his own and spending time outside was a bonus. However, providing home milk delivery eventually became a thing of the past. It is gone, along with so many other services that were a part of our everyday life. In our community, my husband was the last individual milkman who provided home delivery. The dairy continued with wholesale delivery, but home delivery was discontinued. It was the end of an era.

The Senior Class 'Art Project'
By Peg Koehn of Halstead, Kansas
Born 1939

I was raised in a small town in the south central part of our state. It was very hot in the summer and very cold in the winter. Town activities centered around churches and school. Our school did a special activity called winding the May pole during the program called the May Fete at the end of each school year.

Kids had to entertain themselves during the school year as well as in the summer. One boy in our class drew flying saucers on the back of a desk that had come unbolted and threw it out the third story window to see if it would fly. It almost took out the groundskeeper on the way to the ground. Another time some boys caught some smelly fish from the nearby river where they often spent time hunting and fishing. They put them in the refrigerator in the home economics room hoping to upset the teacher. She one-upped them by bringing the fish to science class and having the class dissect the eye of the fish and identify the parts.

In our senior year, we decided our class should do something really memorable. So several boys and a couple of girls decided to paint the water town with a sign that said, "Seniors '57." Needless to say, when the city fathers looked up and saw the 'art work' we were in deep trouble for a variety of reasons: there was much danger in climbing the water tower carrying a bucket and a brush; defacing public property; and the class president's father was the mayor of the town. So someone had to pay for the damage caused by the art. We were in danger of losing the funds we had in our treasury for our senior trip. So we had to get even more creative. We received a clock radio from an elderly gentleman who remembered what it was like to be young and impulsive. We sold raffle tickets and earned enough to pay for having the artwork taken off the tower and still have enough money for our trip. Fifty years later at a class reunion, the people there were still trying to figure out "who done it."

The Good Little Brother
By Owen Burbrink as told to Grandma Peg
(Owen saw me writing my story and wanted to "write down" his story, too. He was four years old when we wrote this.)

All was not well between two little brothers, Wyatt and Casey. They fought a lot. They couldn't stop until one day their mom had another baby boy named Owen.

Something was wrong. It was hard for him to breathe. They took him to a big hospital in Wichita. They put an IV in his arm. Mom cried and Dad went to call Grandma Peg to bring the boys to see Owen, as they didn't know what would happen next. They called a doctor at Children's Mercy Hospital in Kansas City. He said, "Come on down. I'll send my plane." Owen was afraid because he had to leave Mom and Dad and go with the nurses on the plane. But Dad called Aunt Karen, who lived in Lawrence, to meet Owen and stay with him until they could get there. Owen didn't know her yet but she seemed to care a lot for him.

Wyatt and Casey forgot to fight because they had to go back to Grandma Peg's to stay a whole lot longer. Wyatt had to play baseball.

Mom and Dad flew in the car all the way to Kansas City. The doctors said, "Owen is a fighter. We think we can help him. His heart is not perfect, but we can fix it in three stages. First is a little step to give him some time to grow." About a week after the first surgery Mom, Dad, and Owen were able to come home. Wyatt and Casey were so happy to see them they forgot to fight.

Mom decided not to go back to work but to stay home and take care of Owen and the boys. That made Owen and the boys very happy. It lasted for one semester, until the school called and said another teacher had an emergency, and they needed Mom back at work. That's when Mom found Pat and Bonnia to care for Owen. They were very good people. They had taken care of Casey when he was a baby. They were very happy to get to take care of Owen. They loved him very much and took really good care of him.

The doctors said even though Owen was doing well his heart had a problem that would not get better without more surgery. It needed major repair. When Owen was two and a half years old, the family had moved to Newton to a beautiful new home in Stone Creek.

Mom, Dad, and Owen planed their trip to Kansas City for the last time for the really big, final surgery to fix Owen for good. Wyatt and Casey had to stay with Granma Peg again. The surgery went well, and in just a little while they were back home again. Then something went terribly wrong with the drains in Owen's chest. They stopped working, and his chest began to swell. Mom got really scared and took him to the emergency room in Newton. They called the cardiologist in Wichita who called the surgeon in Kansas City who said his plane was on the way. So once again, Owen had to leave his parents behind and fly off to Kansas City with the nurse.

Mom and Dad called Grandma Peg to get the boys and the race to Kansas City was on again. It didn't take long for the doctors to get things straightened out and Own was home again, safe and sound.

Adventures in the Snow and on the Ice
By Nancy J. Pauls of Newton, Kansas
Born 1936

The snow had been falling, but now the sun was shining. I had begged mother to let me go outside to play. She said I could not go outside while it was snowing, but now the snow had quit so she dressed me up warm in my brown woolen snowsuit. I called to our rat terrier dog "Sport" and we were off on our little adventure. My mother told me to stay in my own yard and not to go over to the neighbor's yard. I tried to always be obedient, but it seemed that on this certain day I had other ideas so (when mother was busy in our yard) Sport and I ran across the first yard going west of our house on S.E. 6th Street in Newton, Kansas. I saw in the next yard a Fish Pond with ice on it. In those days, people could have Fish Ponds in their yards without a fence around the pond. I had been pulling a small sled and I thought it would be fun to slide around on the ice. Sport began to bark. He was a smart dog and maybe he knew that the ice was thin. I thought he was just enjoying himself and so I crawled on to the ice. I was not quite half way across the pond when the ice broke. Into the water, I went with the sled. If it had not been for our faithful dog, I might not have been here today. Sport stood on the bank of the pond and barked loud and my mother (who was in our yard) heard him and came running. I know that mother carried me home sopping wet, took off my wet snowsuit, and put me to bed. The result of my adventure was probably a bad cold, but not any worse

Nancy Hiebert with the family dog, Sport

result.

A Dog's Life

In my teenage years we had a black dog that had come to our house one day and my parents decided that we could keep the friendly dog. We decided that the name we would call the dog would be "Blackie." The dog was not a pure bred, but he might have been part German Shepherd. Our dog, Blackie, had many experiences in his new home. One of his sad experiences was that he had been chasing after the paperboy. The boy had always tried to throw the paper right at Blackie. One day my brother came out of the house when Blackie was chasing the paperboy and he gave Blackie a scolding. Blackie ran into the house and I went over to him and gave him hugs. I was sad for Blackie and when my father saw me give hugs to Blackie, he told me that everything would be "Okay," but I did need to know that Blackie was scolded because he was not to chase after the paper boy. I remember that Blackie must have thought that our father was a real pal because at the supper table all he needed to do was to put his head on Daddy's leg and he would be given food to eat. Blackie gave and received lots of love in our family.

Nancy Hiebert with her dog, Blackie

The Blizzard of 1938
By Elva Unruh Kunze, of Hutchinson, Kansas
Born 1938

Arthur Unruh and Maudie Hinderliter were married August 21, 1935. In 1938, they lived just north of Cleveland, KS on a dirt road. Their first child was due April 3, 1938, which was Maudie's mother's birthday. I was that child. The nearest hospital was in Kingman, a town eight miles away.

A blizzard blew in burying everything in snow and drifting the road shut. The house was not windproof and soon the attic was packed with snow. My parents knew if it melted there, it would ruin the ceiling. My dad took a bucket and climbed up into the attic. He filled the bucket with snow then handed it down to my mother. She, nine months pregnant, took the bucket outside, dumped the snow, then brought the bucket back in to my dad. They repeated this operation over and over until they had removed over 100 bucketfuls of snow from the attic.

The sun came out and the snow melted. At 5:30 on Easter Sunday morning, April 17, two weeks after the blizzard, I was born in the hospital in Kingman, KS. Around six months later my parents bought a small farm in Cleveland, and I grew up there until I was a junior in college. My parents then sold the farm and moved to Hutchinson, KS.

Priceless Memories
By Jeanette Unruh Nightengale of Montezuma, Kansas
Born 1941

Growing up in southwest Kansas afforded many cherished, unforgettable memories. Living on the farm in Haskell County with my parents, four brothers, and six sisters had its challenges that we often supposedly refer to as The Good Old Days. I was born in 1941 in the bedroom of the house I lived in until I got married. My grandmother delivered me since she was the community's midwife.

My parents lived to a ripe old age, Dad being a few weeks shy of 102 and Mother 97 years. My parents often told of the hardships unbeknown to us at the time, the times endured during the Great Depression and the reverse Kansas weather. Dad told of the time when he and his older brother hitched up the team of horses and spring wagon and traveled a fair distance to get a load of coal for their family. On the way home, they found themselves in a severe snowstorm. They were unable to see anything. They finally let the horses have the reins and hoped for the best. The horses actually knew the way home and brought them safely home.

Dad was very industrious, being a dairy man, farmer, and stockman. I remember the time when Dad's dream became reality. He was convinced there was water underneath his farm and attempted to test and later drill to satisfy his determinations. After an unsuccessful try, he hired a crew who came with homemade drilling rig and actually struck water. This irrigation well pumped 1,200 gallons per minute for 34 years. The cost for the pump, motor, and gear head was $5,000.00. His well was the third irrigation well in Haskell County, found in 1946.

We were taught to live off the farm. Mother

always had a big garden and a large flock of chickens. A neighbor once said Mother grew more in her garden than Dad did in his fields. Mother made the family's cheese, butter, and cottage cheese. She had a flock of geese. The spring of the year was "geese pickin' days." I remember having to hold the goose's strong neck and its powerful wings while Mother held the legs and plucked the downy feathers, which later provided us with soft downy pillows. I still have one today.

Speaking of chickens, I recall going to the brooder house an hour before dinner to catch our noon meal. Pan-fried country fried chicken was a favorite, along with fresh potatoes and veggies. The time came when the pullets needed to be moved to the hen house. This was done after dark, when the pullets had gone to roost. Dad used a homemade chicken hook to catch them and my sisters and I carried them to the hen house. Oops! Something black and white was spotted in the far corner! Oh, no, that meant caution! Spooky girls and skunks don't go together. There was only a few chickens left inside and the smell seemed to be getting stronger. Dad with is chicken hook and a loaded gun cautiously entered the brooder house to remove the culprit. My sisters and I kept our distance, as the risk was too great. Dad got it! Very slowly, he pulled out a black and white rag.

The Old Barn that stood across the road in the pasture was the place where my brother and I learned to milk by hand. Hobbles were used back then that hooked over the cow's back legs and then clamped tight to prevent kicking. They were used as a safety feature. A friend once said, "He'd hobble a cow even if she had only one leg." Sitting beside Old Roan on a homemade milk stool, this 12-year-old country girl can still recall the warm, squiggly feel that sent jitters through her body as she tried to pump milk out. Seeing Old Roan's big eyes as she turned her head was an indication she also had qualms about the strange experience. The milk was poured into ten-gallon milk cans and hauled in a little red wagon to the washhouse and then placed in a cement-cooling tank filled with cold water. This milk was sold as Grade C milk.

There was a creek beside the Old Barn that ran through our pasture. We spent many happy hours fishing in the summer and skating in the winter. On a beautiful spring day, it was a perfect, peaceful setting to sit beside the creek and fish while the cows were grazing in the distance. The only threat was a very cantankerous Holstein black bull who was often in the herd. Two of our Aunties, both largely built, loved to spend hours beside the creek. It so happened one day that the big black bull came bellowing toward them, causing quite an excitement. Dad told my sister she should watch out for them, should they have trouble. He then sent her out to the creek on our little 8N Ford tractor to rescue them. One Auntie said she'd outrun the mad bull and headed for the Old Barn. The other auntie tried her best to get on the tractor but never succeeded. Dad soon noticed their predicament and came to their aid. Where did the other Auntie disappear to? My sister checked to Old Barn and called, "Where are you, Auntie?" A faint voice was heard, "I'm up here!" There she was hanging on to the rafters and bracing herself on the cross boards with blood running down her arms from the protruding rusty nails. Large in size, one can only imagine how she managed to get up there! Adrenaline must have kicked in, without any acrobatic practice. The Old Barn with its sagging roof soon became a weathered landmark.

Later, Dad erected a new milking barn and Old Roan graduated to an upper level with concrete flooring and nice white stanchions. We then used De-La-Vel and Surge milkers. Also, we upgraded enough to sell Grade A milk. There were six stanchions on each side in the new milking barn. All the cows were again hobbled. The milking went smoothly until somebody made a mistake and opened all six stanchions at the same time without removing the hobbles. Watching the following breath taking experience as the "cow-a-roos" danced out of the barn was a scene I'll never forget! After retrieving the hobbles and seeing the cut up, bloody legs the lesson was learned. It only needed to happen once!

Then came the blizzard of 1957. We were milking 25 cows, including Old Roan, Sally, Blitzen, and Thunder, to name a few. The blizzard was so severe with blowing snow and high winds up to 75 or 80 miles per hour. All transportation was blocked, and there was no electricity, no communication, and no water, only melting snow. Snowdrifts were as high as 15 feet. We made steps up and over the banks to reach our chickens. We could reach down to remove the light bulb from our yard light. Dad was worried about the livestock and especially the dairy cows. They needed to be milked but how? After one and a half days, we bundled up, formed a chain by clinging to each other, and reached the barn safely. We could only relieve the cows somewhat, all by hand. The other livestock took shelter in the Old Barn. Upon checking, Dad noticed the barn was sagging and ready to collapse! There were snowdrifts up to the eaves, which blocked 60 head of livestock inside. My 16-year-old brother risked his life to try and save them. He managed to chop open a space the width of one cow, and then found a crawl space to coax the livestock out. All it took was one steer to jump out and the rest were more than glad to get out and head for the other shelter shed. By the next morning, the total loss was one baby calf, and you guessed it, the Old Barn died.

Lingering memories will live on as long as I live. Today there would be those who would consider the old, weathered boards as priceless. They probably could be found, lining the walls in expensive, elaborate homes. No, the memories of my growing up years on the plains of Kansas cannot be bought with dollars or cents, neither can they be buried in the wind blown fence rows where thistles pile high, but will live on and can be told to the generation following.

Charlene Dickerson in 1950

Free Love Puppies
By Charlene Heim of Haven, Kansas
Born 1943

In 1950, it was a different time. It was a happy, carefree time and I felt safe and secure in our small Kansas town.

I loved the way my dog, Blondie's long, wavy ears swayed back and forth as she ran. Blondie's two fat puppies, with their short legs and floppy ears tried to keep up with their mother. Ever since they were born, I called them my "love puppies" because they were so lovable. Blondie jumped up and licked my cheek when she wanted to play, but I didn't feel much like playing that day.

I knew that once again I had disappointed my parents. I had promised to try to find homes for my love puppies, but as usual, I hadn't tried too hard.

Now my parents' words were ringing in my ears, "dog pound." I felt all squishy, like I might get sick. I had known from the very start that I couldn't keep the puppies. They were just so cute that somehow I just kept pushing "the pound" out of my mind. Mama reminded me that unless homes could be found for them, they would soon have to go to the dog pound. Ads had been placed in the paper, but no one seemed to want a puppy, not even if it was called a "love puppy."

Suddenly, I had such a good idea! I will take them up and down the block, and when people saw how cute the love puppies were, they won't be able to resist.

My sick feeling went away and now I just felt excited. I ran into the house to clean up and comb my hair. I gathered my blond curls up on each side of my face. They formed "puppy-ears" and I giggled that I looked like my puppies. In the garage, I found a big white box and on each side of it wrote "FREE LOVE PUPPIES." I put them in my red wagon and pulled it out into the back yard to find the love puppies. I put Blondie on her leash, the puppies in the box, and the four of us started down the street.

I saw Mrs. Schultz and asked, "Mrs. Schultz would you like one of my free love puppies?" She smiled and said, "No, dear, I'm too old to take care of a puppy."

At the next house, I had to stretch to reach the knocker. "Mrs. Staffer, would you like one of my free love puppies?" "Your puppies are darling, but I have all I can do to take care of my new baby."

Every house I went to, the answer seemed to be the same. I felt like crying, but instead, I patted Blondie on the head and headed on to the next house. There I saw Steve and Karen playing in their yard. They came to see what was in my box. Once again, I asked if they would like one of my free puppies. They ran into their house to ask their mother, but came out with sad faces. "Mama has to think about it," they told me.

I was really sad that not one person took one of my precious love puppies. I decided to ask one more person and then we would head back home. I rang Mrs. Chain's doorbell. "Mrs. Chain, unless I can find homes for my love puppies, I'll have to take them to the dog pound. Would you like one of my precious puppies?"

She answered, "Sweetie, I don't want a puppy, but I might know someone who does. Let me call my sister and see if she still is looking for a puppy for her little boy." I crossed my fingers and waited while she called her sister. It seemed like a long time till she said, "If one of your puppies is a boy, she'll take it. She'll call later and see when she can pick it up."

I thanked her and said I would save the boy puppy for her. I knew they would love him; after all, it's a "love puppy." I took Blondie and the puppies home. At least mama would be happy I found a home for one of my puppies.

Mama was waiting on the steps for us. She said, "Mrs. Stucky called. She and her husband decided to let Steve and Karen have a puppy. Isn't that wonderful news?"

Soon I would tell her the rest of the news. I would tell her how I had saved both love puppies from the pound and found good homes for them, all in one day! Best of all, I had never given up, and that made me feel good inside. I felt good and sad at the same time. I felt that I just needed to give Blondie and her puppies each a special hug right then.

I still remember the feeling of pride that I had finally worked at finding my puppies a home. I feel fortunate to have grown up in a small Kansas town at a time that felt safe for a little girl to go "door to door" peddling her love puppies.

The Little Village Grocery Store
By Sharilyn Reifschneider of Garden City, Kansas
Born 1947

Rozel, Kansas was the small town where my parents and neighboring farmers sent their kids to school, attended church, and shopped for their weekly groceries, miscellaneous supplies, and gas. We lived twelve miles from this quaint little village out on the plains of Kansas, where hard work was known as a religion, was taught to be respected, and was admired for what it produced.

Growing up on a farm in the 1950s during the Eisenhower years with parents who had endured the Great Depression and its deprivations, we seven children were taught at a very early age that money was never to be taken for granted and that nothing was to ever be wasted. Borrowing from, helping out and gossiping with the nearby farmers and their families was a way of life in the country and kept everyone involved and in good company. Most of the farmers in our area were not ones of great wealth, but ones who practiced an honest frugal life of hard work void of frivolities. Keeping up with the Jones' was never a phrase used in the same sentence when talking about these down to earth and humble warm-hearted folk. They lived as best they could with no more than what they needed.

Mom would make a trip into town for groceries about every two weeks, sometimes more frequently if desperately needed. Feeding a large family of seven kids took a lot of grub, which in turn required a sizable sum of money, so the proprietors of the little country market in Rozel were kind enough to extend credit to the local farmers and often times didn't get paid until after a summer harvest was completed and grain sold. And most likely, sometimes they never got paid, but that didn't keep them from continuing to do business with whoever had fallen on especially hard times. Kindness lived in their souls.

This lovely couple, Fern and Alice Kitch, owned the business and was adored by the entire little village and surrounding farmers. They possessed hearts of gold and worked extremely hard seven days a week to keep their abundant inventory stocked with supplies and amenities to serve their loyal customers. A tapestry of fresh cut beef, pork, and dressed poultry was always displayed in the meat case, along with an attractive group of luncheon meats and cheeses. Fresh produce teased the salivary glands of those walking by for a quick look before choosing several of their favorites. Wooden shelves bursting with several brands of canned goods gave the housewives a variety to choose from. Flour was sold in 50-pound cotton sacks, which of course, when emptied and laundered could be stitched into a pretty apron, a couple of tea towels, or sometimes even a little girl's dress. Nothing was ever wasted in those days and the term 'recycle' was just a normal way of life in a farming community. They were masters of frugality and improvisation, using and re-using anything their creative minds could offer.

A plethora of other items filled the corners and shelves of this little market as well. Since it served mainly a farming community, they offered snow shovels, snow boots, sleds, flannel shirts, overalls, handkerchiefs, work socks, pitchforks, work gloves, garden utensils, and a few bath and body items. They stocked kerosene, lanterns, candles, flashlights, batteries, camping gear, and many other items needed in the event of lost power or a bad storm. It was one stop shopping at its best – a mini Walmart. It preceded Sam Walton.

A band saw and meat grinder were stationed on a big thick wooden table behind the meat counter to provide continuous fresh cuts of meat, and many times would be fired up for a shopper standing by requesting a certain thickness to his steak or pork chop. I can still see that huge meat grinder spitting out the hamburger and sausage to be weighed, packaged, and marked accordingly. The word "fresh" hung in the air. Hanging on a hook beside a wooden encased thick freezer door was a heavy winter jacket and a pair of gloves for whoever held the job of going for the meat.

The walk-in freezer was where the beef, pork, and poultry were stored until the meat counter needed to be restocked, and it also had baskets to be rented out to customers for their personal meat storage as well. I remember thinking how good that freezer would have felt on a sultry hot summer afternoon, knowing full well it wouldn't have taken but just a few seconds to cool off.

Old creaky wooden floors that had become worn and scuffed by hundreds of shoes and boots over the years gleaned a smooth shiny surface and were broomed and oiled probably on a weekly or bi-weekly basis. Pendant lighting from the extremely high tin ceilings hung above. Windows across the front showcased the latest and newest items, sometimes the object of attention for many youngsters if a new wagon, catcher's mitt, or shiny toy were being displayed before the holidays. Marketing is the oldest profession.

One of the best memories of this country market for me was the sound of the adorable swinging screen door snapping shut after a customer walked in or out during a cool summer morning or evening. Several of those old style-ceiling fans were always slowly swirling to keep the air moving during the intense hot summer days, but any little breeze swept in by the screen door was always a welcome relief, too. I will always love the sound of that screen door popping against the jam as it bounced a few times before coming to a solid cohesion. Flies were a constant buzz in the summer time, although a fly swatter was usually tossed here and there for those who wanted to help keep the count down, and I suppose there were even a few mice that scurried across those old wooden floors at night seeing what little tidbit or crumb that could find before the stumbled upon a hidden trap. Old buildings always shared their space with a few unwanted little creatures, but no one ever seemed bothered much by it in those days.

Since this was an old, drafty building void of much insulation, the winter days could usher in some pretty frigid temperatures so customers would always want to come for groceries donning a heavy sweater or light jacket, both of which the proprietors wore almost every winter day. Winter shoppers were always kind enough not to linger long at the door to keep as much warmth as possible inside where it was needed and likewise in the summer to keep the pesky flies from swarming in. And most likely, a few kids got their ears occasionally bopped by their parents for not minding this advice.

This little country store also had its own distinct smell and I loved it. It was a conglomerate of oiled wood, brewed coffee, sweet confectionaries, rich tobacco, and fresh produce. Candies were displayed in bulk and sold by the pound or sack, or sometimes just by a kid's cupped hand, and peanuts were sacked and sold by the ounce or pound, not counting a few that were sometimes enjoyed while perusing. Bushel baskets full of apples and oranges could be found nestled on the floor waiting to be critiqued, fondled, and sacked by the hands of those who knew the quality of ripeness. Everything was fresh in the true sense of the word. Expiration dates were not needed.

Flimsy plastic sacks were unheard of; paper sacks were the norm, and cardboard boxes that the food items were shipped in were carefully unpacked and then offered to customers who had considerable amounts of groceries to cart home for their large families. And of course, both the paper sacks and cardboard boxes were then utilized or recycled into some other use over and over at home, or sometimes just saved and used for the next trip to town when the kitchen needed restocking.

Since computers were virtually unheard of in those days, the manner of checking out customers was done by hand, literally. For those customers who needed to charge their items, an employee used a lead pencil and quickly wrote each individual item on a four by six lined receipt book, jotting the price beside each item, being mindful to first insert a carbon sheet in order to produce a copy for the customer and leaving the original for the store. Since many large families were being fed in this farming community, there sometimes would be two or three full shopping carts of groceries to be recorded and boxed for some shoppers. For those who paid cash, their grocery items would be punched in using one of those old cash registers. This process took a fairly long time before the shopper was free to tote it all out the door, always with the assistance of one of the employees or one of the proprietors, and always accompanied with a sincere expression of thanks and sometimes a quick update of that particular family's health, latest wheat crop, or which kid just graduated. Personal service and genuine thoughtfulness were always practiced faithfully in those little country towns, leaving each and every customer with a sense of warmth and an eagerness to return.

The owners of this quaint little market lived in the back of the store and were good friends with my parents, so we children were allowed to enter their private area if accompanied by one of our parents. Their residence consisted of a tiny kitchen, a really teeny tiny bathroom, and a fairly large bedroom that served also as their living room, but this was all they needed since most of their lives were spent in the front running their business. I remember walking to the back with Mom and seeing piles and piles of cardboard boxes stacked to the ceiling in every corner available, ready for their much appreciative customers. If it happened to be a slow day when we went grocery shopping, we would be invited back to the little kitchen for a bit of some new delicious sweet dessert of some kind and a drink of choice, coffee for Mom and soda pop for me. I loved sitting back there and listening to the idle gossip as Mom and her friend giggled and visited for a while before they both had to get back to their business at hand, Mom carting up her groceries and her friend tending to her customers. It was a beautiful friendship and never taken for granted. It was a rare visit to the market that I wasn't offered a few pieces of candy right from the bin, and of course had to withstand a little teasing of some sort as well.

I also recall a few evenings when we would drive into town for Mom and Dad to enjoy a few games of cards with these dear friends after they closed their business for the day, and I would fall to sleep on their bed listening to the shuffling of cards as they all took hits of the popular drug of the times coffee while teasing and laughing the night away, no doubt releasing some pent up tension from their busy lives.

We all have good and bad memories of our childhood. Some of the warmest ones for me will be when I mentally travel back to that dear couple and their little grocery store in the village of Rozel, Kansas. God rest their kind souls.

Lost in the Neighbor's Wheat Field
By Melvin D. Pauls of Newton, Kansas
Born 1936

I might not really remember this event and only know about it from hearing it told many times. We had just moved to the farm. I was about 3 years old and probably was bored with nothing to do while Mom, Dad, and older brother, Vernon were busy. I had my dog, Rover to keep me company and we took off together to explore the countryside. Of course, I needed to find out what the land looked like at our new home. We were "really not lost" but (as the story goes) my older brother Vernon saw the heads of wheat moving in the field about a half of a mile to the East from our farm. Perhaps he could see Rover leaping up and down, Hey! If Rover was there, then Vernon was quite sure that "little brother" Mel must also be there. Vernon rescued me from being lost. I'm sure he yelled, "I see him, he is in the wheat field."

A City Girl Milking a Cow

I remember one of my daily chores was milking the cows. I always had fun squirting the milk at the cats that were always waiting for milk to drink. During my sophomore year at Bethel College, I brought my girlfriend, Nancy to see the farm. This was probably for a Sunday dinner, because Nancy remembers that the meal was a delicious roast of beef (Mom did not like to make steaks, but she really was good at doing roasts) and I had told my Mom that Nancy liked creamed peas. Nancy thinks her future mother-in-law sure wanted to have just the right meal, because years later I told her that we never had creamed peas. Mom usually made a pea soup from the fresh garden peas. My older brother, Vernon wanted his future sister-in-law to experience the "Joy" of milking cows. Vernon brought out the three-legged stool and showed the city girl just how close to sit to "Whitie" the cow. He said that he would step back a bit so he could take a picture.(I do have a copy of that picture) The picture shows the cow being milked, but about one second later the city girl was knocked on the ground by " Whitie " the cow. Hey! Did the cow know the milker was so green at milking or did the click (or flash) of the camera scare old Whitie? Nancy says she still thinks that Vernon knew exactly what was going to happen and was just waiting to

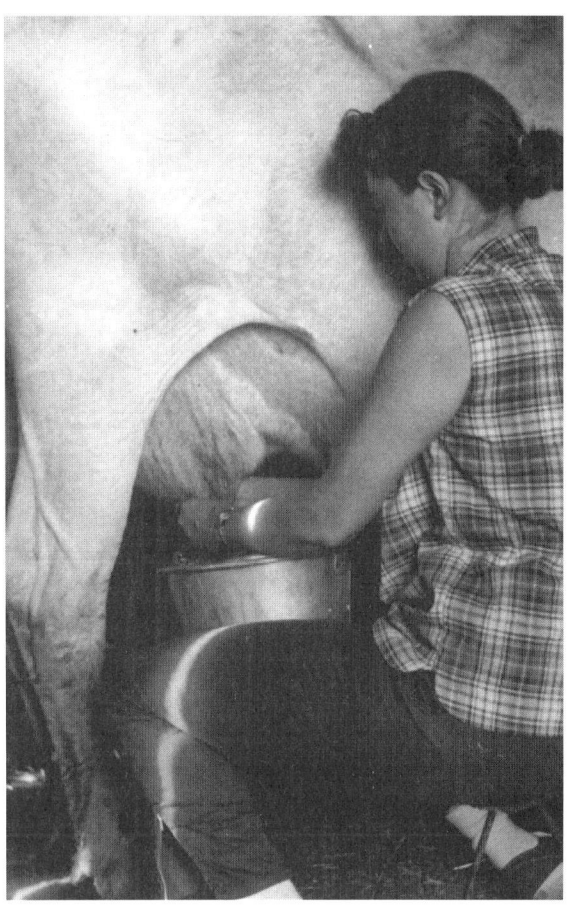

City girl, Nancy Hiebert

get a "Good Laugh ".

The Big Kite

My brother Vernon (six years older than I am) was always into building something and he did not want his "little bro" in the way. Vernon was in the garage working on a big, big kite. Hey! I only wanted to see what he was doing, so (although I was told to stay away) I still went into look at the kite. Vernon told me to "Get Out " and I did leave, but not before I just happened to step on the kite and broke part of it. Vernon said it was (I know it was not) on purpose.

The Brave Batter

If I was going to become a good pitcher for the Conway, Kansas Baseball Team, I (of course) needed to practice. Whenever Mom was not there for me to do those dreaded "in the house" chores, I always persuaded my 6-year younger brother to come into the pasture ballpark. It was most of the time against his will, but he became a brave batter for my fastball. I had made a pitcher's mound and a backstop from chicken wire. Sometimes an old grain bin was the backstop until a siding board got broken. Dad said "No more baseball in the yard."

The Old Outhouse

The Old Outhouse was about 75 ft. from the house to the North. In the dark there were (in my imagination) many scary things. I was sure there were probably some "Gremlins" hiding in the bushes waiting to jump out at me, so I was scared to go to the "Potty" at night and (if I absolutely needed to go when it was dark) I would run just as fast as possible.

Floating Down the Arkansas
By Art Gomez of Scott City, Kansas
Born 1941

I'll never forget the summer of 1952 and the floating adventure trips we used to take on the flotation devices engineered by my good friends, Harley, Dean, Butch, and me. After reading the story about an adventurer crossing the ocean on a raft called Kon-Tiki, we tried to emulate the explorer by making rafts by taking downed trees and tying them together with twine, rope, and wire. None of the rafts were stable enough, and they were also a little too heavy to float down river since the river had started to recede due to flow being diverted to Lake McKinney for irrigation purposes. There were stretches of river that had deep pools, making it a great place to fish and swim. The river was our life, and the countless days and nights that we spent along the sandy shores of our Arkansas River made for memories that would live forever.

We always tried out the prototype rafts at the Kid's Pond. The Kiwanis Club had made the pond and stocked it with a variety of fish so kids could have a place to hone their fishing skills and at the same time keep kids off the streets. There were times people would complain about us being on the water making too much noise, and several times a policeman would show up and have us drag our raft to shore and make us dismantle our project. It never failed that the officer called to remove us off the pond would make fun of our handiwork and kid us that the pile of junk wouldn't float even if it were out in the ocean. Our rafts were too heavy and cumbersome, so we had to get back to the drawing board.

Harley was the guy with all the bright ideas, and one day out of the blue he showed up at the pond with a huge black rubber tractor inner tube. "Wow, where'd you get that huge tube?" we all asked. "Down at Fansler Tires; my dad took me there and he bought this tube for a dollar, and they even patched it for him."

We took turns floating on the huge tube (that was taller than me if I stood next to it) and found the tube could carry four of us if we sat opposite each other. "Let's take it over the hill and try in in the river," said Harley, and we all helped roll the huge tube over the sand dune and flopped it into the river and immediately it began to float downstream. We all piled on, and soon we were downstream about a half mile when we realized we would have to carry the tube back to our launching point. That was when we learned we needed to carry the huge tube back on our heads as if we were on safari. We also learned walking in step made it easier to carry.

Plans were made to make a river trip to a small town downstream from Garden City, and as we traced the river on a map with our fingers we found Pierceville, Kansas, twelve miles southeast of Garden City, was our destination. We all sat down to calculate how long it would take to float down stream and the provisions we would need to make the journey. The excitement shone in our sunburned faces as ideas were tossed around naming the items we would take with us. The most important thing for our trip was each of us had to have a hunting knife with a scabbard that would be threaded on our belts to keep the knife secure in the event we fell overboard in deep water.

Friday night was our planning night, and after the long conversation, we finally had the list of items each one of us would take. We folded our notebook paper notes into tight squares and stuffed them in our jean pockets and headed for our respective homes. We were all excited about rounding up our provisions and the trip items needed to insure a trouble-free adventure.

My mother thought we were loco-boys for floating down the river to be bitten by mosquitos, flies, and whatever other bugs would leave welts after being bitten. My mother wondered what we were going to use to carry water, how we would keep our food dry, and what we would do if a thunderstorm brewed up. I assured her water would be available; we would drink from the river, which we often could and did. She folded some tortillas into the shape of a triangle and wrapped them in tin foil to keep them dry; two small tins of Underwood's Deviled Ham and a healthy chunk of longhorn cheese were going to be my survival food for the trip. The other guys had beanie-weenies, Bond bread, candy bars, soda crackers, and Harley topped it all off with 2 cans of Spam. We were ready for anything and everything.

Harley's dad had made a plywood bottom for the tractor tube and had drilled holes around the edge, which he used to thread clothesline rope in order to lash the bottom to the huge inner tube. We all thought Harley's dad was the coolest guy, and we all helped lash the bottom in place. It wasn't waterproof, but it would hold our stuff and his dad loaned us a waterproof canvas bag that accommodated all of our gear. He helped us load the huge inner tube, and we all jumped in the back of his old Ford pickup, and he drove us to the Highway 83 Bridge south of Garden City where he helped unload our rubber raft. The last thing Harley's dad said to us was, "Be careful boys and don't get into any trouble; your mothers will be upset."

We marveled how well the raft floated, and that day the river seemed to be a little deeper and the current was moving a little faster. Butch made the comment that perhaps it had rained in Colorado, causing the river to swell a little more and all agreed it was a good sign. We pulled the raft back on to the shore, and we set out to cut some stout tree branches to use as steering poles to keep us away from the riverbank for fear of our raft getting punctured by a rock or a busted sharp tree limb. Poles were at their ready and again we nudged the huge tractor inner tube off the shore and into the clear running water of the Arkansas River. With whoops and hollers, we were off on our river adventure, feeling lighthearted and confident that this was going to be the best trip ever for our summer vacation from school.

It was midmorning when we left, and it wasn't long before the topic of our conversation drifted to "when do we eat?" We had floated long enough that we couldn't see the Coop elevators anymore, and we decided it was a good time to steer our raft onto a sand bar and grab some lunch. We secured the raft to a tamarack tree with a length of rope and everyone agreed it was time to eat. We sat under the shade of a huge cottonwood tree on the warm sand as the shimmering sunlight sparkled through the cottonwood leaves. We were having a "gangbusters" good time.

Harley asked me, "What are those flat round things you're eating?" "Tortillas," I answered, "want to try one? My mom makes them out of flour, water, some baking powder, and a little lard." As Harley took a tortilla from me, the others watched to see the expression on Harley's face as he took a bite. His eyebrows went up and said, "Dang! Those things are good with Spam."

Then everybody wanted one, and I gladly passed them around so they could sample my tortillas. From that day forward Butch, Dean, and Harley were regular guests at my house to eat refried beans, pork chili, and warm tortillas with a little butter on them to make the taste buds go nuts. We all shared with each other the goodies we had brought to eat. I became a fan of Spam that summer. I still like Spam to this day, fried with eggs for breakfast…and of course, warm tortillas have to be included. We ate like kings and shortly the reason for being there took hold. We gathered our gear and once again, we were rafting down the river, headed to our destination.

There were cows in pastures along the river and they seemed curious enough to raise their heads to see what the commotion was all about as we passed them by. Horses were encountered in the river with the water up to their bellies, and they just stared as we drifted by. We even encountered some girls swimming in the river, and they all ran and hid in the bushes since they were swimming in their unmentionables. Butch wanted to stop and fraternize with the girls, but we talked him out of it since the day was getting on.

Things were going great until we approached a fence someone had stretched across a narrow portion of the river. Dean said we could make it since the fence was partially underwater, and we could clear it easily… famous last words. No sooner had Dean said that, and we heard a hissing-bubbling sound and immediately knew we were in trouble. We made it past the barbed-wire fence ok and headed for a sandbar to check the damage. There was a small gash just under the watermark, and as the inner tube was deflating so were our hopes of making it any further downstream. We sat there in silence for what seemed ages until Harley piped up and said, "Hey guys this was just our dry run or should I say our wet run." We all laughed until our sides hurt and eyes were wet with tears until the reality set in that we were at least ten miles downstream from Garden City.

The sun slowly set and evening came upon us ever so quietly, and then the sky overhead broke out in a kaleidoscope of stars. We found the Big Dipper and Butch pointed out the North Star and how you can find it by drawing a straight imaginary line from the bottom of the outer cup to the top star on the outer cup pointing to the North Star. Now and then, a meteorite crossed the sky, adding to the beauty and mystery of the galaxies we were witnessing. Our shirts and jeans had dried, and we made ready to spend the night under the open sky while the rustling of cottonwood tree leaves sang their lullaby. The fire burned late into the night until it became a glowing bed of red embers and the only other distraction was the occasional croaking of a bull frog on the opposite bank of our Arkansas River.

Now at seventy-two years and gray-headed, I walk the length of the bridge south of Garden City, Kansas crossing the Arkansas River and I stop mid-river to look to the west and then to the east, to see nothing but a dry riverbed. The trees are gone with the exception of a tamarack here and there and lone sentinels of cottonwoods that somehow have survived the lack of water since the river is no longer a river, but a place for ATV's to speed up and down the riverbed kicking up rooster tails of sand. I still miss the days we spent on the Arkansas River. The feel of sand between my toes and the smell of the river, and the friendships made; along with the stories connected to it have lived on as river adventures that have been passed down to grandchildren and others that will lend an ear.

The Failed At Home Operation
By Noah J. Lewis of Haysville, Kansas
Born 1930

One of the things that happened that I think of most is when my brother, Louie Russell was about eight years old; he got a sore on his ankle. I don't know what caused it, but it would not heal. They had this old Doctor come out to the house and check him. It just got worse so they decided to operate on him right there on the kitchen table. I think he had two doctors from Little Rock, Arkansas, who helped him. Dad was the anesthesiologist. He told how he poured the either on the mask. It almost put Dad out too.

They made all of the kids go and stay down at the barn. He finally woke, up, but they wouldn't let him drink any water. He was begging for a drink. Dad said he wouldn't drink either until Louise could.

The operation did not work because it never did heal. They operated a second time, still didn't heal. After we moved to Oklahoma, I think Louie was about seventeen or eighteen the sore was still there. Dad had tried to get him to have it operated on, but he wouldn't do it. One day when he was putting the bandage on it, he saw something in the sore, so he pulled on it and worked with it till he pulled a piece of bone out about two or three inches long, I sat watching it. It was then he said, "I will have it operated on again." This time they went to Joplin, Missouri to the hospital. They cut his leg from the knee to the ankle. This time it healed up.

I think God was with him, to be operated on under those conditions and have a sore for all that time, and not get an infection.

Adventurous and Carefree "Farm" Kids
By LuAnn Jamison of Caldwell, Kansas
Born 1953

I grew up in the small farming community of Caldwell, KS in the 1950s and '60s. My grandparents owned a small farm about 10 miles from town and one summer in particular I remember my sister, cousins, and I got to spend a whole week at the farm. Our ages ranged from about 10 up to 16 years old. Although the older cousins spent most of the time up at the farmhouse or finding an excuse to use their newly acquired driver's license to run errands into town; we younger ones were more interested in spending our time wandering along the creek bank; swimming and fishing in the mud holes.

Our grandmother made us matching

swimsuits; the younger girls got brown and white polka dot "bikinis" while the older girls had pink floral print ones. She hand-stitched our initials on each of the tops and bottoms so we could easily tell them apart. We literally lived in these suits as each day we had a new adventure waiting for us down at the creek. There was a small rowboat that was dubbed "The Sir Gregory" after one of the older girls' secret crush. We'd pack sandwiches and snacks and spend the whole day rowing up and down the creek. The first day or two we were leery of what lurked under the murky water but by the end of the second day we were accustomed to sharing our swimming hole with turtles, snakes, and the occasional cow that wandered down from the pasture to get a drink of water. Some days we'd decide to go "skinny dipping" just for a little excitement and just because we knew, we could get away with it.

One day our older cousins surprised us with the fine idea of making our muddy creek bank into an "official" beach. They enlisted our help in hauling boxes and boxes of sand from the sand banks along the nearby Chikaskia River back to an area next to the bridge that our little creek flowed under and we had our own private beach! We painted a sign on the side of the bridge naming our new area "Bikini Beach." While the older girls rolled out their towels to sunbath and listen to their transistor radio like one of those popular Annette Funicello's beach party movies; we younger ones were more content to continue swimming and rowing up and down the creek in the "Sir Gregory". It never occurred to us how dirty that old water was as we sank down in the muddy bottom, covering our feet and ankles with that black old "gook."

We ran up and down that creek bank from sun up to sun down. As long as our grandparents could occasionally catch a glimpse of us from the farmhouse. We were totally free to do as we pleased. Each evening we'd mosey up to the house, hose our bodies off at the outside faucet, eat supper, and climb into our sleeping bags either on the living room floor or in the backyard under the stars, anxious to start it all over again the next day. I'm sure if our parents had any idea that we spent that whole week without taking a real bath, they would have had a fit! It's a good thing that we stayed outdoors most of the time because I'm sure we stunk to high heavens!

That summer visit to the farm was one of my most favorite childhood memories. We spent an entire week exploring the outdoors, just enjoying being adventurous and carefree "farm" kids.

16 Short Rings
By Joyce Stark Morse of Tempe, Arizona
Born 1943

Farm life was what I knew and loved. Being Daddy's helper in the barn, driving a tractor during harvest, playing in the woods, or riding a horse provided a wonderful childhood. Our farm was five miles from Corwin, Kansas where I attended grammar school in the two-room country school. I also helped Mother with farm chores like feeding the chickens, mowing our large yard, planting flowers, or cooking for as many as 17 harvesters. Lots of our extended family lived on nearby farms. We attended a country church and went to the Sale Barn on Tuesdays.

In 1957, because of my dad's severe asthma, we sold our farm. At our farm sale, I stood at the window and cried and said, "Someday I'll return and buy this farm back." Of course, that never happened. At 14, a new life was waiting for me in Tucson,

Duane, Joyce, and Doris Stark

Arizona. But I still take joy in my childhood and have often visited the "Anthony/Corwin" area. I subscribe to the Anthony Republican newspaper "just to stay up to date on the happenings."

Two stories came to mind when I saw the flyer, "Help Write This Book." It was probably around 1950. It was a very hot summer Sunday afternoon. We often entertained the preacher's family after church or had relatives for dinner, but this Sunday was just our family of five. Mother insisted we all take that dreaded Sunday afternoon nap. Suddenly, our phone started ringing, 16 short rings, the emergency ring. Mother jumped up and ran to the party line phone that hung on the wall. She heard Rachel, the central operator, say, 'There is a prairie fire on Ralph Stark's farm." That got our attention since that was us! Sparks from the steam engine that ran along our pasture had started a fire on our dry land, and it was spreading fast. Daddy ran to the barn to start filling up milk cans. My brother started filling sand bags. Mother got the truck out. My sister and I were not allowed to go to where the fire was because as usual we were told we were too young. Neighbors began arriving with their trucks full of milk cans of water, sand bags and shovels. The wind was pushing the fire hard and tractors started plowing around farmhouses. The fire moved past our farmhouse, jumped the creek and kept going to some degree for three days. No farm homes were lost, but a lot of profitable land was jeopardized. This is my memory of our prairie fire.

When I was ten, a cow fell on Daddy's leg, while he was hand milking her. This caused a compound fracture followed by weeks in the hospital. One winter day he was home recuperating in a wheelchair and we three kids were at Corwin School when a storm came up. By early afternoon, it was snowing hard and the Principal dismissed school. Again, the central operator was called, and the 16 rings went out to all the families telling the parents that school had been dismissed. We boarded our school bus and started our route with Mr. Dir. The storm became a blizzard. Mr. Dir had dropped off several students at their homes before we hit a snowdrift and could go no further. Unfortunately, for me, I had not worn gloves or a scarf that day. We had passed the Crow farm, a half mile earlier, so Mr. Dir decided we would all walk back to their home. We were in grades from 1st to 8th. By the time we invaded dear elderly Mr. and Mrs. Crow's farmhouse our hands and feet felt quite frozen. The only room they were heating with their wood burning stove was their large kitchen/sitting room, even though they had a nice size home. Mrs. Crow immediately started heating water over the stove, letting us take turns putting our freezing hands into it. There were more than a dozen of us, but they took us all in and tried to dry out our shoes and coats. We were "cozy" in that one room with Mr. and Mrs. Crow and their hired man, Chester. Mrs. Crow went to work knowing she was going to have to feed us and sent Chester to the cellar to fetch canned jars of food. How she did it I'll never know, but at suppertime, we were all eating a wonderful meal. Now it was bedtime, so she started "making up beds" for everyone. I think I slept in a full size bed with a feather comforter with two or three other girls. The boys were on the floor in the living room. None of these rooms were heated, we had blizzard temperatures. I do know that I never got warm that whole night. I do not believe they had an indoor bathroom, but using a "bedpan" was not new to me.

The next morning we had a full breakfast. We had bacon and eggs and I especially remember the biscuits and gravy! Everyone got full. How did this grandma feed that many people without notice or a grocery store? Amazing!

Of course, when we three kids did not show up at home at the expected time, my mother started to feel panic stricken. Daddy was confined to the wheelchair, and Mother could not leave even if she wanted to with all the snow. Mrs. Crow kept going to the party line phone. All evening she tried to reach Rachel, our central operator. The phone lines were down. She just kept saying, 'The children are safe." Rachel was able to hear one of these calls. She put out the emergency rings to all the concerned families repeating, 'The children are safe." That is all I believe my parents knew throughout the rest of the night. During the night, the storm passed. After breakfast, Chester rode their horse to another neighbor that had a four wheel drive jeep. Slowly they were able to get to the Crows' and start delivering children to their homes. We were at the end of the route, so we did not get home until late afternoon. By then our parents were no longer afraid for us because they had more information. They were very happy to have my brother, sister and me home safely. We were happy to be home too, but I fondly remember this as a grand adventure.

Going from a two room country school with an 8th grade graduating class of five to a class of 500 in 9th grade was quite intimidating. I am so thankful I grew up on a farm, but also grateful for my experiences and opportunities from living in the city.

I have lots of other memories of my wonderful Kansas childhood, but these are the two I choose to share. I was called by my given name in Kansas, Joyce, until I was 14. Shortly after we moved to Tucson my name got shortened to Joy by a teacher, so in Arizona I am Joy.

Joyce "Joy" LaDonna Stark Morse

My Childhood on a Farm
By Alberta L. Kingsly of Conway Springs, Kansas
Born 1929

I am an 85-year-old mother, grandmother, and a great-grandmother. My letter contains my life in the 1940s.

When we were growing up, we had an outhouse. We also used gallon cans for our potty upstairs, and of course, with 12 kids we had to take turns bringing them down, emptying, washing, and rinsing it out every day.

We had three bedrooms upstairs, my four brothers had one room with two beds, and we eight girls had the other two rooms, one with two beds, and one with one bed. We had to sleep three in a bed, which was great in the winter for there was no heat upstairs. Mom and Dad had a bedroom downstairs. We had a parlor where we had an organ. My mother played and taught me to play and read the notes and we also sang a lot of German songs. My Mother could really play the polka music.

My Dad used to sit in his chair right by the radio and listened to Fibber Megee and Molly, or a baseball game.

We had a party line phone; we always knew who had a new baby or the latest gossip.

We had a windup phonograph, and played lots of old songs on it.

We had a washing machine with the wringer and two tubs to rinse clothes. We hung our clothes on the line.

We had a windmill for the water, best darn water I ever tasted.

Mother always made our clothes, everything but underwear.

We always had a wooden icebox; we had to buy ice for.

We had to carry our water from the well in a clean bucket for drinking in the house and a sink where you had to sit a bucket under the drain, which had to be emptied quite often. We took baths in a washtub, we had to heat the water, and we took turns taking a bath, all of us in same tub.

I got a spanking or rather a hit across my hands because I wouldn't talk, because we talked a lot of German at home So when I started school I couldn't talk a lot of English, so I wouldn't answer the Nun, and I got whacked across my hands. My favorite teacher was Sister Redempta in my 7th and 8th grades.

We had a blizzard one year to where my Dad took us to school and church in a horse pulled wagon in over 5 feet of snow. We couldn't even see the fence posts.

In winter, we butchered beef and pigs. Mother canned some of the meat but Daddy would make sausage and we got to clean the guts and help stuff them. We had a long rod in the parlor and we would hang our sausages in that room, it wasn't heated.

Our farm chores was to milk the cows by hand, we had six to eight cows. My older sister could handle any cow, even the one who would kick the bucket over, and milk would fly all over. One evening she had enough (as she put it), she grabbed the harness from the wall and way laid that cow, the cow never kicked her again (no one else could milk her). We also had to go into pigpen every night and pick up corncobs to use to burn in our wood heating stove. We also used wood and coal once in a while for heating. Since we had cows we didn't need a milkman, we separate our milk in a separator, got cream and made our own butter. We also had chickens for eggs and raised baby chicks for fryers. We kill and clean six fryers for a meal and during harvest, 8-10 fryers.

We grew our own potatoes; we had to follow Daddy to pick them up as he dug them up. We grew everything including spinach (ugh). Daddy told us it would grow hair on our chest and then we all stated eating it. I love it still today. Daddy use to cut wheat and bind oats, with a binder to make bundles. He told us he would give us each a penny if we go shock oats. We were happy to, but was very hot and itchy. We got our penny for every shock we put up and there were a lot of them, 100 or more. I would drive the horses hitched to the hayrack and haul shocks and hay from the field. One time I was driving the farm wagon with wheat, I was waiting for load and it cracked a loud thunder and those horses took off for home. They would have gotten there, except my cousin Carl got them stopped in front of the barn door that was closed. Thank goodness.

Mischievous we were at times, my younger brothers, sister and I would go into the hayloft and run around to play tag and other games, until we would get caught, it would scatter the hay and fall down below. We had two horses (work and riding), one day the three boys and I decided to ride down the lane in a field. I rode Bert (he was gentle) with one brother, and other two brothers rode Tops (he was little antsy). As I was racing down the land, I fell off, didn't get hurt, but a little sore. Of course, the boys were laughing. We kids always had fun playing and working together.

We used to have a softball game in our pasture about every Sunday in the summertime. Three of our neighbors and all their kids would come. In the winter, we had snowball fights. Oh, such fun with our extended family.

My Dad said I was very inquisitive and I asked where the doctor delivered me, He told me the doctor had to leave me in the mailbox, which was a half mile from our farm, because there was such a bad snow storm and he couldn't get to the house. I believed that till I was a lot older. My birthday is May 31st. My Dad nicknamed me Hoover, because I was born the year Hoover was elected President. Daddy said I was stubborn like him.

My Grandma had a car with a rumble seat and we all got to ride in it when she came to visit.

Our family time was every evening, we would kneel down and pray the rosary, Daddy would lead, and we all answered. As we got older, we got to take turns leading. Oh, we had so much fun with our large family. We were taught to be kind, polite, respectful to everyone, and to honor God.

Grandma Alma Bell Powers Greiner and the Snowstorm
By Marilyn Newman of Elgin, South Carolina
Born 1939

My name is Marilyn but they called me Bonnie until I went to high school. I was born in 1939 and the third child of Ted and Vera Patton of Scott County, Kansas.

I would like to tell you about my "grandma" Alma Bell Powers Greiner. My wonderful grandma was born in 1887 and lost her mom at age three and a half. She and her sister, Anna, age one year, were separated and raised by relatives. Anna was raised by the Powers side and grandma lived with the Peck family.

My grandma married Frank Greiner and had two sons (LeRoy and Clifford) and three daughters (my mom, Vera, Dorothy and LaVerna). Frank died at an early age and my grandma had to support her youngest daughter, LaVerna.

After her children had their own families, she would divide her time with each. LeRoy and Dorothy lived in Boise, Idaho, and

LaVerna lived in the Chicago, Illinois. area and my mom who lived in Scott County. Clifford died at the age of 28 from a tonsillectomy.

Usually she would spend the summer months with us. I was always so excited when the time came for her to stay with us. We would drive to the train station in Scott City, Kansas, normally late at night, and wait on the station plat form and watch the "red" light turn to "green." Then we would watch her get off of the train and wait until they brought her suitcase. Here she is with this old battered suitcase (which I have) and a big smile and lots of hugs and kisses. I would get to spend time with my "grandma" for the whole summer—I loved having her here. Then before you knew it, it was time to take her back to the train station and wait for that "red" light to turn "green" and she would be gone again.

While she was with us, I was her little helper and she had a bed partner. I would help clean out the trash (leaves) that would blow up into the wild yellow rose bushes that were around the house. They were always so thorny and we would always come out with our arms all scratched up. But they would look so nice when we were finished.

She would work outside all day long helping my mom plant a garden, etc. We always watered by irrigation and the ditch would always have this wonderful row of blue flax flowers growing so happily along the edge. What a wonderful memory.

She was also always trimming the trees and bushes. We had a fruit orchard so there were lots of branches to prune. But once she went too far- and cut off one of my sister's and my favorite thing to play on. We had lots of big, big cotton wood trees and this particular one had a very long, low hanging, dead branch, nice and smooth—we would do tricks on it. Then one day after all these years, she decides it should be cut off. We were sooooo mad about that.

We had an old brooder house that we had as a playhouse and she would clean it and fix it all up every spring. It would get so dirty during the winter months and that would be one of our favorite jobs.

One year she had gotten a job in a potato chip factory in Boise. I was so excited when she told me that she knew how to make potato chips—I loved potato chips—I was so impressed—my grandma knew how to make potato chips. She had very little education, so she worked many years in the school systems in the lunchrooms.

Marilyn with her Grandma Greiner in 1943

I remember the many times she would sit me on the dresser and curl my hair in "rags." Now I wish I knew how she did that. I always had pretty long hair and naturally curly so she liked making me look like a cute little girl.

As long as I can remember, she had "white" hair. She always wore an apron and she always made herself a new bonnet every spring out of the feed sack material (which I have) and which they made so many things. She didn't think you should let the sun get on your body let alone on your face. She would always give me a bad time because I tried really hard to get a good tan every summer.

My grandma loved children. She

Marilyn, Vera, Alesia, and Grandma Greiner in 1965

practically raised four of her grandchildren while their mother worked. She would never turn a child away no matter how difficult they would be.

One time when I was probably 8-10, she got really sick. My mom wanted me to go with her to take her to the doctor, which was about 15 minutes way. I refused to go so my younger sister, Kay, had to go. I found out later that I had broken my grandma's heart because I refused to go. I had been afraid to go because I thought she was going to die and I just didn't know what I would do if that happened. She didn't die but my grandma never forgot that day.

When I got married and had my first beautiful little girl, she would just come running when she would see my car. She would always come in and say, "Where is that pretty little brown eyed baby." She passed away shortly after my daughter, Alesia, turned one.

My grandma was so special to me. Even today, I think of her so often. To a little girl I had the best grandma that any little girl could ever have. And I think children really miss out when they don't get to have a good relationship with a grandparent. I know mine was VERY SPECIAL.

There were a couple of songs I remember her singing. One was "Bell bottom trousers, coat of navy blue, I love a sailor and he loves me too." And "Oh the moon shines tonight on pretty red wing"...(an Indian song). It would be wonderful if someone had the music to either of these. She also liked "My Bonnie lies over the ocean," and "Oh Suzanna."

The Snowstorm

A very memorable snowstorm. I think it was in 1956 or 57. We lived on a farm just a few miles from Shallow Water, Kansas.

It snowed and snowed...when it finally ended our home had snowdrifts completely to the roof. My cousin, David, had to crawl out of the kitchen window, which was on the east side of the house—the front door faced the west—to even get out of the house. Once he was out, he dug the snow away from the front door so my dad could get out. We had lots of animals so the first worry was how to get to them.

We had a "wind" break, about eight feet high, and the snowdrifts completely covered it. You couldn't see it—you just knew it was there. Anyway, the first thing that had to be done was to get water and feed to the animals in the various corrals.

My cousin and my dad dug the John Deere tractor out and then they were on their way to getting everything else uncovered.

Of course, we didn't have any school for many days and we had a wonderful time walking and playing on all that snow. When it finally melted—what a mess. Then we couldn't go anywhere because the roads were too muddy. It was still a "fun" time for a kid.

The Boy and the Blazefork
By Henry Pauls of Henderson, Nebraska
Born 1943

By most any measure, it is a small stream, even marked as an intermittent stream on topographic maps. That is true. The occasional passerby may not know that in spring or early summer the Blazefork would become a raging river spreading out to a quarter mile wide carrying torrents of water and mud. Then in late summer, it may only run in a trickle or not at all. Instead, one would find pools shaded by cottonwood, elm and willow as well as sand cherry bushes. These pools were often the last bastion for bullhead and carp as well and bluegill waiting for a late summer rain to swell the stream just enough to provide fresh water and the opportunity to swim freely.

The Blazefork has its origin in wheat fields several miles east of Windom. For some fourteen miles, it is an undulating stream winding its way to the south and east seeking the lowest places in the watershed of fields and pastures. South and east of Conway there is an abrupt change in its character. From the irregular creek with an occasional tall cottonwood shading deep pools, it suddenly becomes a manmade ditch. A deep V shaped channel gouged by huge ditching machines. From that point on the Blazefork runs for the next forty some miles alternating between being a sun drenched wide open ditch running in straight lines and right angles and a curving and ox bowed, tree lined stream. At last, it makes a few frenzied bends before converging with the Little Arkansas River between Hutchinson and Wichita.

Were that all we knew of the Blazefork this would be a mundane and average tale indeed. The real story of this little stream is in its natural beauty, and ferocity, its geography, its ecology, its people and their experiences.

I am one of those people. I was fortunate enough to experience that stretch of the creek just above the beginning of the V ditch. Here, during the 1950s, this land retained characteristics of an earlier time.

During my pre-teen years, the world of my free time was that wild and largely untamed mile of the Blazefork near the end of its course as a creek or "crick" as it was often called by locals. Here among the tall cottonwoods and shaggy willows with a quiet stream running nearby a young boy could roam unfettered by every day cares.

In the early years, I never got far from the farmyard some two hundred yards from the streambed. Those times were spent throwing sticks into the muddy little creek and watching them bob and twist as they disappeared downstream. On occasion, a leopard frog or crawfish would peek my interest.

As I grew older, birds also caught my attention and I noticed they were a colorful and attractive part of the wooded stream habitat. I learned from my brothers at an early age that the Blue Jay and Brown Thrasher were residents of the thicket, tree, and hedgerow while the Meadowlark and Field Sparrow were never to be found on our farmyard or even in trees of any size. They were prairie residents nesting on the ground or in low-lying bushes. The Red Winged Blackbird was a crossover, nesting in low buffalo berry bushes near the creek in sunny areas, but also spending time on fences and occasionally in trees singing a wonderful and shrill "shir-ree." The most wonderful time of a young farm boy's life was to be working at a quiet job like mending fences in the warm springtime sun near a creek or grove of trees. One could hear the warm sounds of the Brewers and Yellow Headed Blackbirds making their contented and busy chatting songs with each other. It was like they were grateful for this one day, this one hour in the sun with their friends, near this creek watching and gossiping about this youngster in blue jeans so busy pulling on wires. They may have been busy as well but not too much so to observe the Red Tailed Hawk circling overhead. A natural enemy who could quiet a verbal flock of blackbirds and send them skyward in a cloud swooping and diving to a new place in the sun.

During my pre-teen and teen-age years, I spent many an afternoon at the "Red Rocks." A steep cut bank resulting from years of the Blazefork making a sharp turn in the pasture exposing a colorful escarpment of red and grey shale. Layers of reddish shale and hard clay in hundreds of layers from a pencil line thickness to much heavier layers up to an inch thick. Sometimes the thin layers of shale held iron oxide. Appearing gold in color, my younger sister, and I were certain we had struck it rich. Closer examination by older siblings soon dashed our hopes. A hard lesson in Midwestern reality. Undaunted we turned our interests to practical things and soon found that these layers of shale provided just the right stuff to make dams, waterfalls and all manner of watery impoundments. Clear little estuaries, which served as holding pens for prizes we could own, small Buffalo Carp and Minnows.

Fishing the Blazefork was a common past time for our family. Early summer flooding meant a new population of fish moving up stream. This provided an excellent opportunity for attracting fish into fish traps baited with spoiled chicken entrails. Large Channel Catfish as well as other species ended up on our dinner table. With fresh potatoes and vegetables from our garden, it provided a wonderful meal. Later in summer, the creek calmed down and would run a fresh stream several feet across in wet years. This was the best time for fishing and a young boy would take every opportunity. Late afternoons or evenings after working was a perfect time to dig a few worms, find a cane pole and head for the deeper pools. Fishing was enjoyable and an educational experience in spite of the constant whine of mosquitoes. How to hook the worm, how deep to fish, how to wait patiently, what to look for in the silent movement of the bobber and how to make the deft jerk to hook the fish were all skills learned by watching older brothers and through experience. One of the wonderful aspects of still fishing is that there is time to take note of the things around you. Sunset time would be time to notice the silent glide of the Great Horned Owl on a hunt for mice or the soft coo of a Mourning Dove resting in a high branch of the cottonwood. The variable song of the Mocking Bird mimicking other birdcalls. A raccoon silently appearing downstream, nonchalantly gazing about while washing his searching hands in the water. A really tranquil time and place for a young person to grow.

As summer gave way to fall and chlorophyll left the leaves of the cottonwood, elm, and willow, the world of the Blazefork responded with brilliant yellows and less striking browns, subtle reds and browns. Long Indian Summers characterized this area as the quiet pools gathered the falling leaves in preparation for winter. Reddish brown milo fields in the creek bottoms gave way to tan stubble fields and as the temperatures dropped rain and snowstorms often developed. Rabbits and squirrels took cover in the underbrush and trees with occasional coveys of quail and isolated pheasants. While fishing dwindled as the pools were fished out and awaited spring floods to restock the waters it was still a great time for hunting and exploring. I put the two together because that is so much of what hunting means to a boy, looking for things, rabbits, squirrels, birds, animal tracks in the snow, anything of interest. I seldom hunted for specific game. Outside of rabbits, game was not that plentiful. But just wandering, spending time alone, outdoors, sunshine, wind, clean air and open space.

Tolerant and friendly neighbors allowed my passage through their pastures at will and made these times possible. Countless fall and winter afternoons saw the sun nearly set before I reached home in time to help Dad with the chores. Sometimes the result of my wandering was a rabbit for the dog or cats to eat but many times the only and really true reward was the time I had spent in the solitude of the creek, noticing the progress of the ice covering the pools, the tracks of rabbits and pheasants in the snow or discovering a badger den in a corner of the pasture.

Our neighborhood was generally a friendly place. Everyone waved with a brief but friendly greeting when meeting another person on the roadways. People often shared in tasks such as silo filling, hog butchering and fence repair. Disasters always brought people together with plowing bees when rows of neighborhood tractors turned over an entire eighty acres in a single afternoon. Doing one another's chores when a rare and well-earned vacation opportunity arose for a neighbor was also a common occurrence. Being part of a community was just a part of life in those days and helped mold who we were. The people were connected to the land and each other during my boyhood days on the Blazefork.

The Tavern Kids
By Beulah Simcox of Hanston, Kansas
Born 1934

I was born under the name of Beulah Irene Johnson on August 14, 1934. My daddy's fortieth birthday was a week later on August 21 and mother was 25 years old on January 9. I was born in Sweetwater, Texas. Daddy said it was Bitter Creek until the Stork dropped me in and after that; they had to name the town, Sweetwater. Daddy was Bill (William Edward Johnson). Mother was (Linnie Irene Moore Johnson).

We moved to Springfield, Illinois from Texas, when I was about three years old. I remember crossing the Mississippi river in a Model T Ford, entering Springfield and arriving at the house at 2829 Lowell Avenue.

We lived in a two-story house with two rooms upstairs. We lived four blocks from the end of the bus-line and four blocks from Fred C. Dodd Elementary School. We were children of the Great Depression and our country was at war as I began going to school. I enjoyed school and my friends there. I dearly loved playing baseball in the schoolyard. We all loved baseball. Daddy played on the St Louis Cardinals baseball team when he was about twenty years old (maybe 1918). He said that they were the same as a Minor league team in those days.

Mother and daddy rented half of our house out, while we lived in the other half and a young couple lived in the back of our house. We shared with our renters a two-story barn, a two-seater outhouse near the alley, a fenced chicken house, and a garden area. We grew much of our food. Something I learned at about six years of age, was that one kernel of corn would grow into a plant that made more corn.

Our neighbors to our north kept an acreage beside our house in vegetable garden annually. When I was in first grade, our neighbors had the front part of their plot full of FLOWERS. Oh, they were breathtakingly beautiful! I stopped by on the way to school one morning, to pick a bouquet for teacher. The bouquet of Bachelor Buttons wilted as I picked them. The more I picked, the more they wilted. Suddenly, there was daddy, home from deliveries (his work). I realized I was way late to school. I cried... Daddy said that it would be OK, and walked with me to school, visited with my teacher and helped me out. But when I had trouble learning to read in third grade, he said that if I didn't pay attention in class and improve my reading, he would spank me; which he soon had to do, and I decided to myself that I would listen to what my teacher said in class and do as she said until I could read correctly to daddy. Well, you see, daddy helped me to learn to read. Another important thing, my teachers taught us children to respect and obey our parents.

My parents never dressed in jeans. Mother and I wore dresses and daddy wore casual trousers. On Sunday, we attended the Salvation Army Church within walking distance from our house where the gospel of Jesus Christ was taught. That lady wore a navy blue bonnet that I thought was pretty. I enjoyed going to her house to visit. She had a lovely flower garden.

Then, mother grew a big fat belly and soon, I had a baby brother. All of that year, I helped mother, ran errands, filled the bucket at the well for water and lifted what I could. Billy (William Edward Johnson Jr.) was born on March 17, 1939, St. Patrick's Day. He had blond curls all over his pretty little head.

Cabinets, water closet, icebox, a coal cook stove, and the dining table were in our kitchen. When the iceman came with ice, he was met by all of us kids on the block, begging for chunks of ice. The coal-man delivered coal into the basement. Our washing machine had galvanized tubs and wringers. It was so much better than having to wash all the laundry by hand, using a scrub-board. When we gained a radio, I listened to Jack Armstrong, Superman, and The Inner Sanctum (The Shadow Knows) in the evenings and we could listen to the News.

Several good things for me happened at once. Our renters moved away, but a Mexican family moved right in. They were parents with teenagers. They moved in and the oldest son Sebastian, went into the Army. Raymond soon graduated from high school and joined the Navy. Mary was still in high school. She and I became friends and spent a lot of time together.

A new family moved into the house across the street. It had been a store and house attached until it sold to this family and it became a tavern and house attached. There were seven kids in the family. They were called "the

The Johnson Family

Richard and Beulah Simcox with their children

Tavern kids," but they were fun to play with and became good friends. I had previously found other neighbors, and Mildred, Donald and George were fast friends, so now I had Jerry and Jenny (twins), Alice (who had one brown eye and one green eye), and Walter and Wally (twins). Anna was the older sister and she was attached to Fritz, her boyfriend, and they lived in his car. John was the older brother who was not interested in our play. Altogether, I had seven kids to play in the street with. During the war, we had no cars or gasoline, so we skated, played ball and slid on old metal coke signs, on snow in the streets, during the winter.

The "Tavern kids" and I went to the movies on Saturday. We rode the bus to downtown Springfield, and passed Abe Lincoln's Springfield home on the way to town. It cost 10 cents to ride the bus and 10 cents to buy the ticket to the movie. Candy & pop were 5 cents each.

Mother kept a swing for us on the Cherry tree and one day daddy built a 2-wheel scooter of "one by four" boards and painted it for me to ride on. I put one foot on the step and pushed it with my other foot. The wheels were a pair, and with one push, the scooter would travel quite far. I was popular because I allowed my friends to ride it too.

I had best friends from school, who lived past the bus-line and North, on Lowell Avenue. Carolyn lived with her grandparents and Jane lived with her parents and they lived about half a block from each other. By fourth grade Carolyn, Jane, Mildred and I, joined the Girl Scouts.

Daddy was a salesman. He kept others well with his meds. At that time, our medical doctor came to our house when we needed him. Daddy sold herbs and elixirs. He kept a small shop at home and built a large route to neighbors in the community and we all stayed well and healthy. He ordered things in from Kentucky. There were no drugstores except in downtown and many customers used daddy's meds, so we earned a living.

In time daddy thought that, I was big enough to ride a two-wheel bicycle. One of his customers had some good used boy's bicycles for sale. Bicycles were not available new because of the war effort. So, daddy bought two of them, painted the smallest one for me, and fixed the other one up for one of my Texas cousins, Royce, whom he thought needed one. Daddy thought it would prove good exercise for me to master riding that boy's bicycle, and he was right. Mother would pack a lunch for me so I could go adventuring. I never went far - to the park or far enough to park under a shade tree and eat my lunch! My bike came in handy when Billy left the yard to play somewhere else, and I had to hunt for him. That's when I traveled on that bike! Billy could ride on that bike bar to bring him home. Do you suppose he ran off so he could ride on

Richard and Beulah Simcox on their 50th wedding anniversary

my bike? Hm

The second time Mother was in an expecting way, I worked hard to help out and the "Tavern kids" also worked hard because their mother was expecting and we were concerned about our mothers. The "Tavern kids" began to ride the bus to the Baptist Church downtown. We were all praying and taking life seriously because we had neighbors and uncles serving overseas in the military and we believed that Jesus loves us and He would help us to win the war if we prayed and did our part. I began to take Billy to church with me then, since I thought he was big enough. I had a friend named Donna just two blocks away, and invited her to go to the Salvation Army Church with me. She then came to church faithfully, and brought her little brother. I was glad I invited her. Mostly, when inviting others, they said, "You're crazy."

Billy and I soon had a baby sister, Snookie (Mary Louise Johnson). Born on June 30, 1942. Mary had red curls all over her pretty little head. I missed out! My hair was brown, not curly.

Our parents went to work at the ammunition factory, I baby-sat, and we were doing things for the war effort. We collected things such as cooking oil and bacon grease that was used to manufacture arms and munitions. I went around the community with my wagon, collecting newspapers and magazines and they were packed in trucks at the school and hauled away. We had open air movies at the park and the side of the community building was our movie screen. We paid for our tickets with scrap metal that we had laying around. Once, we went to a movie with an old coffee pot. Each of us carried one piece of the pot to see "Bob Hope's Busy Day." They often showed a good movie at the park for free. We could walk down the alley straight to the park and sit on the grass or quilts. We also had a lending library at the park. I worked at the library at times. The community building was busy with activities all the time, (pre TV)

I wonder why we have not been rationed in these recent wars. For many things, we had to have a stamp and buy a limited supply of: such as sugar, flour, meat - needed to feed our military men; who were sacrificing their lives for us. I could have one pair of school shoes a year, for the sake of making enough boots for our soldiers. We all wanted to get in on doing our part for the war effort; wouldn't we do that again for God and Country?

The finis of this story is the end of WW 11. The news came over the radio that Germany surrendered in the afternoon of my twelfth birthday, August 14. I had a chocolate cake and was happy enough, but that news made us ecstatic! We hurriedly dressed for town and walked toward town. When we got to the bus-line, there was a huge crowd of people moving toward downtown Springfield. The only time in my life, I ever experienced and saw anything like it!

We were thrilled to be there, slapping each other on the back, hugging, dancing, laughing, and crying all the way to town. It was miles to town from our house, but we were carried along in the happy throng. I think when the Bible speaks of the multitude of the redeemed in Glory, that is what it will be like. We were home again by 2 AM and still rejoicing. I don't remember sleeping, but surely, we got some shut-eye that wonderful day.

The Circle, Once Broken
By Mardia "Dinky" Meece of Norwich, Kansas
Born 1953

My life spent here in The United States of America is surely something for which I am, and will always be, truly thankful! It's a privilege to be part of Kansas' history, living the period from early 1950's to present 2014. "My name is Dinky, pinned on me at age three." When I was a child, there was no worldwide communication or media scaring the bejeebers out of us daily. We listened to news and talk shows on our real wood cabinet Philco radio with no television to watch. We had limited indoor plumbing, which meant one washed their hands in leftover dishwater most of the time. Grandma did her dishes in two small pans filled with boiling hot water from a kettle. And no central air, we had a swamp cooler, that grandpa washed with bleach to prevent the unit from corroding and bacteria forming which would have made us sick.

When I was five, Saturdays were set aside to help at Cook's farm in Norwich. Pearl Cook, my grandma's younger sister, purchased her farm in 1959, for the purpose of raising livestock. It's one-hundred-sixty acres was planted with prairie grass and lots of Mexican stickers. Aunt Pearl was thankful for her sister and brother-in-law's help, and gave us beef and food from her garden, which was the best of her crop. Grandma canned the vegetables and we always had plenty of beef and fresh vegetables. I know Sam, my grandpa, did get some cash when they sold off some cattle, a very common practice to pay ranch hands.

The only structure on the Cook's farm barely allowed shelter from rain and extreme weather. A tiny shanty, built in case of rain, sitting in Canton Township, part of Kingman County. "It will forever be a piece of me."

The three of us little girls would spend the whole day in a field without electricity, batteries, or a phone within four miles of our location. We played jump rope, jacks, and built a fort under a large tree for shade. That was it! Grandma called us for lunch; we would help by getting water from the hand-pumped well and of course, get each other wet in the process. Once on the blanket, we would say our prayer and sit with our grandparents until everyone was finished eating. In the afternoon, we could follow grandpa down to the pond and check it out for fish and tadpoles.

As we traveled from city to country, year after year, songs from the radio kept going through my mind. Music like: "Everything is beautiful, in it's on way...," "Let it Be," or "Close to you." When thinking about the noise in the car, I can't forget complaints made during our journeys, mostly out of boredom, "Are we there yet?" I well up inside, with tears of happiness and enjoyment in my heart, mind, and soul. Knowing I will soon be older, on my own, and pray I will have all this, as I'm older. A farm of my own! We traveled an hour one way. Watching the sunrise from the back window of my grandparent's car showed off several colorful

They sold the farm in 1972. That weighed heavy on my heart for years, yearning to own a piece of paradise in this area of my own. Tales told by my grandpa would make everything seem so much more vivid and thrilling. He lit the room. He could whistle very well, like tunes from Hank Williams Sr. and Grandma's favorite gospel hymns.

Sundays meant getting in a pretty little dress, with shiny little shoes, and going to church with my family. We were raised Southern Baptist in the Bible belt of Kansas. Brother Dorein, the preacher of Olivet Baptist Church, in Wichita really knew how to keep his congregations interest. "By age eight, he had mine!" Willingly and faithfully, he officiated all my aunts and uncles weddings. I admired Bro. Dorein for his leadership. My beautiful mother and wonderful grandma taught Sunday School there at his church. The year is now 1961.

BK is three, Pattycake is almost five, and I'm seven... On Saturday mornings, before sunrise we ate our breakfast, and got ready for traveling to the farm. This was a challenge for my baby sister, too short in the saddle, her chin fit slightly above the edge of the table. When she sneezed, she re-opens her wounded chin, wearing a reoccurring cut and Band-Aid for at least a year, this became a serious matter. Grandma tried to prevent it, adding a phone book under her butt, sitting her on an inverted Dutch oven, but "it still happened!" Intelligent and beautiful, inside and out, BK is fifty something now, and my baby sister is the most thoughtful person you will ever meet.

We take pillows, toys, and blankets, ready for an hour ride to Norwich. Pattycake, my middle sister, needed lots of room in the seat. She sprawls out to go back to sleep. I cradled BK, as she loves to cuddle, while Pattycake took over half the backseat. Patty was the independent type; she enjoyed her freedom and made her own choices. Today she runs a daycare and is a full-time caregiver to our 99-year-old grandmother, our father's mother. She's a very loving and caring woman with the patience of Job, never losing heart or faith in God.

Family reunions are a thing of the past for most groups including mine. Each and every summer, my family would gather up in a park for a potluck feast. We played horseshoes, badminton, and volleyball. At mealtime, everyone bowed their heads for what seemed like thirty minutes while aunts and uncles praised God. Elders would have wet eyes and huge smiles.

We attended Wichita public schools and completed any homework before play. Using the supper table for studies, grandma kept us nearby. She checked our papers and approved them before we could escape outside. She would assist us with our work while fussing around the house and fixing supper. She picked up grandpa at 6:00 P.M. sharp. We had to be in the backseat of her Rambler {automobile} on time, homework completed, and most of all, be ready to travel by 5:15 P.M. Grandpa liked it quiet on the way home. All questions, any conversation, everything stopped when he got in the car. Grandma would look at us in the rearview mirror and smile.

Sam, my grandpa, worked at a foundry most of his life, worked long hours and plenty of them. Arriving back home during the week was exciting because mother would be there, home from work. She would set the table; heat up food prepared by her mother, and sweetened iced tea in glasses for her girls. "We never picked up silverware before prayer." We were encouraged to tell any concerns of the day, in case we needed to pray about that, and listened to what the elders ask God for. They thanked Him for each day. By age eight, I was delighting my family with corny, kid-like prayers. It took years to get comfortable with opening my heart to God and to my family members.

Mealtime consisted of rice or potatoes most of the time. Meat was served at suppertime, fruit, and Kellogg's Corn Flakes for breakfast and vegetables at lunch. Snacks would be a half-cup of milk and half of a sandwich. Bread back then was fifteen cents a loaf and they sold a new product called Franco-American Spaghetti in the can. Grandpa said, Lillie, his wife, could "save her money" and make much better food here at home.

My grandfather was very talented for a poor kid from Texas with a third grade education. Grandpa would embellish things to improve his stories, by adding his take on things, the details made it truly fictitious. He could leave a room belly laughing, in stitches, in no time. He enjoyed pulling pranks, innocently little ones, acting foolish to tease his wife, and making grandma roar from the outcome. "Yes, they were saints!"

Grandfather was seventy-six, and I was thirty-one years old when he passed. We laid one of America's finest to rest that day. Part of my grandmother was buried with her husband of fifty-seven years; their lives were filled with pure love and honest devotion.

Then, just four years later, Grandma Lillie died. My mother and both her parents have passed away. Our young lives were well orchestrated, happy, and controlled mainly by Mrs. Lillie. We had a family that showed deep love for each other, truly respecting everyone's differences. My wonderful, caring, and beautiful grandma was the best counselor on earth. She kept a tight ship, but was always ready to save us from anything life offered! Now they are angels in heaven, looking after the book of life, waiting for our names to be called up yonder. With this period, our journey ended. I started missing the bonding of country life.

I married my high school sweetheart. Two years into our marriage, I delivered my beautiful and thoughtful daughter to the world. Two years after that, my softhearted, handsome son was born. Still missed the country life, thinking, "I'm going to do this!" My children offer me courage and strength and I remained very positive. Sadly, like many first marriages, mine failed to work after a while. Now it's 1993, I was single, stayed that way for several years, and worked at an aircraft company. Refusing to give up, I continued asking God in prayer for things I need. Always thinking, my new family of grandchildren would know what life is like on the prairie.

My dear mother passed away February of 2002. She was my anchor in life and I miss her deeply.

I met a loving man right after my fiftieth birthday in 2003. By Thanksgiving of the same year, we knew we were in love. He grew up in southern California, but he loves farming. Thing I've laid awake praying about for years came true. We bought a 27-acre farm, a lovely corner plot in Bennett Township, just four miles from all my childhood memories... We purchased a tractor and renamed my husband "Farmer Fred." Every day is a fun, getting dirty and sweating is more fun when one can jump into a hot shower afterward. . My dream came true!

Mother and my grandparents would have loved this place. We named the farm Six Penny Farm after a joke made by a friend, that "ole' Freddie can squeeze six pennies out of every nickel." On this farm, we planted a fruit orchard, a vineyard with three types of grapes, and many trees. Some trees weep and some stand tall and straight. Room for everything! Families will eat from my vegetable and fruit gardens the rest of my days. Everyone is more than welcome here. We may never achieve self-sufficiency, but we do supply our table with plenty of top quality fruits and veggies. And we do celebrate some good weather evenings with a fire to cook on and keep warm by. "The good life."

I'm retired now, and working indoor during winter months so I can spend spring, summer, and fall months mainly outside. I wish I'd paid more attention back then, when my elders told me things concerning life, on how to grab life by the horns. It's my turn to stand up and be the matriarch of my family. I feel doubtful anyone is listening. Life today is harder than it should be, given all we have. God bless the miracles of life. I'm a truly blessed soul that made a full circle, doing well at sixty-something... Gardening, planning family outings, praying to God for my eternal home to be even better than this. My life has been a whirlwind sometimes, but, in God speed, it rewarded me greatly. Country living is the life!

Tarpaper House, Swimming Pools, and School Days
By Betty J. Lehr of Park City, Kansas
Born 1930

Betty with her parents and her younger sister in 1936

I was born on October 24, 1930 on our kitchen table by the light of a kerosene lamp in a farm house in Haverhill, Kansas We moved to El Dorado, Kansas, about 9 miles north of Haverhill in a few years and I started to kindergarten when I was four years old. You could do that then if you would be five by the end of the year. I would become five in October. During my kindergarten year, we moved to Oil Hill, Kansas, 2 miles west of El Dorado and my life began. One day I came home from school to find I had a baby sister. I didn't ever know my Mother was pregnant. Oil Hill was a booming oil town in the 1910s and 1920s. It was considerably smaller when we moved there. Most of the homes were owned by Cities Service Oil Company and you could rent one for $9.00 a month if you worked for Cities Service.

Unfortunately, my Dad worked for a private garage and did not qualify. Our house was covered with tarpaper. You could hear the mice running in the walls. We drove the flies out by waving T-towels and shooing them out the door. We got heat from a wood-burning stove in the dining room. My sister and I slept in one bed in the dining room and our grandfather slept in the bed next to us. The room next to the dining room was the kitchen. We had running water but could not drink it. We hauled our drinking water. We could only use the tap water for washing clothes or taking a bath. Our bath was a metal tub in front of the kitchen stove. When we washed clothes, we had to put alum in the water, skim off the top of the water, and then slice P & G soap for the detergent. We had an icebox. When we finally got a refrigerator, I was so disappointed that it was not full of ice cream, pop and all the other things it showed in the magazines.

On the other side of the dining room was my parents' bedroom and front room. Outside, was our 3 hole outhouse. One hole each for Mom, Dad and children. Our town had a Fire Department but I don't remember it ever being used. We didn't have police but I guess you could have called the Sheriff if you were in trouble. The only trouble we had was at Halloween when the outhouses got turned over or moved. It was a peaceful town, with two grocery stores, a restaurant, a filling station, a garage for car repairs and The Cities Service Offices. The town had two sets of phones, one for Cities Service employees only and another that went to other towns. We had neither. I finally got to talk on a phone when I was in second grade as part of my schooling. For entertainment, we had a swimming pool, croquet court and a nine-hole sand golf course. The swimming pool was much better after they put in a filter system and refused to let you take your dogs in the water. It cost 5 cents to go swimming or you could get a season family permit for $1.00. We were surrounded by oil fields. In the summer, we would find a small stream in the fields and follow it until it became a nice creek. That was a whole day's fun. The only people we ever saw were the men servicing the oil wells. School was the most wonderful thing in my world. It was a half mile to school and I came home for lunch most days.

On good days, I could walk, skate, or ride my bike. On a heavy snow day, we would walk on the highway that went through town to avoid falling electric lines. If it was a really bad day, I would take a sack lunch with a liver loaf sandwich. The farm kids took their lunch every day and their favorite sandwich must have been bologna. I still can't stand the smell of it. Walking to school was safe because there was a Mother in every home. Sometimes they were outside visiting. If you needed help, they were there. Women didn't go to work much outside the home until World War II. At recess, depending on the time of year, we had jumping rope, jacks, and hopscotch plus the usual swings, merry-go-round, baseball, etc. Our school had three buildings.   T h e small one had kindergarten through fourth grade, the larger one had fifth grade through eighth grade, a music room, art room, a library and the Principal's Office. In between the two buildings, there was an all-purpose building. It was our gym. Gym classes started in first grade and showers were added in second grade. The building was also used for movies (some of them silent) meetings and various entertainment. On Sunday, it was used for non-denominational church. We had wonderful teachers. Our fourth grade teacher used to read classical books to us. We said the Pledge of Allegiance to the Flag and the Lord's Prayer every morning. We went to the teacher's house in the evening and she popped corn for us, played the piano and we had lots of conversation. Our sixth grade teacher was a full-blood Indian man. He was married with two children. We would go to their house of an evening and play with the kids, work in the yard or just visit. He had a mounted collection of butterflies, moths and other insects, which were always fun to learn about. Once, he took the whole class fishing as a reward for our class work. He taught us for two years and we got our first knowledge about laws.

We had mini-trials when someone misbehaved. Our teacher eventually got into politics. His son was Head of Indian Affairs when he grew up. Shirley Temple was big when I was young and I had several things with her picture on it. My Mother would steam my hair over a teakettle trying to get my hair to curl but it was too straight. Finally, she started taking me to a Beauty Shop for permanents. That was not fun, with all the electric wires attached to your head and the length of time it took. Sometimes your head would get burned; I had to wear white high-topped shoes in the lower grades. We only got new shoes when school started. In second grade, my Mother dyed my shoes black and I was so embarrassed by them, I would sit on them or hide them anyway I could.

A big thing then was getting free things at the movies that included dishes, comic books and other things. You could get in the movies

Betty with the bandana on her head, her 6th grade classmates, and Indian teacher in 1940

on Saturday for a bread wrapper. Since my friend's family owned the restaurant, we got to go often for free. The depression was in full swing. If we ran short of grocery money, my Dad would send me to the restaurant to borrow a dollar to tide us over till payday. The restaurant owners had geese loose in their yard and they would bite me on the backs of my legs. Girls didn't wear long pants then. Sometimes my Dad would take our last five dollars and play poker to win enough money to get by on. Once we got a bean order, which meant getting a free sack of groceries from the government. You were given a ticket and could work off the grocery amount when they contacted you. They never contacted my Dad but he carried the ticket in his pocket his whole life to remind him how hard times were then. One of my jobs as a child was going into the Pool Hall in El Dorado to get my Dad when my Mother had finished shopping and was ready to go home. The cigarette smoke was so bad that you could hardly see. Breathing was hard also. The Pool Hall was full of unemployed men with time on their hands.

When the Second World War started five of my uncles joined the various branches of the service instead of waiting to be drafted. My Dad and his brother were too old so they went to work at Beech Aircraft building airplanes. My Mother went to work for the Cities Service Offices as a telephone operator so we could finally rent a Cities Service house. It did not have an inside toilet so we still used an outhouse. We moved a few years later to the main street in town. Still had no outhouse but the last two houses had showers so we could at least bathe. This house was across the street from where my Mother worked so it was nice to have her so near. Needless to say, my sister and I preferred having our Mother at home.

There were three things I wanted as a child, a bicycle, a piano, and a wristwatch. I got the used bicycle in grade school. When I was in eighth grade, I got a really used large piano. It didn't look like much but it had a good tone and I loved it. I took piano lessons in El Dorado. The only problem was I either had to ride my bicycle or hitchhike the 2 miles to El Dorado. I got in the car with people I didn't know and once shut the door on my finger. When my piano teacher saw how much pain I was in, she sent me home and I didn't have to pay for the lesson. The lessons cost 50 cents. After a couple of years, they went up to $1.00 and I had to quit. I knew enough music by then to enjoy my piano and I was enjoying other things also. Since our Oil Hill School only went through eighth grade, we were bussed to El Dorado for ninth grade school. A fun time for us in the summer was getting to go to El Dorado with friends to "run around." On one of these excursions, we visited a portable skating rink that was only there in the summer. I saw a young boy inside skating that I was really attracted to. I thought if I ever had a son, I would want him to look just like that.

My friends came back looking for me and we left. In my sophomore year, we moved to El Dorado. I was so happy, no more bus rides, I had many school friends there, and best of all we had an indoor bathroom! Our house was small with two bedrooms. I think the main attraction for this house for my Dad was the fact that our back door was just a few feet from the back gate of the High School Football Field. I don't think he ever missed a game as long as he lived there. I had a great time with my High School friends. When I was a senior, the senior girls were all dating sophomore boys for some reason or other. One of my best friends was dating a sophomore boy and decided to call it quits. She asked me if I would tell him. I didn't know him and had always been timid around boys as I had no brothers, but I told her I would. The boy turned out to be the same boy I had admired at the skating rink a few years before. He was so easy to talk to and we started dating. We were married three years later. We have been married almost 64 years. We have three boys and two girls, none of whom look like him although they do have his good traits. We have added 13 grandchildren and 31 Great Grandchildren. Life is good.

An Amusing Miscommunication
By Ruby Waltner of Freeman, South Dakota
Born 1931

Many years ago, I worked as a nurse in our small town 20-bed hospital. The night shift demanded we were our own maintenance crew, as there was none there at night. We had an antiquated phone system at that time.

If one phone was not put back on the cradle properly, none of them worked.

This particular night, that is exactly what happened. We had no calls coming in or going out. The other nurse on duty asked me to remain at the nurses' station while she went room to room to discover the culprit. She would come out of each room either shaking her head or saying, "Not this one."

Her last room to check was the nursery. She went in and came out saying a bit too loudly, "The one in the nursery is dead, too!"

Feed Sack Garments
By Janice A. Pauls of North Newton, Kansas
Born 1939

Normally you would not think of a dusty, noisy feed mill as a place to shop for dress fabric. However, during the 1940s that is exactly where my family obtained material for dresses, aprons, curtains, pillowcases, etc. Although cotton sacks were used long before the '40s to ship farm and food products, they became really popular when synthetic fabric appeared on the market and the price of cotton dropped. The women would have to remove the printed labels on the material. In around 1925 when the manufacturers realized how popular the cotton sacks had become, they began making colorful print sacks with easy to remove paper labels.

When I was growing up in central Kansas in the '40s, my father worked in the local feed mill. When he started bringing chicken feed home in these colorful, printed sacks, my mother would request a certain number of each print so she would have enough fabric for her sewing projects. I still fondly remember the green and white ivy pattern that Mom turned into curtains, a skirt for my vanity table, and a matching bed comforter. I have to admit though that I eventually grew tired of having only feed sack dresses and longed for one purchased from the store.

Our family actually had an advantage, too, because sometimes farmers who had a large operation would come to the feed mill and ask my father to empty a variety of feed sacks to grind and mix the grain together in the mixer. They then loaded the loose grain and mash into their large farm truck and drove away, leaving the sacks behind. Apparently, either their wives were not interested in sewing or the men just didn't want to be bothered with the sacks. In such cases, my dad would bring the unwanted sacks home for Mom to wash, take out the chain stitching, press, and store for future use. Years later after my mother had passed away, I cleaned up her house and still found some plain white sacks, and enough border printed fabric for several pillowcase sets. I hemmed the white sacks, embroidered a pattern on them, and they became wonderful, absorbent dish towels.

Although paper bags eventually replaced the cotton feed sacks in the 1950s, the mystic of "vintage" fabric still exists. Today you can occasionally buy fabric in stores that is reminiscent of a past era.

Outhouses and More
By Howard L. Underwood of Derby, Kansas
Born 1932

The things I remember as a kid growing up in the 1930s in Dodge City, Kansas are many. First, to come to mind is going to the outhouse in the cold winter mornings. Our outhouse was a typical two-holer with the standard issue toilet paper of the times—the Montgomery Ward catalog. (We had moved up from using a corncob by this time.) Comfort wasn't a factor back then. The catalog was only used as a necessity. The hole over which the outhouse sat had to be re-dug every few years, and by my

Howard, Arlus, Phynon, and Leona in 1939

Howard and his brother, Arlus in 1945

early teens, this chore always fell to my older brother (by one year) and me. My dad worked on the Santa Fe Railroad and only came home on the weekends. He expected us to have the new hole completed in a few weeks, and he always checked on our progress. We did a good job for a task we only had to do every couple of years.

That wasn't the extent our hole digging, though. My dad eventually put in an indoor bathroom. No more hauling water from the outside pump to fill a washtub for baths! My brother and I had to dig the trench for the plumbing. It was worth it, though, to avoid those cold winter trips to the outhouse!

Outhouses played a major role in our entertainment on Halloween. My brother and I, along with several of our friends, would go around tipping over outhouses in the 1940s. Sometimes an owner was ready and waiting for the Halloween hooligans to show up. One time the owner was inside the outhouse. When we walked up, he came out with a shotgun and fired into the air. We scattered! Other times, the owner pushed the outhouse to the front of the hole, knowing we would be coming up from behind it to tip it over. Then we would be surprised and have to catch ourselves before falling into that disgusting hole! Usually though, we just pushed the outhouse over and left it lying on its side. This was our version of trick-or-treating. My dad planned ahead for this adventure by laying our outhouse on its side. This way, the troublemakers wouldn't damage it by pushing it over. My dad didn't know for sure that I was one of "those kids!"

I always claimed that I set the record for tipping over 17 outhouses one year! As far as I know, that record still stands since the outhouse became obsolete with the coming of modern times. Who would have thought that the lowly outhouse could provide so much entertainment!

I remember one of the schools we went to was a one-room school in Fort Dodge that had first through sixth grades. There were six

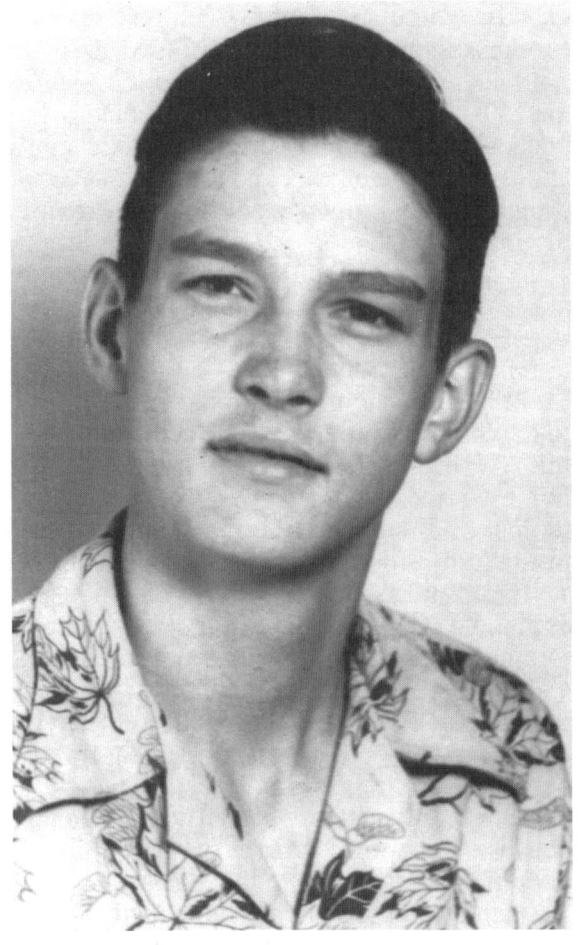

Howard L. Underwood at age 15

rows, front to back. Each grade had a row. My sisters were in the second and fourth grades. My brother and I were in the sixth grade as well as the only other student, my girlfriend. That was my whole class. Me, my brother, and my girlfriend!

When I was in the sixth grade, we lived on a farm outside of Ford, Kansas. I lived in a three-room house with my father, mother, brother, and my two younger sisters. Talk about crowded! You can only imagine! My parents and siblings all slept in the one bedroom. I had a cot in the living room and felt I was living in the lap of luxury. I had a whole corner to myself! There was no electricity or indoor plumbing in this house. We lived here for a little over a year before moving to Dodge City.

We had a telephone with a crank back then. We had to turn the crank a certain number of times to call our neighbor. Our signal was four rings and a friend of ours was two rings. It was a party line, and when you made a call, you could hear other people picking up their phones to listen in. So much for privacy!

The school in Ford had a lot more students, and each grade had its own room. I was into reading then, and read all of the Thomas C. Hinkle books that I could find. I didn't really enjoy my time at school in Ford, but I liked living on the farm.

Even with the hard times we had to endure, we enjoyed life. When I look back, I am thankful that we all had our health and we all turned out well in spite of the abject poverty and hardships.

Life on the Farm
By Samuel Walter Scott of Bloom, Kansas
Born 1923

I'll be 94 come this August. Here are few of my stories growing up in Bloom, Kansas my grandparents are the pioneer founders of Bloom. My mom was an only child, and she said that it could get really lonely with no one to play with. She told us about once when she was a child a wagon came through Bloom. It was loaded with six or seven kids. Anyway, that was a bunch to her. So she tried and tried to buy one of those kids with the pennies she had saved. But the lady said she could never part with any of her children. My mom Anne (Albright) Scott was so upset she cried all night.

One day my brother came home from school and we were playing near the barn when I heard the cow bawl. I was sure she was in the hayloft, and sure enough, she was. We filled the steps going up to the loft up with hay. She got to eating there and went right up to the loft. Closing the door at the bottom, we led the cow along the side of the stairway and pushed her over into the hay. We crawled down where you feed the cows, opened the mow door, and said, "Come on Bossie." There she came sliding out.

One day, four or five cousins and my brother and I were at my uncle's farm south of Bloom. We saw he had a stripped-down buggy with no body or brakes. We fastened a rope to the axle to steer it by hand. About four of us would get on the seat at a time. We would place it at the top of one of the canyon rims and give it a hard push. It would drop eight to ten feet. We would go to the bottom of the draw in a hurry after we would bottom out in that drop. No one ever got hurt. Then we would drag it back to the top, and away we would go again. We had no helmets or kneepads, just pure raw fun in the great outdoors.

Once at a church camp we fixed up a barrel with ropes coming out of both ends. It was tied to poles on either end. We then saddled the barrel, and a man stood at each end by the poles and moved the ropes like we were riding a bucking bronco. Not many could ride the barrel. That evening two or three men came, unsaddled the barrel, and then threw the saddle as hard as they could, "This will stop anyone else from getting an arm broke!" One of the boys tried his best to tell them what happened. A boy from camp went to town, borrowed a mule from someone when its owner was not at home, and rode him on a gallop. He stopped quick, and the boy went over the horse's head and broke his arm. The little boy knew the truth about the story, but didn't tell.

When I was younger, I went to a house sale and came home with a Shetland pony. I picked up a 92-year-old man in Minneola. He said he could find me a buggy. We went to his farm, and he had a sod house in good shape all but one corner. I bought his stripped-down buggy for $5.00. Soon I had harness enough to drive the pony. Each day at four o'clock, I was at Bloom to give the kids a ride. They never got enough rides. When I got older and didn't have a pony anymore, I used my Wiggle Mower to pull it around. Kids would stand in line to get a ride. I do miss hauling those kids; they were the best days of my life! Thank you to the boys and girls for the good times we had.

Cow Milking and Homemade Toy Making
By Sister Alvina Miller, O.P. of Great Bend, Kansas
Born 1918

Peasant farmers were common in the 1900s, and many came from the Volga German area in Russia. My paternal grandparents were born in Russia. My mother's entire family was born in Russia. Some came in the 1800s, others in the 1900s. Adam and Albina Miller came from Russia and settled in Catherine, Kansas. They were married in there in 1915. A few years later, they moved to a farm given to them by their grandfather who was a homesteader. He had bought much land for $5.00 an acre. Each of the children received a piece of land when they married.

Adam and Albina were farmers. Before moving to the farm, they build a house and other buildings needed for the animals. The four-roomed house was home for them many years. It was also, where they raised their children. The children were born at home. The doctor came from Victoria and delivered the children. All kinds of animals were gotten for the farm—cows, horses, pigs, chickens, ducks, and turkeys. These were needed for the family to make a living. Turkeys in particular always built their nests in hiding. Then, some weeks later, they came home with a new family of little turkeys.

The milking of the cows was done by hand. It was then brought to the milk house where it was separated. The separator had a large tank on top that held the milk. The cream and milk were separated by centrifugal force. To get the right thickness of the cream, the turning of the handle fast or slow determined the result. All of the equipment had to be washed after every milking, morning and evening.

Farmers planted mostly wheat, for that was what was sold to get money for making a living. When harvest time came, usually in June, the wheat was cut and thrown into a header box. Then it was carried to a certain place where it was stacked until August. Then it was threshed. Grandfather Jacob Mueller and his sons went from one farm to another and threshed the wheat. There were 12 children, so it really helped when the brothers worked together. Adam then took a load of wheat in a wagon drawn by horses to Victoria. That was a 14-mile trip and took almost all day. When dad returned, he usually brought a sack of candy that cost 5 cents.

There was no indoor plumbing, so water had to be carried from the windmill to the house. Some was put in the large reservoir at the end of the large coal cook stove. It was used for washing dishes. In the summer, a three-burner kerosene stove was used. Laundry soap was made with the scraps of fat left over after the butchering. When the butchering was done, Adam made three kinds of sausage—blood sausage, liver sausage, and beef and pork mixed sausage. The casings used were the intestine of the pigs. They were cleaned and used for stuffing the sausage. Nothing was thrown away—the kidneys, heart, liver, and everything else was used.

Beer was made at home with hops that were grown in the garden. The malt was bought. A capper was used to cap the bottles. Mother canned meat and also put some in a large crock barrel poured lard over it. It kept for a long time. The bacon and hams were soaked in saltwater for a length of time and then smoked and wrapped with cloth and newspaper. They were then hung in the hayloft of the barn. They could be used anytime we needed them. They were very tasty compared to what we have today.

The family had no car, so we went to church on Sundays with a buggy drawn by a horse. Of course, it was very cold at times. One time on the way home, which was four miles, the horse fell on the ice at the bottom of the hill. That scared me so much that ever after, Mother held her hand over my eyes when we arrived.

The children made their own games. Chinese checkers was one. It was made with a large cardboard with the lines drawn. Buttons were used instead of marbles. In the summer, we made our own horse toy from the bones of the animals and a large empty can of sardines.

There was a small house next to the windmill. On the top was a large water tank. Inside the house was a large tank that held water in which we kept our cream, milk, and butter, and other things that needed to be cooled. The water came from the well, into the tank, and flowed out the other end into the garden.

There were embarrassing times. My parents had gone to town while we were in school. Some girls tempted us to use lipstick, which was forbidden at home. We came home, and in a short time, my parents arrived early and caught us. We were told never to do it again. That was a no-no.

Our little country church was torn down. There had been around fifty families. We worshipped every Sunday with the Holy sacrifice of the Mass. At 2:00 in the afternoon, we sang Vespers.

The farm was sold and all the buildings were torn down. In my mind and heart, it was a great loss because that was the home of my childhood. Another memory that stayed in my mind was when my aunt Rose Miller died. She was in her twenties and was laid out in our home until the funeral. I remember Grandpa was out in the yard and I heard him cry aloud at the loss of a young daughter who had one small child, Leota. My parents raised her, so we grew up like sisters.

I never had a sweetheart because at an early age I decided to become a Dominican Sister in Great Bend. I attribute this wonderful grace to the prayers of my mother when she was rearing me. She asked God for a special grace for me. This has been a most wonderful life for me. Nothing ever could have taken its place.

Growing Up in Protection
By Lavon Wiersig of Alva, Oklahoma
Born 1941

Country life in Kansas was a good life in the '50s. I have many good memories growing up as a farm girl nine and a half miles southwest of the small town of Protection, Kansas. We had five miles of dirt road. We kept

Lavon and Lavona Hazen (twins) in 1944

those roads busy going to school and church activities. School activities I was involved in were band, pep band, vocal groups, Kayettes, speech plays, junior and senior class plays, football and basketball games, and track, along with school dances and parties. I am a 1959 graduate of PHS.

Our family sometimes made trips to Dodge City, Woodward, Pratt, and Hutchinson to shop for special things we needed. We built a new home and moved into it in 1951 when I was in fourth grade. Our house was built on a hill, so we could see far away. I remember looking out our living room window and watching storms, and even tornadoes. We were glad we had a basement to go to.

It was so much fun having family gatherings in our new country home. I had older siblings Eugene, Irene, Lila, Melva and my twin sister Lavona, One brother, Ora Lee, age 15, was a sophomore at PHS when he died of ruptured appendicitis in 1945. Our family would come home for holidays and other special times. It was a happy time playing with nieces and nephews. Our house was often filled with good food, laughter, and fun. Melva was a junior when we moved into our new house. She soon went away to college.

Lavona and I had farm chores to do when we got home from school. We gathered eggs and watered the chickens. We were sometimes reluctant to reach under the hens on the nest to get the eggs, as one time we encountered a big bull snake in the nest. That scared the wits out of us! We also had a rooster that knew

Lavon and Lavona Hazen in 1947 at the farm

we were fearful of him, and he chased us! I remember the excitement of finding those larger speckled eggs, which the hens sat under. It took 21 to 28 days for baby turkeys to hatch. Lavona and I also walked down the pasture to bring in the cows for milking. One time we tried to help our daddy out so he could take us to a school activity. We were hand-milking Betsy the cow and were so proud! We had almost a bucket of milk when the cow kicked the whole bucket over! Our hearts were sad but our daddy understood and we got to town early.

In the summer, we helped with wheat harvest. We had a large garden and we still made time for softball practices and games in town. One summer my sister and I filled our pails full so we wouldn't have to make so many trips from the well to the chicken houses. That may have been the reason both of us had appendectomies that summer! We both had broken arms earlier in our lives. I had fallen off a table and Lavona fell from a tree.

Daddy shipped cattle to Kansas City by rail and Mother, Lavona and I got to go with him by train to the big city. We would get on the train at Pratt. That was a big highlight for us to ride on a train and to see the sights of a large city. Daddy would go to the stockyards while the rest of us shopped. Our parents made sure we got to do something special in the evenings. We attended a Kansas City ball game and we even saw an opera. Staying in a big hotel and eating in a large cafeteria were big things to us, being from a small rural town.

Living in a small town, we made our own entertainment; it was fun. When I was in high school, we would have dinner parties and invite dates. I remember Lavona and I planned the menu for a meal and our mother would prepare the food. She was a wonderful cook. Lavona and I set the tables and made centerpieces. After the meal, we would visit and play games. We had parties at many houses of friends. We often entertained friends and had dances in the basement of our house. One Saturday, we invited a group of girls and our sixth grade teacher Miss Bernice Anderson out to the farm to ride horses. Mother made a good lunch for all of us. We also attended movies in Protection, Coldwater, and Ashland.

Lavona and I rode the school bus. We were the first ones to be picked up at 7:30 in the morning and last off at 4:00 or a little later. There were times when we got to stay in town after school until Mother picked us up. Our favorite place to go for a drink was Jones Drug Store where we could get a coke for 15 cents and a candy bar for five cents. Now that was a real treat! Paul Edmonston was our school bus driver for many years. Sometimes my mother would have wonderful homemade cinnamon rolls ready when we got home from school. She would often come out and share some with our bus driver, too.

We had an unexpected school bus sleepover in the early '50s. A heavy snow was falling when our school bus began taking children home from school. When we got to the house at the first bus stop, the snow was coming down heavier with blinding wind and drifting. Our bus driver made the decision that we all unload at that house. There were 15 to 20 kids on the bus. Our parents were notified that we would spend the night at Jim and Leona Williams' house. They had three daughters, Kala, Sharon, and Vicky. What a surprise that must have been for that family of five when all of us unloaded to spend the night with them! They graciously made us all feel as comfortable as possible. There was no electricity, so blankets were used to keep us warm. Mrs. Williams made us all supper. That night we played games and we gathered around their piano while

Leona played and we all sang. It was a noisy household, but fun and comfy, Mrs. Williams gave us girls gowns to sleep in. We slept all over the floor. Breakfast was made for us the following morning. We were happy when we learned the roads were cleared for us to go on that morning. That was a night I shall never forget. I'm sure the Williams family was also thankful when they could resume their normal life without a noisy busload of kids.

I graduated from NWOSU in Alva, Oklahoma with a teaching degree in 1963. I received a call from a former Protection superintendent in Garden City, Mr. George Cushman, asking if I would be interested in teaching there. He knew my older siblings and family, but I didn't know him. I felt it was an honor to be asked by someone who had ties to Protection, Kansas. I found out that my fifth grade teacher Miss Clara Thielan was also a teacher there. I taught in Garden City three years and had a special bond with these people. It was a nice experience for me teaching there and being around former Protection residents. I married a boy from Alva, Oklahoma and that is where we have lived since moving from Garden City. I taught a total of 37 years in Kansas and in Alva.

Farm life and living near Protection was a wonderful experience for me and I wouldn't trade it for anything. We had a good home life, good schools, and fine teachers. All these things helped build a strong foundation for my success later in life.

Dancing with Doorknobs
By Jackie Carol Smith-Lamkin of
Hutchinson, Kansas
Born 1950

I always tried to get my dad to write down his stories for me, as some of them were quite funny. One story he used to tell involved his older brother, Wally. They were visiting my Great-aunt Alma in her home, and she used to raise chickens. She asked them to go outside and get a chicken for dinner. She sent them both out with a big knife to get this chicken. She stood in the doorway watching. They caught the chicken, and since Uncle Wally was three years older than my dad, he was wielding the knife and Dad was holding the chicken. According to Dad, a man was driving by in his car and stopped. He yelled, "Stop! You boys are murdering that poor chicken!" Uncle Wally was sawing with the knife instead of chopping! The man got out of the car, chopped off the poor bird's head, and said, "You're welcome!"

Then there was the time that my grandparents put the kids in the car and drove to my Great-uncle Frank and Aunt Flossie's house for Sunday dinner. When they got there, no one was home, so Grandpa went out and killed two chickens himself. Back home they went. Later, Uncle Frank called and said, "Why didn't you go on in? We had dinner waiting for you. We had to go somewhere quick."

I can also remember that my grandpa

Lavon and Lavona Hazen in 1958

would always tell me that to get rid of moles on your skin you should coat them with rancid linseed oil. That would cause them to dry up and fall off. I always asked him how old linseed oil had to be to be rancid. I remember that my Grandma Bertha Lee told me that one day I would grow up and marry Elvis. I would cry and cry and tell her, "But Grandma! I don't want to marry Elvis!" I also remember watching American Bandstand on Saturdays and, as no one would dance with me, I would dance with the front doorknob!

I still remember the very last spanking I ever got. I was in the sixth grade and in the girl scouts. I told my parents I wasn't going to the meeting that day, but changed my mind and didn't call to inform them. Believe me—after that spanking, I always remembered to call. My daughter, who is now 44 years old, still calls me right before she comes to Kansas and right as she gets back to Texas.

I was in grade school when Barbie came onto the scene, I can remember the clothes were very pricey. Mom and Aunt Thelma made me a lot of clothes for my Barbie. They were actually pretty cool clothes—better than the store-bought ones!

I remember in junior high at Central Junior High I made the mistake one day of telling my friends that I liked pickled beets, as the school was serving them that day. By the end of lunch, I must have had over 100 pickled beets on my tray, as all the kids in my class walked by and deposited their beets on my tray. I can remember saying, "Okay guys. I can handle a few, but this is really stupid!"

I remember a dream that I used to have quite often. My neighbors had a dog named Sport. He was pretty old, and I remember in this dream he was chasing me up the street. I would run and then jump really high. When I would come back down, he would catch up again, so I would run really fast and jump really high. This went on three or four times, and then I would be home. I don't really recall Sport ever chasing me at all. I don't know what that dream meant!

As my dad was a fireman, I can remember going to the station and getting to slide down the fire poles with him. I would also get to play volleyball with the firemen. What a great time! Being a kid in Hutchinson was pretty great most of the time!

The Memories Branded into my Soul
By Jeanette Elder of Garden City, Kansas
Born 1934

On June 2, 1934, two tiny baby girls were born in the little town of Leoti, Wichita County, Kansas during the height of the "dirty thirties" to a young couple, Thomas Albert and Mary Ellen (Langley) Askey. What a shock this was to them, as they were expecting another large 11 ½ pound baby boy like their big brother Raymond. Instead, they got a six pound baby girl, Jeanette LoVonne, and a five and a half pound baby girl, Jean LaVerne. These twins were born at home, as this was the custom at that time. Dr. Nowell delivered the babies. My Daddy was co-owner of the Askey-Turner Garage in Leoti, and Daddy worked on the doctor's car to pay for our delivery. That was the bartering system in those hard times. My daddy's mother, Lena (Diem) Askey assisted the doctor as a midwife, as she had helped with births in the past. After everyone quieted down from the shock of twins, the doctor asked the family if there were any twins in the family. My mama said she had twin cousins. At last, my grandmother Askey said, "Tommy, you had twin brothers who died at birth." What a shock, as he had never been told about this. My grandmother Askey was a very quiet woman.

Mama had to hang wet sheets on the windows to keep the dust out. The dust in Kansas made Jean very sick, and so Daddy realized that he had to get us out of the dust storms for Jean to survive. Daddy got a job in Peoria, Illinois with Avery Farm Equipment and moved us east. Later we moved to Shelbyville, Indiana. Daddy worked as a lathe operator in a defense factory. In the middle of the 1940s, we moved back to the Langley Ranch and Farm 18 miles northwest of Leoti, Kansas. The Langley Farm was the Homestead of Malachi and Ellen Clara (Goodchild) Langley. Malachi was from Chippingham, England and Ellen Clara was from Moulton, England.

Ray, Jean, and I attended Jumbo School. How the school got the name of Jumbo, I'll never know. This was a one-room school, and our teacher was Miss Marita Snowbarger. Ray was in the eighth grade, Jean was in the fourth, and I was in the fifth. What a shock coming back from Shelbyville, Indiana to use an outhouse! The kids at school thought I talked funny. I guess it was my Hoosier accent! My Aunt Anna had also taught in a one-room schoolhouse in Wichita County, Kansas, and her favorite story was of her toilet paper disappearing so quickly from the boys' outhouse. The culprit was finally caught when he came back from the outhouse trailing toilet paper across the room of the schoolhouse. The kids weren't even scolded when they all laughed. No more extra loss of toilet paper! The other shock I got was seeing a horse stable in the schoolhouse yard. The stable was no longer used, as this was the 1940s. Now the older kids got drivers permits to drive "Old Clunkers" to school!

Miss Marita was fresh at the job, and so she allowed us kids to ice skate and sled on Buffalo Wallow that iced over in the winter. We also ran out during school when a B29 Bomber flew over! We also learned a bible verse each day. I still remember John 3:16: "For God so loved the world that he gave his only begotten son that whosoever shall believe in him shall not parish but have everlasting life." Can you imagine that today? Heaven forbid! All of us drank out of the same cup from water in a crockery jug, and none of us died from some dreaded disease!

At recess, the boys played jack knife, marbles, and baseball. No one got fatally injured! The girls played jacks, jump rope, and baseball. In the winter, we played fox and geese and made snow angels. My first love was a boy who was two years older than me. His name was Charles Brown. He used to leave notes to me in an empty lipstick tube hidden in the stable. On one note, he drew a picture of an ocean. It was signed "With oceans of Gurgle Gurgle" (you know what) Charles. He also gave me a box of chocolates with my valentine, Wow!

We took a lunchbox to school. One day Jean and I forgot our lunches, so Mama got in the car to catch us and give us our lunches. I was driving that day, and Jean said, "The Brown kids are behind us," so I floored the gas pedal. (Daddy had put a governor on the engine to slow it down.) When we got up to our 40 mph top speed, the car was weaving back and forth on the dirt and sand road, and the car behind us couldn't pass us. Lo and behold, when we got stopped in the schoolyard, it was Mama screaming at us in our families maroon-colored car! She handed Jean our lunches. I am sure she was not a happy camper on her drive back home. Besides teasing me about my Hoosier accent, the kids couldn't understand that I didn't know what a garden hose was. We had plenty of rain in Illinois and Indiana, so we had no use for a garden hose.

Jumbo School students in 1948

My next one-room school teacher at Jumbo school was Mrs. Ann Schrader. What a change! No going out to play except at recess. Where was her sense of things that made all of us students happy? Nonetheless, she was the best grade school teacher I ever had. We learned our lessons well. At recess, she taught us girls to knit. I never got past the potholder stage. Mrs. Schrader was an expert knitter. She made sweaters, gloves, scarves, socks and baby blankets, which were all very beautiful. I'll never forget my part in the Christmas play we put on when I was in the eighth grade. There were not enough boys, so I played a boys part! I was Ben and Ella Brown was Em. I had my long hair under a hat and wore men's clothing. My line was, "Here Em, have a piece of hoar-hound candy." The crowd roared! Yay!

Oh how I hated to get up in the winter. I had so many blankets piled on me to keep me warm that I couldn't even turn over! We had a water bucket to drink out of, and many mornings it was frozen over. I had a chamber pot in my room, but had to run to the outhouse in the mornings. Brrrr.

Like all the other mothers, Mama made our clothes out of chicken feed sacks. None of us felt underprivileged. We had no idea what a clothing brand was. We took eggs to the grocery store to trade in for cash for groceries. Jean and I gathered the eggs. There was always one grouchy hen that pecked us! We dropped our cream can off at the depot to be shipped to Kansas City, Kansas. This money also helped to buy groceries. We also raised a huge garden. Mama canned green beans and tomatoes. She bought Colorado peaches to can. They were yummy, as was her peach butter. Aunt Mable Askey canned beef and made the best beef and noodles I've ever eaten.

Uncle Earnest Langley had a turkey gobbler that chased Jean and I to the house more than once. He called us "City Babies." But it certainly wasn't fun anymore when he was under the hood of a truck and the gobbler hit him in the back hard enough to knock him head first into the engine! He rang the turkey's neck!

My Uncle Fred Askey, like his sister Anna, taught in a one-room school in Wichita County Kansas. Like many other young women, my mama, Mary Ellen Langley, also taught at a one-room school. This was right after she graduated from high school in Leoti, Kansas. During a blizzard in the late 1920s, Mary sent her students home as soon as the storm began. On her way home to the Langley ranch, the blizzard got worse and she couldn't even see where she was going. She ran into a barbed wire fence, grabbed a hold of it, and followed it home. Mary didn't last long as a teacher. A dashing young man, Thomas Albert Askey, came into her life. They fell in love, got married, and she got fired from her teaching job. In those days, it wasn't acceptable to be married and also be a teacher. Her sister Bessie Langley taught at the last sod schoolhouse in Wichita County, Kansas.

So, like an arrow in the night these long forgotten memories have flashed by me once again. It has been so much fun remembering all of them. It is strange that I can't even remember what I went across the room to get now, but like the Lazy L Bar brand of the Langley ranch, these memories are branded inside my very soul. If I listen hard enough, I can even hear my Gram Langley singing "Daisy, Daisy" in her sweet English voice echo across the Kansas prairie.

Snowstorm 1948
By Joan Goering of Hutchinson, Kansas
Born 1928

Glen W. Goering

Glen played the clarinet in high school band. The week after graduation, that would change forever. World War II was being fought. Many able-bodied men were gone, and Glen was helping the neighboring farmer with wheat harvest. In those days, that involved two machines—the combine, and then the tractor to pull it. Glen's job was to ride on the combine to put it in gear and to raise or lower the platform to conform to the terrain.

Machines did not have many of the safety features required today. When the combine unexpectedly went into a badger hole, Glen grabbed at whatever he could to keep from being thrown off. That, unfortunately, was the sprocket chain of the combine. His hand was badly mangled. He was rushed to Hutchinson where his hand was put in a cast and packed with Sulfa. The "wonder drugs" were just being developed, and so penicillin was not yet available. In five weeks, the cast was removed. The hand was healing, but his clarinet playing days were over. He no longer had enough fingers to cover the holes.

The healing of his hand continued over the next year, but Glen was very self-conscious about it. He kept his hand in his pocket most of the time. Friends joked with him to help him to accept his problem. "Just think how much time you're going to save the rest of your life without those fingernails to clean!"

The war was continuing. Glen needed something to do. He worked at several things and did well, but saw no future in them. His mother, always looking out for him, got him interested in teaching school. Teachers were needed and were in short supply. Glen went two quarters at Bethel College and got a provisional certificate. He was hired as the teacher at Wolf Creek School, in rural Inman, a one-room school. He taught eight grades and 16 students.

Being teacher at a one-room school is an overwhelming responsibility. Glen enjoyed it but felt inadequate. He taught at Wolf Creek two years and then took a job as seventh grade math teacher and coach at Hugoton in far southwest Kansas. He would have 50 students in his homeroom. What a change! Hugoton was a wealthy school district, being the center of a large natural gas field. Pipelines extended from southwest Kansas all over the nation. People here were either gas or pipeline workers, wheat farmers with large acreages, or people working for them supporting the agricultural economy in some way.

Glen had two college friends teaching at Moscow, about ten miles from Hugoton. He had gone by train to visit them, so he had an idea what this wide-open, flat, treeless country was like. It was 200 miles from home and that girl he had met in summer school and planned to marry. His car was getting unreliable. He had hitchhiked out to Hugoton for his job interview. In order to supplement his income and get that car he needed, he also took on the job of a school bus driver. Every morning at 7:00, he would run the 31-mile route over roads that were for the most part through large wheat fields. There were no fences and no ditches, just wide-open country dotted here and there with a farmhouse.

On Monday morning, Glen and his two buddies had met at Liberal and, as was usually the case, had spent the night visiting. They could talk for hours. They really hadn't planned it that way, but they never got back 'til the morning. Glen got in his bus wearing the sports coat he had worn the night before. It was getting cold, the skies looked ominous, and snow started falling.

At his first stop, the parents, worried about the weather, would not let their children get on. The snow was really coming down now. At the next stop, again the children were not allowed on the bus. Glen called in from there to ask the Principal whether he should go on. He was told to run his route as usual. "Go on, you Sissy." Glen went on. Soon he was in whiteout conditions, never really sure if he was on a road since there were no ditches or fences as guides. Finally, the bus simply drowned out in a snowdrift.

Here he was alone. He was glad those parents had kept their children home. He had been told for safety's sake never to leave the bus, but he knew he could never stick it out alone. Surely, he could find a farmhouse nearby. So out he went into a nightmare of snow. He went on and on into the blinding snow. He was not finding anyone, anything, and no shelter. He was not dressed for this. His face and hands were freezing. He had to find shelter. Then the wind let up just a bit. It looked like a building ahead, but maybe he was just imagining it. He stumbled to it and pounded with his arms. They were so frozen that he didn't feel it, but he knew it was solid. He had found something. A young man came around the corner and helped him inside.

It was a little one-room shack, about ten by twelve. On one side of the room was a bed. On another wall was a gas cooking stove, which provided the only heat in the place. It was cold inside, but he was out of the wind and the snow. Living here were the Dugans, a young couple, kids really, only 13 and 14, and their baby boy. The only other occupant of the room was a pet rooster, which was in the corner of the room, but he had the run of the place. The couple had come from Arkansas and were allowed to live here since the young man was working for one of the big wheat farmers.

Glen had found help when he needed it, but these people needed his also. He was the older, experienced person they could rely on, and that gas stove was a problem. It was connected directly to the gas well outside. That meant the occupants of the shack had to be constantly alert because the wells often would freeze off and then come back on. If not taken care of, they might be asphyxiated. Someone had to watch the stove all the time. Now there were three to share the watch. There was no place to sit but on the bed. As Glen thawed out, they sat and talked. Each one took a turn watching the stove while the other two rested. There weren't enough blankets to really keep warm so two would stay together with the baby, little Johnny, sharing their warmth while the other watched the stove.

The storm blasted on through that day and night. There was no food and no milk for the baby. They had some flour. They mixed some with water to feed the baby. The next day the storm continued on and on. They were exhausted and hungry. The old pet rooster was sacrificed so they could have something to eat. Glen took a drumstick. It was so tough he could hardly bite into it, so he threw it under the bed.

Glen told story after story to pass the time. Finally, the third day dawned, cold and clear. Glen was so hungry that he found that drumstick he had thrown under the bed and gnawed at it. Baby Johnny was getting along with his flour water better than any of the adults.

They thought they heard something. Glen looked out. There from Panhandle Eastern, the pipeline company was a truck. The men were working their way toward them. The crew would stop occasionally to probe the snowdrifts with pitchforks. When they reached the shack, one of the men said they didn't know there had been a shack built there or that anyone was living there. Glen asked if all the schoolchildren were safe. He replied, "Yes, but we lost a school teacher." "No, you didn't." Glen identified himself and the crew radioed in the news that he had been found. He was two miles from the abandoned school bus. "These people are out of food and there is no milk for the baby."

After Glen was delivered back into town, they brought back sacks of groceries to the Dugans as well as the overcoat Mr. Dugan had sent with Glen. The principal who three days before had insisted Glen continue his route was in tears because he was so glad to see him.

Some valuable lessons were learned. Years afterward, whenever there was a question of whether to call off school because of the weather, Glen would ask the experienced bus drivers. They always seemed to know. The next summer Glen married and he and his bride spent their first year together at Hugoton.

Two years later, Glen read in the Hutchinson News that John Dugan of Hugoton was in the polio ward at Grace Hospital. John Dugan of Hugoton? It had to be little Johnny. He knew about that polio ward. He had visited it many times years before when his mother had polio. Families were not allowed in the ward, but you went around to the courtyard on the east side and you could visit through the open windows.

Glen drove into Hutchinson, and sure enough, there were the Dugans. As usual, down on their luck, they hadn't eaten in two days. This time it was Glen's turn to come to the rescue. He saw to it that they had food and money for their future needs. "After all, they had next to nothing but what they had they shared with me."

Little Johnny recovered and the Dugans moved back to Arkansas. Glen kept track of them for several years. Oh, yes, The Dugans added to their family. They had a little girl. They called her Glenna.

Covered Wagons and School Paddles
By Ralph E. Nutter, Sr. of Valley Center, Kansas
Born 1917

I was born three miles North of Protection, Kansas in 1917. While I was still a toddler, we moved to a place about three miles south of Coldwater, Kansas. While we were living there, Mom raised a lot of chickens. One day a rainstorm came up and my sister, brother, and Mom were trying to get the chicks in the hen house before any harm came to them. There was a lot of standing water in the barnyard at the time. Lightning struck and knocked my sister down. My brother got to her and carried her to the house. I remember her legs turning black from the knees down. Mom had her set by the stove and put her feet in the reservoir of warm water on the stove.

Poppa went to town one day and bought a .410 gauge single shot shotgun that used the short two and a half inch shells. Mom needed the gun to protect her chickens from chicken hawks, which were getting to her chickens. She shot a chicken hawk out of the air with this little gun, which was quite a shot.

One day Poppa and Mom were gone and my oldest sister and I were at home. (She was 18 years older than me.) I got into a cupboard that I was not supposed to be in and found a pretty bottle. The bottle was so pretty that I drank some of it. The contents turned out to be iodine. It scared my sister when she realized what I had done. She knew she needed to do something. Mom sold milk and cream in those days, so she got into the cooler where the milk and cream were kept and made me drink a lot of cream. The doctor said it saved my life.

We moved from this place to a farm just north of Douglas, Kansas when I was about five years old in five or six covered wagons.

Ralph Nutter in 1919

We took turns walking, riding, and driving the cattle. At night, we slept in the wagons. Mom's wagon was the lead wagon and had all the food in it. Mom stayed with the food wagon because she didn't want us kids to piece on it. We stopped in the city of Kingman for about a month and then headed on for Douglas. Poppa had bought Mom a nice piano, but the rain ruined it on the way so we left it behind. I don't remember where we left it. My oldest sister was the only one in the family that could play the piano. Poppa and my brother could play the violin. I played the guitar and violin. None of us could read music, we played by ear only.

Sometime after unloading the piano, we made a stop at Riverdale, Kansas. It had rained and rained, so we stayed at the grain elevator waiting for the rain to clear up. We ran out of food, so Poppa went to Wellington, Kansas to buy more groceries. Just before reaching Douglas, we had to ford the Walnut River. One of the wagons got stuck in the river and we had quite a time getting it out. The water was probably about one or two feet deep at the place where we were crossing.

One of the things I remember from our days at the Douglas Place is that Poppa built a croquet field down in the draw. We would all go down there to play croquet. We rented the farm, and so when the owner sold it we had to move. We moved quite a bit. We moved to another place North of Douglas on Highway 77, one block from school. I was in the fourth grade when we lived there. We then moved four miles south of Augusta to another rented farm. We stayed there for several years.

The farmland that Poppa was working had a lot of oil wells on it. In those days, the oil wells had engine houses and huge water tanks used to keep the engines cool. I learned to swim in those water tanks. I went with some of my cousins to play in the water tanks. As everyone was swimming, I was just going around the edge holding on to the edge and not venturing in farther. Two of my cousins watching me do this said "You are going to learn to swim today." The two of them picked me up and threw me out to the middle of the tank, and then made sure they moved away from my reach. They told me to swim! I splashed around and kicked until I finally figured out how to move in the water and was able to get back to the side of the tank. I was probably ten years old or so. I was able to swim from then on. The water in those tanks was always warm because it circulated through the engines and back into the tanks.

When we lived south of Augusta, I went to a four-room school in a place called Brown Town. The school had four rooms with one teacher and two grades per room and a gymnasium. I had five older sisters and I was spoiled. I would pout at home; it worked on my sisters. One time at school, I was trying this and the teacher came up to me and put her arm around me to console me. I shoved back in the chair causing the teachers arm to hit the back of the chair, breaking her watch all to pieces. She did not blame me; she said it was her fault.

I managed to get the class into trouble once because of a paper wad. The teacher was writing on the blackboard with her back to the class. I put a paper wad in a rubber band and shot it. It went right past the teacher's head, grazing her in the process, and then bounced off the blackboard. I ducked my head down like I was studying something; the teacher turned and asked "Who threw the paper wad?" No one said anything, but the whole

Ralph and his bride of 59 years, Iona Mulkey, in 1940

class turned and looked at me. I remember that everyone had to take tests the rest of the day because of me.

I also got my first and only spanking in school while there. I was spanked for sassing the teacher. I don't remember what I said; I just remember it was for sassing. The teacher took me to the gym and had me bend over one of the bars around the edge of the gym between where the spectators and players would sit. Then she swatted me three times with a paddle. I could hardly sit in the seat when I got back to the classroom. I never did anything to get a spanking again.

Another thing I remember at this school happened at lunchtime. The teacher was gone for some reason and all of us were eating our sack lunches in the classroom. We knew the teacher kept her paddle in a desk drawer. It was a wooden paddle about 18 inches long with holes drilled in it. It was made for her by a high school kid. We all had pocket knives, and while the teacher was gone we took our knives and all took a turn cutting and slicing the paddle up, leaving the splintered pieces in her drawer for her to find. I don't remember her finding it or what the punishment might have been.

We moved two miles west of Valley Center while I was still in the seventh grade. Poppa had a work/saddle horse that he bought from a rancher. It had been trained to work cattle. One day the cows had gotten out and I hopped on the horse bareback to go after them. As I was bringing the cattle back, one of them decided to take off on its own. Since that horse was trained on a cattle ranch, he took out after the stray. Because I had jumped on bareback, it was all I could do to stay on as that horse worked the cattle. The horse ended up getting all of them back home. I managed to stay on his back, somehow.

My older brother worked in Ellinwood in the oil fields. He had me come up and go to work in the fields with him as a roustabout. During my days as a roustabout in Ellinwood, the crew I was working on was asked to go work on a rig North of Claflin. It was wintertime and the temperature was negative six degrees Fahrenheit. We worked through the night, and it was one of the most miserable nights I ever spent on any job. We were pulling the casing on the rig we were working on. Our hands would get wet, and in those cold temperatures, the water would freeze on our gloves really fast. We would spend about 15 minutes working, pulling the casing, and then we would have to go in and stand around the stove until our gloves thawed and we warmed up a little. Our crew traded off all night—outside 15 minutes and then back inside for 15.

Another time I was painting oil derricks. I would climb the derrick about 85 feet in

Ralph with a restored tractor in 2007

the air. I would hang on to the bucket and the derrick with one hand while I painted with the other. I was thrilled to be finished with that job.

I have lived all my life in Kansas. I am a retired Cessna Aircraft worker and live close to two of my children, with the third just a 40-minute drive away.

Pepper Takes the Cake
By Melody Elsworth of Pretty Prairie, Kansas
Born 1953

One afternoon, my mother had just finished all the dishes from lunch and baking three Bundt cakes. Two were for a funeral dinner the next day. My dad came in from working at the sale barn. He wanted to lay down on the divan and watch TV and rest. Mom came out and told him she had baked three cakes and they were cooling on the kitchen counter. She was going to get her hair done at the beauty shop, get a few groceries, and then come home, unload the groceries, glaze the cakes, and then they would get ready to go to the funeral home for visitation. She would be home in two hours.

Pepper, our Dalmatian, followed my dad in the house. Mom tried to get him to go outside, which he didn't want to do. It was 92 degrees outside. My dad told my mom, "Leave him alone. He's not hurting a thing. It is hot and we need to rest." Again, Mom told Dad about the cakes that were cooling and to keep the door shut that led to the kitchen. She then left to do her errands.

My dad and Pepper climbed up on the couch and took a nap. Sometime later, my dad got up to go to the bathroom. When he returned to the divan, he forgot to close the door that led to the kitchen. He got back onto the divan with Pepper. Soon, my dad was in a deep sleep. Pepper smelled the cakes cooling and decided to go investigate the kitchen. He helped himself to the cakes, and then returned to the divan with a content belly.

When Mom drove in an hour later and opened the door, she found my dad and Pepper asleep. The door to the kitchen was open and on the floor was a big cake mess. She then yelled and Dad woke up and said, "What did you want, Wilma?"

Our Dog Pepper
The year was 1970. Our childhood Dalmatian had died of old age the year before. My mom made it clear that we were not getting another dog. One night, my dad came home from Southern Kansas with a Dalmatian dog and a black eye. His story was that he was loading cattle and pulled the gate back too fast and it hit him in the face. The auctioneer took my dad home to "doctor" his eye. The auctioneer had this Dalmatian that took a liking to my dad, so he gave him to my dad.

Well, my mother was not happy and she knew that his story wasn't completely true. So the next week my mom went with my dad back to the auction barn and got the real story. My dad had gotten drunk and got into a fight. That is how he ended up with the black eye. The auctioneer took him home to sober up. While he was sobering up, my dad asked about the Dalmatian. His name was Pepper. The auctioneer's wife was a beautician, and she had remodeled their beauty shop with a black and white interior. She had black sinks and white counters, and her floor was black and white. Her scrubs were black and white. Her car was white, and the auctioneer had a black truck. This was the only reason that she had gotten a black and white dog—the Dalmatian.

Dalmatians always follow moving vehicles; that is why they are the firemen's mascots. Pepper would see kids riding their bikes and he would take off and follow them into town. Then they would have to go look for him. He wouldn't stay home. Howard decided to have the vet castrate the dog to see if this would help. It just made him do silly things, and he still followed the kids on the bikes. My dad told Howard, "I'll tell you what. I'll trade you a cow and a calf for that dog. Howard knew his wife Ida would be mad, but for a cow and calf, she could get over it.

When my mom and Ida got together, they were ready to keep the dog and get rid of the husbands! Mom told Ida to come with Howard to our sale the next week and she could take Pepper home. When they came to our house and saw how content Pepper was to be around kids, she said, "I just can't do that." Pepper stayed on our lambing porch and went everywhere with my dad or with us kids. He was getting a lot of attention and never ran away.

A few years later, my younger sister Traci decided she was going to take Pepper as her 4-H project. Whenever Pepper saw me take a bridle out, he knew I was going to ride my horse. He would follow me all over the pasture. As Traci worked with him to sit, stay, and lay, I always had to stay away because he would think I was going to ride my horse.

As time got closer for the 4-H fair, Traci kept working with him. He was really obeying her very well. The day of the dog judging, I didn't go to the fair. I knew it would ruin her hard work. Traci and Pepper went along and were doing very well. He kept his tail up and was very obedient. Then the judge came and announced, "We are going to do breeding for our last part of the show. I will pick the two top dogs." Mom went over to Traci and told her that this was it for them. She told her to just step out of the judging. She and Pepper did a fine job, but Pepper was neutered, and so they would be out.

The lady judge came up to Traci and told her to get back in line, so Traci and Pepper obliged. She then moved them closer to the front. She came up to Pepper and began feeling and rubbing him, checking his muscles conformation. Then she moved him closer. Mom and Dad just looked at each other. What was she doing? Another judge came up to Traci and asked her if her dog was intact. Traci didn't know what he meant, so she said, "He looks okay to me." The judge just snickered and walked off.

The lady judge soon had Pepper and another dog at the front. It was a little late in the competition by now for the K-State judge to change her mind in front of everyone. They gave two grand champion trophies, one for the overall grand champion and one for obedience. Never before had that happened. It was supposed to be Grand Champion and Reserve Grand Champion. Of course, Traci didn't go on to the state fair to compete. We and everyone in town had a good laugh over the lady judge from K-State.

Don't Get Cheated!

I was a substitute teacher for the third grade a few times two years ago. We had fun. The only problem that we came across was the fact that the whole class could not figure out how to multiply! They could divide, but they struggled learning their multiplication tables. To help them out, I told them a true story about when I was in the third grade with my brother. This is the story:

"Our dad was an auctioneer and owned and operated a livestock auction barn in the 1960s. At the beginning of school, we were learning our multiplication tables just like you're doing now," I told them. "The first of October, the sale schedule turned to daytime, starting at lunch. The whole morning, farmers would come in and bring their livestock. From 10:00 AM until 1:30 PM, the lady that operated the café was busier than a one-armed paperhanger. She would make a dinner for the week, usually homemade chicken and noodles, roast beef dinners, etc. it was similar to hot lunches at school. Then she'd serve pie for 15 cents per slice. They were wonderful. A lot of Dad's customers said they mainly came for the meals. The lady worked at the Catholic school as a cook. Life was good until the sales turned into day sales.

My brother would come home from school, head to the auction barn, and start pestering Mom for money to get something to eat and wanting to help. The lady that ran the restaurant told my brother, "I've got a job for you." She went to the storage area and took out two wooden cases, set them on the seats, and said, "See all those pop bottles people have drank out of? They are setting on all of those seats. If you will go pick them up and put them in these cases, I will give you a big piece of pie." My brother jumped at the chance, and so he went and filled the cases for a piece of pie.

Everything was going good until it got closer to spring. One day my brother brought home one of his friends, Brian. Brian informed him that Miss Rose, who owned the grocery store, paid two cents for a pop bottle. He went around town and picked up bottles and was making a fortune! My brother told him to come with him and he'd show him where pop bottles could be found!

One Saturday, they went all over that barn and picked up four or five cases of bottles. When they turned them in, all they got were two pieces of pie. Brian was mad. "Next week I am taking these bottles to the store," he said. That's where we stopped the story. The class and I did our math. How much were bottles?

Two cents each. How many does a case hold? 24. What is 2 x 24? 48 cents. How much was a piece of pie? 15 cents. So how much should they have gotten paid for the bottles that they had gathered the week before? .48 x 4 = $1.92. .48 x 5 = $2.40."

That is where I ended the story. I told the students that my brother and his friend were taken advantage of, and that I didn't want anyone to take advantage of them in the future. Of course, they wanted the rest of the story. This led to a showdown.

My dad told my brother, "If you can figure that out, do you want to make money or do you want to keep messing around with pop bottles and pie?" My brother said, "I want to make money." My dad told him to be up and dressed on Saturday at 0700. He would take him to the stockyards and show him how to make money. That is how he became involved in the sheep business. My brother is 60 years old and I don't think he has been cheated since!

Carolyn's mother, Hazel in 1951

Growing Up and Growing Old in Kansas
By Carolyn Arpin of Hutchinson, Kansas
Born 1944

I grew up on a farm in Kansas in the '40s and '50s. From dawn to dusk, the farmer and his wife had to endure hard work, but it was very satisfying and rewarding. To a child today it would be considered boring because there were no cell phones, no texting, no computers, video games, etc. We used our imagination and made toys out of whatever we could find that would work. We were one of the last families around to get a television. We would listen to shows on the radio such as Amos & Andy, You Bet Your Life, or The Herb Shriner Show along with listening to music. On Sunday evenings, we would sometimes go to my aunt and uncle's house to watch the Ed Sullivan Show. I remember I was always envious of all of my cousins because they had a nicer house than we did and had a television.

In my early childhood years, we had no running water. Therefore, we had an "outhouse" and took our Saturday night baths in a galvanized tub in the kitchen. By the time I was in grade school, we had running water but we still didn't have an indoor bathroom. I can remember the outdoor shower that my Dad rigged up for us. It was wooden and three-sided. He put a big barrel on the top. We would take a garden hose and fill it with water. After being in the sun all day, we would have hot water for a refreshing, relaxing shower at the end of the day.

Farming then was much different than it is today. With the huge machines today they can cover more ground in a half an hour than it took back then in one sweat-stained day. My dad was a crop farmer. His days were long because he would farm for the day then work the evening shift in Hutchinson. I remember he would get up early and go to the field before eating breakfast. My mom would fix him something and we would take it to him. One of his favorite things to eat was that I can remember was bacon and peanut butter sandwich. He would take a bite then smile and always say, "Umm, umm! That's good!" Guess that is why I like them to this day!

One of the most exciting and important times in the summer was harvest time. My sister and I would help my mom fix a big

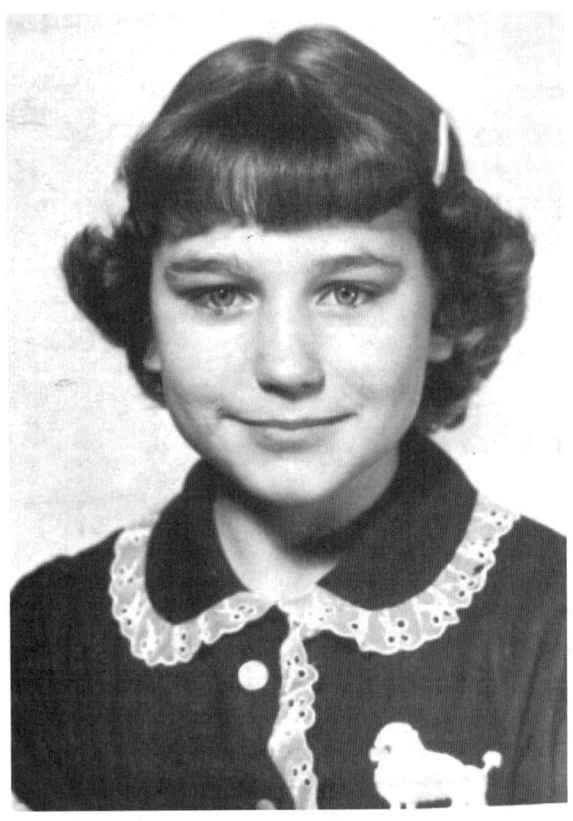

Carolyn at age 10

meal for lunch for my dad, brother, uncle, and his hired help. After eating, my dad would lie down either on the floor or outside under the big oak tree for about a 30 minute nap before going back to the field. In the afternoon, we would take them a snack and either homemade lemonade or iced tea. While they were taking a break, us kids would take our shoes off (if we even had any on) and climb up into the bed of the truck, which was loaded with wheat. We would let the wheat go between our toes, and it felt so good. My Dad would always take a jug of water with him. It was a glass gallon jug and he would wrap a burlap sack around it. He would fill it with cold water and then soak the sack with cold water so it would stay cool until he came in at noon. Then he would soak it down again.

My mother was very busy with all the things that go with being a farmer's wife and a mother. She did our laundry with a Maytag wringer washer and three tubs for rinsing. If you weren't paying attention, the wringer would "eat" your fingers, which I can tell you wasn't much fun. Then, of course, there was no dryer, so everything had to be hung outside on the clothesline. In the winter, the clothes would freeze so stiff that they would stand up on their own. Everything smelled so fresh after drying outside. Back then, it seemed like we ironed everything. We would sprinkle them with water and let them sit for a while. We would then iron them later. If you didn't get to them soon enough they would mildew, so then we'd have to wash them again.

We always had a garden. My mom would can the vegetables and fruit. The house would get pretty hot because we didn't have air conditioning. She made the best applesauce and apple pies from the apples off of our tree. I loved that tree and was always climbing it. She was a very good seamstress. She sewed on the old treadle machine that I learned to sew on. My sister and I never had a store-bought dress until we were in high school. Our dresses were not just simple dresses. She always put extra touches such as many buttons for trim, yards and yards of rickrack, and etc. With the leftover material, she would always make our dolls matching clothes. She also made our flannel pajamas with matching doll pajamas, of course. I still have some of those doll clothes today that she made. And oh, I can't forget those stinky, smelly "Toni" permanents she would give us. The only thing about them that I liked was the paper dolls that came in the package.

My paternal grandparents lived only a quarter of a mile from us. We could see their house from ours. My grandmother was always busy cooking, making lye soap, or washing windows. She did this almost every week in the summer. Heaven forbid if someone saw

Carolyn's grandparents, Russel and Gertie Showalter in 1961

her dirty windows! She was known for her homemade chicken and noodles. They were the best in the country, and everyone talked about them. She also made very good cookies and cinnamon sugar pies for the grandkids. There would always be some in the pantry for us.

My grandfather was a quiet man and never had too much to say. He had a wooden leg, but that didn't slow him down. I would always know when he was going to work in the field because I could hear his "Johnny Pop" (John Deere) popping until he was done in the evening. My maternal grandfather died in the '30s, so my grandmother was a widow quite young. She was a very special person in my life as I was growing up. She lived alone and never drove. On many occasions, she would come to stay at our house for several days. My sister and I shared the same bed, so when she would come to our house we would have to give her our bed and we would sleep on the sofa. We didn't care because we loved having her there with us. Then she would go spend several days at our cousin's house. She had 24 grandchildren and all were very special to her as she was to each of us. I remember getting together with all the aunts and uncles and cousins on many, many occasions. I remember on Christmas Eve at her house everyone would eat and exchange gifts with the person whose name we drew. She had a diary that she kept from 1954 to 1958. I have that diary, and I often pick it up and read it. It brings back so many wonderful memories.

Quite often, all of us would get together on Sundays after church at one of our houses and have dinner. After we ate, the adults would visit all afternoon and us kids would go outside and play. Sometimes we would all take a picnic lunch and go eat and play in the water at the Ninnesach River at Castleton.

Christmas was always exciting, as it is for every child. When I went to bed, I would be so excited I could hardly sleep. That was always the longest night of the year. We usually got a toy and a game or book. We were always happy to get anything because our dad would tell us that he could remember when he was a little boy he didn't get anything.

Each year at Christmastime, the church that we attended would give everyone a sack of goodies which included an apple, orange, nuts and hard candy, like ribbon candy. I was so excited to get that sack; I would make it last for weeks.

In those days, our bedrooms were not heated, so in the winter before going to bed my sister and I would warm our pillows by the stove. When they were warm (sometimes hot), we would grab them and jump into bed before they got cold again.

We had a lot of snowstorms and blizzards. In 1953, I was in the third grade. It was the day before Thanksgiving. We were at school and it started snowing and blowing that morning. The roads were drifted shut and the buses could not get us home. Our aunt and uncle lived across the road from the school, so my sister and I stayed with them. Our brother stayed with another family. Our dad was able to come get us on Friday. I was awful homesick for Mom and Dad, especially since it was Thanksgiving and I couldn't be with them. Several years later when I was in my early teens, we had a blizzard. My mom and brother were stranded in Hutchinson, My dad, sister and I were home. Our neighbor and his wife had gotten stuck in a snowdrift near our house and were not able to get to their house. They spent the night with us. My sister and I had to fix supper for all of us. Lucky for them, we had plenty of eggs. We fixed scrambled eggs and fried potatoes.

The only animals we had on our farm were cats, dog, and chickens. Through the years, we had several chickens that we named. The ones I remember were Brownie, Specky, Blackie, George, and Liberace. The bantam roosters had spurs and they were always so "cocky." They would ruffle their feathers and chase us. One time one of them was chasing me. As I was running, I went under the clothesline and jumped up. I grabbed a hold of the wire and was hanging there kicking my feet until he gave up. You always had to be on the lookout when you were outside. In 1952 the movie *Wait Till the Sun Shines, Nellie*, starring David Wayne and Jean Peters was being filmed in Hutchinson and surrounding areas. Some of it was being filmed at Castleton. Many of the local people were hired as fill-ins for the movie. Both of my parents, brother, and sister were in the movie, but I was too young. I do remember going to Castleton as they were filming it and I got to ride on a trailer in a parade. In 1955, the Santa Fe Railroad ran its last doodlebug train. A long-time resident of

Castleton bought tickets so all of the children there could have the last ride to Hutchinson. That was my first train ride and I remember being so excited.

Many, many miles were put on my bicycle, as I spent hours on it every day. Our dog Petey and I would take off and go around the section on those gravel roads. He would have to sniff every bush and row of trees, hoping to scare up a rabbit. Somehow, he would always beat me home. Don't know which one of us enjoyed the ride the most.

Kansas may not have the "Majestic Mountains" or scenic oceanfronts, but it does have the "Spacious Skies" and "Amber Waves of Grain." It also has beautiful sunrises and sunsets. I will always cherish the wonderful memories of growing up and growing old in Kansas.

Hula Hoops
By Dana Davidson of Harper, Kansas
Born 1954

My sister, Jeffy, and I were in elementary school when hula-hoops became all the rage. Our dad, who was the fire chief in our small mid-western town, felt those tubes of plastic were too pricey, and as he often did, he set out to make, build, or invent something similar. He took two black plastic tubes, cut off two small lengths of dowel rod, encircled the tubes, and plugged up the two ends. Voila! Instant hula hoops!

One of them was slightly larger than the other, and being skinny little girls, we both preferred the smaller one. We actually fought over it, as we fought over most everything back then. After only a few days, Daddy was tired of hearing us fighting, so he spanked us and sent us to our twin beds in the room we shared. While we were laying there crying, he brought the hula-hoops in and broke them in front of us. I remember laying there, being so sad about our hula-hoops, but being even sadder that we had upset Daddy and all of his good efforts on our behalf had been wasted.

What I didn't know until later was that Daddy had gone straight to Mom, told her that it was too hard, and that he was never going to spank us again. True to his word, he never did! He also went out to the garage and put our hula-hoops back together. They were waiting for us when we were released from our beds. If memory serves me correctly, we never fought over those hula-hoops again—at least not in Daddy's presence!

Homemade Toys and Clothes
By George Roets, Sr. of Goddard, Kansas
Born 1930

My parents couldn't afford to buy many toys or clothes for nine children, so my brother, a year older than I, made our own toys. We found pictures of horses in catalogues and magazines and cut them out. Then we drew them on cardboard and cut them out. We put a piece of wood between two horses to make a team. We used string or twine for harnesses and reins. We had a small wagon that we hitched the horses to. For corrals, we used sticks and twine.

Mom sat up nearly all night after being up all day. She was sewing dresses for four girls and shirts for five boys. Many years she used kerosene lamps to see with.

Sneaky Fortune Tellers
By John A. Harding of Medicine Lodge, Kansas
Born 1940

Traveling circuses and carnivals were very popular in the 1940-50s. In the year of 1955, a carnival came to our little town of Augusta, Kansas. They had a few rides for the kiddies, but mainly the fairway had booths that were good at taking your money with little chance for a prize. My best friend and I rode out to the carnival on my motor scooter. You could drive a scooter on a "learner's permit" at 14 back then.

After arriving and "gawking" as they called it back then, Butch, my friend was enticed to visit a fortuneteller's booth. It didn't hurt that the fortuneteller was young and very cute. After getting Butch inside the tent, areas on the body were felt that made Butch think he was going to have some good fortune for a 13 year old! After leaving the tent, Butch discovered his one and only 50-cent piece was missing. (She had left a nickel.) Going back to get his money, he was told that she did not take it and that further more he needed to move on.

Butch was so upset that he had been duped; he kept looking for a way to get his money back. After some time, Butch noticed the Gypsy fortuneteller going out to the outhouse that was provided by the carnival committee. After going in the outhouse, the fortuneteller closed and locked the door to do her business. Butch ran up from behind and pushed the outhouse over, with the door facing down. (I may have helped him; as this point in my memory is a little foggy; after all, I'm 73 now!) Anyway, hearing the lady screaming, two carnival men came running. They were able to catch my friend Butch, and down in the outhouse hole he was thrown!

Later, as we met in the parking lot, Butch wanted a ride back to his house in town. Butch was my best friend, but Butch walked home!

My Grandparents' Old General Store
By Dorathe Wiltshire of Pratt, Kansas
Born 1922

I was born in 1922 in a very small town in south central Kansas where my grandparents had a general store. Although we lived on a farm nearly 40 miles from there, we visited often, and spent many happy times in that old store Hinshaw and Hinshaw. The ceilings were so tall and covered with ornate metal. There were shelves lining both sides of the store filled with canned goods, bolts of cloth, sacks of sugar, and many wonderful things! Neat rows of shoes of all sizes were placed on the floor beneath the shelves.

Along the back of the store was a long wood counter holding an old cash register and a scale. The meat case had a glass front so we could look in at the cheeses and meats from that part of Kansas. Crackers were packed in boxes so they wouldn't break, and huge barrels or sacks held potatoes, flour, and pickles. There was a barrel of peanuts free for the eating. All the shells thrown on the floor helped keep the wood floor oiled.

The store was heated with a potbellied stove, around which old men frequently sat, telling their stories. Of course, there was no indoor plumbing, but the outhouse was pretty handy! An old wooden crank telephone hung on the wall.

Although I was too young to help much, my "job" was to line up the candy (so I could easily see it!) and dust the cans. I also helped candle the eggs in the back room. There was a black box with a light in it and a hole. The egg was placed before the light to see if it had been fertilized. Many milk and cream cans were lined up in this back room.

I have so many wonderful memories of the hours spent in my grandparents' store. It was placed on the National Register of Historic Places, but nothing was more important than the love, security, and happiness we felt there!

Small Town Celebration: V-Day
By Gwendolyn E. Rice of Caldwell, Kansas
Born 1926

It was a hot August day in 1945 in the small town of Caldwell, Kansas when we heard on the radio that Japan had surrendered! World War II was ending. Several of my friends and I got together to go downtown where people were gathering with excitement over the news. We were almost 19 years old and had already graduated from high school. I was teaching in a country school after getting an emergency certificate, as there was such a shortage of teachers during the war years.

After watching the people in our town, who were going crazy, we loaded up in my friend Madelyn's car and her dad drove us through some neighboring towns to witness their celebrations. They were the same as our townspeople in the streets, yelling, laughing, crying, throwing firecrackers, dancing. Wow! Everyone was so excited! We drove through Arkansas City Winfield, Oxford, and Wellington before getting back to our hometown at about midnight. Things in our hometown were still going strong!

I received a letter from my boyfriend two days later. He was in the Navy, stationed in the Pacific Ocean. He was the radioman aboard the ship and was the first to get the news that Japan had surrendered. The other sailors didn't believe him at first, but suddenly the skies lit up. Ships were sending rockets in the air and shooting guns. They were coming home!

There may have been bigger celebrations in the big cities like New York and Chicago, but none could be as exciting as our small town in Kansas as we waited for our men to come home.

The happiest day of my life was the day my sailor stepped off that train home from the war. It didn't take us long to get to the justice of the peace to get married, as did many of our friends. We contributed to the start of the baby boom by having eight children.

My sailor was buried with military honors at a small cemetery by Corbin in 1994 after 48 years of marriage. So even though the day my man came home was the happiest day of my life, the day I lost him was the saddest. I relish the many years we had together and was always proud of his service to our country.

The new house after the fire

House on Fire!
By Galen P. Yunker of Caldwell, Kansas
Born 1951

My family lived on a farm north of South Haven, Kansas in the '50s, '60s and '70s. There was my mom and dad and us eight kids—six boys and two girls—a great big Catholic family. My brothers and I loved sports. We played football, basketball, and track. Our mom and dad never missed a game. My mom, June, was the loudest cheerleader at every event.

One cold day in February, I had just played in the "B" team junior high basketball game and I was sitting on the bench during the "A" game watching my older brother play. I noticed our school superintendent came in and said something to my parents and they quickly left. I soon found out our whole big two-story house had burnt to the ground while we were at the ballgame. There was nothing left. It was a terrible feeling to look at that burnt heap and not knowing which way to turn. I also remembered that I had just received a basketball for Christmas and it probably had burned up, too.

The townspeople of our little town came together and each family took one of us kids in with them. I felt pretty lucky to be taken in by a rich farmer with a son my age. His mom took me clothes shopping and I had more stuff than I ever had.

After some time, we were told of a big white farmhouse for sale over around Perth, Kansas. So my dad was able to buy it and we had a big old moving day. They hoisted that house up on trailers and it was moved 12 miles to the location of our old house. It was quite a sight as people pulled over and watched as that house was moved down the middle of the road. My two brothers and I were sitting on the house, helping out somehow, I am sure. It was double the size of our old house and we were in hog heaven in this big beautiful house.

I was too young or uninterested at the time to understand how this all came about. I do remember at the next two home basketball games the cheerleaders carried around big white sheets so the crowd could throw money in them. It all went to us. I am sure there was also a fire "shower" for my folks, but as a kid, I don't remember it. I just know the people in our community took our family in and helped us get re-established so we could once again be all together.

That beautiful farmhouse still stands five mile north of South Haven. We are happy to know that another big family with 12 kids moved into that house after we all grew up and moved away. Mom was always thankful we were all in town at the ballgame that horrible day and no one was hurt or killed as the fire raged. I will never forget that day back in 1963 when as a twelve-year-old boy I lost my home and my only basketball.

Flowers and Fun on the Farm
By Rachel Witte of The Villages, Florida
Born 1931

I have memories of flowers and fun on our farm in the late 1930s through 1947 with my parents and four sisters and one older brother. There are so many happy memories of growing up on a 160-acre farm that my dad worked for the owner, but I'm going to concentrate mostly on the flowers we had.

My only brother and older sister were in the Armed Forces during World War II. My mother created a large 'V' in our front lawn visible by the many people driving past our farm. She planted it with red, white, and blue flowers and in the middle created a large star that also had red, white, and blue flowers planted in it. It truly was lovely, and people would slow down to admire the flowerbeds. I don't recall exactly what the flowers were, but we younger girls had a lot of weeding to do—and Mom made sure we knew a flower from a weed! We enjoyed the task and loved being outside. Mom loved pansies and made a round flowerbed for them nearer the house. Those, too, had to be weeded. Between the large 'V' and the pansies was a row of peonies. It was a beautiful yard.

Mom planted a large vegetable garden after Dad plowed it and spread fertilizer with the manure spreader. (Ahh that is what is referred to as "pure country air!") Along with the vegetables was an area toward the right front of the garden where there were moonflower plants. Mom did not put them on a trellis, so they crawled along the area and took up a sizable space. As we played in the lawn at night, we could smell the sweet moonflowers.

The play consisted of several games, one being Poison Tag. There were three or four of we sisters playing, I being one of the two youngest. We condensed the play area bordered by the driveway, the 'V' flowerbed, and a row of three trees. The "Itter" chased and tagged someone. Where that person was hit, they had to keep one hand on that spot as they ran and tagged. If you got tagged on the head it was okay, but if you got tagged on the ankle—oh! That was a different situation. Needless to say, the lower part of the body was where the "Itter" aimed. There were lots of laughs and some tears.

Another popular game was "Mother May I." We lined up and had to go from one designated line to another by asking Mother. We requested steps like "giant" steps, "baby" steps, "scissor" steps, or "zigzag" steps. The first one to get to the finish line won. So we took turns asking questions like "Mother, May I have three giant steps?" She gave a yes or no answer.

We also caught the illusive fireflies. Those evenings are special memories as our mother sat and enjoyed our laughter in the cool evening air.

Well, back to the flowers. The last one I will tell about are the lovely-smelling lilac bushes. Their flowers made such lovely indoor bouquets. These bushes were in a special spot, right beside the outdoor, three-holer toilet. Wish they could bloom all year! They often housed a robin's nest, so it was fun to make that trip to the toilet. As we sat, we would go through the "wish book"—the Montgomery Ward catalog. Those pages were also used as our toilet paper. We thought everyone used that in their toilets, so no shame or problem.

In May when Decoration Day came, we would make bouquets of lilacs and tulips. Each of us had a bouquet and would go to the high school where there would be a program honoring our Armed Forces. The band would then march to the cemetery and many of us followed. There we were instructed to place the bouquet on soldier's graves along with a flag. It was very meaningful and a pleasant memory.

The Big Red Barn
By Rose Alderson of Nickerson, Kansas
Born 1943

Some of the best memories of my childhood are of playing in our huge red barn. We spent most of our summer days in its cool dust and shadows. We had a big swing that we could take up to the haymow. Taking a giant leap, we could swing far out of the giant doors and into the sunshine. We also loved to jump out of the haymow windows onto the soft grass. When tired of swinging, jumping, or games of hide and seek, I spent the rest of the day in my "playhouse" in one of the empty corncribs.

Every morning and evening Bossy stood patiently while being milked, and when there was a new calf, we first laid eyes on it in our barn. Our cats feasted on warm milk and mice in that friendly barn. And each spring they had their kittens in its secret hiding places. Oh my, it was a place of such wonders.

We did "naughty" things in the barn also. We were strictly forbidden to walk the rafters, but we all did it anyway. Most of the rafters were only a few inches wide, but there was one bigger board that spanned the top of the barn from one side of the haymow to the other. If we had ever fallen, we could not have survived. The first time I walked those rafters, I was about six. We knew we weren't supposed to do it, which made it even more thrilling! I almost ran along the rafters, but when I had to jump down into the soft hay, I was too afraid! I begged my siblings to "go get Daddy." They knew very well we all would be in for it if he found out what we were doing. My older brother paid me a dime to jump. That was big money. I happily accepted and closed my eyes and jumped. Spankings avoided!

We also made tunnels with the hay bales. This was also strictly forbidden because of the danger of the bales collapsing. We had so much fun! And the worst injuries any of us sustained were merely skinned knees and elbows and splinters in our feet.

My biggest memory is of our hide and seek games—one in particular. At the very top of the barn was a huge wooden box on a platform. It was the perfect hiding place. The summer that I was seven, I climbed into that big wooden box. No one would ever find me! Soon I heard a strange noise. SSSSS! SSSSS! What could it be? Finally, I turned around and saw the biggest snake I had seen in my entire life. I jumped out screaming and hollering. My sister abandoned her hiding place and came running but she was mad as an old bull when she found that it was "only a snake."

"I thought you were really in trouble," she yelled. "I thought you were hanging from something by your fingernails. That was just an old bull snake." She went on to tell me that she was hiding in the best hiding place she had ever found and I had ruined it. Luckily, she soon forgave me and we called to our old dog, Cap, who killed most every living thing including skunks and snakes. That poor bull snake that was just being a snake didn't have a chance. After Cap killed it, my sister and I put it on a stick and dangled it in front of the few cars that passed our house.

So many memories of that barn! My husband and I still live on that farm and still enjoy that barn. When our kids were teens, they hosted many barn parties. We would check every 10-15 minutes to make sure that everyone was upright and behaving. We didn't learn until years later that they paid our youngest to be their "lookout" and warn them when we were on our way!

Today our grandchildren love that barn as much I did. They are the fifth generation to play (both allowed and forbidden play) within its walls. At least 100 or more children have played in and loved that barn. The initials of many of them who are long gone are carved in its walls. Recently my cousin's son came from California just to add his initials to his father's, grandfather's, great and great-great grandfather's. If those walls could speak, what wonderful stories they would tell. May it stand forever!

The Dry and Lean Days
By Ms. Helen Farney of Kiowa, Kansas
Born 1928

I was born on a Monday morning, October 8, 1928, which was a washday at our house. My mom and dad had four girls and four boys all born at a farm in Oklahoma during the dust bowl days. We did not have running water, electricity, or any of the things we have today. There was no money; we raised all the food we ate: chickens, pigs, a large garden, potatoes, and we made our own soap. We bought only sugar and flour with the extra sour cream and eggs we had. We raised crops of wheat, barley…when it would actually rain. We had lots of dirt storms and experienced rainstorms and hail that also ruined our crops. Machinery consisted of hand and hard labor.

I had a very good mother who took care of us children and a father that worked very hard to raise us all as Christians. We went to church every Sunday and Wednesday nights on dirt and muddy roads. One old car held all of us. We had one truck and got by. We each had our chores to do, and also had a simple wonderful

House built in 1900

life that is not seen today. We had time to go fishing and swim in the creek behind our house, and eat at picnics, unlike today. Everyone today is on their cell phone and in a hurry. There are seven of us still alive today. Four girls are in their eighties and the boys are 89 to 70 years old. One brother passed away from cancer at 49 years old. My brothers: two are farmers and one was captain of American Airlines.

Our folks did not participate in the Cherokee Run, but bought our farm from someone who did participate. My dad had to borrow $3,000 from an uncle so he could get a loan to buy the farm. Dad made sure he paid back every dime of that borrowed money and loan. He worked several jobs, plus farming, and driving the school bus. Most of my family lives fairly close; one sister lives in Oregon, one in Texas, and the rest in Kansas. We are a very close-knit family and get together as much as possible. I have two children, five grandchildren, and eight great-grandchildren and one on the way.

I took care of my Dad, who died of cancer (age 89), and my mother, who died after having hip surgery. (She was 92.) I not only was a farm wife, but for a few years when crops where bad (no rain for many years), I also worked at a bank. Later on, I also worked with sick and dying people at the hospital. With what I earned, I purchased antique dishes. I later opened an antique store with my husband's help. We had a lot of fun going to auctions and working together. Huber died in 1996 of cancer, and a few years later, I had to close my store after 28 years due to my bad health. After having back, heart, eye, surgeries, I now live with my daughter. I was fortunate enough to live in the Farney homestead—a large brick home—for 63 years. I raised my children there and had bridal and baby showers there as well. I also hosted many dinners for family and friends and always had an extra bed if needed.

At this time, my son and grandson farm the 540 acres of land for me. I've had a wonderful life. We were poor, but didn't know it. Everyone else was poor also. When I was a child, I craved chocolate candy, so I would go to the kitchen and mix sugar, cocoa, and cream, stir it up, and it was delicious.

Dust Storms of the Thirties
By Justine Sullivan of Lakin, Kansas
Born (not stated)

It is difficult for any of my family members to remember specific details about the numerous dirt storms that occurred in the thirties. The people of this time period spent approximately eight years in a haze of dirt and dust, and like the dust, the stories have seemed to merge together to make a giant cloud. Depending on what was happening at the time, some stories are more vivid than the others. Sitting on my grandfather's lap listening to him recall the harsh and scary conditions, a couple of his stories were imprinted on my mind.

My grandfather, Walter, was born and raised in a small community in southwest Kansas. He was born in 1927, and spent the majority of his youth surrounded by dirt storms. The first major dirt storm he remembered was during his first year of schooling, and it was a terrifying experience for him. While playing outside during recess one day and looking out onto the open plains and vast horizon, a mountainous black cloud could be seen rolling along the ground. The air was completely still and you could see birds frantically flying for their lives ahead of the black mass. None of his classmates or his teacher had ever seen anything like this before.

In order to escape the unfamiliar and ominous cloud, they all desperately ran into the one-room schoolhouse. The cloud enveloped them and the brutal wind was blowing hard enough that the ceiling seemed to shake hysterically and bounce up and down at least two or three inches. The air in the classroom filled with choking dust, and my grandfather was afraid that the wind was going to blow down the schoolhouse. As the wind blew, it grew darker and darker. This was before the Rural Electrification Associations (REAs), so there was no electricity, and it became so dark that you could not see your hand in front of your face without a lantern.

Luckily, the schoolhouse remained standing, and he stayed at school until the dirt storm blew over. He could not remember how long he sat in the schoolhouse along with his terrified classmates and teacher, but it seemed like it lasted forever. This would prove to be the first of many dirt storms that plagued the southwest Kansas plains for years to come, and an event that imprinted itself into the many avenues of my grandfather's vast experiences in life.

Another occurrence that my grandfather recalled with the dirt storms of the thirties that stands out in my memory from the many stories that he had so eloquently shared with his children and grandchildren over the years occurred when he was a little older. Being the eldest son of a farmer/rancher required that you start helping out on the farm at an early age. When he became old enough, he started to drive the tractor and listing fields. One of the advancements in tillage practices that came out of the thirties was to plow deep furrows and ridges with a lister plow. The rainwater would be caught and stored in the furrow, so it could soak into the ground instead of running off the field. Then the farmer would come back and split the ridge, and make a new furrow where the ridge was and a new ridge where the furrow was. This would prevent the ground from losing moisture and would capture the water from rains that they prayed would come in the future. This was a slow process and the tractor moved only about a mile an hour through the field.

One day while he was listing a field, he looked up and saw another one of the rolling dirt storms headed right for him. He was more familiar with dirt storms at this time, and he knew he had no time to escape, even though he was less than an eighth of a mile from home. He barely had time to shut down the tractor and grab a jacket he had with him for the cool mornings. He narrowly managed to escape becoming enveloped by the murky cloud by lying down in a furrow beside the large rear tractor wheel. The storm hit, and he could see only a few feet. He lay down in the furrow and covered his head and shoulders with his jacket. To prevent himself from choking on the dust, he had to breathe through the cloth of the coat. He said it grew as dark as night, and he had no concept of how long he lay there, but it seemed like an eternity.

The storm finally let up enough to allow him to see maybe 20 or 30 feet, but the wind was still blowing strong. He had never seen such a joyful sight as when he saw his dad struggling to follow the row through the field to find the tractor. Together they used the furrow to get to the end of the field and then follow the end of the furrows in the direction of the house. They finally found the fence to the corrals and were able to use it as a guide to get home. He was one happy boy to be in the safety of the farmhouse.

Everyone who experienced the black dirt storms agree that the winds in the storms were different than the usual winds that often blew through the Great Plains. The winds seemed to sweep along the ground and stay low like they were being held there by high pressure above. The wind would roll along the ground stirring up the soil and moving it in great quantities. It is amazing to think of what the people during the thirties lived through. Even living in southwest Kansas now, I have experienced dust storms that have rolled through, but I cannot even imagine the shock of seeing the giant black clouds that swallowed the landscape back then. One thing is certain; it made some great stories for my grandpa to share!

Diddie Lynne, Danet Kaye, and Deedle Ann
By Jeri Myers of Mulvane, Kansas
Born 1948

There are three girls in our family: Jeri Lynne, Janet Kaye, and Jean Ann. I am older by three and four years. The little girls are 14 months apart. When Jean Ann was learning to talk, she could not pronounce 'J's. So our names were Diddie Lynne, Danet Kaye, and Deedle Ann.

In 1956, that would make us eight, five,

and four. Elvis Presley's movie, "Love Me Tender," came out. Now, we all loved Elvis, and my mother was also a big fan. We could sing his songs, and I especially loved "Love Me Tender." My mother planned a big surprise one evening and took all three girls to the Miller in Wichita to watch the movie. We never got to go to movies, so this was a big deal, and the Miller was a big theatre. We sat in the balcony on the front row.

Well, as you know, Elvis Presley dies at the end of the movie. I was heartbroken and I started to cry, rather loudly, according to my Mom. Then, to her horror, I was sobbing uncontrollably. She kept saying, "It is just a movie; it is just a movie! He is not really dead." My sisters would pat me and tell me the same thing. Mother finally couldn't hide her embarrassment any more. She ducked her head and managed to get all three of us out of the theater. Of course, I was still crying. We got in "Old Pinkie" (our pink Ford station wagon) and the little girls lay down in the back for the ride home. Mother turned on the radio hoping to distract me. About ten minutes later, there was Elvis Presley on the radio singing "Love Me Tender." Janet Kaye raised her little head up from the back and said, "See there, Diddie Lynne, I told you he was still alive."

When I was 15, my Dad decided to raise rabbits. Not just a few—but 350 of them. We moved to this old farm five miles from town. My sisters were ten and eleven. The farmhouse was over 100 years old. It had no electricity, no running water, and no indoor plumbing. But, the farm boasted a huge barn for the rabbits! Dad put in the electricity. We then had a man come out and use a willow branch to "witch" for water on the property. We followed him around, thinking, yeah, right; he is not going to find water. But his branch went down, and they drilled for water, and sure enough, we got running water for the house. I think they called this "dowsing" or "divining" for water. Still there was no indoor bathroom.

We also had goats that would eat the mulberries from the mulberry trees. When Mother would milk them, we had purple milk or homemade purple ice cream. Old Nanny tried jumping a barbed wire fence one day. She caught her stomach on a barb and ripped a long tear on it. My Mother yelled at me to go in the house and get her a needle and thread, the scissors, and peroxide. We flipped the goat on her back and my Mother proceeded to stitch her up and disinfect her.

Jeri's parents Madge and A. D. Humphrey with their family

My sisters shared a bedroom upstairs. The whole wall on one side of the room was a honeycomb. Bees had been making honey there for years. Honey oozed down the wall and made a mess. We had to call a beekeeper who came and got the queen bee and then all the other bees left, too.

One day, the Little Girls, as we used to call them, came running down the steep stairs screaming at the top of their lungs. They had caught a garter snake in their room. They were carrying it downstairs in a milking pail with a record on top of it, and with a knitting needle stuck through the hole in the record. That snake was not going to get away from them! We also had a family of skunks living in the cellar basement of the house. They were usually pretty docile. If they got up on the ledge of the basement wall, our little dog, Sugar Babe (part Dachshund and part Beagle) would smell them through the floorboards and she would scratch and claw at them. They would in turn get upset and spray. The house would totally fill up with skunk

Jean Reusser, Jeri Myers, and Janet Hand

smell.

My mother was a teacher in Mulvane, and I was a cheerleader that year. We went home after school to eat supper before the high school basketball game. We just got in the door and Mother was making sandwiches, my sisters were getting our milk, and I was upstairs putting on my wool cheerleading uniform. The skunks started screeching and hissing at Sugar Babe and Mother yelled for us to grab our sandwiches and milk and get out of the house NOW! I ran down those steep stairs, missing some along the way. By the time I grabbed my milk, the smell was so horrible, it hurt not only your nose, but your eyes. We jumped in "Mr. Green Jeans" (our green Oldsmobile station wagon) and Mother floored it toward town. The milk was so "skunky," we couldn't drink it. The sandwiches were a disaster. We got to the ball game (Why didn't we have Febreeze then?) and jumped out of the car. We ran in to the game. The cheerleaders were practicing in the foyer of the school. I joined them and immediately someone said they smelled a skunk. I was mortified! But, I carried on like a real trooper. I said Mother had run over a skunk on the highway and the smell was in the car and I guessed on us, too!

A family story passed down over the years is one my dad tells. He was the last one born in his family of nine brothers and sisters. Almost all of his brothers and sisters were out of the house by the time he was five. Aunt Irene was still in high school and had several girls over to spend the night. They wanted to make a cake, but had no milk. This was probably in the 1930s. No grocery stores were open at 11:00 PM. So, the girls ran across the dirt road and hiked over the neighbor's fence, opened their shed, milked their cow, hiked over the fence again, and ran across the road, and finished making their cake.

How did you wax and polish your floors in the '50s? Put three little girls in the bedroom to play, move the furniture out, get on your hands and knees, and apply the wax paste. Let it dry. Get out an old blanket, put the little girls on it, and swing them around on the floor until it shines! To get up close to the walls, put socks on the girl's feet and let them slide around the edges!

The Blizzard of March 1957 in Southwest Kansas
By Leonard Hitz of Garden City, Kansas
Born 1942

It was Friday March 22, 1957. We had experienced at least five years of drought in western Kansas. I remember dust storms in the 1950s similar to those told to me that occurred in the 1930s. But those in the '50s were not as severe; they were still so dusty that the sun was blocked out when they rolled in.

The crops had been small and money was precious to a farmer in those days. We milked cows and sold the cream in a five-gallon cream can to Fairmount Dairy in Dodge City. It took a week's worth of milking and separating the cream to get a five-gallon can full of cream. That can of cream brought in from $8.00 to $10.00 and was what the folks used to buy most of the groceries we needed once a week. We always stopped at Dillon's in Dodge City on our way back to the farm.

The night of Friday, March 22, 1957, we were having a school dance in the community building of my hometown of Kingsdown. During the evening while the dance was going on, it started raining outside. We all went home excited after the dance because it was raining. The dance ended about ten o'clock that night, and by morning, the rain had turned to snow sometime during the night. We did the milking and the normal chores for morning, but later in the morning, the wind started to blow hard. By night, we were in a full-blown blizzard.

REA had gone through in 1949 and we had electric power traveling over the high lines, but sometime in the afternoon of Saturday, March 23, we lost power. The lines had blown down. Our home was heated by one propane stove that sat in the middle of the house, and that was all we had for heat. Mom and Dad dug out the kerosene lanterns and candles that were kept on hand for such emergencies. Since our cook stove was electric, we had no cook stove to prepare meals on. Dad was able to hook up a small two-burner propane stove that Mom could cook on. When night came, all we could do was read by kerosene lantern or go to bed.

When the wind started to blow on Saturday, we never ventured out of the house except twice to find our way to the car shed to listen to the news on the car radio. Remembering stories of people getting lost in blizzards and freezing to death, Mom was very worried when we went out. She thought that we might get lost in the wind and storm and not make it back to the house. Visibility was next to zero, but we knew our way to the car shed which was just a short distance across the driveway. We were able to get there and listen to the news on the car radio, and get back to the house safely. With this in mind, we never got out of the house again until Monday, March 25th at about 3:00 in the afternoon.

The blizzard had drifted everything shut. We could not get to the barn to milk because the south side of the barn (where the door was) was completely covered. You could walk to the pitch of the barn roof and never know you were on the barn. The same thing happened to the chicken house, but the chickens were okay.

Our biggest concern was finding our cowherd. They had been in a pasture two miles west and one mile south of our home when the storm hit. So on Tuesday morning, the 26th, after digging our tractor out of snow bank and getting it started, we headed out to find our cows. In those days, no one had four-wheel drive vehicles. The tractors were not at all like they are today. They were relatively small horsepower and fairly low to the ground. As we headed west, we found the going slow because all the roads were drifted shut and we had to slowly bust our way through the drifts. By backing up and hitting the drifts as fast as we could, backing out again, and hitting the drift again, we were able to eventually break through the drift. We repeated this until we finally made it through the drift and then on to the next one.

As we past our nearest neighbor to the west, he got his tractor and went with us to look for the cows. Then we met a second neighbor who had two tractors and he joined our search for the cows. When we finally found them, they had drifted south with the storm. They had drifted about four or five miles in the blizzard. We did have some that died because they could not withstand the stress, but for the most part, the majority of them survived. The saving grace was that the temperature never got much below freezing, in the mid-twenties, but had it gotten real cold we could have lost a lot more of the cattle, and possibly all of them. We found our cattle in a draw south of Highway 54 east of Bloom, Kansas. With the help of the neighbors and four tractors, we got the cattle home and fed. It took the whole day to get them back.

Until the power was restored we could not use the restroom in the house. No electricity to pump the water, therefore no water to flush the stool. We had just got rotary dial phones a couple of years earlier, but they did not work because the lines were all down due to the blizzard. Mom cooked on the small two-burner gas stove for several days and we just went to bed early rather than staying up. Until power was restored, we had no electricity and no TV. But oftentimes when the TV did work we could only receive signals from three TV stations and oftentimes they were impossible to watch due to snowy pictures. Of course, we all had to have a tall outside antenna to get any reception at all, and if it wasn't turned in the right direction to pick up the signal, you did not have TV at all.

The thing I liked most from this blizzard was the fact that we could not get to the barn to milk the cows. They dried up and Dad decided that we would no longer milk cows. This blizzard did break the drought and it started raining that summer. Rains came from then on to break the drought. Crops started producing once again, and the grass in the pastures started growing again.

The blizzard of '57 even had trains on the Rock Island Railroad stranded and life stood still for a while. It will always be a vivid memory in my life. As coincidence would have it, we had a similar blizzard 30 years later on the same date in 1987!

Surviving the Dirty Thirties
By Dorothy Richardson of Wellington, Kansas
Born 1930

In late 1930, I was born in a farmhouse southwest of Caldwell, Kansas in the same bedroom that my dad was born in 31 years earlier. His parents participated in the Cherokee Strip Run in 1893 and settled one mile inside Oklahoma, as that is where there wagon broke down. I was eldest of four children—two brothers and one sister. We had neither electricity nor telephone. Our house was of wooden frame. Four rooms, three bedrooms and the fourth was a kitchen, bathroom, and living room combination.

Our grandmother, my dad's mother, lived with us. She was quite a character. I never saw her take a bath, brush her teeth, or change clothes. We have no pictures of her, as she wouldn't let us take one. She was about five feet tall, approximately, 140 lbs., with grey hair that she wore combed hack in a bun in the back. She knelt on one knee, held the bucket with her left hand, and milked faster than the rest of us with two hands. She worked hard until she had a stroke milking a cow. She only lived about six hours after the stroke and died at age 77 in her own bed at home.

Dorothy, Bob, Doris, and Herb in 1938

She sewed her long dresses and aprons by hand, out of grey chambray material. She only went to town twice a year when she went to the doctor and bank. She pulled her own teeth and was fairly well until her stroke. When she went to town, she dressed in black, full length with a velvet hat. After the threshing crew finished, she would empty her ticking bed and refill it with fresh straw. The pillow spanned the bed and was filled with straw, also. All four of us took turns sleeping with her. One night was enough, as the straw was scratchy. She was busy every day, fixing fences, doing chores, raising turkeys, hatching the eggs, and making shelters for them. One time she came running and yelling. The bumblebees were after her. Guess she contacted a nest as she was building the shelters.

She was somewhat of a superstitious person. In the dry seasons, she hunted a snake, killed it, and hung it on the fence. Surprise; it usually worked. It would rain until she took it off and then the rain stopped. She despised the prairie dog. They were undermining our pasture. She rolled rags and tied them in a small ball, then dipped them in a liquid she called Hokey Pokey. My oldest brother went with her as she dropped each one in the hole and then pulled the dirt in, covering the hole. Eventually she ridded our pasture of the critters. She thought the farm animals would step in the hole and break their leg. As the potatoes grew, she took a butcher knife and dig around the plant until she would find enough fresh potatoes for the family.

We kids dressed up one Halloween as witches by wearing her clothes and riding a broom, and boy did that make her mad. Every time she got mad, she "moved out" and into the granary. But that wasn't

Dorothy, Bob, and Doris with their pet turkey gobbler

the only time she got upset. Another time I remember she got upset was when my mom got curtains. She moved out whenever mom got anything new. When she "moved out," she would eat raw vegetables and wouldn't have anything to do with any of us.

When we were children, we had a pet turkey, Gobbler. As we played outside, this turkey played, also. We would lie down on the ground and this bird would walk on us, over us and all around us, playfully. We wanted a horse to ride. All we had was two workhorses, so we coaxed, petted, and fed them until one day my brother decided to try and get on one. He bridled the black one in the barn, got on her, and out of the door she went. Finally, she settled down and he and my sister rode double thereafter. Her name was Daisy. The other horse was grey and I think her name was Nell. My little brother and I rode her. As they were work horses, and were very big; our legs practically were straight out.

On Saturday night we took turns bathing in a square washtub behind the potbelly stove, youngest to oldest. Mom would add a teakettle of hot water now and then. I was number four.

We attended the Sunnyside School, two and a half miles from home. It had one room and grades one thru eight with one teacher. We walked to school every day carrying our books and lunch. When it was muddy, our feet got so heavy. When it was cold, Mom made us wear long brown stockings, long underwear with our brother's overalls on top. When we got to school we took off the overalls, rolled up the underwear, and rolled down the socks. We were girls with dresses! One time I remember, when I was in the first grade I was swinging high and jumped out like the boys did and tore a three-corner hole in the back of my dress. The teacher sent me to the house about a quarter mile north and the lady stitched me up.

Our school only lasted eight months of the year and the only day off was Christmas. We were the only students in school when we came down with chicken pox, so school was dismissed, and our teacher took a vacation. That's the only year we received perfect attendance. All four of us took our turn with all the childhood diseases. We even had the seven-year itch. Mom would stand us on a chair and rub us with something that smelled terrible. No, it didn't last that long, but it was awful. I attended the east school one year with four boys. I was the only girl. When I graduated eighth grade I had to pass the state exam before high school. This was my favorite teacher.

When growing up we played in the barn, climbed trees, or made our toys from things on the farm. We swam in the horse tank (nude). Company drove in one day and we had to stay in until they left. We had stripped in the chicken house a hundred feet away. We decided to run away one day and moved to the barn. We took cereal from the house, milked a cow to get milk, and then made our beds in the hay. There was an old buggy in the barn. We smoked the stuffing in the seat. We also pushed it to the top of hill and one guided with a rope and one pushed while the other two wrapped ourselves inside spokes for a ride down the hill. We went swimming in the red mud ponds in our underwear. The red Oklahoma clay always stained them. Our poor mom. I have wondered how we ever grew up safe and sound.

Our mom was always working. She cooked on a three-burner gasoline stove, making all our bread and food. She had three children before getting a washing machine. On washday we pumped water, carried it in and put it in a boiler to heat, and then put it in the washing machine. Also, the rinse tubs had to be filled then carried out. Before she got a washing machine, she did all the laundry on the washboard. She was my favorite person.

I remember the "dirty thirties." It got so dark the chickens went to roost. It sifted through our windows and doors. The only way to clean was with a broom, which just

Vicki, Marvin, Randy, and Dorothy Wyckoff

made more dust. We stuffed rags in all the cracks of the windows, but it didn't seem to help. Every morning the windowsills were full. It drifted in the ditches and covered the fences in places. We also had blizzards, but we escaped the tornados.

My dad was a farmer and we helped when we were big enough, from putting hay in the barn to scooping wheat into the granary. We also took our turn on the tractor and binder. Then we shocked the bundles and learned to drive in the field. There were also chores like milking, feeding chickens, and gathering eggs. We also had turkeys, guineas, geese, and calves. I can still see Mom picking feathers from the geese. She made our pillows and featherbeds with the feathers she collected.

Our trips to town were usually on Saturday. Our folks took cream and eggs to sell, and this bought our groceries for the week. We kids received a dime each to spend. We never saw a movie until we were in high school. One time, Dad loaded the cream in a pickup to go to town. He went around a corner too fast and it upset, spilling both cans. How do you clean 20 gal of cream from a pick-up? No hose. We would have ice sometimes if Mom put the card in the window. She turned it to how many pounds we wanted. We had a choice of 10-25-50-100. Mom had him put it in a washtub, covered it with newspapers and quilts. This would keep on the porch a week. That was our only refrigerator.

Our daily thing was to get to the outhouse, talk, and wish from the catalog. We had a double-holer. Also, we got to listen to the radio if the wind had blown enough to charge the battery. We liked to listen to Inner Sanctum and Lone Ranger. It was the only way the folks had to hear the news. This was wartime so we always had to hear news. We also had a wind-up record player with cylinder records.

I lived on the farm until I was 16 years old when my parents moved south of Wellington. My parents are gone now, but as I look back I don't know how they managed all of us. My two brothers are gone now, also. My sister and I remember all the good and bad times. We live a hundred miles apart, but visit on the phone and go visit once in a while. She raised six children and I two. Both have lost our husbands; I have lost two but we have our churches and our faith and are doing fine.

All the Things I Remember
By Nora Ellen Allender of Norwich, Kansas
Born 1929

The stock market crashed in 1929 and Richard Byrd put the American flag on the South Pole. That was the year I was born. After 85 years, I'm still living in Kingman County, Kansas, where I have lived all my life. I attended school at Adams, Kansas all 12 years and Friends University in Wichita, Kansas two summers.

We lived on four different farms on the same section, which was 80 acres each. We just rented them and finally bought the last one after living there a few years. This was during the depression years. Several banks went out the year I was born, which was 1929. After the depression and dust bowl days and during World War II, a plant opened up west of Wichita, Kansas that made airplane parts. It was called Aero Parts. Several farmers who were past the drafting age got jobs there and formed a carpool to go to work. With money scarce, this way they could afford to drive. We lived off our farm, raising chickens. We had our own eggs to eat and also hatch in an incubator so we could restock our old laying hens. We had turkeys where people from Wichita, Kansas came to our farm and bought them for Thanksgiving and Christmas dinners. We sold them to make a living. My aunt and uncle had a flock of 400 turkeys. We had guineas and geese. My mother, sister and I would drive the geese in the barn, shut the doors and catch them to help our mother pick feathers to make feather pillows.

We had cows so we had plenty of milk to drink, to make ice cream with, and to use in other ways. We had a separator to separate the cream from the milk. When the cream got to the stage to churn, we would make our own butter. From the cream that had soured, we would make cakes. Cottage cheese was also made from cooking the soured milk. None of this was bought in the grocery store, as they did not have these food items in those days. People bought eggs and milk from farmers. There were no mixes and very few cold cereals. On Saturday evenings, my father would take the eggs to a small town grocery store and trade it for groceries we needed.

We raised pigs and butchered them for our own meat. My dad would cut it up and put it in a wooden barrel in a brine solution to keep and sometimes use a sugar cure. They would render the fat for lard to use in our baking. We also used to make our own soap for washing clothes, of which we had to add lye to it when it was cooked outside on a stove in a boiler. We always had fruit trees on our farms, so we canned our own fruit. We always had a vegetable garden. The vegetables were used on the table and canned for use in the off seasons for several months. Very few things did we buy from the store.

A farmer that lived nearby planted sorghum feed. We went to his place and saw where he processed it into sorghum and bought some to use for cooking purposes. We raised wheat, so in the fall, my father would fill the trailer and we would take it to Oxford, Kansas to have it ground into flour. It was put in white cotton sacks. When we got home, it was put in a large barrel in a back room where it was cold and to use for the year ahead. This way the mice couldn't get into it. The flour sacks, when empty, were unraveled at the seams, washed and hemmed to use for dishtowels, as we didn't have dish drainers in those days.

During the drought years, we would herd the milk cows along the township roads on the grass. A lot of them were two track roads and there seemed to be a lot of grass there. Since we only had 80 acres the pasture, grass went fast, as it was small. We had a horse I rode to watch the milk cows along the road, then go by a creek where they drank water before heading them back home as we only had a hand pump well and not a windmill to pump water.

We always had a large garden. The vegetables were used on the table and canned for the winter months. Very few things did we buy from the store. We had no refrigerator, just iceboxes until two and a half years after I was married. A man would bring block ice around in the summertime to the farm homes. The people who had an icebox would put it in the top. There was a drain tube to the underneath side and a pan was put there to catch the melted ice. The bottom section was used to put food in. Bananas were hung in a cluster at the grocery store and they broke off what you wanted. The cheese was long and six inches round (Longhorn) and they cut off what you wanted. No sliced cheese in those days of any kind.

When things were scarce during the '30s and early '40s, the little chicken feed was put in large printed sacks; that was our sewing material. When empty, the seams were unraveled, washed, and made into dresses, as females didn't wear slacks in those days.

We had no electricity; no bathrooms. We had an outhouse and used catalogues for toilet paper; our school did this, also. The houses were heated by wood and coal, so only the kitchen and living rooms were heated. We used kerosene in lanterns for light. There was no television and only had radios in later years. Our school had a barn where we put our horse that we rode to school. My brother and I (and later younger sister) rode the horse to school. We would meet a family a half mile down the road and one of us girls would ride in their cart with those children. It was pulled by a horse, also.

We had a telephone about the time I was five or six; then none thereafter. We used kerosene for cuts and injuries, as we could not afford a doctor and castor oil for illnesses. We had a woodstove, so I helped run a crosscut saw to cut wood and axe to split wood. Also did this after I was married. My job also was to gather eggs and feed chickens on the farm. As soon as I was old enough, I milked cows as long as I lived at home. Sometimes my boyfriend had to wait on me to get through before we could leave on a date. I helped plant our garden and worked the ground during growing season. We also had a large potato patch. I would help pick them up when they were dug at the end of the growing season.

Our swings were made of old tires and boards and hung from our trees. I helped shock wheat when it was cut with a binder. Later that year, it was threshed with a threshing machine. There were a lot of men to fix dinner for as they had a hayrack pulled by horses to haul the shocked bales to the threshing machine. At mealtime, they would wash their hands out by the water well in a wash pan as there were several of them and no room in the house to do this. Of course, no running water and sink.

We had a wringer washing machine and two rinse tubs. We would hang the clothes on a line strung between trees in the yard even in the winter when they would freeze dry. Our cats would have kittens and my siblings and I would each claim one. They were fed skim milk after separating it. There were also a lot of snakes on the farm.

While attending Friends University, I would ride a small passenger train that came through our small town to Wichita on Sunday afternoons for class during the week. After school on Friday, I would ride a local bus to our small town and my folks would pick me up. This was at the end of World War II and there was a shortage of teachers as a lot of men were lost and others had not gotten home yet. So the government passed that you could go to college and get eight hours and teach one year. I did this for two years.

My paternal grandmother would come from the big city to our place and stay for a week or two in the summertime. We would take her to a neighbor of ours that was a schoolmate of hers back in her days to visit. She told of wearing long dresses with aprons in her days to school. One day they found some kittens on the way home and they put them in their aprons and took them home. When they got home, her father told them they were baby skunks.

The women in our community had a club that would fix boxes of food and necessity items to send to the service men in World War II. J.C. Penney, Woolworth, Kresses, Gambles, Firestone, 5¢ & 10¢ Variety Store, and Ben Franklin were some of the stores people shopped; no Alco, Dollar Store, Wal-Mart or big chain grocery stores. Towels cost 50¢, and they were not heavy ones like today, suckers were 1¢, bread 10¢, milk 15¢ a quart. We didn't have saran wrap, aluminum foil or plastic bags. We did have wax paper (saved from cereal boxes) and waxed sandwich bags. We took our own lunches to school every day.

Our family couldn't afford to drive to Wichita, Kansas but once a year. We made our own clothes and only had one pair of new shoes a year, which were purchased before we started school. This pair was worn for every occasion.

Memorable Times of the Past
By Eugena "Jean" Burdorf of Cheney, Kansas
Born 1936

I was born in 1936 at home in Goddard, Kansas. My parents were Dick and Almyra Ayres. I was the last of 16 children. My folks raised a granddaughter (Louise) eight months younger than I. We also had a dog, Trixie, a terrier. She wouldn't allow a snake or mouse in the house.

We never saw a doctor except for broken bones. Our remedies were; castor oil, mustard plasters, skunk oil tea, mentholated chest rubs, and bed rest to heal. We owned a Philco radio with about six broadbands. Dad would scan the bands for news of the war. They had six sons who served in every branch of the service. Louise and I would hurry home from school to listen to Roy Rogers, Gene Autry, The Black Hornet, and many more. That old Philco was well used. Around 1943 to 1946 the city of Goddard had outdoor movies on Friday and Saturday night, which cost a nickel. They showed the movie on the side of the city building. Seating was on the ground or your own chair.

We had a wringer washer with the handle to make the washer go. One of my older brothers, Bill, learned to how to do electric wiring in school. He put a motor on the washer. Mother was so happy; she couldn't believe it. In the winter, the washer was moved into the kitchen, but the laundry still had to be hung out on the line. When it was below 32 degrees, the clothes would freeze-dry. Dad wore overalls; we would bring them inside and let them stand-alone until they thawed and fell. Louise and I thought that was so funny to see the overalls standing with nobody holding them up.

Our source of heat came from an old potbelly stove. To cook we had a three-burner coal oil. The use of this was to put the coal oil in a glass bottle and set it in a holder that fed into the burners. Around 1946, Dad put in a propane tank and got a propane-heating stove and cook stove. Again, mother thought she had gone to heaven! My dad and mom had a cream station in Goddard; Dad would go to the farmers' house and pick up their cream four days a week. On Friday then he took it to Wichita Stephens Dairy Co. In the summer, he let Louise and I go along. We would stop at the Sunshine Bakery and get a big sack full of broken and over-baked cookies for 25 cents. I remember my dad did the cooking and mother would sew our clothes. She would get used clothes, cut them up, and remake them to fit us. She mended everything. She had an old treadle Singer sewing machine. My brother,

Bill, put the motor on the washer, put a motor on the treadle, and made it electric. Mother had that machine as long as I can remember. One Christmas my older sister got Louise and me a big doll. The next year mother made clothes for our dolls.

Harvesting wheat in the Goddard area

We girls walked everywhere, including to school, which was about a mile. In the year of 1943, we put on our snowsuits and went to school. So much snow had fallen that we walked on top of the snowdrifts that were higher than the fences. Louise and I got to school took our snowsuits off and sat down. This was second grade. The teacher took one look at me, took me to the coat closet put my snowsuit on and sent me back to my mother at the cream station. While walking to school I had broken out with chicken pox. I stayed home for two weeks with chicken pox. When I went to school, I again was sent home. The whole first and second grades had been exposed.

Our school wasn't one room but one building with 12 grades. First through eighth were located on the north side. The grades ninth through twelfth were on the south side above the gymnasium.

My mother was born near Lestershire, New York. Work was hard for her father to find. His wife died when her last brother was born, and her grandmother helped raise the children. Her father had a cousin that ran a hotel in Cheney. She wrote and told him he could get work in the wheat harvest. Around 1908, by this time the grandmother had died. They came on the train. Mother was born 1892 (died in 1994), she and her sister two years older; they were tied with ropes to their waist then to their fathers waist to keep them from getting kidnapped by the white slavers. The two boys were also tied together.

My mother stayed in Kansas and married my father at 18. The rest of the family went on to Redding California. After my father died in 1955, the family got together and flew her to California where brothers George and John picked her up and took her to see her family for the first time in 45 years. When Mother was 100, we told her we were going to have a birthday party for her 100th birthday. She said "Oh no; if I was that old I'd be dead." My grandfather John Ayres homesteaded north of Cheney Kansas. He made the Kansas territory run when Kansas was opened for settlements; if you settled on the territory, you got 160 acres of land. It was in the family until the government built Cheney Lake in the early sixties, now it is in the lake.

I fondly remember our neighbors—the Perez family. Shorty and Juanita were like second parents. Shorty came from Mexico to work on the railroad. They lived in a boxcar on the sidetrack. They bought some land from my dad. Shorty built a house using discarded railroad ties. Louise and I were always welcome for tortillas and beans. If there was an activity at school after dark Shorty (after working all day) would walk his children, Louise, and I to and from and get us home. They always had a garden with lots of jalapeno peppers. In the fall, they were picked and hung upside-down in the attic to dry.

During the depression of the 1930s, there was a government program: WPA. At that time, was when Lake Afton was built. After WWII, there were a lot of hobos that would ride the boxcars. They went west for winter then back east in the summer. My dad said they were soldiers that come back from the war and had a war problem. Dad would cook a dozen hard eggs every morning. If a hobo came to the house, we were to fix an egg sandwich and another in a bag to go. We had a water pump and they could wash up and drink, also had a bar of soap for them to use. Dad said if they could go to war and fight for us, the least we could do was to give them something to eat. Louise and I were ten and twelve years old and stayed home alone because Mother was a cream tester at the cream station. Not one time were we molested or afraid of those hobos.

After the soldiers came home from the war, they started going to Lake Afton for weekends. There was no place close to get ice for their coolers, so my dad built an icehouse. On the weekends, Dad would make three trips a day to Wichita to get a load of ice. Mother, Louise, and I would sell the ice for $0.50 per 25-pound block. Sometimes people would be waiting for him to get back.

We loved Thanksgiving. A lot of the older brothers and sisters would come with their children. A lot of my nieces and nephews were about the same age as Louise and I. We got goodies that we usually didn't get; pie, cake, and fruit cobbler. Dad always cooked a large turkey with oyster dressing. He would get a live turkey from a farmer and dress it himself.

I've been told that when I was born I couldn't tolerate cow's milk so dad got ninny goats for milk. There was an old bachelor (Bailey) that lived north of us less than half a mile. He would take a bath in his coal and wood shed. He took his clothes off except his long johns, (which he would wear all year) only in the house, and then go to the shed with clean long johns. Well one evening he went to the shed for a bath; our goats got loose and wandered off. By chance, they came across Bailey halfway from his house when he saw the goats and they chased them. He ran four blocks to the windmill on Main Street and climbed the windmill. The next morning storeowners began to come to open and found the sight, Bailey up in the windmill in his long johns, and Dick Ayers' two goats below. Someone came to our house and told my dad about the situation. Dad took Bob and John to get the goats and Dad took Bailey home. The windmill had a cement water tank on north and south sides. When farmers came to town with their horses, they could water them at the windmill. It was there in 1955 when Dad died.

I also remember the party line phones. In town, they had rotary phones. My sister Rose Meredith lived on a farm and was on a party line. Her phone had a handle on the side to call. Each party on the line had a ring; two long ones and one short, etc. There was also a ring for the operator. When I married in 1958, we were on a four-party line. We lived four miles north of Cheney. It was the late 1960s before we had a one-party phone. Unless you were making a long distance call, you only needed the four numbers.

More about the cream station: To keep the cream cool, Dad had a very large cement tank with cold water pumping in and a drain hole to drain the water. When the cream came in from the farm, it was weighed, tested, and put in ten-gallon cans, and then into the tank. On Friday when the cream was taken to Wichita, Louise and I were allowed to play in the water.

I remember we bought war bonds in school by buying stamps and sticking them in a book. It was $25.00 dollars per book, and we'd turn in the book of stamps for a bond. I remember the ration books for sugar, flour, and other things. Also during the war, the government would send the family a gold star for each son in the service and a silver star for each son-in-law. We had six gold stars and four silver stars in the window of the cream station in Goddard, Kansas.

As I mentioned before, we had an outhouse toilet. At Halloween, our toilet was always turned over. My dad got tired of putting it back up and put in a cement base and built a new outhouse. It was never turned over again. Our toilet paper was the Montgomery Ward and Sears Roebuck catalogs. We didn't like the slick pages; we could spend time in the toilet to look through them. We called them "wish books."

This story I was told. On Halloween some Goddard teen boys the Wilson's lived south of the school. The Wilsons had a small herd of sheep. Somehow, those sheep were put in the school gymnasium. Another Halloween story that happened a few years before the sheep disaster, some older boys took apart a Model A Ford and put it back together in the principal's office. No one was proven or admitted to doing the deed.

The Revenge of the Skunk
By Laura Ann Schrag of North Newton, Kansas
Born 1931

As newlyweds 50 years ago, my husband and I rented an old farmhouse for $10.00 a month. It had no indoor plumbing, only an outhouse. One summer night we were awakened by the odor of a skunk. Elmer got his gun and went out in the moonlight. As he raised the gun and took aim, his pajama bottoms fell to his feet! He fired. The skunk crawled under the outhouse and there she died, either from the bullet or what she witnessed and got her revenge. The outhouse was all but unusable for some time.

Work, Eat, Sleep, and Repeat
By Faye Klinge of Syracuse, Kansas
Born 1937

I remember outhouses. Hot in summer and breezy in the winter. Smelly chamber pots used mainly in the winter. My job was to empty and clean them every morning. Getting lost in a blizzard. Had not chopped enough wood for the heating cooking stove. My dad had to find me. Never turn your back to the wind. My brothers making tractors out of a 6" 2x4, four wooden spools for wheels. Matchbox garages and stick fences. Locking my mom in the house so I could gather the eggs I put them in my pocket and broke them. She caught me and after sitting in the chair awhile, I made the remark, "I can't figure out how you got out of the house." That stopped my egg gathering. Being chased by a bull and ending up in the rafters of the milk barn and my brother Jack saying not true bull wasn't mean. Next morning he got chased out of the corral. Bull went to market. Playing in the rain. Stomping in rain puddles, making angels in the snow, snow forts, and snowball fights. Snowstorms so bad you climbed out of the upstairs window to get out of the house. Travelers stranded and spent couple of days. Hadn't gotten to the store, ran out of food, ate boiled potatoes and water gravy. One farmer down the road got his tractor started, hooked on a sled and picked up the farms along the road into town. The owner of the only store in town raised the prices on the merchandise. Pitching bundles of wheat into a thrashing machine. They had to put in a certain way or it would clog the machine. When we got tired one bundle accidently went in wrong. Then dad had to crawl up into the machine and unclog it. Saturday night baths started with baby first and ended with papa last. Hot water added as bath cooled down. Times were hard and the work was hard. Too tired in evenings to do much but eat, sleep, and do all over the next day.

The Ghostly Cave
By Cathy Boles Amara of Huntsville, Alabama
Born 1956

My favorite story my father, Dr. Boles, would tell of his hometown, Wilmore, Kansas was of a man the town called "Dow-Slam-It." He was the town hermit. This bearded man frightened the children when they first met him but found him a good friend when you were accepted into his world. He wasn't always a hermit he had at one time been the town butcher and was called Henry Baldwin, before he took up "hermiting."

One year, "Dow-Slam-It" decided to change living quarters and picked an area the town called the zoo, as the site for his new cave home. The area for centuries had been the gathering and camping place of Indians. It was in this area that the children of Wilmore would search for arrowheads and other Indian artifacts. I took as a child searched for pieces of arrowheads finding a few. Dow-Slam-It picked a spot in a hillside facing south towards to town. His friend, Frank Stout, helped in the excavation of the dugout and planned to live with Dow-Slam-It. When the cave was complete, a serious complication arose when the two of them unearthed a long dead Indian. The Indian had been buried in a sitting position with his arrows, bow, and other items arranged around the skeletal remains. As the skeleton became exposed, Frank thought he was seeing a ghost. In fright, he dropped his tools and took off running towards town, vowing never to return. Nothing Dow-Slam-It or anyone else could say or do could sooth Frank's fears and induce him to return. Dow-Slam-It finished his cave alone and was its sole occupant.

The cave was made of poles laid across the excavated area to form a base to hold other boards, which closed off the openings between the poles. The entire roof structure was finished off with soil piled in such a way as to make a rounded mound to facilitate water run-off. Dad said Dow-Slam-It invited him in to see the finished product and it was a pretty good cave. Dad said he couldn't see any ghostly presence. When Dow-Slam-It pointed to the spot where they had unearthed the Indian, but said he would not have liked spending the night alone in the cave. Dad said that over 50 years later the state historical society sponsored a big archeological dig in the area. They referred to the cave as a historical cave site. His response was, "Historical my eye, it was Dow-Slam-It's home of the 1930s."

My Tonsillectomy
By Helen L. Murray of Newton, Kansas
Born 1923

When I found an envelope in my mailbox a few days ago asking for a story about something that had happened to me, in the same mail I received a copy of my hometown newspaper in which was an article that said, and I quote, "Helen Farrar had her tonsils removed Tuesday at the Wallace hospital." I decided to write my story.

I grew up in Norwich, Kansas. It was a small community in Kingman County. Our local doctor's name was Eugene Wallace and his motto was "My Ford is always ready." It was a shiny black sedan. I remember folks back then said, "If you want a Ford you can have one in any color as long as it is black." I was seven years old when I needed to have my tonsils removed. I remember the feeling I had when Dr. Wallace gave me the shot that put me to sleep for my tonsillectomy. It worked quickly. I was out like a light. The next thing I knew, my dad was sitting beside me, and I was in a hospital bed.

Before long, a nurse brought me a small dish of ice-cold orange flavored sherbet. Of course, it hurt to swallow, but I could eat it slowly. Later a nurse gave me a five-stick pack of Yucatan chewing gum and encouraged me to chew it. That helped to heal my sore throat. Dad took me home and I soon forgot about my successful operation.

Party Lines in Rural Areas
By Elinor Keesling of Newton, Kansas
Born 1922

Party line phones were both a joy and a bane to subscribers. To rural subscribers especially, they were a joy as they could contact businesses, friends, or relatives without having to drive to do so. But they were a bane because nothing you said over the phone was private. The phone itself was a box-like contraption they mounted on the wall. It had a speaker that projected out of the center. The receiver hung on a hook on the left side attached by a long cord. When you lifted the receiver, the hook went up and made the connection. On the right side was a crank that you turned to call "central" or the phone office. The operator would answer, "Number please" and then call the number you asked for. If the person was on your party line, you could call them without going through the central office.

Each family had its own number of rings, one long, one short; two longs; one long, one short, one long; all sorts of combinations and everyone knew everyone else's number. You could lift your receiver and listen even if it weren't your number and many did. I can remember when my future husband would call me. We never said anything we didn't want anyone to know. It made it more difficult to hear when others lifted their receivers so you might have to ask them politely to hang up. Most people cooperated. Once in a while,

Papa, Ernest and Helen

someone might ask you something several days later that made you know they had been listening in.

The style of phone changed in later years and we had a desk type phone. It rang, only at your house. But one lady discovered that if she placed her phone on her TV and turned the TV on, if someone else's phone rang, her picture would turn snowy. Then she would pick up her receiver and listen. We soon realized that and if you heard a receiver being picked up, you might say, "Okay Mrs. Hornbaker, please hang up your phone."

There were usually 10 to 12 parties on each line. It could be helpful in rural areas. If lightning would strike a building or haystack and the farmer needed help, he would ring a very long ring. Everyone knew they were to pick up the phone and listen. Then many would come to assist in putting out the fire. Just before we were married (I had been teaching at Sylvia, Kansas and my parents lived at Plains, Kansas) the trains went on strike and all mail was carried on trains then. So we couldn't make our final wedding preparations by mail. So my husband-to-be would drive 10 miles into Sylvia from his parents' farm so we could talk on a private line. Party lines made life much better for those living in rural areas especially.

Two Little Girls Left Behind
By Ruth Saranko of Valley Center, Kansas
Born 1931

When my sister and I were six and ten years old, our parents decided to move to Louisiana. There was not room in the car for all of us so my sis and I stayed with our grandparents. Our grandma and grandpa lived on a farm, milked cows, sold eggs, and farmed wheat for a living. Our grandma was a shy little lady who wore long dresses and had a bun on her head. Grandpa had a good sense of humor. She milked the cows (each cow had a name). He would then cool the milk in the milk house and take it to the ice cream plant in Hutchinson. Sometimes Sis and I would ride with him because we always got an ice cream bar at the plant.

Sometimes Sis and I got to go to the pasture and bring up the cows to be milked. We had to cross a paved road so one of us would stop cars so the cows could go across. After all, we couldn't stop the cows once they started across the road. Grandpa took the milk cans to town in an old box style car that had the passenger seat out to make room for the milk cans. He also had a one-gallon can by the gearshift that he spit his tobacco in. there were tobacco stains running down the side of the door on the outside. Our grandma would never ride in that car. She had her own 1938 Buick that was kept in the barn. My uncle would drive it to town for her, which was a rare event.

My grandma was a great cook and once won a contest for the best pumpkin pie but could not produce a recipe so she didn't get the prize. She cooked from scratch and never measured anything! The hobos from the railroad behind our house would come up and ask for food. Grandma would fry some egg sandwiches and give them a quart of milk. We ate a lot of fried chicken. Grandma would wring their necks but my uncle had a tree stump and axe that he used. I wanted to try it so I held the chicken by its legs and put its head on the stump. I only got it chopped part way. The blood squirted and I screamed and let go of the chicken. It ran around with its head flopping over, and then died. I never wanted to try that again!

Our grandma was a little paranoid and always put a rag over the mouthpieces of the wall telephone so people could not hear us talking in the house. We liked to see her comb her long gray hair. She would bend over and comb it towards the floor then twist it around and around and it would settle down on the top of her head as if it belonged there! I guess it did!

We had no toys to speak of so my Sis and I used our imagination. We put sheets over chairs and made us a house to play in. outside we would get buckets of sand from the lane and put it on the sidewalks and make towns and streets and trees out of sticks and cars out of cardboard. We cut pictures out of the catalogs and used them to play with. When our parents left us behind, some people felt sorry for us, but Sis and I know, it was one of the best times of our lives. A year later, our parents returned so we went back home, but grandma and grandpa were very special people to us.

A Time of Simplicity and Poverty
By Martina Stegman of Oxford, Michigan
Born 1933

I am writing from the time I lived in Rush County in Bison, Kansas. I lived on a farm all my childhood days till age 14. I was number six in a family of eleven children.

Our family home was a house of one large front room where we cooked, had an icebox, and ate around a large table. There were three bedrooms: one for my parents, one for the seven boys, and one for the four girls. Those seated on one side of the table along the wall sat on a bench. In this room, there were games on the floor for the small children in the evening and the older ones tried to listen to the radio (like the *Grand Ole Opry*) or read the newspaper. The younger members were often cautioned not to be too loud. Often the ball rolled and hit the bottom of the icebox opening where a pan was placed to catch the melted ice above. So we needed to wipe it up! In this icebox, there usually was some beer for the farm workers or anyone else. Growing up I didn't know children could not or should not drink beer. I did on a hot summer afternoon; took a few swallows and capped the bottle for anyone later!

Most family activity happened in this big family room! On a cold winter's night when a pig gave birth to her litter of pigs, she often was not able to feed them all. So my father would bring two or three into the house in a box so we could feed them on a nipple placed on a pop bottle, preferably a "grapette" bottle because of its small size. This was a delight, needing to take turns to feed or over-feed those babies! This was the case too when the mother sheep died and left baby lambs to be fed and kept alive.

In the early morning before school, my older brothers were out in the cold barn milking cows. I being about nine years old was asked to go to the barn to get a pail of milk for breakfast cereal, which was always expected to be warm! Only later in life, I wondered why people served cold milk for cereal? Also in my morning jaunt to the barn, I was asked to go to the brothers to ask them how many pancakes they wanted to eat. My mother made the pancakes as big as a large plate. It was not unusual for the order to be as many as three for the high school boys!

We had a rotary phone. Ours was one long and one short ring. We knew our neighbors rings, so when our older neighbor's ring was ringing more than usual, we presumed there was severe illness or maybe even death in the family. Sometimes people even would listen in on the conversation to see what the problem was.

In the summertime, we would live mostly in a smaller house called our summerhouse. This house had two rooms: a large room for eating and recreating during the day and a small kitchen in another room. We had no air conditioning, so on a very hot day, we would hang a wet gunnysack (wetted in the stock tank) and hung it on the window to allow the cool air to blow threw. It was amazing how comfortable this would be for as long as the gunnysack was wet. This gave the younger set some activity and help around the house. This arrangement also allowed for improvements, such as painting in the larger house to take place. Very dutifully, we pulled all the shades during the hot summer days so this house would be cool to sleep in come evening. This house too did not have air conditioning.

On Valentine's Day at our country school of three rooms, grades 1-8, it was an eventful time to exchange Valentines. We would keep our Valentines from year to year. When it came time to think of exchanging Valentines, we would find our bag of the year before, erase the names, and decide who to give this valentine to this year. This was acceptable in our school and time of life! Imagine the poverty and simplicity!

During the war, WWII, our school was eligible for commodities. The meals were prepared with what the commodities allowed and these were far from the taste of mom's cooking. I remember being cautioned by my teachers not to be wasteful, and so I would put what I could not stomach in my napkin and throw it into the outside toilet! I remember one item being chocolate rice.

Paying My Way in 7th Grade
By Allan T. Kimmell of Topeka, Kansas
Born 1925

I was born at home on May 18, 1925 in Cherokee, Oklahoma. I was only called "A.T."

or just "T," as my grandfather Bernard was "A.T..." He was my mother's father; I was the third son of Robert and Etta Kimmell. They had married in 1915 and ended up adopting my oldest sister in 1918. They had been told they couldn't have children.

Vivian and her parents lived in an apartment upstairs from a bank where my mother was employed. She had been visiting them daily until both of baby Vivian's parents died the same week. Both died of flu. Grandfather suggested that the baby girl be adopted by my parents. Who would have known that five children would be born later? Bob in 1921, Charles in 1923, A.T. in 1925, Doris Jean in 1928, and Margaret in 1930. We all lived in a small bungalow type house that was built by dad and his mother prior to 1915. The house was on a corner number of lots with plenty of room for a coalhouse, a garage, and a big garden. A big front porch and a partial enclosed back porch, three bedrooms that had room for dad and mother in the largest, Doris Jean and Margaret in the middle one, and a front one for Vivian. Us three boys lived and bedded in the back porch. In winter mother heated bricks in the oven and wrapped them in towels or papers for us to take to bed for warmth.

I started in the 1st grade in 1931 there was no kindergarten. I started bringing animals home, the first were two little Billy goats, given to me by a nice guy who owned a goat dairy. Dad and I sat on the back steps and he told me we had no feed for them, I thought they could eat tin cans. Finally, he offered me a nickel to take them back to Mr. Woods, so I did. Later I owned dogs and cats, steer, calf, and finally a small flock of registered sheep. The sheep sold when I enlisted in the US Navy. I finished the 8th grade in 1939, wearing a tailored suit, Justin cowboy boots, and I paid for all this with $1.00 down and $1.00 per week! Hamburgers cost a dime and movies also.

No one was surprised I ended up becoming a veterinarian. My dad gave a heart to heart talk when I was in the 7th grade. He told me that he and mom would furnish me a home and daily meals but all other costs I needed to pay for them myself. From about 1937 till I left home in early 1943 I paid for my clothing and my other costs of living; I paid my own way. My life was pretty well organized by working for my Bernard's Dairy and going to school. I was limited on all other activities, but it worked out okay. I missed both grade school and high school sports, so I lacked much relationship with other guys my age. My job became very important to me. A grandfather who really believed in the president's social security program started taking a few pennies for me to be a member.

Both of my older brothers were members of the US Army, 45th Division and were mobilized in September 1940. Both ended in Army or Air force service through the entire World War II. I waited until I was 17 years before I learned I could graduate from high school and was able to get both parents to sign me in the US Navy Reserves. I finished school in December 1942 and was enlisted in early March of 1943. At a Navy base I learned to eat beans for breakfast, march, tie knots, wash and pack uniforms and bedding, and become homesick.

My job within the dairy was a seven-day a week affair. Up every morning with my mother's assistance. I was the runner from the delivery truck with a needed delivery to each houses front or back door area. I rode on the running board on the rider's side or my uncle drove through the streets of my hometown with the rider's side window down, I could

Vivian holding A. T. with his brothers Charles and Bob in 1927

reach in and find exactly the quantity of milk products that was carried and the empty glass bottles set by the customer was returned to the truck. Saturday and Sundays required me to pasteurize, bottle, and refrigerate the milk for Monday's delivery, both to residents, grocery stores, and cafes downtown. Often I was late getting to school.

During gardening season, my father grew many vegetables like potatoes, corn on the cob, onions, peppers, tomatoes, radishes, and even cantaloupes. My sister Jean and I had a wooden wagon we pulled up and down many streets and knocked on doors to sell our produce. All income went home to dad. My father was paid with "scrip" instead of money during those terrible years called "The Dirty Thirties." Scrip could be used to purchase things in certain designated stores, like we could buy groceries or drugs but could not be exchanged for money.

All of us remember the dust storms that came in air from and that were south or southwest of us. Some storms were very dark or red in color and some lasted for a short period of time, but some continued to blow for quite a long time. Our flock of chickens occasionally thought it was the night and so they went to roost!

My Lifetime of Learning
By Maurice B. Craghead of Dodge City, Kansas
Born 1926

I was born in the winter of 1926. Officially, I am a high school graduate, however I have spent a lifetime going to schools, part-time, while earning a living to some 40 years on more aircraft, electronic, teaching, supervisory, etc. schools, which were required for my trade, as an Electronic Technician for a major Airline. Then I taught electronics further on at a Junior College level. I have accumulated five federal licenses and I am mostly self-taught, so studied for those licenses on my own.

I was born and raised on a small farm in the Western Kansas Plains, about 16 miles north of Dodge City, Kansas. During the 1930s, there was no money. I was 6 years old. This became known as the "Great Depression" and we were right in the middle of what was known as, "the Great Dust Bowl." To begin with, the people all raised cattle because the buffalo grass was solid and plentiful, before that stock market crash, but the farmers could make more money from plowing up that sod and planting winter wheat. My dad was a cattleman. Still, grain elevators sprang up in every small town, so more people plowed up more land. Dad was forced to go along. So they raised more wheat. Then the drought came. There was little rain, and the crops failed to produce. Those winds swept the prairies bare and the topsoil blew away leaving just hard bare ground. So this created much more hardships, you could not see day from night for two weeks. One day the wind would blow from the north, the next day from the south. The dust so thick you could not see to go from the house to the barn, so we strung a wire to the barn, to find the barn. The dust drifted, like snow does in the wintertime.

In the early days of this great depression, which was started with the crash of the stock market in 1929. From as far back as when Kansas was still a territory, the Indians had warned these new farmers that if they plowed up these open plains that it would blow away. Still those young farmers, in order to put out more production from their land, plowed up the sod. This sod in many cases was used for building sod houses since there were few trees for building wooden homes.

There was no money, so we survived by work and breathing dust, with bandannas over our noses. There were no oil breathers on the autos and tractors, they hadn't been invented yet, and the dust served as grindstones and ruined the engines. Luckily, my dad had a good team of draft horses, so we were still able to farm. We raised our own cattle, which gave us meat, milk, cream, cheese, and butter for feeding the hogs who gave us sour cream, which we sold at the creamery in town. With the money from the cream, we used for buying staples, clothing, and other necessaries. New shoes once a year, otherwise we went barefooted.

The wind blew; we rode saddle horses to school, two and a half miles one way. We were three boys riding the same horse. Dad didn't worry, because he always said, "Teach them to ride and all they had to do was stay on the horse and he will always take you home, blizzard or dust storm." Our school was a one-room schoolhouse and we lived some 14 miles

Maurice in the middle and his brothers

from the nearest town (Jetmore, the county seat) and Dodge City, just 16 miles south of our farm. Our teachers only had a high school education, with one summer school to teach them how to teach. Yet we, the students, had to compete with the town schools, and take the same final test as everyone else in the state did.

Every one of we boys had our special chore. Me, being the youngest from the time I was two, since we had no plumbing or electricity, I was assigned the job of carrying water from the well to the house; carrying coal, and kindling to my mother who cooked on a wood/coal burning cook stove, and for the heating stove. If the axe was too heavy, they gave me a hatchet. If the bucket was too heavy, they gave me a gallon bucket. We had an outdoor privy.

Thousands of farmers gave up and packed up trailers and headed west to California and Oregon. Those of us who did not leave suffered the consequences, by breathing dust and fighting the drought. These dust storms lasted until I turned about 12 years old. Then, just 6 days after I turned 14, the Japanese bombed Pearl. We were now at war in Europe and in the Pacific. All three of we three brothers wound up in the war before it ended. Dad had been a wounded WWI Veteran. My oldest brother joined the Army immediately and was called into the field artillery just after the first of the year in January of 1942. He ended up in the Army Air Corps. He flew in B-17s over Europe and was shot down over France, but survived the crash landing with disabling injuries. Later he received a medical discharge because of his disability, and he received 50% disability for the rest of his life. My second brother finished high school in 1943 and then joined the Army Air Corp also, as what they called an "OLT" (On the line trainee). This was an emergency replacement program for the replacement of pilots who had been killed in combat. He was later discharged as surplus after the surrender by both the Germans and Japanese.

I finished high school in 1945. I was drafted into the Infantry following WWII, "Battle of the Budge." Two weeks later, the Germans surrendered. The war in Germany was over. Because of an injury to my feet, I was washed out of the Infantry, sent to the Army Air Corps and was sent on to 11 weeks of radio repair school in Truax Field in Madison, Wisconsin. Then the very weekend we finished the first 11 weeks of radio fundamental course and a new course was scheduled to begin the next Monday, the Japanese surrendered in the Pacific. The war was over.

Because I had taken typing in high school, I was now drafted to become a Discharge "Clerk Typist" in the personnel office. After most of the former AUS, (Army of The United States) were discharged, I was assigned as a clerk typist in the personnel office. We discharged thousands of veterans based on a point system. I received my discharge about a year later, on October 12, 1946. But that radio school started my life's career with Continental Airlines. Here I spent 25 years as an Avionics troubleshooter and supervisor of aircraft maintenance. I retired from Continental Airlines over 30 years ago, on April 1, 1982, at age 56.

My Special Hometown
By Patrick Sandoval of Greenwood Village, Colorado
Born 1950

What makes my hometown, Garden City, Kansas, a special hometown? Well some will laugh, but I'm really serious that my hometown has some special features, or at least I remember that it did. First of all, we had a drainage ditch that went through the middle of most of the city. It was rare that I ever saw much water in that ditch. Did we really need that ditch? Perhaps it had to do with a major flood we had in 1965. That flood was just like an Irwin Allen movie. There was a hill called "Thrill Hill." If you drove over it fast enough, it gave you a thrill.

In the center of major wheat and cattle country, we had Penny the Elephant, who happened to live at the Lee Richardson Zoo. If you went on a hayrack ride, you made new friends saw a million stars, plus shared hot chocolate and a warm fire at the end of the ride. You always cruised the bypass now and then, even when nothing was happening. Dragging Main Street was a great way to spend your evening in order to meet someone new. Five Points was the only place in town where five streets came together. Whose idea was that?
We had a feedlot called Brookover's Feed Lot. Who was the clown that created the expression, "Smell the money"?

Near the corner of Main Street and Kansas Avenue, you would find the only Dairy Queen in the city. Knowing where the Dairy Queen was located was a must, especially when you needed a hot fudge sundae. In 1959, seven miles west of Garden City, was the small community of Holcomb, Kansas. Two recently released convicts, Richard Hickock and Perry Smith, murdered farmer Herbert Cluter, his wife and two children. Truman Capote and his friend, Harper Lee, came and researched a book that we now know as *In Cold Blood*. Rural America was changed forever. Some say it was the end of innocence in the Midwest.

Garden City actually had two processing dairies (Meyers and Gardner's Dairy) within two blocks of each other. They both had great dairy counters where you could get ice cream, sandwiches, and great malts. Both of these dairies employed a lot of Garden City families. We actually had two other great spots to have a bite called The Creamy and the A&W Root Beer Stand. The A&W featured servers on roller skates that brought you a delicious mug of root beer and a grilled cheese with French fired pickles on the side.

On Main Street, you could go to the State Theater. Its name was impressive. It was the State Theater not the City Theater, not the County Theater, but the State Theater. Midnight movies there were quite interesting on Halloween night. Who threw that firecracker? Let's not forget Saturday morning Christmas movies at the State Theater. Each year those movies and cartoons were provided by the downtown merchants. They would have drawings for free gifts for all the kids that held on to their ticket stubs. I once won a Sunkist pocketknife. I thought I had just won the lottery. In Finneup Park, the younger kids could meet Santa and get a free bag of candy.

Parades, yes we had great parades. I almost forgot the annual Christmas parade with the marching bands from surrounding communities, not to mention Santa Claus in a big, black, old Cadillac. Garden City always had a nice parade for our annual fiesta. Wow, it was so fun to go to the fiesta in September to see your friends, listen and dance to old Mexican rancheros, as well as enjoy all the great food that was being served at each of the booths.

The end of harvest, usually in late July, meant that many farmers finished cutting their wheat, yet started looking ahead to planting their next year's crop. So in August, the Finney County Fair, plus a rowdy carnival brought many families together from all over Southwest Kansas. The farmers were able to swap stories with other famers, plus see the latest tractors and new implements. The carnival brought great rides like the Farris wheel, Tilta Whirl, and chance booths, which guaranteed a winner every time. I can see those colorful lights, smell the popcorn, and taste that pink cotton candy as if it were yesterday.

Each October we had Merchant's Night (Oktoberfest) in which all the downtown merchants stayed open late. The fun part was they always had three local bands playing in the middle of Main Street. Louie Garcia had a great Rock/Latino band and Ray Hudson and the Rhythmaires played old country western. The third band was always a new surprise. Halloween was a night that I think our parents dreaded the most. Why? Because it was the night that we would come home with many large pillowcases full of homemade popcorn balls, caramel apples, and other assorted candies that we would enthusiastically devour.

Fire, did I mention fire. We had great bond fires right on Main Street. The Garden City High School Marching Band would play great fight music. After the cheerleaders got our hearts thumping the wildest thing happened. Everybody grabbed hands and made a human chain. Some people called it the whip, others called it the snake. We all weaved back and forth down Main Street running like crazy people escaping the blob. Somehow we all ended up at the stadium to watch the homecoming game. A special thanks to the GC Volunteer Fire Department for putting out that fire.

I remember going to see Garden City High School's great championship team of 1962. There were hometown heroes like Doyle McGraw, Richard Masoner, Scottie Davis, Rodger Stoner, and my brother, Richard Sandoval. One other person on that championship team was one of the greatest high school athletes I have ever seen. His name was Mike Johnson. Mike was one of our neighbors on First Street and a classmate of my older brother and sister. Mike became a Kansas High School All American football player. This Garden City native continued his football career at the University of Kansas, playing two of those years next to KU's legendary, Gale Sayers. Mike graduated from the University of Kansas and then was drafted as a running back for the Oakland Raiders. Mike Johnson was traded and played three years for the Dallas Cowboys with greats like Don Meredith, Bob Hays, Walt Garrison, and Mel Renfro. I hope someday, my hometown will recognize Mike Johnson for his lasting contributions to Kansas's athletics.

Yet, I still remember rednecks in the high school stands shouting their racial slurs at Mike Johnson. In the 1950sand '60s there was still a lot of discrimination against African and Mexican-Americans in Garden City, Kansas. Mexican-American GIs returning from the end of WWII had to fight a new war for themselves and their children. I remember as a Mexican-American having to sit upstairs at the movie theater and in the choir loft at Catholic Mass. Dances at the Civic Center in middle school were where you were told, "to dance with your own kind." After the giant city pool was finally opened to all citizens in 1947-48, there was no way minorities were allowed into any of the private pools. I had many wonderful teachers and coaches that made me believe I could accomplish anything, yet I had one teacher that gave us pet names such as "Slant Eyes" and "Jew Boy." I still can't believe that this same person retired as a "Distinguished Educator." I remember taking a wonderful girl named Nancy to get a Coke after school. The next day her brother, a good friend, and track teammate, approached me the next day, "Pat, you and I are best friends and I really like your older sister. Please, please don't ask my sister out again. Pat, you don't understand, but our parents are in the Klan." The discrimination in the '50s and '60s was both overt as well as covert. Those were the realities of that time. Garden City has come a long way since then.

Garden City also was a hot spot for great music and dancing. Man, we had The Keg, one of the best beer joints I can ever remember being in. The Keg was all painted in black light, which depicted the Universe. The National Guard Armory brought in bands like the Fabulous Flippers, Big Brother, and the Holding Company, and many, many more. Let's not forget those homecoming or prom dances at Ben Grimsley Gym. It was so fun to be on the planning committee to decorate that old gym. Ben Grimsley Gym also held many basketball and wrestling events for both the high school and junior college. One night, that old gym was host to pro wrestling (WWF) and the fans got to see Texas Bob Geigle in person.

Did Garden City, Kansas have a drive-in? Does Warren Buffet make money? Yes, we had The Garden Drive-In. It was a great place to sneak into even if you had the money. Bad, bad kids. The drive-in had Buck Night, which was good on dad's wallet. The children always enjoyed the playground in front of the main screen. I remember the wonderful aromas going into the concession stand. You could smell corn dogs, hot dogs, hamburgers, popcorn, and sip on a big old coke. You could watch your movies in your car, on your car, next to your car with a blanket, or from the back of your truck. If the movie was good or bad, it was never as good as the massive lighting storm taking place behind the screen. Best of all, was making out with your honey. Oh, Bubba!

Garden City's free swimming pool was the largest free swimming pool in the United States. It was built during the great depression by the WPA in the 1930s. Garden City, Kansas must have had only had 2,000 citizens then. Exactly 2,000 people could have easily fit into that pool. Man that was some serious digging. Nothing like watching a cute lifeguard strutting their stuff. Do you remember the smell of swimming pool chlorine, baby oil, or the taste of chewing Sugar Babies? It's true at the end of summer, they would drain the pool and while it was draining, they would let the elephants come and swim, letting them cooling off after another hot summer day.

Now don't get me wrong, Garden City, Kansas wasn't perfect. In the '50s and '60s, Garden City had only one radio station called KIUL. It was a good local station for farmers needing the daily agricultural reports. They played rock and roll music in the afternoon from 3:00-5:00 p.m. Thank God for WLS in Chicago, KOMA in Oklahoma City, and Wolfman Jack broadcasting from the mighty 250,000 watts, XERF 1570 AM in Ciudad Acuna, Coahuila, Mexico. I did clap for the Wolfman and always will. God rest his soul.

Well, I hope you got to grow up in a special American hometown like I did. Thank you Garden City, Kansas. Perry Como used to sing a great song written by Burt Bacharach called "Magic Moments." Those magic moments seem brighter after all these years. Garden City, Kansas you were very much like the great book, *The Learning Tree*, written by Gordon Parks. I did learn so very much about what is good in life, but not perfect. Bless all of you who got to share my little town. Remember to smile; you might be on Candid Camera.

Rita's mother, Velma Lorene Thompson Gooch

The Dirt and Dust Storms
By Rita Anne Mills of Hugoton, Kansas
Born 1943

My story starts out by what my parents and grandparents told me, because I was only about nine months old at the time. My brother, Mike Gooch, was three years old. Our mother had put us both down for our naps and my daddy asked her to take him down the road about a quarter of a mile to bring the cows in to be milked. My mother, not wanting to wake us up, turned the coal oil stove off and proceeded to take daddy down to bring in the cows. When she arrived back at our home, smoke was billowing out of the windows. Frightened, she ran into the house and grabbed my brother and me and ran out of the house to return to the field to fetch my daddy. By the time they arrived back at the house, it was blazing so fiercely, they couldn't enter to save anything.

We lost everything that day, except the clothes we were wearing! My brother says he remembers standing in front of the house and watching neighbors passing buckets of water to one another in an assembly line, trying to consume the fire. My mother thinks that when she turned off the coal oil stove that some flames must have leapt up and caught the kitchen curtains on fire, which caught the house on fire. They were just so thankful that she hadn't taken daddy farther down the road and couldn't have got my brother and me out of the house. When I got married and had my own children, she warned me never to leave them in the house alone to do a chore or even to drive down the road to get my mail. She learned a lesson the hard way.

My mother made most of our clothes when we were younger. I remember my Grandma Hanner taking scraps of material from the dresses my mother made me and making a sunbonnet quilt for my bed out of the material leftover from my dresses. I still have that quilt today and I will always cherish it. My older cousin, Joyce Drew, from Rolla was older than me, so I always got a lot of her clothes, which she had grown out of. My Aunt Gladys would bring boxes of her clothes and I would love it. It was just like Christmas. Her clothes were always store bought and not handmade. I would spend hours trying them on and standing in front of the mirror.

Three years after I was born, my mother had us a baby brother. His name was Joe. I thought he was the cutest little guy. I used to dress him up in my baby clothes and pretended he was my little sister. He didn't always like that, but I sure had fun. Years later when he saw the pictures, he really became angry. As the three of us grew older, my daddy would clean our big horse tank out and fill it with water and that was our swimming pool. I remember after a few weeks, we were sliding on green moss in that swimming pool. Who said you had to have chlorine? Our cousins would all come down and we would have a ball in that old tank and climb up in the barn loft to try to find a new bunch of fuzzy little kittens in the hay. Then we would go out in our windbreak and make hideouts and play for hours. I have so many memories of living on the farm.

My older brother and I attended all eight years of grade school in a one-room schoolhouse. We never had more than 18 to 20 kids in our whole school. I think we had about four teachers in those eight years. I remember some names. Mr. Gillette was the first teacher I remember. I remember if the boys were acting up, he would flip his ruler on the back of their ear, and they would straighten right up. I remember Peaches Johnson. I really liked her. I remember a Mr. Bradfield, but don't remember his first name. I also remember Mrs. Garner, but don't remember her first name. Back then, you always addressed them as Mr. or Mrs. I guess that is why I don't remember their first names.

We had two rooms off the schoolroom. They were called cloakrooms. We would hang our coats in lockers and put our lunches in there until noon. The boys had a cloakroom and the girls had a cloakroom. If someone brought soup for lunch, we would put it on the floor furnace to keep it hot until lunch. We had outdoor toilets; we called them outdoor Johns or outhouses. Along about our 7th and 8th grade years, we got indoor toilets, running water and all. We thought we were in tall cotton then! The teacher would call each grade, one at a time to a recitation bench to teach our subjects, starting with the 1st grade and ending with the 8th grade. We were taught reading, writing, arithmetic, English, history, science, and music. We had two recesses that we would play kick the can, Andy over, Red Rover Red Rover, and run races and practice for track meets. At the end of the year, we would go in to Hugoton to the grade school and all of the country schools would compete against each other in a track meet. At the end of the year, all of the country schools would have a school program at the Hugoton High School. We would have piano solos, vocal solos, and some would read or recite a poem. Then the whole school would sing a couple of songs. That was always a fun time.

When we finally got a telephone, they were party lines. Several other people could listen to your conversations that you were having with friends. I didn't like that very well unless it was me listening in to someone else's conversation. Ha. It went both ways I always said. You sure never had any secrets, that's for sure.

We had chores we had to do. We had to milk the cows before we went to school. I hated milking because my younger brother always liked to play around, and instead of milking, he would try to hit the cats mouth with a stream of milk. He would always make a mess and I would have to end up milking his cow and mine, so we wouldn't be late for school. After we milked, we would separate

Michael Berry Gooch, Joseph Eugene Gooch, and Rita Anne Gooch Mills

Rita's family in 1991

the cream from the milk. I would help mother churn the cream into butter. I liked to churn. It was fun to watch it turn to butter. I thought that was cool. I remember staying all night with my piano teacher's daughter. I came home telling my mother all about this good butter they had for breakfast. I said, "It tastes better than our butter, you need to find out what they put in it." Later I found out it was oleo or margarine. My mother said, "That wasn't butter that was a butter substitute." I didn't care I thought it tasted better. My mother got a kick out of that.

I had to gather the eggs. Sometimes I waited too long and the old hen was already sitting on the nest with the eggs under her. I would have to reach under her to get the eggs and sometimes get pecked because she didn't want me fooling with her eggs. I finally figured out that if I took a stick with me and held her head down with the stick, then I could reach under and get the eggs, and she couldn't peck me. I remember a little Banty rooster we had, his name was Billy. I should have named him Bully. I hated it when he was out there when I went to gather the eggs. He would chase me around the chicken house until I went into the hen house, then he would finally leave me alone. When he died, I actually cried. I don't know why. We always raised chickens, so when I got older I would help mother by killing the chickens, dipping them in hot water, and plucking their feathers off. Cleaning and cutting them up wasn't my favorite part, but I sure enjoyed my mom's fried chicken all winter.

A bad memory was the horrible dirt storms that would roll in on the horizon, so black and dark. One evening our family started to Liberal to take in a movie for the evening. We got several miles down the road when my daddy turned the car around and we headed back to the house. He saw a dirt storm moving in on us. The dirt hit before we got home. We couldn't see anything and then our car died. Daddy said, "I'll have to go to the house and get the jeep and come pick you guys up." He tied his handkerchief over his nose and mouth and followed the ditch to find his way to the house. I was terrified! I knew he would get lost and we were just going to die out there on that road. After about an hour, he returned and was I glad to see him. Getting back home safe and sound made me one happy girl.

I'll never forget that we had a horrible blizzard one year. When it started snowing, you couldn't see anything. We had baby chickens that had to be fed and watered in the brooder house. My daddy tied several ropes together and tied them around my brother's waist. He told him to feel along the house and then find the fence that went around the chicken house and follow it and if he felt like he was lost, just tug on the rope and he would pull him back to the house. My brother didn't have any trouble. He got them fed and watered and got back in safely. It was fun because we didn't have to go to school. Mom would pop popcorn. We would play Chinese checkers and other games and put puzzles together. It was just good ole family time. When the snow finally quit, we had drifts that we could climb up as high as our REA lines that brought electricity into our house. I've never seen a snow like that since.

We washed our clothes out in the well house. It wasn't too far from the house. We had an old wringer washing machine and then we would hang up our clothes on a clothesline outside to dry. On top of the well house was a supply tank that held our water for washing, drinking, etc. The windmill would pump the water up out of the ground and then we had a pump that pumped the water into the supply tank. The top was open, so once in a while we would have to remove dead birds from our water in the supply tank. I don't know how we didn't get really sick drinking that water. We always had dogs and cats as pets. I always liked dogs better than cats. It was always sad when we lost one. We would bury them and have a funeral for them. We had quite a pet cemetery.

Memorable people in my life were my family, grandparents, aunts and uncles, and cousins. I didn't have a sister and I always wanted one. My cousin, Sheryl Gooch, lived down the road south of us about a half-mile. We would ride our bicycles or horses to one another's house almost every day. We were like sisters. Her mother, my Aunt Rachel was like my other mom. We never got tired of playing together. One day we found a skunk and we taunted him until he finally sprayed us. Our mothers wouldn't let us in the house until we took a shower in the well house. Then we thought we would try our mothers' cigarettes out behind the chicken house. They caught us and were we in trouble! We never tried that again.

The Magic of Yankee Stadium
By Donald C. Lipprand of Winfield, Kansas
Born 1935

I was born and raised on a farm at Bunker Hill in Russell County, Kansas, in 1935. I was the 3rd of 6 children. When I was 18 years old, in 1953, I was invited by a couple my family knew to go to New York with them to an eight-day religious convention, which was being held in Yankee Stadium. My father gave me $100.00 to take care of expenses, so I got to go. On the first day of the convention a pretty girl, her mother, and two younger sisters from Saskatoon, Saskatchewan sat beside me and the couple I was with. We arranged to meet each day of the assembly so I got fairly well acquainted with her and her family. After the assembly was over, we wrote for two years. We never had a phone so our only contact was by letters. Two years later, in the summer of 1955, we decided to meet again. By then I had my own car. My grandmother and I drove to Vancouver, British Columbia to meet again. We decided to get married; it took five months to get the necessary papers so she could come to the United States to live. She came to Kansas in November 1955 and we got married December 7th, 1955. That was 58 years ago and we are still happily married. Each year since our marriage, I have taken my wife home to see her family. Her parents are both deceased, but we still go each year to visit other members of the family.

Betty and Don today

Betty and Don in 1955

Jackolopes
By Lowell Wayne Jones of Johnson, Kansas
Born 1934

I Lowell Jones and my sister Gwendolyn Jones lived with our parents and a brother and another sister both older than us. We lived about fourteen miles southeast of Johnson, close to Sandaroy Creek in 1936 Gwen and I followed a small dog that we had away from our house to the creek area during that time a bad dirt storm came in. We could not get back to the house and my parents could not find us. They hunted for us all afternoon with all the neighbors. At about night one of the neighbors heard the dog barking, he found us under some sagebrush plants we were using to hide under from the dirt storm. We never followed the dog off again. I was two years old and my sister was three years old at the time.

My grandparents lived on the other side of Sandaroy about one mile from our house from their house we sometimes could see balls of light just above the ground. The older people called the lights jackalopes when they started drilling gas wells they stopped glowing.

Some people used to think it was the gas pressure that would come out of the ground and glow.

Don't Go Near the Railroad
By Lloyd H. Yoder of South Hutchinson, Kansas
Born 1937

I grew up here in central Kansas, my great grandfather moved here from Ohio in the 1800s. An Amish man with his family, after a number of years he moved back to Ohio, one of the boys my grandfather stayed here because he had found the love of his life here. Mary Miller, things were real tough back in those days. My grandparents had seven boys and two girls.

My dad Harry Yoder was the fourth in the family. They lived seven miles southwest of Hutchinson. A new highway went through from Hutchinson to Pratt and two railroads on the north side of their farm, Rock Island and Santa Fe, with a lot of trains going.

Two of my uncles moved to Oregon and got married, leaving the Amish.

Years later when they came back to visit grandpa was still living in a little house on the same farm with Albert on of his boys and the whole family would get together and have a big dinner on the farm.

I was about eleven years old and my dad had always said don't go near the railroad tracks, well, after dinner two of my cousins said let's go watch the trains and that was just too much for me. I went with them, we put pennies on to have them flattened, well one of the boys started throwing rocks at the train so I did too, well, and my rock hit a window, now who would have thought a boy forty-two inches tall could throw a rock that far? Well, I did, I came from a family of six children, three tall, and three short, my dad was six feet tall and mom five feet seven inches. My older brother, now deceased, grew to forty-eight inches tall, like I did; younger sister is forty-two inches tall.

Well, scared as I was I hid in the barn, later that afternoon the security officer came by and because the whole family was on the lawn he stopped, and asked, and of course, one of my cousins ratted on me. Someone came to the barn and said somebody wants to talk to me, well, he questioned me, and I had to admit to it. He made me promise to never do it again. (Oh yes, sob, sob). Well, my dad had to go in and pay for the window, $6.75 cheap. It was a small window; it only broke the outer window of a restroom. I was told there was a lady on the commode and I scared her half to death. Now I wonder what went on inside that restroom.

The officer had the rock because only breaking the outer glass it fell down and lodged between the inner and outer glass. My dad was never hard on me and I wondered why until later in life in one of our reunions at reminiscing time the story was told how three of my uncles took a bar of homemade soap and soaped that same track and a train was on the side track a mile away and came down just starting up, well you guessed the rest it took one hour to go one third of a mile back and forth and the boys were in that same barn laughing their heads off and my dad was one of them. I got caught; they didn't so children don't go near the railroad tracks.

Be sure your sin will find you out.

Void of Any Present Day Conveniences
By Betty Elaine Koehn of Galva, Kansas
Born 1929

"Two boys and two girls" were the wishful words spoken by my 5-year-old brother, that night before Christmas, as he looked into a basket where a little baby lay. But alas for poor brother, it wasn't a boy. It was a girl. He probably thought if a family already had two girls and a boy, it was only natural to have another boy. So, perhaps he was a bit disappointed. Later in life, he made the remark "that if it hadn't been for his 3 sisters, he would never have had to be spanked."

The rural Hesston, "Maple Grove Country School" was presenting their Christmas program that evening and my sister, wanted her Mother to come too, because all the girls had embroidered handkerchiefs for their mothers and planned to present them with these precious gifts that evening, but her mother chose not to go. Perhaps she was already feeling signs of impending childbirth. My mother was a rather heavy woman and probably wore a large dress plus a big apron and my 8-year-old sister didn't have a clue what might be going on. That night she had to come downstairs to get a drink for her little brother. When she got down stairs, there was a bed all set up in the living room and Mother was lying in it. There hadn't been one there when she went to bed, so she said, "Mom, are you sick?" Mother told her to look in the basket, which she did, and with that, she spun around and ascended the stairs at record speed. Pretty soon, three children were coming down to look in the basket.

I was born December 24, 1929, on my Grandpa's farm, located one mile north of the Meridian Church, rural Hesston, Kansas, and lived there until I reached the age of four. At that time, we moved to my other Grandpa's farm at Halstead, Kansas and that is where I grew up. I had two sisters and one brother. We lived in a rather large two-story house that had a canopy of grape vines on the west side of the house, which provided lots of shade in the summertime and it seemed cool under there. A pump was also located there. Just a short distance south was the first refrigeration as such that I remember, a deep well that had a bucket tied to a long rope, so if you needed to have something kept cool, like butter, milk, eggs etc. you put them in the bucket and let it down, deep down into the well to be kept cool, and when you needed one of these items to prepare a meal, you went to the well, opened the lid and pulled on the rope and brought the bucket up. There was also a "spring house" a short distance to the west where water from the windmill ran through and cooled the milk after milking time and then from there, the water ran to the stock tank for the cattle to drink. I'll always remember the wonderful orchard, where I loved to play. At one time, my grandpa had planted many apple trees, different kinds, and in the fall, he would sell boxes full of apples.

I grew up in a time just after what we call "Horse and Buggy Days." My mother used to tell of a time when they would see a strange light at night, like a ball of fire and it would come up close to a buggy, as it was going down the road and when it would get almost up to the buggy, so close that you could see the shadow of the horse, it would disappear and appear again a distance behind them. Lots of old timers saw this light. This even happened to my mother as she was driving her horse and buggy down the road one night, but it was never known to hurt anyone. It was said to have originated from a deserted farmstead down the road.

Old farmhouses were rather drafty and cold in winter and hot in summer. Sometimes, in a snowstorm, snow would drift in around the windows and would be lying in a drift on the windowsill and the windows would be so frosty you couldn't see out. Bedrooms were icy cold and your breath would rise up off the pillow in a cloud of vapor. We'd get out of bed and run to the dining room to get dressed behind the roaring heating stove. My dad would get up early and build a fire in the heating stove and then in the wood burning kitchen range so my mother could fix breakfast.

These farm homes were void of any of the present day conveniences, bathroom, water heater, faucets, central heating, and air. So, of course, going out into the pitch dark evening to the formidable "outhouse" was quite a challenge, for a little girl. A lantern would have to be lit and my older sister would have to be persuaded to "please" go with me. She was usually kind enough to go. That time, in general, was a quiet time, no streamline trains, jets or big machinery, just the sound of the birds, dogs, pigeons crooning in the hayloft, roosters crowing, the cows mooing, the whinny of a horse or the delightful song of the meadowlark. It was a time when "gross" meant 144 or 12 dozen and the word "cool" meant that maybe you should wear a jacket. "Hippie" indicated a broad backside. Drugs were something you would take for a headache or a bad cold. It wasn't uncommon, if you had a cold, to have to sit with your flannel wrapped around your neck, drinking some kind of hot toddy. You would probably break out in a full blown sweat and, of course, that was supposed to do wonders for your cold!?

We found pleasure in just simple things. Nearly everybody was poor, so there wasn't much of what we call "peer pressure" today. I remember going shoe skating on a nearby frozen pond in the winter, taking the sled with us. Of course, there were no ice skates, perish the thought, or at least not for us. I would feel so sorry for my mom and dad because they couldn't go too. They acted like they didn't even want to go, and I thought it was so much fun. Sometimes on a snowy winter night, my mother would make "snow ice cream." We would go out and skim a bunch of fresh, clean snow off of a snow bank, no fall out, and she would add eggs, sugar, and cream to it and beat it up and "yum" it was good.

The following incident was related to me by my oldest sister. One day, when I was a few months old, my mother's sister came over to take my mother cherry picking and wanted her to drive her car, Model T, so she got behind the wheel. My sister was taking care of me, but wanted to go along to the orchard too. Since I needed a diaper change, she laid me down at the end of the sidewalk to complete the job. All at once, she saw this car coming straight for her, and she just barely got out of the way in time, without any time to pick me up. The front wheel must have hit the edge of the sidewalk with such force that the front wheel jumped over me. Then instead of the back wheel running over me, the car veered off in a half circle and came to rest at the woodpile. My mother was not used to driving a Model T and she pulled or pushed the wrong lever. I was taken to the doctor immediately and he checked me over thoroughly but could find nothing wrong. Miracle!

The Great Depression of 1930-1940 was a very trying time for most people, especially when it deepened in 1932. This was followed by a horrible drought two years later, which turned the entire state into a dust bowl. Many banks across the country were forced to close and people lost their money, farms, and homes. The sky was literally choked with dust as top soil took to the air.

By this time, we had improved greatly with our refrigeration. We had a wooden ice box. One side held a 50 pound hunk of ice and the other side held the perishables. What a treat it was to get the icepick and go to that hunk of ice and chip off a little piece to just suck on. Of course, I really didn't want my mother to see me doing this. I'm sure she would not have approved.

When someone died, the Undertaker would go to the home and dress them for the funeral and pack them in ice until the funeral. There was no embalming at that time. My sister remembers that they put pennies on my grandma's eyes to keep them shut. She was taken to the church in a horse drawn hearse. It was a wagon type rig that had a seat quite high where the Undertaker sat and drove a nice looking team of horses. My sister remembers that when they opened her casket at the church, some moisture had collected on her face, so the Undertaker pulled a red bandana handkerchief out of his back pocket and wiped her face.

Harvest time was always special. My dad cut the wheat with an old binder and a team of horses. Then the bundles of wheat had to be shocked. It was always exciting to hear and see the big old steam engine pull the threshing machine into the lane and out to the field to thresh the many shocks of wheat. My mother, grandmother, and aunts always fixed lots of good food for these men, plus taking a lunch out to the field in the afternoon. We had a little Shetland pony and a little cart and the thresher hired me to take the hard-working men the bundle haulers and the threshing crew, a cold drink of water from the windmill once every hour. I had a jug wrapped in a gunny sack and I would get cold, fresh water from the windmill and they all drank out of the same jug and were refreshed! He paid me a dollar a day, which helped me buy a new bicycle at the end of the season and I was so thrilled. I remember it was green with "balloon tires" and a basket on the front. Butchering was another fun day for me. I liked to watch them make the sausage. My one problem was that unless they butchered during the Christmas vacation I couldn't go to watch. I HAD to go to school, no playing hooky. We would always have some kind of fresh pork for supper that evening.

I'll always remember long, winter evenings when the snow was blowing and drifting and I secretly was hoping we would be "snowed in" by morning and wouldn't be able to get out to go to school. My dad would be sitting on one side of the table, reading a book to the family and mother would be on another side either cutting out quilt blocks or darning socks, with the lone kerosene lamp in the middle of the table as the only light. Some evenings, usually around Christmas time, instead of reading he would be drawing cards, depicting old-time winter scenes, horse drawn sleighs, and barns, Old Mill streams, etc. with his many fine pointed pens and different colors of ink. I've wondered what he could have done today with all the modern fine pointed, different colored pens, or ballpoints that are available. He would have never had to worry about the ink blotting.

Tell Me a True Story
By Gwen Wilson Brooks of Dodge City, Kansas

When I was a little girl, I would love to crawl up in my daddy's lap and beg him to tell me a true story. As a young boy, he had come to Kansas with his parents and a company of settlers from New York. At that time people could stake a claim if they promised to plant trees. They built a "dug out" in Hodgeman County, north of Hanston. He said his sister made "mud pies" on the earthen floors.

Life was hard for homesteaders and my grandfather left his wife and children to go work on the railroad. My dad became the "man-of-the-house." He had gone to school only three years and now his job was to herd cattle. He said one time he came upon another herd with two mean looking cowboys. They told him that his dog had stampeded their cattle and they were going to cut off his ears!

One time he told me that he took his little

Louis Bishop Heimer and his wife, Edna Lee (Cowan) Heimer in 1954

sister, Jenny, with him. They took the cattle to a rocky hill near where the Mennonite Church is. A rattlesnake bit her. He had to carry her and get the cattle back. He then walked eight miles to get Dr. Bowie, hoping he could save her. She had crawled up on a trunk and gone to sleep. However, it was too late. They buried her the next day. Years later my dad had her remains taken to the Marina Township cemetery.

In those days, an important social event was a "Box Supper" girls would decorate a box and fill it with a lunch for two and the box would be auctioned. Dad said his girlfriend secretly described her box, so he would know which one to buy.

Even with his "limited" education, Louis B. Heimer and his wife, Edna, owned and operated a General Merchandise store in Hanston from 1909 to 1954. The Hanston State Bank is now located on that corner.

Their only son, James, died at the age of thirteen in 1929. Through the years my parents supported the schools and churches. My dad was the Mayor of Hanston for many years. They were truly pioneers.

I still own the Homestead. As a girl I remember days when we had outhouses and no electricity. It was a custom to turn over those thrones on Halloween. I remember when we could buy a quarter's worth of gas and drive around the "Mile Square" and out to "Pike's Peak." We had some severe blizzards and sometime "Dry Draw" would flood.

My first grade teacher was Miss McClean. She was a role model for me and that is one reason I became a teacher. Another teacher I remember was Mr. Hirschler. He made me wear a Red Ribbon all day because I climbed to the top of the Merry-go-Round. He also told me "A whistling girl and a crowing hen will always come to some bad end!"

Sheep Loving Youngster
By Ruby Ashcraft Deaver of Fowler, Kansas
Born 1930

The days have come and gone to my memory of farm life in Kingman County, Kansas.

Before old enough to go to school, my love for baby lambs made good toys and friends.

When the sun shone bright I would lay in the long narrow ewe feed bunks and let the little lambs suck on my fingers, and I took my nap and my mother would hunt her long lost daughter, she most always knew where to find her, in the sheep pen sound asleep with little lambs sucking away on her fingers.

Later when shearing time came along in the spring and the mommas were penned and the lambs in separated pen, after each ewe was sheared and turned loose in another pen I would place her lamb without a miss to its mother. Remember the mothers didn't look the same without wool.

In later years, I helped my dad block the ewes and rams for County Fairs and yet later my bottle fed lamb, Peanuts, was Grand Champion, and showed him at Kansas State Fair and lead the last livestock parade in front of Grand Stand in 1947.

At this show, I met the love of my life and nine months later married for sixty-two and a half years.

My love of sheep ended at the Jr. Livestock Show in Wichita, Kansas where my lamb followed me to Douglas Street and back up the ramp in the forum to the sheep quarters then to the auction ring.

I said good-bye with lots of tears. After graduation, I was married to my State Fair lover and moved to western Kansas, Fowler, with my husband Jim.

Great memories of my sheep loving parents, Harry and Alice Ashcraft.

Growing Up in Southwestern Kansas
By Vernon McMinimy of Charlottesville, Virginia
Born 1930

I was born and raised near the line that separates the western third and the central third of Kansas. Our home was 13 miles north of the Kansas and Oklahoma line. Dad raised cattle and wheat. Home was one-quarter mile south of a very small town called Sitka. The population of Sitka, at that time was about 65, maybe 70 people. Today it totals 2. You can still find it on a road map but it really doesn't exist. My early childhood included the great depression and the dust bowl. I don't have much recollection regarding the great depression. I do remember the dust storms of the dirty thirties, however, there was much more good than bad in my childhood.

A few years ago, the family had a reunion at the home place, and one of my grandsons, who was there for the first time, commented, "How can anyone live here?" Well, I did, and had a wonderful time doing so. I had a dry creek one-quarter mile east, and a wet creek one-quarter mile west. About a dozen boys

Ruby and Peanuts in 1947

within three or four years of my age were in the area and 1800 acres to work and play in. There was a small swimming hole in the wet creek where we would go skinny dipping to our hearts content. When it rained it was a day off, and you could construct an earthen dam in a little ditch, which held water for a while. The area is semiarid so a rainy day was a day to celebrate. I couldn't understand the concept that a rainy day was a gloomy day. Rain was GREAT! I had horses to ride, no charge. Cattle to take care of, milk cows to milk. Horses, cows, and occasionally one of the milk cows calves to feed and care for. In milking the cows, cats were always around so you could squirt milk in their mouths. With practice, one could get pretty good at squirting and hitting the target. However, it did somewhat cut down on the milk production. One time I broke one of the milk cow calves to ride, I named him Lazy. In the evening when it was time to bring the milk cows in from the pasture, I would ride ole Lazy out in the pasture to bring his mother and the other milk cows in for feeding and milking. One day I was riding Lazy around the corral where the milk cows were resting. Lazy's mother was laying on her side so I rode Lazy behind his mother put my leg out to touch her back; she saw me do that and got up very quickly, Lazy jumped away and I fell between them and broke my arm.

Taking care of the farmyard animals was called "chores," which you did morning and evening every day of the week. It wasn't work; it was "chores." We had chickens so one of the chores was to gather the eggs every evening. My older brother and I on occasion would throw a hen up in the air and watch it flutter to the ground. We stopped doing that when one we threw up came down headfirst, didn't flutter, broke its neck, and died. Not all the eggs the chickens laid were laid in the chicken house, but were distributed around the farmstead. One day some of the boys from Sitka, my brother and I gathered about two dozen of those we found around the farmstead and took them to the grocer in Sitka. We offered to sell them to Jake, the grocer, he said he wouldn't give us money, but, would give us a bag of candy. You can't get a better deal than that so we gladly took the candy, went to the wet creek, and consumed the candy. What a deal. A few days later dad found out what happened. He went to Jake and apologized for what his boys had done and said he wanted to set it right. Jake told dad not to worry, he said the boys gave me rotten eggs, and I gave them wormy candy. Even trade.

We had this mare I rode when we rounded up the cattle, or just rode out to check and see how the herd was doing. When you saddled her, she would make her belly bigger so after you rode a little while you needed to stop and tighten the synch or else soon you would be riding sidesaddle. I failed to stop and tighten the synch one time and ended up on the ground. I was in the sixth grade when we had her bred to a palomino stallion that belonged to a cousin of dads. The product of that mating was to be my horse. When the colt was born, she was a beautiful palomino colt. I watched her grow up, running and kicking her heels in the air. I loved watching her. I named her Beauty, she was a beautiful horse. Beauty was two when we broke her to ride. I had a wonderful summer riding that horse around the area, and a few times, I rode her six miles to my cousin's place, and my cousin and I would play in the canyons fighting the Germans. It was our country, so we always won. Late that summer I went into the barn and Beauty was staggering around, so I called dad. He came and saw how Beauty was acting, went to the house, and called the veterinarian. The next day the veterinarian came by, examined Beauty, and said she had sleeping sickness. Gave us some medicine and said to keep her moving as much as possible. I did that, but she got worse. The vet would come and see Beauty almost every day. In spite of all the attention and medication Beauty died. Years later, I asked dad how much the veterinarian charged for his services. Dad said that he didn't charge anything; he just didn't want to see that boy lose the horse that he loved.

One summer one of the farmers in our area broke his leg around harvest time. So most all the farmers in the area agreed on the days to come to his farm, harvest the wheat, plow his fields, and do what was necessary until he could return to work. Sometimes there would be as many as six tractors in the field at one time. With that many in the field it doesn't take long to finish the field. On those days when many gathered to do the work, the farmers' wives would come with food for the workers. Farm families did this in addition to harvesting their own wheat and plowing their own fields.

Years later, I left home for college, married, had children. We lived in various urban areas. I always felt sorry that I couldn't give my children the toys I had growing up: a dry creek to the east and a wet one to the west. So to my grandson, that's how anybody can live there.

Lake City
By Ivan Harris Phillips of Pratt, Kansas
Born 1925

We moved from a ranch in Southwest Barber County in 1927 to Lake City a population of about one hundred people. We were very poor but did own our own home of about 1100 sf. I had a brother and a sister who were older than me. Our home was not modern in anyway, yes an outhouse, no electricity, no running water, wood burning stoves. One pair of work clothes and one pair of school clothes.

I finished high school with seven friends when I was seventeen. I worked on farms and oil fields until I was eighteen. Shortly after I became eighteen, I was drafted into the service where I grew up quickly. I was a member of the Army Air Corp, and became a gunner on a B-24 aircraft. To make a long story short I went to the south pacific as a crewmember of a Recon Squadron of course the war was over about three months later so we were lucky. We flew our mission from Palawan Island to Borneo, where several crews were assigned to map Borneo. After the war when I was a flight engineer, we flew to Australia and photographed airstrips and cemeteries for a couple of months.

My first vehicle was a 1928 Model A pick-up, which my dad had bought from Bell Telephone Co. for about $50-$70, which was a lot of money in those days.

We didn't own a car until I was seventeen when I sold the pick-up and bought a 1929 Oldsmobile for $75.

Back to when I was fourteen years old and a sophomore in high school, I worked on public works, scooping sand to a concrete mixer for forty cents an hour, forty hours per week, and went to school one day per week.

Nancy Phillips and her son, Ivan Phillips in 1944

Then they found out that I was only fourteen.

I attended the largest one man owned Rodeo when I was about eight or nine years old. The owner was M.F. McClain or as most knew him as Mac, and he was a true cowboy with tobacco juice seeping out of the corners of his mouth. Mac stood about six feet tall and always wore tall cowboy boots with his trousers in the boot tops. By the way, the rodeo grounds were just south of Sun City, which was a pretty tough Gypsum Mining Town. You never wanted to say anything about anyone while there. Because they're about all related and you could get you're a___ whipped.

My first girlfriend lived in Sun City, which is six miles west of Lake City, and I have walked this many times a night going home.

Carrie Nation lived in Barber County and there is a memorial there for her. My dad saw her crush a joint in Kansas City, Missouri, but as a very small lad, I did know Bill Horn, but as a stagecoach driver, he got notoriety. He was the one who kicked Carrie Nation off the stage way out in the country. You see she slapped the cigar out of his mouth.

There is no Lake at Lake City. The pioneer that settled there was a Lake and I'm not sure which one, and there is only one there now Russell B. Lake III.

At Medicine Lodge, there has been a re-enactment of the Indian Peace Treaty, but I don't have the particulars.

Rural Route #1
By Wendel Chalfant of Hutchinson, Kansas
Born 1939

I was born the third child of four siblings. Our family lived in several houses in Hutchinson before Dad and Mom bought an acre of ground two miles west of the city and moved us to a house in the country at rural route #1. Although it was only two miles from Main Street I later learned, it can be a long way to walk.

It was a small two-bedroom house with no insulation in the walls, no bathroom, and only a freestanding gas stove to heat the entire house. Air conditioning consisted of opening the windows and screen doors. There was a small, unattached garage, a chicken house and an outhouse. As I recall the toilet was a deluxe model two holer. Dad eventually added a room to the rear of the house and remodeled one room into a small indoor bathroom but it was several years after we had moved in. I was probably only about three years old but I remember how huge this place seemed and how tall the weeds were above my head. The house was so cold in the winter that Mom used to heat bricks on the stove and wrap them in a blanket and put them in bed with us to keep warm. The house was located on a short country road that had no name and for years, we had no address except for Rural Route #1. The road was always muddy with huge mud holes to play in. Everyone had a mailbox in a group that was located on Old Highway 50 at the corner.

Dad was a carpenter and Mom was a stay at home housewife until Dad was badly injured in an automobile/bus accident. Mother went to work in an egg factory located on South Main Street in Hutchinson. My grandmother lived with us and was my primary educator until I started elementary school in September 1944 at North Reno Grade school. There was no kindergarten class at North Reno at the time. It was a public school located at West 17th Street and Wilshire Blvd., Hutchinson, Kansas, and is still there.

The school consisted of two buildings, one small building for the 1st through the 3rd grades, and a larger building for the 4th through 8th grade. The larger building was divided into two large rooms separating the 7th and 8th grades from the elementary students. The larger room also consisted of a small library and a stage. The stage was used for a variety of activities including school plays, PTA meetings, movies and election voting. Hot lunches made from surplus military rations and milk was served in the basement. There were also two outhouses, one for the boys and one for the girls. I remember them as very smelly and very cold.

The walls on one side of the classroom and the front walls were covered with huge blackboards where we did a lot of our assignments. The blackboards also served quite efficiently as a disciplinary tool. I remember too many times writing on the board "I will not talk during class." However, our teacher believed in increasing our vocabulary and would have us write something more expressive like "I shall refrain from discussing unnecessary subject matter during classroom activities." Write that 100 times on a blackboard and you learn that keeping quiet during class is a true virtue. After writing the statement 50 to 100 times then we were required to erase it all and wash the blackboard with clean water twice to prepare the board for the next day. Then we had to dust all the erasers that were used during the day. This was all done after school was dismissed. Then we had to walk home. It was at the teacher's discretion to what type and how much discipline you were assigned with many variations. Putting you in a dark cloakroom for long periods of time would probably be frowned upon today.

One of the most exciting memories would be the walk to and from school. I have often told the kids and grandkids I walked ten miles to and from school. Just to set the record straight it was only one (1) mile. Sometimes we would catch a ride to school but rarely would we get one coming home. Can you imagine your grade school child walking to school today or catching a ride with whomever? However, to a grade school kid in this day and age it would seem like ten miles. It was quite the road. The road was dirt with one section completely covered with huge cottonwood trees on both sides. We had each part of the road named with descriptions such as, dead dog hill, the swamp, dead man's run, etc. At the start of the road, there was a huge junk yard complete with every little boy's fantasy. The old cars, trucks, and tractors, kept us busy for hours. Fortunately, there was no junkyard dog but we did have to deal with a mean old man that owned the place. It was fun to hide from him but very scary when he would almost catch us. We played a lot of "kick the can" along the way. Mostly it was just get a can and see how far you could kick it all the way to school and back. Tore the heck out of our shoes and I remember mom yelling at me to "stop kicking those cans, those shoes don't grow on trees."

I think almost all the 7th and 8th grade boys ended up cutting asparagus for a local farmer, Mr. Hubert Morgan. Every afternoon in the springtime, he would show up in his pickup truck and haul a truckload of boys out to his farm. He had two large fields of asparagus planted in long rows. We used razor knives to cut the asparagus and he would mark a measure on your hand to make sure you didn't cut the asparagus too short. You would cut a bundle in your hand and carry it over to a "box row" unless you were lucky enough to get a "box row." It was back breaking work and you could make up to 50 cents an hour if you worked fast enough. Many bloody fingers and aching backs later we would load up in the pickup for our ride home. If the weather was warm enough we would head over to a big irrigation ditch for a quick swim in our "skinny dippin" suits. Mr. Morgan would pay us once a week in silver dollars or 50-cent pieces. You were doing very well if you made $10 in a week. He gave an incentive that if you didn't miss a day of work, Saturdays and Sundays included, he would take you for an airplane ride in his private airplane. It took me 3 years but I finally got to take my first airplane ride in his little Piper Cub.

Dad and Mom always planted a huge garden of tomatoes, beans, squash, peas, corn, lettuce, cabbage melons, fruit trees that required copious amounts of water to make things grow. We, my brother and I and all the rest of the neighborhood kids we could Tom Sawyer into helping, dug a large well with casing by hand. Dad rebuilt an old Willy's engine, hooked up a pump, and created a powerful irrigation system. When it came time for irrigating, we would dig ditches to the garden and flood them by building streams to all the plants. It was a lot of work but playing in the water and mud made irrigation day a fun time. At the end of the growing season when the fruit began to spoil, we would have rotten tomato fights.

Mom canned all the vegetables that came out of the garden all summer long. I still remember the sweat dripping off Mom's head in that hot little kitchen as she prepared jars and cooked up the veggies to put in them. We ate canned vegetables all winter.

It was always exciting when I learned we were having chicken for supper. That meant a "chicken killing" was coming soon. I don't think Mom had it in for any particular chicken. She just picked one out and then stalked it with her special built chicken hook. Once it was snagged, the unlucky chicken would be grabbed by the head, violently twisted about three times until the neck snapped, a foot placed on the broken neck and the head pulled off. The chicken would flop like crazy for a while but I think it was dead long before the flopping began. Then we would dunk the dead chicken into boiling water and pick out all the feathers. I still think about chicken a little differently when shopping now at the supermarket.

I have never cared much for watermelon but could not resist the thrill of going "melon stealin." There was this huge melon patch not too far away from where we lived and on a moonlit night nothing could beat sneaking into that patch with all the snakes and other creepy creatures that might be lurking about, find the biggest melon and carry it off. Since I didn't care much for the taste of watermelon, I would find a nice ripe cantaloupe. They were much easier to carry anyway. We never got caught but got the hell scared out of us a few times when the owner was waiting in his car looking for poachers. Luckily we saw him before he saw us.

The Arkansas River ran only about one

half mile south of our house and we spent many exciting hours swimming, fishing, camping, hunting, and whatever else you could do in and around a river.

Sometimes we would hitchhike to town. Along the way we would pick up any discarded pop bottles. If we were able to find six of them we would take them to Mammel's grocery store on 1st and Adams Street and redeem them for two cents apiece. That would buy us a ticket to the State Theater for an exciting afternoon movie starring Tom Mix, Hopalong Cassidy, or the Durango Kid. Downtown offered many exciting adventure choices with the Fox, Strand, Midland, and State Theatres, the YMCA, The Penny Arcade, The Karmelcorn Shop, Kresses, and Woolworths just to name a few.

We did not have a TV set when I was a youngster. I think dad finally bought a black and white set about the time I became a teenager. I watched mostly westerns, Paladin, Maverick, Have Gun Will Travel, Wagon Train, Gunsmoke. We really enjoyed The Honeymooners, Father Knows Best, 77 Sunset Strip, Perry Mason, and Arthur Godfrey. We played a lot of card games, Canasta, Pitch, and Poker. Our most popular board game was Monopoly. Our entire family would sit around and listen to radio dramas like The Lone Ranger, The Green Hornet, The Shadow, Innersantum and comedies, Abbott and Costello, Burns and Allen, Fibber McGee and Molly, Bob Hope and Jack Benny.

We didn't have any timesaver appliances and everything was done by hand. I remember a big thunder storm once left our yard covered with large hailstones which we quickly gathered in baskets and used to make homemade ice cream. We had a small Oak icebox to keep food cool. It was powered by a 50-pound block of ice on one side of the box with the rest of the box used for keeping butter and milk cool. It also had a water cooler with a spigot. It now sits in our dining room storing video tapes and games. All of us kids had specific responsibilities and everybody chipped in to work around the house. Laundry was done in the basement on a two wringer Maytag and carried outside to be hung and dried on a clothesline.

Southwest Kansas
By Barbara C. Campbell of Liberal, Kansas
Born 1942

Many times my thoughts go back to the little farm house on the hill in Kansas. That's where I was born in 1942, and I grew up there with two brothers and one sister.

There were many interesting things for kids to see and do as we grew up in the 40s and 50s.

There was the big old dusty barn with the cows coming in and out. Later on there were my older brothers horses he was paid to train. Daddy told us to be sure and stay out of that barn when they, the cows, and horses were in there! Sis had been kicked in the head when she was little, so I always did stay out when I saw them.

The haymow was too full of dust and dirt and little hay to play up there anyway!

We had a tiny little garage built for a 1912 Electric Car, I think! All our buildings were built in 1918. Back of that garage was a little room I claimed for a playhouse. Daddy poured a cement floor and put in a real door and window on the South side. That was the side on the corral.

The cows could come up and look in! One day one tried to come in! I kept that door shut after that.

Summer days on the farm

Barbara and her siblings

The chicken house was too full of packed down hay and dirt to play in there.

I loved the garden next to the chicken house to the north. It was fenced with a picket fence just like the yard.

Daddy spent a lot of time in there growing things. He grew the best big luscious red tomatoes in there.

There were rows of asparagus, rhubarb, squash, radishes, cucumbers, onions, corn, and melons. Years later, when daddy's health was bad he planted it all in grape vines.

Today that garden fence and all no longer exists. It's nothing but hardpan dirt out there. The barn went down and the chicken house was torn down and carted away. Time takes care of everything.

The road ran by the front of our farm. We had a long driveway. Daddy poured that with white rock and kids rode up and down with our tricycles and bicycles. One day when my little brother was about five or six, I gave him a big push on his tricycle! Just at that moment, I heard a vehicle coming over the hill from the west! I just knew he was going to get hit! And I had pushed him out there! Little as he was, he guided that trike into a quick right turn and avoided disaster! Whew! We didn't tell daddy about that!

Daddy also told us to stay out of the pasture when the cows got close to the farm. Also not to play or swim in the Buffalo Wallow when it was full of water after a rain.

That spring daddy took the boys on a train ride to see the mountains! I'd heard him discussing it and thought that naturally I would go too! One morning they sneaked out and left me! I ran after them and cried to no avail. I was so mad about being left out; I planned to go swimming in that lake! That afternoon when it was warm, I went down there and got in! After a couple of hours, I went home. Then in a while, I began to get a bad headache! Mom put me to bed and I didn't get up for two weeks! That was one bad headache!

When daddy came back, I couldn't remember what had happened to me! He took me to the doctor; he didn't know what tests to run, now we know that an amoeba causes the sickness! Don't let your kids swim in dirty water ever!

The Galloping Gourmet of the Third Grade
By Shauna Labo of Saraland, Alabama
Born 1963

Growing up on the farm in Comanche County, Kansas was a rich delight! Some of my fondest and favorite memories of Kansas were rooted in 4-H program experiences. Daily chores included riding our horses to round up our wooly critters that needed tending. After chores, came dinnertime. My family definitely enjoyed testing my creative culinary concoctions. It did not take long before I was affectionately labeled the "galloping gourmet" of the third grade. Thankfully, my grandmother, Hazel Murphey, taught me much about homemaking, as my mother was of the undomesticated sort, to say the least! To her credit, farming was her forte!

My culinary creations began with demonstrations of how to make eggnog, a muscle drink, for school and 4-H projects. Later they blossomed into bigger and better experiments. One of my favorite memories was trying to make a Baked Alaska. It started out with all the necessary ingredients, except one, which was the one thing to make it into a flaming festive fare, the liquor. My family was not big on liquor, so I dared not ask about trying to obtain it. This, coupled with the fact that Comanche County was a dry county, there was no liquor readily available! So, I ventured forth to the local grocery store in search of a substitute, something with alcohol, to test it out! I actually found that peppermint extract's content came the closest to 100% alcohol. So I tried it! The Baked Alaska was a flaming success, however, due to the amount of alcohol required to make it a fiery feat, the pungent peppermint perfume wafted all throughout the house. Since then, I've not been highly fond of peppermint!

By 1980, when I was 17 years old, I decided to make a cherry pie for the county fair 4-H competition. At first, I made two pies, one a lattice-top crust and the other a full crust. I was being very creative as I had meticulously laid out the latticework on one pie and carefully crafted a 4-H emblem for the center of the full-crusted pie. Whichever pie looked the best was the one I was going to take to the fair. Unfortunately, the full crust pie burned on the edges, so we attempted to eat it. Much to our surprise, it was terribly tart! Suddenly, it donned on me that I must have forgotten to put in the sugar! So, to double check the lattice crust top pie, I stole a cherry from it to test its flavor. It was tart too!! Oh no! Knowing this, my pie was destined for disaster unless there was a diet/diabetic dessert division! Alas, I made yet another pie, this time with sugar!

At the county fair, my final cherry pie won the Grand Champion prize! I was so elated! Back then, the food exhibits were judged and kept on display for about three days in a building that was not air-conditioned. On the final day of the fair, we decided that we'd celebrate our hard-earned efforts with an "After the Fair" snack to enjoy the Grand Champion pie! Much to our surprise, after being re-cooked in a building for three days, the grand champion pie had fermented! We tried feeding it to the dogs and they would not even touch it!

My current success as a homemaker is largely due to the many experiments I had during my childhood, trials with a few errors along the way that my family survived! I took great pride in becoming creative when, at times, life lent lemons; one just makes lemonade, doing with what was available at the time. Many thanks to all my family members for being my guinea pigs while laughing and living to tell about it.

Small Town Girl

I was a small town girl that graduated from high school as co-valedictorian of a class of nineteen students in Protection, Kansas! Nine years later, in October 1989, I moved to Manhattan, Kansas and became the Riley County 4-H Agent. This was my ultimate dream job! I was continuing a long-time family legacy that my grandfather began when he became the first Greeley County 4-H Agent in Kansas back in 1930. Manhattan was where, in May of 1992, I met my future spouse-to-be.

When my husband and I planned to get married, my parents were adamant that we get married in Comanche County so that my grandparents would be able to be present for the occasion, since traveling was not an option for them. Destined for the heartland of rural America, this was going to be a "small-town" wedding, and conversely I was marrying a "big city" boy from Burnsville, Minnesota, which is a suburb of Minneapolis.

My family was known for its wedding day shenanigans, so I did everything in my power to thwart any efforts that might end up deterring us for our big day. Unbeknownst to everyone (except the bride and groom of course), we stashed our car in a garage in Pratt, Kansas at the limousine owner's house who we hired to pick us up after the wedding celebration. Upon our car drop-off, we had the limo driver take us into Greensburg, Kansas where both bride and groom had differing plans of how to get to our destination of Coldwater, Kansas

David Labo preparing to take his bride, Shauna Murphey for her first ride as his wife

for the rehearsal and wedding. As the bride, my plan was to meet up with one of my bridesmaids in Greensburg who was going to take me into Coldwater. My future husband was supposed to meet one of his groomsmen at the tuxedo shop in Greensburg, and then they were supposed to go on to Coldwater from there. The limo driver dropped off the groom at the tux shop and then dropped me off at my bridesmaid's home. Lo, and behold, the groomsman failed to meet the groom, so the groom ended up calling his future father-in-law to come to his rescue, for a ride from Greensburg to Coldwater. Thankfully, during the trip to Coldwater, no questions were asked about why the groom was stranded in Greensburg with no ride to Coldwater. Indubitably, my father suspected something was awry…but he kept his mouth shut!

When everyone was present for the rehearsal, my brother started quizzing everyone about where our car was. He even threatened one of my bridesmaids to tell him where our car was; after all, his mission was to turn our car into a mess. Aside from the bride and groom, not a single soul knew where our car was at except the limo driver! My brother's threats and mischievous plans foiled; he had to resort to other motives to prank us on our wedding day.

Coming to small town rural America that is Coldwater, Kansas, from the big city of Minneapolis, Minnesota, the first question from the groomsmen upon arrival in Coldwater was "where is the nearest ATM machine?" The town folks quizzically responded, "What's an ATM machine?" After the rehearsal and dinner, the groomsmen had planned to hold one last celebration of their own for the groom, asking residents "Where is the nearest liquor store?" Their response was "This is a dry county. We have no liquor store. Isn't that a good thing?" So, needless to say, the groom's party had to drive an hour to Dodge City to find the nearest ATM and liquor store!

When all was said and done, the wedding concluded. The bride's brother could only muster up a wheelbarrow decked out with a string of cans and slippery (Vaseline) handles. The bride's first ride was from the church to the reception hall a few blocks away in her "homemade chariot," thanks to her brother! After the reception, dinner, and dance, at the appointed hour as precisely planned, the bride and groom quickly disappeared into the limo that suddenly appeared, all in a move that stunned the entire wedding party, the immediate family members, and all guests. It was much like a Cinderella fairy tale come true, where the "small town" bride and the "big city" groom lives happily-ever-after, after their real chariot, a horse-powered limo, takes them off into the sunset across the plains of Southwest Kansas!

"Eye to the Sky"
By Arlie DeFreese, Jr. of Garden City, Kansas
Born 1955

Friday, June 23, 1967 for me started out as a typically hot, muggy, southwest Kansas summer morning. I was two weeks shy of turning 12. But instead of sleeping in and awaiting a day of fishing, I was up at 5:00 AM with my dad getting ready for a day of work hauling milk. During summer months dad drove a semi-truck delivering milk to several outlying towns from our hometown dairy.

It was exciting for me to help him; I loved riding in the big truck. But it was very tiring also, as I was the one who brought all the empty milk crates back to the truck and loaded them. They were heavy metal then, not plastic like today. Dad bought me lunch every day for helping, plus any "sodas," I might require. But the time we spent together was priceless.

That day started out normal, but by 10:00 PM that night, our world turned upside down. Driving north coming home that evening at about 7:00 PM my dad looked to the west and noticed a large black cloudbank building in the distance. He turned on the radio and we learned we were in a "tornado watch" until 10:00 PM. Living in "Tornado Alley" we took such notices seriously, and this cloudbank looked particularly menacing. I remember dad saying, "We might be in for it tonight."

When we got to town, we fueled and parked the truck and headed home to a hot meal prepared by my stepmother, and a hot, refreshing bath.

After supper and a bath, the three of us gathered in the living room to watch TV. I was laying on the rug on the floor. Dad was in his favorite chair, but his focus was not on the TV but on the storm that had started to rage outside. Our house faced east and had four large elm trees in the front yard. Our house was also a "raised" house meaning we had a basement but the top half of the basement was above ground. We had a huge concrete porch with six steps climbing up and leading to the front door. We had a clear storm door on the front and dad got up because he said he saw the trees bend way over in the wind one way and the next second bend the other way, and then start to suck straight up in the air! He was watching through the storm door when he turned and made the announcement "we had better run for the basement." At that moment, all of the windows in our house blew out!

My stepmother and I made it in the basement, dad only made it halfway down when the roof of our house lifted off and one wall fell in, sending concrete blocks tumbling down on top of dad, and knocking him the rest of the way down. The roar was deafening, everything was swirling. I thought it was the end of the world.

After a short period of time the wind lessened, but still blowing very hard, and the rain was coming down in sheets. My dad, stepmother, and I were completely caked with dirt, mud, and bits of insulation stuck on and all over us, and my dad had a very sore shoulder from the concrete blocks. Dad had to talk to us loudly so we could hear him over the roar of the storm. He told us to make a run for our garage, which was detached from the house 30 feet away and still intact, because he was afraid the rest of the walls of the house were going to cave in on us. He told us to be careful of the "hot" power line that was down and "dancing" on the ground between the house and the garage.

I went first, and when I got to the garage I slid under the folk's car parked inside. The car was bouncing up and down slightly and I will never forget the feeling of the rear differential bouncing up and down on my lower back. Just as I got under the car, the rear glass blew out. My stepmother got under the workbench, and dad stood at the open garage opening, we had no garage door at that time. I asked my dad from under the car if we were going to die and he said, "No, son, we will be okay. All this will stop in a couple of minutes." And he was right. It calmed down to just a gentle rain and we all came out to a scene of devastation.

Dad was muttering about losing the house but his other concern was where did the pick-up go? He had parked it bumper to bumper against the car in the garage, however, now it was nowhere to be seen. There was a major drainage ditch about 750 feet north of our house and he just figured it was picked up and dropped in there.

The neighbors around us, who basically had no more damage than broken glass, all came running to help us in any way they could, they were carrying what possessions of ours they thought they could save by putting them in their garages or houses.

Dad was more concerned about getting to his mother's house that was a mile away on the south side of town. She was 84 years old and lived alone.

As we all walked around to the front of the house, we were shocked to discover dad's pick-up. The tornado took it backwards 100 feet to the blacktop street, twirled it around several times, and then backed it up between four elm trees right up to the front porch. All while still in gear and the emergency brake on! The driver's door suffered damage as it hit one of the trees on the way past. The glass was broken and it would not open, otherwise the pick-up looked perfectly fine. The next day we counted the black swirl marks on the asphalt and determined the truck spun around four complete times before being backed up to the porch.

Saying thank you to the neighbors, the three of us climbed through the passenger door of the truck, it started on the first click, and off we went to grandma's house. It took a while the first half-mile because of downed tree limbs and power lines, but the second half-mile you couldn't tell there was even a storm that had hit! We learned later only the north half of town was hit.

We walked in on grandma and almost scared her silly from the way we looked. Dad explained what had happened and we all three used her bathtub to get clean again. My stepmother slept on the couch, and my dad and I on the floor with pillows and blankets.

The next day one of dad's many friends and his wife offered us their basement to live in while our house was rebuilt. It took three months to rebuild our house, and by the start of school, I had just moved into the basement of our newly remodeled house. How cool! I always wanted my own room in the basement!

We lost most of what we owned that night, but we ourselves, survived. I still rode the truck with my dad the rest of that summer, and at the end of summer, he bought me a small portable TV, and also a small, vinyl reclining chair for my bedroom, so I could watch TV in comfort. These were his gifts to me for helping him all summer. My dad was a good man.

This incident gave me a life-long appreciation of storms. The night the tornado hit the north side of our town dozens of homes were demolished and there were two fatalities. I have been a trained storm spotter now for thirty years. I have seen many tornadoes. I also have unfortunately seen the aftermath of very large and brutal tornadoes, and have volunteered many hours in aiding in clean up afterward. I like to think I have been instrumental in helping to get plenty of notice to people in the path of advancing storms. Living in "tornado alley" means every year you prepare, and keep an "eye to the sky."

Once every year or two I have a recurring dream of that night when I slid under the car in the garage as it "bounced" up and down hitting my lower back. When I wake up I'll look at my back in the mirror, and I swear to you, I'll have a red mark across my back, in the same place I did the day after the tornado in 1967!

My Brothers and the Farm
By Mariella Sawin of Lyons, Kansas
Born 1928

My brothers' first memory of this young sister was probably the next day after she was born following a Thursday night delivery. Moma said their excited words were, "now we won't have to dry dishes anymore." I can't even think how disappointed those brothers must have been when I wasn't standing at the large square draining pan by Saturday, and had to wait several years for that time consuming miracle to occur. All this to fill the void after the oldest sister earned a certificate to teach in an elementary school away from the home.

Undoubtedly, my first memories of

Mariella's father, Edward A. Tobias with James Tobias in 1940

Robert included the times he and Jim would play toys, games, and sometimes "dolls" with me. Can you imagine the doll conversations? And then all eating meals together at our square kitchen table. Jim and I sat "on the bench" with Robert sitting at his own side and Raymond on the south side with Cecil, when he could be home from his work for a day or two. We were all entertained, well, maybe not me, with the funny and scary faces that Raymond would make across the table at me, and the family news happenings of the day. It must have been quite noisy!

I was blessed with wonderful "in-house" teachers. My mother taught me how to embroider designs on tea towels before I started to school. And how to run her treadle sewing machine to make doll clothes while waiting to grow up enough for first grade. Since my legs couldn't reach the treadle, I learned to make the machine work by turning the smaller top wheel by hand, and then my brothers stepped in for me to be outdoors and help them with small tool delivery. This is when I became the family "tool runner" with only a call of "Toots." I learned all the hand tool names, the uses and placement in the shop. It was only troublesome when the boys calling me sounded like the squawk of a chicken and I didn't respond with any tool. But there were benefits too, my long skinny legs grew muscles; remember the pain of a Charley horse in one's leg? I could run fast and jump high enough to receive a few coveted blue ribbons in our county track meets for country school students.

All my brothers could have been professional whistlers, but it seemed Jim taught me the most, probably because he was the last one home as I became older. Of course, he had to "stay in" during recess for whistling in class at Union Two! As a high school freshman, Raymond walked the almost two miles west to the highway to catch a ride with another student. Moma said she could hear his whistle as he came over the high railroad track, so she knew he was safe, and would soon be home.

One wish my two youngest brothers didn't teach me was how to swim. I'd guess that after numerous days of begging they were sick of me. Anyway, Robert and Jim walked me to this good-sized place in the creek; both picked me up and without any fan-fare, threw me into that deeper water hole. I think they were in cahoots. That was the end of lesson one. The second lesson was never discussed, by me anyway, and I still can't swim!

The grown boys in the family enjoyed other recreational pursuits around the creek. If the ice on Cow Creek was smooth enough they would skate there. If not, they knew of ponds with ice "as smooth as glass" that would be fine on near zero temperature days. They also had beautiful knitted sweaters for dress up skating; I think that probably meant girls were involved. I also had a lovely knit sweater, in an old photo, but no skates, they told me I was too little for clamp on skates on regular shoes. I was "too little" for most things!

They built a sled of their own design that must have been pulled by a tractor. Metal, I think, shaped like a bobsled, but when it hit a tree on the side of the driveway and there were injuries, I don't remember them using it again. It was a fancy one and fast!

There was always fishing through the ice on the creek. A real production and fun for everyone. The most momentous experience was quite a bit later in 1945. It was a very cold Christmas Eve morning, with no wind. Beautiful! Jim, Pope, and Mr. Weihe were ice fishing because the news from Mary in the hospital was "wait and see." Then a phone call asked the men to return to Lyons immediately. So I was the "runner" once again, with almost shoulder length hair, wet from shampooing and going out the kitchen door on the run. My hair froze in long strips of ice before I ever reached the end of the sidewalk and clattered all the way on this important round trip. The noise of cracking icicles all around my ears was deafening and very cold, but Jim and Mr. Weihe arrived at the hospital in plenty of time for the birth of Larry and Jerry. Were fish caught that morning? I don't remember seeing any.

Before we leave this "too many stories of the creek," I must mention one brother's hand fishing into the piles of brush under the water. He seemed to have no fear of swimming snakes, snapping turtles, and most important those catfish that he was determined to catch. I learned later from another nephew that he knew to leave the biggest ones alone because of the danger. But some other family members experienced these adventures first hand, and they have their own special memories, and I remember with great respect, carrying the gunnysack for him once!

Like most Cow Creek youngsters, we consumed vast amounts of fish, caught legally or not, jellies, and juices from sand hill plums and wild grapes growing on vines circling the trees near the creek. Pies from elderberries, mulberries, Dutch Shoo Fly and green tomato pies, our own meat and garden and Popa's favorite, fried crispy and crunchy chicken's feet, and gizzards. Yikes! There was lots of ice cream, sometimes the freezer was cranked as we sat on the basement steps. Ice was from the stock tank or purchased as blocks at the

Raymond and Robert searching for more cereal boxes in 1920

275

Mariella's family homestead on the Creek

"ice house" on West Taylor Street after church during the summer. And always crushed in a gunnysack for faster freezing with crushed salt from the local salt plant. Family Thanksgiving dinners were followed by the young folks attending Lyons High Football games against another school, on Stahl Field.

As you can tell, most of the recreation was made by sheer ingenuity, and scattered around all chores, milking cows, fieldwork, haying jobs, and the busy summer wheat harvest. Those "boys" could build or fix anything, very talented and very intelligent. They could shimmy around the top of the empty silo to fasten the blower pipe in place for chopped cane, called ensilage for cattle feed. That's when Moma said, "I couldn't watch them through the window." The top of the silo was also the best for photo shots of the creek flooding all around the farm buildings.

And we had family rituals, like polishing shoes every Saturday and cleaning the ears on the way to Sunday school. That was always accomplished in the car with a white handkerchief and spit from the front seat, and to be finished by the time we reached that high railroad track. It almost felt like a sin if it took any longer. Maybe Popa was driving too fast! I asked Robert about his a few years ago, and with such a startled face he wondered how I knew. How could I forget, the noise of that procedure reverberated from one corner of the car to the other. That must have been the beginning of full-around sound.

All the boys came back home from their work, to help with seasonal jobs as often as they could. You've each heard many of those stories, like finishing cutting wheat by moonlight and helping to paint the peak of a house and on and on. Now, there are no Twin City tractors with lug wheels and no workhorses. Tractors and combines are computerized and have a GPS. Wouldn't my brothers and their father be shocked!

Robert greatly expanded my worldview way beyond our life on the farm, and with so much energy, ideas, and challenges to give everyone who shared a tiny bit of his life. Of course, Moma was always pleased and grateful every time he arrived in Lyons, by car or plane! He and others were one of Dr. Marion Trueheart's predictions fulfilled to her that "since she thought she couldn't be a missionary herself, there would be others in her family to do some of that work for her." What a blessing, and indeed, there have been several of our parent's grandchildren and great-grandchildren who have done Christian work on other continents. There have been many more who have found their personal niche of love and caring in their own church and community to serve others in a myriad of positive ways.

I still remember my parents and myself driving "all the way" to Enid, Oklahoma to visit Robert and Phillips University. We probably also carried his laundered clothes rather than mailing in his brown canvas suitcase that week. Perhaps it was a parent's invitation visit, I don't remember that part. I missed him when he went away to school, and of course that was only the beginning of his world travels.

I missed other brothers also, when they were gone from home to be active in World War II. Robert was sent to areas in Central Europe to aid churches and congregations in being rehabilitated from war damage. Two other brothers, Raymond, and Cecil were part of building airports in the States and on islands in the South Pacific. Jim, my youngest brother, was a Navy fighter pilot also in the Pacific area. Their teenage sister became their father's helper on our farm and it was a special joy to work with him those years. When Japan surrendered on August 15, 1945, our special friends, John and Beulah, came to our home that evening to celebrate quietly the feeling of blessing and relief from those circumstances of war. But it didn't feel like a real celebration since several of our neighbors didn't have sons able to return home. I still remember that evening with many mixed emotions of both love and caring, and it was so special to have friends in to share those feelings. Our family was so fortunate.

My belief now is that each one of us would like to take a warm Sunday afternoon, walk to the footbridge over the creek, and just enjoy the peace and quiet of the clear moving stream as it was in those days. We could also watch the minnows darting around in the water and see the sand pebbles on the bottom, maybe even a small turtle at the water's edge and a snake slithering by near the top of the water. Yikes! But, oh that's right; Robert said it wouldn't hurt me.

Thanks to all my brothers, for those wonderful memories of our growing up together on the farm.

Life on a Southwest Kansas Farm
By Jean Hicks of Newton, Kansas
Born 1933

I was born to Floyd and Vira Meador Winsted on September 19, 1933 in Satanta, Kansas at the home of my uncle and aunt, J.B. and Eunice Winsted. Doctor J.B. Ungles was the physician who delivered me. There wasn't a hospital in Satanta. I joined Joan, six years older. Seventeen months later Joy joined us. Reports were that Joan thought we were pests. If Joy and I argued around daddy, he made us face each other until we could say, "I'm sorry." We always ended up laughing.

Our home was fourteen miles from town because our grandfather Winsted had homesteaded it. Father and Mother moved there in 1926 as newlyweds after living with the Winsted's for a year in Floris, Oklahoma. The farmstead consisted of an old two-story house, a windmill, bunkhouse, and a wooden grain bin. The nearest neighbor was one mile away. There were no modern conveniences. Instead of indoor plumbing, there was an outhouse. It was made of wood and was a "two seater" (had two holes). We used old catalog pages to clean ourselves after finishing "the job." The outhouse was many yards from the house so a pot was available at night. No one wanted to clean it! After several months, a new hole had to be dug so the outhouse could be moved. A large new hole was dug using the dirt to fill in the hole from the old outhouse after the "house" was moved. Lime was also added to the old hole. To move the house required a tractor with a chain. Daddy smoked cigarettes once in a while. Joy and I thought that looked like fun so once we sneaked a cigarette and some matches to the outhouse. When daddy came in from the field for lunch, he saw smoke coming out of the outhouse. At the table, he asked if we enjoyed our smoke. It took us many years before we figured out how he knew what we'd been up to.

When Joy and I were old enough mother put pans of water on chairs so we could do dishes. We were to gather eggs. Sometimes we would get an egg to add to our mud pies. If the ram was in the chicken house during hot weather, he wouldn't let us in. Sheep ran loose on the farm to eat weeds. We helped mother "dress" chickens when butchering day came. Our job was to pick the feathers off. She never complained but I am sure she had to re-pick them herself. When the chicken showed up fried for dinner, we were glad to eat it. I was often reminded of a family Thanksgiving dinner at my grandparents when I asked for

Jean's parents, Floyd and Vira Meador Winsted

the turkey to be passed saying "you might as well hurt a lot as a little."

We had a crank phone. Several families had phones on the same line so you could hear everyone's ring and listen in on their conversation if you wanted to by just picking up the phone. Our ring was 3 longs and 3 shorts. Daddy was the only man in the area with spikes to climb the telephone poles for repairs.

Mother had a wringer washer with a step-on crank, which required daddy to start. Water was pumped by the windmill to a storage tank. From there the water was heated in the house and carried to the bunkhouse about 20 yards away where the washer was. After the clothes were washed they were carried to the clotheslines to be hung, but first the dirt had to be wiped off the lines with a cloth.

When the dirt blew hard, which it did often, mother put wet towels over the windows to keep out the dust. In the summer, she did the same to help cool a room with the breeze blowing through.

In the winter, we cut paper dolls out of a catalog. If the large stock tank froze over, we put a rope on a scoop shovel. One sister got to ride the shovel and the other ran around the tank pulling it. One morning Joan, Joy, and I went out to play. Mother said don't play on the tank because the ice is too thin. Joy was the smallest so we thought it would be okay if she rode on the shovel. She got on the scoop and promptly fell in the water. We took her to the bunkhouse, where a hired man had previously lived. There was a small heater there. When Joy's clothes were dry, we went into the house as if nothing had happened.

Mother greeted us with "did you get her dried out?" We often played like we were fishing in the tank with wire hanging from a nail on a long stick. Didn't catch a thing!

When I was eight daddy had me help feeding cattle in the lot. He put the pickup in second gear and I drove while he threw feed off the back. He planted a cattle feed crop that grew to approximately five feet tall. The field of feed was harvested into bundles by the farm equipment. The bundles were put in teepee shocks to dry. Joy and Jean tried to drag the bundles, but they were too heavy for young girls. It was left in the field to dry before being brought in to use as cattle feed later. We got a lot of exercise chasing the field mice that ran out of the bundles as they were dragged to the shock.

Vira, Floyd, Joan, Jean, and Joy Winsted

Joan was mother's household helper. Joy and I helped to can beets, peaches, green beans, and other garden foods. After the food was canned, it was stored in the pantry under the stairs. We used this as our grocery store in the winter, with Joy and me taking play money for the goods when mother needed something. If we actually had to go to the grocery store, we went to Satanta where we also rented a meat locker to keep the meat frozen after we butchered, since we didn't have a freezer at home.

If we wanted to shop for clothing, we drove to Garden City, 35 miles from the farm. One of the stops Joy and I insisted on during these trips was for tamales being sold by a man with a sidewalk cart. This was a new food to mother and she wasn't sure it was a good idea.

We seldom were sick but if need be mother

put Vicks on our chest and throat and pinned a rag to our pajamas to keep it off them. To treat my earaches mother put oil in a spoon and heated it with a match, then dripped in my ear. One night she left the match under the spoon just a tad too long! When it was time for vaccinations, Dr. Ungles painted our arms with Merthiolate so the shot wouldn't hurt. One day I climbed up on the cabinets to get the thermometer because I wanted to play with it. I dropped it and it fell to the floor and broke. I picked it up and put it back in the box. Several days later mother asked me how I broke the thermometer. Our hired man said if something goes wrong, I might as well confess because I was going to get blamed for it anyway!

The only radio program I remember was "Fibber McGee and Molly." We listened to the radio, which was in the living room. The radio sat on the table next to my dad's chair. We laughed often at the programs and it was a fun family time. The radio wasn't used much except Tuesday nights. One day the neighbors came to our farm and said "Pearl Harbor has been bombed." The adults rushed to turn on the radio, I didn't know what Pearl Harbor was, but I knew it was sad. I went to my parent's bedroom and cried.

We played outside most of the time. Cats were dressed up like dolls. We rode horses from the time we were big enough to put a bridle on one. We had races when we got big enough to saddle the horses. Jinx was the first horse we rode because he was smaller. We put a bridle on and both Joy and I would ride bareback together. If a rabbit jumped out in front of us Jinx would balk or jump and Joy and I would fall off every time. He would stand there and wait while we tried to get back on. Later our horses were bigger and we rode with a saddle. The horses were so gentle that we could saddle them by walking under them instead of around the horse. One fun game was to grab a tumbleweed and run with it while it tumbled across the prairie. Sometimes it was too windy to hang on to the weed. We also thought riding on the open cab combine was fun. The tractor pulled the combine to cut the wheat. Daddy had a large stick with a rag tied to it to keep flying ants away from us. He would swing it to keep them away.

Joy and I would dig a hole, put paper and small twigs in the hole, set it on fire and then place mud covered potatoes down on top of the embers. This was covered with dirt and let it cook. We never ate a tender potato, and probably not a clean one, but we thought they were delicious.

Driving to my Meador grandparent's home in Anthony, Kansas was a treat. We wanted to go fishing with granddad and he always said, "You whippersnappers can't be quiet." We enjoyed playing with our cousin and visiting our uncles' hardware store, grocery store and boot shop.

My Winsted grandparents remained in Floris, Oklahoma, in the panhandle. The main attraction there was a player piano. One sister would sit on the bench and watch the keys and music. The other sister was on the floor pumping the pedals. That piano is now on loan to the Haskell County Historical Museum after being restored. Flossie, my aunt's cat, was a fun playmate. We dressed her in doll clothes until we couldn't find her. Later we discovered that she was hiding from us in the bedsprings. I would jump on the bed and Joy would pull on her tail trying to get her to come out. Not such a willing playmate after all.

Our one room schoolhouse, Busy Hill, was two and a half miles from our home. Mother drove us to school and we walked home. When I was in first grade the older kids dared me to kiss a boy at recess. I wrestled him to the ground and did it! He cried and wouldn't go in to class so the teacher had to fetch him. We played running games like Red Rover and Whip Lash, but I wasn't ever on the end to "crack."

There were six to ten kids, all grades, and we all played together. One day we all got on top of the coalhouse just to sit and talk. The merry-go-round was always fun and we played baseball. Lunches were prepared at home and carried to school until the lunch program was implemented. After that all I remember getting for lunch was powdered milk and dried eggs! We never had homework; you did your work while the teacher taught the kids from another grade. Our school hours were 9:00 -4:00. The school year was eight months so the farm kids could help with summer chores and farming. The teacher lived with a family who farmed ground near the school. There was never more than two kids in a class in our school and not all grades were represented. I remember there being about 10 kids at the school.

Box Suppers
By Letha Roets of Goddard, Kansas
Born 1938

I attended a one-room country school. It had one classroom (eight grades were taught by one teacher) and an entry room where students hung their coats and hats and left their lunch boxes. A large wood stove was at the back of the classroom.

One Saturday night a fundraiser called a "Box Supper" was held at the school. For the box supper, ladies decorated boxes in many ways. They were beautiful. Inside the boxes was a meal prepared by the lady the box belonged to.

The boxes were then auctioned and the men bid on the box that he liked. The highest bid won the box and the lady that the box belonged to was obligated to eat with the buyer of her box.

To make it more interesting, the bidder didn't know who the box belonged to and the lady didn't know who might buy her box.

Lost Shoes
By Verene V. Eason of Newton, Kansas
Born 1926

It was springtime on the Peter H. and Lena (Wedel) Jantz farm, which was located east of the Eagle Chief Creek in Oklahoma southwest of Cleo Springs. We had to walk to school in town, which was 1 1/2 miles from our house. We usually walked home with our neighbor's children. There were 13 children in the Pierce family and there was another boy, Joe Clark, from another family just south a little way from the Pierce's.

One afternoon, my Dad hired two of the Pierce boys. Gene and Carrol, and Joe Clark to help my sister, Elvera, and I hoe weeds out of the row crop, which extended west near the creek. After we had hoed several rows, we decided to go over to the creek looking for clamshells and pretty rocks. We also skipped rocks on the water. Then one of the boys said, "Let's go across to the other side." We all took off our shoes and waded across, it wasn't much more than ankle deep. I don't know how long we were over there, but when we thought we had better get back, the creek had come up and we couldn't get back where we had crossed. We started walking north hoping to come to a road with a bridge. When we saw a swinging bridge, it looked very scary and old, but we took a chance and got back across. When we got back to where we had left our shoes, they were nowhere to be found. We went home barefooted. We got scolded but the Pierce boys got a big whipping.

Riding in a Rumble Seat
By Ellen Sullivan of Branson West, Missouri
Born 1923

My folks lived on a farm four miles from Haven, Kansas. This is where I went to High School. There were only 29 in my class, but we had fun. One day as I was leaving school, a young man named Milton asked if I would like to go out to eat with another couple to Hutchinson, Kansas. I said yes, because I thought that would be fun. I didn't know I would be riding in a rumble seat.

When we got to the restaurant, the waitress came to take our order. Milton and I ordered chili. The waitress asked if we wanted beans in the chili, and Milton said we did since we were riding in the rumble seat. A rumble seat is part of the car in the back that folds down and this makes a seat. It is open air, no roof, but it wasn't raining when we were riding in it.

The next time I am asked to go out, my first question is what kind of a car do you have?

Butchering Day
By Iris McIntosh of Lakewood, Colorado
Born 1938

One story that comes to mind from my youth is of the butchering days on the farm in Rawlins County, Kansas. I was a small child, but I still remember well the procedure that was used. A small hog was selected for priming. This meant that they were fed a different kind of feed, for proper fattening. Butchering was always in the wintertime. After the hog reached the stage for slaughter, my dad would use a sledgehammer to kill the hog with a blow to the head. Next, he would slit the throat area to bleed the hog out. A barrel of scalding water was already prepared beforehand, and the hog was put into the water butt-first to scald off the hair. Sharp knives were used to dress the hog out by removing all the inner organs. The carcass was then cut in two halves. A pulley was attached to two legs, and then put on the wooden windmill tower to cure out. After several days, more sharp knives were used to cut off the various cuts of meat. Pork chops, hams, and loin roasts were the most common. The hams were rubbed with a seasoned salt and taken to the cellar to be placed on metal racks for later use. Pork chops and roasts were cooked down, and then put in jars with grease covering them. Sausage was made, and also put in jars covered with grease for later use. Even the brain and tongue was used to make headcheese that was formed in a loaf in the natural aspic of the head, and then it was sliced off. Those slices made really good sandwiches! The feet were pickled, thus the only wasted part was the snout. With no refrigeration or electricity, this was the preferred method of processing pork.

School Gyms
By Larry Miles of Round Rock, Texas
Born 1941

High school basketball games and church activities were the primary sources of social interaction during the winter months in those days.

Usually there were two games a week (Tuesday and Friday nights.) The families in the small farm communities would gather, root on their team and visit with each other. That interaction occurred not only within the communities but also between the communities. It was unusual to drive more than 30 miles for a game.

The size of the gymnasiums was the reason for the closeness of these gatherings. Most would have difficulty in seating more than 200 spectators. Our gym at Milton would accommodate folks one deep on a bench around three sides of the court. The fourth side was the stage for plays and other activities at the school. There was a balcony with seating on three sides about three deep. The top row of seats in the balcony put your head at the same level as the bottom of the roof trusses. The circular arc of the top of each free throw circle intersected the mid-court jump circle, the court was that short. The out of bounds stripe along the edge of each side and the ends were within two or three feet of the feet of the spectators. In the case of some other schools (Zenda, Bluff City, etc.) the out of bounds line was within six inches of the wall and all the seating was above the floor and the wall. Zenda was the smallest with seating I believe only on one side of the court. Milan, Bluff City, and Norwich had seating only on one side of the court with a stage on the opposite side. At the Milton gym, a long high arching shot could be in danger of hitting the roof trusses. Argonia, Adams, and Norwich (after the mid-fifties) had the best gyms.

The gyms were also used for most community gatherings such as school banquets, wedding showers, family reunions, etc.

Those were the days.

Outhouses and Chamber Pots
By Grace McLaughlin of Coldwater, Kansas
Born 1933

Living on a farm in the 1930s with no electricity meant outhouses were a necessity. In the summer, the outhouse was hot, smelly, and full of flies, wasps, mice, spiders and sometimes snakes. The wind was blowing dirt through the cracks in the walls (This was in the "Dirty Thirties" Dust Bowl days in the area.). You didn't stay any longer than necessary. Before using it, you checked for flies, wasps, spiders, and such. We had a hand sprayer with something in it to kill those pests. You gave the place a good spraying.

Toilet paper was an old Sears or Montgomery Ward catalog. When you sat down, you ripped off a page or two, folded them up, and rubbed them together until they were softer, before use.

In the summertime, we didn't use the chamber pot unless someone was sick. Everyone went to the outhouse. On dark nights, we could use a flash light or lantern.

The wintertime was different. In the daytime, you needed to put on your overshoes, coats, and hats. Cold winds were blowing snow through the crack in the walls. Western Kansas had a lot of snow in the 30s and 40s, and you hoped the drifts weren't too high on the path there. In the outhouse, you needed to brush the snow off the seat. Needless to say, in these situations you started before you really had to go. Again, you wouldn't stay any longer than necessary or your rear would be like a frozen rump. You didn't have to worry about varmints except maybe some mice.

To keep the outhouse odor free, we had a sack of lime in the corner. Every day we would throw a one-pound coffee can full of lime down the hole.

We lived on Highway 160 in western Kansas. In the '30s and '40s, we had a lot of tramps or hobos walking to find work. If one would use the outhouse, Mother would mix up a bucket of lye water and give the outhouse a good scrubbing. She didn't want us to pick up any bugs the people might have.

The chamber pots were used mostly in the wintertime and at night. As I got older, about five or six, it was my job to empty the pot every day. Rinse it out and then give it a scrubbing with hot water and homemade lye soap. You can't know how glad I was in 1948 when we got R.E.A. (Rural Electrification Association) and finally an indoor bathroom.

A Fun Game in a Simpler Time
By Marilyn J. Albright of Hutchinson, Kansas
Born 1945

The game we used to play was located on a farm that no longer exists. My aunt and uncle moved, and the land reverted back to the owners after 1966. After the barn and outhouse mostly disintegrated, the remaining pieces of usable lumber were sold. The house was literally moved to Hutchinson, Kansas. It was originally a hotel for the town of Pretty Prairie, Kansas, as the latter used to be located three miles west and two miles south of its present location. The town moved to where it is now due to the arrival of the railroad. Oddly enough, the tracks were all taken out in the last approximate ten years, and the wheat crops are once again trucked to their location

Sam, Darrell, Janette, and Marilyn

for milling.

Unnamed Game

My brother and I, plus three of our first cousins from an uncle's family are the oldest five grandchildren in our family (from the maternal side), so we would often play together as children.

On numerous evenings, as our parents were inside visiting, the five of us would play outdoors in the yard. I don't know if our game had a name but we enjoyed it.

After dark and with the yard light turned off, one person was chosen as "It" and the remainder of us formed a line and held hands. We closed our eyes and slowly started forward reciting:

   Star light, star bright
   First star I see tonight
   Wish I may, wish I might
   Make my wish come true tonight.

Sometime during the poem, the person who was "It" would jump out and scare us. We would scream and laugh and then do it all again.

While recalling this game, I realized how simple people lived, requiring no equipment in this instance. We had a lot less material items but were generally happier.

Drunken Hogs
By Bob Hessman of Dodge City, Kansas
Born 1935

When I was about 11 or 12 years old, the years were 1946 and 1947, I was going to a one-room school about ¾ of a mile from home. My sister and I rode a horse to school. I also had a trap line approximately ¾ of a mile beyond the school. I was setting traps for possum and skunk. One day, I told my teacher that I would like to check my trap line during lunch hour and she agreed.

That day was very successful. I had caught three skunks. I always carried a gunnysack on the saddle horn to put whatever I caught. When I got back to school, I was not even allowed to get off the horse. My teacher yelled at me and told me to go on home. My sister had to walk home.

I didn't understand why my teacher was so upset, but when you are exposed to a skunk, after a period of time, you cannot smell it yourself. This all took place about 6 miles west of Dodge City, Kansas.

Mom and Dad understood, because Dad had trap lines before I came along. We had a system to draw the smell out of your clothes. I had a sheet of tin that I would put my clothes under and overnight the smell would be gone. The worst part was running naked into the house and jumping into a washtub of vinegar and tomato juice "flavored" water! This was very stressful when there was company.

I had another trap line on the Arkansas River, where I went after mink, muskrat, beaver, and coons. Sometimes the beavers would build a dam and back the water up and cover my traps to the point where I would have to reach under the ice and water to check my traps.

Once I shot a duck, only breaking its wing, I jumped into the water, which proved to be a big mistake that duck could swim faster than I could run in knee-deep water. I finally gave up, got on my horse, and rode 1-mile home in frozen clothes.

Even though it was unpleasant at times, I basically bought my first car with skunk money. At the end of trapping season, Jan 31st, Dad and I would remove the pelts from the stretcher boards and pack them into a burlap bundle and ship them to Sears and Roebuck. In about 2 weeks, I would receive my check.

I think my teacher and the rest of the students were glad the trapping season was over!

About this same time frame, Dad told me to remove a fence that he no longer was using. This meant digging out the posts by hand with a posthole digger. I discovered that I could nudge the posts with the truck bumper and the post would loosen up and I could pull them out a lot easier. However, the truck was a 1929 Chevy and the bumper was not very strong. So, when I bumped the post with the end of the bumper it bent back toward the tire.

So, when I drove straight the tire would rub the bumper. When I was driving home, Dad saw me driving in circles and I knew right away I was in deep doo-doo! We had a cellar where we stored potatoes and canned food. A local beer distributor had brought out several cases of beer that they could not sell. When spring rolled around Mom wanted the space for her canned goods. Dad told me to feed it to the hogs. It was a hot day and the hogs were thirsty, so they drank a lot of beer. After a while, they started to fall down and lay on their sides, squealing and kicking their feet. It was pretty funny. Soon Dad showed up and began giving me what for until he got tickled, too!

Life on a farm was often funny, lots of hard work and I loved every minute!

The Lady of Harper
By Brian M. Ede of Harper, Kansas
Born 1948

My family relocated to Harper, Kansas in 1957. The State was building the new blacktop here and since we lived on the west border of town, I got to see a lot of the construction. We weren't a high roller type of family. Dad left in 1960, which was a good thing. Mom worked at the local post office, and I worked wherever there was work. I got to know most of the rural people, driving tractors and throwing lots of hay bales, lots. We did pretty good. Back then, there wasn't Government aide for single moms. She would have turned it down anyway. A pride deal.

Grade school and high school passed and I tried college at Wichita State in 1966. I think that was the year it was changed from WU to WSU. No matter, I wasn't college material. After 3 semesters, the war called, and my buddies and I quit and went to enlist. Of all things, this guy flunked the physical and came home. Linda and I were wed in 1968 and remain 45 years later.

My first real job was at a gas station on the main highway for a guy named Hoover. He taught me well as far as customer service. Any vehicle that entered our drive received a total workout of windows being cleaned, under the hood service, tires checked, and maybe some gasoline. He was a great boss.

With growing pains, Linda and I opened a muffler and alignment shop west of Harper in 1977. For almost 30 years, we serviced a fairly large radius of customers. In 2005, I had a lung infection that sidelined me for about a month. Coming back to the shop, I could see the change. Muffler shops were becoming a thing of the past. I sold the equipment to a local mechanic and the building to a couple of investors. The last 9 years have been as a counterman at a local auto parts store. It's warm in the winter and cool in the summer. Quite a climate change.

Memories…I guess my fondest would be of our fountain. I call her "The Lady" as she sits in the heart of Harper. She has a lot of history being installed originally by a woman's group in the early 1900s. A second lady's art group removed her and put in a brick structure with waterfalls. It was a failure.

In the '80s, our local chamber took on the project of bringing back "The Lady." I put my heart into this project. The fountain was brought back and the chamber presented it to the city. It was an emotional day.

I wanted the fountain to remain in its location so I took on the task of getting her on the State Historical register. This was accomplished so she should be safe in the center of our town. She's a focus point. If you come into our town and ask for directions, most will say, "Well from the fountain you need to go… "She's The Lady."

The gist… The summer the fountain returned, the chamber had the yearly free feed downtown. This was during the County Fair and an annual occurrence. They opted to have an evening ham and bean feed instead of the afternoon meal at the city park. This being for the meal to be enjoyed around the presence of "The Lady" with stories and conversation. It worked other than the temp was 105° when the feed began and 106° when the last person was served.

Several of us members were sitting and recovering from the heated deal when a woman came up to me. She said, "I have 3 things to say, the fountain is the wrong color, it is too hot, and there wasn't enough sugar in the cornbread." I thought for a second and replied, "Well, Mary, I can fix the fountain, and I can fix the temperature, but I can't fix the cornbread." I have no idea why I said it but will always remember it. We all looked at each other, including Mary, got up and went our ways.

By the way, "The Lady" is always in our city's heart if yer interested.

Going to Grandmother's House
By Geraldine Stufflebeam of Hutchinson, Kansas
Born 1929

My name is Geraldine Stufflebeam. When I was growing up, we lived on the edge of town. We had to go to the outhouse to the bathroom. We had a chamber to use at nighttime.

My parents used a lot of home remedies for colds or other things.

We took baths in a washtub. Mother used the washtub to do the washing and the washtub for baths on Saturday or when you needed a bath.

Geraldine Stufflebeam at age 13

Mother sewed our clothes on the sewing machine that had a foot pedal so the mound would work.

I went to a one-room schoolhouse. I walked to school about a mile, even in bad weather.

We had an icebox. The iceman would bring a block of ice if the ice card was out that we wanted ice.

My parents had a wood stove that was used for heat and to cook on. We chopped wood and brought coal for the wood stove. When I got older, we got a wringer washing machine.

We didn't have a phone. We went to the neighbor's to use the phone.

We didn't go to town but once a week, for we always had a garden.

I remember going to Grandmother's house and sleeping on a feather bed mattress. She had kerosene lamps, as she didn't have electric lights. In the wintertime when you went to bed, she would heat a brick to warm your feet.

I remember playing house and wearing Mother's dress.

There Is No Santa Claus!
By Francis "Frank" Moore of Pasco,
Washington
Born 1947

I was in the third grade. My nephew Jim and niece Linda were both about two years younger than me. You could say I was the baby of the family. Or you might say, "Oops!"

The one-room school where we all attended our first eight years of school had a Halloween and a Christmas Program every year. These "recitals' gave children a chance to get up in front of people, their parents and pretty much the whole community to show what they had learned. There was always a short play or skit and some singing too. There were boxed meals at Halloween that were made and auctioned off. The money went towards buying bags of Christmas candy that everyone got during the Christmas program. Santa Clause always came and gave a bag of candy to each kid.

During the Christmas Program the person playing Santa Claus, just happened to be our neighbor Orval, who had a big chest and belly. The assembly was gathering and my brother Robert was escorting my five-year-old nephew Jimmy to the men's out door toilet before things got underway. There were out door toilets, one for boys and girls behind the school building itself. They were passing some parked cars when Jimmy saw ole' Orval out beside a pickup truck in the Santa Suit but with no hat or beard, puffing on a cigarette. Jimmy didn't say anything to his Dad about what he saw and my brother Robert didn't think he'd gotten a glimpse of "Santa."

The next week Jimmy, Linda, and their cousins were both at our house while their mothers went Christmas shopping. With four nieces and nephews around my age, it was great to have playmates for the day. Today trouble was brewing between Jimmy and Linda though. Mama could hear the ruckus from the kitchen. "There is no Santa Claus!" Jimmy said, "Yes there is too!" Linda retorted. "Nuh-uh," Jimmy said, "I know there's no Santa Claus I saw him at the school and he was just our neighbor in a red suit smoking. And he was no Santa Claus!" As Linda started crying, Mama left the kitchen and came to the rescue. Although Mama assured them Santa was real, she could tell Jimmy wasn't convinced.

She had to figure how to get the grandkids to believe in Santa Claus again. And after some thought she came up with a plan. My brother Charley would make a perfect Santa. The kids wouldn't expect him on the farm since he went to the high school in town and only came home for weekends. In a small Kansas farm town like Lakin there was no school bus but he'd be home for the holidays in time for the ruse. Charley would be Santa Claus. Of course, Charley thought it would be great fun. My teacher Miss Chloe provided the school's Santa suit, so her sister Margie, who was also Jimmy's mother, could help her mother-in-law. And so it was arranged, Mom got Charley to play Santa. The only hitch in their plan was when I spotted the suit and Mama had to let me in on the secret.

Christmas Eve came along. The tree was up and there were lots of presents under the tree. The presents were usually clothes and other basics but presents were presents in my book. The whole family was there. The house was fairly packed. Mom, Dad, Robert, Margie, and their children Jimmy and Denise, Walter and Fern and their kids Linda and Kenny; Dick and Dorthey, CW and Ruth, Charley, Aunt Golda, Uncle Orval and Aunt Hazel and me, . There were four grandchildren, two were five, and two were still very small. We had a great dinner and finished up with a cake. Everyone was stuffed. The whole family had crowded into the living room to open presents. My Mom let on she still had a couple of things to do and was in the kitchen, where she had a gunnysack full of presents for her grandchildren and children. My brother Charley was in the bathroom attached to the kitchen, getting into the Santa suit. He could get out of the backdoor without being seen with the gunnysack in hand. Everything was going well. The plan was for Charley to come around the back of the house and in the front gate to get to the front porch. It was dark and the only lights for miles were the ones shining from the bedroom windows.

We were in the living room when, here comes Santa Claus with the sleigh bells jingling, yelling, "HO! HO! HO!" at the top of his lungs. Well, Mom hadn't thought about our three farm dogs when she'd put together her scheme and my brother couldn't see the new trees Mama had planted just behind the house. Gallon-size Folgers cans covered the trees to protect them from the rabbits. From the back of the house we heard a string of "Ho Ho Ho's," punctuated by a loud crash and then the sound of the dogs barking furiously and running towards the back of the house, where a red-garbed figure had knocked over some of the Folgers cans. Mama came to the door of the living room, "I think I hear Santa coming kids. Do you hear him?" For a moment, there was silence, and then Charley, hollering at the top of his lungs, "Ho, ho…Ah, what the hell? G!@# d@#$ son of a b@#$%*." The children's eyes were all as big and saucers and mine as well. My other brothers and sisters were all looking at each other trying to figure who was missing. It was at that time that Charley rounded the side of the house and promptly fell over another tree and coffee can. By this time, the dogs had gotten to him and were biting at the gunnysack and at Charley himself. We all crowded in the door to get a glimpse. The kids got to the door to see "Santa" struggling to his feet and kicking at one of the dogs, yelling, "Get the hell out of here you dogs." What a site! The dogs were after Charley in earnest now, not realizing that their best friend was the man in the suit. He'd get a few more feet and knock into another coffee can, cussing and kicking and swinging the gunnysack at those darn dogs.

As Santa climbed up the steps, Mom opened the screen door and got Santa into the house. "Santa" was quite a sight with his pants coming down and pillows sticking out everywhere around his slender body. , But the kids didn't notice a thing except Santa Claus had come to Grandma's house. By this time, all of the older people including my Dad, Aunt Golda, Aunt Hazel, and Uncle Orval were laughing so hard they could barely contain themselves. CW fell off his chair he was laughing so hard. Somehow, my Mom kept a straight face. Santa went around to each child, calling them by name and asked if they had been good. And then he dug a present out of the gunnysack with their name on it. Then he went around to all the brothers and sisters and spouses and asked the same questions to them. Finally, everyone got themselves composed to go along with the Santa Claus deception.

Finally, it was time for Santa Claus to go deliver more presents, and the whole thing started all over again. The dogs were waiting for the man in the red suit. They were trying to bite Charley and he started cussing the dogs and kicking at them. The dogs finally realized that the person they were trying to bite was their best friend. They backed off, standing there barking. My brother went out the front gate but this time went the other way around the house, to get back on the back porch. All the little ones were chattering about their gifts from Santa and excited by what had happened. Charley finally appeared out of the bathroom a little worse for wear and sweat still rolling down his face, but the children were fooled. Jimmy didn't argue whether Santa was real again; Mama's plan did the trick. This was a Christmas that I will never forget.

Soda Fountains and Free Movies
By Ellen Pulliam Young of Isabel, Kansas
Born 1945

Jumbo Hill was a couple of miles north of Sharon, Kansas. My grandparents said the major battle fought by the Calvary from the Medicine Lodge Stockade had took place

Rose and Barbara

there at that location. When driving north of Sharon several weeks ago, to my surprise I saw Jumbo Hill is no longer there. It has been leveled.

My aunt gave me her bicycle when she got married! It was a real treasure to me. Every week in the summer, my cousin and I would ride our bikes to Jumbo Hill and back to Sharon. We had sacks on our handlebars and collected pop bottles. We were nine and ten at the time. We each spent five cents after selling the bottles. Big mugs of root beer were five cents at Spears Drug Store.

With the soda fountain, booths, and pinball games, Spears Drug Store was a favorite gathering place for everyone. It was very busy on Thursday evenings during the summer. Everyone got a treat from there, even if only a one cent lollipop.

On Thursday evenings during the summer, the outside wall on the north side of the locker was painted white. The area to the north was vacant. Everyone, young and old, came to watch the free show. They brought blankets, hay bales, lawn chairs, or sat on the ground. A show was projected on the white wall. It was a great time for all the community to get together.

When I was very young, an elderly lady stopped by the farm. She said she had lived there when she was a little girl. She was happy to see the large tree. She said she had played under it. Many children have played under it over the years. Our parents are both gone now; Dad lived to be 91 and Mom 89. Our great-grandchildren now play under the tree. That lady also told us the house was a Pony Express stop.

When digging the foundation to add three bedrooms on to the house, Dad uncovered the iron bars to the jail.

The most important thing I remember about Sharon is all the good families that have and still live there.

The Runaway Horse
By Elsie Regier of Newton, Kansas
Born 1918

The Depression was in full swing in the early 1940s. I had finished two years of college and had applied for a teaching job at our rural school. I was hired to teach ten children in five grades. My dad offered me his horse and buggy for transportation, which I gladly accepted. Our neighbors also went with horse and buggy. On cold or rainy days, we had curtains to snap in the front of the large opening in the front of us, and we kept cozy and warm. We also had a bearskin blanket to keep us warm. It had a wool backing and long black hair to keep the cold out. The schoolyard had a small shed for the horse to relax and protect it from the weather.

One spring day the horse was nervous! Something spooked it. The children had left already, so I untied the horse, got in the buggy, and started for home. The horse, being spooked, started to run. She took the corner of the first mile to town off too fast, upset the buggy, throwing me into the ditch. The horse kicked her way out of the harness, freed herself from the buggy, and ran home as fast as she could.

She met my folks, who were returning from Newton, at the end of the driveway. Mother noticed a wild look in the horse's eyes as they met in the driveway. They came right after me. I had started to walk home and was thankful they came so quickly. Our neighbor just came by and offered to take me home, but I said my folks were coming! Now that was faith! Now here they came. They had been in Newton and just returned to meet my horse at the end of the driveway. I was so glad they came.

We picked up the mail and I had a letter from my sweetheart, who lived 15 miles from us. He told me we had an invite to our aunt and uncle's place for Sunday evening supper. That made me happy! The next morning, my brother, Art, took the reins, and we took the same horse and buggy, and the horse obeyed him and behaved. No more runaway!

The Jesse James Gang
By Nancy Ashworth Douglas of Larned, Kansas
Born 1944

Jesse James

I remember my mother, Velda Abrams Ashworth, telling about a very unique experience her mother had as a little girl. My mother's parents were Robinson James Abrams and Myrtle Ary Abrams.

One night they had visitors come to their home. This occurred either three miles north of Lewis, Kansas or near Fellsburg, Kansas. These visitors were none other than the infamous Jesse James Gang! As a little girl, Myrtle and her siblings were very frightened as the gang came into the house with their guns. The children were sent to bed in an upper loft bedroom. The James Gang demanded grain for their horses. My maternal great-grandparents, John Anderson Ary and Julia Etty Ary, also fed the men and then retired for the night.

When they awoke the next morning, the James Gang was gone, much to the relief of all in the household. The felt very fortunate, as these could often be very dangerous men. However, they were known for their "Robin Hood" qualities of being kind and generous. This was confirmed when my great-grandfather went to the barn the next morning and found they had left money in the feedbags to pay for the feed and the meal my great-grandparents had provided.

I have often marveled at this true tale handed down by my ancestors to me. I can hardly imagine the fear my grandmother and her sisters must have experienced!

The Blizzard of 1957

In 1957, our family experienced a blizzard and ice storm that greatly altered our normal lives. The Myrl and Velda Ashworth family, who lived north of Macksville, Kansas, lost electricity for six weeks. Many power lines and poles were down, and in those days, it took a long time to replace them.

Though our home life changed, we were very fortunate to have everything we needed. We had a coal oil furnace so we had heat. We had a windmill outside our basement door; we manually pumped water and stored it in cream cans in the pantry. We had an old gas stove in the basement which hadn't been used for many years, but now provided us a means of cooking our food.

In the evening after my dad and brothers milked the cows and separated the cream, we prepared our meal and carried it upstairs where we ate by lantern light. Then, with no electricity and thus no TV or radio, we created our own entertainment. We popped corn and played cards at the kitchen table, retiring to bed quite early, usually by 8:00 p.m.

We had a freezer in the basement, but in those days, we did not have generators to provide electricity to keep it cold. As the weather stayed quite cold, we took the food out and put it out in the snow banks. When we knew it would no longer keep, we cooked the food and shared it with neighbors.

Another unusual situation we had to deal with was taking baths. It took a long time to heat water to warm the cold pump water in the cream cans. As a result, several people usually ended up bathing in the same bath water. Those were the days when families did more things together, and we certainly increased our togetherness during the blizzard of 1957!

We were grateful we had the resources to meet our basic needs of warmth and food, and thankful for the safety of a good home and good parents who taught us to be prepared and willing to share with others.

Store Bought Dresses and School Chores
By Sister Cecilia Ann Stremel of Great Bend, Kansas
Born 1943

I was the youngest of four children. The others were all born at home, and I was the first born in a hospital, St. Anthony's in Hays,

Kansas. We lived on a farm three and a half miles east of Loretto, a German Russian settlement.

By the time I was six years old my sisters were off to high school, a boarding school in Wichita. So I had "big" chores like gathering the eggs and keeping the chicken trough cleaned and filled. I didn't mind gathering the eggs, except for the hen who insisted on setting under the roost, way back in the corner. So I used the chicken hook to shoo the hen off her nest and then crawled under the roost to get them.

Another chore was to close the chicken house at night when it was nearly dark. It seemed like miles to reach the chicken house, so I'd run as fast as I could out to close the door and even faster if I heard the coyotes off in the distance. I never saw one but was so afraid of their howl, and I knew if the chicken house wasn't shut, they'd get the chickens.

Homemade Clothes and Toys

Oh yes! My mom was a wonderful seamstress. In the spring when we went to La Crosse to Schwab's to get our chicken feed for the baby chicks, I got to go along and help pick out the bags, because that cloth would be for a new dress for school. At that Mom made her own patterns cutting them from newspapers. I would look at the catalogs; we got three – Sears Roebuck, Montgomery Ward, and Aldens. I would show her what I liked, what collar or ruffle, and she made it. She made my older sisters' clothes too, so parts of theirs they outgrew or they didn't want, she just put together one for me. My first bought coat was when I was 14 years old.

When I was about seven years old I got my first bought dress. We had a wonderful harvest that year and usually took some wheat to the elevator in Galatia to sell it. Well, that year, the elevators were full as was our granary. So it was piled on the grassy area (buffalo grass) in the yard. When we were able to take it to town to the elevator and it got picked up there was quite a bit in the grass yet. My brother, who was six years older than me, and I were to rake it up and the money we got for it we could have. When it was taken to the elevator I got $3.00 for my amount, or so they told me. So I got out the catalog and picked out a dress, an aqua and red plaid and white trim dress that did not have a tie belt but a red plastic belt with a buckle. Did I think I was "hot stuff."

The next bought dress I got was when I was 15 and was leaving home to enter the Convent.

We went to a two-room school, four grades per room. In the "little room" (grades one through four) our playground had a merry-go-round and swings, but most often we played group games, for example drop the handkerchief, elephant steps, red rover, here we go around the mulberry bush, etc. In the "big room" (grade five through eight) it was mostly softball with the two room outdoor toilet (boys on one side and girls on the other) or our back stop. Only in the seventh or eighth grade do I remember a basketball goal and some volleyball.

Going to a two room schoolhouse, we also helped clean our rooms each day. We were assigned chores each week. For example, we had to ring the bell at the end of recess (a hand bell), clean the chalkboards, clean the erasers, take the trash out to the barrel, etc.

We also played a lot of kick the can and hide and seek at night when several families visited each other at the farm or in Loretto.

As for phones, we had the wall phone when I was quite young. Our ring was two longs and a short ring. I don't remember much of it, because following a storm the lines were all down and it didn't work. It hung on the wall for a long time. When I came home at Thanksgiving of my freshman year, we'd gotten a desk phone, but it was used very sparingly and only for emergencies.

Horrible and Happy Days
By Connie Taylor of New Canaan, Connecticut
Born 1935

I was born on a farm between Newton and Wichita, Kansas in 1935, the daughter of Belma Bare Taylor and granddaughter of Eva McMinimy Bare.

My grandmother lived in Protection, Kansas in the most charming house I have ever seen, even to this day. I loved to go there to visit. I took my roller skates, which fit on the soles of my shoes and had a key to adjust the fit so that they stayed on. I remember being allowed to roller skate all around the

Doug and Connie Taylor

sidewalks of Protection. Grandmother's house had a big bathtub, big enough to float in, which I thought was wonderful! The house I grew up in until I was seven had no indoor plumbing or indoor toilet at all. I remember the outdoor outhouse, but I think that at least for my brother Doug, three years younger than me, we mostly used an indoor potty. Grandmother's house had electricity. We had none on our farm until 1941, when I was six.

On our farm, we had two large barns, both with hay in the haymow. Dad raised hogs in one, but then cholera spread through them, the pigs were gotten rid of, and the barn they were in was torn down. I remember it was said that we could not have pigs there, on that soil, for at least 20 years.

Along about that same time, at the end of the 1930s and just before the Second World War, for at least two farm work seasons, a man walked in from the road wanting work. I was so excited the second time he came because I remembered he had taught my brother and me to sing, "You scream, I scream, we all scream for ice cream." My brother was probably only one or two and doesn't remember it. I still, to this day, feel excited and happy when I think of that. The man, who looked rag-tag and scruffy and my parents called an "old hobo" as I remember, never came into our house. I only remember him being in the yard. I'm sure he slept in the barn in the haymow. I think my mother gave him his meals to eat outside. He probably cleaned up in the water tank.

There are so many things to remember at the end of the 1930s and the early 1940s. There were the lingering effects of the Depression. My mother always said if my dad said he needed to go to town she had to wash the dress she was wearing, because she only had one dress. There was no rural electrification where we lived until 1941 when I was six. I remember putting perishables, milk, meat, etc., down in the water well in a bucket on a rope to keep cool. I remember getting our first refrigerator. I remember some of the Dust Bowl and putting wet towels in the cracks around the window and hanging wet sheets over the windows. I remember going to a one room schoolhouse for all eight grades and having teachers who were hardly any older than the older students, and in which the school year started after Labor Day and ended in the middle of April.

And then, of course, I remember the Second World War, with rationing and very little travel in to town. Since we were as isolated as we were, I had thought I wasn't affected much emotionally. But about nine years ago, I happened to be traveling several hours in a car with XM Radio, and it happened to be the anniversary of the end of the Second World War in Europe, and they were replaying radio programs originally broadcast on that day, and I burst into heavy, sobbing, uncontrollable tears.

Those days were filled with so much emotion, wonderful and horrible and in between.

Crepe Paper Roses and Chicken Care
By Dell Spurgeon of Protection, Kansas
Born 1931

On July 26, 1931 I was born, the second daughter to Quannah and Goldie Hauth. I was born at home in the east end of the panhandle of Oklahoma. It had been called no man's land in earlier years, and the nearest town was Clearlake. It had a grocery store, a hardware, a blacksmith shop, and a telephone office.

We were all on what is called a party line, and our calls all had to go through the local operator. Each party had a separate number of rings, but anyone could pick up the phone and listen in anytime if they chose to do so.

We rented six different homes in the area. By the time I was in the seventh grade, I had attended four different schools, and with the exception of one, all were within eight miles of Clearlake.

We had our own cows, chickens, and pigs, so we would take our own cream, eggs, etc. to sell in exchange for feed for the animals.

Mom always grew a big garden and canned all kinds of food for winter months ahead. We children worked in the garden with her. We learned the different kinds of plants and which ones were weeds to be pulled and which were vegetables and left to grow. We learned where and how to hoe and how to make or draw a watering ditch between the rows of food plants.

There were very few cars, as I recall. Most of us traveled by horse-drawn wagons or on saddle horses or walked. It wasn't too long before a gas station came, bringing more cars into the area.

One of my first memories was the day our house burned down. I was probably four years old. My father was working on the WPA, building roads. He would take a team of horses and the wagon on Monday and come back home on Friday. Mom had gone to the barn to milk the cows and left orders with my older sister, Fay, to keep an eye on the kerosene cook stove, as she had water for washing heating on top of the stove in a large boiler. Mom had instructed Fay if the stove should catch on fire to come and tell her. And it did happen! Fay got me and DeWayne, just two years younger than me, and put us on the cellar door. And after telling Mom, Fay headed across the pasture to the nearest neighbors. She put out a general ring on the party line. By the time Mom got to the house, the fire was so advanced she could get nothing out, nor could she get to the phone. People came as soon as they could.

It was about seven miles or more to where Grandpa and Grandma Hauth lived, so we stayed with them for a while.

No one had much of anything to share, but nearby neighbors gathered up what they could spare and helped us out. My mom told me of a neighbor who was feeling bad because she had nothing to give but a box of old rags. Mom told me it turned out to be so very helpful, as in those days we had no Kleenex, paper towels, cleaning cloths, etc.

We soon moved into Uncle Walter and Aunt Lona's house, as they had moved to the state of Washington, where he worked on the big Vancouver Dam. This house is where we were living when I nearly died of pneumonia.

We were taught at an early age the necessity of work. From the time we could carry a quart or more of water in our little buckets from the windmill to the house we learned the value of work. All of our wash water and bath water, as well as water for cooking and drinking, had to be carried by hand into the house.

Mom made most of our clothing. I wanted to learn to sew very eagerly, so Mom patiently taught me how to make doll clothes by hand, sewing before starting school. She later taught me how to use the old treadle sewing machine.

My sister preferred cleaning house to kitchen work like cooking, washing dishes, preparing food, etc. When I had a choice, I took the kitchen work. I had a terrible time trying to mop the floors, just couldn't get all the streaks up. I would have to go back and mop it over and over until the dirt streaks were all gone.

From Feathers to Fry Pan

Caring for the chickens was always a chore that I deeply enjoyed. I was always interested in them. God made everything in its own special way.

Hens never lay more than one egg a day. Their best time of egg laying is in early spring. As the temperatures rise, the hen's body temperature also rises, and she has an instinct to want to set on her eggs. If she has been with a rooster, and she is allowed to sit on her eggs for about three weeks, there will be baby chicks from the fertilized eggs. Mama hen faithfully turns the eggs with her feet and beak to keep them all just the right temperature. When the chick is mature and ready to be hatched, you can actually see the chick's little beak pecking its way through the shell while stretching and kicking its way out. You can sometimes hear them peeping in the shell before they hatch. It is necessary that the chick break its own way out of the shell. The chick gains strength while working its way out. If one tries to help it out of the shell, it will be weak and puny and may not live.

Chicks grow fast and the baby down changes into feathers. By the time they weigh two to three pounds, it is time for fried chicken.

I had to learn at a young age how to prepare a chicken from catching, beheading, and de-feathering it before removing its entrails, cleaning it thoroughly, and cutting it in pieces before it ever reached the fry pan. I had to learn to cut the chicken at all the joints and dip them in flour or a seasoned mixture before putting them in a hot skillet of hot oil or grease. The pieces had to be turned often to keep them from burning.

It was a great feeling of achievement to place that platter of golden-brown, mouth-watering chicken, along with mashed potatoes and gravy, vegetables, salad, etc. on the table. I will be forever grateful to my mom who taught me how to do it all.

I hope my real life saga of taking the chicken from feathers to fry pan has not been too shocking, but it was indeed a part of my young life and on into adulthood as a cowboy's wife.

My First Real Job

My first job away from home was for our mailman and his wife. This was just before I turned eleven when school as out. His wife was afflicted with what was then called "milk leg," which caused her to be bedfast most of the time, and they needed someone to stay with her and get her water or food or whatever she might need. They had wanted Fay, my older sister, but she already had a job. My mom told them that even though I was not very big, she thought I could handle the job. So he came and picked me up to stay with them. They were both very surprised with what I could do. I swept the floors, did some cooking, washed dishes, made my bed, and helped her in many ways. I tried to keep things picked up and looking nice and neat.

Since it was getting close to Decoration Day, she was feeing sad because she could not go anywhere to get flowers. I told them if they could get me some crepe paper and a few things I would need, that I could make crepe paper roses. So he bought all the things I needed. I was able to make all she needed.

That launched me into my first business as the next year she asked me to make more flowers for her and also for others who bought them from me. That continued until I got married. So from that small beginning, I made many dozens of roses each year.

One Room Country Schools

We always walked to school and were joined by many other kids who walked with us, as there were quite a few people living in the area.

I remember during the winter months we were met at the school by a friendly teacher. She arrived early enough to clean the ashes out of the coal stove and start a warm fire to get the room heated for us. Sometimes we would all stand around the stove to get warmed up before starting our classes.

Our school day started with "The Pledge of Allegiance" to the America flag and would you believe, part of the time had Bible reading and prayer, depending on the teacher.

Because we had no inside water fixtures, our restrooms were two little buildings outside the school and were called outhouses. Our bathroom tissue was usually the *Sears Roebuck Catalog*.

We would average from 12 to 20 students with grades from first to eighth with one teacher for all. We all brought sack lunches. We would play outside at noon and recesses. We would play softball and hide and seek, and a teeter-tooter, a merry-go-round, and swings were always on the playground.

We had various community activities through the year, such as spelling bees, Halloween parties, Christmas programs, Valentine parties, and box suppers, where the women and girls would make attractive boxes with the food inside, and the men and boys would buy the boxes and eat with the owner of the box. Usually at these there was entertainment from students, helping us to learn to perform before an audience. This helped to raise money for the school. There were cakewalks with outside speakers and sometimes students. We would have musical programs or other things nearly every month.

The last day of school we looked forward to a picnic other than at the school, sometimes by a creek or grove of trees. There were not many of those in our area.

I recall Mom telling me of a surprise blizzard during my first year of school at Clearlake. Those of us that needed to go east made it to the nearest home about a mile away from the school. They had a full house that night. The party line let our parents know where we were. They had plenty of food, and we were kept warm and dry until the storm ended and our parents could pick us up.

The Dirty Thirties

How well I remember Grandpa and Grandma Hauth telling about the black Sunday afternoon when all of a sudden they could not see anything. They got caught away from the house at the time of this terrible dust storm and managed to get to a fence and held on to it until they reached the house.

It must have been the same day my husband, Windy, and his brother, Bill, and mother, Viola Johannsen, were doing chores. Mother Johannsen kept talking to the boys until they were all able to take hold of hands until they found the clothesline, and Mother held on to the line and them. It was so dark they could not see anything. Pappy Emil and some of the rest of the family were in the house. He thought to light a kerosene lamp and put it in the window. It wasn't until they were very close to the house that they saw the lamp burning, so it did help them to find the house.

Liberty School's students in the mid-1940s

The Way it Was as I Remember
By Ruby A. (Bare) Swanson of Brookings, South Dakota
Born 1933

When the telephone on the wall was first installed, it must have amazed everyone. It was more than a tool for practical use; it was means to socially connect with neighbors and relatives. Everyone was on a party line, perhaps as many as eight or ten on one line and there were as many lines as needed. If one wanted to make a call you first had to listen to be sure, the line wasn't in use. Everyone on the line had their own ring. Our number was 13F3, which was 1 long and 3 shorts. A long was 2 full turns of the crank on the side of the telephone and a short was only 1/2 turn of the crank.

My aunt, Gertrude (Booth) Baxter, was the first switchboard operator in Protection, Kansas. No one called an operator by her name; she was known as 'central.' We signaled central by ringing one long. If we wanted to call someone on another line, we had to go through central. Also if the clock had stopped, central was the one to call to get the time. Central recognized everyone's voice in the whole system and knew the latest news. If a general ring was issued, then everyone was to hurry to the telephone to listen; perhaps there was a pasture fire, family illness, or farm accident. This is how I heard of President F.D. Roosevelt's death. Mother was making bread and asked me to take the telephone call.

Something we had to cut down on summer heat was two homemade water coolers in our living room. Excelsior was put between screens, which fit on the window frame. Along the top was a rod with little holes in it, so water would filter down through the excelsior and with the hot south winds blowing through, it would make a nice cool breeze inside the house, and we were very comfortable.

I attended a one-room country school with a cloakroom, just inside the door, where coats were hung & the lunch buckets were stored until mealtime. Liberty School was one mile north of the home place. My great grandfather, William Wesley McMinimy, provided one acre of land for the school. I was in school when we had smaller enrollment in the 1-8 grades then when my older siblings (Marguerite, Chet, and Robert) attended school there. I had one classmate, Leo Thielen, and with only 8 to 10 students, not all grades were represented. Two teachers, I remember, were Miss Jackie Peacock and Miss Doris Anne Dorsey. Jackie had been a high school classmate of Marguerite and Chet and Doris Anne boarded at our neighbor's house, Sam and Lois Frantz, during the school week.

In the mornings, weather permitting, was

when students gathered close to the flagpole to raise the flag. The Pledge of Allegiance was then recited before going indoors for classes.

The school had an outhouse for the girls and another for the boys, a wood burning stove, and a cistern to pump to get a cool cup of water, and only a merry-go-round and teeter-totter for playground equipment. A favorite recess game was playing anty-over, which was tossing a ball over the schoolhouse to the other team. If the ball was caught, everyone ran around the school and the one carrying the ball tried to tag a player of the opposite team. If successful, that person became a player for your side. Other fun games were hide and seek, tag, hopscotch, jacks, jumping rope, but my least favorite was baseball. I could never hit the ball and I was usually in the outfield chasing balls that seemed to always go across the road in the ditch full of weeds.

In grade school, I tried riding a horse to school. Trigger did not like going on the road under the railroad bridge, so I would get off the horse and lead him. I finally came to the conclusion it was easier to just walk to and from school. Trigger was probably happier anyway not to be in a stall at school all day.

These are just a few of many memories I have of living in Clark County, Kansas.

Life on the Farm
By Dale Klenke of South Hutchinson, Kansas
Born 1946

I was born in 1946, grew up on a farm south of Spearville, Kansas. My Dad and Grandmother raised me and my two brothers as my mother died when I was 2 years old.

We learned how to do lots of chores, feed and water livestock and chickens, milk cows, butcher, drive tractors and wheat trucks, shock feed and put up hay bales. We rode our bikes 4 to 5 miles to play with neighbor kids on dirt roads. Sometimes we'd ride to town and see a movie for 25 cents. We learned how to hunt for jackrabbits and pheasants.

Radio was our entertainment; we played baseball, shot baskets and tossed footballs in the yard. Dad put up a windmill tower with antenna when I was 10 for our first black and white TV. We only got two channels. Howdy Doody, Lone Ranger, Cisco Kid, Bob Hope, and Ed Sullivan were our favorite shows.

Saturdays were laundry days. Heated water on stove, poured into washer. When clothes were washed, they were put through ringer and into a tub in rinse water. Then back through ringer and put on clothesline. In winter, we strung clotheslines inside the house.

In 1957, we had a big blizzard. Snow drifts 10 to 15 feet high. We helped Dad dig a tunnel to barn (3 football fields away). Dad got out tractor and dug path to stock tank so cattle could get water. He dug path to chicken house and worked all day moving snow. There was no school for a week. Since our road was not plowed us three boys rode on the tractor to a better road and rode to school with neighbor kids for a week.

Before we got TV, we would listen to a lot of baseball games on radio. I remember I carved a baseball bat out of a fence post. My brother was trying to kill a skunk with a fence post so I got my trusty bat and killed it. Grandma was mad. She made us throw away our clothes and take lots of baths. We had to give dog baths also. Our two dogs were great. One killed a rattlesnake once. The rat terrier was playing in a wheat bin as we were scooping wheat into a grain auger. He got his legs caught in auger and we had to put him down.

Halloween was great fun for mischief. My friends and I tied a cow to the Mayor's front door, put chickens in high school, and dragged out houses into the streets. Once my younger brother got caught and was put in old city jail. My buddy hooked a log chain to the bars of the back window and pulled down the back wall with his Dad's truck, breaking Randy out of jail. In Junior College, one of my buddies' bet us he could climb a water tower with a keg of beer strapped to his back. He got up about 15 feet and keg slipped out hitting concrete below and showered us with beer. This was dumb, as we could have killed the poor guy. I had to pay $50 for damage to keg but it made a good milk stool with a pillow on top.

Once in high school my buddy and I killed a coyote. We hung it on the steps pole inside the Kinsley Coyotes' team bus during a basketball game. We never got caught for this stunt.

In summer, Dad would take us to visit our other Grandma. She lived on a farm north of

Yates Center, Kansas. Grandpa milked 20 cows by hand. He used kerosene lanterns, as there was no electricity to barn. Milk cans were put into a tank with large blocks of ice until truck picked them up. Livestock could drink their water but humans could not. Grandpa would hitch his team of horses up to wagon and take us 3 miles to one room schoolhouse well for water.

We took baths in round washtub with water heated on stove. They had no indoor bathroom so we used an outhouse. Grandma had an old party line crank phone. She would make us pajamas out of feed sacks that had nice prints on them. We would pick berries for Grandma to make pies.

Dad would take us to Colorado Mountains every 3 or 4 years and to visit relatives. He'd take us to Dodge City every July 4th to the drive-in movies and see fireworks.

My favorite Christmas was at age 10. My brother and I got BB guns. We took flashlights to the chicken house and shot sparrows that were roosting in rafters.

We had no microwave, dishwasher, dryer, or air conditioning. We learned how to separate cream from milk and make butter. Grandma had a large garden and we helped her can vegetables and fruit.

I remember when one of our friends stayed overnight. We dared him to pee on the electric fence. It was funny but he got real mad.

I played basketball and football in high school. My graduating class had 25 students. Later on, out of the 12 boys in my class, 10 of us served in the military.

Life on the farm was simple but I wouldn't trade it for anything.

Growing Up on the Farm
By Bill Temaat of Monument, Colorado
Born 1939

I was born August 16, 1939, to a German family, living about 20 miles east of Dodge City, Kansas.

There were seven children, born to Bill and Helen Temaat, six survived, and one died shortly after her birth.

I am the youngest of the six surviving. We lived in one of the oldest rock houses in Ford County with approximately 500 sq. feet of living space on the main level and then an upstairs attic where my four brothers slept.

We did not have running water, electricity, and of course NO bathroom. We had a two holer, about 100 feet from our house and that is where we went to the bathroom, cleaning ourselves with the Penny's catalog, doing the best we knew how.

I slept in a pull out sleeper with my sister who was about five years older than I was. Since we slept in the living room, we could not go to bed until our company went home.

When it was time to study, we read by a candle or dad lit the kerosene lamp that put out so much more than a candle, but after an hour or so, it too faded out until dad pumped up the kerosene and then another few minutes of BRIGHT light.

In the summer of 1945, when I was six years old, my older brother, Norbert, and I were unloading a truckload of wheat. We had the lift, on the truck, in the air, and then the wheat rolled out into a hopper.

When we were finished unloading the wheat, the elevator was run by a John Deere motor, which had a flat belt, about eight inches wide. Since we were through, Norbert said we should take off the belt, but it was quite tight, so he said, "I will take off the spark plug, and you take your foot and push the belt off." Well, me being six years old, trusting of my older-smarter brother, I put my foot up to the belt and just as soon as I did, it grabbed me and twisted my foot around the pulley.

I knew I was hurt, but did not know how bad, but was crying. Norbert said, "Go to the house." Well, I could not walk, so he put me into the truck cab, and drove me the 200 feet to the house. Mom and Dad saw how bad it looked, so they took me to Dodge City, Kansas, to the hospital where the doctor decided my right ankle was broken, and needed a cast.

They put this terrible smelling stuff called ether under my nose and I was out in a few minutes. When I came to, I felt terrible, not only because of my broken ankle, but probably more so, from that ether.

When we got home, Dad made me a set of crutches; I hobbled around the rest of the summer.

Then in 1947, my Dad and brothers and other friends, built a new house with eight rooms, a "hotel" to me. The first night we slept there, I found out what it was like to turn on an electric light, flush a stool, take a bath in a tub, and we thought we were living like kings.

The house was built out of scrap lumber; my brother Tony dug the basement with a small Farmall tractor with a small scoop. It must have taken several weeks to dig, going in to get a scoop full, backing out, and putting the dirt on a pile to use for backfill.

I was of course too small to help but have very vivid memories of it being built. I recall the guy who did the drywall, with sheets 2 feet by 4 feet and then taping each seam. His name was MaTheny and the guy who did the wiring was Ira Hickman.

When I grew older, I helped with the chores, milking nine cows by hand with flies, cockleburs, manure, and water dripping from the cows, all going into the same milk bucket. Then we took the whole milk, to a separator, to separate the cream from the milk. The cream we sold to a gentlemen, named Bud Heiland, in Spearville, Kansas, and the skim milk we fed to our 30 or so pigs.

From the nine cows, we usually got about 30-40 gallons of milk twice a day. Then in 1953, Dad bought a milking machine and boy did that make things easier. Just put a strap around the cow's belly, hook the machine up and sit there and watch. We could milk two cows at a time, so what took a couple of hours before, we could now do in about 30 minutes, plus no more manure, flies, or cockleburs in the milk.

After doing the chores, feeding 500 chickens, 30 pigs, and 10 little calves, we ate a good breakfast, and then off to school 4.5 miles away in the old 1928 Ford, a classy ride to say the least. One day, while my older brother, Tony, was driving, the brakes went out and we hit a rock wall about five feet high, and two feet thick. Yep, that stopped us, and broke the milk jar that we were taking to the nuns in Windthorst. I guess they had dry cereal that day. Sorry sisters!

From then on, my life got easier, going to school, playing baseball, football and basketball from the fourth grade all through high school, and then on to St. Mary of the Plains, where I played basketball on a scholarship.

I had a chance to play baseball with the Yankees, but my dad needed me on the farm, since I was the youngest, to help with the harvest.

Grandad Gorilla
By Claire Ryta Thompson of Milan, Kansas
Born 1948

My first memory of "the farm" was one of white sheer curtains blowing in the warm breeze of my grandparents' bedroom as we rested at mid-day. Their days started early and there was no air conditioner, so a little rest in the heat of the day was a good idea. The house was quite small and consisted of four rooms with an enclosed porch along the back. The kitchen was the center of life there and I remember Grandma Ruth cooking on the wood stove. She also heated water for our baths on it. The rectangular galvanized tub was brought in from the porch and placed in the larger bedroom. Then everyone took turns bathing. I recall Grandad Claire bringing home a newborn lamb to spend the night in a box near the stove on a bitterly cold evening.

My grandfather would "wash up" in a basin inside the back door and we gathered around the table in the center of the room.

Claire's mother, Wanda Forrest in 1948

Claire Ryta Thompson

One meal stands out because my two younger brothers and I had gotten to ride in the back of the manure spreader that morning. My brothers kept tossing rocks at the metal reel that flipped the manure out onto the fields. Grandad had warned them to stop several times, but they had to throw just one more. As he turned to tell them to stop, that rock flew back and hit him square in the eye. His bruised and bloody looking eye cast a grim mood over that meal. Another time, the two spent hours setting "gorilla traps" along the tree row of the farm. They would pull a small sapling down and then pile large rocks on them. The "gorilla" who lifted off one of the rocks and got smacked by the sapling was once again, our Grandad.

I loved all the farm animals from the milk cows to the chickens. Grandma would put the feed in and move the board to hold the cows head in place, put on the cow kickers, and tuck in their tail. Then she would perch on a T shaped milking stool and milk the cows. I was allowed to take my turn even though I was quite small. The cream separator was in the kitchen and I wasn't allowed to have anything to do with that, as Grandma was very particular. The cream was then separated from the milk and could be made into butter. There were two chicken houses, a larger one for the egg layers, and a small red one, which housed the bantam fighting hens, which were really just pets. Excess eggs and milk were traded or sold on their weekly trip to town.

Wash day required getting the washer set up on the back porch and heating water to use. I was never allowed to put the clothes in the wringer but it sure fascinated me. Then of course, the clothes were hung on the line to dry and they smelled so good when you brought them in.

One summer, my dad told us we were going to the farm because he had a surprise for us. I could barely wait as I was hoping it was the horse that I prayed for each night. We stood waiting in a line and then my dad rode out from behind the outhouse sitting astride a burro with his feet nearly touching the ground. That burro was our getaway ride when we pretended to rob a bank although it never traveled faster than a slow walk. It would walk to a sticker patch and then buck you off. As soon as you started sliding down his side, he'd just stand there. Once you were on the ground, he'd follow you around like a dog. We named him Ike after the current President. Ike thought he brought the cattle up to be milked each evening. Once when my brothers were riding him, the cattle finished drinking from the pond and started off without Ike. He bolted to catch up, dumping them in the pond. They were left sitting in the edge of the pond howling and my Grandad laughed.

I went back to photograph the remains of the farm recently. It was much smaller than I remembered. Small trees filled the yard where we used to sleep on an old spring bed. As a child, I thought we were so far from the house on those starry nights but it was just a short distance. It brought many poignant memories to mind and old feelings of content in just the simple things.

The farm is located 3 miles north of Argonia and 1/4 mile east. My father was born there in 1931, the youngest of five boys. He was delivered by his Aunt Mitt who was a midwife and also "doctored" locals, including setting broken bones. My mother's parents, Claire and Ruth Raine lived there from 1945 until the late '50s. I was about 10 or 11 when they moved to Argonia.

Learning to Swim
By Robert Peterson of Grayson, Georgia
Born 1942

It was 1957 and I was 14 years old. I lived in a farming community in western Kansas where all the boys learned to drive tractors at a very early age. Some of them were driving double-header tractors when they were only 10 and 11 years old to help their dads on the farm. Most of us had an old car and could drive if we had a licensed driver in the car with us, but most of the time we didn't. We just drove around and eluding the local cop was an easy thing to do. I don't think catching us was one of his priorities because a lot of the kids lived in the country and used their cars to drive back and forth to school and help on the farm. Most of us, however, didn't know how to swim!

Our closest swimming pool was at another city 45 miles away and that was just too far for us to drive. We had to get there by going through another small town and we were enemies of the boys in both towns. We played against them in sports and you were considered a traitor if you became friendly with one of them. We didn't want them in our town either, not only because of the sports rivalry but because we didn't want any of them dating the girls in our town and they didn't want us dating any of the girls in their town either. That was just too much, if they did, a fight was sure to ensue.

Although I'm sure our town's fathers didn't take any of that into consideration when they decided we needed to learn how to swim and it gave us something to do during the summer months when school wasn't in session. Plus it was good politics. Look what they were doing for the kids! Anyway, the school furnished a couple of school buses and we were bused the 45 miles to the swimming pool one day a week, it was a big deal to us. We loved to go there and play all afternoon in the swimming pool; we were also given swimming lessons. The swimming classes were broken down by age and one's ability to swim. The goal was to reach the advanced swimming class.

Going back home was also enjoyed by all the kids, we would talk of course about swimming and once that wore off we would more often than not sing "99 Bottles of Beer on the Wall" over and over the rest of the way home. I'm sure it drove the bus driver nuts but we had fun.

Unfortunately it was difficult for some kids to make the trip and there was always some who couldn't go because of other commitments. Fortunately we had caught "swimming fever" and we wanted to swim. With the lack of swimming pool availability, we devised our own method of learning how to swim. We used a local irrigation pond. It was fairly close to town meaning we could drive there without using a lot of gas. Lord knows we didn't have any money for gas and we were not supervised. We could do what we wanted when we wanted, it was ideal!

The pond was approximately 75' x 75' and had a high embankment on all sides. There were even some small plants growing in the embankment because of the moisture of the pond. The water was about 7' or 8' deep. Perfect! There was also a raft. Someone, I'm assuming the owner of the pond had made a raft. It was constructed using six 55 gal drums. There were three drums on each side. They were sealed and laid down on their sides and held together via a wooden platform on top. The raft floated in the water so that the platform was about 8 inches above the water level. This allowed us to swim up to the raft and pull ourselves up onto the raft without much difficulty.

The trick was getting to it since it was generally floating somewhere near the middle of the pond. If you couldn't swim, you had a problem. Someone who knew how to swim would get the raft and bring it to the bank so the non-swimmers could get on. We would use our hands and paddle out to the middle of the pond to sunbathe and/or swim. Of course boys will be boys so once we got to the middle of the pond we sometimes played "king of the raft" and would try and push each other off the raft. It was at that point, sink or swim, we quickly learned how to "dog paddle" and could get back to the raft that way. Once there, we would pull ourselves up onto the raft, we did this until we got tired or we saw a snake. It wasn't unusual for a snake to go slithering by us when we were swimming to or around the raft. We would just splash water on it and it would go its way and we would go our way. It's scary when I think about it now.

We would go to the pond during the summer months a lot. It was a quick way to cool down and have fun doing it. And once you have "dog paddling" down, it's a simple step to learning how to do an overhand and/or breaststroke with a little help from your friends. We all learned how to swim in the pond that summer. We just improved our swimming techniques at the swimming pool far, far away.

Tribune, Kansas is Home
By Helen Gilger Glenn of Las Vegas, Nevada
Born 1926

On a cold winter night, my life began January 20, 1926 in Cimarron, Kansas. My first seven years, I lived on a farm near Ingalls, Kansas with my parents and siblings.

I was one of five children, who on March 1, 1933, moved with our parents to a dry land wheat farm seventeen miles southwest of Tribune, Kansas. Several miles from us, were our nearest neighbors and a one-room country schoolhouse. At that time, very few acres were plowed for farming .There was nothing between us but a beautiful prairie of buffalo grass.

At first, my father built a one-room adobe house. As there was no ceiling, a platform was made in the rafters for the boys' bed. We girls' bed was made up on a mattress that during the daytime slid under our parent's bed and pulled out for the night. To make more living space, my father cut the west house window into a doorway, put a "cook-shack" there, partitioned it in half and that became we children's bedrooms. Our furniture was orange crates, covered by curtains Mother made from pretty chicken feed sacks.

Water is the number one priority for sustaining life on a farm. We were blessed when the drilling company hit pure, clear, cold water the first try. A small barrel was installed on ground level. This was used as our drinking water, carried into the house using a galvanized water bucket. Pipes from the barrel lead into a trough inside the small building, beside the windmill; we called the "milk-house." Here, in waterproof containers, we could keep our milk, homemade butter, cheese, and anything that would spoil, for several days. The pipes from this trough lead outside to the livestock tanks. We had the usual farm animals. Cows, horses, pigs, chickens, turkeys, dogs, cats, etc. Our barn was more like a shed than a big red barn you usually see. Times were getting hard and the Depression years were upon us.

Pat and Helen in 1942

Laundry days were an unforgettable experience. We had a mail order washing machine, when not in use, was kept in the "milk-house." On washday, it was rolled into the main house. As we had no electricity, it had a loud gasoline engine that gave off so many fumes the front door had to be left open. Water was heated on the wood stove and poured into the machine that held homemade soap. After the clothes washed, they were put through a wringer into a galvanized tub of rinse water, then into a second tub of water that held a blue liquid to make clothes whiter, then into a basket carried to an outside line to dry.

This didn't take long in the Western Kansas wind. Even though washday was busy, I looked forward to the nice clean clothes and the cornbread and beans we had for supper.

The Jim and Mabel Gilger family in 1935

The country schoolhouse (South Prairie View) was located nearby. All eight grades were taught to less than 15 students. I went here from the first grade until the seventh, when it consolidated with the town schools in Tribune, Kansas. I studied while riding the bus, as the route was long.

In 1939, I was 13 when my sister was born. Even though we were poor, as everyone was at that time, she was the most wonderful baby anyone could ask for. All of us needed and adored her. We now had someone to care for, love and play with.

I was 14 when a neighbor boy wanted to take me to a movie. My father said I could date as soon as I learned how to make biscuits as good as Mother's. I made biscuits and more biscuits until I finally passed the test and got to see the movie "Gone with the Wind" with my friend. (He lost his life in Germany during World War II).

The Dust Storms of the dirty '30s are vivid in my mind, as to the reality of living through them. I remember how our family survived many storms, of which some people have heard or read about but find hard to believe.

One morning I remember waking up to the sound of tractors, seeing my father staring out the window in disbelief as he said, "Someone is plowing up the pasture land" preparing it for farming. For a time this was no problem as long as there was rain. Then the dry years came and with the Western Kansas winds, so did the dust. There was no grass to hold the ground from blowing and the crops weren't growing.

At first, the dust only blew occasionally and just locally. Then the storms started rolling in from a distance. Large, dark rolling clouds of dust would come through, lasting a few hours or a few days. One never knew. Sometimes you could see them coming and at other times, they were upon you before you knew it, turning daylight hours into nighttime darkness.

When a storm was raging outside, the family sat around the table, with a coal-oil lamp in the center, furnishing the only light we had, playing cards and eating popcorn. Mother made popcorn popper out of new "fly screen" - folding it like an envelope and sewing the seams together with a piece of the screen. Over the hot wood stove, she could pop a dishpan full at one time, pour homemade butter over it and we were ready to wait out the storm. Dust was coming in throughout the house.

Before we went to bed, Mother dampened bedding sheets, putting them over the head of our beds. She would also stuff rags around the windows and doors, but nothing could keep the fine dirt out. When morning came, we started cleaning out the dirt that had sifted in, using a large shovel to scoop it out. If a storm came up during the night, you could see where your head had been lying with dirt all around it.

As the storms continued, the farm was beginning to suffer the effects. Fences were being covered by mounds of dirt. The blowing thistles would lodge in the fences, causing dirt to pile up making drifts compared to blizzard snowstorms. Out buildings were getting filled with dirt. No crops were able to grow. There was dirt everywhere and no rain in sight.

In 1938, my father moved the family to

The Gilger homestead in 1942

Canon City, Colorado. He continued living on the farm and planting crops. Within a year, all of us wanted to move back, as the rains had settled the dust and the crops were looking good. The drought years appeared to be over for the present time.

In the fall of 1940, I entered the Greeley County High School in Tribune, Kansas. I enjoyed everything about school especially the classes, teachers, and classmates. I remember December 7, 1941, when our principal called all students together, telling us of the Pearl Harbor attack on America. At the time, I didn't realize the impact this would have on my life.

Older boys were drafted or voluntarily enlisted in different branches of the service. World War II was upon us. Now younger boys were enlisting. Many of my classmates enlisted, never to return. This was a sad time for everyone. We Americans rallied around our troops, thankful for the freedom they were fighting for.

Hired men to help my father on the farm were hard to find. My younger brother and I were his helpers. I became his tractor driver, pulling the combine or other equipment. I could also scoop wheat, helping to load the truck before driving to the elevator in Tribune.

I graduated from High School in 1944. Continued living on the Greeley County farm until 1946, when my father made our final move to Canon City, Colorado - leaving what he proudly called "Our Family Homestead" forever.

At the age of 88, I have been away from Tribune, Kansas many years but till refer to it as "Home" There were some hardship times but also wonderful memories of living in Greeley County Kansas and that is what is important. This is my story. It is my intentions for you to have enjoyed it, as I have in reminiscing and writing it.

Paper Dolls and Homemade Clothes
By Joan Irene Farney Dunn of Hutchinson, Kansas
Born 1928

My family moved from a farm home to a small town in Reno County, Kansas in 1934 when I was six years old. I was the youngest of five children. At that time our town consisted of a main road that ran north to south and east to west for approximately five to six blocks each direction from the central point and made up the business district: two gasoline stations, a mechanic's garage, a restaurant, a drug store and soda fountain, a grocery store, a United States post office, a telephone exchange office, two churches, a lumber yard, a movie theater, an ice house, a one through eighth grade school building, a four year high school building, and a large gymnasium. The Rock Island Railroad came through the south part of town, and there was a depot and two large concrete grain elevators along the tracks. The large steam engines on the freight trains and passenger trains were very noisy. We also had a public croquet court in the center of town that was a favorite gathering place on Saturday nights when the "country folk" came to town to shop and to visit for the evenings. How we created a lot of our own entertainment is another long story.

Outhouses
Oh how I hated them. I would put off going until the very last minute, because there were always wasps flying around and they (the outhouses) were really smelly!

Radio Programs
We always had a radio. However, the static was so bad. I remember my dad sitting close to the radio trying to hear *Fibber McGee and Molly*, a favorite program, or a baseball game.

Phones
Oh yes, the party lines: each phone on the line had its own number of rings. One could listen to the neighbor's news and gossip. Our phone hung on the wall, and you had to stand to talk and hold the receiver to your ear. No phone messages were ever private!

Wringer Washers
Monday was always washday. The first thing, early in the morning, to get enough hot water to fill the washing machine heated in the reservoir on the side of the wood burning cook stove. The wringer was hand propelled and the larger articles such as bed sheets and bath towels had to be folded and guided through the rollers on the wringer. I remember I wanted to help at a young age, and Mother was afraid I would get my fingers in the rollers. All of the laundry items were hung on several wire clotheslines that graced the backyard. All items were hung with wooden clothespins, the

spring snap kind, and the slip over ones, to air dry.

Homemade Clothes

Various feeds were sold in large sacks that were very colorful with floral or plaid or stripes and checkered designs. This was a source of cheap material for making dressed, blouses, shirts, pillowslips, tablecloths, etc.

Toys

I remember my brothers making miniature hayracks and wagons from small scraps of lumber given to them at the lumberyard.

We were lucky enough to be given a pair of roller skates (not roller blade shoes). These were metal skates with four wheels that fastened to our regular shoes and were adjustable to fit different sizes of shoes. They had a large key that tightened the clamps and a leather strap to go around your ankle.

We had a wagon we could pull each other or propel it with one leg in the wagon and the other foot pushing.

Bag swings were popular and easy to make. A gunnysack was half filled with sand, a sturdy rope was attached to it, and it was hung form a large tree limb.

Dolls

The Sunday newspaper edition had a comic section in color, and one-half page of this section had dolls and clothes to be cut out. The *Hutchinson News Herald* was published twice daily in Hutchinson, Kansas and was transported by rail to the depot in Langdon. Local children were hired to deliver these early morning and late afternoon to all subscribers living in town and place the paper inside the screen door.

As I reflect back on my childhood days of growing up in a small town that did not have much to offer in the way of entertainment I realize I learned a lot about being responsible for my own actions, because everyone knew everybody and everything that was happening and who was doing it. I did a lot of walking, no tricycle, or bicycle to ride. A few boys and girls to play with. We did a lot of walking around town, singing, catching fireflies in jars and watching them light up. As we grew older and in later years in school we all played softball, tennis, volleyball, basketball, last couple out, and took part in track meets with other area schools.

My brothers had the paper route for several years to earn a few dollars to help pay for schoolbooks and supplies. I was their substitute much of the time before school and after school, because they took part in all athletics and had to practice. I was offered a job at the corner drug store with I was 13 years of age and worked every summer and after school and Saturdays and Sundays during the four years of high school. I clearly remember running the two and a half blocks to the drug store after school dismissal and after all school evening functions so as to beat the crowd that would gather there for an hour or two. I had many interesting experiences there and having had a responsible job for four years really helped me in getting a job with a grain company upon graduating from high school.

I Love Garden City
By Sue Knight of Garden City, Kansas
Born 1943

I grew up at 105 N. 4th Street, Garden City, Kansas. My mom did not work or drive, and Dad worked at the sugar beet factory and the state highway. My mom did not work outside the home; she was a great mom. She raised eight kids, six girls, and two boys. My mom passed away in 1965 of cancer. She was from a family of ten kids.

My dad worked hard and played some softball. When he was younger, he worked part time at the Blue Bird Cabin on Fulton Street. They sold lunchmeat, cheese, beer,

The Knight family

The big pool

pop, candy, chips, and gas. He passed away in 1980.

I can remember going swimming without shoes or towels so that they wouldn't get stolen. We would run from the tracks to the first shady spot to cool our feet.

We had a wringer washing machine in a one-room basement. We would have to carry the laundry upstairs to hang it on the line. We would even hang underwear with two clothespins. Our mom made our pajamas and slips out of white flour sacks; the ones with prints were used for our dresses.

I was the third to the oldest. I don't remember much of my older sisters' lives at home. My sister, Connie, was a year younger, and we were very close. We lived in a small house and shared a bedroom. We always had plenty to eat and got one thing we wanted at Christmas. We played outside a lot, even after dark, hide and go seek and kick the can. We were about three blocks from the zoo and the biggest free concrete swimming pool. We would swim almost every day. The zoo didn't have much at that time, a brown bear, a polar bear, some birds, and I think the biggest thing was Monkey Island.

During my teen years, we had two theaters downtown, the State and Ritz, the drive-in, and the skating rink. We had A&W Root Beer and Dibbers. Going downtown on Saturday afternoon was the best if we got all our chores done. We could walk all over by ourselves without worrying of anything happening to us. Downtown on Main Street there was two shows, a bowling alley, two Renick Drug Stores with fountain counters, a Woolworths Store with candy by the pound and a lunch counter for hamburgers, shakes, etc., a Duckwalls 5&10 cent store across the street, and Myers Ice Cream with music, which was cool. I worked at the Garden City Laundry on 8th Street folding sheets for motels.

When in junior high school on 8th and Kansas Avenue, around from the Tinker Shop north of there was a store, I can't remember the name, but they sold hamburgers, pop, school supplies, and had a jukebox. I would use my lunch money to play music. I loved to dance. Elvis, Ricky Nelson, and Big Bopper were my favorites.

On Main Street, there was a teen hang out called Pop Baringers for kids to hang out playing pool and listening to music. None of the boys would dance so us girls danced with each other and had fun. I told my grandson a way to get a girl was to learn how to dance.

We would drag Main Street, go to the Dibbens Drive-In, go around back, and go to Time Square, which was the empty space behind the old Sears Building on 8th Street. There was a clock above the radiator shop, and we would park a while, and then do it all over again. We would see kids in the skating rink. Arthur Hammond was the bouncer or whatever there. He sure was a good skater and danced on skates.

Connie and Sue

We had one big, bad blizzard, and it was hard to get around. We would go to my cousin's farm once in a while, but I hated it because they had an outhouse. When we had a sore throat Mom would make us gargle with salt water, put Vicks on our throats, and wrap an old sock around our throats for the night.

My teenage years in Garden City were the best. The kids nowadays don't know what fun is. I quit school my sophomore year and went to work at the Garden City Laundry on 8th Street. It was next to Tom's Tavern. I started folding sheets for the motel, and then went to packaging uniforms for guys. That is where I met Jim Knight, a driver. We had a lot of fun there, too.

Jimmie and I married in 1960. He was in the Navy. We moved to California and had two kids, Shelly and Terry, and then came back home and had another daughter, Shannon, in Garden City. I have been here ever since. I love Garden City, Kansas.

Homemade Rumble Seats and Rotten Egg Mud Pies
By Rebecca Otter of Larned, Kansas
Born 1935

I grew up on a 360-acre farm in northwest Kansas in Norton County. My parents worked hard to raise 12 children. They also taught us how to work.

I remember helping my mother do the laundry during the summer months. She heated the water by starting a fire in a barrel on which was set a large iron kettle filled with water and homemade lye soap in which the diapers were boiled to get the stains out. The first washer I remember was a half-moon shape with a wooden handle that stood straight up on the front side. The opening on top was a sliding door. Holding the handle, we would swing the washer from side to side to wash the clothes. Later we had a wringer washer, and we thought we were uptown!

Oh yes, the Saturday night baths! Baths started early, right after supper, with the younger children so they could get to bed earlier. Being the second oldest it was sometimes very late before I got my bath. The bath water was heated on the wood burning stove in a boiler tub and then carried to the bathtub in the bathroom. The bathtub was one of those with the clubfeet. There was running water but only cold water from the cistern, which was filled from the windmill on the hill north of the house.

My mother made all of our dresses for school and for Sunday, some from flour and feed sacks. Watching her sew fascinated me, and I wanted to learn early on. I would sneak some material from the rag box to make doll clothes while my mother and father went shopping in a town 30 miles away.

My school was a two-room school, one room for the first four grades, the other for the fifth to eighth grades. There was no kindergarten, so we started with first grade. One day, before I was in school, I went to town with my father, who stopped at the town grocery store to get some smoked herring for my older sister's lunch. He sent me to take it over to the school, giving me instructions to knock on the south door, because that is where my sister would be. Well, I walked around on the outside of the building and couldn't find the south door, so I went in the only door to the school, and sure enough, there was a south door in the hallway. I knocked on the door and Sister (the teacher) answered. I held the sack up to her and said, "Here is some stink fish for Eulalia's (my older sister) lunch." I left and went back to meet my father at the store. That evening when my sister arrived home, she was very upset with me for embarrassing her in front of the whole classroom!

My father owned a Model A Ford coupe, a one seater, when he married my mother. The oldest child would sit in between them and the youngest would sit on my mother's lap. When numbers three and four came along, it got a little crowded, so my dad took an old spring seat from an older car, cushioned it, covered it, took the lid off the trunk of the car, and placed the spring seat in the trunk. Viola! We now had a rumble seat! Well, guess who got to ride back there. The three oldest, all girls. Needless to say, we were embarrassed to ride back there. What would our friends say? You know what they said? "Gee, that looks like fun. I wish we had one of those!" There were times when, on the way to church, we had to knock on the window to get my dad's attention to let him know one of our hats flew off, and we needed to stop and pick it up. When the weather was cold, we covered up with blankets.

There were always farm chores to be done: milking cows, herding cattle, feeding pigs and chickens, gathering eggs, bringing the work horses in from the pasture, cleaning the chicken house, hoeing the garden, and helping to put up the hay. But there were also some fun times. A small creek ran through our property, so when the work was done, we got to go play in the creek on hot summer afternoons. My dad always checked the creek for the good swimming holes before we went. We didn't have swimming suits, so we just found some old clothes for the occasion. That worked for us. Playing ball was another family game, which we all enjoyed. My mom and dad both played ball with the town teams.

We had no air conditioning, except the outside air coming through a wet blanket my mother hung in the doorway. We studied by kerosene lamps until I was in the fifth grade. That's when we got electricity and a radio. Food was kept cool in an insulated icebox with a big chunk of ice in one part and a drain pan on the bottom. I think the ice was delivered from a nearby small town. There was no commode in the bathroom, but we did have an outhouse. That was a good place to go after dinner and stay long enough to get out of doing dishes.

My grandparents played a big part in our lives. My paternal grandmother lived in town. My grandfather had died when my dad was a small child, so I never knew him. We would go to my grandmother's house often after Sunday Mass, and when there was a blizzard and we couldn't get home from school. My maternal grandparents lived on a farm, so it was always fun to go and play on old machinery and buggies with a lot of our cousins. And of course, there was always good food and plenty of it. I remember especially the homemade churned ice cream with fresh strawberries from the garden.

Besides being fascinated with sewing, I also liked to watch my mother bake and cook. She made homemade noodles and dried them and covered them with a dishtowel on her kitchen worktable. I would often sneak a noodle or two and take them outside and wrap them around a mulberry and try to bake them in the sun. It didn't always work. One time I decided to make mud pies with some rotten eggs I found in the middle of the chicken coop. I didn't think anyone knew about it, but my mother asked me where I found the rotten eggs. She could smell them on me!

Playing in the Farm Buildings
By Georgia Thomas of Kansas City, Missouri
Born 1930

My story has to deal with the buildings on the farm. Each one had its purpose, and they each have a story to tell. I can relate some of these stories.

We lived in a nice, big farmhouse. There were nine children, six girls, and three boys. We were all born in that house. One interesting thing was the room we were born in depended on the time of year we were born. I only remember when my baby sister was born. We were quickly shipped off to my aunt and uncle in the middle of the night during a blizzard on February 18th.

Climbing on the roofs of the buildings on the farm was a real challenge for my younger sister and me. We managed to climb them all. Now, the barn was a real challenge that was nearly our demise. The roof was rather steep, and two thirds of the way up we started slipping down. Luckily, there was a cable along the edge of the roof from the lightning rods on the peak of the barn. We were able to grab and hold onto the cable and slowly get ourselves down far enough to reach the gate that we used to get up on the roof. Right down below us was the bullpen.

The pig shed was a smaller building, and it had a fun roof to slide down. We wore the shingles smooth and holes in our pants.

Some of the other farm buildings had a dual purpose. Growing up, my sister and I loved to sing and dance. We were going to be movie stars. When the hay was used up in the hayloft in the barn, the bare loft was a great dance studio.

We had dairy cattle and sold milk to a dairy. We milked the cows, morning and evening. After each milking, the floor had to be scrubbed clean. The floor was concrete and made a wonderful skating rink for us when we wanted to skate.

The milk house was close to the milk barn.

The grainery

There was a trough in the milk house full of water. The milk cans were in the trough, and the milk was poured from the milk buckets into the milk cans. Our job was to stir the milk in the milk cans with a special stirrer to get it cool. The milk was picked up early every morning. In the summer when the milk was gone, we played in the water in the troughs.

The brooder house especially had a dual purpose. A brooder house is a shed or barn where baby chicks are raised until they are old enough and start to grow real feathers. The building was concrete and had a glass southern exposure to help heat the shed.

Early in the spring, the baby chicks came in the mail in special boxes, and we all went to the brooder house. We took each little baby chick and dipped its beak in some water to get it to drink and then let it run. They were so soft.

I learned a lesson from baby chicks. In some of the corners of the boxes, there would be a little small chick, and the others would be pecking on it. I'd call it bullying, however Mother explained to me the pecking order. Animal behavior is a dominance hierarchy, seen especially in domestic poultry that is maintained by one bird pecking another of lower status. A study suggests the birds are smart enough to gauge another's status, even in other groups.

When the chickens developed into hens and started laying eggs, they were moved to the chicken house, where there were nests to lay eggs in, and roosts were made so they could roost and sleep. Then another job we had was to gather the eggs from the nest. We took the eggs to market on Saturdays.

Black snakes were attracted to chicken houses for the eggs. The snakes swallowed the eggs whole. We were always afraid of the snakes in the hen house. We also raised chickens for the meat. They were called fryers.

You've heard the expression "running around like a chicken with your head cut off." That is something to watch and a little scary when you are a kid. You chop their heads off and they do jump around until they stop bleeding. I learned to clean and dress chickens. Mother showed us how to cut up a chicken in 12 pieces. Maybe it was because there were 12 of us to eat every meal. My mother's dad lived with us so that made an even dozen.

My grandpa was a blacksmith. His shop was a lean-to on the south side of the granary. Grandpa mainly sharpened plow shears for the farmers in the area. I loved to watch Grandpa heat the plow shear in the forge to a red-hot glow, and then he'd pound the shear with a special hammer on the anvil to a sharp edge. Grandpa did a lot of work with iron.

In the winter of 1945, the brooder house was changed into an infirmary. I contracted scarlet fever and was quarantined for six weeks, and since my dad had had scarlet fever when he was in the Army, we moved out to the brooder house. So that way everyone could go to school, and we could continue to sell milk.

My school friends and family came to visit me from the windows on the south side. I remember I had checked out <u>Lassie Come Home</u> from the library. Mother had to bake the book in the oven before the library would take it back. The other papers and magazines had to be destroyed. I collected movie star magazines and pictures; it was hard to burn them. I missed six weeks of school. I never did catch up in algebra.

My dad preserved some meat by salting, curing, and smoking it. The process took place in another building, in a closet like in the washhouse. Laundry was a big ordeal, and it took days to do the laundry for 12 people. Mother also did a lot of canning. The washhouse was used for a lot of things. Much later, it became a garage.

In the backyard next to the washhouse was the root cellar. It was another wonderful place for snakes and spiders. In the spring, most of the food was used up, so we had to clear out the cellar, especially for shelter. We lived in the tornado alley in Kansas. My mother was really afraid of storms. We spent a lot of time in the cellar on blankets in the potato bins.

The cellar was like a big berm in the backyard and was a great place to play king of the mountain on. Another game we played which involved a building was Annie, Annie over. It is an active game of tag involving throwing a ball over a building. In the game two players or two teams of players stand on opposite sides of a small building, in my case the brooder house. With a cry of "Annie, Annie over!" the ball is tossed over the roof of the building. The kids on the other side of the building try to catch the ball. If they catch it, they run to the other side of the building and try to tag someone out by throwing the ball at them. It is a very active, fun game. We sometimes played over the main house. According to the Kansas State Historical Society, this game was played in the schoolyards in the late 1800s and the early 1900s. My mother taught in a one-room school in Sedgwick County, Kansas in the later 1800s.

With so many sisters, we played a lot. The granary was another building that was used for storing grain, and it was fun to jump into the wheat from the rafters. The granary was used for a playhouse when the grain was gone.

It sounds like we played a lot, but we had to work first. We learned to hide from our dad, because he could always find something for us to do if he saw us playing.

My memories on the farm are wonderful, and I wouldn't trade living on a farm for anything.

Chili for Uncle Fred
By Beverly J. Davis Smith of Hutchinson, Kansas
Born 1938

I was born April 21, 1938 in Abilene, Kansas. My father was a telegrapher for the railroad. My mom said he was always popular, because he knew all the important news first. People would go to the railroad station to learn about important news as it came over the line. Him and his friend, Woody Seat, started our local radio station. He even played his violin on the air.

When I was eleven months old, he died of a ruptured appendix in Hutchinson where mom had taken him for an operation. We were in Des Moines, Iowa. Mom brought us, my brothers, and me, to live with her family in Hutchinson, Kansas. Living there were my grandparents, a crippled aunt, an older bachelor uncle, and my youngest aunt. My uncle was like a family keeper, taking care of everyone and everything. The youngest aunt was the caregiver and homemaker. They all took us in and cared for us.

She, Mom, told me of the sorrow she felt on the train; three children and her husband in a casket in the baggage car.

One of the first things I remember was the whole household listening to the war news on the radio. They were trying to figure out where the five uncles who were in the war were.

Later I learned Uncle Fred led troops into Berlin. He told of using German marks from the Berlin bank for toilet paper. He admired General Patton. Uncle Daryl sent a wooden shoe to me. He had been a frogman. They were divers who looked for mines before ships came in. They sent toys and kimonos from Japan, wine from France, and crystal, a surgical field kit, a Luger, a Swastika, and a belt buckle from Germany. One of them sent a torn silk parachute, and Mom made my cousins me and blouses. I think she made underwear out of the rest of it.

Hutchinson Naval Air Station was 13 miles from our house. The whole area had to have a blackout when there was an alarm. Everyone would come out and stand in the yard. Grandpa made sure everyone turned off all the lights. It was every eerie.

My grandma and her friends would set on the front porch drinking tea, gossiping, watching the kids, and knitting olive green caps, gloves, mittens, and scarves for the soldiers. They could fill a basket in a day.

My mom worked at a bag factory during the day. Some evenings she would go to the Red Cross to roll bandages. She worked very hard and raised us with no social security or welfare.

Rationing was a big topic for the adults. Coffee, sugar, tires, and gas were bartered every day. A lost needle stopped the world until it was found. Needles and stockings were in short supply, too.

When I was five, my brother came home from the barbershop. He was blowing a big pink ball of bubblegum. I had never wanted anything so bad in my life. Grandma asked him to take me to the barbershop to get bubblegum. I guess bubblegum went to the war, too. The barber gave me the gum after asking how many of my freckles he could have.

We didn't get a telephone until I was about eight years old. Telegrams were sent for important news. Our house was kind of a clearinghouse for family news.

The day the war was over was like nothing I had ever seen before. Everyone was laughing, crying, jumping, kissing, and hugging, even strangers. Luckily, all my uncles came home to us, and I got to know and love them.

One memorable day was when my Uncle Fred came home. It was summer and very hot. My mother made a big pot of chili. Everyone groused that it was too hot for chili. She said she had a feeling, an urge to make it. We had just sat down at the table and a duffle bag flew across the floor. Uncle Fred was home, and he loved her chili. He said he smelled it clear down the block. When Mom was born, Uncle Fred was three years old, and he told them she was his. He had always looked out for her.

When my grandfather was young, he had some money. He bought a lot of lumber, put it on a train, and moved from Baltimore to Tribune, Kansas, to start a lumberyard. He had heard there were no trees in Kansas. Him and five of his six sons were cabinetmakers. When the Dust Bowl came, they came to Partridge, Kansas and then to Hutchinson. He met my grandmother in Tribune.

My grandmother thought that castor oil would cure any stomachache. We learned never to let her know if we had a problem. My knees were always a mess from skating on concrete. They poured peroxide, they said, on my knees. I think it was Clorox. It hurt so bad. When I got sties in my eyes, everyone would grab me and hold me down so they could put Argerol drops in my eyes. I hated that.

One day I decided to help my aunt wring out the wash. I ran my right arm through the wringer right up to my armpit. They put the arm in a sling, and I learned to use my left arm. It still comes in handy sometimes.

Elvis, I loved him then and love him still. I will never forget that first *Ed Sullivan Show*. That's okay, my husband loved Doris Day.

My mother had a Model T Ford. She was tiny and had a hard time cranking it. She sold it and got a little coupe with a rumble seat. My brother, four years older, and I usually sat there. She claimed we bickered or giggled too much. We were distracting her from her driving. She hated to drive.

I am terrified of snakes. When I was about nine, a group of neighborhood kids were fishing off the railroad trestle by the salt mine. I don't remember what I did to the next-door neighbor boy, but he chased me all the way home, hitting me with a snake. For years, I ran in my sleep and kicked whoever I was in bed with.

When I was 12, I went to Attica, Kansas with my new sister-in-law. Her little sister and I were about the same age. Her dad was the janitor at the school. He had arranged for Nan and I, with three other girls, to help farm wives during harvest. We all rode a huge draft horse from farm to farm, following the harvesters. We did dishes, peeled potatoes, babysat, cleaned house, took food and drinks to the field, etc. To get on and off the horse we stood on porch rails. It was really exciting to me, and I made a lot of money.

When I was nine, we moved from Grandpa's house. We lived many places in town. I think my mom missed the moving she did with Dad. When I got married we bought a house, and I have parked here for 58 years.

My husband looked so much like our milkman it was weird. He had never met him. One evening we were out with friends. Someone mentioned our children looked a lot like the milkman. Everyone was laughing. He didn't know what was going on until we told him he looked like the milkman.

Thanks for the memory trip.

A Trip with My Grandmother
By Mora L. Weber of Hutchinson, Kansas
Born 1933

I was born in 1933 in Hutchinson, Kansas, population about 35,000, and I am now 80. I do remember a lot when I was five and a little bit at age four. My family of four was very quiet, so I learned early on to entertain myself with paper dolls, real dolls, and later, movie magazines. When I was about eight or nine, I listened faithfully to the half-hour radio shows *One Man's Family*, *Fibber McGee and Molly*, *The Shadow*, and some others I don't

Mona Lee Weber at age 2

remember.

One day when I was five, I played with a little girl from across the street who was all broken out with chicken pox. She asked me if I had had the chicken pox, and not knowing what it was, I said yes. Mother found out and waited for me to break out, but I never did. Our doctor told her I must have a natural immunity.

My brother, who was six and a half years older, had his bedroom in the basement. I wasn't supposed to go down there, but I did. I discovered he had lead soldiers that he would melt and make more lead soldiers. I got in trouble over that.

I remember at age five standing on a chair on Sunday mornings to have my straight hair curled. She would put the curling iron in the flame on the stove; I hated that curling iron, but for a few hours, I had curls like Shirley Temple. I still hate curling irons.

Riding in our car once in a while on a Sunday was a big treat. It had a running board. We went to Carey Park. The entrance had a fountain that shot up colored lights. Sometimes we would stop at the RB for root beer. Little mugs for children were free. I think that was when I was four. I told my mother, "When I be five, I will be a big lady." Entertainment at that time was simple.

My brother, Stamey, was talked into taking me to a movie. We saw "Dr. Cyclops," a horror movie, and I spent most of the movie under my seat. I had nightmares after that, and he never again took me to a movie.

I remember the boy I played with, Dee Dee, when he put our cat in the clothes chute on the second floor to the basement. Mother and I were using the washing machine. It was a wringer type and we had no drier. The cat came down, scratching and howling all the way to the basement. The cat wasn't injured, but I sure laid into Dee Dee.

Sunday dinner was always at my grandparents' house in Hutchinson. I played with cousins. Everyone smoked then except my grandmother, Mammy. I think this is why I never became a smoker. My grandfather, Pa, came up behind me on the stairs and said, "Boo, I'm a big, black bear." I said, "Pooey, I'm a hop toad." He was a lot of fun and died much too young.

Grandmother Mammy

A big flood came here in 1939 and Mother came, picked me up at school, and told me to take my shoes and socks off. Home was just a few blocks away. It was a big adventure. At home when I saw canoes go by, I said I wanted to go out and play. It was Cow Creek and the Arkansas River water, but my brother said there would be snakes in the water. I didn't go out.

While in grade school we all played hopscotch, hide and seek, and jacks, and we rode our bikes and roller-skated. There were no fast food places, so I had bread and butter, maybe sugar, and an apple. There was no television, of course, so only one girl was on the heavy side.

My grandmother, Mammy (Lois Stamey), took me on a train ride to Colorado. She made sure each of her granddaughters had a one on one trip with her. I was about 12 and soon was excited about riding a train. The dining car was special; there were waiters in black and a white towel over their arms. After the meal, the waiter brought bowls of water. I picked mine up and started to drink and then Mammy said, "No, these are finger bowls to dip your fingers in to clean up after the meal."

On that trip, we saw ice skaters practice at the ice rink at the Broadmore Hotel in Colorado Springs. We spent the night at the only lodge in Green Mountain Falls, west of Colorado Springs and didn't have bathrooms, just a chamber pot under the bed. Mammy called the slop pots. I woke up to see her sitting on the sink, using it as a toilet. I asked her why she didn't use the slop pot, and she said she had to go so little and didn't want to use it.

I don't remember saying this, but my mother said I said it at the age of 15 or 16. I said I was going to the University of Michigan and Ann Arbor to major in music (piano), get married and have four kids, and then teach piano. That is just what I did.

Butchering Hogs
By Mark McIver of Santana, Kansas
Born Unknown

As I remember my life growing up in Satanta, Kansas. I was born in Satanta in a one-room house. My older sister and an older brother, we moved north of town in 1934 and lived there for nine years. We went to my grandpa's southwest of Satanta as much as possible on Sundays.

We grew up learning to milk cows and other chores. One of the highlights was butchering hogs. They butchered one for the family and two for market. They made lye soap and stuffed sausage and smoked ham and bacon.

Mr. Hoon ran the pool hall in Satanta and I worked for him setting pins, as he put in two bowling alleys, just about this time World War stated called duckpins and small balls. We walk to school and home each day.

When Working Was a Privilege
By Virginia C. Winter of Conway Springs, Kansas
Born 1923

I am one of thirteen children born on a farm seven miles south of Haven, Kansas, to John and Elizabeth Ast on March 6, 1923. We lived in a five-room house with three bedrooms. One of the bedrooms had three beds, and we slept three in each bed. Of course, we had no running water. I remember the excitement when we got a real bathtub! Before that, we used a square, tin tub, where three kids took their baths before the water was changed.
And, yes, I remember outhouses. We had a two-seater with two levels and a half-moon carved on one wall for ventilation. We had a wood-burning stove (coal was too expensive) and had to gather kindling wood the night before to start the fire in the morning.
We raised all our food, including a large plot of potatoes, which we dug up in the fall and stored through the winter in our cave, together with canned fruits and vegetables, and eggs, which Mother would gather in her apron. My dad culled chickens to make extra income. We bought flour in 100-pound calico sacks with patterns on them. My sisters and I would each claim the patterns that we liked best, and Mother would make our dresses from that material.
On cold nights, we would warm bricks in the stove and put them in our beds to keep our feet warm. Warmed bricks would also go in the buggy we would take to school in

Ost, Kansas. The school-aged children would pile into the buggy, and, with my brother Vic taking the reins, our horse Topsy would pull us the seven miles to school, where we would shelter him in a shed and feed him at recess. We were from the W.P.A. age, and Dad always said working was a privilege. That's what we did from sunup to sundown just to keep food on the table and clothes on our backs.

Halloween Stranger
By Arlys Kraus of Pheonix, Arizona
Born 1941

I grew up in a very small farming community called Protection, Kansas. One of four siblings; I had a twin brother, Arlyn; a younger brother, Jerry, and an older sister, Donna.

My dear dad worked for the State of Kansas Grain Inspection Department. Therefore, he traveled from early Monday morning to sometimes very late Friday afternoon. My precious mother was, for the most part, a stay at home mom, who always had fresh baked cookies or some kind of treat waiting when we got home from school.

Those were the days when you could go to bed without locking your doors. Crime was unheard of then.

However, one Halloween we were passing out treats and this big figure, dressed for Halloween came walking in with some kids. He sat down on our sofa. The kids all left, but there he sat, and sat, and sat. Mom kept asking who it was, but got no reply.

I stayed at night with an elderly lady who was uncomfortable to stay by herself.

The mystery guest at our house that Halloween turned out to be one of her sons, Ralph Moore.

Circle Skirt Mishap
By Shirlee Hoopes of Anthony, Kansas
Born 1932

When I was in high school in 1948 and "circle" skirts (It was a full circle at the bottom,) were in style, some friends and I went in the "fun" house at the summer carnival that came to town. As you came out a big puff of air would blow up. A friend went out first and it blew her straight skirt and her hair up. I decided she stepped on a button on the floor-so I made a run for the opening and jumped over. Well, my skirt went up over my head and when it came down the ticket seller was laughing his head off-and so was everyone-but me. Funny now, but not when I was sixteen. The ticket guy was the air button-dumb me.

My husband is eighty-four years old now but when he was in the sixth grade in the country school, his lady teacher asked him to drive her car to get her paycheck from the school board member that lived about three miles from the school. Being a farm kid, he knew how to drive-but to take her car and go alone! She trusted him, and he could do the task. Wouldn't happen today-even in the country.

Pet Skunk
By Gail Schroeder of Sedgwick, Kansas
Born 1941

This is a true story form Sedgwick, Kansas about a happening concerning the Schroeder boys, Gail and Earl.

It was the early 1950s and my Brother, Earl and I had a pet skunk (deodorized.) One night he got out and got himself shot and killed. The shooter thought him wild and therefore stinky. His death caused us much grief, because he was a good pet.

Anyway, a couple of years later, while sitting on the front porch across the street from Pollard's Horse Barn, we saw a mother skunk and four youngsters come out of the barn and go into a driveway culvert. We watched this happening regularly. HA HA! Here is our skunk replacement. All we have to do is catch and deodorize. Instant pet, and a couple leftover to sell and pay for the vet to de-pew them.

The plan: Get the lawnmower out; add oil to the gasoline so it smokes badly. Take mom's vacuum cleaner and remove the flexible hose from it to attach to the exhaust on the mower and blow smoke into the culvert, and then catch skunks as they come out the other end.

SIMPLE HUH!

After much arguing, Earl manned the smoke hose and I had to catch the skunks as they came out and get them into a gunnysack, held by Earl.

The first one out I caught by the tail and into the bag, success, a piece of cake! Two more catches, all right we had three in the bag, very next out, was mother skunk and I had to catch her quickly before she could spray us. Grabbing her by the tail, I threw her into the air, yelled "Run" and we did. She came down running also, luckily in the opposite direction.

Well, we had three baby skunks young enough they couldn't spray yet. We already had the old rabbit hutch converted to a skunk house. They were eating good and growing fast.

One morning, dad stopped by the cage to check on them and got sprayed. He wasn't very happy and opened the door and let them go.

This wasn't much of a financial success and we still didn't get a new pet skunk.

The Wooden Ice Chest
By Anna Jane Goetz of Kingman, Kansas
Born 1926

Lois, my daughter wanted me to tell about my memories of my childhood. There was quite a few but at this time; I remember raising the lid to the wooden ice chest. I was warned about not doing it but somehow I would open it and it would fall on my fingers. I didn't obey very well and my fingernails were black and blue. I don't remember mom getting mad or spanking me but I should have been.

I can remember the man bringing ice to put in it and how I liked to pat it! The container for the ice was a wooden chest and was too heavy for me to raise it and get to the ice. I was about four or five years old at this time.

When I was about six years old, Grandma had creeping paralysis. I loved to push her in the chair to see the rabbits in the pen. The chair got too close to the little hill and she tumbled out. I can still see her in my mind, how helpless she was as it was too much for me to handle and she fell out of her wheelchair. My mom and someone else came to the rescue.

Hokey Pokey at the Windmill
By Anna Mae Pracht of Goddard, Kansas
Born 1937

Born to Art and Mary Becker, I am a sibling of eleven children. My sister, Mary Katherine (Becker) Cruz wrote a story about our family to you about the early days of our family.

I just remember everyone had to pitch in and help with all the work. I remember how all the neighbors were there in good times or bad. When anyone had extra work like harvest, filling silo, mowing, and baling hay or cutting wheat or whatever needed to be done. We had a very caring and loving neighborhood. One neighbor, Gayle Gregory would come over just to throw us kid in the horse tank.

We went to Saint John's Catholic School at Clonmel Kansas about five miles south of us. We went there all through grade school. It had only two rooms; first through fourth in one room and fifth through eighth in the other room. About three families would carpool. Each family would take a turn taking us to school.

We went to the grocery store in Goddard. It was owned by the Hubbard family. They would let my dad charge groceries. After harvest, he would go in and pay the bill. Many times Grandma Hubbard wouldn't be able to

A stormy evening in Kansas

find the bill.

There was a windmill and a horse tank on the main intersection of town.

When I was in high school at Goddard, we would go downtown and hang out. Joe and Grace Doss had a restaurant where you could get pop and sandwiches or snacks. We would go to the windmill and do the hokey pokey around it. Lots of fun. I wish they would have never taken it down. That would have been a great historical mark of Goddard, Kansas

Band played on. Even now when I see the bell ringers at stores around town, it brings memories of those sights and sounds when I was a kid.

Now that the mass merchandisers have lured shoppers away from downtown shopping, it is sad that this and future generations won't get to experience the beauty and excitement of that era. In my opinion, those '40s and '50s were the nicest times to be in our hometown.

Our Hometown
By Tom Walters of Lakin, Kansas
Born 1942

My hometown of Hutchinson, Kansas was a city with a great shopping district. It was large enough to have dime stores such as Kressses and Woolworths along with Sears, Wards, Penney's, and Anthonys. These stores, along with local clothing, hardware, and other specialty stores, made for a sizeable downtown area. The town had three indoor theaters and three drive-ins. In the 1940s and through the 1950s, the Hutchinson Naval Air Station helped swell the population. It might have seemed strange to see sailors strolling along the streets so far from the ocean, but it seemed normal to us.

My parents' faith was one that did not celebrate holidays as other religions did. So there would have been no reason for me to have been downtown during the evening shopping hours except for an activity that my parents participated in. During that time when so many people were downtown, they stood on street corners with their religious publications. I would be sent up and down the street, handing out tracts to passersby. That allowed me to see all the fantastic sights I otherwise would not have seen. I have to admit that I spent more time looking and enjoying than I did handing out literature. Sometimes when I would see that I was far enough away that my parents wouldn't notice I would step in one of the stores to catch the sights and smells there.

My parents always chose to stand at the corner that was directly across the street south of the corner that the Salvation Army

Good Times and Sad Times
By Flora Erickson of Chanuk, Kansas
Born 1926

When I was six years old, I was the only one in the first grade in a one-room school. My teacher had long red hair, and she let me brush and comb it at recess and lunch hour. I felt like I was privileged.

We lived one mile from town and always walked to school and church. My Grandmother Edmondson lived in town, so I stayed with her a lot. One cold winter day, I was the only one out of five children who wanted to go to school. I walked that mile in thirty below zero weather. I am sure my parents did not know it was that cold. Instead of going to school, I went to my grandmother's house, and she soaked my feet and hands in cold water. That is the remedy for frozen feet and hands.

When I stayed with my grandmother, she let me drink coffee if I didn't put anything in it. Needless to say, I didn't get to drink it at home.

My mom and I were the only ones in the family who went to church. Usually it was just me; as she was so busy taking care of a big family. I was baptized in that church, but it has since burned down.

We lived in Iowa, and when it snowed, we made igloos to play in. It was so cold the igloos didn't melt for a long time.

One morning when I was eight, I was walking home after staying the night with my grandmother. One of the neighbors called out to me that I had a little sister at home. I didn't know what she was talking about, as back then we didn't talk about anything like that. I was pleasantly surprised when I got home, and there was this cute little baby, my little sister.

One time my brothers and I tried smoking corn silks under a culvert. It didn't work very well and made us sick.

Back then, we had to wear long underwear to keep us warm. Sometimes when it warmed up, I would take mine off before I got home, and I would get scolded for this.

My brother, Jobe, and I were both sick with what my mother thought was the flu. He got deathly ill, so they took him to the hospital. He had acute appendicitis and died within a few days. I will never forget this, as it was so sad.

Skunkus was His Name
By Linda Walters of Lakin, Kansas
Born 1945

I was raised in Hutchinson, Kansas in what I refer to as the good ol days. It was a time when we shared family time; you know meals together, watching television as it became a household item, and funny stories my very "unique" daddy told me. One I remember vividly was about Skunkus.

Daddy was born in Oklahoma in 1907. Times were hard, and there was no extra money. So if the kids wanted some candy or to be able to go to a movie, they had to earn the money themselves. My dad pictured himself a line trapper. He would set traps, hoping to snare small animal, such as rabbits, beavers, squirrels, and even skunks. Since this job was very important to him, he didn't mind being a bit late to school in the event that he had been lucky enough to have a full trap. If so, he would remove the victim, swiftly remove the pelt, and reset the trap. As a result, more than once he was tardy to school. This was not particularly worrying to him, as being a scholar was not his dream. After all, he did have his own business.

As he grew to adulthood, he carried on that work ethic and ran his own successful business. Oh, I forgot to mention, if his prize turned out to be a skunk, he would carry that fragrance on his clothes to school. On more than one occasion, he was sent back home to bathe and change clothes. Well, that made for a rather short day at school, and it caused his classmates to give him a new name, "Skunkus." I asked him if it bothered him, and he said, "Not one little bit. I don't know why they did that though, because I don't think it was a bad smell." In fact, he said, "You know, to this day I'd rather smell a skunk than the best bottle of perfume money can buy."

I'm not sure if I feel the same way, but I will say that when traveling down a road and encountering that familiar aroma, someone will speak out and say, "You know, sister, I'd rather smell a skunk than the best bottle of perfume money can buy!" It always brings a smile to my face and a warm, fuzzy feeling to my heart.

Thanks for who you were in my life, Skunks, and thanks for the extraordinary stories you brought to life as I was growing up. I love you and I miss you!

The Sunset
By Alfred Rohr of Derby, Kansas
Born 1930

I grew up in a small town in mid-west Kansas, population approximately 1,000 people. There was no major entertainment for the young people when I was growing up.

During my school years, I and four or five of my close friends started exploring for things to do. We found a small swimming hole on the far west end of town. The location of the swimming hole as the sunset in the west made it look like it set in the water. So the swimming hole was called Sunset. It became our weekend meeting place with all the things we needed. We made sandwiches at our homes, and then filled bottles with water for our lunches there. A small stream running over rocks not far from the swimming hole kept our water cold.

A tree with a limb hanging over the water was ideal to attach a rope to for swinging out over the water and dropping in. We would swim for a while, and then we would lay on the bank, talking and making plans for our futures. Then we would go back in the water.

There was a cave on the east side of a hill. It had three rooms, one large room we could stand up in and two smaller rooms big enough only to sit down in. We kept our clothes there until our day was over.

During the winter months, the water on the

swimming hole froze, so it became our hockey rink. We used a tin can for the puck and tree limbs that resembled hockey sticks, resulting in many skinned shins. To warm up after the game, we went into the larger cave and started a fire with broken tree limbs. That turned out to be a mistake, because when we got home, our parents thought we had been smoking grape vines. It took a lot of explaining about why we smelled like smoke.

I and all of my dear friends have grown and are scattered all over or have also faded into their sunsets. Whenever I go back, I go to check out our old swimming hole, The Sunset. It has since dried up, filled with trash and tree limbs, and is no longer a swimming hole. It is gone, but the memories will always remain and our time together will never be forgotten. The town has grown and now has a large swimming pool in the center of town. But the children today will never have the opportunity to have the experiences and enjoyment we had swimming in The Sunset. It is gone but never forgotten.

Kansas: A Great Place to Grow Up
By Connie O'Bleness of Idaho Falls, Idaho
Born 1933

I don't remember having any chamber pots. We had an indoor bath in the house. We also had an outhouse for the men who worked for us.

In our home, we had rules for using the party line phone. If you wanted to make a call, you would pick up the phone to see if someone was on the line. If you heard someone talking, you were to hang up! Not everyone was good about this, and gossip would spread like wild fire. Before World War II, you might hear German being spoken when checking to see if anyone was on the line, but when the war started there was no more German spoken.

Washday was a very long day. We had a washhouse with two big, oval tubs. Our water was very hard. Mother had to put lye in the heated water in the first tub, and then move the water to the other tub. Early on, Mother had a washer with a gas motor that Father had to start. Once they arrived, my mother loved detergents that worked in her water. Later, she had an electric washer and dryer. Life was good!

We had homemade clothes, sometimes even made out of feed sacks. The women picked out the prints they wanted. After the feed sack was empty, the cloth bag was made into a dress or shirt. Mother made cloth rag doll for me.

We had two schools, a smaller one-room building, and a slightly larger five-room building. Our one room school was for first and second grades. The larger schoolhouse had third through fifth grades in one room, and then sixth through eighth grades in another big room that was also for storage. The larger building also had a small library and a coat closet. The room you came in to had a stove to provide heat. Outside there were two outhouses and a coalhouse. It was all pretty small.

My father brought home a prairie dog as a pet for us. He had one when he was a kid. It was fun to watch it eat a marshmallow! Unfortunately, it didn't last too long. It started to make a nest in one of our chairs. I remember pouring water down holes to flood out tarantulas. When the spider would appear, we would run away screaming!

There were plenty of farm chores. I remember the hens would peck at my hands when I would try to gather eggs. I got even with them by enjoying stewed chicken for supper. Since I was the only girl in the family, I got to work with my mother in the kitchen while my brothers were out working the ranch. Mother and I had a wonderful time. We cooked for the extra men at wheat harvest time. One year, due to my grandmother's health, I cooked for the harvesters all by myself; not bad for an eighth grader.

When I was young, we had an icebox on the back porch. I remember going to town for the ice blocks. They would slide along a chute and were then picked up with large ice tongs. We didn't have a milkman. Well, rather we did; it was my father, a bucket, and a cow!

In the small town of Sitka, Kansas, they had a gas station. The pump was different than they are today. First, you had to pump the gas up into a glass tank to measure it, and then the gas could flow from the tank to fill the car. Behind the gas station was the blacksmith's welding shop.

It was important to my family to keep up-to-date with the world. We took two different papers every day. The local State College Extension Service also kept the farm families up on the newest products and techniques for raising crops and cattle. A lot of new products were tested there. The 4-H program kept the children up-to-date as well. Kansas was a great place to grow up.

In the early 1900s, once a year the small towns would go to the other towns with their bands to advertise their town.

Chautauqua was also a big event in the small towns. It showed off local talent. The main speaker was a national person, and then others would perform. My grandmother gave readings. For many years, my aunt traveled with Chautauqua all over the United States playing the piano.

Other families chose western music, but in our home, the music was always classical. That was our family's favorite. We had a wind up record player. My favorite record was "Blue Moon" by Vaughn Monroe. We would listen to the radio. I remember *The Jack Benny Show*.

Saturday was a day when people came to town to shop. We would visit people in their cars that were parked in town. Saturday was also a day for movies. There were six churches in town. Everyone had to go to church to keep them all going!

A farm house with a country kitchen and outhouse

The Kansas Schoolhouse, Good Old Days
By Lorene P. Gnaedinger of Lady Lake, Florida
Born 1932

It was called the Dust Bowl in 1930. The farmers in Kansas lost the topsoil from their fields. Rain was needed to soak the ground to prevent the wind from blowing the black soil away and into the farmers' homes and other buildings. Even wet sheets and towels by doors and windows couldn't keep out the dust. Baby beds were covered with wet dishtowels to help the children breathe safely.

President Franklin D. Roosevelt, FDR, began the Great Plains Shelterbelt Program in 1934 to help the farmers. Trees like cedar, olive, evergreen, and Chinese elm were planted in rows ten feet wide and half a mile long. These trees served to slow down the strong winds that dried out the soil and even blew it away. The shelterbelts were constructed during the Depression days of the Nineteen Thirties by the WPA, Works Project Administration.

One-room schoolhouses were still common in Kansas in the Nineteen Thirties. District 13 School was located between the small towns of Claflin and Ellinwood in Barton County. The teacher in District 13 educated the children from eight families.

The simple wood frame school building was rectangular shaped with a slanted roof and chimney. In the back of the room were long nails on a board for hanging caps and coats. Above the board was a shelf for lunch pails, and nearby was a long table for school projects. Near the main door was a stand for the water pail with a dipper. The students' personal water cups were lined up next to the water pail.

Outside the school was a drinking water well with a pump. Farther away from the school were outhouses, one for the girls and another for the boys. Each had one hole with a wooden cover. Near the hole was an old mail order catalog that was used for toilet paper.

Andy, Andy, over! Let the ball come over was a favorite recess game. After picking teams, one group went to the east side of the school and the rest to the other side. The west side team then chanted, "Andy, Andy over, let the ball come over." The east side team then threw the ten-inch softball over the slanted roof. If the west team caught the ball, they would run around to the other side and tag a person with the ball. If successful, the west team gained another player and returned to their side with the ball. Then the east team chanted, "Andy, Andy over, let the ball come over," while watching the roof for the ball to come over. At the end of recess, the teacher would ring the brass hand bell and the children would return to their studies.

Softball was another favorite recess activity. The ball field had many gopher holes in the ground. When the gophers were active, some of the older boys carried buckets of water to drown the gophers out of their holes.

The teacher's wooden desk was in front of the room facing the students. In the back corner of the school was a large black stove, which burned coal for heating. On very cold days, a mother would sometime make a pot of soup. The pot sat on the stove and heated during the morning. The teacher and the students then enjoyed eating the hot soup for lunch and dinner.

Lunch pails usually contained homemade cookies and homemade bread with butter, jelly, eggs, or sausage. The families did not have the money to buy fresh fruit.

Most of the school year, the children walked to school with their siblings and neighbors. The farms were all within a two-mile radius so it was an easy walk for the children. Actually, the children had to walk at times when the dirt roads were bad. Cars could not travel the roads when the ruts were too deep and wet from rainy weather. Deep snow also hindered car travel.

Both boys and girls wore hand-me-down coats, hats, and gloves. The boys wore hand-me-down bib overalls with shirts made by their mothers from flour bag fabric. The girls wore hand-me-down dresses and those made by their mothers. Much of the fabric came from beautifully designed flour sacks. In the store in Claflin, the clerk took the list from the shopper and brought the items to the counter. The women could then select the flour bag design they wanted.

The teacher taught reading, arithmetic, geography, spelling, and penmanship. Some years all eight grades were not represented. Sometimes older students listened to younger students read. Students who completed their homework were rewarded by being permitted to do a project at their desk or at the project table in the back of the school. Paper Mache maps, clay relief pictures made with scraps of wood, fancy pillow covers stitched with yarn, and pig shaped breadboards were some of the favorite school projects.

District 13 students received a sound educational foundation. Fifteen of the seventeen students who attended District 13 graduated from college.

The Thirties were hard and challenging times for the rural families in Kansas. The children learned how to work and be responsible. Looking back, they were the "good old days."

Adventures were Plentiful
By Lester Seuser of Timken, Kansas
Born 1930

I was born in 1930 on a western Kansas farm at the start of the Great Depression. As time passed, I became aware of the economic difficulties. We always had plenty to eat. We had chickens, eggs, milk, cream, butter, hogs, and sheep, and Mother grew a big garden. She canned with a pressure cooker to preserve food. With time, we had a butane refrigerator and butane lights. Then with more time, we had 32-volt lights and an electric motor to run the washing machine.

We always had chores to do. My brother, Jim, and I pitched the upright silo empty in the winter. A few times, we threw out too much silage, and it plugged the chute at the bottom. I had to climb over the top of the chute and down the outside to empty the chute from the bottom. The silo was built so that it could be climbed anywhere on the outside. I climbed all over it just for fun. I was instructed to be careful and I was. That was the safety lesson.

Anything that was purchased was carefully scrutinized. Flour was bought in 50-pound bags. The bags had different prints on them. A desirable print was chosen. It would be made into a tea towel or some piece of clothing. My brother and I decided we could contribute to the clothing efforts by making our own garments. We had gunnysacks in the barn. They had held cattle feed and were just lying around. We turned them open end down and cut the corner off for armholes and an opening in the middle for our head to go through. Then a safety pin at the crotch completed the design. Then we put them on. Our creation was a terrible failure. I have never worn anything so itchy.

Jim and I had a cousin, Gordon. He

expanded my horizons. Gordon was three years older than I, and Jim was two years older than I. Gordon was there on visits, and we had many adventures. One Sunday afternoon while he and his family were visiting, he asked my dad if we could drive the Ford Model A coupe, and dad said no. Well, we got in it. Gordon drove, Jim rode passenger, and I climbed behind the seat. I didn't have much room, but I was only six or seven years old and fit behind the front passengers. We headed up the drive toward the railroad tracks with both sets of parents in hot pursuit. Gordon drove into the edge of the field, and we piled out. Well, we got a licken' and I didn't think I deserved it since I was only an accessory to the crime and so young and innocent.

In another of our adventures, we played with matches and set dry patches of grass on fire north of the house. We put the fire out by taking off our pants and beating the fire out with our pant legs. Mother complained about our sooty pants legs. So we turned our pants inside out and beat the fire out with the insides. We had black legs, but our pants looked clean. Problem solved.

On one of our grass burning episodes, we set grass on fire, and it was more than the three of us could handle. We had to call for help from our folks and our girl cousin. Eight of us fought vigorously to extinguish that fire. We almost had it out, and Gordon set another fire. It was worse than the one just concluded. I don't think we got a lickin' for that. Everyone was too tired.

We had plenty to do with chores, school, 4-H, and church, but we managed to find time for extra-curricular activities. One of these was to make homemade black powder. The ingredients were readily available at the pharmacy. We spent the powder in homemade pipe cannons. The construction was simple: we found a piece of ¾ or ½-inch steel pipe and closed one end with a cap or welded it shut. After that, we tamped a bunch of black powder in through the open end and tamped wadded newspaper on top. We found a rock about the height of the blowtorch and placed the back of the cannon up against a tree so that the tree absorbed the recoil. Then we aimed the blowtorch against the powder-filed part of the pipe cannon and ran behind a building. We had no fuse or touch hole to ignite it, and it took two or three minutes for the powder to ignite. Generally, we used no projectile. There was one memorable exception. We found a half-inch iron rod about four inches long. We thought it would be a worthy projectile. We loaded the cannon with an extra-heavy charge of powder, tamped in the newspaper, and pushed the rod in the end. We aimed the cannon at the door of an old icehouse, a relic of camp meeting times. The door was wood and thick. We figured that would stop our shot. It didn't. Inside the icehouse were odds and ends. Our projectile cut through a roll of steel wire, a hoe handle, and the metal frame of a hand rake. We never found the rod. We were ecstatic; Dad wasn't. Our cannon blew up, tearing a chunk out of the snout of his blowtorch. I guess he didn't look inside the icehouse. We heard nothing more about it.

I made my last batch of black powder shortly before I went to the Army, and I left a cupful or two in one open can in the shop. I was the welder in the family, but Dad wanted something acetylene welded. So he got a neighbor over to weld. He looked for some welding flux and saw this open can. He heated up his rod and stuck it in the can. He asked me when I came home what I had in that can. He said it shot up to the ceiling, and he fell over backward.

Adventures were plentiful. It was rewarding. Luckily, we had good health and few accidents, for which I am thankful. I gave the blowtorch to a grandson.

The Family Homestead
By Anna Schlereth Looney of Jetmore, Kansas
Born 1947

My name is Anna Schlereth Looney. I live on the Schlereth home place that was homesteaded by my Great Grandfather, Joseph Michael Schlereth in the mid-1880s in Hodgeman County, Kansas. There was a witness that said, "Yes, he knew Mr. Schlereth and yes there was a house on the land with five windows and a door and yes there were other buildings on the land and yes, he knew Mr. Schlereth to be a fine man." Dated 1885 (I do not remember the day or month.)

My Grandfather, John Michael raised

Buildings around the Schlereth homestead

his family in this house also. The Buckner Creek runs through this farm and I remember grandpa charging one dollar a carload for people to fish.

Then at Christmas-grandfather would have us grandchildren all line up and he would give us each a dollar!

None of my grandparents-six children did much fishing-they were too busy working.

My grandparents-John Michael and Anna Schlereth raised six of their own children and several cousins. There were lots of animals on the farm and the grandchildren helped at times.

I remember gathering lots of eggs and putting those eggs in wire-coated baskets and placing the baskets inside a bucket of water. The bucket was then placed on a platform that gently agitated the eggs. After the eggs were cleaned and air-dried. My sister, and I Elaine would put the eggs in thirty dozen cartons. Grandpa would then load those cartons of eggs into his Plymouth, I think it was a 1946 Plymouth, and take those thirty dozen cartons of eggs to the restaurants, and cafes, and grocery stores and sell them for extra money for the farm. I believe Grandpa quit selling eggs to local businesses when grading the eggs became necessary. He felt like investing in the equipment would not be worth it.

At this farm, there were lots of haystacks. We grandchildren would have contests to see who could throw the ball over the haystacks. One of my cousins, Darrel Burkhart dug a hole in the dirt, then put newspaper over it and then sand over the newspaper. Then called his brother, Larry to come. Darrel said he had something he wanted to show Larry. When Larry came running, he fell into the hole!

I remember Grandpa putting a large piece of fat off of a roast beef on a fork and shaking that fat towards me saying, "You need to eat this-it is good for you."

I remember when Melvin Bredfelt, the propane man would deliver propane to the farm. He would give each of the grandchildren a package of Dentyne gum. We were so tickled!

There were a lot of picnics and gatherings on this land, oftentimes the house was cleared out, Grandma would play the piano, and other neighbors would play guitars, violins, sing, and dance.

My father, Raymond George Schlereth, thought we would run out of water. Our family was allowed a bath once a week and we were allowed to wash our hair once every two weeks.

In my younger years, there were no cell phones, no computers, no disposable briefs, or diapers. No dates on food purchased. No curling irons or flat hair irons. Most all clothing was starched and ironed.

Boyhood Serves as a Training Period
By Ken Patterson of Wellington, Kansas
Born 1944

A part of learning that takes place in any environment in any era has to do with the four-step process of going from not knowing what you don't know to knowing what you know. Growing up in a farm south of Anthony in the '40s and '50s was indeed a period of country living that separated town folks from country folks. We had a family of eight growing up in a primitive two and a half-bedroom home with no electricity, no indoor bathroom, no running water, or any kind of gas stove. The good thing about circumstances that seem unbelievable in today's world is that one is forced to find joy and satisfaction in what you do have, not knowing what you don't have.

We always milked, by hand, seven to eight cows every morning and after school, subsequently separating the milk to get cream to market twice a week in town. In addition to milking, we had bucket calves, pigs, goats, chickens, ducks, and horses to assist with the family provisions. We enjoyed homemade ice cream (by utilizing frozen ice on the pond), homemade butter, cottage cheese, and an abundance of fresh meat. What we didn't have early on was refrigeration, due to lack of electricity in our home. We used the traditional icebox together with a storm cellar for maintaining fresh produce.

In the fall of 1950, while pumping water from the cistern, as we didn't have a well, my sister and I noticed smoke coming from the home. This was created by a fire that would necessitate major reconstruction and electricity. Shortly after, I remember especially one of my dad's buying trips to town when he came home with a toaster and radio to go with our new electric lights.

Probably even a greater absence even worse than electricity was the absence of running water in our home. Bathing was a major ordeal, which involved pumping several buckets of soft water from the cistern, heating it on a wood or coal stove, and then using a galvanized oval tub for a series of family baths. You wanted to be one of the first ones; Mom would be the last.

Going to bed early was never a problem due to lack of a television, lights, etc. Waking up, especially in the winter, was challenging, as the bedrooms were unheated. Sometimes the temperature in the rooms could reach less than 20 degrees. The beds were kept warm by heating bricks on a wood burning stove and then wrapping them in paper and a large sock and placing them under the covers to warm a resting place. Normally once the comfort level was reached, we would not move until Mom beckoned us to arise for our chores.

Needless to say, a primitive house led to primitive ways and mice, snakes, flies, and mosquitoes were frequent guest in our home. There was no way to chase them out, so we had to co-exist. We didn't have to like it but we did have to learn to live with it.

One of my visual memories of youth was about 1960 or 1961 when I was in high school. We were covered with a large January snow, as much as 12 to 20 inches with blowing winds. Needless to say, the east to west roads were closed for days with no school and animal care became critical. Our home and barns were separated from a good part of the pasture area of the farm where a large part of our stock cows were kept. In order to provide protein (cubes) and hay for them, cow feed had to be hauled ¼ to ½ of a mile by horseback, as no tractor would start. This took most of the day, and I hardly had time to miss school. I'm not sure the horse understood her importance to the operation, but riding her bareback was a warming experience for me.

As a boy growing up under these conditions, this time served as a training period to man up, but my four sisters and my mom braved the same challenges. I often think about how it may have scarred or haunted their rise to normalcy. Anyway, the truth is it probably made us all better; we just would prefer not to do it again. My mom, at 96 years old, still remembers the good old days fondly, though one might wonder how because her youth in the '20s and '30s, was certainly more trying.

Another interesting chapter in life in the pre-1950 era is the relived stories of summer storms that came in unannounced in the middle of the night. I can never forget being awoken from a deep sleep to take a trip to the cellar, a distance of six to eight feet from the home, to sit out the remainder of the storm and be afraid of the lightning and thunder that would accompany every such trip. Fortunately, we were never in the tornado's path, but as a youngster, we were forced to get acquainted with the dark, musty cellar, lit only by a kerosene lantern, packed together while Dad or Mom watched the scary storm clouds out the open door. The comfort of a warm bed to the threatening danger of an eminent storm; this was a journey that symbolized daily life. Circumstances do and will always change. Comfort zones will always be tested, and life on the farm had and will prepare you for the reality of life.

The conditions created by growing up poor on the farm do have lasting effects in later life. Most of us are proud to have lived that life but also profess to always craving to have more and to keep what we accumulate. Perhaps we get this from our parents: save, don't throw anything away, especially food. There are starving people who would love to have what you want to throw away. So we become hoarders, seeking to fill the emptiness we had in our lives early on.

In truth, I did learn early on that there was

more out there than I had experienced and as I have climbed the ladder, I am humbled to have enjoyed the climb. The 21st century necessities, education, and technology but will forever value honesty, humility, integrity, and hard work. The good old days may not have always been good, but certainly, there was a lot of good in them.

Tom's Peanut Candy Bars
By Martha Stroup of Hutchinson, Kansas
Born 1947

Marsha, Nona, and Martha in 1950

I was born in Hutchinson, Kansas in December 1947. I am a twin (girl) and had an older sister and a younger brother.

When I was around eight to ten years old there was an ice cream store across the street (It was called Joy's) from where we lived. When the Tom's peanut man came to stock the ice cream store, my sister and two neighbor girls would talk to him and tell him we all ate Tom's Peanuts so he would give us all peanut bar candy. To this day, I still love those things. We all thought we were the only kids in town that got free candy. We also got ice from the iceman.

All of us girls in the neighborhood would make mud pies and would act like we would bake them in an old icebox in our backyard. One side was our oven and the other side was a refrigerator.

The Kansas State Fair was selling chameleons with a string tied around its body and a safety pin on the other end so you could pen it to your shirt. One year my older sister got one, but she was afraid to touch it. But my dad made a cage for it anyway. One day it got out and none of us girls wanted to catch it, so we had to go down the street and get a neighbor boy to come and put it back in the cage. I think it cost one or two dollars.

In the early 1960s, we got a TV with a remote control. One day, my little brother was playing with his metal cars on the floor in front of the TV and it went off. My mother wasn't sure how to turn it back on, so she called the repairman. When he came out, he said the TV had been turned off by the remote and she didn't think to try using it to turn the TV back on. Come to find out my brothers toy cars hitting together would make the TV turn off from the sound waves.

A lady from our church would keep the city's alligators in the winter. She would let them walk around inside of her house. When us girls were over there she would put them in the bathtub so if we had to "go" we would go together so someone could watch the alligator while the others could go potty. One day she let a salesman in and he would not leave so she excused herself, and went into the bathroom to set the alligators free, then she returned to the front room and in a little bit the alligators came slowly walking out and that man ran for the door as he saw the reptiles.

My Mother and Aunt would go to her house to care for the reptiles when she went out of town, us girls hated that, because sometimes we would have to help feed them. The neighbor would floor one corner of her basement and we would have to stand on the steps and throw the food down to them.

We also had an old car in our backyard and we all would play like we would go on trips all around the country. We would also go to the drive-in movies in it. That old car went a million miles without ever leaving the backyard.

Out There Upon the Farm
By Clayton Sadowski of Newton, Kansas
Born 1928

I sat one day having thought about "Out there upon the farm"
If I wrote a poem about it, it would certainly cause no harm.

Many thoughts went passing by,
As I sat there thinking just how I'd try

The many happy and sorrowful times I remember well,
Though they were many years ago and some are hard to tell

My mind meandered back and forth, thoughts of long ago
Wondering where to begin this story that seems to entrap me so

So please bear with me and the horrible poetry and charm
As we start our long old journey about "out there upon the farm"

Do you remember the oven on the kitchen stove so old
And how it warmed your feet when you came in so cold

Direct to you from Kalamazoo the name I remember well
And all the wood we carried to it was almost too much to tell

The pot-bellied stove in the dining room with ashes on the floor
My how it would crack and pop and sparks fly out the door

The register there above it, which heat went passing through
To warm the old cold bedroom in which it would never do

The big thick feather beds you snuggled in to keep warm
Is one thing I remember most about "Out there upon the farm"

The kerosene lamps with chimneys all smoked and black
Would give off a little light if you were not a sitting too far back

Then came the Coleman lantern that was oh so bright
Providing all the mantles were all working right

The electric lights that finally came were just a sight to see
As we kept flipping switch's knowing it really couldn't be

    Way "Out there upon the farm"

With cows to milk and wood to carry and all the chores to do
You sometimes thought that Mom and Dad were always picking on you

Go get the cows I remember Dad would say
And I knew when I left the barn they would be far away that day

Remember the stools we used when we went to milk the cow
And all the alfalfa we threw down to feed them from the old hay mow

Milking cows was sometimes fun
As we'd squirt the cats and make them run

Putting up hay was quite a day for we'd let the hay door down
I knew every time we did it, it would come crashing to the ground

The slings of hay would come flying in the door
And I knew the guy a tripping it would land up there upon the floor

Harvest time would start in June and a cutting we would go
As we hooked up to the binder and tripped them bundles in a row

Cutting wheat and shocking it I hated with a passion
For I knew that following it, the next thing came a thrashin'

Pitching bundles and scooping oats is what really made you bitch
For when you got through a scooping it boy how you would itch

Fill the jugs and get the burlap wet, so they would all stay cool
Do not play in the new straw pile for if you did you were a fool

    Way "out there upon the farm"

Remember all the weeds and sour docks we

would have to hoe
Then we would go beg and plead with Mom so a fishin' we could go

She'd argue and fight with us but finally she'd give in
But we'd go back to hoeing weeds for we knew it wasn't right for us to win

The old Galloway engine and how with it we'd sometimes play
And if you worked it right it would sometimes start and it would run all day

The peaches we used to pick and then go climb a tree to eat
You'd thought we were a bunch of monkeys with some sort of treat

Remember the new bike we got and riding it was so much fun
And the turns we had to take and you thought that yours would never come

  Way "Out there upon the farm"

Remember the cookies you'd always get for taking Kater's their mail
It was a half a mile down and half mile back but they would never fail

Saturday afternoons when Dad would go to town I remember still
Waiting out there upon the road to see him come over the hill

For in the car was always a sack of candy to divide
It was one for me and one for you and you hoped the divider never lied

Also in the sack was another Saturday treat
A loaf of boughten bread and a bunch of bologna meat

The lunches we used to take to school of lard and homemade bread
Was almost as bad as the mile and a half to school we always had to tread

How many of you remember how Dad and Mom would say
Don't put your tongue on the cold doorknob or that's where it'll freeze and stay

  Way "Out there upon the farm"

How many of you remember Sundays, it was going to church or at least give it a try
And on the way home we'd stop at Charleston's and a block of ice we'd always buy

Put it on the bumper and you thought for sure it would turn to mush
But there was always enough left to put into a gunny sack to crush

Put it in the freezer with a little salt to burn
Then you start to crank on it till it was hard to turn

Then pull out the dasher and eat from it before it all would melt
And you never got your share, at least that's how I always felt

Remember all those wonderful meals we used to have out there
It was sauerkraut with pickled pigs feet and ears and they still had a little hair

Oh yes, there was also milk muose, flincin and cu tuffa calsions
It wasn't that they tasted bad but they gave you the convulsions

Remember shooing all them flies from the kitchen with towels that weren't too clean
And how they'd all get back in through the hole in the window screen

The battery powered radio seemed like we'd never get our fill
It was *Gang Busters*, *The Lone Ranger* and *Lux Family Theater* with Cecile B. DeMille

The old John Deere and cutting wood and how that blade would sing
I sometimes wonder yet today if that's what makes my ears still ring

  Way "Out there upon the farm"

Remember those hot summer days when the sun was bearing down
And how that powdered dirt would burn your barefoot feet and make you hop around

And when you came in from plowing all day and you were hotter than sin
You'd hop into the Model A and go to the pond to take a swim

Then after you had cooled off and night was setting in
You'd go upstairs to go to bed so you could start sweating again

Then winter would come and with it all that snow
Remember all the paths we'd scoop so to the barn we could go

The drifts were deep and roads were blocked and cars sometimes got stuck
And Dad would take his team and pull them out and sometimes make a buck

The rabbits we used to catch when the ditches were filled with snow so deep
We'd poke into the holes they made and soon out one of them would leap

When it got so cold at night that Dad would drain the Model A
The hot water and blankets he'd have to use to make it run again the next day

   Way "Out there upon the farm"

Do you remember them darned old clucking hens and how they'd always peck
It would hurt so bad you'd want to wring their dirty pecking neck

I bet there aren't too many of you that really can recall
Of herding chickens into the chicken house when it turned cold in fall

Why do that I'm sure some of you might say
Because if their combs would freeze the hens wouldn't lay

Remember when we kids were ornery and the rules were sometimes bent
Mom would get mad at us and say, "Vat gbish due matter mitder kleenakint"

Remember how Mom could make a meal with nothing in the house to fix
But she could do it every time cause that was one of her many tricks

When things were going bad and you thought that you were losing
How the troubles went away when she pulled you to her bosom

I remember when we got older and we'd tease and put our arm around her
How I now look back and wished I'd hugged her a little longer

And all the work she had to do with never a complaint
Well, that is why within my heart I know she is a saint

   Way "Out there upon the farm"

And all the noise and fighting that went on inside that big old house
All Dad would have to do is holler "Boys" and it became quiet as a mouse

His big old brawny hands seemed like they always had a sore
From wrenches slipping or banging on a door

How he could work that razor on a piece of leather strap
I remember watching many times, wondering how he did all that

How he could roll a cigarette when it was rough as it could be
Though the Velvet can was jumping all around was just a sight to see

A quiet gentle man with never much to say
But if you searched for him in Heaven, you'd find him there today

I will always remember how poor we were and how hard it was to make ends meet
We never had many fancy clothes to wear but we always had something to eat

It seemed the only dresses Mom ever had is the ones she had to make
From the print material from chicken feed sacks, now that's poor, for goodness sake!

All the dirty clothes Mom had to wash with that lousy homemade soap

And doing it all in that old Maytag washer that went popity, popity pope

The eggs and cream we took to town on Saturday afternoon or night
Was all the money we had a come'n in to help us in our plight

But through it all I can't recall of really suffering and doing without
Except all the things that money could buy and those were the things we didn't know about

I think of us all as we sit here today, wondering just what might be changed
To live it all over again, no thanks, even if it could be arranged

But to take just one penny for all that you learned would be wrong
For what would you have if you couldn't think back about the things that helped you along

Just look at us all and what we have done, not one of us has to confess
Of putting a bad mark on that farm, only a mark of success

So when I drive by out there yet today I'm always looking around
To see if I can find the thing that made us all so sound

But in my searching it finally dawned on me and now I'm content and warm
For all that it was, was the life we had out there upon the farm

So I guess the journey's over and we'll all come back somehow
But maybe the thoughts and memories we have are a little more treasured now

There are many more stories and thoughts that each of you could have told
And they would all be different as you let your life unfold

But I do know this and I say it without alarm
That these are my thoughts and memories of

"Out there upon the farm"

Colored Snow
By Calvin L. Barnhart of Pratt, Kansas
Born 1946

I was born in Pratt, Kansas in the year 1946. I grew up on a farm southwest of Pratt. It did not seem like we had much. We did not even have a television. Oh yeah, we had plenty to eat and to wear and all that kind of stuff. Dad was trying to pay for a newly purchased farm.

I did have a bicycle and I really did enjoy it. I rode it a lot. That seemed to be a way of entertaining myself. My bicycle was a used twenty –six inch Schwinn Black Phantom, that dad bought at an auction for ten dollars. I acquired a speedometer for it somewhere along the way. My goal was to see if I could put one hundred miles on it the first week. I attained that goal! That proved to be a lot of riding up and down mostly country gravel roads. I was not allowed to ride on the main highway coming south out of Pratt, which passed us to the east, just one mile away.

At the same time, we had farm neighbors, living one and one half mile west of us, down the same road we were on. They had a son, Van, approximately one year older than myself. We became very good friends while attending the two-room schoolhouse, that was a long side the road between our house and theirs.

These neighbors had a television! My friend's favorite show was "Disneyland,"

Calvin Barnhart on his twenty-six inch Schwinn

which aired once a week. For a period of time, I was often invited to their house to watch that particular show with Van. Whenever I could go, I would. I would ride my bike to their house, in the evening. It did not matter whether it got dark, or not, before coming home, because my bike was equipped with battery-powered lights, front and rear. As a result of all this, television was not a complete stranger to me.

A huge moment came my way one day in 1957, if I recall correctly. Van's grandparents lived some thirty miles west of Pratt in Greensburg, Kansas. His grandpa was also the mayor of Greensburg, at that time. The news came that they had just purchased a new color television. The day the television was to be delivered and set up, Van, along with his family, planned to go out in the evening to watch two shows to be aired in color.

I could hardly believe it, but I got invited to go with them! Oh, was I ever excited! It was not just the television. That, of course, was the biggest attraction, but secondly, the thought of visiting in a mayor's house was nearly as exciting. That seemed about as big to me, then as if I were going to the White House to see President Obama today.

The anticipated time came to go. We got there in plenty of time. We all gathered around the set to view the first show in color. But, they could not get it to come in, in color. They worked and worked with it. They made every kind of adjustment to it they could think of, but all they could get was colored snow! Therefore, we watched both shows in black and white, before returning home. It was truly a big disappointment, but not all was lost!

The house we were in seemed like a mansion to me. It was so big and stately looking. It was definitely different than what I was used to back on our farm. Actually, the house was just a big old square, brick, two-and a half story home, very nicely kept. Unfortunately, it was pretty well destroyed in the Greensburg tornado of May 4, 2007, some fifty years after I was privileged to visit there.

And incidentally, I need to get started restoring that classic old bicycle of mine. You never know when the next colorful episode will come my way, or should I say black and white?

Time Takes All but Memories
By Carol J. Stone of Hutchinson, Kansas
Born 1934

This story was written by my husband, Bob Stone before he passed away July 8, 2012.

I, Robert Lynn Stone, was born on July 3, 1932 at my Grandma Stone's house in Rolla, Kansas to William John and Ethel Fay Stone. I weighed in at ten and one-half pounds and have been rather large ever since. Carol says they probably didn't have scales in those days, and the doctor just lifted me and estimated!

If I could have chosen when I wanted to be born, I couldn't have picked a worse time. Dust storms were ravaging the Midwest, and farmers like my dad were unable to raise crops and had little money. The Great Depression, where people were jobless and had no hope for the future, was also in progress in the United States at this time.

The Dust Bowl encompassed parts of several states, including Kansas. The causes of this sudden disaster were threefold: a shortage of rain, poor land conservation practices followed by farmers, and high winds, which were always prevalent in this area of the United States. It was said that grass in the flint hills area was as green and normal as ever, while in western Kansas there was just total devastation.

Young children were particularly vulnerable to the fine dust that infiltrated the houses. Their lungs were not fully developed, and breathing this dust caused bronchial diseases such as pneumonia and asthma. I was told that when I was young, wet rags were spread over the crib to trap the dust before it was inhaled. According to some sources, 20% of the children living in the Dust Bowl died of lung congestion in the period from 1931 to 1939.

Dad was a school bus driver, and I always begged him to let me ride the route with him. Sometimes he took me, and I would sit on a little jump seat right by the window. I always went to sleep before we got back home.

In 1937, it was still not raining, and the dust was still blowing in Kansas. My folks made the decision to move, because they were afraid I would die of dust pneumonia if we remained here any longer. I remember Dad loading up our most needed household possessions, some farm implements, our tractor, and one cow, and we moved to a 160-acre farm near Ellinwood, Kansas.

I had just turned five years old and was very immature, but Mom decided to send me to school since Jean was an eighth grader and could look after me. What reasoning! In a normal situation, I probably wouldn't have been ready for first grade a year later, let alone going when I was five. I did enjoy school, but I mostly played and never had a great deal of one-on-one time with the teacher. While the teacher was busy with another grade, she would send one of the older students to work with me. I was the only first grader that year, and I remember sitting on the teacher's lap to read. She was always praising me, which I liked and never got much of at home. It seemed to me that there was a better relationship between students and teacher in those days, because there was just one big family atmosphere.

A dust storm in 1934

The country schoolhouse was located about three miles from our farm. I do remember walking home from school on nice days with other kids, but usually we carpooled to and from school.

During the winter months, Dad fed hogs for two farmers in the area and received one dollar a day for his wages. I remember Dad working for another farmer in the area pitching hay. One night he came home and seemed to be in a good mood. He called us all into the kitchen, and under the kerosene lamp showed us a five-dollar bill that he had earned that day. My sister and I had never seen a bill that large before. This amount of money was much more than the going wage, but the farmer told Dad that he was a good worker, and he wanted to reward him.

During wheat harvest, Dad worked for Mr. Miller and in return, Mr. Miller harvested our wheat. Sometimes my mother and Jean and I would go to the Millers' farm, and Mom would help Mrs. Miller (Bertha) prepare lunch for the harvest crew. Counting our family of four, the Miller family of eight, and two or three hired men, it made quite a group for lunch. We all sat around one very large table in the dining room without air conditioning or fans of any kind on very hot days. The menu was always fried chicken, mashed potatoes and gravy, and several vegetables from the garden. There were no napkins on the table; instead one damp washrag, controlled by Bertha, sufficed. When we needed to wipe our hands or face, we raised our hand and Bertha "chucked" it to us. When we were finished, the rag was tossed back to Bertha. The rag was used frequently, and I never saw it washed out during the meal.

Saturday nights were the only time farm families went to town. Everyone looked forward to this night, grownups and children alike. My parents would do their grocery shopping and then sit in their car with friends and watch the people go by. The kids would find their friends and walk up and down the streets. I never had any money to spend, but neither did my friends. Sometimes we would look in the gutters to see if we might find a penny or even a nickel, but it didn't happen often. My Grandma Stone lived in Rolla, and sometimes she would send me a quarter or half-dollar for my birthday. My folks would let me take a nickel or dime of that money to town to spend. The thrill was deciding what to buy.

In the fall of the year, many farmers would get together and cut wood at each farmer's house. This wood supply was to last each family for the winter. Our only source of heat and cooking was from this wood. I remember it being a huge pile, as large as an outbuilding, but maybe it looked larger to a small boy. My job each day after school was to bring to the house three of my little wagon loads of wood. This in reality was probably a thirty-minute job, but between playing with the dog and just messing around, I always took two hours. I would stack the wood too high on my wagon, and it would fall off several times on the way to the house.

Our farm had about a ten-acre area of nothing but live trees, dead trees, and tall weeds. In the summer, when the weeds were tall, Dad had Jean or me drive the old milk cow down to the acreage to graze. There was no fence around the "woods," so we were to crawl up on an old dead tree and keep an eye on the cow. If the cow strayed from the woods, we were to bring her back to the corral, assuming she had enough to eat. Sometimes the cow had other ideas, and I had to get Mom or Dad to help drive her home.

The Worman brothers, Durwin, Richard, and Bennie, lived about a half mile from us at Ellinwood. I always considered them experts at making beanie shooters, or what kids today call slingshots. I would take my beanie shooter and some rocks and go to the woods to shoot at birds. I never remember hitting any, but the Worman boys were good shots. Durwin Worman, the oldest of the brothers, was later killed in World War II.

Dad received word from friends near Rolla that it was raining again in the Dust Bowl area and planned our move back to our farm near Rolla for February or March in 1939. I didn't mind moving back, because I had friends that I still remembered there. I remember nothing about the move except that we had a 1934 Chevrolet car. We had only moved our basic necessities to Ellinwood, so it wasn't a real chore to move back. Jean wanted to complete her freshman year of high school at Ellinwood, so Dad worked out a deal with Dave and Bertha for her to stay with them and their six children until school was out in May.

I still remember the terrible sight of our farmstead when we drove into the yard. Sand dunes were as high as the eaves of the house on the north and west sides. There were no fences around the corral, all being buried by thistles and dirt. Dad backed the truck up to the back door, crawled up in the attic, and started scooping the fine silt from the attic onto the kitchen floor and then into the truck. The entire house had to be scooped and cleaned before we could move in. You really have to have great respect for people who lived in this type of environment or question their sanity. Remember, at this time we still didn't have electricity, butane, running water, or a telephone. The old two-holer was still standing out back. All it needed was a catalog, and it was ready for business.

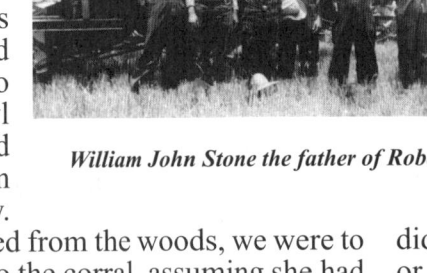
William John Stone the father of Robert Stone is 5th from the left

I started school at Rolla in March, after moving back from Ellinwood, and was one of 15 students in the second grade. It didn't take long for the teacher to find out what I didn't know. I had missed a lot of basics necessary for completing second grade. At the end of the year, the teacher told my parents that, "Bobby doesn't know what it's all about and should repeat second grade." I really didn't mind, because I knew that I wasn't doing well and couldn't do what the other students were doing. Also, all of my friends would be in second grade with me the next year. Remember, I had started a year before they did, and now they would catch up with me.

The Rolla Schools served the children hot lunches at noon. A bowl of bean soup, a piece of cornbread, and a half-pint of milk cost five cents. I am sure we must have had some variety, but this was one meal that I remember. It sure beat the cold sandwich in the country school.

I once saw this inscription on a sundial at a nursing home where my dad spent several months until his death; "Time takes all but memories." How true! It makes me wish I had listened more carefully and asked more questions when my elders told stories of life in earlier times. Reliving my life has brought back memories, some foolish, some serious, some happy, and some sad, but such is life. I smiled a lot and cried a little as I reminisced. It was fun reliving memories through the pen and some in-person contacts.

The Gate of Inspiration
By Galen R. Boehme, Ph.D. of Offerle, Kansas
Born 1944

The Scar of 1957

The scar reminds me of the blizzard of 1957. March 1957 had been a pleasant month for me as a 13-year-old sixth grader and farm child, as the weather had been warm enough for a number of outdoor activities, including the planting of potatoes and other cool weather vegetables.

That month, I had already experienced two or three instances of stomach pain that the doctor thought related to an appendicitis issue. But the doctor said for me to continue my normal activities, as the attacks were short-lived. Consequently, my father and grandmother decided to take a seven-day trip to eastern Kansas. My mother, my two-year-old brother, and I would take care of the feeding of our one hundred head of cattle. A sufficient amount of baled hay and sorghum was in the cattle shed to feed the cattle while Dad would be absent. The trip would allow my grandmother to visit her daughter and family in the Topeka, Kansas area. My father would spend time at the collegiate basketball games in Kansas City, Missouri.

On Sunday night of that last week of March, a blizzard blew in and literally paralyzed the area. Snow piled into drifts at least ten feet high in the corrals. Highway 50-56 that runs in front of our farmhouse became non-travelable, as drifts covered the road. The local newspaper reported that during this time frame, a Greyhound bus with 27 adult passengers and two children became stalled four miles east of our farm. Stranded motorists filled the local motels; farmers became trapped in reaching their cattle. Over 100 telephone lines in the area went down. Power was disrupted because of the fallen lines. On Wednesday of that week, a road department crew spent the entire day in opening the highway from Kinsley to Dodge City, successfully opening the road to only one lane of traffic. (*The Kinsley Mercury*, March 28, 1957, p. 1)

During this storm, I became acutely ill with appendicitis, staying in bed as I suffered severe pain. Mother and my brother fed the cattle, dragging the bales of feed from the cattle shed out into the open area for the cattle to eat.

On the day that the storm broke, Mother walked one-half mile to the Offerle Coop and persuaded two of the employees to use the company's pickup to take me to the Kinsley Hospital for medical care. Only one lane of traffic was open. We noted telephone lines down the entire distance. Our local doctor, Dr. Schnoebelen, met us at the door of the hospital. He knew that the appendix had to be removed, as he sensed that the appendix had broken open, a sign that gangrene could soon set in. The surgery had to be completed even though the hospital was operating on very limited power. The Kinsley power plant was the only source of power for the community, as the electrical line between Kinsley and Hutchinson was down. The next day after the surgery, my father appeared at the hospital room, amazed at what had occurred during his absence. He had taken the first train available from Kansas City to Offerle.

On April 1, Dr. Schnoebelen removed the stitches. He said, "This is not April Fool's joke. Your appendix is gone, and you are on the road to better health. The incision scar will always remind you of the blizzard of 1957."

Dr. Schnoebelen remained our family doctor for at least another 40 years. Every time that he would give me an examination, he would look at the scar and say, "That scar looks like my work. Is that the scar of 1957?"

Opening the Gate

A quality teacher opens gates for the students. Mrs. Hazel Dowd, a "unique" piano teacher serving the Edwards County area for several years, designed her house and her property around an "opening wooden gate" that consisted of three parallel wooden boards and a diagonal 4x6-inch brace.

In 1989, she sent me, her former student, a penciled sketch of her home with the gate in the wooden fence surrounding the house emphasized. "You came through the gate so many times before playing the beautiful 'Lotus Land' at our high school commencement exercise. I thought you would enjoy this picture."

Mrs. Dowd was my third piano teacher in six years, far more exacting in her demands than the other two, but she provided me with the discipline that I needed to develop the piano skills that I have continued to use for the last 55 years to enrich the lives of individuals attending worship services, celebrating special occasions such as graduation, weddings, and funerals, or residing in nursing homes.

My first meeting with Mrs. Dowd was on a warm August day in 1961 when I stepped from my car and searched for a way to enter her house, which was surrounded by a thicket of tall evergreen trees and precisely spaced Ponderosa trees. The only visible entrance to the yard from the east was through a wooden gate. The piercing chords of Rachmaninoff's piano version of "Prelude in C-Sharp Minor" drifted across the air, so I knew that I was in the right place even though I had never physically met this lady before. My mother had previously made the necessary arrangements by telephone.

After entering through the gate, I gently knocked on the front door, a weathered, deep brown stained door containing a glass window the size of a legal-sized envelope. The music stopped and before me soon stood a rather slender, middle-aged woman wearing dark framed glasses. Her reddish-brown hair was in a bun. She spoke ecstatically, welcoming me into her home, gesturing excitedly as if I were a former schoolmate rather than another student.

Mrs. Dowd immediately began explaining the procedure that I must follow for each lesson. First, we must give utmost respect to the piano, hers a light-brown grand piano with ivory-white keys. Her piano carried status, as her piano rested on the only rug found in the house. If I came early for a lesson, I was to enter the house through the back door and sit in the small waiting room to the right of the kitchen. Before my lesson actually began, I was to wash my hands in the sink. "I want to prevent any child from contracting a serious disease from my piano keys," she told me.

Mrs. Dowd then explained the uniqueness of her home. Her father had built the house in 1945; he had chosen the materials wisely, as the government had frozen building materials during the World War II era. Her home had three distinct sections. The front part was constructed from discarded lumber from property nearby. The center section came from an outdated schoolhouse moved into Lewis from approximately ten miles south. The attached garage was fashioned from a horse barn. The limestone for the chimney and the fireplace came from an Episcopal Church no longer open. Inside the house were no curtains or window shades. The woodwork was either painted dark brown or left in a natural, unvarnished condition. The bookcases on both sides of the open fireplace in the piano room were filled with literature considered the classics.

Each Monday evening lesson began with a cheery "Hi, there!" Mrs. Dowd would then record in an orange notebook that I owed her "another buck and a half" for the lesson. She would then discuss some piece of news of interest to her after I said that nothing unusual had occurred at school. One bit dealt with three delinquents loosening the screws on the piano lid last week at the local Christian Church. "Just luckily," Mrs. Dowd concluded, "the pianist discovered the prank when she began to lift the lid before the Sunday services. And do you know what? My 80-year-old dad had to go down to the church and reinsert those screws himself."

My turn to perform came next, playing the assigned scales, as well as reviewing the Beethoven or Bach selections "somewhat mastered." Each week it seemed that she added another penciled comment to the score. "See that FF there? Add some majesty to that part of the selection. Add a ritardando to this section. That is why I have underlined it. Now start memorizing. How do you know when you have apiece memorized? It's when you can play the selection on the kitchen table – without looking at the music. I also want you to work on the timing. That is what a metronome is for. Use it."

I frequently left each session more displeased with myself than when I had arrived. Mrs. Dowd could tell easily when I had not practiced at least one hour a day. But she believed in me. When opportunities came to perform publicly, she made the necessary arrangements for "us" to practice on the performing piano before the actual performance. "Us" is the correct term, as she would be there to critique. "You must know in advance the feel of the piano before you actually perform for an audience," she repeatedly said.

To me as a high school student, Mrs. Dowd was an individual of unbelievable contrasts. One of my lessons was on a sub-zero evening. Instead of finding a warm, comfortable home, I found intense cold throughout her house. Mrs. Dowd explained the reason: the local power company had disconnected the gas meter in order to do repairs. "However," she added, "I could burn wood in the fireplace, but I just can't stand the smell of burning leaves!" While I followed her instructions in removing my winter coat so that I could play the piano more easily and skillfully, she snuggly wrapped about herself a heavy winter coat and sat rather relaxed in a nearby rocking chair.

Mrs. Dowd frequently said that a "good musician never remembers how much one owes for lessons," but she never forgot to give me a statement of her charges for lesson every two months. She considered herself to be a good musician. At times, she appeared more miserly than frugal. For refreshments at one of her student concerts, she gave us nickel candy bars as well as paper cups. "Use the cups to get water from the restrooms," she said. On the other hand, she once opened a secret drawer for me one evening and showed me her newly-purchased pair of gray shoes. "And to think I paid $10.00 for these. They blend well with my Sunday outfit," she admitted.

The gate to musicianship that Mrs. Dowd has opened for her students still remains open even though she passed on in 1997. She unlocked for me a desire to perform with precision, with enthusiasm, and with pride. Perfection comes with discipline, even though other individuals may say the discipline is too demanding. When the skill has been perfected, opportunities will abound for serving. Mrs. Dowd served me. I tried to serve her by being the organist and the pianist for her funeral service. I memorialize her each time that I now perform in public, opening for someone a gate of inspiration and encouragement.

We Are Who We Are
By Mary Ann Buller of Coldwater, Kansas
Born 1942

No Name

Stories usually have another story with them, another story within and quite often, you have to peel several stories away to get to the one you want. Each story has the ability to stand on its own and sometimes they are circular in nature, leading back to the beginning story.

Halstead is a small town located in Harvey County, along the Little Arkansas River in south central Kansas. It was largely founded by conservative Russian Mennonite immigrants who brought over the hard winter Turkey Red wheat, establishing a farming community in 1877. The town was named in honor of Murat Halstead, a respected Civil War correspondent and newspaper editor.

Standing on the east bridge leading out of this picturesque little town looking to the west, a dam close to the bridge provides a waterfall in the river. A measuring board is mounted on a tall pole in the north side of the riverbed, close to the dam. Looking on down the river, you can see a swinging bridge that leads into the park on the north side of the river. This park, covered by a canopy of trees, is used for amusement rides during the annual Old Settlers Picnic. This east bridge leads the traffic north out of Halstead. The locals call it the Hertzler Road on Highway 89. The antiquated square cornered elevator located on the south side of the river close to the bridge has the writing, The Biggest Little City in Kansas. Behind the elevator is the Warkentine House. The Warkintines had an old mill around the Halstead area. Along Main Street, some of the dated brick buildings are mixed in with modern renovations. Other old buildings have been torn down and modern ones built, including the schools. Some of the streets still have brick pavement. Old trees surround the two story houses with wraparound porches in this nice little historical town.

Like most towns, it had to survive when the country was at war, through depressions, recessions, and growing pains. Several manufacturing plants have come and gone. It had its moments of fame with the Hertzler Clinic, Halstead Hospital, and the old-fashioned horse and buggy doctor, Arthur Hertzler, MD. A school for registered nurses was also located there. Some noted people that came from Halstead were Jim Roper, a Nascar driver; and Adolph Rupp, a NCAA basketball coach. The primary location of the movies *Picnic* was filmed back in 1955 and *The Parade* in 1984. Halstead was reputable for its flooding, but none of this is the story, except for the flooding, which leads to it.

On the corner of 801 and North Street where the old water tower used to be, there is a dirt road SW 60th, right before you cross the west bridge heading north. Go one mile west, past the old farmstead of Elmer Unruh, and you will come to a T in the road. Turn right, known as the South Old Settlers Road, and go one mile north; you will come to a dead end when the road turns west. There is no road going east, but if you go east through the field ¼ of a mile, there is a low indention in the ground where the slough originates beside the Little Arkansas River. This slough comes down behind Elmer Unruh's house and meanders south through the next section and crosses the county road, on the road west out of Halstead towards the Grace Mennonite Church. A little east of Popkins Hill it cuts cross Clyde Young's farm to 801 South Halstead Road leading to 96 Highway. It circles behind the high school and the new Halstead addition, continuing to and crossing the 803 road, making its way through the land two miles south and one mile east of Halstead, where the slough dumps into the Arkansas River below the levee. This slough runs when there is a heavy rain or when the Arkansas River is flooding. Otherwise, the slough has minimum water in it with its fragmented stale pools of water, which attracts insects for the frogs who consider this their home. The slough has *no name*. So what is important about this? It involves a devastating flood back in July 1951.

The Little Arkansas River was starting to rise, and the people anxiously scurried out to the east bridge by the measuring board to see how high the river had risen. The dam was under water and the foaming swift current put out a surging roar as the tree branches slid by, slapping against the underside of the bridge. You could see the slow encroachment of the flood. On the north side of the river, the river was flooding the park, houses, and the paved road out to the cemetery, and it was soon closed. It was time to start sandbagging, as the river started to flood over

Uncle Dar C. Buller's home

the railroad and move downtown. Rowboats were eventually going up and down Main Street. All this took its toll on the *no name* slough, and quickly the little bridge without bannisters west of town towards Popkins Hill was under water. *No name* was getting deadly.

A proud grandfather with his fourteen year old and eight year old grandsons was riding horses and came to Popkins Hill where *no name* crossed the road. The eight-year-old boy was riding double with his fourteen-year-old cousin, who was also with them. On sure-footed horses, they started crossing the flooding bridge. The exact details are a little obscured with the passage of time, but it seems like the cousin's mount lost its footing and the eight year old slid off the horse and fell into the water and was swept downstream by the current. The cousin was able to stay on his horse until the horse drowned about a hundred yards downstream. He grabbed some bushes and held on until two local men, who had just arrived on the scene, rescued him. The other fourteen-year-old boy was also rescued by the two local men. Another tidbit lost in time is how the grandfather got across the slough, except we do know that at least one horse, maybe two, survived.

The call went out for help. Telephone operators manually operated the switchboard and sent the message over the party lines. One long ring meant everyone was to answer, and soon the town and country friends and neighbors responded. Several brought boats, nets, etc., knowing it would probably be too late, the search began.

An ultra-conservative Mennonite man with his family stood in the crowd with his balding head and beard. Someone yelled out that they thought they saw the eight year old's head bobbing in the water. This Mennonite man turned to look at the plain dressed woman with a covering on her head. A poignant look was exchanged that spoke volumes. Whether it was the fact that they knew the pain of losing a little child by an accidental death or that, they had a little girl the same age as the little boy in the slough, the man reached into his overalls and handed his billfold to the woman. Surveying the layout of the slough, he walked to the edge of the slough and jumped in to the swift rushing water and started diving down to the bottom, again and again. Another Mennonite man also joined him. Unfortunately, the heroic acts were in vain. The body was found two days later, entangled in some bushes caught in a fence a long way downstream. Who was this *no name* Mennonite?

He was my father, the Mennonite man who had a little girl (me) the same age as the drowned little boy. My father had grown up several miles northwest of Halstead in a now more than century old house along the Little Arkansas River. The river was his playground, and he knew all about swimming in dangerous currents, whirlpools, and where the deep fishing holes were. He knew where he could set his animal traps for food. Later on in his married life, he lived there again for a few years with his wife and children, including me. What was unusual about this? Who his father was.

His father was one of the Russian Mennonite immigrants to help establish the farming community around Halstead in the late 1800s and the early 1900s. His father purchased a homestead where my father grew up with his siblings back in May of 1907 along the river. It had originally been owned by the Santa Fe Railroad. My father is like all of us; we are who we are.

The Ole Red Barn

Driving by an old deserted farm, my eyes automatically gravitated towards the dilapidated old barn. The upper half of the door was missing, and an owl flew out of the opening. Up in the loft, the door was hanging on one hinge and the peeling painted boards showed evidence that it was once red with white trip. Had this barn ever teemed with life like I remembered the ole red barn of my childhood?

You would smell the hay bales when a person stepped into our barn to milk the cows. Feed would be scattered in the trough by the stalls, the cows' heads held in place by the stanchions. As soon as they started to eat, hobbles were placed on their legs to keep them from kicking. Sitting on a three legged stool, someone would start milking them with a gentle squeezing pulling down motion, and release on the swollen teats. Soon the pails of milk would be carried to the milk house. The milk area and where the horses could eat was divided by an aisle. Towards the back of this was a ladder to the hayloft, the playground for the children.

The muffled sound of little kittens meowing let to the discovery of a kitten's nest among the hay bales. The wild barn cats would move the little kittens after we found them. The tamer cats that hung around the house would leave the kittens in the same spot and these little kittens would become tolerant of being dressed with doll clothes.

Bales of hay were stacked on each side of the loft, leaving a path down the middle of the floor. Our imagination could run wild as bandits chased us up and down the hay bales and we escaped by grabbing a rope that had been hung and knotted over a rafter. We would swing to the other side of the loft, landing on some bales. Tunnels were formed by the older children and the game follow the leader was played. The unsuspecting younger children, thrilled to be asked to play with the older children, would crawl as fast as they could after the leader. The barn was filled with screams of terror as the younger children fell off a deliberately made ledge within the tunnel. The rafters rang with laughter as we sheepishly crawled out of the tunnel. Tag was another game, which would end when our older brother got tired of it.

A bale elevator would be backed up to the open loft door. Hay bales would be manually lifted with a bale hook requiring physical expertise and placed on the elevator. Two chains would clank and chug as they moved the bales to the top, where they would drop off in the loft. Someone would have to stack the bales neatly, an art of its own. Fresh hay would permeate the barn again and the play would start all over.

A very special 'thank-you' to my sister Marjorie Schmidt, who helped me with the legwork for putting my story together.

First Time Sewing
By Lois Timmermeyer of Wichita, Kansas
Born 1932

I'm writing this on my eighty-second birthday. My mother would make me feel so good when she would tell me about the day I was born-April 1932. The apple tree outside the bedroom window was full of blooms, and the four hundred baby chicks were outside chirping. The doctor told her he had something new to help ease the pain-Ether. I was the ninth child of fifteen, so I felt very happy she didn't have the pain she had with the first eight.

One year there was only four of us going

Lois Timmermeyer's parents, George and Sophia Leis

Lois and Robert Timmermeyer in 1954

to school a little over ten miles from the farm. My dad bought a Model A Ford with a rumble seat. My older sister was in high school and she didn't want to hold my brother, two years younger than me, cause he would wrinkle her skirt. So I had to hold him on my lap. When the weather was nice, I would have him sit inside and I would ride home in the rumble seat.

It was probably in 1937 when lightning struck the huge barn on the farm. My dad jumped out of bed and hit his head on a door partway open. With blood running down his face, he started yelling for everyone to get up and get dressed. We only had kerosene light, no electricity in that area. He told my oldest sister to grab a sheet and start getting clothes for all of us in case the wind blew sparks or anything towards the house. There was a lot of hay and grain in the barn and it burned for days. Sometimes it would really flare up and my mom, dad, older brother, and sister would carry buckets of water from the stock tank to throw on it. It completely burned to the ground.

My folks bought chicken feed in colorful cloth bags and baking flour in white cloth bags. I had many school dresses made from the colorful bags and mom would make our underpants out of the white bags. One day she was sewing a pair of underpants and she told me to go to the basement to get potatoes to fix for lunch. I was scared to go down the pitch-dark basement so I didn't go. She told me again and I still didn't go. This is the only time I remember not minding my mom. So she got up from the sewing machine, threw the material at me, and said, "You sew it." I had no idea how to sew on the old treadle sewing machine, but I tried. Some of the seams were probably one-half inch wide and others almost ran off the material. I told mom, I'll peel the potatoes if you sew it. So she did. By the time I was in high school, I was sewing my skirts and blouses. When I was twenty-two, I made my own wedding dress and veil. A couple of years later our ladies group at church helped a mission group in South America. They were wanting white dresses for girls to wear for their first communion. So I took my wedding dress apart and made two dresses with the satin and lace. They went sent to South America. We heard back from them, they were really happy to get them. I was very happy to do something useful with my wedding dress and veil and not wonder what to do with it in the years ahead.

My teacher in the fifth and sixth grade was Sister Irene Hartman. One day I handed in a paper and she said I had two words spelled wrong. I said, "I had the right letters." She came right back to me with, "How would you like your name-Lois Leis," spelled as "Soil Lies?" She even mentioned this in a Christmas letter I received in December 2013.

Moving Around
By Simon Korbe Jr. of Leoti, Kansas
Born 1931

It all started with my grandparents, both sides immigrated from Marienthal, Russia to Victoria, Kansas. They were all German who spoke no English; from there they went to Wallace, Kansas. I was born in Wallace, Kansas in Wallace County on August 2, 1931. I had two brothers and two sisters.

Sheep at the Billbe Ranch

My first memory was of the dust storms, "The Dirty Thirties." Mother would wet a bed sheet to put around the table and all of us sat underneath it. Black Friday, Uncle Herman came from the fields over two miles away. He would have to bring the reigns into the house and hold on to the horses until the storm was over. My Uncle Alex and dad were too far from the house so they lifted the wagon box off the frame and turned it over and sat underneath it.

We didn't live very far from our grandparents. My grandfather gave me a little bird that would wind up and peck and my little sister a doll that would wind up and crawl. Those toys can be found in the Museum of the Great Plains located in Leoti, Kansas.

I started school in a little white schoolhouse in Logan County. I knew very little English, because we spoke German until my grandparents passed away. The schoolhouse was closest to Twin Buttes.

We lived out on an old farm close to a lister. I will never forget one day, I crawled on top of the lister because a big old rattlesnake was trying to bite my feet. Dad had to light the lister on fire to burn the snake out. I can remember dad filling a quart jar full of rattles.

We moved to the Billbe Ranch, where dad looked after sheep for Mr. Price. Then the blizzards of 1948 and 1957 ended the sheep in western Kansas. When that happened we then moved to the Blau Ranch in Logan County, we went to school at the Rock Schoolhouse and the Snowbarger kids drove a horse and buggy to school about seven miles, all winter long. We moved around a lot, after only one year, we moved to the Hock Master Ranch in Wichita County. They had a grove of Mulberry trees. We would climb the trees and eat the mulberries. We worked for Herb Barr and walked about a half a mile to school. We lived on Ladder Creek that was in 1936, all the creeks and rivers ran water all year round in Western Kansas. The best thing I remember was the fishing on Ladder Creek all summer long. We moved to Leoti in 1937, we had to milk six cows every day and separate the cream before walking to school and every Saturday put the cream can in the wagon and haul it down to the creamery to sell or trade for groceries. The jackrabbits were so thick, on Saturdays, the town folks would build a big pen, and sometimes up to two hundred-fifty people would show up. One Saturday, I know they killed over twelve hundred jackrabbits.

I remember using the old crank phones; you would have to dial three short numbers then five numbers and then sometimes five than three numbers, so we didn't use the phone much, way different than today when people go everywhere with their phones.

Every Saturday night people would come to town to do their shopping and sometimes would stand in the streets visiting till midnight.

On Grandpa Dechant's place, there were two dirt hills. One of which we believed there was an Indian Chief buried because we would find all kinds of beads.

Mom had a washing machine; it was a wooden tub you put your clothes in. She used a handle to agitate them before running them through a ringer that was also hand cranked, and then she would carry them over to the clothesline.

Both black and white would attend the Little Eagle School, and there were never any problems. There was never any segregation; everyone was just part of the community that grew to be... now they are all gone.

Remembrances of Yesterday
By Lavona Hobson of Valley Center, Kansas
Born 1941

I remember my favorite thing to do after school was to go to Jones Drug Store and get a Cherry Coke and a Snickers candy bar. Sometimes eating hamburgers and fries at Kathy's Café.

Growing up was so much fun being a twin and having a twin sister as a best friend.

We remember finding Christmas gifts early like trikes in top of the barn, and dolls on top of closet in bedroom.

We hid in the garden once when the minister came to visit as we had clothes on we didn't want to be seen in

I remember peddlers coming to our farm. We didn't answer the door but us kids looked out the window upstairs and they walked around our house and saw us so we hid upstairs. Once someone stole some of daddy's turkeys that he had loaded to take to sale.

We once kept my nephew, Merle Hazen, and mother was fixing someone's hair and we discovered we couldn't find Merle. We

The Twins
Levon and Lavona Hazen

searched the farm so worried and finally found him asleep on the floor under the kitchen table where we all were.

Once I lifted the garage door for mother to back the car out and a rattlesnake fell out of the door and fell out not far from me. I was scared to death! My mother got out of the car, got a hoe, and killed it!

Sometimes we would get in the cattle tank to cool off.

For entertainment, out on the farm, we would have a bull chase us and run to the gate or have turkeys chase us.

We were excited to see harvesters come in summer. We would take them garden vegetables and share with them.

My twin sister fell off the dining room table and broke her arm. She dared me to climb a tree and I did and fell out and broke my arm. We had appendix surgeries two weeks apart.

We played "Ante" over the garage, and house and "Hide and Seek."

We would gather flowers and take to our mother for bouquets.

We received one special gift at Christmas each year. Some I remember well were skates, trikes, dolls, and watches.

Mother would go to the stores, and draw a pattern of a dress and go home and cut out of newspapers and sew dresses for us. We dressed alike all through school.

We rode the school bus and was first ones on and last ones off.

In my high school years, I worked in a grocery store for Loma and Joe Harmon. That was fun.

I remember getting to ring the school bell in our old two-story grade school. I remember once someone left water running in the girl's restroom and I did not do it but, was accused of it and had to sit in the corner for it. It broke my heart, as I didn't do it.

When we twins were born, mother belonged to a club that gave her two baby baskets for us. I remember Mother telling us she cried when she found daddy had nailed them up in the chicken house for chickens to lay eggs in.

There were red wild flowers that grew all around. My twin sister and I would pretend

The family of Albert and Edith Hazen in 1960

we were selling them for tomato plants.

I remember big snowstorms when snow was to the roof. One Memorial Day, we had floodwater everywhere.

We were on a party line and had to wait till neighbors got off the phone to use it.

We always looked forward to Saturday nights as we would go to town and my parents would sell eggs. I remember going to Sitka to the grocery store and we loved to get sliced bologna and cheese and eat it sometimes on the way home.

Every Sunday aunts, uncles, and cousins would come over or we would have picnics or meet at a creek. I remember I almost drowned once and was so scared.

We had a sad thing happen to our family. We lost our brother only fifteen years old with a ruptured appendix. We twins were only four years old at the time.

It was so much fun growing up in the small town of Protection, Kansas and going to school there.

The Shack
By Jane Schmidt of Wilmore, Kansas
Born 1951

Though I was born in 1951, "The Great Depression" and "Dirty Thirties" were still fresh in my grandparent's minds; World War II, brothers fighting in wars overseas and rationing of food and supplies was still fresh in my parent's minds. We lived in a house that by today's standards would be considered a "shack." Built in the 1880s, many a child had grown up there, including my dad who was born there. It had no indoor bathrooms, only cold water plumbing in the kitchen and very little to no insulation in its walls. What electricity we had was generated by a wind charger that my dad and grandpa contrived. It charged a large battery on the outside of the house. When in good repair, and when the wind blew, we had feeble flickering light from ceiling bulbs. But we had no electrical appliances. The reliable source of light was from kerosene lamps. And our heat source was a large propane gas-heating stove in the living room. With no air conditioning or fans to circulate the air, we kid's spent most of our summer days outdoors.

Daddy worked two to three part time jobs, as well as farmed my grandpa's quarter of land on which we lived. Mother was a homemaker in the true sense of the word. She cooked all of our meals. She washed clothes on a wringer washer that had a loud motorized tub and hung the clothes outside to line dry. In the winter, of course they froze stiff! She also sewed most of our clothing on her Singer treadle sewing machine.

Mother heated our bath water on the kitchen cook stove and we bathed in metal "washtubs" on the north porch, which was enclosed but not heated. This room also served as the laundry room, housing the washing machine.

Having no television set, Mother or Daddy usually read us stories in the evening after supper, by lamplight, from books checked out from the town's library. My favorite stories were those of *Thornton W. Burgess-The Old Mother West Wind* books. Oh what delightful stories they were!

We had a large radio in the living room. It was amazing when viewed from the back as it was composed of many, many tubes! It was always on it seems. There was a program out of Dodge City that was broadcast at eight a.m. called The Southwest Shortie Show. My brother climbed aboard the yellow school bus that took him off to school and I stood in front of the radio and "danced." My mother and her two sisters sometimes went to Dodge City to sing live on the radio. I can remember often drifting off to sleep with The Star Spangled Banner closing down the day's broadcasting.

We also had a big wooden telephone hanging on the west wall of the kitchen close to the pantry. An awkward looking contraption, the mouthpiece was a part of the box, but the earpiece was a bell shaped device on a cord attached to the box. The thing had to be "cranked" to reach the operator. We were on a party line and everyone's "number" on the line rang into our house. Our ring was two longs and two shorts. The switchboard was located in town and the local operator knew everybody's business; if you needed to know someone's whereabouts, just ring the operator!

Daddy milked a cow and Mother churned butter. We also had chickens and a few heads of Angus cows. We refrigerated our food in a propane gas Seville refrigerator. If mother ordered anything from Sears Roebuck or Montgomery Ward, it arrived in town by train. So we got to go to the train depot to see the stationmaster and collect our package. What fun!

We lived only one-half mile west of town (Mullinville.) The old Santa Fe railroad grades ran just north of our house, and, the two trestle grade build-ups, sans tracks, located on our property were one of my brothers and I's favorite places to "explore" and play. One summer morning we told mother we were going to the grades to play. We soon grew tired of playing "King on the Mountain" and tromping around on top of the grades so we decided to walk over to the neighbors to see his pigs. Still not wanting to go home, the day being so fine, we walked on over to the cemetery. Did we stop there? Oh no, we hiked all the way into town to see a cute girl in my brother's class who lived on the last west street in town! Deciding to take the highway home, because it was now our shortest route, we were at least smart enough to walk on the shoulder. At that time, a new Highway 154 was being built and there was lots of activity to occupy our attention. We had just set our feet homeward in earnest when we spied daddy's green Ford pickup headed out to the grades, looking for us no doubt. Wildly flailing our arms to get his attention, we started running as fast as we could knowing well we were in deep trouble. And boy were we ever! It was probably the worst trouble we'd been into- ever.

Another time, we carried the strap on skates grandma had given us for Christmas all the way to the grades thinking it would be great fun to roller skate down their deep sides. Had the slopes been smooth, and without stickers, there might have been a better outcome to the adventure. But alas, we arrived home dirty, skinned up, full of stickers, irritable and most of all, highly disappointed that our big idea of the day was a big fat flop.

I haven't mentioned our two-seater outhouse for a reason-it was a hot, stinky, full of flies in the summertime and bone chilling cold in the winter. And to top it off, there was a knothole in the roof. The center had fallen out so there was a real hole. Someone could easily climb the fence to the top of the chicken house and only a small leap took them to the top of the outhouse, where they could peek down at you as you went about your business, or could drop things down the hole at you.

We moved from this "West Place" in the fall of 1958, having survived the disastrous blizzard of 1957 in this house with no modern conveniences. Physically this place no longer exists but the memories linger in our minds.

Family Living
By Aden E. Nettie Keim of Haven, Kansas
Born 1949

I grew up on a Jersey dairy farm, southwest of Hutchinson, Kansas. There were six girls and one boy in our family. So us girls helped with the farm work, milking cows, and working in the field. We also had a big garden every year, with a big strawberry patch. We also sold strawberries. With nine in the family, Mother wanted to freeze a lot for our own use.

We had a U.M.M. tractor, which we did most of our farm work with. Later we got a 930 Case tractor. We enjoyed using our new tractor. We also bought an old K.T.A.M.M. tractor from our neighbor, when he sold out and moved to town. We used it to bale hay. Our Ford tractor, we used to mow and rake hay. Dad and our neighbor mowed hay helping each other. Us girls raked hay and drove the tractor to bale hay. Dad and our neighbor were on the wagon stacking hay; they were good friends and visited while working together. Dad had lots of patience in teaching us to work in the field. We farmed for an older widow lady, she wanted her things done right and dad always tried to please her and they got along well.

Us four oldest girls attended a one-room school. My oldest sister graduated there. I attended in the first and second grade and have fond memories of the good times we had there. There were no bathrooms; we used outhouses one for the girls and one for the boys. A hand pump was used to wash our hands and get a drink from with a cup, east of the schoolhouse. There was a big barrel where water was kept right inside of the schoolhouse entrance, where we got a drink when it wasn't convenient to go outside. When I was in the first grade, we had one teacher for the grades from one to eight. When I was in the second grade they fixed the basement for the seventh and eighth grades, then we had two teachers. We carried our lunchboxes and often walked to school, if the weather permitted. We also had a cart we hitched to our old horse, Minnie and drove it to school sometimes. We had two and a half miles to school. When the weather wasn't nice, the neighbors took turns taking the children in the neighborhood to school. A new school was built around 1958 and three to four one-room schools were combined. We had buses for transportation then.

When we came home from school, we had chores to do. Feeding calves, and helping with the milking. We also had chickens and sold eggs, by the case, which were picked up by a man that had an egg route. It was our job to clean the eggs; we scrubbed them with a brush, which looked like a block of wood with sandpaper on it. One evening my sister and I were to clean the eggs and everybody else went to bed. The kitchen door was closed so the others wouldn't be disturbed from their sleep. With a family of nine, we had a two-bedroom house. We had an open porch on the south side, so we were sitting right on the inside of the screen door, with a hook to lock it. We were so scared somebody would look in and see us, so we hurriedly cleaned eggs. We were glad when we were finished, and safely crawled into bed. That never happened again! We were taught to be wise and do our chores earlier.

In the summertime we herded the cows along the road, they ate grass and weeds in the ditch. While doing this we were hoping our cousins living one and a half miles north of us would come play with us. We were sure they were coming if we saw a little speck of something. It usually turned out to be our imagination! This taught us to be patient herding cows. We enjoyed life and were thankful for what we had.

Trips to Hutch were few and far apart. Often we went with our horse and buggy, or our neighbors took us with their vehicle. When we drove out with the horse and buggy, sometimes we took a baby calf along to the livestock sale. We put it in a gunnysack with just the head sticking out. We left it at the sale and went to do shopping along Main Street of Hutchinson. There were plenty of stores along Main Street to do our shopping Sears, Wards, Woolworths, Kress, Penny's, Ben Franklin, Self-Service Anthony's, Shoe stores, Fabric stores, Beardlees, House of Fabric, and more.

We left our horse and buggy on the south end of Main Street and a little west in a barn and walked to do our shopping. On the south end were Dillions, Smiths Market, and Mammels where we got groceries before going home. It took all day, so we had lunch at a little hamburger restaurant or we got things

Elmhirst School students

Grandma's kitchen

at the grocery store to make sandwiches and usually we got the little pint Jacksons ice cream containers. We each got one and just ate out of that .Such a treat! We had to take turns to go along to Hutch with our parents, usually two of us, so we'd have room for groceries, etc. Dad loved fig bars so he always got some to eat on the way home. Sometimes when our two oldest sisters went along, us younger, ones would stay at Grandpa's (Mother's parents,) which was very special. Grandma baked her own bread in a wood burning stove in round pans. She used everlasting yeast. You started your dough the evening before and put the everlasting yeast in that was kept in a little jar in the fridge. Next morning, you took out a jar half-full to keep for the next baking. Then added more flour to make your bread.

Grandpa cooled their cream from their Jersey cows in a tank of water pumping from the windmill. The cream was separated in an old boxcar. They hauled it near the house to cool in a ten-gallon cream can in a two-wheeled cart. They sold cream and fed hogs with the skim milk. They had a hand pump in the kitchen for their water. Later they had running water at the worktable.

We had electricity at our house before Grandpa did. There was a snowstorm, and we were out of electricity. With a dairy, this wasn't too handy if you depended on it. Dad went to Grandpa's to get water in ten-gallon milk cans, from the hand pump in their kitchen. The milkman couldn't come to pick up the milk. We got out the oil lamp and used it. There was no school and we put puzzles together. What fun! Of course, I'm sure our parents had more worries than we did. Mother often helped with the milking.

In 1958, we enlarged the open front porch and enclosed it. On the west side of the house, we put in a new kitchen. Dad had helped tear down a house in Hutchinson and we put the worktable from that house in our kitchen. This gave more room for our growing family, which we really appreciated. In 1964, an upstairs was put in on the east part of the house. We hired a carpenter to do it; he was a strong man and carried heavy things up the ladder. We had a frolic one day; friends and neighbors came to help, by evening the roof was on the upstairs. Our neighbor lady called it in and it was published in the *Hutchinson News* She got a tip for it. In around 1965 to 1966, in the fall we put in a bathroom on the north side of the house. Now we had a good sized house and enjoyed the new additions

My Dad loved history. I called him our walking history book. He was a young man when World War II started and there were many stories he told us at the supper table. Also when he was a boy at home and the Hobos stopped at their house by the railroad. They'd work for a meal or bed. The Hobos had a sign they placed near a farm where they were treated well, so they often had Hobos come to their house. One Sunday eve, a Hobo came to their house and he slept in the barn. One of Dad's brothers came home from a youth gathering. Usually he gave his horse some hay from a haystack in the barn using a fork. That night for some reason, he decided not to. The next morning he found out that a hobo was sleeping on the haystack. So they felt a guiding hand told him not to feed his horse that night. Dad's mother died before I was born so I never got to know her. . Grandpa was a widower for over thirty years. So he was at our house for meals sometimes, which we greatly enjoyed.

In the winter, we butchered beef and hogs and he was always helping. One year we did this during Christmas vacation from school. Most of us, children were sick with a stomach flu. He came into the living room and teased us; you all look like sick chicks. He thought we ate too much candy over Christmas. That at least made us smile.

We'd often go visit him on a Sunday evening. We'd sit quietly and listen to the grownups talk or run out in his yard with a picket fence around it, and watch the traffic on Highway 61 and the trains going by. Often it was bright moonlight in the summertime when we'd go with the horse and buggy. On the way home, Dad would sing. One song I especially remember was "When there's Love at Home."

After supper, we'd read one to two chapters in the Bible together with an evening prayer. I thank God that we were privileged to have Christian parents. They taught us to respect authorities over us, parents, teachers, ministers, etc. Dad died in two thousand at the age of eighty. Mother is still living at the age of ninety-two.

Hollyhock Dolls
By Mary E. Yoder of Hutchinson, Kansas
Born 1930

First of all, I want to thank the Lord for letting me be born into a Christian home. We were taught to love and honor the Lord. We grew up in an Amish home so life was simple. My folks were married in 1927, and lived in Indiana till 1936. So I have some memories from Indiana. Dad raised mint, so he had a mint still, and processed peppermint oil. He always rented as long as I was home, so remember moving three times. First move was coming to Kansas in 1936. I was five and a half years old. We moved several miles northeast of Partridge in Reno County.

Mary and her classmates

There were six children by then; three boys and three girls. I was the oldest girl, two older brothers, and one memory of Indiana was when my youngest sister was born in 1935. We were not told a baby was coming, so I really thought the doctor brought her in his little black bag. I remember him coming one evening in his Model T Ford, going into the house with a black bag. Dad gave us children strict orders to stay outside, but we tried to look in through the porch windows. Of course, we couldn't see anything, but we thought we heard a baby cry. Sure enough, after the doctor left, Dad came out and invited us in to see the new baby.

My two older brothers went to school in Indiana, but I was seven years olds before going to school. I could hardly wait!-, and I loved going to school. We went to East Eureka School. It is still at the same place, but made into a home now. It had one main room. Two cloakrooms and a little library room. The cloakrooms each had a little room at the end with a stool (non-flushing) so no outdoor facility. One for the boys, and the other one for girls. They did have a window, and the teacher put in something to keep it from smelling. In all the homes, we lived in there were no bathrooms, so this was quite an upgrade for us. (We had to take our baths in the living room or pantry, and always had an outhouse.)

The schoolhouse had a basement with a furnace for heat. We used to put food on the register to heat it in the wintertime.

There was a little barn to keep horses in as some pupils came with a buggy, or a wagon with benches inside, as they had quite a way to walk. We walked to school, one and two-thirds miles, till about the last year. The boys were old enough to drive a horse, so dad got an older racehorse named Dewey. He was a safe horse, so all six of us children piled on a single buggy. I think two stood on the back, and off we went. A neighbor once tried to pass us, and with Dewey's racing blood, he was not about to be passed! He sped up and the neighbor was left behind we still chuckle about that.

My favorite teacher? I only had one teacher, Mrs. Florence Stallman was my teacher, and she believed in letting her pupils take several grades in one year. She was a good teacher, but I only went to school five years for all eight grades. I started in September 1937 and graduated in April 1942. I remember the lilacs were blooming, and we went to Poplar School to take our eighth grade exams. It was a neighboring school that we had gone to for spelling bees, etc. Another girl and I were quite competitive, and we almost tied but I did get the top grade in Reno County that year. Like I said, I loved school, and it was easy for me, but we didn't have nearly as much schooling as they do now. I don't remember any homework. It was in the Depression era, and my folks didn't have much but we always milked five or six cows and had a couple hundred laying hens. Mom always had a garden, and canned fruit and vegetables so we never went hungry. She was a good cook.

Dad helped a neighbor for one dollar a day with his farming. We moved west of Partridge in 1942, and then he got more land to farm, and could do a lot better financially.

While we were still living at the first place, we had a lot of fun in the summertime. The boys had two pet bantams named Cocky and Biddy. They made a harness for them and a little wagon for them to pull, and then they caught a grasshopper, and enticed the chicks to pull it, by dangling the grasshopper in front of them. We also had a stock tank close to the house. The barnyard was fairly close, and we had goldfish in the stock tank that we liked to watch. We had hollyhock flowers and we would make hollyhock dolls to float in the tank, by taking a flower and a toothpick, and the bud for a head, the flower for a skirt.

Mary's grandchildren, Abbie, Elsie, and Evan

In Brother's Memory
By Phyllis Haltom of Coldwater, Kansas
Born 1936

This memory of my brother who was killed October 1944 in Italy during World War II is very vivid still today as it was when it happened. My brother, Everett, was 13 years older than me. Everett was a senior in high school, and I was in the first grade. We were close, and he always was there to take care of me.

President Roosevelt said he wouldn't draft boys out of high school. The boy called up in front of my brother decided to go to school to become a minister. My brother's name was next in our county and was called to go for a physical for the Army in his senior year.

My dad and all of my uncles volunteered to go to the Army so Everett could finish high school. All were rejected.

Before Everett was 19 years old, he was sent to Italy to fight. He was a strong Christian and carried a small Bible over his heart.

In a battle, all of the men in his unit were wounded. Everett was the only one not wounded, so he went for help. He was shot in front of the Army hospital tent in the back by a German sniper and killed in the line of duty. All of the men in the unit survived.

I was six years old when he was killed.

We got the telegram that Everett was killed on a Monday, washday. I still remember my dad and mom crying. This changed the lives of my parents, two brothers, me, my relatives, and the community.

To this day, I still cry when his name is mentioned or I think about Everett, 71 years later.

Pea Pods and Exploding Beans
By Wilma Kinser of Medicine Lodge, Kansas
Born 1934

There were eight kids in our family, five girls, and three boys. The two youngest boys were four and six years older than I was. The youngest three girls were close in ages, being two years apart and 16 months apart.

Daddy had built a wooden bench for four of us to sit on at the table. I would sit on one end of the bench, and one of my brothers would sit on the other end. We would take a pocketknife with two blades, open the blades, and position them so they would make a right angle. Then we would throw the knife at each other, and it would stick in the bench. The different way it landed with one blade stuck in the bench would be worth so many points. The game was called mumbly peg.

We were playing it one evening, and I left my hand on the bench, and the knife landed on the back of my hand and went in. I screamed and Mother took the knife away from us and told us we could not play anymore. My brother was really unhappy at me, because Mother took the knife. I was only about five or six years old.

I remember on washdays the washing machine would be rolled into the kitchen, and there would be two big tubs of water to rinse the clothes in. The last tub of water would always be blue. Mother would take the bottle of bluing and pour just the right amount in the tub to make it the right color. Then she would run them through the wringer from the machine to each tub of water. The wringer would swing just right so we could guide the clothes into each tub.

But washing clothes wasn't near as much fun as when summer would come, and we would go to the truck patch and fill five or six gunnysacks full of peas. Then Mother would get the washing machine out, and we would pile peas on top of the machine. One of us girls would help Mother feed the pea pods into the wringer, and the other two would stand on the other side of the wringer with a bowl each and catch the peas as they came out of the pod. If you fed the right end into the wringer, the pod would pop open and the peas would just roll out, and the pods would fall into a container for the trash. What fun we had shelling peas. It didn't take long to get them all podded, and it was such fun. Now snapping beans was a whole nother ballgame.

Daddy would buy ten bushel of peaches each year at the same time. We would come home after school, and they would be stacked in the kitchen and on the porch. We had a big kitchen and dining room. All of us would come home from school and help can peaches until bedtime. Mother would can during the day alone, but we knew we had to help until they were all canned.

We weren't particularly fond of snapping beans, but at least we didn't have to do them all at once, because Mother raised them in the garden. We owned the lot just west of our house, and almost all of it was the garden.

One day we were canning beans, and Mother had just put the jars into the pressure cooker and put it on the stove. We sat down to eat supper, and the pressure on the cooker got too high and blew the lid off the cooker, and we had beans and glass everywhere. They were all over the walls, the stove, the floor, and the ceiling. No one was hurt, because we ate in the dining room. It was a huge mess. Mother never canned green beans in the pressure cooker again. She would cold pack them after that.

We were always thankful when canning season was over, but we were very thankful for the jars of food.

Riding the Doodle Bug
By Patsy Kaye Miller Wilson of Kiowa, Kansas
Born 1945

My life's journey began at 10:25 p.m. on Sunday, January 28, 1945 at Achinbach Hospital in Hardtner, Kansas to James Edwin and Verda Louise (Liggenstoffer) Miller. I was joined in the nursery on the 29th by twin cousins. Donnie, the little boy, died on the 30th. This was to be repeated in the Miller family by another sister of my dad's 14 years later with twins born on January 29th and the boy dying on the 30th.

I had an older sister, Sharen Ann (four years older) and a younger sister, Peggy Sue (19 ½ months younger). We were blessed with a second set of parents, our Uncle Eddie (Edwin James, a first cousin of my dad's) and Aunt Panny (Frances Jule, an older sister of my mom's). I gave her the name Panny when I couldn't pronounce my Fs, so Fanny became Panny. She was known from then on as Panny by family and friends. They had no children after she had a tubal pregnancy, so they helped raised us three girls.

We lived in Burlington, Oklahoma until 1946 when my dad went to work for Schupbach Implements, the local John Deere dealer, and we moved to Kiowa. I have many wonderful childhood and school memories, along with Miller, Liggenstoffer, and church family gatherings.

Riding the Doodlebug from Kiowa to Burlington to Grandma Miller's with my sisters or vice versa with no parents along is one I really treasure. The Doodlebug was a small train that ran from Kiowa to Enid, Oklahoma used by city shoppers and shippers of freight. Kiowa had a main line Santa Fe rail going north to Chicago and southwest to California. A lot of people rode to Wichita to shop and cattle were shipped to Wichita and Kansas City for selling. We thought we were so big with no parents along, with a clickity clack of the train we headed south going over Uncle Ed and Aunt Panny's railroad place (quarter) plus looking west from it you could see the red barn place (quarter). Drinking water from cone shaped paper cups from the water bottle tasted so good.

Years later the red barn disappeared as my nephew was working that quarter's ground on a tractor, a summer day with numerous dust devils, the barn was lifted and exploded into pieces. Though he denies it, I think to this day he surly filled his pants.

Life in Attica
By Martha Jeanne Howe Wakefield of Omaha, Nebraska
Born 1949

I was six years old when my family moved to a little town called Attica, Kansas. A Mobil plant was built near Attica, so a lot of families moved there for a job. I have so many wonderful memoires of life in our small little town, going downtown on Saturdays for a drawing for money at 2:00 p.m. to see whose name might be drawn! My parents would give us kids ten cents, and I would go buy a nickel Coke at the Bauman's Drug Store. That's where everyone went to hang out. At Christmas, everyone would get a number, go around the stores, and see if our number matched a prize. I won two times: a snack set which I gave to my grandmother Judy for a Christmas present and one other year I won leather gloves (I think) with zebra lining. I won those at the prettiest store in town,

Joann's. I thought I was big stuff!

Attica also had a rodeo every year and had a rodeo queen contest, swimsuit, evening dress, and all! I was chosen to be the rodeo queen when I was 16 years old. That was a huge highlight for me in my life. My sister, Judy, was a runner-up a few years before me.

My family was my dad, who worked for Mobil, my mom, who worked a lot of jobs during my time in Attica, and my sister, Judy, the oldest. She was three years older than me. And my sister, Linda who was a year older. I think we lived in five houses during our days in Attica. The last one was the one we lived in the longest. It was by the city park, which was fun. I could walk over and roller skate on just a slab of cement going round and round.

We also had a wonderful woman who was our neighbor and a caretaker for elderly people in her home. She had never married. She had a large tumor (I think) on her hip, and this was a great way to support herself. I will never forget her. He name was Julia Berry, and she was so loving and kind to me. She taught me how to hook a rug and how to crochet. I remember sitting in her small kitchen and watching her make jelly and can vegetables. What was really beautiful about Julia was how she took care of the elderly who lived in her home. She also had a cellar at her home in the yard where she put all her canned vegetables and tornados! We spent a lot of time in that cellar running over to Julia's cellar whenever there was a warning of tornados. My dad would always go into the house, get Virginia, and carry her down to the cellar. She couldn't walk.

One of the years in Attica was a day of competitions. I so remember I won the record of Elvis Presley's "Blue Suede Shoes" for winning at jacks! I also competed in the hula-hoop contest.

My parents owned the theater in Attica for a while. My biggest memories are walking downtown to go to the movies and seeing someone run over our dog, Sailor. That was terrible. I was probably six or seven. Also, I got to drink the leftover orange drink!

Attica at one time had free movies every Monday night. The screen was a big canvas attached to two telephone poles, and a couple would have the projector in the back of their pickup truck and would sell popcorn and candy. The one movie I really remember is "Midnight Lace" with Doris Day and Rex Harrison. Very scary. We would lay on blankets or you could sit in your car. That was a fun time.

We only had one policeman in our little town. His name was Fred. He always seemed so kind. On Halloween if you were caught doing something you weren't supposed to do your punishment was to be put in jail for an hour or to ride around with him for an hour. Big punishment!

Well, there are so many great memories for me in Attica. I haven't missed a reunion yet. I love going back and seeing everyone. Thank you for creating this book and letting me go down memory lane.

A Quiet, Entertaining, and Good Life
By Evelyn Olson of Monte Vista, Colorado
Born 1923

During my childhood, Ransom, Kansas had a population of about 250, and it has remained that size. I graduated from high school in 1940, attended Fort Hays University for four years, and taught high school English in Ness City, Kansas for two years. Then I married and came to Colorado.

Although we had running city water, which labeled it a modern house, we had an outhouse on the property, as did many of the houses. Schools had functioning restrooms.

Telephones not only were of the rotary variety, but also most of them hung on a wall. Often there was a high stool nearby, in case one wanted to sit and visit. Party lines were common, with four to eight people to a party. Each person had his own combination of long and short rings. My grandmother's number was 43C, a long and three shorts. One, rang Central and told her either the number or the name one wanted, and she would ring the right party. One time a woman called everyone on her line and told them to leave the receiver off the hook at eight that night. She had a guest who was going to sing "The Holy City" and others could enjoy the music.

There were also soap opera programs on daytime radio. My mother enjoyed one called *Betty and Bob*, but I was too busy playing outdoors to sit still and listen. Probably the program was aimed toward clean-minded adults, for the word 'pregnant' was never used. Information was conveyed by a hint. My dad and grandfather would hover around the radio in the fall to hear about World Series baseball.

I grew tall while quite young, so it was hard to find appropriate clothes. My mother usually sewed my school dresses, and sometimes she made matching underpants.

My favorite teacher came along in high school. Her name was Myrtle Houghton, and she treated me like an intelligent young adult and not a silly kid. Because she was an excellent teacher of English, I became an English teacher.

During the 1930s, Kansas was part of the Dust Bowl; a cloud of dust would appear on the horizon and soon visibility would be diminished for hours. The dust was as fine as flour, and it got into everything. People became ill with dust pneumonia. Trees survived, but perennials and bushes often died.

I always had dogs and cats as pets. I taught one cat to ride on my back. When my parents refinished the floors, the cat found their backs a good place for rides. My parents found the cat to be an unwelcome distraction.

My dad and his uncle told stories about herding cattle in earlier days. The stories sounded wonderful to me; now I wonder if they were embroidered for my pleasure.

For family entertainment we often went fishing at a nearby pond, and on warm summer nights we had wiener roasts outside for supper. Then we slept on quilts spread on the grass.

Life was quiet, entertaining, and good in Kansas in the 1930s for a healthy child.

Swiping Some Boloney
By Estol Coen of Hutchinson, Kansas
Born 1931

This is a story about life on a farm in the 1930 located by Neola, halfway between Hutchinson and Pratt, Kansas.

Life dawned bright and early on the farm. There were all those cows to milk! Grandma Rose, who was heavyset, would shuffle to the kitchen to stir up her sourdough pancakes and

Estol's parents, Geneva and Fred Sherman

cook bacon and eggs for Sonny, her husband. He was a man with quick wit, and he didn't talk a lot. Rose had a way of 'ruffling his feathers.' She would yell, "Sonny, it is past time to change your underwear!" He wore those long johns most of the year.

In the spring, she would pester him to hurry up and plant potatoes. They had a large garden and worked very hard. They had a wood burning stove in the kitchen and one in the living room a kerosene stove and kerosene lamps before electricity. Their son, Fred, his wife, Geneva, my sister, Florence, and me had to move in with them after 1931 because of the Depression. It was a huge farm with horses, cows, chickens, and pigs.

There was a windmill to run water to three tanks through a long pipe. When the wind didn't blow, they used a gasoline motor to pump the water. There was a long wooden box that the water ran through to the pipe that led to the tanks. They kept some groceries in the box to stay cool, such as baloney. When Florence and I would get hungry between meals, we would swipe some baloney while no one was looking!

There was also an icebox in the house. It

was fun when the iceman came from Turon with big chunks of ice in his pickup truck. He carried them into the house with giant ice tongs. It was also fun when Welch's Grocery Store truck came. Florence and I were treated with candy bars! It was always a happy day when the mailbox had a check for the cream that we sold. The building where the cream was separated from the milk was called the well house.

It was an exciting time when a hog was butchered. They would string it upside down to a tree with thick chains and large hooks. Rose would cut up the fat, make pork rind cracklings, and fry the pig brains with scrambled eggs.

Rose was a professional at raising plants and chickens. The setting hens were kept in a special building with a special yard for when the chicks hatched.

Florence and I had the privilege of gathering eggs in the long chicken house. If a hen was still sitting on the nest, we held her head so she wouldn't peck us as we reached under her for the egg!

Nearly everyone in the country had outdoor toilets and pots for the house to carry back and forth.

The Day to Wash Our Clothes
By Sister Diane Traffas of St. Catharine, Kentucky
Born 1935

Even now as I approach my eightieth year of life, I remember with great clarity, and now also with great gratitude, the Monday morning special operation at our farm. It was simply called, "This is the day to wash our clothes."

My mom, God bless her, would go around the house into each bedroom emptying all the hampers of the soiled clothes of the past week for ten children, sort them out into piles of like colors and like fabric textures, roll up her sleeves, and knuckle down to insure clean clothes for the week to follow. What a never-ending task!

First of all, she would have to heat the water to pour into the machine before she applied her foot to the motor lever. This resulted in the God-awful noise of starting up the ole Maytag and filling the washhouse with fumes and popping noises. The water and the clothes inside the tub would gyrate and slosh back and forth, washing away the dirt and grime on overalls, shirts, socks, and, in a class all by themselves, the bedclothes.

About half an hour later, the machine automatically went silent, and we knew it was time for the next procedure, which was to dig into the rinse water and pull out the garments to run through the wringer. The wringer consisted of two hard rubber cylinder rollers that pressed together and rolled at the same time, succeeding in squeezing almost all the water from the clothes. It was a long and arduous, if necessary process, because these clothes were being prepared for the next step – a trip to the outside clothesline for drying.

With clip-on post clothespins, whoever was lucky attached them to the wires extended across the yard for just this purpose, to dry the clothes. It was thought that the sunshine and fresh air gave them a special scent and made them last longer. While that may have occurred, it also occurred on numerous

Estol with her grandma, Rose Sherman and Florence

occasions that Mom nearly froze her fingers as she hung clothes in the dead of winter.

When finally they dried, someone would bring the clothes into the house, where they were separated by "clothes that just needed folding" and another pile, which was labeled "clothes that need ironing."

By now, it was noontime, and it is anyone's guess how, in addition to this weekly Monday morning routine there appeared on the table a wonderful feast of fried chicken, mashed potatoes and gravy, and corn or green beans, and sometimes good ole apple pie. When I think back, it is not hard to make my mother a saint.

Buckner Valley School
By Shirley Hoskinson of Dodge City, Kansas
Born 1947

Buckner Valley School was built in the late 1920s or early 1930s. My grandparents, Edward and Mary Stapleton, donated a corner of their land for the school. It was a typical one room, rural school, as there was one teacher who taught students from the first through the eighth grades all in one classroom. At one time, there were 26 students in attendance. My grandparents' farm was ¾ mile from the school, so my dad, Walter Stapleton, and his siblings would walk or ride horses to attend school. My dad said he could walk the distance in four minutes.

From the time, my dad attended until the time I started school, there were only a few improvements made to the building. The coal-burning stove had been replaced by an oil-burning stove. The last improvement was electricity being added in 1951 or 1952. We still had the wood desks, with the inkwells, and the wood seats. There were a couple of bookcases filled with reading books, encyclopedias, and a dictionary. The American flag was pinned to the wall above the slate board. A larger, wood desk for the teacher was placed at the front of the classroom. Just inside the front entrance, there were a couple of small rooms to hang our coats, a cupboard for lunch bags, and a washbasin with a pail of water.

Outside the school building was the usual playground equipment, old hand water pump, two outhouses, and the coal shed. One of the neighbor ladies, Gladys Hessman, planted several flowers to brighten up the grounds.

In August, my mom would take my older brother and me into the county superintendent's office to get our schoolbooks. Mrs. Eichman was the county superintendent and her office was located in the courthouse at Jetmore, Kansas. Mrs. Eichman always knew which books we would need according to our grade level and the state requirements.

School days always started after Labor Day in September. We would only take a few days off to celebrate certain holidays, so our school was out for the summer in April. We enjoyed school, as it was fun and a wonderful learning experience. We were taught the basic education of reading, writing, mathematics, history, and how to use the dictionary and encyclopedias.

The country schools would have holiday programs and other activities to involve the whole community. Students would memorize lines to a play or poem, and then perform their talents in front of family and friends. My first grade teacher, Miss Tieben, was so proud of me, because I had memorized a long poem for our Christmas program. When it was my turn to recite the poem, I was so shy and spoke in a whisper so no one heard a word. I think that was the same time when Santa Claus came in wearing my daddy's shoes.

We would sometimes have a box supper to help raise money for the school. Ladies, young and old, would pack a lunch in a box, and then decorate the box to attract a man. The men and boys would bid on the boxes in hopes of having supper with a special lady. I was in third grade and found out my great-uncle, Elmer, was going to attend our school program and box supper. I adored Elmer and asked him to buy the box that I had decorated. I was so proud to share my lunch with a special man.

We would take an educational field trip in the early spring. I can remember going through the sugar beet factory, the Coca Cola Bottling Company, the milk producers company, the potato chip factory, Lee Richardson Zoo, Boot Hill and Horse Thief Canyon for our field trips.

Recess time was never boring, and all the students were actively involved in some game. We would play baseball, fox and geese, Annie over, hide and seek, drop the hankie, and hopscotch. There were times the boys would torment the girls by locking them inside the outhouse or coal shed. The boys would catch bull snakes and put them in the outhouse or inside the school.

Buckner Valley had finally served its purpose as a school and closed its doors in 1958 or 1959. The old school still stands on a corner in southwest Hodgeman County, Kansas. It is now a local landmark and home to the birds and wild animals.

How Hutchinson Helped Win the War
By Lolita (Bonnie) Baker of Hutchinson, Kansas
Born 1933

Thank you so much for allowing me to participate in your storytelling project. My kids keep asking me to write about some of my lifetime adventures. I am almost 81 years old, and I have had a wonderful, satisfying life.

My four children have married and produced 13 grandchildren for me, and they, in turn, have presented me with 14 great-grandchildren.

Most of my lifetime has been spent in this small city that I love called Hutchinson, Kansas. For two years, however, I lived in Sasebo, Japan as a US sailor's young bride. And I was a Fulbright Exchange teacher in Southampton, England for one year. I also lived one year at the Alameda Island Naval Air Base near San Francisco.

My travels have been throughout Europe, the Holy Land, India, Hong Kong, Mexico, and Canada, as well as 47 of the United States.

I hope you find my story about how the Hutchinson folks helped win World War II interesting, unique, and just the type of article you were looking for. It was a joy to recall those young life experiences.

Shortly after the United States entered World War II, our small farming community, Hutchinson, Kansas, became significantly involved in it.

It was 1942, when the US Military was ordered by the government to construct a naval air base just south of Hutchinson. Most of the farms were owned by Amish Mennonites. They were conscientious objectors and they would never fight in a war, but they cooperated as they sold their land to our government for this project.

About 1,000 Navy men arrived in September of 1942, but the airbase was not ready to house them. So the 4-H building at the Kansas State Fairgrounds was used for their barracks. Our family did not have any extra rooms, but some of my friends with big houses got to have the officers stay with their families.

By 1943, Hutchinson was well entrenched with military men, but they were not all citizens of the United States! Now, a group of German Prisoners of War (POWs) were being 'jailed' in the 4-H dormitories at the Kansas State Fairgrounds. Why here, you might wonder: because the young German men replaced our farmers who had been drafted. Each day, busses distributed them out to the farms to work in the fields. These young German POWs found many commonalities of Kansas farmers and German farmers. Something unusual happened! When the war ended, many Germans brought their own families to Kansas and established farms here in the rural Hutchinson area.

In 1943, I was a gregarious, patriotic girl student at Roosevelt Elementary School. Every Friday my classmates and I faithfully brought our coins to school to purchase stamps for our war bond booklets. When the booklet totaled $18.75, it could be exchanged for a real war bond. In ten years, it could be redeemed for $25.00. My parents used that money for my college education!

One day, our school principal, Miss Casebolt, entered the classroom with the surprise news that the students had purchased enough war bonds to buy an Army jeep. We followed her out to the playground and there it was! Every student got to take a turn riding in it with the soldier driver. How proud we were that day!

Twice a month, I joined my friends for the Junior Commandoes meeting at Mrs. Long's house. Sometimes we baked cookies for the older USO girls to present to the servicemen who rode the troop train through Hutchinson. In our neighborhood, we went house to house to collect kitchen grease, which was used to make Army ammo (I think). We also collected silk hosiery and rubber elastic for use in parachutes. The lack of elastic posed a problem. Our underwear had to be held up by a button instead of an elastic waistband. Yes, there were some embarrassing moments when the button accidently slipped out of the buttonhole.

During this wartime, many grocery items were rationed. Families were issued government food stamps to sparingly purchase meat, sugar, and butter, etc. Because fresh vegetables were sent to the troops, many families exchanged their back grass lawns for a Victory Garden of vegetables.

Gasoline and tires were also rationed to civilians. Automobile factories were busy producing jeeps and other military vehicles, so there were no new cars. People rode bicycles to school and to their work place. Fortunately, my dad owned the bicycle shop here!

Our extended family planned a reunion in Enid, Oklahoma. Dad saved gas coupons so we could drive the 120 miles to join them. Dad would drive slowly and stop often to let the tires "cool off." Finally, one more bridge to cross and we would see our cousins. But the bridge had washed out from a flood. Solution: we ate our picnic on the north bank, and they ate their food on the south bank while we yelled stories to each other across the river!

When the war ended in August of 1945, several teenaged boys made a big bonfire in the parking lot of the grocery store next door to my house. They had firecrackers to explode in it, so I found my leftovers and punk from the Fourth of July and went out to join them. The celebration was halted when the police arrived and the big boys took off running down the alley. There I stood with my string of firecrackers and smoking punk. I thought sure the police were going to throw me in jail, but they just told me to go home. I quietly sang to myself, "God Bless America!"

Family Shenanigans
By Trulin Kinser of Medicine Lodge, Kansas
Born 1931

I came from a large family. There were 14 children, eight boys, and six girls. We were from 11 months to 3 years and 9 months apart. I have one nephew who is about two years older than I am. All of us, with our parents, were only together once in our entire lives. The oldest was born in 1909 and the youngest was born in 1935.

One of the oddities of the family is that six of the children were born with extra toes, fingers, or both. Most of them were able to be removed surgically at birth without too much trouble, but sometimes, especially the toes would be positioned in such a way that it would ruin the confirmation of the foot to have it removed. Sometimes the extra appendage would be on one foot and not the other so they might have 11 toes instead of 12, but the foot would be perfectly formed.

There is mention in the Bible of a giant who was killed in battle, and he had six fingers and six toes. This is a genetic thing that is passed directly to the next generation. If you do not have it you will not pass it on, and all of the children in a family will not have it. Also, none of the boys had a mixed family. They either had all girls or all boys.

At present, there are still eight children living, with the oldest being 103 and the youngest being 79. The oldest brother lived to be 101.

My brother just older than me and I were riding bareback together in the sand hills, about one half mile from home. I was approximately nine and he was eleven. My brother got off to open and shut the gate. When he went to get back on the horse, I was too little to pull him up so we put plan B into action. He climbed up on the top wire that was fastened to the post, and I rode up close enough for him to jump across the back of the horse to be behind me. When he jumped the pressure pulled the staple out of the wire, and he flipped head down and in the fall the top of the post caught the crotch of his pants and left him hanging with his feet in the air and his head toward the ground. He could not reach the ground with his hands so he was just hanging there. I was laughing so hard, I couldn't push him up high enough to get him unhooked. He did not see any humor in it at all. Finally, I was able to quit laughing long enough to get him off. I always wished I'd had a camera for a picture of it.

We would dare each other to put the wagon up on to the peak of the roof of the barn, get in the wagon, and ride it down. The backside of the barn had the roof to the lean-to fastened to the roof of the barn and the roof was much flatter. It was about 24 or 25 feet wide and was the full length of the barn. The challenge was if you went off the edge you landed on the pile of straw and manure from cleaning out the barn stalls. It was on the backside of the barn, and you could only see it from the house from the window of the very back bedroom. Mother could not see it from the rest of the house, but an aunt and uncle lived about one-fourth mile from us, and they could see the back of the barn very well. She never let Mother know what we were doing until we got older and told her.

We were all fascinated with flying, and we would get up on the windmill tower and jump off the second brace up on the windmill. It was 18 to 20 feet above ground. We would jump and flap our arms, trying to fly. Mother could not see the windmill from the house, again, except from the back bedroom. We never broke any bones or got hurt seriously enough to tell her or for her to find out. We would land in a pile of sand which at that time there was plenty of. That was another thing we confessed when we got older.

We were raised without any boughten toys, so we found a lot of other ways to entertain us. One of the games we enjoyed was called root the nail. We would take a pocketknife and open the blades at a right angle. We would hold the longest blade against our chin and flip our head, releasing the blade, and it would flip toward a wet mound of sand we had fixed. We had to stand at a certain distance from the mound. We had three tries, and the way it would land would be a certain amount of points, and you added up your points. The winner would put the point of the nail in the sand and would give it one pound with the handle of the knife, and the loser had to kneel in front of the nail with his hands behind him and pull the nail out with his teeth.

We lived in an area that was really sandy, and we would dig holes deep enough to bury someone up to their crotch standing up with both feet in the same hole. Then they would try to wiggle their feet and legs, trying to get loose. The more you wiggled, the more the sand would slide down and pack tight. There were times when we couldn't get loose, and we had to be dug out.

Snowstorms and Learning to Read
By Hildred Schmidt of Walton, Kansas
Born 1932

Sand Creek School, a one-room school, in Marion County was where I attended third through eighth grade. Third and fourth grades were taught by my sister, who was approximately 12 years older. I was her custodian who cleaned the chalkboards, erasers, swept the floors, carried out ashes, and got the coal from the coal shed/outhouse. This building became a milk barn in the community, a half mile north of my home. The schoolhouse was moved to Moundridge and became a home. My sister's first year of teaching was in a two-room school named Waldeck where she taught the lower grades and was my first year in school. She had books at home that previous summer to prepare. She let me use her books, and I remember thinking that I needed to know how to read because I was going to get to go to school! I followed my parents, sister, and brother all over the farmyard to learn the words I did not know! The result was my first grade teacher at Wareham School in Marion County stopped my dad after the first day of school and told him I was no first grader and wanted to put me in the second grade. My father said no but agreed to let me do first grade work the first semester and second grade work the second semester.

Dogs are my favorite pets. My first dog came from a neighbor and was killed on the road next to where Dad was working in the field soon after I got it. My dad was waiting for me when I got home from school. He knew I would be devastated and had already found out that another neighbor had puppies, so he took me to pick one out! That was a black and white English shepherd I named Grandpaw because one foot was mostly white. The next dog was a black and white border collie we called Fritz and he got to be about 17 years old and mostly deaf and was killed by a propane truck. The next dogs were English shepherds, Pal and Sandy. Sandy was killed by a speeding car and Pal died some years later from cancer. The last dog was Penny, a sable and white purebred English shepherd with long hair. She was very intelligent, understanding over 50 commands or phrases. She had a stroke and about two years later her teeth were getting bad so we got some canned food for her and got the contaminated food and she died a few days later at 16 years, 6 months, and 8 days old. We understand that this food was from China and sent on purpose.

The first radio in the family was a crystal set put together by my brother. It had to be close to the window with the antenna out, which he strung out to the barn. It was very difficult to get it exactly on the station. I liked to listen to the programs called *The Firestone Hour* and *The Telephone Hour*.

We grew up on two farms, both in Marion County. One was my mother's home place nine miles west of Peabody, the other about 4 ½ miles east of it. After her parent's estate was settled, they bought this farm and moved back after three years. It has been in the family for over 100 years. In 1966 my parents, sister, and I had a new house built. Soon after that, the old outhouse became history.

In the Fifties when I was in college at College of Emporia, a big snowstorm prompted the college to dismiss us early for Thanksgiving vacation. Many of us from both colleges made it on the train in Emporia. There were so many of us the aisles were packed with students sitting on suitcases! The train had to move slowly. I had arranged to get off at Peabody where my sister was teaching. She brought tall boots to the station for me, had bought chains for her car, and bought extra groceries and supplies because my parents, brother, and a cousin staying with them could not get to the grocery store. All the roads were blown shut, so we ended up staying in my sister's apartment until the highway was cleared. We got to a mile east of home, parked the car, unloaded suitcases, packed the food we had in them, and walked on the road to the half mile, then cattycorner through the field and pasture to our house. Meanwhile my brother went out hunting and got a jackrabbit, which my mother had prepared for their Thanksgiving meal.

We had a league musical event in Lyons where I was teaching the day of the Hesston tornado. The rehearsal was interrupted by tornado sirens, and we all had to go to the storm shelter inside the high school building. When the news came through, the Hesston students were given the option of staying for the concert that evening or going home. They opted to go home and the concert was presented without them.

Hildred Schmidt at the Wareham School District 28

In 1947, my brother was a student at Bethel College. He had volunteered to go to Europe on a cattle boat, bringing relief to suffering people after the war. The day he was to leave it started to snow heavily so my dad took him to the train depot in Newton, leaving mother and me at home to do the chores, milk ten cows, etc. The weather got worse and worse, but mother wouldn't let me help her milk the cows, because she wanted me to stay inside to answer the phone in case dad called. For a teenager it was a long difficult evening! Finally, dad did call. He had gotten to his mother's house about three miles from home. The mile going east of Highway 15 was so snow packed and the snow blowing so hard he had to scoop out a car length, move the car, scoop out again, etc. for about a third of the mile. Then he went south to Grandmother's house. I don't remember whether he walked or drove that quarter of a mile.

My brother didn't make it to his destination on the east coast on time. They had to wait for another boat. This boat carried mules and went to Greece. He took his chemistry assignments along and studied on the way back and his understanding chemistry instructor let him do the experiments after he got back. On the way back, the ship, Woodstock Victory, was caught in a rough hurricane but survived. Some years later while vacationing, we spotted that ship in the harbor in San Francisco. He got to get on it and about didn't make it off the ship as it was leaving the harbor!

Party line phones and rotary phones, we had them. If there was a message for the community, the operator would ring a long ring and give the message. There were some people who would eavesdrop on your conversations so we were careful what we talked about.

We had a wind up record player, a washer powered by moving handle back and forth to a Maytag with gasoline motor with a wringer, homemade clothes, some from feed sacks, and a battery powered portable radio. My brother and sister had homemade toys. We all helped with farm chores: shocking, threshing, trucking wheat, oats, etc., filling the silo, driving tractors, cleaning up machinery, shingling, gathering eggs, picking mulberries and currants, mowing the grass, from cutting by hand to push mower, to gasoline powered push mowers to riding mowers.

Music Lessons and Female 'Tom' Cats
By Alice R. Uphoff of Hutchinson, Kansas
Born 1925

My name is Alice Uphoff. I live in Hutchinson, Kansas. I was raised in a little town of Florence, Kansas. The following paragraphs were all from when I was a child at Florence. A few of my remembrances I will try to bring to you.

I was born in 1925 at a little town of Florence, Kansas, 15 minutes before my twin sister was born. A birth of twins was a rarity back in those days. I was the fifth child of seven children born in the same house that our mother was born in back in 1882. Eight of the grandchildren were also born in the same house.

The first was the running water that we had. You took a bucket, ran to the well, pumped the pump handle until the bucket was full, and then you ran back to the house with it. And being well water was it ever cold!

When the electricity went off in a storm, we would all sit in front of the wood burning stove, watching the flames through the isinglass windows of the wood burning stove door. When the lights were on, you really could not see the flames. This is why we kids were never really afraid of storms.

Daddy gave guitar lessons in Florence, Marion, and Cedar Point. The ones I remember him giving lessons to was the Weidenbrenner boys and their sister in Marion, Ralph Linnens in Cedar Point, John Edwards, and George and John Dresher. He gave mandolin lessons to their sister, Mary Margaret in Florence. Paul Dresher, their dad, had the shoe repair shop in Florence, and he repaired all our shoes in return for his children's lessons. Mother also taught piano to Mary Margaret. This was also supposed to be in return for shoe repair, but she never left after a lesson but what she left a fifty-cent piece on the end of the piano.

Mary Margaret got good enough to play the organ at the Catholic Church. The year she was to play for the midnight Mass at Christmas, she especially asked Mother to come to the Mass just to hear her play. She asked Mother if she had a hat (at that time all ladies had to wear a head covering when entering the church). Mother said she did so she did not have to borrow one from Mrs. Dresher.

Back to Daddy's trips to give lessons. On one of Daddy's trips to Marion, we stopped on the way home to go swimming in the Cottonwood River. Mother went in, too, holding her dress up and wading in almost to her knees!

Whatever Daddy set his mind to, he pursued the project until he was an expert at it. He was an expert on the guitar, mandolin, clarinet, writing music, composing, and transposing music, all self-taught and in the study of the Bible.

Daddy always shaved on Wednesday and Saturday nights. Wednesdays had to be done early, before he went to I.O.O.F. Lodge. He always used a straight razor, setting at the dining room table with a shaving mirror, a cup of soap, a shaving brush, and a piece of newspaper tucked under the shaving mirror to wipe the used soap and whiskers on. Sometimes he would put some soap on our faces and pretend to shave us using the backside of the razor. And of course, he always had a razor strap handy to sharpen the razor on. And I still have a razor strap hanging in my bathroom now in memory of my dad!

The oleo we bought (we couldn't afford butter) was white with a little packet of coloring with it. If you wanted yellow 'butter' you had to kneed in the coloring into the white oleo. It really did not change the taste, but the yellow 'butter' sure was a lot better than the white 'butter.' The boxes the oleo was in had doll furniture printed on the inside of them. This was a gimmick to get people to buy that brand of oleo. We, with Mother's help, of course, would carefully cut them out and assemble them for doll furniture to play with.

In preparation for Sunday, all shoes had to be polished on Saturday night. I can still see them in my mind, lined up from the biggest to the smallest, waiting to be shined. We only had one pair of shoes apiece so they had to look their best (for whatever that is worth) on Sunday. I do not remember having a new dress for Easter, but we always had new Easter shoes. After wearing the same shoes all winter, we were ready for new shoes by Easter.

The back bedroom was the only room in the house large enough for two beds, one for the girls and one for the boys. Mother and Dad were a little leery about letting the boys sleep in the basement. With a little coaxing from the boys, they decided to try it, and it worked out real good. Then we girls had a room of our own! We still only had one bed so we three girls all slept in one bed, with me in the middle because I was the littlest.

My oldest brother was still at home, running the projector at the movie theater when Mother fell down the basement (primary department) of the church one Sunday. By 3:00 p.m. her arm was hurting so bad that she finally consented to go to the doctor. She had refused to go until then, because that would cost money that she thought we did not have. Sure enough, her arm was broken. She baked the bread for the family and she worried about how that would get done. I mentioned that Bill was still home. He took over the job of baking the bread for the family of seven kids, Mother, Dad, and Grandpa, and he got pretty good at it.

The 6th Street where we lived was the sledding hill of the town. And we had a lot more snow than we do now. My oldest brother had friends that lived at the top of the hill in what we thought was a mansion. It was a big house. She was afraid they (the kids) would get her house dirty, but they (the kids from all over town) were always welcome at our house. During sledding times, our house would have wall-to-wall (or so it seemed) newspapers to catch the snow and drips and whatever else the town kids brought in. As I remember the older boys never went to her house in good weather, but her boys always came to our house.

When we got to about the second grade Mother decided it was time for my twin, Alta, and I to learn to play the piano. Our big sister had learned from Mother, but Mother thought we would learn better from someone else. So our sister agreed to clean house for Mrs. Mader in exchange for lessons. So we started our musical education. But you know what they say – practice makes perfect. Who wanted to be perfect anyway? So after a while this effort went by the wayside. However, later in high school, I realized I made a mistake in not continuing the lessons! So I started on the piano again. Later I became the organist and pianist at the Abbyville Christian Church for 18 years, then the pianist at the Chase Christian Church for another four years until they disbanded.

Whenever we discovered a leak in the house, Daddy would give one of us kids some wires and put us up in the attic. When we saw daylight through the roof, we would stick a wire through the hole. Daddy would put a shingle there. And it always seemed to work! No more dripping in the house. The back bedroom had a flat roof, and every two to three years Daddy would heat tar to a liquid and mop the tar onto the roof.

As a child, we always had a cat. We had several cats. My brother, Bill, brought a kitten home and asked Mother if we could keep it. Mother said no, we couldn't afford to feed another mouth. Besides, not only this cat but there would be little ones, time after time to be fed and find good homes for. Bill assured Mother that it was a 'tom cat' so there would be no litters to worry about. So she relented. Bill named the cat Mickey after his best friend, Keith Mickey Shelton. Bill and his friends spent a lot of time at Keith's radio shop. Well, after a time Mickey proved to be a female cat and of course, did have litter after litter of kittens. By then everyone was attached to the cat and could not let her go. It was standing joke for years to come that Bill's tomcat had kittens. And we always seemed to find good homes for the little ones! Fritz Alders Dairy took a lot of them. And Mother was happy for that because she knew that they would always be well fed!

There was at time after I was married that we had so many mice (one was too many). Mother offered us the services of Mickey, because she had proven to be a good mouser. So we took her to the farm in a basket with a lid on it. When we got home and took the lid off the basket, Mickey ran and we did not see her again, on the farm, that is. Six months later she appeared back at my folk's house. She was fat as could be and her fur was so soft!

In 1943 Florence had a flood. It was four to six inches in the house. Mother and Daddy stayed in the house to be there when the water went down so as to sweep out the flood silt with the water. They heard something at the door. When they went to the door, there was Mickey! She had swum through the floodwaters to get home. The folks were so happy because they thought she had drowned in the flood. Mickey lived to be 23 years before she died.

I could tell other stories about living in a small town, but that will have to do for now.

Fourteen Years of Age
By Marion L. Hearn of Stafford, Kansas
Born 1931

Dear Alesia,

So you're 14 years old. Have you ever thought of what your life would have been like if you didn't have electricity until after your 14th birthday?

Well, that was your Grandpa Hearn's age when they got electricity on the farm where he was born. The power line was on the west side of the road, and it carried electricity to the town of Hudson a few miles north. For some reason the power company wouldn't cross the road to furnish electricity for those living on the east side, but after four or five years

Marion and his twin, Melvin sitting on their grandfather, T. E. Tuchwood's lap

they finally did. Dad's niece's husband, Gib McVey, wired the house, and when he was through and the electricity was turned on, the folks turned on a new electric radio and they were given the news that President Franklin D. Roosevelt had died. It was April 12, 1945. For that reason I've always remembered that day in history. The folks didn't think of getting any light bulbs and Mr. McVey only had a 200 watt one that we used that first night. Man, was it *bright* after what we had been using. The radio we had before then was one that was big enough to have a car battery in the back of it. I don't remember how long the battery would last before taking it to town to have it charged, but it lasted for several weeks.

I would like to bring to your attention some of the things I recall about growing up in those conditions.

Though you never knew my identical twin, Melvin, you will note that from time to time I will use "we" and "our" because it is still a part of my life. Once a twin always a twin. We were born March 18, 1931 in the farmhouse, which was my home until your

Grandma Wanda and I were married October 24, 1952. Melvin spent the rest of his 58 years living in the same house in which we were born.

Our source of light at night was the coal oil lamps, which didn't put out much light. They had to be kept full of oil, and the glass chimneys had to be cleaned quite often, because they would put out smoke part of the time and would smoke up the glass, especially if they were turned up too high. We later had gas lanterns that had two cloth mantels and a little pump-to-pump up the pressure that put out much more light than the coal oil ones did. That was the kind of light that we studied by, put puzzles together by, and played cards, checkers, and caroms by. Caroms was played by shooting little rings with your finger into corner pockets.

I remember one Christmas the folks gave us some little army tanks that when pushed along on the floor they would shoot little sparks from the gun barrels. We'd go into the bedroom, get under the bed where it was dark enough that the sparks really showed up, and push them back and forth to each other.

Another time we were given little cars with rubber wheels, and we'd lower the oven door and play with them on it, and one time we 'parked' them in the oven and shut the door. The next time Mother used the oven she didn't look in it, and as the oven was getting hot you could smell hot rubber. That was the last time we played with the cars on the oven door, but then they didn't have wheels anymore.

Another year our Christmas gift was a little tool box that had a pair of pliers, a hammer, and a saw in it. What did we do? We took the saw and sawed the handle off the hammer! That was a no no!

Our Christmas gifts consisted of a toy and some clothes; usually a pair of gloves, overshoes, or some other needed item to wear.

We always looked forward to coming into town to Grandma and Grandpa Tuckwood's for Christmas dinner. She always gave each of her many grandchildren a crisp new one dollar bill and a new handkerchief. Grandma and Grandpa lived in the white stucco house at 611 West Broadway. Grandma and I moved into town to 221 West Broadway on October 16, 1982.

Thanksgiving was also a memorable one as we always had dinner at Uncle Jess Tuckwood's. Then there was the annual football game between Stafford and St. John that many attended.

In the wintertime we would bring in a wood stove, which as stored in the wash house during the summer. There was wood to chop and carry in and then the ashes had to be carried out. I remember Dad chopping the wood with an ax, as we didn't have chainsaws then.

With no electricity to run an electric pump we would go outside to the well, which was close to the house and pump water by hand and carry it into the house in a bucket, and it took several buckets full a day even when conserving it in many ways. What was carried in had to be carried back outside, so none of it was wasted.

We didn't get to town but a couple times a week, on Saturday night, to buy groceries and to go to church on Sunday. The only thing that was bought was flour, sugar, fruit, cornmeal, and salt.

We had our own chickens and eggs. Dad would buy 300 baby chickens in March from the Stafford Hatchery on West Broadway, and that building has just been torn down this fall. The man that ran the hatchery always gave Melvin and me each a little black chicken. We would take the baby chicks out to the farm and put them in the brooder house, which was a small building with a brooder stove, which the chicks could get under the big cover to keep warm. They soon became big enough to grow feathers, and when they got a little older we would catch them and put them in the larger chicken house where they grew to become old enough to lay eggs. Then we would gather 180 to 200 eggs a day. The eggs were brought into town and sold to a farmers produce where they were either shipped out in trucks or taken to the Santa Fe Depot and shipped out by train. We ate many or all of the male chickens, or roosters, when they reached three or four pounds. When they reached that stage we would take a day and dress or clean 65 or 75 of them and bring them into town to the storage locker where we could stop by and get them as needed.

The chicken house and brooder house were both built by our father and his brother and since we didn't have electricity all the boards were sawed by hand with a hand saw.

Bother buildings are still on the farm, though the brooder house is in bad condition and the chicken house is used for storage.

We had our own meat supply from the cows and pigs that were butchered and ham and bacon was hung in the wash house to cure out after 'curing salt' was rubbed on them and left to cure for two or three weeks. We ground, seasoned, and stuffed our own sausage.

There was a lot of fat that was trimmed off the pig that was rendered, and that process consisted of putting it in a large cast iron kettle over a wood fire out in the yard, and it was stirred several times when it was cooking and we would put the lard in five or six gallon stone jars and set them in the cellar where it would keep through the winter. A lot of lard was used to fry chickens, steaks, porch chops, etc. After frying meat several times, the grease would be saved to make soap with. I remember stirring lye, which was a white powder and came in a can, into the melted grease. After stirring a while it would thicken, at which time it was put in a round dishpan to be broken or cut into pieces after it had cooled. Mother would usually put a chunk about the size of a large bar of today's soap into the washing machine, which was run by a gasoline motor. Remember, we didn't have electricity. When several loads of clothes were washed what was left of the chunk of soap was kept to use the next washday, which was always on Monday. Tuesday was ironing day.

Not having electricity we would have a bucket hanging in the well mainly to keep butter in. It wasn't long until we got an ice chest that was set in the dining room that would hold 100 pounds in one side, and we'd have our butter, milk, and eggs in the other side. There was a drip pan under the icebox that needed to be emptied as the ice melted. If it was not emptied in time and ran over then the floor would get scrubbed. We got our blocks of ice from the icehouse in Stafford, which was in the same building that the State Farm Insurance is at the present time.

When Melvin and I got to be eight or nine years old Melvin would drive the tractor to pull the combine, which Dad would stand on a platform to operate it. I remember when our hired man would bring the wheat to the granary in a wagon pulled by a team of horses, and he'd scoop the wheat into the bins. We learned to drive the tractor at an early age. It was a John Deere D that had steel wheels with lugs. Later Dad put rubber tires on it, which was quite an advancement. Melvin and I put a battery on it and one headlight so we could run it after dark part of the time. The first truck Dad got was a used Model A, and he traded a milk cow for it.

In the summer we spent several afternoons with Jim in a group of trees quite a ways west of their house in which we had a rope tied to a branch that had a sack of wheat straw tied to it and a ladder propped up against another tree close by. We'd climb the ladder and jump off onto the sack of straw and swing for quite a while.

After getting electricity Melvin and I started saving dimes to buy an electric train, which we'd wanted for a long time. When we were juniors in high school we had saved $19.00 worth of dimes, which was enough to buy the train. We mounted the track on a 4 by 8 piece of plywood and all the family enjoyed it for a long time. I still have the train but it doesn't work anymore. I also have the box it came in, which is about as valuable as the train, which I have been informed is worth over $200.00.

By the time we had enough dimes saved up we had other funds that we purchased the train with and kept the dimes, which was the beginning of several years of coin collecting. I always said that Melvin collected the coins, and I kept them in circulation.

Hope you enjoy the memories I have thought of, and I want to wish you a happy 14th birthday and many more with much success in the years to come.
Love,
Your grandfather

Just Stick Around
By Richard L. Sandoval of Beaufort, Missouri
Born 1943

A brown boy watched as a black man with his sleeves rolled up plowed the huge spring garden spot with his proud mules. Black, black earth turned over smoothly and effortlessly in the wake of his bright and shiny blades. The fresh, moist, rich odor filled the western

Rich and his sister, Virginia in 1946

Kansas air as the dark man softly clicked and talked; his mules seemed to read his mind and plowed without the need for instruction.

That fall with all of the garden gone, two suntanned children played around that summer's burning garden brush – the boy browner than brown and his sister very fair. As in America's cultural script where minorities are frequently the victims, she said, "You be the Indian and I'll be the cowboy, and I'll brand you." Of course, he agreed, and she picked up the burning stick and kept that scripted promise.

He watched his young, handsome father with beautiful hazel eyes and muscular arms as he turned the crank on the green Model T with black running boards. He tried and tried again and would quickly run to the key. When old cars were cranked and the engine caught, the key had to be turned on simultaneously. Dad was not fast enough to be in two places at once. Finally, in exhausted desperation he said, "Son, can you try it? Be careful; that crank will kick back. It can break your arm." The little boy grabbed the cold, dark, heavy metal, turned with all his might, and jumped back quickly. Much to his astonishment, it fired (started).

"It's just soda pop." Or so the sisters and brothers said. "Let's put a hose in the barrel and you suck it out." And so they did. He sucked it through the hose. Oh, no, he couldn't breathe! "Call Mom! Call Dad!" What can it be? Dad, the hero man, came. In his arms, he placed his son on the handlebars of his bike and rode him to the doctor, our friend.

Four children slept in our rollaway cot, our ship, our African Queen. But then, there was no more room for the fifth among all those crossed-legged sleepers. The oldest was pushed from the nest to make room for all the rest. There was a place at Grandma's house. Back and forth and back and forth. Which place was home?

The tub – hot tub, cold tub. How many children can you rub in the tub for the Saturday night bath?

The First Street Neighborhood, Seven-Day Adventist, Catholic, and Protestants. White people, German people, black people, and brown people. Dirt fights and rock fights. Mother always said, "Don't bring your fights in here. You get over it and all be friends again."

"The casita," the little house. Let's play Doctor. Pretend we are married, a first kiss. So we kissed, a young miss and the suntanned child boy, and it was so sweet. But then the sky fell in that next day when Betty Ireland – or

Rich Sandoval at about five-years-old

was it Englishman – announced her parents' view: "I washed and washed until I washed all of you off of me." A heart was lost; a heart was broken. If you are brown, just maybe stick around.

That first day of school, I remember it well. It was just yesterday. She held my hand, that most perfect Madre. We walked up the step of Hutchinson Elementary, now gone. The squeaky wooden floors, the smell of crayons and freshly varnished floors. Into the classroom, we stepped to wooden desks with fancy metal scrolls down the side and flip top tops. Real ink well, too.

Truant I was that first year and played in dirt piles all day in front of my mom's best friend's house. A spanking I got and swore never to skip again. I remember my dad saying, "This will hurt me more than you."

Jane and Dick; Dick and Jane. I hated them both – and their families, too. I memorized that book, or at least the first and second pages. But then they knew – Dick and Jane – and my classmates, too. I couldn't read in the first or second or third. Held back and a failure.

Angry, bully, tough guy on the outside. But crying on the inside and no place to hide. My friend saw my misery and said, "Fess up. You're nothing but a bully, bully, bully. And you've got to change." I said to myself, I can change; I will change.

So we played – black kids, brown kids, and white. We learned not to fight, but to play and race. Football, soccer, basketball, softball, track and field. We discovered a special brown role model, a coach named Mojica. We learned a champion could achieve without a fight and to play with all our might.

"This is KIUL Radio." That was the local station. They played Bozo the Clown, Snow White, and other children's stories. Children were guests and the announcer asked, "Where did you get that beautiful tan?" And I said, "That's not a tan. I'm Mexican and Mexicans are brown."

Life magazine came to Garden City, to our school. It was for National Education Week. Tommy the Lion was in our classroom, too and the photo they took became quite famous. We were all stars, but didn't know it. The winds had changed.

I first learned to really read in the fourth grade. <u>Squanto and the Pilgrims</u>; I remember that book still. He was a brown boy like me.

Perhaps that is what kept my attention. My fifth grade teacher asked on a Friday, "Do you have a library card?" "No," I said, and she gave me an article on Huskies to read over the weekend. I read it. On Monday she said, "Did you like the story? Can I help you get a library card?" "Yes," I said. I read and I read shelves of books, but that is not all it took.

My sixth grade teacher said, "You are my card (someone with a sense of humor). You have the special sense of humor, and there is in you something quite exceptional. I have heard your father is a good speaker. Would you ask your father to come and speak about being Mexican American and about Mexico?" He did and he was very good.

The sixth grade teacher helped me to learn and to understand. It's in every one of us to be quite special. She helped me to believe in myself.

Mr. King was a teacher, too. Born a slave, he said. Became a free man and a farmer and quite successful. But life had taught him to be very careful. But still he gave his land and all his farming equipment to his sons. And all was lost at a great cost. But the black man taught the brown boys about life and work and drive. In another time, he might have been a football star, a pro. He taught us how important it was to know to learn and with all of life's success to never forget caution.

Mrs. Price was a teacher, a graduate of the famed Tuskegee Institute. She was not allowed to teach, her color wrong. But in Garden City, she taught in her home using her books and the piano. She taught about life and how to rise above the strife and life's barricades and how to succeed. Her students – brown boys and girls – became writers, photographers, newspaper people, educators, and musicians. Should we just "stick around?"

New Life
By Evelyn Crockett of Offerle, Kansas
Born 1932

A newborn, calf is very wobbly on its feet
Facing a brand new world to meet
It matters not how large or small
They always seem to take the first fall
Our children were like that too
But Mom and Dad were there when they

were blue
Because growing up is hard to do!
They taught us how to tie our shoes.
And count to ten by two's.
A little child is like a beautiful rose.
All started from a bud, small and compact.
Even to the smallest freckle on their nose!
Let their love stay true to us,
When we are wrinkled and old.
Because love is more precious than any wealth or gold!

Potato Chips, Ice Cream, and the Party Line
By Diane Berry of Hutchinson, Kansas
Born 1943

When I was growing up in Sterling, Ks. The elementary school I attended was across the street from the Sheriff. In his garage, he had a huge black pot, fired by an open burner on the bottom. He made potato chips. At recess, we were allowed to go over to his house and get a small brown bag of chips for 5 cents. Of course, the bag was dripping with grease but those were the best potato chips ever! This was in 1951.

I remember gathering around the radio to listen to the Jack Benny show. & Roy Rogers and the Singing Cowboys. And some scary ones I can't recall the names. In the summertime, we always had a big bowl of ice cream as we listened to the radio.

When my husband and I were dating, we had the old crank wall phones and an operator would answer and say "Number Please." When he called me, we were always interrupted by the operator, needed to get off the line as someone else wanted to use it. Back in those days, everyone on the party line could hear your conversation.

How fondly I remember the ice cream plant. I could walk to it and get a nice chocolate covered ice cream bar for 5 cents.

When I was in high school I worked at the local cafe, had to wear the white nylon uniform and hair net. Jukebox was 5 cents, coffee 5 cents, and steaks around $4.00. I was only making $.40 an hour but I made good tips.

I keep telling my children and grandchildren I wish I could turn back time for a day and let them see the world as it was in the '50s. They'd never make it!

Duck Hunting and the Skunk
By Dave Ackerman of Canon City, Colorado
Born 1948

As a farm boy growing up in Southwest Kansas, I always loved to hunt. One day during my high school years, my best friend and I decided to go duck hunting. With no large bodies of water in our area, our favorite hunting method consisted of sneaking up on small pasture ponds. This particular cold November day we had already struck out at a couple.

At our next pond, we crawled along the pasture draw towards a small earthen dam and immediately became excited as we heard ducks quacking. Our excitement increased as we slowly crept to the top of the dam and peaked over. Our patient pond hopping was rewarded with the sight of a flock of green headed mallard ducks.

We looked at each other; jumped to the top of the dam, and began firing at the flock as it flew off. As we shot simultaneously, one duck spiraled to the ground on the other side of the pond. (We decided we had both shot at the same duck!)

Unlike a wounded pheasant that can hit the ground and run, we knew the duck should be easy to find, so we took our time as we walked to the spot where we thought it had landed. As we approached the heavily weeded draw to locate and retrieve our duck, we heard the weeds rustling. Thinking we had found the wounded duck, my friend leapt right in the middle of the tall weeds and received the surprise of his life. This particular "duck" was black with a white stripe down its back and a tail lifted straight up in the air. He received the full blast, and it didn't take long for the smell to hit.

He took off running at high speed escaping the skunk but not the odor. Fortunately, we had driven his pickup, and he hopped into the bed of the truck. Holding my breath, I jumped behind the wheel and took off driving to his house as fast as I could. We skidded into the yard and ran to the door only to be greeted by his mother who refused to let him in the house.

He'll have to tell the part about how they got the smell off his body. I went home thankful he was the one who made the leap. The truly sad part of this story is that we never did find our duck.

Godly Grandparents
By Joan Clayton of Clovis, New Mexico
Born Unknown

My godly grandparents had a great influence upon my life. I loved to hear Granddaddy pray in that little country church. On bended knees, his prayers came straight from his heart. I don't remember the words but I do remember the humility.

In the summer, the ladies used those pretty paper fans on sticks with flowers on them. No one knew anything about air conditioning.

I can almost taste Granny's pickled peaches and fried chicken. My job was to catch one of her pullets and pick the peaches for Sunday dinners. "No one can cook peach cobblers like Sister Farrar," the visiting revival preacher said.

Granny made pallets for my younger brother and me under the big tent revival. My nurtured soul drifted off to sleep amidst those grand old church hymns. Granny's early morning rendition of those same songs, the smell of bacon frying and the soft goose feather bed made me think heaven had to eat Granny's house.

Granny had one of those wall telephones. Her ring was three rings and one short. That didn't matter. Granny eavesdropped anyway. She shushed me to be quiet before she quietly took off the receiver. That was how all the news spread in that little town.

Granny always sang when she churned in that dasher crock with that funny looking stick with crossed boards at the bottom. Her cow gave lots pf cream and the butter always came to the top.

"Bossie" had a bridle and Granny would lead her to a good place around her house that had lots of Johnson grass. Then she staked Bossie with a long rope. About noon, she brought Bossie to the water tank and then took her to the shade of the barn.

I can almost taste that milk with crumbled up cornbread in my bowl.

I have Granny's butter mold and I wouldn't part with it for anything.

Many times the all of us cousins met my brother and me at Granny's. Being the only female among them all, I tried to be "The Brat's Boss," but I had a larger cousin who packed a harder punch.

"I'll be the preacher this time!" My robust cousin shouted.

"No!" I persisted. "It's my time. Just cross this line."

"Okay kiddo!" Then we boxed.

I picked myself up saying, "Then I'm going to be song leader." "Who cares?" the gang retorted.

"We're singing, "When we all get to heaven what a surprise that will be." So I sang at the top of my voice while my chorus half-heartedly chimed in. Granny smiled behind the door.

It all stopped when we heard the big black puffing train engine coming. We hurried to wave at the engineer. We counted the cars and slugged it out if we disagreed.

Hot and thirsty we marched to the filling station and drank strawberry soda for only a dime. .a treat we tried to make last a long time.

I could never understand then why Granny went around saying, "Mercy! Mercy!" Now I know.

Every once in a while we had "I Double Dare You" day. The rules said it had to be bigger than the last time we played it. I dared them to jump off the barn like Superman.

They sneaked some of Granny's nice clean big towels that she had washed at the country laundry where sometimes the winger went around and around when someone got their sheet wrapped in the winger. My cousins wrapped the towels around their necks and jumped. Amidst their groaning, they got in my face and said, "Okay kiddo, now it's your turn." They huddled together making all kinds of fun about me while trying to think of something daring. They thought of all kinds of things but I would say, "No that's too easy," "Thing of something harder: Finally they approached me with a "gotcha" look.

We double dare you to climb up the

windmill and walk around the fan on that little porch up here.

"Any sissy can do that. Is that the hardest thing you can think of?" I proudly strutted around them. Then I climbed up that rotten old wooden ladder like Jack in the Beanstalk, but inside I shook with fear. Once at the top, I paraded around the fan and took a bow. I sat down a while, acting like the windmill had become my throne, and my cousins were my peasant subjects. The truth of the matter is I was too scared to come down. A neighbor saw me and ran to tell Granny. The boys ran and hid. Somehow, I managed to come down as Granny said, "Mercy! Mercy!"

My grandparents' house still stands in that sleepy little town. We stopped and looked at it recently. I wanted to go inside and become a child again, feeling the same childhood excitement. Maybe Granny's calico apron or even the aroma of gingerbread still remained. I thought I could almost see it in the photo of my mind.

A house with love in it, that's what it had been for me. A precious memory that time can never erase.

"Don't go yet," I pleaded with my husband, "Let me look just a little bit longer."

My grandparents gave me love, faith, and courage. I learned what heaven must be like.

Going back to my childhood summers in the Depression reminds me today what is really important in life.

Being content with what you have with those you love is the only way to be happy.

Lesta Freeman with her dog, Pal in 1948

Some of my Favorite Memories
By Lesta Freeman Esser of Riverton, Wyoming
Born 1946

Memories certainly become more precious as life is zipping by! I always loved school and started out in a one-room schoolhouse in the country. My teacher, Mrs. Clawson was the best. I began first grade at Mingona. I listened in on the older grades as they had their lessons and learned from the other kids. We didn't have much playground equipment but I do remember a merry-go-round. We played games instead like Red Rover, marbles, and baseball. There was certainly no grass. Oh, how I loved special events, like the holidays. At Halloween, Mrs. Clawson set up different stations. Like guessing how many beans in a jar and bobbing for apples. I just thought that was so fun. We had an evening family masquerade party. My mother dressed up and coached me not to give away how she was dressed. My daddy let her out down the road from school and she walked the rest of the way to conceal her identity. I was so excited I could hardly contain myself! Christmas time was very special and a community affair. We put on a big program and Santa came when it was over. We all got a brown sack filled with an orange and candy. I loved those chocolate drops.

We lived in the country for several years. That was great except for the snakes. I hated the big bull snakes that lived under the wheat granary. I would go to gather eggs and the snakes would be eating the eggs, so scary. My little dog, Pal, would try to protect me. The snakes weighed more than him but he was still very brave. We were lucky to have inside plumbing but we still had to haul water because the well couldn't keep up. I learned how to conserve water. My Mother and I also went to town once a week to do laundry, usually on Saturday.

We also did grocery shopping. Saturday evening was a social time as people parked their cars on Main Street and visited. When we first had television, the stores that sold televisions would turn them toward the street so people could sit in their cars and watch!

When I was young, polio was such a scare. My folks were so afraid I would get the disease. My daddy wouldn't let me swim in the local swimming pool because he didn't want me to get exposed to the disease with all those people. People my age were living their life in an iron lung. I can remember the day the news announced an immunization for polio. Soon after, we stood in line on Main Street to get the first vaccine not on a sugar cube. The waiting line wrapped around a whole block as we waited our turn for the miracle.

Turning sixteen only means one thing, getting a car! I was lucky that my uncle was the best car salesman in the country. He found me a great car, a 1955 black Chevy. I was so excited. I think the price tag was $450 in 1962. My daddy told me I had to clean it every Friday and he gave me $2.00 a week gas allowance. Of course, gas was $.20 a gallon. Fortunately, I had no wrecks or no speeding tickets.

Cousins, I had lots of them. We had great family times and excursions together. Probably one of my favorites was the 4th of July. We would gather at my uncle's farm for a wiener roast. He had a small creek that ran through his place and the adults would build a big bonfire by it. We would eat hot dogs and marshmallows. Then we would impatiently wait for it to get dark enough to do fireworks. The kids only got to do sparklers and the men lit the dangerous stuff. One of my daddy's favorites was the 'Roman Candles'.

Before we went to church, my daddy would always wash the car. I don't think we ever drove a dirty car to church or to a funeral. After church, my daddy and I would drive to Medicine Lodge to buy a Sunday newspaper at the local drug store. I would also get to buy a comic book and a 'Cherry Mash'.

Times have changed but lots of memories remain. I haven't lived in Kansas for 45 years but part of my heart still belongs to the Sunflower State.

Riding Cows
By Howard Hamilton of Wichita, Kansas
Born 1922

I was born February 22, 1922. I really don't remember that experience. My earliest memories are events and experiences that go back before I was turned four years old.

I remember going with my older sisters to play in an old house across the road from our farm home. Inside this old house, most of the plaster from the old lath and plaster style walls, and one of those walls had wide spaces between the laths. To me it was like a ladder. This was probably about August of 1925. The weather was warm, and as we returned home, we went up on the front porch. I remember my brother Richard, born January 2, 1924, was napping in a cradle there with a cheesecloth mosquito netting to protect him from the flies.

In that summer of 1925, I remember my mother cutting fresh corn from the cobs and spreading it on newspapers on the floor by an open window upstairs to dry. This was an alternative to canning to provide food for the winter months. I also remember Mother putting curds in an empty cloth sugar sack and hanging it on the clothesline to drain the whey. This was a way to prepare cottage cheese.

Our parents had a Model T Ford, which our mother would drive occasionally. I remember her taking us children to visit family. All I remember is crossing a railroad track when the engine died. Everyone was excited and concerned about getting the car off the tracks before a train came.

I used to play with a little red wagon. I also played with an orange crate, which I laid, on its side making the hinged top swing open like a gate. I'd open that "gate," walk through, and then close it, just as I'd seen my daddy walk through a gate.

In the fall of the year, I remember going with my sister Inez into the apple orchard where she picked dollops of hardened tree sap from the trees. We would carry them in our pockets for watches like daddy had.

Sometime during the fall, I remember going with my three sisters down the very muddy road to the highway to get a butcher knife, which had been left in a newspaper box as a premium for our daddy allowing an advertising sign to be put up on the fence along the highway.

As winter came on, I remember our mother's long-time friend Mrs. Corfield helping our mother made flannel nightgowns for us children. This event probably stuck in my memory because in playing around their rocking chairs I fell on a rocker and cut my forehead, leaving a scar that I carry to this day.

Probably the last of my memories prior to our move to a different home in March of 1926 was of my dad taking my mother to see the farm we were moving to. I was taken along and I remember my dad holding me as he was pointing out some things of interest to my mother, specifically the spring fed stock tank where the water flowed from a pipe in a constant, never-ending stream with no windmill, as we'd required before.

My brother Richard and I were close in age and size and most things we were involved in, we were involved in together. One time on the farm, I suspect it was in early spring as the sheep had not yet been sheared and had a heavy coat of wool, we decided we would treat ourselves to a good ride down the hill from the sheep shed to the far side of the lot in which the sheep were kept. We could maintain a good hold on their wool. They gave us quite a ride, about as exciting as any bronco or bull ride in a rodeo.

It so happened that our dad was working in a field about a quarter of a mile away. He saw what was going on, and before we knew it, he was right there and put a stop to our activity. It was really a good thing because the weather was quite warm and our thoughtless actions would have proven quite detrimental to the sheep.

I believe it was during the summer of 1928 that Dad traded the old model T Ford touring car in on a 1926 Chevrolet touring car. We were all excited about getting the "new" car. Our mother had driven the Ford some, but when she started to drive the Chevrolet, she had a problem with changing from the foot pedal system of the Ford to the gearshift of the Chevy. When she tried to shift from first to second gear, she got it into reverse. This upset her so much; I don't think she ever drove a car again.

The fall of 1928, I experienced my first day of school. My mother dressed me in short pants and shirt and carrying my lunch in a one-half gallon syrup pail, I walked the two miles to school with my three sisters. There was one other boy, Bobby Reatherford, in first grade with me. I had some trouble with a bad temper, probably because of being teased by my sisters. Bobby also had a bad temper and on this first day of school, one of us bumped the other on the slippery slide at the bottom. We were immediately in a fight and had to be separated. I think we had at least one fight per year during our elementary school days.

That school was an old one-room country schoolhouse with a big round furnace and outside toilets. The old coal furnaces, when shut down to control the heat output, would sometimes build up a gas. Then when the gas ignited, there would be a minor explosion. I remember the furnace "blowing up" during class and there being a roomful of smoke and soot. I thought it was kind of exciting.

1929 was a good year for corn production and we had a big harvest. I remember the corn huskers coming in at noon and again in the evening with full wagonloads. It was interesting to me to watch them scoop the corn into the corncribs, which were eventually filled nearly to the roof. I was seven years old and learned that year how they measured the amount of corn harvested. Each inch in depth in the standard wagon box was equal to one bushel of corn. The standard wagon box sides were forty inches and with extra sideboards, a full load was fifty bushels. One hundred bushels was a pretty good day's work for a corn husker, who was usually paid by the bushel.

It was probably at the time of springhouse cleaning that Mom would sort out the worn-out clothes that were beyond repair and we would burn them with the other trash. First though, we had to salvage any usable parts. Any good parts from old bed sheets were saved to make handkerchiefs for the next winter, or for any other use that might be found for them. Portions from pant legs or shirttails were saved for patches. Buttons were removed for possible use on new clothes Mom would make for us.

Another springtime ritual was taking up the living room carpet, hanging it over the clothesline, and beating it with brooms or bed slats until the dust was pretty well beaten out of it.

One of the duties Richard and I had as

young boys was to herd the cattle as they grazed in the wheat fields after harvest to keep them from wandering into the corn or alfalfa fields. In one part of the field was a low area which was overgrown with a thick, waist-high growth of weeds which were known to us a "smart weeds," so-called because if you rubbed your skin with them they would make it "smart" or burn. These weeds were full of blossoms that very heavily scented the air with a fragrance very like that of clover or clover honey. May times we rode horses to herd the cattle. Of course the dog invariable accompanied us and spent much time chasing rabbits. Often, near the end of the day, when the dog chased a rabbit, and as soon as he caught it, we would take it away from him and we'd have fried rabbit for supper. Sometimes while we were herding the cattle we would jump on the back of one of the cows. Some of them didn't seem to mind, but others would give us a ride that would rival the bull rides in a rodeo.

Love at the Filling Station
By Evelyn Mace of Johnson, Kansas
Born 1930

Our schools before 1953 had classes like typing, shorthand, bookkeeping, business math, and now we don't have these classes. The typing classes have been replaced by computers. The computers do all the work—bookkeeping, business math, etc. Shorthand is no longer used. Home Ec. is no longer a class in the high schools either.

Technology has changed in our churches. It is possible to have a recording of the services on DVD's every Sunday morning. When members of the church miss a Sunday, they can pick up a DVD and play it at home on a DVD player. Churches have screens placed in the front of the church so that words and songs can be placed and can be read by the congregation.

It used to be when you get gas at a filling station; only men put the gas in their vehicles. They also checked the oil. There was a time later when the opposite sex started doing the same work.

I had a teacher when I was in the third grade and I remembered she was my favorite. She showed us students the movie "The Wizard of Oz." That movie has been very popular ever since.

Before we had TV, we used to listen to the radio Sunday mornings in our dining room and lay on the floor with our funny papers and follow the radio as they read them.

In 1969, we finally got a black and white TV and then purchased a color TV that was gotten for our Grandpa to watch the same year.

I remember when I was growing up, we washed clothes on Mondays using a wringer washer and rinsing in another tub and hanging the laundry outside on a line. On Tuesday, we ironed our clothes. Today we use automatic washers and dryers to do our laundry.

We went to the movies in a theater and paid 25 cents for adults and 10 cents for children to get in. We bought popcorn as we entered the theater to eat while we watched the movie.

The dirt storms in 1954 were terrible and somewhat destructive. We watched the storm come in from the north and when it got to town, we prepared for it by putting towels around the windows and doors of our house and then stayed inside until the storm went by. It was pretty scary for a while. It was remembered by everyone.

Our children had lots of pets. There was a dog, lots of cats, several ducks, and a goose. We had used our baby bathtub in our back yard for the ducks and goose to play in. It was quite the entertainment for everyone.

Talking about my first love, I met a man who was putting gas in my car at a filling station and we got acquainted and we started dating and finally got married. We ended up owning a service station and a tire shop.

When we had a big garden behind our house, we had lots of green beans and our kids were made to pick them when they were ready to pick. They were made to snap them also. They didn't like the job so when no one was looking, they tossed the beans over their shoulders back into the garden. They got into trouble over not snapping them.

Red Rover, Red Rover, a game throwing the ball over the roof of the garage of the house to the player on the other side was quite popular. Marbles and hopscotch was played a lot.

My parents used to tell us when they used

to get their milk from the milk truck and when it was delivered to the front door of their house. They used iceboxes then. They always went to town to pick up ice at the icehouse on Main Street here in town.

I remembered my parents telling stories about when they went camping with their friends at a lake several miles south of town. There was a swimming hole that they found to go swimming in but it was not a place for swimming. They did it anyway. They got caught and had to pay a fine of $ 25.00. That ended the trip there and they never did go back.

Washday on the Farm
By Carolyn Kay Mohler of Scott City, Kansas
Born 1941

I was born in a country home on March 13, 1941. I never did ask Mom where that home was located. Then we moved to a farm, which Dad purchased. Again, we moved to a much larger farm, which was also purchased. We still own it. The farm is located just a few miles southwest of Shallow Water, Ks. It was a big step for Dad. To me, there was lots of space and a big house. I was 4 years old.

Our farm was a very busy one. We had several horses, lots of cows, a few pigs, and lots of chickens, and turkeys. Plus, two large dogs and many cats. We also had a large garden.

My mother, worked just as hard as my

Bonnie and Carolyn with Baby the colt and Wayleigh the dog

Carolyn and Bonnie

Dad. While Dad worked in the fields, Mom was outside taking care of her many animals, yet she fixed three big meals every day.

I have many fond memories of living on that wonderful farm, but I will tell about washday.

Washday was on Monday—all day Monday. There were seven of us, dad, mom, grandma, and four kids. My brother was the oldest, then 2 sisters, then me. The baby of the family. I loved helping mom with all the chores. So, naturally, I helped on washday.

Our washing was done in a separate building, called the "washhouse." Within that building was a double car garage, a bedroom for grandma, and the room where we washed the clothes. That room was also used to separate the milk, cut up the chickens, and house the deep freeze.

We had a white Maytag machine with a finger-smashing wringer. The machine was filled with warm soapy water from a nearby sink. The drain was located in the middle of the floor. To rinse the clothes we had three galvanized tubs. One filled with warm water, the other two with cold water. The wringer swiveled around to all three. We three girls wore a lot of dresses and white blouses, so there was always lots to wash.

The clothes were washed in soapy water then rinsed two times in the double tubs. The white things were washed first then rinsed in the tub filled with the cold water which bluing had been added.

Mom used Mrs. Stewart's Liquid Bluing. I loved to watch the blue swirl around as mom poured it into the cold water. After the white items were washed, the colored ones were next, and then last would be Dad's very dirty overalls.

My most favorite part was sticking the clothes through the wringer. The machine was electric so the rollers were always turning. Mom was always worried I would get my fingers caught, but I never did. I was very cautious; I knew it would have really hurt.

The clotheslines were behind the washhouse. There were four long wire lines. My sister, Bonnie, remembers hanging up the many pairs of socks and handing clothes pens to grandma. The pens were in a cloth bag with an attached wire so it could slide along. One of my jobs was to wipe each line with a wet rag removing the dirt that always managed to stick to the lines.

My sister and I loved to play between the bed sheets that were draped over the lines. Inside was so nice and cool. Of course, our mother didn't much like it for fear we would pull them down. We usually waited until she wasn't around.

After washday, all those clothes had to be ironed. In the '40s and '50s, everything was made out of 100 % cotton. No dryers or fabric softeners to take out the wrinkles. I didn't help with that very much. I decided it was too hard! Mom thought she would solve the ironing problem by purchasing a mangle. It was a big Ironrite mangle that took up a lot of room. It was difficult to use on small parts; like sleeves and collars. It worked great on large pieces such as tablecloths and curtains. But, they weren't washed that often. We found out it wasn't all that it was "cracked" up to be.

We always had nice clean clothes, not really thinking how much work it was. My sister and I just thought it was a lot of fun.

Our poor mother!

Laundry, Now and Then
By Lorraine L. Lovette of Wichita, Kansas
Born 1929

When I sit and reflect on my childhood, it brings to mind my growing up on the plains of south- central Kansas, and the influence of both my mother and father. Stories of those times spring forth far more readily than did water on those dusty farms.

Wonderful, wonderful summer! We could hardly wait until school was "out" and shoes were "off." We had waited for this with great anticipation. We could stay home all day and see what was really going on there.

The last day of school was exciting. We cleaned out our desks and checked the cloakroom for stray gloves, hats, and scarves. The teacher saw that we all had a stack of our "gold star" workbook pages and art papers. I always had lots of art papers, but was a little shy on "gold star" spelling pages! Things that had been so new & shiny at the beginning of the year were, by then, just plain shabby. Even my ruler was the worse for wear and I hadn't measured all that much. The pencil box, my very great pride and joy, was scuffed and the lid-snap didn't always catch well anymore. I paid special attention to sharpening all of my pencils because I knew that we didn't have a pencil sharpener at home.

The teacher handed us our final report card as we filed out the door. It was inside a sealed envelope, and we were admonished to give the envelope directly to our parents without opening them ourselves. Naturally, everyone peeked once we were out of the teacher's sight. Standing in little clusters, the cards were passed around to prove that we were successful scholars! Of course, everyone passed. I only knew one person who was "held back" and that was because of being too young to start school in Kansas.

We then lugged our belongings to the school bus and climbed on for a last, rowdy ride home. Our lunch boxes were full of crayons and our spirits soared. It was summer at last!

We handed our mother our grade cards as we whooped through the door and ran directly to our "play room" to stash our belongings. We immediately returned to the kitchen and stood in front of Mother smiling broadly, waiting for her to pretend to be amazed that we had passed to the next grade level. There was much hugging and kissing and our cards were passed on to our dad at suppertime. His reaction was much less dramatic. He expected us to do "OK" and gave us a smile and a hug.

My little brother and I played imaginary games all day. We climbed every tree and building on the farm, including the house. We rode our pony or walked to the river just a quarter-mile away. We watched the minnows swim around. We splashed water and ran along the sandbars. There was a little grove of trees between the house and the river. We climbed every single tree either coming or going. I can't remember ever falling out of one of those trees.

The first big decision was dependent upon our mother's discretion. "Can we go barefoot today?" She would take the question under serious consideration and seemed to call upon some invisible oracle for a determination. When the good news came, we whipped off our shoes and stockings and ran out the door.

The sensation is still clear, it was a focus of activity in the summer...bare feet! My feet could feel every grain of sand, every crack in the porch floor, the soft, smooth feel of the living room rug. How could one go outside with these delicate feet? There were rocks and stones and sand and "stickers" out there just waiting!

But in a couple of days, we were running around like Aborigines. A sandbur or "devil's claw," nature's aggravation for the livestock, could slow us down a bit. At least once during the summer one or the other of us managed to step on a rusty nail and had to go to town so the doctor could give us a tetanus shot and avoid getting "lock jaw." We had no idea what this dreaded "lock jaw" was but we were happy for the ice cream cones that followed the shots.

We rode with Dad on the farm machinery and followed him through the barn. When it was time to cut the wheat, we rode in the big, metal box on the combine and let the wheat cover our feet and legs. Sometimes we chewed it like gum. We got hot and dirty and loved every minute.

Sometimes, when it was especially hot, my dad would pull a hayrack up beside the house, then he would put some old bedsprings on the wagon. Mother made soft beds with an assortment of feather-filled mattresses, sheets, pillows, and blankets. We would all lie on the big bed and listen to the crickets, listen to the wind in the cottonwood trees, and look at the constellations in the sky.

Sometimes Daddy would tell us about "the old days" and we fell asleep thinking about Indians that used to live there.

Summer was one long, carefree experience. We invented our days as we moved through them. We never heard the word "bored." Our world seemed endless and endlessly appealing. We thought summer was made for kids like us.

It was not so carefree, however, for the adults. The big screened-in porch off the kitchen was a focal point of activity, especially in the summer. Washday was every Monday and an exciting day for us. Mother had a Maytag washing machine kept to one side of the porch until she moved it to the center and arranged for the big operation. The washing machine had little wheels on each substantial, but slender, leg. The hard part was filling the washer and rinse tubs with water.

Our water was at the windmill and that was approximately half a city block from our house and had to be carried in buckets. Water that was used in the washing machine had to be hot, so Mother either heated it in a copper boiler on the kitchen stove or built a fire under the big black, iron kettle that sat in the yard near the outside porch door. The iron kettle method was preferred in the summer time because it kept the heat out of the house.

The laundry was sorted into large piles beginning with the sheets and other white things. Next, came light-colored clothing, then came dark things and, last of all, the really dirty things including Dad's bib-overalls, rugs and rags. Rags were used for those tasks we use paper towels for today.

Wooden benches were placed to the back and left side of the washing machine. Three square, galvanized washtubs were set on the benches and filled with water. Hot water was poured into the washing machine, warm water in the tubs.

Now came the moment of truth. Would the washing machine motor start? It was a gasoline motor and there was special measuring can with a long spout and the gasoline was carefully measured and poured into the little tank. The motor had to be "kick started" with a sturdy foot-pedal. It usually took several tries to get it going, but when it started, it was loud and lovely. We knew things were as they should be and all was right with the world for Mother.

The first tub sat on the right side of the washing machine and was used to soak the dirtiest laundry items. My dad's overalls went into this tub along with rugs and "rags." The overalls started out every day shiny, ironed, and clean but Dad was a magnet for mud, dust, and any other general farm "mess."

The tub to the back of the machine was the "first rinse" and the water was warm. The tub on the bench to the left of that tub was the "second rinse" with cool, but not cold, water. Can you visualize that very sturdy old washing machine with a bench and two square tubs at the back and a tub to the right?

Now, it was time for Mother's homemade lye soap. The soap had been cut into large bars and stored where it was protected from rain or other moisture. She took one bar of soap and whittled it into a big pan of boiling water and stirred it until it turned to a liquid consistency which she poured into the hot water of the washing machine and started the agitator. The sound of rhythmic agitation and the fragrant clean aroma of that hot tub of soapy water was wonderful. The first load of laundry went into the washing machine and the "sloshing" laundry hailed the beginning of another successful "wash day!

The wringer was placed on the upper left-hand corner as you faced the washing machine. It had two heavy rubber rollers that squeezed the water out of the fabric as it was fed between them. The wringer could be swung around to accommodate the tubs of rinse water.

The agitator was stopped and the laundry was moved from the hot, wash water, through the wringer into the tepid, first rinse water. Laundry that was moved from the washing machine to the first rinse was handled with a strong stick about two-and-a-half feet long, usually cut from an old broom handle. There was a certain amount of dexterity required for this maneuver or you found the end of the stick going with the laundry through the ringer.

Moving clothes from the first to the second rinse was easier to handle. No stick was necessary. The cool, last rinse had just a drop or two of Mrs. Wright's Bluing added to make the whites really sparkle. Then the laundry went into the laundry basket and was on its way to the clothesline.

Everything was hung on a wire clothesline to dry. However, the clothes to be ironed were first placed together in another basket for starching. Mother boiled the starch, poured it into a big pan, then dropped each garment into the starch mixture, and wrung it out with her hands before it was hung to dry.

After drying, we carried the starched clothes into the kitchen and spread them on the clean kitchen table. Mother had a bowl of clean water. She dipped her hand in the water, shook her hand, and sprinkled every item to be ironed the next day after it had been folded, rolled, and placed in a lined laundry basket.

Then, of course, the water had to be emptied and the washing machine cleaned, dried out, covered, and rolled back into place. The big square tubs and the copper kettle were also washed out, dried, and hung on the wall. Mother, who never wasted anything, had already used the "clean" rinse water to mop the porch floor. The rest was dumped on the sandy yard outside the house and was soon soaked away. What could we do with the rest of the day?

I am awed at my Mother for spending that effort for her family every week during the winter and summer. I remember that she was happy and sang as she went about her work. I'm proud of my mother for many reasons, but washday had to be a challenge. "Don't play in your school clothes," was a wise work-saving directive.

Today, I really enjoy doing laundry and I'm sure it is because it is so easy. There are no buckets of water to carry, no lye soap to make or whittle, no stick to lift heavy, wet laundry, no bluing to add, no starch to boil, no clotheslines to wash off or gasoline powered washing machine to start! Mixed with my recreational laundering is a sincere appreciation for my mother's loving efforts.

The Good Ole Days
By Jim Hammeke of Burns, Oregon
Born 1934

Living in the 1940s era there were many unique things the way we lived and enjoyed life. The following thoughts are a few of what I recall.

A very important aspect of life was that we were on our own for the most part. Since money was hard to come by, we had to grow our own food. Also, we had to do the work by ourselves. We did have cream and eggs to sell so once a week someone would come by and buy our spare cream and eggs. Everyone in the family was involved in this. We kids all had our daily chores like milking cows, feeding hogs, and chickens. In the summer, we also weeded and watered the garden. We did not have to be told to do these things. They were a given.

Also at a very young age, we helped in the fields working the land and harvesting the crops. Some days did become exciting. I recall one summer day when we were harvesting wheat one of those Kansas afternoon storms blew in unexpectedly. We quickly dumped the wheat from the combine into the truck and took refuge in the truck. The wind blew so hard and kept shifting; the wind was so strong we had to keep turning the truck to keep it from rocking. Most of the wheat blew out of the truck by the time the storm ended. After the storm past and we were on our way home, we noticed the wind had bent one of the big oil derricks in half. Our winter weather could also get nasty. More than once, it would snow and cause large drifts across the road. That meant we got to walk to school. They didn't have the equipment to clear roads they have now. We had a mile to walk but my recollection was that we didn't mind it that much. Another storm we had in the winter was a very strong blowing snowstorm. It blew so hard that we had a 10-foot high drift so we could walk right up on the roof of the chicken house.

Jim and Rover in 1949

The home of Jim's parents, Tony and Laura Hammeke in 1938

We did have our enjoyment by playing simple games. One was hopscotch in which we drew the squares on the cement pad by the water pump close to the house. The object of the game was to skip from one square to the next and then turn around and hop back without going out of the lines. We also played marbles a lot. We drew a circle approximately 3 feet in diameter. We placed 1 marble in the center of the circle. We then took turns shooting a marble with our thumb trying to knock the marble from the circle. We would play this on smoothed ground outside. When you knocked a marble out of the circle, you got to keep the marble.

We did have a piano but I don't remember if any of us could play it. We had paper rolls with holes in them. The piano had pedals and when pedaled turned the paper rolls and because of the holes the piano played songs.

We did have the new mode of communication, the telephone. It was a party line with eight households on it. Each house had its own rings, longs and shorts. As an example, it could have been 2 longs and 1 short. To ring some on the line the telephone had a hand crank. A long was like 2 turns and a short was 1/2 to 1 turn. If someone was talking on the line and you wanted to make a call you could break in and ask them to hang up. It worked sometime. To make a long distance call you had to call an operator and they would dial the number you gave them.

Working in the field for 10 or 12 hours presented a problem. You would come home dirty and did not want to carry all that dirt into the house. We built a small temporary building approximately 6 feet by 6 feet. We put a 55-gallon drum on top with the top cut out. We attached a sprinkler head on the bottom to make a shower. Since the top was open, the sun would warm the water during the day. It was a one temperature shower, some days a little cool. We did enjoy the shower rather than sitting in a tub of dirty water.

One farm in our area had a huge shed but was left empty because they had no equipment. The rats made it their home, hundreds of them. They would also venture over to the house basement where they separated the cream from the milk. They would rinse the separator and leave the water in a bucket. The rats would occasionally drown trying to get a drink.

An additional source of pastime, which also provided some food, was hunting turtles in the creek. We wore old shoes with the toes cut out. This was to protect the toes from being bitten by snapping turtles. One person would drive the pickup alongside the creek and either one or two would use pitchforks to throw the turtles into the bed of the pickup. These were snapping turtles so you didn't put you hand in the water. To kill them before getting them ready to cook you had to be very careful as their mouth would close and never open once the head was cut off. They were excellent eating after being cooked like fried chicken.

We did have a dog "Rover," a black collie with a white collar. He was a gentle dog but big enough to keep strangers away. We also had many cats. They kept the mice out of the barn. Because farmers didn't neuter cats, at times we ended up with many cats. The one animal I enjoyed the most was our Shetland pony. My brother and I would ride him 3 miles up the road to play with our cousins. We would spend a few hours with them and then come home. We had an old time flatbed buggy that we hooked him up to and venture into the Cheyanne Bottoms. It was a very light buggy so he could pull it easily.

Since there were a number of us in the family, washing clothes day was a very busy day. First, we had to bring water from the outside pump to put it on the wood burning kitchen stove. After it heated, we carried it to the washhouse and put it in the wash machine. We used a gas motor to run the machine. For soap, we used lye soap, which we made. After washing, we manually turned the crank on the rollers to get the bulk of the water from the clothes. The clothes were then hung on the clothesline to dry.

I had many good times with my grandpa as I got to stay with him a couple days at a time. One time we were going out to get the cows from the pasture as it was milking time. The pasture was about 1/4 of a mile from the barn. As we got to the barn, he told me he was a little tired and that I would have to get the cows by myself. The only reason I wanted to go was to be with him. I did go and I never held a grudge.

Dust Storms, Grasshoppers, and Picture Shows
By Doug Fisher of Haven, Kansas
Born 1927

In 1933, I was six years old and in the first grade. I lived on a farm outside of Peabody, KS and went to a one-room country school 3/4 of a mile away from our house. I walked to and from school every day, despite the weather, all through the winter.

We moved to Florence when I was in second grade in 1934.

One day at school, we saw a dark cloud coming and the teacher sent us all home. She took me out to the corner of the road and told me to start walking in a straight line. I couldn't even see my hand in front of my face because the dust was so thick and black. She told me to stick out my right arm and when I got to the end of the block, to turn that way because that's where my house would be. Somehow, I made it home!

The dust was so bad that everything was ruined. The fences were covered and there was just nothing left for the animals to eat.

When I was in 5th grade, we moved back to the farm outside of Peabody and raised horses. We saw another big cloud coming across the section, but this time it was a cloud of grasshoppers - not dust there must have been thousands of them. They started attacking everything and our chickens started eating them one by one. There were just too many of them that the chickens got scared and they all ran into the henhouse to hide. We ran inside to get away from them and when we came back out once they were gone a few hours later; the grasshoppers had chewed off all of the harnesses on all of the horses. They came from the north and swept south and destroyed everything they could find. Even the trees were bare. We didn't have any newspapers or radios at that time, so we really didn't know what was happening or why they were there. The news was all spread by word of mouth.

I really wanted spending money but my parents had no money to give me, so I started to trap animals and sell their skins for extra money. I woke up every day at 4 AM to trap minks, muskrats, skunks, and possums. I would skin them myself and stretch out the hides. Then I would sell them for 15 cents each - some were 10 cents, the really good ones sold for 25 cents. I used this money on Saturday nights at the picture shows. Then I'd have enough left over for an ice cream cone.

For after school snacks we didn't have any extra food, so we would eat leftover pancakes from the morning's breakfast. We would cover them in sugar and honey and roll them up for a snack.

Every day before school, I would run my traps and milk 3 cows, and then we had more chores after school. Sometimes my teacher would send me home from school when I got there because I smelled like a skunk.

The school principal would swat us hard in his office when we would misbehave. He would use a paddle. As a 6th grader, I drove myself to school in a 1932 Chevy. My first car I owned was a 1927 Model T that cost $17.50, a fortune. I would drive two girls to school every day, and I charged them each $1 a week for gas money. One of the girls, Betty Homan, became my wife a few years later.

When I came back from the war, Betty said, "I've been waiting all this time for you so either we have to get married or call the whole thing off!" So I said, "Okay, then let's get married." It didn't really matter one way or another to me.

We had a double wedding with her brother and his wife, and then went to Wichita to the Blue Note the night of our wedding where we saw Rosemary Clooney perform. The next day we traveled to Colorado Springs for our honeymoon. The room at the Broadmoor cost us $1.50 per night. We went out to eat for the first time ever, neither one of us had ever eaten out. We spent 50 cents on our meals and thought it was the greatest thing ever.

When I went off to the war, I got on a ship in San Diego and took a 7-day trip to Pearl Harbor. I didn't even know what a ship was; I had never even seen one. I was seasick the entire time until the exact moment we dropped our anchor. They wouldn't let you stop working so I had to carry around a 5-lb bucket with me for the whole week. Then I was never seasick again.

We sailed the Pacific Ocean and went into Hiroshima right after they dropped the atomic bomb. There was nothing left but children screaming for their parents. We couldn't do anything to help them. It was all such a bad memory. Then we went to Tokyo and I used my 5-cent packs of cigarettes to buy kimonos and Japanese war medals that I still have today. We weren't supposed to take them off the ship so I taped the cigarette packs to my underarms and between my legs, so that I could use them to barter with the Japanese people.

Finally, when my ship was in the Marshall Islands, my commander told all of us men to undress completely naked and stand on the bow of the ship. They dropped 2 practice bombs, one from the air and one from a submarine, and they needed to see what the effects of it would be. So we stood there naked when all of a sudden, the strongest gust of wind you can ever imagine came and knocked us over. It wasn't just a gust of wind - it was the radiation-filled air sweeping across the water straight at us. Then they told us to get dressed and go back to work. I wonder how much affect that level of radiation has had on me all these years. There is no recorded history of this ever happening because no one wanted anyone to know. I am 87 years old.

My Name is Not Bill of "The Bill Thing"
By Gordon Beaushaw of Halstead, Kansas
Born 1952

My grandfather was a burly railroad man who always wore striped, bib overalls. He smoked big cigars and a pipe. Prince Albert went in his pipe and he bought cigars by the box full. He was all no-nonsense. In his younger days, he had served in WWI as an infantry doughboy and I still have a photo of his company that was taken back in 1919. Maybe he developed his way of thinking and rough personality based on military experience or maybe his upbringing made him tough. You know, survived the dirty thirties!

He had a beloved old cat named "Oscar" and he did treat him really, really well. "Oscar" was missing the first joint on one of his front legs. He had gotten it caught in a trap made for varmints and such early in his life. He had healed up nicely after the loss except where his foot was supposed to be, there was this bare joint bone sticking out and he would click, click, click when he walked across the old flowered linoleum, which covered half the house. No carpet here and the remainder of the floors were wood. I couldn't handle him on jumping up in my lap with that bone just sticking out and touching me, YUK! Grandpa loved that old cat and treated him nicer than any human I knew.

He worked in a small Kansas town doing, who-knows-what for the railroad. Being a 10-year-old boy at the time, I had never asked him exactly what he did and I'm not sure I would have known what to ask anyways. All I knew is that he would sometimes take me down to watch the trains rumble through town. Yep, big excitement in Formoso, Kansas. He knew when the slow ones would be passing through, and especially when the fast ones would be barreling through.

He showed me a neat trick which involved defacing American currency which I assume now is not a problem at least when it happens to a penny. When the fast train was scheduled to barrel down the tracks (you could hear it coming by putting your ear down on the rail), he would have me spit on a penny and place in on the train track. Spit would make it stick for a little while. We always did this routine next to the elevator because the rocks were whiter there and also spread much wider at that location. Two important details I need to share right here, 1: No spit means no flat penny, 2: Lighter, whiter colored rocks made the darker penny easier to find after the flattening process (that penny sure could fly sometimes). I tested his expertise on these two items many times and it seems he was right! That enormous train would flatten that penny just like those new-fangled machines you see at theme parks. You know the ones you put a penny in one slot and two quarters in another slot and then turn the crank. You get a flat penny with a nice picture on it. My railroad penny was just flattened and curved somewhat and only cost me, you guessed it, a penny. No pretty picture although the resemblance of Abraham survived somewhat intact, sometimes.

Grandpa's town had a small grocery store and I swear that Howard, the guy that owned the store, still ran it and looked exactly the same 30 years later. That's just crazy.

Grandpa would give me and my sister (little brother hadn't come along yet) each an old Alka-Seltzer bottled stacked full of pennies and nickels. Mostly pennies if you know what I mean. These bottles were, yep, made of glass and were tall and skinny. They stacked the Alka-Seltzer tablets in those glass bottles one on top of the next. We might get up to 30 cents in generous bottles and sometimes the bottles were only half-full. That great little bottle would be presented to me and would subsequently be taken down to Howard's Market. We would come back with a heavenly assortment of candy in a little plain brown paper bag. That bag was chocked full of delicious penny candy. Did I mention it was heavenly?

Grandpa and Grandma lived without indoor plumbing. No piping to various sinks and stools and such. The house had four rooms and none of them was a bathroom. They did have a well pump inside the house located right next to the deep, porcelain coated kitchen sink. There was always a bucket there full of the last water pumped and at-the-ready to prime the pump next time water was needed. Yep, water only came in COLD. Grandma wanted one of those water closets but Grandpa refused.

Stick with me, I'm going somewhere! Back to "the Bill thing"!

Grandpa would always say to me, "Bill, let's go water the horse". That was secret guy talk for, I need to go relieve myself, ya wanna go with? For number one relief we didn't bother to run to the outhouse, we just stepped out the back next to the shoe scraper buried in the ground, and "watered the horse."

Yep, "Bill" was the name Grandpa had given me because he didn't like the first name I had been blessed with by my parents. I was told by my folks to just put up with it. Grandpa had slipped up only once and accidentally called me by my correct name. But with a short grin and a look of perplexity, he went right back to "Bill" quickly without missing a beat.

In my later years I thought that to be very strange that he didn't approve of "Gordon." My gosh, his real name was "Elmer." Who would name there kid "Elmer" anyways? He had a longtime friend and the best buddies were known as "Jum" and "Jigs." Grandpa's nickname was the former. I thought how can you handle "Jum" and "Elmer" and then think "Gordon" was so bad. And what's up with "Jigs" anyway.

We visited Grandpa and Grandma about twice a year or so, once I began remembering things. These visits included some in summer don't-cha know. Grandpa was always trying to toughen me up and would save the lawn mowing for me. He loved those new-fangled, crank-up, gas lawn mowers. Not the rotary kind but the ones with the blade underneath the deck. He didn't like to pull that starting rope though so he went for the crank-up version. You just kind of wound it up until you couldn't get the spring to go any tighter and then popped the button to turn it loose and it did the cranking for you. If only lawn mowers would always start on the first crank. I now realize that cranking was easier than pulling the rope. But to a 10-year-old boy, either starting style seemed pretty tough.

It was one of these potential mowing foray assignments that a rebellion welled up in my innards. I had always been accommodating, I had held my tongue, and I had been very nice about the "Bill" thing. I guess I was finding myself and I just wanted to test authority some. Who knows about the minds of 10 year olds and how they decipher things?

One beautiful morning I was outside playing in the front yard on one of these grandparents visits and I heard the name "Bill" being yelled repeatedly from my Grandpas lips out the back door. I quickly decided not to answer, OOPS! My reasoning was that if he couldn't call me by my right name, he must not be calling me! This was perfect 10-year-old wisdom. Everyone else in my entire world called me by my correct name and had never even thought of calling me anything else. Why couldn't ole "Elmer"?

I heard a few more calls emanate from the backyard and decided to hide just in case he brought his enquiry for the missing "Bill" to the front of the house.

Sometime later, I was cornered in the front yard by an angry "Jum"/"Elmer." He grabbed me up by the arm and turned me around and the following conversation, obviously somewhat short ensued, with him doing most of the talking.

Grandpa, "Bill, why didn't you come when I called you?" Gordon (Bill), "My name's not Bill"

Grandpa with righteous indignation and much force he stated, "As long as you're here at my house, your name is "Bill."

Bill (Gordon), as Grandpa walked back into the house I said low enough one more time so as not to be heard, "MY NAME'S NOT BILL"

Well, we got the mowing done that afternoon and I don't ever remember having the conversation with my Grandpa about that "Bill" thing ever again.

So I guess the statement, "perception is reality" was true in this case. MY NAME IS BILL! Depends on whose point of view it is mostly, I guess!

At least "Grandpa", "Elmer," "Jum" didn't call me "Oscar". Although I might have been treated a lot nicer if had!

Fulfilling Childhood
By Marilyn Jean Davis of Clyde Hill,
Washington
Born 1936

My birth in 1936, sandwiched between the beginning of the Great Depression and the start of World War II, was overlaid with the Dust Bowl days. I was born in Dodge City, Kansas, and raised on a small wheat farm three miles south of Ensign, a town of about two-hundred; I was surrounded by a close-knit family of grandparents, aunts, uncles, and cousins - all living nearby.

My earliest memories occurred when I was two years old, watching Dad bringing in the coal bucket in to fill the coal stove; and the other, moving to our "new" house 1/4 mile away, begging to ride in the back of the Model T truck with Mama and the furnishings, but my dad convincing me to ride up front with him to watch the breakable items in the glove compartment.

Everyone had an outhouse, and I was so proud ours was a "two-holer" and everyone else's was only a "one-holer." When I was small, my girl cousins and I had companionship during our young lives when nature called. At no other time did two people use it at the same time, so why it was built that way in the first place, I never knew nor did I ever think to question it.

Once a week Dad brought in a large, galvanized tub, in which we bathed. My brother first, to my dismay; I was next. Then, my mother and finally my father with water reheated from a teakettle as the water cooled. The rest of the week, we washed ourselves morning and night from water in an enamel pan using a washcloth. Once a week our hair was shampooed, and, once a month my mother applied olive oil to my hair, wrapped my head in a hot towel for a while, followed by a shampoo, so I enjoyed glossy, shining hair, partly due, also to the nightly ritual of brushing it 100 strokes.

We, of course, were on a party line. One of the women, and we knew who she was, on our line listened in to all our conversations as we could hear the "click" as she picked up her receiver. I was forbidden to mention this. Small towns shared every bit of information, and Mama told me this woman must have been lonely to need this experience.

We had neither indoor plumbing nor electricity until I was 11 when REA came through the area. Before that, Dad rigged up a wind charger, with bare light bulbs lighting our main rooms, with Coleman lanterns to supplement; and propane heated our main rooms, with the bedrooms remaining unheated. The windmill pumped water into a storage tank for our water supply. Our house was cooled during summer months with excelsior stuffed in a chicken wire frame, which hung outside one of our south windows with water from a hose dripping through it from the top. The prairie wind did the rest.

At six, I started first grade in the two-room Ensign Grade School with grade 1-3 in the south side and grades 4-6 in the north side. A garage-type door between the rooms was occasionally raised to share music. There were only two of us in the first grade, and probably no more than 20 pupils in the three primary grades, so we all overheard and absorbed all lessons taught. One of my proudest moments as a first grader was frantically waving my hand in the air when the teacher asked the third graders to spell "turtle." No one in the three grades responded except me. My delight knew no bounds that I knew the correct answer! But, I also recall my disgust that same year in attempting to form perfect printed letters in penmanship on pale, yellow, ruled paper embedded with tiny bits of wood scattered throughout and having the pencil lead hit one of those pieces, ruining the perfection. I swore when I grew up I would buy no paper with pieces of wood!

School began at 9:00 a.m. and let out at 4:00 p.m. with an hour for lunch, which was a full, heavy meal. Our cook, Mrs. Tedlock, lived across the street from the school, and, she, being the mother of one of my uncles, had

Marilyn with her parents, Lloyd and June Sutton in 1936

no reservations reporting to my mother if I did not eat all my meal. Prior to school, breakfasts at home were bowls of hot cereal on a rotated basis of oatmeal, rice, malt-o-meal, and cream of wheat. The snack after school was always a glass of milk with crumbled up white bread and sugar added. Our suppers were light meals.

In the fall of 1944, our family moved to San Antonio, Texas for the year. The cultural shock to me was extreme. In my tiny Ensign school, my schoolmates included both Mexican and Negro children, so I had not been exposed to racial prejudice. To my bewilderment, I discovered that first day in my new school that separate drinking fountains and separate bathroom sections were religiously observed. With heart-pounding anxiety, I used the facilities, panic-stricken, fearing I may not have made the right choice even though they were well marked. I quickly realized if I drank nothing each day, I could wait until I got home after school to use our own bathroom, a routine I followed for quite some time as I vividly remember running home after school in desperate need, and a couple of times not quite making it in time. I was eight years old.

Other new rules included children having to respond to adults with "No, Sir," "No, Ma'am," or "Yes, Sir," "Yes, Ma'am." I broke that habit when I returned to the Ensign Grade School when my schoolmates laughed at me! My mother was appalled when she later learned we were all routinely checked for head lice while at that Texas school.

I recall rationing during World War II, particularly of sugar, coffee, and rubber, with my parents using a coupon book to redeem grocery items, and I took a dime to school each week to buy a war bond stamp. One of our car front tires had a big bulge on the side of it, which greatly embarrassed me. During the war, my dad bought a box of colored globe Christmas ornaments with hangers made of paper instead of wire, which I still enjoy each Christmas.

We rarely went to the doctor, as aspirin was given for fever or headaches. Cuts were doused with alcohol or hydrogen peroxide and then smeared with iodine. Because I loved roller-skating on the school sidewalks, my knobby knees were always bright red due to frequent falls. For sore throats, Vick was rubbed onto the neck, a rag was tied around the neck at bedtime, and it was removed the next morning. Unfortunately, no matter how hard I scrubbed before going to school, I left a trail of the odor of Vicks throughout the day. Dentist visits were a must, so I can thank my parents' vigilance on this issue as I still have most of my teeth to this day.

Evening activities included playing card games like Old Maid, Authors, rummy. We also played checkers, jacks, and the piano. When I was nine, my folks bought us the complete set of <u>The Books of Knowledge</u>, and growing up, my brother and I spent hours devouring those pages. Outdoor activities of my brother and me was serving as restaurant or grocery store proprietor or customer, using play money, and grasses, weeds, grains, etc., and dregs of discarded condiment bottles to make different ingredients mixed with mud pies. We also built miniature "farms" in the yard.

My early farm chores included gathering eggs, setting the table, helping with the dishes, and, as I grew older, hanging and gathering clothes from the clothesline, which my mother had washed in a wringer-type washing machine, and ironing with a heavy, gas-powered iron. Scalding and plucking chickens for Mama to cook for dinner was my job, and, to this day, the smell from a dentist drilling into a tooth brings back that same odor. But, my most hated job was washing and rinsing the seemingly thousands of milk separator discs each day.

My grandmother accompanied us each Saturday when we went to Dodge to shop. Mama changed from her daily cotton housedresses and Dad from overalls into trousers. Self-sufficient, we always had a vegetable garden, milk cows, pigs, steers, and chickens for food and eggs, and Dad butchered to supply our pork and beef. Mama's canned beef still makes my mouth water just thinking about it. Dad shook a quart jar filled with our whole milk to make butter.

Rain, snow, and dust storms play a part in my memories. My mother and grandmother were flower gardeners. My mother even had a greenhouse. I grew up surrounded by all kinds of trees, bushes, and plants, some exotic, giving me a deep appreciation and knowledge of botany. Later, dust storms stripped the leaves of everything in its path, leaving deep drifts of dirt lining our fences and tumbleweeds piled high. One severe winter blizzard drifted the snow so high we walked right over our detached garage. Wheat crops were destroyed by hot summer winds, which cooked the grains, with hailstorms or grasshoppers causing severe damage, usually right before harvest. A good memory after a rain was gathering tadpoles from the ditches, watching them grow into frogs; then, turning them loose.

Each summer we vacationed in the New Mexico or Colorado mountains. One highlight as a child was viewing a skeleton of a dinosaur in the Denver Museum of Natural History.

It was a rich and fulfilling childhood. Western Kansas was a great place in which to grow up.

Dumplings and Potatoes
By Christina Bongartz Bollig of Wakeeney, Kansas
Born 1929

I was born August 28, 1929 in Trego County, Kansas, the oldest of six siblings—three boys and three girls. Mom always said I caused the stock market to crash. It was only a few days after I was born when it crashed. I don't see how a tiny two-pound baby could cause such an event.

We lived on a rented farm about 26 miles from the nearest town, which was Ellis. So you see we were quite alone out there, although there were relatives nearby. Everything we used, ate, or wore had to be made or raised on the farm, as there were very few trips to town, with the exception of going to church on Sunday. This trip was made if at all possible.

I remember one icy, cold morning we were sure there would be no church that morning, but dad said, "Get ready, we're going." So we all piled into the Plymouth and headed down the road, after going about 400 feet, the car spun around in the road making a complete circle heading back home. Not a word was said but we headed back home. We drove back home into the yard and around the windmill and away we went to church.

The nearest school was a mile and a half away. A one-room school with all eight grades, no kindergarten. My first grade teacher was Carol Newcomer. His job was not only to teach, but to make fire, carry in the coal, clean the schoolroom and see that water to drink was available. On nice days, or even some not so nice days, we walked to school. On cold snowy days dad took us by car or in the wagon pulled by our team of one black and one white horse. When we walked to school, we had to walk past a pasture of our neighbor who raised Galloway cattle. (They were black with a white belt around their body). Anyway, there was always a big bull in the pasture along with the cattle. He made a point of walking to the fence "bellering" which scared us half to death. Needless to say, that half mile was covered pretty fast.

Our cellar was our grocery store. Everyone always said you could feed anyone with all the food down there. Every spring we planted gardens everywhere. All this food was canned or dried. The squash were stored in the granary under the wheat in the wintertime. That way they would not freeze. Mom had the first pressure canner used in Trego County. She had to take lessons on the use of it from the extension agent so that it could be used safely. One year she and a neighbor lady canned over 300 quarts of corn plus the other vegetables from their gardens. My family worked with the extension office often. I remember having chicken demonstrations at our place using our chickens to teach neighbors how to raise, cull, and feed chickens. To this day chickens are one of my special animals.

Our neighborhood was always having parties. If anyone had a birthday, there was sure to be a party somewhere. The evening was spent playing cards and eating. Everyone brought food so there was always a table full of goodies. Finally, a family moved to a farm about a mile from our place that had a big barn on it. So soon, there were barn dances. Most of the children in this family played instruments, so no other musicians were needed.

Our farm had one good source of water on the place, just a deep well windmill. This water was only good for the cattle to drink, so all of the other water was hauled in from a pump a half mile away. Many hours were spent pumping water. My sister and I used to take turns pumping by jumping up and down and reciting poems or songs. Each one had to do the whole song or poem on their turn. With no ample supply of water, no water was ever wasted. The rinse water from doing the dishes was used to scrub the kitchen floor. On washday, every drop was put to some use—the last being to scrub out the outhouse.

In our neighborhood, neighbors helped each other so if someone needed help, dad would be gone to help. On those days mom would ask us kids, what we should have for dinner (the noon meal)? In one voice she would hear, "dumplings and potatoes." So that's what was fixed. Dad did not care for dumplings and potatoes so that was our chance to eat them. These were boiled and then fried in homemade butter. Oh, so very good! I'm not sure how many calories. Guess we didn't care.

Most of the toys we had were homemade such as a wheel that we rolled around with two slats nailed together in the form of a "T" or stilts. Many were the falls from those until we learned how to use them. Another great favorite was bones from the feet of decaying cattle that we used as play animals. We made corals of sticks and twigs so that we had our ranch. This seems like a weird plaything, but several years back, my sister, who was a psychologist, called to have me send her a box of bone animals that she wanted to use in her profession. Never did find out if this helped her patients.

Olive Ann McCormick

My Growing Up Memories
By Olive Ann McCormick of Kingman, Kansas
Born 1940

We didn't have electricity until 1949. We had lights with mantles and used kerosene. We had to change the mantles as sometimes they tore, as they were very fragile. Also, wash the globes on the other lights. We lived in a 4-room house, kitchen, living room, bedroom, and back room. Each room had an outside door.

My parents had an icebox. The iceman would bring ice to our home. On Saturday, my parents went to town for groceries. We (children) stayed home. We didn't want to talk to the iceman. We put the sign in the screen door. How many pounds we wanted, 25, 50, 75, or 100 lbs. We put the money in the dish on the kitchen table. We hid in the bedroom. Years later, my father purchased a gas refrigerator. We had to put gas in it and start it to make ice cubes during the summer.

We didn't have running water. We pumped water and brought it to the house in a bucket to drink, cook, and do dishes. We had to heat our water to do dishes and etc. We had a kitchen cabinet and cook stove. The kitchen floor was not even and we would have to work to get it sat even on the floor. Mom had an oil-heating stove that she would use in the winter to cook oatmeal on. For breakfast mom would fix eggs, bacon, toast, oatmeal, juice, and their coffee. I had hot cocoa or postum made with milk.

My mother got her wash water hot on the stove. We had a washer that you had to step on it to get it started, as it was a gasoline engine. You wash all your clothes in the same water. Starting with tea towels, sheets, whites, lighted colored clothes, towels, dark clothes, jeans, and rugs. We had two rinse waters and one had bluing in it.

Mom made lye soap to wash with. We hung clothes to dry on the clothesline. In the winter, the clothes froze dry.

We had a wood stove in the living room that was used in the winter. Dad would get up in the morning and start the stove. Ashes had

378

to be taken from the bottom of the stove with a small shovel. Ashes were taken out when they were cool.

A radio stand was north in the living room outside door. The radio had an antenna out north east of the house by the rose bush.

The washstand was inside by the back door and in the summer, it was on the east end of the porch where you could wash your hands. A bucket was on the stand with a dipper to put water in the wash pan, soap, and a towel to dry your hands. Then you would throw the water in the flowerbeds.

We didn't have a bathroom. We took baths on Saturday evening in the living room by the wood stove. We all used the same water. Just kept adding hot water to the tub.

We washed our hair in the dishpan in the kitchen. Sometimes we would go down to the creek east of our home and get water from the creek. We also caught rainwater and strained it so we could use it to wash our hair. The rainwater was dirty coming off the roof. The water made your hair soft. When we used well water to wash our hair mom would put some vinegar in the rinse water to make our hair soft.

We brushed our teeth with salt water and usually did it outside unless it was winter.

We had a pot in the bedroom to use at night. You would take it out in the morning and empty it and leave it out all day to air. Had to remember to bring it in at night. The outhouse (toilet) was out back. Catalogs were used as toilet paper. (National Bell Hess catalog.) Mom would put lye down the outhouse so it wouldn't smell.

Our bedroom was cold in the winter. We had two beds in the bedroom. I would put a brick or flat iron on the stove in the morning. Before I went to bed, I would wrap the brick or flat iron in a cloth and put it in the bed where I laid. Then when I went to bed, I would put it at my feet. Had so many blankets on you could hardly turn over. In the summer, we would sleep outside. It was cooler then in the house. If it rained, we would roll the mattress up and take it inside the house. It was neat looking at the stars and moon at night. Once in a while, you smelled a skunk.

We would take our eggs and cream to town. They would take our cream and put it in test tubes and check it. My mother would purchase flour in sacks. (Cloth) When she got enough that was alike, she would make us a dress. In later years, a man came and picked up our cream at the house. We churned butter on Saturday. We even made homemade cottage cheese.

When I gathered eggs mom said to look in the nest before putting your hand in the nest as snakes like eggs.

When I had the chicken pox, a baby chicken was born. My mother brought it in the house and put it in an oatmeal box. When it grew bigger, we put it outside. It would come to the kitchen door and want inside. It would go to our back room and get in the dirty clothes box and lay an egg. Then she would go to the door and want out. I had named it Junior but we changed it to Junior Etta.

I don't know how my father knew when a storm came up at night. He would get us up and we would put our coat and shoes on over our pajamas and go to the cellar. We sat on cream cans and empty egg cases. Dad would keep checking outside the cellar door to see if it was clear so we could go back into the house and go to bed. Dad also had an ax down there in case something fell on the cellar door then we could get out. The cream separator was in

Olive Ann's brother, Gale Beck and his herd of sheep

the cellar. Dad used it morning and evening after he milked the cows. There were shelves down the cellar that mom put her canned vegetables and fruit on. There was a small table down there that we could put things on. We kept the eggs down there to keep cool. When it was clear, we would go back in the house to bed.

When the roads were bad, dad would take us to Sunday school with a horse and wagon so we wouldn't miss Sunday school.

We use to walk on stilts. Yes, we fell off but it was fun. I had a kitten I would bring in the house and dress up in doll clothes. I had a white bunny rabbit for a pet. I would let her out to hop around in the yard. I never had pop or store bought ice cream when I was growing up. We made homemade ice cream with a crank freezer. Mom served liver and onions once a week so we would get the iron we needed. We had soup beans on washday.

One year we went to Nebraska for Thanksgiving at my Uncles. They had a four-room house and lived on a farm in the country. We arrived on Wednesday like some of the other relatives. One bedroom, grandma slept in one bed and I think my aunt slept with her. The other bed, four of us girls slept width ways in bed. I ask my older brother where he slept and he said he slept under the kitchen table with another uncle of mine. My other brother and some of the cousins went and slept in the barn in the hay. The next morning there was snow on the ground. I remember there was an egg case setting on a stool by the kitchen stove the next morning and eggs were being fried. My uncles like to play cards so there was always a card game going on. Some of the relatives went and stayed with other relatives.

I rode in the bin of the combine when cutting wheat. Had to be careful not to get in the auger in the bin. I rode on the fender of the tractor. There was a handle to hold on to so you wouldn't fall off.

Sometimes on Saturday evening, my mother and I would go to town to the movies. I didn't like western movies with shooting so I got under the seat. My father would go and visit with the man that run the shoe repair shop.

I didn't have a telephone until I got married.

I am the youngest of seven children.

Getting Clean was a Chore
By Joy Kline Moser of Topeka, Kansas
Born 1942

Memories, I have wonderful memories of growing up in Southwestern Kansas in the "old days." Not the "really old days" but the days when my folks had children, the days just before, during, and after World War II. And in a way, even before that, as we lived in the country, 30 miles from a town of any size. Even little burgs were about 20 miles away. We grew up in the northwest corner of Hodgeman County, Kansas.
It was wonderful growing up there. There was so much to do, see, learn, and love. My father was a farmer. We had our own little world, occasionally venturing out to where others lived. Our nearest neighbor was about a mile away. I live in eastern Kansas now but I will forever love western Kansas, the people that lived and still live there, the terrain, plants, and animals, and the life that we lived.

Before we got electricity when I was 10 years old, we did everything by hand. We did not have a bathroom. We used an outhouse during the day and a chamber pot at night. Dad built us a neat outhouse, better than anybody else's, that is, anybody else's that I used. Most people's outhouses were little sheds with a door that opened up and two holes cut into boards to allow adults to sit over the holes and relieve themselves. One set of grandparents had an outhouse that had two adult holes so that as a child, it was difficult to balance yourself over the hole. Since I was always smaller than others my age, I was always afraid that I would end up falling down the hole into the smelly bowl movement and pee. Even worse at these grandparents was that there were medium sized white crickets that lived in that mess. I was always afraid that they would come up and bite my bottom. So before I got on the hole I would always look down in the hole to locate the crickets and shoo them away, then make my business fast. My Dad built our outhouse, which was much nicer. First of all, there were no white crickets or other things moving around in the mess. Secondly, Dad made the outhouse holes to fit the people intended to use them. There was a Daddy-sized hole, a Mommy-sized hole, and one that was shorter and sized for all five children. No worries about falling in or getting your bottom bitten. But it smelled too. All outhouses smelled, even the one at our one-room country school.

The chamber pot was another matter. It was in the house, in the bedroom, placed where you could find it in the night. It was white enamel, trimmed in black, like many utility pots and pans were in those days. It also had a matching lid. The problem was that it was hard to find in the night. If you accidentally kicked it over, it was a horrible mess, hard to clean up, and brought recrimination from everyone. They didn't like the smell, wanted to use it too but then had to go to the outhouse in the dark night, and were awake while you lit a lamp to clean up your mess. At least there were no chamber pots in the one-room country school.

We all attended one-room country schools. There were two different schools. For a few years, we attended one made of red brick, which was square and was located in Ness County. For most of the years, we attended a one-room country school located in Hodgeman County, which was made of long limestone rocks and was an oblong shape. There was one teacher for the whole school. The number of children to be taught varied each year but all eight grades were represented. There were a lot of grades with just one person in it, some with no one in it and some with several children. Everyone helped each other to learn. The older ones helped the younger ones to read and, of course, it helped them to improve their reading too. Again, older ones would help the younger ones to learn to spell, figure mathematics, and with penmanship. With only one teacher, she couldn't help everybody so all the children pitched in, a learning/teaching experience. Later my older sister came back to this school and taught my youngest brother when he was in eighth grade.

There was a 15-minute recess each morning and each afternoon. At recess, we played on the swing and slide set or on the old-fashioned wooden merry-go-round. We also played softball and football. Sometimes we played it in the pasture next door running bases or touchdowns out around the cactus. We also played Annie-over throwing the ball over the roof of the schoolhouse to the other side, and many other games. During those times, of course, we played cowboys and Indians. We used the old barn to stable our "horses" and plan how to win. We used the old coal shed for a sometime jail for the bad guys. If we were the bad guys sometimes, the coal shed was the bank to rob so the good guys could try to catch us. We also played these games during the last half of the noon hour, after eating and trading the food our moms had put in our lunchboxes. Sometimes, in later years, we would practice track, learning to run, high jump, and broad jump. I even remember one time when there was a countywide track meet at the grade school in the county seat and the one-room country schools got to compete. We even won a ribbon or two.

We got to perform in plays, pretending, as all children love to do, that we were somewhere else doing something else for just a little while. Everyone got to participate. No one was left out. So theater productions with some kind of costumes and memorized poems were part of what we all learned to do. There was a play at the one-room country school at least twice a year.

The first program was given near Halloween with a Box Supper and later near Christmas with a Christmas party. The Box Suppers were great too, raising funds for the treat sacks for Christmas. Each girl and woman decorated a box filled with food for a supper, which was then auctioned off. The men and boys bought these decorated boxes and got to eat with the unknown maker of the box. The men tried to guess what box was made by the best cook in the community and then bid on that. The boys tried to bid on who they were sweet on. That was after the play was over and everyone could relax. After the Christmas play while again people were relaxing, Santa Claus came and gave sacks of candy with an orange and apple in it to each child there, even those not in school yet.

Our parents generally drove the six miles to bring us to school and pick us up when the school day was over but sometimes we walked home. There was only one farm on this road and it was only about a half mile from the school. Occasionally our folks, in the spring or fall, would bring our bicycles with us to school in the morning so we could ride the bikes home after the school day was over. There was hardly any traffic on the six miles of that road.

The idea was that we should go to school and learn. So our folks drove through the mud, gumbo, rain, sleet, and snow to get us there and back. There are a couple of years that I remember in the late 1940's or early 1950's when the blizzards and snow pack were tremendous. Snow piled high was covered with an ice crust that could hold a lot of weight. With our boots on, we could walk on top of the snow. Not only that Dad took us to school riding in the cab of the tractor, driving on the ice crust over fences and across fields and pastures, stopping opposite the school door in time for classes. He used the same route to come get us after school was over. He did that for several days until the roads were cleared enough for use. In earlier years, the teacher stayed in people's houses but by this time, the teacher lived in an old remodeled schoolhouse south of the school where the barn used to be, so she was there anyway.

Blizzards and snow pack not only affected our schooling but was a big problem when people needed to get to town for something. The lady about two miles north of us was pregnant and due one year in November or December and another time in March or April. Keep in mind that we did not have phones then. A blizzard came twice when she was pregnant and in each of those two years, she had her baby at home during a bad snowstorm. So her husband drove down to our place in a tractor while it was snowing and asked my folks to come help with the birthing. Dad and Mom got in the cab of our tractor and went off to help the baby be born. We kids stayed home. As the wind blew and the snow flew, we watched out the window for their return. After what seemed like many hours and prayers later, the folks returned, the baby was born, and we were all together again.

For all farm people and for most people in those days, you took your bath on Saturday night. Then you would be nice and clean and ready for Sunday and church. Getting your whole body clean was a major operation, especially if you didn't have a bathtub. Mom would heat up the bath water on the stove. Sometimes like in the winter when it was cold, we bathed in a big round washtub (also used for laundry) inside the house. Mom brought hot to warm water and put into the tub, which quickly cooled off. You had to watch to make sure the water wasn't too hot when you got into the tub or when she poured it on you, or you could get burned. In late spring, summer, and early fall, we had a kind of a shower. Those baths were always taken on the porch.

Mom would heat up the water and bring it out to the porch and pour it over us while we soaped ourselves. Then while we shivered, Mom would heat the water again and bring warm water for us to rub the soap around with and rinse with. Sometimes it would take a third heating of the water to get your body washed off and clean. Then you could dry yourself with a towel and get into clothes and get warm again. So Mom would have to heat water for seven people, the five kids and Dad and her. Getting clean was a chore.

Childhood Days
By Karen Matthews Parker of Derby, Kansas
Born 1943

I spent my first eight years as an only child. With no other siblings and only one other young girl in my neighborhood, I spent a lot of time entertaining myself and developing a big imagination. Hours were spent on my rope swing pumping my way through the clouds that resembled the wildest animals or making a fishing pole from a willow stick, string and a safety pin. I would fish in the ditch in front of our house for tadpoles. I observed the transformation of tadpoles into frogs and

Karen's mother

somehow equated this with the development of human babies, and in my longing for a baby sister, I thought my fishing might just catch a baby. Eventually, my impatience overtook the longing, and I left the willow stick upright in the ditch. In time, it rooted, and my mother transplanted it behind the house where it still stands.

My imagination got me in trouble more than once even though my intentions were always good. My father purchased a very used pickup truck. The paint had dulled over the years, so I reckoned it just needed a coat of paint to make it a truck my dad would be proud to drive. I didn't find paint in the garage, but there was a brush and a can of shellac. I began with the drivers' door and ended there also. Painting can be tiring. Daddy didn't get upset, not in front of me anyway, and that old truck's left door remained the way I left it.

There was also the time my mother went shopping, and upon her return, she said she bought me some candy. I ran to her purse pulled out a small blue box with red lettering. Inside I found what looked like chocolate, but it wasn't as good as a Baby Ruth. I helped myself to more. When my mother realized what had happened, she called our doctor who told not to worry "ex-lax" wouldn't kill me, but she would have a very busy little girl for a while.

I remember at one point feeling less than adored by my mother and deciding that leaving home would probably make her appreciate me more. I told her I was leaving and instead of begging me to stay as I had expected, she offered to help me pack. When the suitcase was filled, I didn't have a choice so set out with my terrier to face the world. When my grandmother learned of my fate, she came to offer to take me to her home. It sounded like a good alternative, but I was determined to make my mother suffer so I continued to walk. Two blocks from home there were no more houses only a field laid ahead. With my head down, I walked on. Suddenly, a pair of feet appeared before me. My head rose, my eyes moved upward from the feet to reveal an elderly, bent woman dressed in black. I knew she was a witch! In a crackly voice, she asked, "Little girl, do you know the way to Maiden Lane?" I did, pointed in the direction, and turned to run all the way home. I was truly thankful for that witch's appearance as it gave me my excuse for returning home.

The radio always stimulated my imagination. The sound of Hopalong Cassidy's spurs as he walked along the boardwalks of a western town brought vivid images to my mind. Saturday mornings with "Smilin' Ed and the Buster Brown Gang;" plus Cream of Wheat's, "Let's Pretend," were delightful. But Sunday afternoons piqued my friend Sandy's and my imaginations in a different way. With paper and pencil in hand, we would turn on "True Detective" to hear the weekly description of a wanted criminal. At the conclusion, we would rush from the house and search hopefully for the fugitive to no avail.

The radio also introduced me to becoming emotionally involved with a story. The "Lux Radio Theater's" presentation of "The Yearling" brought me to tears, which I tried to hide by burying my head in a pillow.

In 1950, my father found work at one of the aircraft plants in Wichita. We lived in Beechwood, a government housing project that had been built during World War II when Wichita played a vital role in providing aircraft for the war effort, and housing was needed for the thousands who immigrated to work there. It was a great place to live. I had never had so many children to play with before. I learned to roller skate, ride my Western Flyer bike, and swing from monkey bars. Summer evenings were spent outside with fathers throwing horseshoes, mothers visiting on stoops and children playing "Punch the Ice Box," "Red Light, Green Light," various versions of tag and finally as the sky darkened, "Ghost."

Summer was the time to bring out the Monopoly game. Hours would be spent building a real estate empire to only go bankrupt in the end. I had a subscription to "Jack and Jill" magazine that featured a different play script each month. I'd gather actors, costumes, and props. Since I had the only copy of the script, it seemed obvious that I should also direct. These summers were pre Jonas Salk's polio vaccine. Children would return home for lunch and remain for an hour of rest leaving the neighborhood quiet for a short time.

Fall and the return to school changed our play. We would return to cowboys and Indians, building forts and staging bloodless battles. However, in third grade our teacher

Mrs. Mitchell introduced her class to Laura Ingalls Wilder's *"Little House"* books along with Gertrude Chandler Warner's *"Boxcar Children."* This led to a wagon train of children crossing the prairie and surviving on the food nature provided. On one occasion, a pesky younger girl named Linda tried our patience one-time-too-many. We tied her hands with jump ropes and placed her in a coal bin. Fortunately, for Linda and ourselves, we did relinquish before any damage was done. Those days of imaginative, independent play were the best. I wish children today had time and freedom to play imaginatively as we did.

That fall my wish for a baby sister almost came true. I had been told that my mother was pregnant. Elated I saved my money and bought a tiny pink dress, bonnet, and socks. The morning of September 25, I was awakened by my father with the announcement that I had a baby brother. I felt betrayed! He had to be lying. I ran to the bathroom and locked the door. Dad brought the radio and sat it outside the door. He turned the dial to a local radio station that announced births each morning. There it was, "Mr. and Mrs. Floyd Duke had a baby boy." Eventually, I opened the door, dressed, and sullenly made my way to school. Mrs. Mitchell asked if I had an announcement. "No," I replied. I went to my Aunt Onie's to stay while my mother and brother Johnny were in the hospital. It wasn't until I returned home and saw the precious baby that I was overcome with joy. As for the pink outfit I had bought, Mother let me dress Johnny in it occasionally until he out grew it.

Halloween was a special time. Back then, many housewives made homemade treats. All the kids could count on Mrs. Boren to make popcorn balls and Mrs. Beals would pass out candy apples. Those were the first homes to hit! My mother made my costumes, and they were always special. Our school had a parade and "best" costumes were rewarded. My "old lady" was selected one year. From the hat covering a gray wig to the calf high shoes, everything was just right. Mom showed me how to replicate the walk of an octogenarian using a cane. I think that was what put me over the top.

In 1952, just before Thanksgiving, the Wichita area was hit with a blizzard. Unlike today, there was neither Doppler radar nor automated school fan outs to alert parents of school closings. The students of Beechwood Elementary were dismissed early and allowed to walk home. The wind was driving the snow into my eyes, blurring my vision. Then, I heard my mother's voice calling my name. She must have instinctively come looking for me. My father became stranded in the snow and didn't make it home that night.

At eight I still believed in Santa, but that came to an end on a December day when a boy in my class blasted me with a piece of coal to the head and the news on our way home from school. I rushed into the house and asked my mother if it were true. She answered distractedly, "Yes, it's true." In tears, I went to my room. While lying on my bed critical thinking came into play. If there was no Santa, then there must not be an Easter Bunny! My first experience with confronting life's disappointments had dealt me a double whammy.

I have wonderful memories of Beechwood Elementary School. I attribute my love of books to those teachers who treated books as treasure and who read to us daily with enthusiasm and always ending at a spot that would make us beg for more yet knowing we had to wait until tomorrow.

We left Beechwood in 1954 and a year later, it was demolished, no longer needed. As an adult, I had lived away from Kansas

Karen in her "Old Lady" costume

for over 40 years, but returned to live in the Wichita area four years ago. Office buildings have been erected where Beechwood once stood, but I believe I found the creek that ran through it. The one the wagon train traversed and where the Box Car children picked wild berries for supper.

Cowboy
By John H. Duncan of Liberal, Kansas
Born 1933

This story started in 1943 as my father purchased 10 acres of land with a 30 X 60 adobe barn on it. This barn was built primarily for a hog barn, but the fellow who'd built it decided to go in another direction. Then, a barn must have animals, so we quickly acquired three brood sows, one of which I claimed and one my brother Bob claimed. It was our job to be sure there was feed and water for all three sows. Not too far down the road, we came up with two milk cows, "Brindle and Horny." Next came the baby pigs, 8 or 10 to a litter. Wow, we were really in the hog business now with probably 25 or 26 pigs.

My dad was a member of the Morton Co. Grazers Association, and come spring when the grass greened up, each member could put his grazing cattle on what was called "Government Range." This was a strip of sand hills, sagebrush, and grass, and was located on land that the Federal Government had taken over during the Dustbowl Days. This reached from north of Wilburton, Ks, (now non-existent), to 4 miles north of Rolla, Ks. It was fenced, with a cowboy to ride daily to check fences and watch for sick cattle.

My dad went to the stock sale and bought 10 yearlings to graze. There was a sorry looking white steer that had been down in the truck and could hardly walk. The auctioneer couldn't get a bid, so I bid $2.00, and everyone laughed. "SOLD" called the auctioneer, and I had just purchased my first cow brute. Dad had a friend, Warfield Pate, who owned an old Ford truck. Dad told him to be at the sale barn around 5:00 pm to load our animals. We loaded dad's first, and then had to help my old steer up the loading chute to the truck. Mr. Pate had bought two butcher hogs, which we loaded also. We got home to Rolla, and unloaded the cattle and Mr. Pate's hogs, as dad had agreed to butcher them later. After we had unloaded, it was chore time. I went in and got the milk buckets so we could get the milking done. Dad had fed the sows and pigs and scattered bundle feed in the corral. We milked and went in to the house. What a day for a 10 year old boy!

I finally convinced dad that I needed a saddle horse. We bought Old Buff from a fellow who couldn't buy feed. If I remember right, Howard Winter wanted $50 for the horse, and dad offered $40. The other fellow said no, so we left. I wasn't real happy with dad, and he knew it. That night while we were milking, he explained to me that Howard was out of feed and broke, and would likely take the $40 tomorrow. Now I learned a lesson here. First, don't ever doubt your dad, and second, when the other party is broke, take advantage.

Old Buff was quite a good buy, and yes, the other fellow agreed to sell for $40. This mare was a real kid horse as well as a good cow horse. When it snowed, we'd get a hood off an old car; tie a rope from the sled to the saddle horn, and sledded all over Rolla.

In the late Fall, around September 25, all of the cattle had to be rounded up and removed from the government pasture. I got out of school to help with the roundup. Boy, was I ever a Cowboy now! We started north of Wilburton pushing all cattle east towards the big corral north of Rolla, a distance of 7 or 8 miles likely 3 miles wide. When we got to the corral, most of the cattle went right in, but a few wilder ones gave a bit of a battle.

We had picked up a huge Holstein bull in the roundup. This old boy was on the fight as soon as the gate closed. He had horns 7 or 8 in. long. Somebody had sawed off the tips likely because he was so mean. Nobody knew where he had come from, or who owned him. Price Stout, who was the Roundup Boss, saw that this bull was double trouble and needed to be pulled out of the corral, but couldn't be helped any. He came to dad and said, "Tom, can you handle a rope?" Dad told him that if he was in close, he could do ok. Dad called to me to bring Old Buff over to him, and he borrowed a good saddle, as he didn't think mine would hold the bull. He also borrowed a good rope and he and Price rode into the corral. They were met by a mad bull!

Price lassoed his head and horns, dad scooped up his heels, and they dropped him there. Somebody got a long solid railroad tie and posthole diggers and dug a deep hole just at this bull's head. They planted the tie and by now, Mr. Bull was livid and snorting, but thanks to two good horses and two good hands, he never gained his feet. The men on the horses let a bit of slack and the bull could get to his knees, and after a bit, he stood up, but couldn't move the post. Someone brought a bucket of water. He sipped it and then kicked the bucket with his front leg and destroyed the bucket!

Now that the mad and fighting bull was securely contained, the next question was what to do with him. Each town along the railroad has a good solid stockyard for those ranchers to use while loading the railcars, so the suggestion was that the bull be transported to the railroad stockyards and held until ownership could be determined. There was a fellow in Rolla, Walt Perkins, who had a couple of trucks for hire to haul animals. He also had a heavy two-wheeled trailer made of iron, for hauling mean animals. The next day, he brought the bull trailer to the corral.

While all of this attention was being given to Mr. Bull, all of the other cattle were being sorted and loaded out for home and a likely trip to the sale barn. Our cattle had done real well and my white steer had healed and put on weight and looked good. He probably weighed 800 lbs. and boy was I proud of my first venture into the cattle business. Since we only had 4 miles to go, I and a couple of other cowboys drove them on to our corrals, which were next to the R.R. stockyards.

Then, we got back so as not to miss anything at Roundup Camp. We figured that when they went to load that bull, there would be a lot of action! The driver backed the trailer close to the big post and Mr. Bull didn't like it! With two lariats around his horns and the chain still in place, the post was pulled and the bull thinking he was free, charged right up into the trailer and the tailgate slammed shut! The chain was still around his horns, though a bit bloody by now. The chain was pulled to the front of the trailer and he was again held tight. He was kicking and blowing snot from his nose.

Walt Perkins pulled the bull trailer with a 1939 Chevy pickup, and away they went to the stockyards. Upon arriving, there was plenty of help and too many spectators. When the tailgate was opened to the loading chute, and the chain removed from his horns, the bull was still not happy. He went to the far side of the pen, and then decided to wreck the place! The bull hit the pen wall and didn't damage the pen, but knocked him out for a bit. Price Stout announced that everybody should leave and stay away, as this bull was definitely a killer and anybody that got hurt being around him, was at their own risk. Now, this information comes from dad who rode to town in a car, and I was coming in on my horse.

We had all been warned to NOT go near the stockyards, but being young and dumb, we couldn't resist the temptation. Nearly daily, some town boys went to the stockyards and tormented this bull. He would run at the pen fence, but not get out. Now, we had a nutcase, Buddy, who was a bit braver than the rest of us. He would wait until the bull was at the far end of the pen, and then jump down into the pen and "beller" like the bull. This only made Mr. Bull more agitated and he would make a run at this guy in his space. "Old Cass" as we called him, would quickly climb the fence. He was working an angle to maneuver this bull into the loading chute, thinking that if he could get that close, he could mount and ride him. Cass let it be known that he could ride that bull. He even set a date of next Thursday evening. I knew if he tried, he would likely get killed. I told my dad about this ill-fated deal, and dad talked to Cass's dad.

Everyone in Rolla knew of this most vicious bull, and most moms were scared for their boys. One evening when Cass came in, his dad said, "What's this I hear about you planning to ride the mean bull?" Cass said, "Yea, I thought I'd give it a try." His dad said," Well, guess we'll have your funeral about next Saturday." Cass said, "What? Are you planning to bury me and I'm still alive?" His dad said, "Yes, for now, but if that bull don't kill you, your mother will, so anyway, we are making funeral plans." Needless to say, that ended the bull riding talk.

After the Sheriff tried for 30 days to find an owner for the bull, it was decided by the Grazer's Association that the bull would be taken be sold. Walt Perkin's bull trailer was hired to haul him to Elkhart. He was unloaded at the sale barns and corrals and immediately went through two board fences. Cowboys got ropes on him and held him until his turn in the ring.

The Good Old Days in Kansas
By Katherine Becker Cruz of Westminster, Colorado
Born 1925

One of my earliest memories is from 1930, when I was 5 years old and my family was moving from our home on a farm in Schulte to a farm that my parents bought near Goddard, about 8 miles away. At that time, I had 2 brothers and 1 sister. We had a dog named Blacky, who kept running back to the old farm. My dad had to retrieve him 6 times. I guess Blacky just liked the old farm better. It took several trips in my dad's farm truck and horse-drawn wagons to move all of those chickens, cattle, farm equipment, and household goods. The move took several days.

This was during the Great Depression and many families were having a hard time. There was a drought, no work and little food. When FDR was elected president in 1933, one of his goals was to create work for the public. He did this by starting the Works Progress Administration and the Civilian Conservation Corps (CCC). The WPA affected so many people's lives. They were building new lakes, bridges, and many other projects. One of them was a lake near our farm, called Lake Afton. It was used for recreation, like fishing and ballgames. It was always busy. Now they also have a boy's camp there. 80 years later, it is still very popular today. At the time that it was built, men came from miles around to work on the lake. The construction provided opportunities for men who needed work to support their families.

My dad, Art Becker, did not work on the lake because he was busy farming. He raised wheat, alfalfa, and barley. He also had about 25 dairy cows. He and my brothers would milk early morning and again early evening. After milking, Steffen Dairy would come out every day in a refrigerated truck to pick up the fresh milk. The men would carry it in buckets to the milk house where it was poured into large milk buckets, and then put into large silver vats. The vats sat in cool water, and then the milk was hand-stirred to keep it cool and fresh. We had to keep the milk house clean, washing the buckets and cleaning the vats every day. The inspectors came out to check quite often. I was the oldest girl, and my younger brothers were rascals who liked to tease me. They would yell up to the house for their sisters to come and help. Most of the time it was just a set up so they could squirt us with milk. My sister fell for that trick a lot more than I did- I was wiser! It was the girls' job to help with all the household chores, like cooking, cleaning, and laundry.

Once we had moved to our own farm, our family seemed to grow and grow, just like the wheat and other crops. Every two years or so another baby came until there were 11 of us. One of my sisters died in a tragic farm accident. Some memories are too painful to talk about. Our family then consisted of 5 boys and 5 girls, and we always had a lot of fun, even though there was a lot of work. Sadly, the fun came to an end for a while, when my mother died in January of 1939 from childbirth and other complications. All

The Becker family in 1917

of the babies were home births. The doctor would have to drive about 10 miles to be there for the deliveries. He came by himself or, if needed, his wife (a nurse) came along. He was a great guy, a country doctor, and we all loved him. This was before antibiotics, so his most frequent prescription was "Go home and take a hot toddy" but my dad wouldn't allow whisky in the house! Dr. Beirman practically died on the job, working hard until the end.

My father was a very devout man. He prayed the rosary almost every day and never missed mass on Sundays. We all attended.

One morning there was a knock at the door. It was a neighbor man. He said his wife had had a baby that night and it died. He didn't know what to do, so my dad made a small coffin out of wood and painted it. My mother lined it with satin. I remember seeing the baby before they placed him in it. We held a little prayer service for the baby, and my brother and I were the pallbearers. My father dug a large hole in that family's pasture, where we laid the baby to rest and prayed.

We walked 2 miles to the country school for our education. My dad served on the school board. It was a 1-room schoolhouse; heated by a wood burning stove (the students carried the wood). There was only 1 teacher who taught 1st-8th grades. There were about 15 of us students. Lunch was at noon, followed by recess. We made up our own games, like hopscotch and jumping rope, but I remember softball the most. They always made me be the pitcher!

At Christmas, we only got one toy from Santa and it was hand-made by my parents. There were some better years, when we'd get a purchased toy: a doll for the girls, and a gun and holster or a wagon for the boys. But we were always happy with what we got. We always had a big family dinner with lots of food, and we enjoyed playing with our cousins on Christmas Day.

I got my 1st driver's license when I was 14 years old. It cost me 25 cents at Clearwater, KS. We didn't have to take driving tests in those days. The roads weren't paved or black topped just dirt and mud so you couldn't drive very fast.

In the summer, some nights were so hot and humid, and of course, we didn't have fans, so we'd take our blankets outside and sleep in the front yard. The mosquitos were bad. For entertainment, we'd go to outdoor movies in the summertime. The small towns would show them, usually in the park. The first movie I ever saw was "The Wizard of Oz" in the late summer of 1939. Our mother had passed away earlier that year, and sometime after harvest, our dad packed all 10 of us kids into his Terreplane and drove us to an air-conditioned, indoor movie theater in Wichita. Afterward, he treated every one of us to ice cream. In those days, they had special cones that would hold 3 different flavors.

The last day of school with a picnic and ballgame (boys and dads)

Our dad was such a good man. Although he was struggling to raise all of us, he never complained.

We had a wall phone. It was a party line and about 10 families were on the same line, so when it rang everyone had a different ring, but it would still ring in everyone's houses so they'd all listen in on your conversation.

We lived near a railroad track. A lot of homeless men would catch a ride in the box cars. Many would get off and walk looking for work or food. My mother would always feed them, and some would spend the night in our barn and leave in the early morning. Sometimes she would pack a lunch for them and they'd be on their way. Occasionally my dad would hire some of them for work around the farm.

Times were hard during the war (1942). We were issued stamps to use to buy fuel,

Students on the school's playground slide

sugar, coffee, and other items. Women couldn't get silk stockings and men couldn't buy dress shirts. The clothing stores carried very few, and only in white. There were no colored shirts available. Each person got so many ration stamps per month. We had a large family, so we always had plenty. We'd give some away to people who needed them more.

My Dad worked very hard, and he worked all the time without complaining. Looking west, he could see the dust forming in the sky. It was brown and black. He would get into the car to pick us up from school four miles away, then he and the boys would hurry home to take care of the animals and get them inside the barns. We girls would help our mother hang up wet sheets on the windows. The sheets helped us breathe. The sand was so fine it got in no matter what, but the sheets helped. We hung them on the inside, covering the windows, because no matter how tight your windows were the sand still seeped through. We'd put the sheets flat against the walls, though I can't recall how we got them to stay in place. By the time the storm was over those sheets would be dark black. I don't remember that it hurt my dad's farming. They had to keep fields plowed and cultivated so the sand wouldn't blow so badly. Roosevelt had regulations in place to cut down on the damage, and one was that fields HAD to be cultivated. We didn't get it so badly in Kansas. Those winds blowing off eastern Colorado really hit Oklahoma worse than us.

We never had electricity until about 1940. It was the R.E.A. They ran a line through our field. That was such a happy day for all of us. We had the house wired for it for about a year before it was even turned on. It was such a long wait. The children just about wore out the switches from turning them off and on to see if they worked! Regretfully, our mother didn't live to see us receive electricity, though she was very excited for us to get it.

I was a teenager during prohibition, but there was always a way to buy liquor and everybody knew how. I remember going to dances with other couples and stopping at a house in the country where the boys bought whisky. I didn't care too much for whisky, and most girls didn't, but we'd go along for the ride. We had to turn off the car lights to avoid being seen. The house was dark and the boys knocked on a boarded up window where a person handed them the whisky, but you couldn't see their face. It was spooky! Kansas was a dry state until around 1949, at which time I myself was already a married woman and mother; standing in line to vote with my baby. The line to vote in favor of alcohol stretched around the block.

These memories are all precious to me, but they are just a fraction of what I remember about the good old days in Kansas.

A Band of Angels?
By Walter Perrin of Clallam Bay, Washington
Born 1941

I was born in Hutchinson, Kansas, the baby brother of four sisters. We are descended from homesteaders on both sides of the family. My father's family emigrated from England, homesteading in South Dakota. My maternal grandmother's father and grandfather homesteaded on land in Reno County, west of Hutchinson. Their homesteader shack is on display in the museum in Hutchinson. Great-grandfather Joseph Siegrist emigrated from Switzerland. His parents were from German Swiss stock and Anabaptist persuasion, possibly Mennonite or Amish. He landed in Pennsylvania, part of the Pennsylvania Dutch, soon married, and eventually moved to Illinois where he founded a beautiful farm. Later he and his son, Jacob, homesteaded in Kansas, becoming very successful and acquiring even more land than the original 160 acres. It is recorded that he had 250 fattened hogs ready for market. Leaving the original shack, he built a very nice two-story house one or two miles north, which became my grandparents' house.

Grandma Siegrist married Byron Eastman from New England. Grandpa Eastman was a very intelligent, wonderful man with a great sense of humor. He had a nice voice and loved to sing, sometimes impromptu. He was religious, attended the Methodist Church, and always asked a blessing before meals. Together they were the best grandparents ever.

I loved to visit their house. It was full of antiques: marble-topped dressers, canopy beds, and a grandfather clock at least six feet tall, oil paintings, a piano, and cool objects from China like a real ivory back scratcher carved in the image of a monkey's hand and a beautiful Chinese checkers game. Then there were several guns: double-barrel shotguns, octagonal barreled .50 caliber buffalo guns, and a .32 caliber Remington-Elliot pepperbox pistol that Grandma carried. My grandpa had promised me the guns but they were taken by new family members. There was a wind-up Victrola, a tall Zenith radio, and so forth in the parlor. If you carefully lifted a floorboard in the upstairs northwest bedroom, you could scoop out honey and a honeycomb, for bees had found their way in from the eave and built a huge hive. We kids, along with Uncle Byron, played Annie over at this house.

Their farm had seven cows and three horses, chickens, guinea hens, ducks, geese, hogs, beehives, and peach and pear trees. Honeysuckle covered the front porch and mint grew in the shade of the trees. They had a huge garden, berry bushes, and wild black currents. Grandma always wore a sunbonnet, as she spent long summer days bent over picking off bugs and nursing the plants. Even with doing this, she was still able to cook big meals on a wood stove for the farm workers. Farm crops consisted of mainly wheat, oats, sweet corn, and alfalfa. Crops were rotated, and it was all organic long before that became fashionable; it was just the normal way things were done. The dark, rich topsoil was at least twelve inches deep, and I plowed a lot of it, having learned to drive a tractor at age seven. I loved working on the farm as a kid trying to keep up with the men, pitching hay and operating equipment.

One summer when I was about ten years old, I rose at 5:00 a.m. each morning and ran over to Grandma's house to help with the milking. She would squirt milk from the udder some distance into a barn cat's open mouth. Later the milk would be run through the cream separator. The cream was sometimes traded for vanilla ice cream with the Jackson Ice Cream Company. Eggs were sold to neighbors and relatives, many of whom took advantage of a sweet old lady's compassion and generosity. Many of the promises to "pay later" never came to pass.

I got to drink coffee and eat Cream of Wheat and Danish rolls for breakfast after milking each morning. Grandma would give me a banana to tide me over on the ¼ mile walk home with the admonishment that if I dropped it crossing the highway not to try and retrieve it because of the fast traffic on Highway 61. Grandma, bless her heart, was overly protective. She had borne three children: my mother, the oldest, Byron, the youngest, but the middle child as a newborn baby was dropped on his head and killed when a nurse at the hospital fell asleep holding him. That and the fact that the government had stolen some of her land by imminent domain to build the railroad combined to make her paranoid. Years later, a train on that track killed our twin first cousins.

The telephone was a wooden wall mounted box with a black microphone in the middle of its face, a receiver on a cord that hung in a cradle on the left side, and a crank on the right side. To make a call you would remove the receiver form its hook, wind the crank handle to generate power, and ask Central to connect you to whomever. Grandma always kept a cloth cover over the mouthpiece so she could wash it periodically, being concerned about germs.

I don't think Grandma ever cut her hair. Each morning, she would bend over and brush and brush her long hair, which reached the floor. Then she would twist it into a knot.

Going to town with her was delightful. I would sit beside her in the velvet-covered back seat while Uncle Byron drove the pristine 1938 Buick. Grandma always smelled so nice of lavender and peppermint. She would give me a couple of peppermints form the neatly folded flowered handkerchief. Grandma's cooking was legendary. It was not unusual for her to have five desserts with Sunday dinner. When we worked in the fields she would appear at the edge of a filed and holler, "You-who, you-who" and we would stop for dinner, the noon meal.

The old two-story house my family lived in was actually owned by my grandfather. Counting the long lanes, it was maybe a ¼ mile away from the grandparents' house. We had only wood or occasionally coal heat. My dad was remodeling the house, but since we had no bathroom, we did sponge baths from a basin. The upstairs got very cold. Being the youngest, I got the worst room until my sisters left home. There was no upstairs heat so I could not turn over for the weight of many blankets. My mother rigged a clothesline in my room, and the clothes froze so solid that when I whacked them with my BB gun, it broke off at the stock. My sister, Mickie, always checked on me when she returned form dates or whatever. Upon finding me shivering, she would give me extra clothes to wear and snuggle with me in her bed until I warmed up. Pretty nice of her considering I was such a brat to her. Once while hiding inside a lilac bush I saw her kiss her boyfriend and threatened to tell our parents unless she paid me a quarter! Another time I accidently happened upon her and her girlfriend smoking cigarettes on the roof of the chicken house, and I was paid a nickel "hush money." It's a wonder I didn't become a mobster.

I lived an idyllic life but not having friends close by, learned to play by myself. My sister, Arlie, her friend, and I rode stick horses a lot. Sometimes our third cousins who lived across a field would come over at dusk, and we would all play hide and seek as it got dark.

The one thing that was unique at our house was the outhouse. The WPA had built it, and someone had a real creative bent. When you opened the door both seat lids would automatically raise up and lock open, ready for use. It had a solid concrete floor and base, and there was no way it could be overturned at Halloween

I spent all summer long shirtless and barefoot. I was frequently bitten by snakes, because I accidently stepped on them.

My dad had two horses, a black one named Blackie and a white one named Charlie, also my dad's name. One day one of the boys from the Roper family talked my dad into letting him try to ride Blackie, who was only harness broke. Blackie had no desire to be saddle broke, however, and the Roper boy found out what it was like to have a broken arm when he was bucked off.

My sisters Mickie, Arlie, and I sang on the radio a couple of times. Mickie was 13 and played the piano; Arlie was ten and I was seven years old. We were called the Singing Perrin Kids. The first time I ever saw TV of any kind was in 1951 at a Mennonite boy's home.

I attended the same one teacher, one room school that all four of my sisters had attended before me. The teacher, Miss Anderson, was amazing in the way she kept complete order teaching eight grades in one room. Unfortunately, she didn't seem to be so impressed with me. She frequently compared me to my sisters, saying things like, "You sure aren't as good at arithmetic as your sisters were." Interestingly, I eventually took every math course available to me and consequently knew more math than any of them.

Many of our neighbors in the surrounding farms were Amish. Some of my earliest memories are of my grandma standing in front of an Amish buggy talking to old Noah Mast, an ancient Amish man with a long white beard. Periodically he would visit her. They would converse in Low German for some time, and then he would turn around and leave.

When I was young, I would stick out my thumb and hitch hike a ride in the Amish buggies. I didn't really need a ride, but it was a lot of fun, and they seemed amused.

Not having a baler, we usually put up our hay loose, but there were a few years we had some Amish men bale our hay for a percentage of it. There was always great cooperation between the farmers.

I bought a couple of gilt pigs from Ramon Headings to raise for a Future Farmers of America project and got a guided tour of his house and farm. I was amazed that the chicken houses with their incubators as well as the other out buildings were very modern; having electricity, but the house had no electricity or modern appliances.

There was one Halloween night where some of the Amish boys went with us high school boys to Amish farms and 'borrowed' several buggies. I remember sitting in the trunk of a car and helping to hold on to one of them as we slowly brought them to our high school town of Partridge. Then using amazing engineering expertise for boys, the buggies were lifted onto the roofs of the high school building, the post office, and the drugstore. The next school day the sheriff called the entire lot of us together and chewed us out. We had to bring the buggies down, of course. We were careful, and none of them were damaged.

After drinking several beers, I was driving home on a deserted gravel road and a heavy fog set in. Suddenly ahead in the fog I thought I was seeing a band of angels in a chariot. Was it the beer? It turned out to be eight Amish girls in an open buggy, four abreast in the front seat, and four abreast in the elevated rear seat. They were dressed in white gowns and caps. It was eerie but beautiful. I don't know what they were doing out there so late, but someone said it was a pre-marriage ritual.

Memories of My Parents
By Vita M. Henning of Kingman, Kansas
Born 1936

My parents, Frank Albers and Clara Berning were married in the depression year of 1935. My dad was 47 and mother was 33. She brought some money along with her that she had saved over the years. The place already had running water and electricity but no bathroom. So they used her money to enclose a screened in porch and put in a bathtub and stool. They lived a mile and a quarter east of St. Leo and were the last ones on the electric line and also the telephone line going east. At the time my dad owed the blacksmith shop some money for work done so the owner got worried that this bachelor's new wife was going to spend all his money so he puts a lien on the land to cover his debt when in fact it was her money they were using to make the improvements.

They had a propane run refrigerator and a propane cook stove but they had a coal burning heating stove. They only lived in the kitchen, which was a big room and closed off the rest of the house. They also had a little propane heater in the bathroom but was only used when they took their Saturday night bath otherwise it was also closed off. In 1949, a propane forced air heating stove was bought but we still only lived in the kitchen. The telephone consisted of a sort of box on the wall with a crank on it and place to speak into and piece to put on your ear to hear and when you were done talking could hang it up on a hook. You would have to crank the crank to get the operator and then she would connect you to whomever you wanted to talk. There would be different rings for each party on the party line such as one long and two short rings or two longs and a short and so on.

For an auto, we had a 1930 Model A Ford that would go about 30 to 35 miles to the hour. Whenever we would go even to Wichita, it would be an all day trip. Leaving before sun rise and getting back after dark. In 1949 after they received an inheritance from her Dad's estate and they then bought a black 1949 Chevy 4 door sedan car, a 1953 Chevy pickup with a lift on the bed special made and M &M rubber tired tractor and other machinery. Before that, Dad mostly farmed with horses yet. He did have a caterpillar crawler tractor that he did the plowing with but other things were still done with the horses such as drilling wheat or spring tooth or harrowing the ground. Cutting oats with a horse drawn binder and later trashed with a thrashing machine. He hired a pull type combine hooked on to the caterpillar where there had to be an operator on the combine. My dad would often fall asleep on the tractor and the combine operator would have to throw some wheat at him to get his attention if he was getting off course. They hauled the wheat into the granary with horse and wagon and scooped in the granary by a hired man who lived with us during harvest time. In the winter time, he would haul it to the elevator to be sold which was 8 miles away at Nashville. He could probably haul two loads in a day with the horse and wagon.

In that area of St Leo, each Catholic Church Parish would have a picnic to raise money. It was a big gathering of people to celebrate a good harvest and they would have a big dinner and sell tickets for the dinner. Have bingo, poker, raffle items, and other games and in the evening have a dance all to raise money. All the local parishes would do that such as Cunningham, Zenda, and Sharon and St Leo. One year the Zenda Parish raffled off a 1949 Studebaker 4 door sedan. My folks usually did not go to the surrounding celebrations but somehow was able to buy raffle tickets. In the middle of the night a group of people got together after leaving Zenda and the winner was announced, came to my parent's yard honking their horns and making all kinds of noise to wake up everyone in the house to tell them they had won the car. What a surprise!

We had a fire in the house one year. My Mother had went to church because it was Ascension Day and left us kids at home and Dad was helping a man shear the wool off of the sheep in the barn. I was not comfortable in the house so would go outside to the brooder house and set and watch the baby chicks play. I went in to check on my brother and he was doing okay so went back outside again to watch the chicks play. When mom came home, she went into the living room to go to her bedroom to change her clothes when she discovered the living room full of smoke and a small fire so had me run out to the barn to tell the men. The fire was contained on the couch, which had an electric blanket on it, and it must have gotten a short in to start the fire. The men got the couch outside and put out the fire. Other than the couch, being burned, and smoke damage in that room, I don't believe there was any other damage. The only thing I can think about is that I must have been smelling smoke but did not realize it and that is why I went outside to get away from it.

My dad only had a 4th grade education but was very smart and with no formal training surveyed his own terraces on the land. Terraces were built on land that was hilly or slopping to keep the ground from washing away so bad after a rain. The soil conservation people came out and did the surveying at first and they would run them flat so they would not drain properly and would have places where the water would stand. He was one of the first persons in Kingman County to have terraces. So with my help holding the stick he would proceed to survey the land and built his own terraces so they would drain.

During World War II Kingman County had a draft board and they would pick and choose who would be drafted into the army. In 1945, the board drafted Alois J. (Boobie) Jarmer, a local blacksmith that had his shop in St Leo working with his dad. His dad was getting elderly and not able to do the work much anymore so my dad thought the board should exempt him from serving in the Army. They would exempt a farmers oldest son from going so why not the blacksmith son. He proceeded to give money to one of the draft board members as a bribe. He gave it to the wrong one, to keep Boobie out of the Army. He was turned in, was arrested, and had to spend the night in jail. My brother Ralph remembers a black coup with FBI came in the yard and talked to my Dad and apparently took him to jail then. Boobie served in the Army from April 1945 to August 1946 so his efforts did not work.

Vita's father, Frnak Albers in 1935

My Mom always had a good sized garden and a big potato patch. She planted lettuce, radish, onions, green beans, and tomatoes and other things I don't remember. We also had an asparagus patch and a rhubarb and a strawberry patch that came up every year. We would can the excess. She also went out and found sand plums and other berries to make jelly. She would buy cucumbers to make pickles with. She also canned peaches and pears. We would always have enough to last until the next year came and we could start all over again. She also planted some flowers to enjoy. When she had an excess we would take a bouquet to church that would be placed on the altar for decoration. She could also sew and sewed me dresses out of feed sacks and the boys got shirts. In 1967she got a quilting machine and made 1356 quilts for a lot of people sewing the tops and bottom together with batting in the middle. She made her last quilt in June of

1978 and passed away in Oct of 1978.

My Mom was a good cook and in the summer time we would go out in the yard, catch a couple of roosters that they had raised that spring and proceed to chop off their heads, put them in hot water, then pull the feathers off and clean them up to be butchered, then fried for dinner and she always made pies too as we would have a lot of hired help in the summer time. One thing that never failed to happen was my dad would take a 15 minute nap after dinner no matter what. The hired help would go out and set on the porch and wait until Dad got his nap in.

Dad was our weather spotter. When storm clouds came up, he would spend all hours of the night watching the clouds for tornados and when he thought it would be a bad storm he would let Mom know and she would get us kids out of bed and head for the cellar which was some distance from the house and usually he would wait till the last minute and it would already be raining and we would have to cover ourselves with blankets to keep from getting too wet. Mom always had her bundle of important papers with her. We would stay in the cellar which was a hole dug in the ground with cement on the roof and then ground covered it over the top. They had a small cot in there where we could set while we waited out the storm. It was also the place where the potatoes were stored and all the canned vegetables and fruit and the cream separator and cream were kept. When the storm was over, we could go back to the house.

Our roads were all dirt roads until 1950 when the county decided to improve the road that run in front of our property. They had to do all kinds of grading and leveling and finally put on oil to make a hard black top surface. That was so nice to be able to drive on a nice smooth road to St. Leo and other places.

In 1953, the folks decided to build a new dairy barn and sell Grade A Milk with milk machines and a pipe line to carry the milk to a cooler with 10 gallon cans in it to put the milk into until the truck would come and haul it off to their processing plant. Up until this time, we milked cows by hand. Would separate it and just sell the cream and feed the hogs the skim milk. We would only have 2 or 3 cows but when we started to dairy, we got up to 10 or 15.

In 1954, we got our first TV. It was black and white and we had to put up an antenna on a tower outside. Then we would have to run outside to turn it just the right direction to get reception. Then the reception was so poor it was mostly snow that we saw on the console TV that had a very small screen and we could only get 3 channels in our area. But we had TV and thought it was great.

The Blizzard of 1952
By Pat Reichenberger of Mt. Hope, Kansas
Born 1942

Tuesday, November 25, 1952 began as a wet, balmy fall day. My dad, mom, three brothers, and I got up early to tend to the livestock on our farm near Andale, Kansas. After our chores and a hardy breakfast, we quickly dressed for school, which was 4 1/2 miles away. As we were preparing to leave the house, we noticed the big change in the weather. The wind was blowing from the north, the temperature was dropping rapidly, and the damp clouds began to drop heavy, wet snow. An hour later, as we began to settle into our seats at school, the wet, heavy, and blowing snow was drifting everywhere. Visibility was reduced to zero. Classroom windows were covered with snow on the north side of the school. Truly, a full-blown blizzard was roaring in across south central Kansas. As a 10-year-old farm boy, I was excited. I loved the snow!

Morning flew by and at about 10:30AM, Mr. Kennedy, the principal of our school, knocked at our classroom door. We were excited when we overheard him say school was out for the day. In 1952, our school district had no school buses, so we went to and from school in our 1941 Plymouth, with my oldest brother Dave, who was 18 years old at the time.

As we made our way out of the school building, we could barely see our car. We slowly made our way out onto the country roads and we were frightened by the deep snow and zero visibility. We had gone about a 1/2 mile when we rear-ended another car that was stuck in the snow. We abandoned our car and made our way to our uncle's house nearby. Another neighbor with a new farm pickup truck took my brother Dave as far as he could go, on his way to his farm. My brother nearly died in the blizzard as he trudged through the deep snow before reaching our farmstead.

Meanwhile, back at our uncle's and aunt's house, we were nervously waiting for our uncle to get back home safely from a trip for groceries. Then, about 11:30AM, another schoolmate, Bob Meyer, also stranded in the blizzard, found his way to Uncle Willie's house. When Uncle Willie finally got back, around 3:00pm, he was on foot, almost frozen in the blizzard. He got his heavy coat and asked my brother Tom and Bob Meyer to go along with him on his tractor to pull his car home. I begged to go with Uncle Willie and Tom. Reluctantly, Uncle Willie gave in and the four of us left on the tractor in the raging blizzard. The old tractor was equipped with a front-end loader powered by the power-take-off shaft on the rear of the tractor and heavy cables to move the loader up and down. As a 10-year-old boy, I was unaware of the impending danger as I stood on the cables. When my uncle Willie engaged the power-take-off shaft, my left leg was pulled into and tangled in the heavy cable. I yelled out to Uncle Willie for help. He immediately disengaged the power-take-off shaft and jumped off the tractor to examine the problem. He told my brother Tom to guide my nearly severed leg as he reversed the power-take-off shaft. When my leg was free from the cables, Uncle Willie, with tears streaming down his face, put a tourniquet on my leg, loaded me in the back seat, and began to tow the car to his house. Once there, they loaded blankets and pillows for me and we headed out in the raging blizzard, the tractor towing the car, back to Andale, 1/2 a mile away. After what seemed a very long trek back into town to where the restaurant and bar were located, a few hardy men gathered by Uncle Willie's car to see why anyone would be out in the blizzard. When they looked in the back seat, they saw me and could see blood soaking through the blankets.

The previous several hours had been very uncertain to me as a 10-year-old child. As I lay in the back seat, I had seen and examined the large bone, which lay exposed in the blanket. I was alone part of the time as they hooked the car to the tractor. I knew our family doctor was 13 miles away-an impossible distance in the blizzard and Andale had no doctor. I prayed to God to please find help for us and to let me live through this tragic accident. Now, as the tractor and car sat quietly on Main Street, we at least had the comfort of other people. But, no one knew what to do to help. I could see the helplessness in the eyes of the men gathered there that night.

But, then, they heard the far-off but distinct blare of the Missouri Pacific freight train-apparently the only possible means of finding a doctor and hospital 25 miles away in Wichita, Kansas. By this time, it was about 6:00pm.

One of the men quickly began to trudge through the deep snow toward the train depot with his flashlight. Uncle Willie towed the car to the depot area. The train plowed into the small depot area and came to a halt amid the deep snow. As Uncle Willie and the men gathered around the engine, Paul Tate, the engineer, and Clyde "Woody" Woodson, the brakeman, crawled down out of the engine. The men gathered around them. They quickly decided to load me into the caboose of the old freight train near the red-hot coal stove. Only one other rescued man was there with me, Uncle Willie, and Woody, the brakeman. I finally felt safe when the train jolted and moved forward. As the train chugged along through the night, the large drifts caused it to jerk almost constantly. Pain began to surge through my left leg as we traveled closer to Wichita. I never thought of derailment as I prayed to God to get us to Wichita safely. The train did derail the next day because of the snow, but on this cold and desolate night, we pulled into downtown Wichita about 9:30pm, almost 6 hours after the accident had happened. About 30 minutes later, the ambulance from St. Francis Hospital arrived, loaded me into the back of the ambulance, and took me to "safety"-the emergency room at St. Francis Hospital in Wichita.

At about 10:30pm, a young Doctor Stolz and his crew of nurses came in and began to cut away my "new school" jeans. That was the last thing I remember as they slipped the ether mask over my face.

Wednesday morning dawned calm, white, and beautiful. Only Uncle Willie was there by my bedside. My dad rode the freight train to Wichita on Thursday, Thanksgiving Day, to be with me. My mom was able to come by car on Friday. God truly blessed our family and me. Dr. Stolz and the nurses had been able to clean my leg and sew it back on. It was in a big heavy cast. After several weeks in St. Francis Hospital, and 2-3 months of recuperating with crutches, my leg had completely healed. By late March of 1953, all the snow was gone and only the memories remain.

Growing Up in Small Town USA (Stafford, Kansas)
By Alice Kay Miller of Lenexa, Kansas
Born 1948

I was born and raised in a small farming community located in South-Central Kansas. What might seem a bit unusual is that I lived in the same house all of my "growing up" years in the town of Stafford, Kansas, in Stafford County, on Stafford Street. I had the most amazing childhood a kid could ever have growing up during the late '40s, and the '50s and '60s "time period." (Of course, it didn't hurt that I had the greatest parents and big brother in the world.) And, I do feel that most everyone that grew up there during that time would most likely agree that it was a great place to grow up. To this day, I still consider Stafford to be "home" even though I haven't lived there since I turned 18 in the summer of '66. It was truly the best of times.

To give you a little background of my family, my dad (Gordon) was parts manager at the local Chevrolet car dealership (Wes Lander Motor). That was back when you drove your car up to the gas station and someone came out and pumped your gas and cleaned your windshield with a big friendly smile on their face. As was the case in so many instances with the townspeople from that small community, a person worked their every day job but also wore many other "hats" to help raise their family and to help keep the town running smoothly. It was a community effort. With that, Dad enjoyed being a little league baseball coach and, at one time, was a city councilman and also on the volunteer fire department. My mother (Velta) was a beauty operator and had her own shop in our home called "Velta's Beauty Shop." I still remember the folks adding the shop onto the house when I was in kindergarten so that mother could be at home when we kids got home from school. She also helped down at the funeral home so she made many ladies "beautiful" throughout the years. The folks' main priority was to make a good home for our family and to teach my brother and me how important it was to grow up to be responsible adults. Being able to raise us in that small town environment was extremely important to them as they wanted us to have that freedom but, at the same time, to feel safe in the small town atmosphere.

My brother (Monte) and I grew up in a great neighborhood (with the other neighbor kids) on the west side of town. We did what most kids did during that time... we "played" outside all day long until it was dark or until we heard our parents calling our name(s) to come inside for supper. We played in the dirt a lot; we played Cowboys and Indians; we played cars and trucks; and we rode our trikes and bikes and skated for all hours at a time going up and down the long sidewalk in front of our house. Of course, we liked putting those playing cards on the spokes of our bikes so it would make that cool flapping sound. And, if we weren't playing outside, we were usually inside watching "Mickey Mouse Club" and other similar shows of that era. We also played in our tree house that our dad built in the big tree behind the carport but, along with that tree house, there were some rules we had to abide by. If we broke any one of the rules, dad told us it would come down. Well, needless to say, the tree house finally had to come down because we "apparently" broke one of those rules and dad always meant what

Alice with her parents, Velta and Gordon and her brother, Monte in 1949

he said. Our parents were always very fair but were also true to their word. You could count on that for sure.

Summertime in Stafford was the best! There were always little league baseball games going on up at the fairgrounds and we had the "Stafford" County Fair every summer as well. I also remember going to Brownie Scout Camp in the summer, which was a ton of fun, too. (However, being eaten up by the chiggers was not so much fun.) But, I was usually ready to come home as the week was coming to an end because I missed my family so much. I also remember as a child that during the summertime, my brother and I would get to go to the "Stafford" swimming pool just about every day, which was only three blocks from home. We had a 2-hour time limit because mom didn't want us to get sunburned. So, I remember thinking that if I went from 2-4pm that it felt like it was a longer timeframe than if I went from 1-3pm. (Yes, it's amazing how the brain works when you're a kid, isn't it?) Also, my first job ever was working part-time in the candy stand at the pool when I was 11. Then, as we got older in the summer months, I would cook the lunch and dinner meals to help out mom while she worked in the shop and my brother would work for the area farmers bailing hay or for the City of Stafford doing various jobs. We also had other chores around the house and received a weekly allowance, which wouldn't be a lot in today's standards, but we were happy to get it, nevertheless. Also, the folks would save all year long for our family summer vacation. We would pack up the ole "Chevrolet" and head out on a two-week vacation across the country. We might head west to the Rocky Mountains, or to California to visit my Aunt Alice (and Disneyland), or to see the beautiful Grand Canyon, or down south to the Florida beaches for some summer fun, and many other parts of the good ole USA. Of course, we always had to stop at a motel that had a swimming pool. (Dad knew he might as well keep on driving if it didn't have a pool.) Some of our happiest times as a family were spent on those trips and looking at old vacation pictures all these years later, it certainly brings back a lot of fond memories and some good chuckles, too.

Monte, Alice and Naomi in 1949

We lived in a town where you could walk anywhere and feel safe. If you happened to leave your car door or house unlocked, it was okay. My brother and I would walk clear across town to go to grade school or we'd ride our bikes sometimes. Of course, "clear across town" wasn't all that far but it seemed like miles to me at the time. However, on really cold winter days when it snowed, dad would take us to school. And, back in those days, when it snowed, it usually snowed a lot. It seemed to me that the weather was more severe back then but I also thought of things in a much different light as a child, as you can see. At any rate, I just remember really cold winters and a lot of drifting snow and wearing a lot of hats, gloves, and boots and eating a lot of oatmeal or cream of wheat on those cold winter mornings before heading out to school.

My brother and I both had great friends growing up in Stafford and there were even some kids that we went to school with from the time we were in kindergarten all the way up through high school graduation. We have some great memories of those childhood friends and are still in contact with many of them all these years later because of our life-long ties to Stafford. My brother and I were always busy with so many activities all the way through school as were many of the kids in town. When you grow up in a small town, you are active in "everything" because that's just what you did to keep busy. Certainly all the sporting events were a big part of what was going on in town. The parents and townspeople were such a big support system for the kids' activities no matter what event it was or when or where it took place. Along with my many activities that I participated in growing up, I worked part-time at the local

Monte, Velta, Alice Kay, and Gordon

dry goods store, Ontjes-Harrison, located on Main Street, while I was in high school (and two summers during my college years). I learned so much from that job, which would go with me for the rest of my life.

Of course, we can't forget the teenage years of having that first crush, that first date, or that first sweetheart. Those were the carefree, fun-loving years. And, dragging Main Street was a must! Everyone would drag Main after some game or event, or you would sometimes stop to get a beef burger at Starlight Drive-Inn, or drive by the swimming pool in the summer to see who was there, or you might drive by your girlfriend or boyfriend's house "just because." Oh, and there were the slumber parties, the school dances and school parties, the school plays and music programs, the band and drill team performances, the football and basketball games, the Homecomings, the pep rallies and bon fires, the track meets, the proms, and numerous other events and activities that kept our little town thriving. And, then all of a sudden, it was "graduation day". And, once you approached your graduation, you suddenly realized that this wonderful life you had for the past 18 years, would soon come to an end. You would be heading out into the world somewhere to discover the next phase of your life. No matter how excited you were at the time, reality had finally set in that you would probably be leaving Stafford behind... that wonderful small town of your youth. However, some never left and chose to stay there for a lifetime. Either way, life was about to change. As for me, I knew my future was "out there" somewhere. Even though I knew I would be coming back for many years to come to see my folks in my childhood hometown, I also knew it would never be the same again. My "childhood years" had come to an abrupt end that summer of '66 when I turned 18. I was ready to take on the world with pure excitement along with all the uncertainty and innocence that came with it. I would be looking at my childhood in the "rearview mirror" with such fond memories but heading down the road and looking ahead towards the future with much anticipation.

As I now look back through the years, I can honestly say that I wouldn't have wanted to grow up anywhere else other than in the small town of Stafford, Kansas, in Stafford County, on Stafford Street. Although it has changed throughout the years, it's still where I came from. My "roots" are there and always will be. Yes, it was the "best of times" and now I have the "best of memories" to look back upon as I settle into my retirement years. I had my wonderful parents and big brother to thank for their love and support along with my many wonderful friends and teachers, and that entire community (when I was growing up) for making my childhood an incredibly happy one. It was a true blessing indeed, "growing up in small town USA" (Stafford Kansas)!

Life in Rural Kansas
By Maureen Grandon of Eatonville, Washington
Born 1932

When I was going into second grade, we moved to a farm three miles east and four miles south of Anthony, Kansas in Harper County. My brother, Galen Bonham was five years older, a sister, Joyce, one year younger than me, and a sister, Yvonne is five years younger than me. We started going to the local one-room school, all eight grades, one teacher. It was three miles away. When the weather was nice, we rode horses to school. All the schools had barns and the fathers would stock them with hay. Galen would unsaddle the horse, pump water, and take it to our horse. Tinker was part Shetland but much bigger than a full Shetland. Our schoolyard was on the corner of two lightly traveled country roads and had a shelterbelt of cottonwood trees on the west and north side, One year, Galen and Melvin and Robert who lived in farms across the road decided to build a cabin. So they found two trees that were suitable to hoist a large limb between and make an A frame. So, one of the boys walked home, got a block and tackle and hoisted the limb between the two large trees. Then we little kids found smaller branches and dug them into the ground to form the cabin. Then we found twigs and wound them in and out horizontally between the branches to make it airtight. It was tall enough that I could stand up in, in third grade by then. This was all done during the day when recess and lunch was long over, but no one seems to mind. I left that school after seventh grade and that little cabin was still there although not exactly wind proof, we never went in it after we built it.

Every year the enrollment declined until when I was in seventh grade there were only five kids in school. One in eighth grade, me in seventh grade, my sister in fifth grade, one in fourth, and my other sister in second. When we moved to another farm and Veldora went on the high school, they closed the school.

A railroad track ran diagonally from our school to the main road. The school was one mile east and two miles south of our house. When it was just two or three of us walking home, and the section hands from the railroad were on their way home, they would offer us a ride to the elevator. So we would get on their little platform, which we called a put-put car and get a ride halfway home. It was just two men; they had shovels, picks, and a pointed rod. We thought it was a great trip. Sometimes the man running the road grader would stop and ask if we wanted a ride home. Other times people we did not even know would stop and see if we wanted a ride, Joyce would get on one running board and me on the other, put our arms through the window and we would tell them where we lived. We knew the section hands and the man who ran the road grader, but never any of the people in cars.

The house was a rattle trap house. The kitchen evidently had been just stuck on the west side of the original house; it was a step down from the rest of the house and had no foundation. The house was on a slight hill and the kitchen was always in a state of disrepair. Big gaps would appear between the floor and south wall from time to time. One day when my Mother was alone in the house a rat came climbing up through that gap in the wall, as soon as she moved it scurried back down. So the next day she was ready, she got my Dad's twenty-two rifle and sat very still on the step going into the house. Sure enough a rat came up and she shot him dead right on the kitchen floor. When I got home from school, I had a big rat to bury in the plowed field next to the house. They would no more get one hole covered until another rat found or chewed another hole. That whole gap was eventually covered with big tin can lids. Before it was over, my Mother shot eight rats and I buried every one of them. Of course, we told the other kids at school and did the neighbors kid my parents about that. That kitchen floor had bullet holes all over it, but it didn't really matter in that old house. When we would come home after dark and we had no electricity. It would be pitch dark in the house. The routine was that the first person in the back door would take about three steps over to where the matchbox was on the wall, strike one, and start lighting kerosene lamps. One night, I was the first one in and a rat ran over my foot. I let a yelp and my Dad who was right behind me said, "What's the matter and I said a rat ran over my foot, he said Oh, I thought someone might be in here." So, that is how we were raised, not much fuss about a rat running over a foot.

My Father became very ill one summer and my Mother had to go to the field during wheat harvest along with my brother and one hired man. Since we girls were too small to be left alone with my dad sick in bed, they hired a lady probably in her sixties to stay with us and cook and look after us. The windmill was only about fifteen feet from the kitchen, Joyce and I would climb up the windmill with rocks or anything we could find and throw them on the roof of the house, which had a tin roof. Mrs. Garrison would come flying
Out of that house like a crazy person yelling for us to get down off that windmill. I remember how hard it to keep rocks in our dress tails as we were climbing up almost a straight ladder and only use one hand on the railing to keep our balance. Then we would have to climb up on the roof to get our rocks, my brothers' metal toys, and anything else we had thrown up there. I don't think my Mother ever knew about that, she wasn't going to tell her she couldn't handle us, and we sure weren't going

to tell. My poor Dad was very ill and could hardly get out of bed for that whole summer.

When I was in sixth and seventh grade, we girls rode to school with the teacher who lived just down the road from us. She had a Model A with a rumble seat. She had gone to high school at Bluff City, which was the next little town east of us. One afternoon when I was in seventh grade, she decided we should all go over to their football games that were played on Friday afternoons. So Veldora and I got in the rumble seat, and Joyce, Jerry, and Yvonne, were in the front with the teacher. So we had a great time, we had no idea what the game was about; none of us had ever seen one before. There were no bleachers, just some parents walking up and down the sidelines. I don't think our parents knew anything about going to the game until she brought us all home, no one seemed to mind at all.

The Kansas rural schools were about six miles apart, the idea that no child would have to go more than three miles to school. So there were a lot of one-room schools like ours all over the country. We had a separate superintendent who had an office in the courthouse in Anthony. He traveled around to all the schools; he brought a hand cranked movie projector. The kids would take turns turning it, when one kid got tired the movie would slow down, so then another would take over. Our school had no window shades and it was so bright we could hardly see what the movie was about. I remember one movie he brought was about Tom Sawyer, I don't remember if it had sound, probably not.

We had a different teacher every year until my sixth and seventh grade, all of them except one who had a car and lived in town, rented a room with farmers who lived within walking distance. The teacher was expected to start the fire going, that meant going out in another building and bring in buckets of coal and get the building warmed. Ours had a huge metal jacket around it and it got very hot, we would dry our mittens and gloves after being out in the snow. We also took turns pumping buckets of drinking water; we would raise and lower the flag in all weather. We were very careful not to let the flag fall on the ground and fold it according to flag etiquette. If the teacher could play the piano and most of them did, we would sing a few songs like, "My Old Kentucky Home," Yankee Doodle Dandy," The Blue Danube," "Deep in the Heart of Texas," and many others. Other days we would be required to have a current event or recite a Bible verse. The teachers were expected to sweep the floor. We took turns cleaning erasers, that meant standing outside and banging them together, chalk dust would be all over us. In those schools, there was something going on all day long. When there were several kids, the teacher would have someone reciting something in class all day long. Usually in the morning, the first graders would come up and do some reading or whatever their class was, they would go back to their desks, then the second graders would come up and on and on all day long. I learned to listen to what was going on up front the same time I was doing my lessons. By the time I was in the next grade, I pretty well knew what was going on. With the teacher being busy all day long and when the little ones got stuck on something, they had permission to come around the back of the room and quietly ask an older student for help. That seemed to help pretty well. WE started the day after Labor Day, got off a day in October for teacher meetings, then two days off at Thanksgiving, then only Christmas Day thru New Year's Day. School was finished in early April because the boys were needed to help on the farms.

When I was in eighth grade, we moved to another farm in the area but a different school that was a larger one-room school with more students. In those days, the parents had to buy your schoolbooks. We could never get new ones only used ones because of how much they cost.

I am Maureen Bonham Grandon. I was born November 29, 1932. When I was in first grade, we lived a mile from town and I attended School at Washington Elementary in Anthony. My Mother drove me to school the first day, introduced me to my teacher, Miss Emma Henry. She was very kind and put my lunch on the shelf by the coat rack. When lunchtime came, she forgot about me and instructed all of us to walk home for lunch but to remember to come back since school lasted all day. In those days in my family, we did what any adult said, so I walked the mile home. My Mother loaded me back in the car and took me back to school and Miss Henry was properly horrified.

Lead a Horse to Water
By James M. Hall of Salina, Kansas
Born 1934

Memory tells that this event happened during the summer of 1945.

On the farm home of my grandfather, horses were still an important part of life on the farm. A stock watering tank was kept on the east side of the barn for the horses to get a drink.

My cousin and I had discovered some fishing opportunities in the north pasture and some good bait minnows in the creek below the barn in the south pasture. So, to save ourselves time and effort, we moved some minnows into the watering tank. This plan worked very well and we caught a few fish using the new source of bait from the watering tank.

However, the horses refused to drink from the watering tank because the minnows would nip at the horses' noses when the horses were drinking. My uncle got very upset and cousin and I were in deep trouble for a time.

We learned to think about unintended consequences and what might happen as a result of half-baked ideas being put into practice. Maybe this lesson is wasted on the young. They keep doing dumb stuff just the same. Maybe human nature is just that way.

1926 Chevrolet
By Esley Schmidt of Waverly, Kansas
Born 1926

My days growing up were spent in the country where there was no rural electrification. After dark, light was produced from kerosene lamps in the house or kerosene lanterns to take to outbuildings to do chores. For really bright light, we had lamps that burned unleaded gasoline under pressure.

My parents had a car that was manufactured in the year that I was born. In a picture taken about that time of a gathering called a "crowd" nearly everyone already had an automobile; however, there were still a couple of buggies pulled by horses. Many people had Model T Fords, which had three pedals. One was the brake, the middle one was reverse, and the other one was low, high, and neutral. It was in low when pushed to the floor and high when let out to its maximum. The neutral was in between and could be locked in by means of a hand lever. The Model T had much clearance between the wheels and the fenders and could travel mud roads quite well without getting the mud stuck between the wheels and the fenders, however, with only low and high speed, it was quite slow if the mud was so soft that the engine did not have the power to move the car in high gear. On the other hand, a 1926 Chevrolet such as my parents had, with a second gear was much faster unless the mud was so sticky that the mud would pack around the rear wheels and the car and engine would bog down. In order to prevent that from happening, a bit of ingenuity work separated the rear springs with a couple of chunks of two-by-four lumber and thereby solved the problem.

Despite other hardships that are not generally experienced today, we had good times as well.

Pear Tree Swing
By Elma Ash of Derby, Kansas
Born 1932

I was born in Caldwell, Kansas February 8, 1932 and until I was ten lived on a farm seven miles west of Caldwell and a mile or so north of the Oklahoma line with my mother, father, and younger brother.

We lived on Bluff Creek, where in years past the Indians have lived. Our house had a kitchen, living room with a bay window, and two bedrooms with a walk-in closet between them. Mom cooked on a wood stove and we had an icebox. A loaded rifle sat by the kitchen door, as we had skunks, opossums, raccoons, and snakes that would come around the house.

There was a garden plot and a well with a windmill on the south side of the house. We had a large pear tree in the back yard that had a swing on one of its limbs. My brother and I used the swing a lot.

On the north side of the house above Bluff Creek was the outhouse and a long building with a workshop on the east end and a chicken house on the west end. The barn was west of the house. The stock tank was kept full by a pipe from the windmill. We used the outhouse in the daytime and a chamber pot at night.

We did not have electricity, running water, or a telephone.

There was a pasture east of the house that went down to where the creek curved and ran into Oklahoma. Another pasture to the west was where the milk cows grazed during the day. Pigs were kept near the barn. Wheat, oats, and corn was raised in the fields. My parents sold wheat for ten cents a bushel during the Depression.

The house had a basement dug under it after it was built so it was not very large. Mom had a 100-egg incubator warmed by kerosene burners that hatched chickens for the family and for neighbors. When the chickens hatched, they were kept in the corner of the kitchen in a makeshift pen with newspapers on the floor. My brother and I loved playing with them until whoever they belonged took them home.

Mom grew a garden and canned everything she could so that we were well supplied all winter. We ate chicken and I could cut up a chicken before I was five. We also occasionally had squirrel. Mom would catch channel catfish from Bluff Creek and kept them in the stock tank so when she wanted to have fish, she would use her dip net, catch a fish or two, and fix them for supper.

My brother and I had a bucket of Indian artifacts that we played with. Arrowheads, scrapers, etc. we picked up all along Bluff Creek.

School was about a mile away. It had eight grades, one teacher, and eight students that consisted of my brother, our three cousins, three other kids, and myself.

Icel Lee Russell age 6

I was in second grade in a one-room country school. There were sixteen students from first to eighth grade. During the day blizzard conditions settled in. At dismissal, time parents were there for their children. There was a buggy, a wagon, a homemade wooden sled, and my Grandpa was there for me riding a workhorse. He put me on the horse with him and led my pony. I was wearing a stocking cap with a hole for the eyes and nose. My nose was covered but not my eyes. When we reached home, my eyes were sealed shut. Grandpa carried me to the house and Grandma thawed my eyes with cool water. What a memorable experience!

A Day to Remember!
By Icel Lee Russell of Valley Center, Kansas
Born 1922

I was born in 1922 and my Mother passed away at my birth. My maternal grandparents took me to live on a farm in Wheat Country.

One cold, windy day in February, it had snowed during the night, but I rode my pony to school as usual, two and one-half miles. Clouds were threatening.

Dust Bowl Wedding
By Gertrude Raple of Mt. Hope, Kansas
Born 1920

I was born in 1920 in a beautiful white house on a farm with a barn just like my dad wanted with a creek and pond just right for his ducks and his 13 children to play, ice skate, and go fishing. My dad was a very good farmer, loved the outdoors, worked hard to control the weeds, and worked with all the livestock. He was a very creative man and could fix anything. We had lots of trees around our house and had fun 'playing roads'. My brothers were a lot of help drawing maps as to how the roads should turn, make room for playhouse, all made with sticks, brick, rocks, and string. We were all good at making our toys, as we all knew what it was like during the Depression and Dust Bowl days of the '30s as there just wasn't much money for toys. Dad bought us kids a little red wagon, a toy we could all enjoy giving rides and taking turns pulling it. Sometimes we would haul produce from the garden in a very useful gift.

My mother was the best cook and made some of the best bread, "kolaches," a Bohemian recipe we all loved. She was an expert with no electric appliances—wood burning cook stove, oil-burning lamps.

In writing my memories, I think how lucky I am to grow up during the Depression and Dust Bowl days of the '30s and '40s before all the modern conveniences, push buttons, TV, etc. I appreciate everything I have today.

My early childhood days were fun helping with the farm work, gardening, and flower garden. Dad really had some bad years, but always had plenty of food on the table. The Dust Bowl days were terrible. Some days when the dust came rolling in, it would get so dark; we would have to light the kerosene lights and go in the house. I vividly remember a big dust bowl storm in the 1930s when I was 16 years old. My cousin was getting married in western Kansas. My dad and mother drove us out in a Model T Ford to the wedding. The Mass was beautiful, followed with an outdoor celebration, great food, and lots of homemade beer. My aunt planned and served all the food. Fried chicken, potatoes, homemade breads and pies. We were all enjoying the outdoors. All of a sudden, the weather changed and clouds started rolling in and it got darker. Clouds of dust came rolling in. It was so dark that we all had to go in the house. We pulled all the blinds, then took all the bed sheets and got them wet and covered all the windows with them. All of the guests of the wedding had to stay in house; more than 50 people were staying overnight, beds on the floors. The next morning, woke up and clouds of dust gone, but there was dirt and dust everywhere. My aunt made breakfast for everyone.

I attended grade school eight miles from the farm. My oldest sister took us by horse and buggy. The horse we drove was always afraid of cars and would take off and run when he would see one coming and we would all jump out.

We did a lot of sledding in the pasture up and down the hills. After playing in the snow we would go in with all our wet snow clothes, eat our dinner, and in the evening we would have our taffy pull on the porch outdoors. The colder the better the candy would be.

At the age of 14, I followed my three older sisters' leads and left home to find work in Wichita. Times were tough and I would send money home to help my dad pay the family's bills. My first job was babysitting for 50 cents an evening. Other jobs were at Cessna in the tubing department where "red was for gas and blue was for air". Later in my life, I returned to school to receive my GED.

Corbin Grade School
By Jolene Rice Roitman of Wellington, Kansas
Born 1951

Most of my young life was spent on a farm two miles north and one-quarter-miles east of Corbin, Kansas with my mom, dad, my three brothers, and four sisters. We lived on a 160-acre wheat farm with cows and chickens. Our house was a big, two-story farmhouse with five bedrooms and a huge country kitchen. Mom was a stay-at-home mom and there was always a baby in the house. She always said, "A baby in the house is a happy house." And it was a happy house. Dad was a hard worker.

Corbin Grade School

He farmed, raised cattle, and operated a bulk plant, delivering fuel to farmers. He helped with us kids, often driving in the driveway, dogs barking, in his big gas truck and taking a couple kids with him on a fuel delivery. Oh, and he fixed a cup of coffee and grabbed mom and gave her a hug. He operated on full speed all the time. He came home for dinner at noon every day. A big, hot meal at noon… steak, fried chicken, goulash, cowboy hash, or pork chops with potatoes, vegetables, and ice tea. Then he would take a 15-minute nap… always. No matter how noisy it was. Mom was a beautiful, stylish woman with the latest fashions and dad was very, very handsome with a playful sense of humor and always had a joke ready. He loved to laugh and have fun. And mom was his biggest fan and would always laugh. They loved each other.

We all attended Corbin Grade School in the town of Corbin. It was a two-story, red brick school built in 1909. I think it was a high school in 1909, but in 1957, it had grades one through eight. A "little" room with grade one through four and a "big" room with grades five through eight. There was one teacher in the "little" room and one teacher in the "big" room. Mrs. Isabelle Almack was my teacher when I started school in first grade. There were only about three or four students in each grade and the teacher was expected to teach each grade and try to keep the other students busy at the same time. We started each day at 9 a.m. and ended at 4 p.m. We had a hot meal every day upstairs in the lunchroom and our cook was Mrs. Hess. She was the best cook and made everything from scratch, including homemade potato chips. Every day as we exited the lunchroom to go out for noon recess, we would say, "Good dinner, Mrs. Hess." To this day, our family says this after a good meal. We were taught reading, writing, arithmetic, art, and music. I remember singing all the old songs like "Clementine," "She'll Be Coming Around the Mountain," and "Nick, Nack, Paddy Wach." After school, we would walk uptown where there was a grocery store, hardware store, post office, gas station, and my dad's bulk plant. He would usually give us a nickel to spend at the grocery store. If he was out on an order, his secretary, Beatrice, would give us a dime. Then we could get two things…a candy bar and a pop.

We would have community meetings once a month upstairs in the school where we had a very professional looking stage with a big, velvet curtain. Sometimes we put on little plays, sang our songs in a chorus, or played our piano pieces for the community. The Christmas program was the best. We had a huge Christmas tree, sang Christmas songs, exchanged gifts with our classmates, and Santa Claus came up the stairs shaking all his bells. When we heard those bells and the, "HO, HO, HO" coming up the stairs, it was pure excitement.

I loved growing up in the Corbin community. The Corbin Grade School was torn down in the 1970s. The memories live on…

Sausage Making for Food and Fun
By Richard Robl of Hutchinson, Kansas
Born 1936

"I finally realized why your sausage tastes different from store bought stuff," my brother-in-law told me. "It tastes like meat, not fat!"

That's the very reason we keep making it, along with the great camaraderie of the event. For over a hundred years our German farmer family, who settled in Kansas, has been grinding and smoking sausage using the same recipes. Yup, every year there's serious discussion over the merits of more or less pepper and how long to leave the links in the smoker, but we always return to the tried and true.

All our lighthearted banter brings back happy memories of the hard work we faced every fall once the weather was cold enough to butcher.

I can close my eyes and see, hear, and smell it now. The day before, we take hours setting up all the equipment—grinders, tubs, sausage press, tying table. Everything has to be sterilized with boiling water and bleach. I can still smell the Clorox. My hands are puckered for days! The big day family and neighbors gather to slaughter the hog, roll it in boiling water, then scrape all the bristles off the hide. Some of us work at rendering the lard, putting chunks of fat in big pots to boil, then pouring off the pure liquid that will be used all year to make mouthwatering fried chicken and piecrusts. Others cut the meat into long, thin strips to fit in the big, metal grinder. After grinding it twice, strong young men mix the meat with spices, stirring 50 pounds of cold, raw meat up to our elbows in huge galvanized tubs. When the spices are well mixed, one of the women forms patties and fries enough for everyone to sample. Oh, how we savor the sizzling tidbits! Our recipe has lots of pepper, mustard seed, and coriander. In weeks ahead, when we return the help by butchering at the neighbors', some of them go heavier on the garlic. Every family secretly knows its recipe is by far the best!

Next step is cleaning the casing, scraping the intestines with a knife, and running lots of clear water through them. The older kids stay busy keeping a fire going under big pots of boiling water that, mixed with cold, is just warm enough to keep the casing pliable. Throughout the work, there's lots of teasing and laughter, keeping everyone warm (except for the toes). Even the most reticent of the old farmers cracks smiles and shared a few funny memories.

Turning the press is long, muscle wearying work shared by all the strongest teens and men. We make it easier by lots of joking about the turner's abilities and occasional nips of peppermint schnapps or a tall beer. As the meat streams out of the press filling the casing, we are ready to cut the long tube, twist it into manageable loops, and tie the ends tightly enough to hang from poles ready to go to the smoke house. It takes practice and skill to tie the slippery links tight enough not to break loose. Of course, there are always several dogs alert to the delicious possibility of a "runaway sausage," barking their approval of all our work.

Each farm has its own smoke house, a little building blackened inside by years of use. Every year we save fruit tree prunings to give subtle flavors to the smoke. To ready the smoke house for the sausage, a fire is started, and then covered to smother the flames. More fruit wood branches are added as others burn down. The amount of time the meat hangs in the smoky building determines the pungency and dryness of the link. I always want the strong flavored dry links.

While the meat is smoking, everyone is busy scrubbing the equipment, using the last of the boiling water from the big pots on the outside fire. Even though everyone is tired, all the sausage-making equipment must be dried and oiled in preparation for its use next year.

We end the day thoroughly saturated in the fragrant smoke. Our old barn coats and hats hold the memories of sausage time for the rest of the winter. After several hours in the smoke house, the links come out hot and darkened to a shiny brown. Our evening meal will be home baked bread, homemade butter, and the new sausage.

We must be in heaven!

When the Navy came to Kansas
By Betty Jayne Smoot of Sterling, Kansas
Born 1925

The year was 1943.

I was a senior in Hutchinson High School and was ready to graduate. We knew that a Naval Air Force Base was being built, four miles south of town. Our population then was about 30,000, but we didn't know much about the base except that people were buying up any house or apartments that was vacant of "For Sale" and some officers assigned to the new base were even renting garages to live in.

One day, a lady we knew, came to ask us, my sister and I, if we would like to be hostesses at the new U.S. O. (United Service Organization.) The ladies of the Federated Women's Club were taking on the huge task of providing entertainment, and a home-like place for the sailors and cadets when they were in Hutchinson. There really was no place but the YMCA.

Of course, we wanted to participate. We and our parents were assured we would be in a supervised place and each of our sponsors would transport the girls on their schedule.

The clubroom, at that time was upstairs, over the Lewis cleaners, across the street from the New Courthouse on Adams Street.

There was plenty of room for dancing, pool tables, and a room of tables for board games and of course a very active food canteen. The ladies furnished the pies, cakes, sandwiches, and soft drinks.

It was so interesting to meet guys from all over the country.

Betty and her sister Virginia in 1943

A new group had just come in from basic training in Dallas, Texas. We loved the soft southern accent.

Another group was from St. Louis, Missouri and one guy was a terrific piano player, and could play all evening, and of course, we had seventy-eights with all the many popular groups of the time.

Hutchinson was never the same after that but everything was changing all over the world. We were at war on two fronts.

We dealt with ration stamps. Stamps for limited items like shoes, butter, work clothes, etc., and many things just weren't available. Everything was for the military such as tires and fuel.

But I don't remember anyone complaining about that. Everyone was anxious to do their part for the war effort.

Because troop trains went through our town, we saw the young soldiers and sailors hanging out the windows of the passing trains and waving to us. We wanted to sacrifice anything for them, even in such a small way!

To quote "It was the best of times-it was the worst of times."

But, some of life's wonderful memories!

"The Cowboy Kid"
By Alvera Lacey of Argonia, Kansas
Born 1938

On one hot summer day, my Brother and I went out to play. It had rained the day before as Mother told us not to get in the mud. I was four years old and my brother was six years old.

We wanted to go to the pastures and play in the "buffalo wallows" but, we had to walk through the wheat field to get there and of course, it was pure mud. I guess we thought that we could scrape off the mud before Mom saw us. Anyway, we took off thru the muddy field barefooted.

About one-half a mile later, I stepped in a den of red ants. They stuck to my feet like glue, stinging all the time. We finally got them all scraped off my feet but, they hurt so bad that I couldn't walk. My brother carried me piggyback all the way to the house.

When Mom saw us, she said that she wasn't going to punish us because I had been punished by getting stung by the ants and my brother was punished by having to carry me all the way home. Bet you can bet we never pulled that trick again!

A couple of years later when we should have been wiser, we had a ravine in the field across the road from our house, which would run full of water when it rained. Now, it was winter and it was full of snow. We thought it would be fun to jump into it. We jumped in and it went over our waist. Were we scared, but our arms were free and we finally dug ourselves out, but we never did that again either.

My Father came from Iowa to Oklahoma in a covered wagon with his mother, father, and two brothers when he was one year old and his brothers were three years old and five years old. One day they came to a river, as Grandma needed to wash clothes, they camped, and she began her washing. She noticed that several buggies had passed by dressed in their Sunday best and looking at her strangely. Then all of

Alvera's dad the cowboy

a sudden, she realized it was Sunday and they were on their way to church. Grandma was very religious and would never have washed clothes on Sunday. But I guess it's easy to lose track of time living in a covered wagon with three little boys, they settled on a farm near Pond Creek, where the boys grew into teenagers.

One night, my Dad and his brothers had been out visiting and were coming home after dark on horseback, when all of a sudden they heard a cougar scream. The horse took off like greased lightning; the boys hung on and made it home safely.

They moved to Kansas about this time to a farm near Conway Spring, Kansas.

My father who was nineteen at this time, decided to take up boxing. He was very good and became the featherweight champion of Summer County. His mother wanted him to stop boxing but he loved boxing, until one night he knocked his opponent out and they thought he was dead. His wife and children were crying over him but, he finally came to, and that was the end of "The Conway Kid."

Then Dad and his brother bought a motorcycle with a sidecar and went to Montana to be "cowboys." The owner of the ranch where they found work was a widow and she offered my Dad a permanent job as foreman but, he and his brother were homesick and decided to go back home.

Later in life after Dad retired, he took up horseshoe pitching and joined a horseshoe club. He won many trophies and ribbons.

Halloween Prank: The Junkyard Lock-up
By Gerald Speer of Garden City, Kansas
Born 1938

Dighton is a small town in south west Kansas where my twin brother, Jarold and me grew up and attended high school. Most all the kids called us twin, the older guys in town teased us some by calling us Pete and Repete. I was Repeat. Between us and our school buddies, we were quite a creative bunch.

This story actually starts the night before Halloween when three of our high school buddies were caught doing some early Halloween pranks and taken to jail, locked up for a few hours, then released.

We had three cops that patrolled our town, us boys respected these guys, they were good cops. But tonight we thought we would rustle up some devilment and get even with these cops for throwing our buddies in jail the night before. So I got a hold of all our buddies and told them I wanted to meet them out south of town on a hill that we called watermelon hill. All of us senior boys had citizens band or C.B. radios and we visited back and forth most of the time.

The day before Halloween, I was down at the Radio shop visiting with my friend who ran the place and he told me to tell the guys to be careful on Halloween evening because the cops had him install C.B. radios in their cars. I thought, we'll fix those cops. I got the boys together and we devised a plan to lock them up in the city junkyard, it only had one road in and one road out.

407

At 9:30 Halloween evening, we put our plan into motion. We had a couple of guys setting downtown in cars watching the cops, we also had an couple of guys and myself hiding behind the Texaco service station that was only about 100 feet from the road going down into the junkyard. We had our cars hid behind some grain bins that were close by and at 9:45, we had a couple of guys go into the Texaco filling station to hide the only pair of bolt cutters we knew they had.

While one of the boys kept the attendant busy, the other guy relocated the bolt cutter. Then I got on the C.B. and said, "Hey! Do you guys know what I heard a while ago?"

"What's that?" they answered over their C.B.s.

"I heard that the boys who were thrown in jail last night are really angry and they are going to get even with the cops tonight."

One of the boys asked, "What are they going to do?"

"They told me they had gotten a truck and they were going to go to the junkyard and fill it with trash, then take it to the intersection of town and dump it."

The cops, not knowing that we knew they were listening in on our conversation, headed for the junkyard immediately.

The boys that were downtown watching the cops for us, just said on their C.B., "Okay," which told us boys hiding behind the Texaco station and the other boys the cops were on their way. Man! It wasn't long until we saw a cop car coming down the highway and headed straight for the junkyard as fast as he could go.

When the cop entered the junkyard road, us boys hiding behind the Texaco station ran over real quick and slammed the gate shut, padlocking it, and getting back out of sight again. It wasn't long until the cop decided there was no one in the junkyard and he came back up the dirt road like a bat out of a hot place. We thought he was going to go right through the gate until he finally slammed on his breaks and slid to a stop just a few feet in from of the gate, dirt was just boiling from all around his car. When the dust settled, he got out and saw that he was locked in. We watched as he crawled over the gate and walked over to the Texaco service station looking for some tool that he could cut the chain with. The cop spent about four hours locked up in the junkyard before he got someone to come and help him. By that time, Halloween was well over and that was the last I saw of him that night.

After that, us boys all went back to watermelon hill having a beer and laughing about the whole incidence.

The junkyard lockup was noised about so much that there was an article about it in our local paper and the cops had the C.Bs removed from their cars and were never used again.

Do Up the Wash
By Elinor "Skip" Vasey of Sylvia, Kansas
Born 1932

Since time out of mind, Mondays have been designated to "do up" the soiled clothes and linens accumulated during the week. Back in the 1930s, when I was a little girl in pigtails, I was very impressed with the ritual of washday, and in my memory, I can picture the details as if it were yesterday.

When breakfast was over and daddy had gone off to work, mama would strip the beds, empty the hamper, and head through the kitchen and down the basement stairs with the load. A few families we knew had clothes chutes, where you magically dropped things down to the basement from upstairs. I thought that would be wonderful, because, of course, you could throw other things down there! Our basement had a big room with a workbench running down the middle like an island. On one side was the laundry assembly line. A little shelf on one short wall held a box of Lux soap flakes, a bar of Fels Naptha, and a bottle of Mrs. Stewart's bluing. The long wall next to it had hot and cold faucets with short, black, rubber hoses attached. There was a big, square, galvanized tub set on legs and then came the green enamel Maytag washing machine. It had an agitator with a pole sticking up inside and three blades that moved the clothes around, whipping soap into bubbles. A lid came off and on one side of the machine was an automatic wringer.

An old, wooden broomstick stood on the floor in the corner to stir the clothes in the galvanized tub. It had been used so much that it was smooth and white because of the

Elinor Vasey in 1936

the kitchen stove. We carried the basket out the basement door, which opened to the back yard. On one side of the door outside was a chicken wire trellis against the wall, which was planted every year with sweet peas. I have ever loved their pink and white frilliness and spicy smell.

On the other side of the door was a pulley with a rope clothesline that ran to another pulley on a big pine tree at the far side of the grassy lawn. There was a cloth bag on the line for clothespins, but I preferred to hand the pins to my mother as she needed them.

Later on when all were dry, they were rather haphazardly folded and stuffed into the basket and left to be "mangled." Colored clothes went through the then and I suppose there were about three loads altogether every week. Needless to say, my father came home to a rather sketchy dinner on Monday nights.

Tuesday was the usual ironing day. The wringer was taken off the machine and a round tubular roller mangle was attached. A folding wooden rack was set up beside the workspace to hang the freshly ironed pieces

bluing.

First, the clothes were separated into whites and coloreds. The whites (linens and daddy's white shirts) were put in the tub to be bleached, after rubbing Fels Naptha on "ring around the collar." Hot water was hosed into the tub and the whole batch was stirred with the broomstick. There was a plug in the bottom of the tub and a hose that led to a floor drain.

Things were rung out (I believe by hand) and then put in the washer. Mama seemed to know just how long to leave them in, because there was no timer. There was a drain with a hose in the bottom of this, so the soapy water was drained out, and rinse water followed suite.

Then, wonder of all wonders, the clothes were run through the wringer (which had a little safety bar to push in case fingers or arms got caught), and the things dropped damp-dry into a big, oval, wicker basket with a handle on each side. If there were pieces to be starched, such as aprons, housedresses and doilies, mama cooked up a pan of Faultless on

Elinor Vasey in 2012

on. The operator stood to do the ironing. My arms were too short to do things like sheets and tablecloths, but I was thrilled to iron pillowcases and hankies.

What rigmarole to go through for clean clothes, but it was far above beating sheets on a rock in a river or scrubbing socks on a washboard! How easy we have it now. Turn a couple of dials and empty the lint trap and technology has your laundry done in jig time. Wow—even a man could do it!

Where Were You When You Heard the News?
By Ruth B. Sanderson of Shawnee, Kansas
Born 1929

Fort Riley has always maintained a large presence in Manhattan, Kansas, and by the later part of the 1930s, the number of personnel at the Fort was being increased, partly because of the situation in Europe and partly because military service was one way to provide an income for young men, as the country was still working its way out of the Depression.

My dad had served in the Army in World War and had a definite soft spot for the guys in the service. As a result, on almost any Sunday, one or two (occasionally more) soldiers were invited home to dinner after church. This resulted in a few friendships that were remarkably long—and others that were ended by the war. One of those was Emanuel Baldini, a delightful young man from New York City. He was a most talented piano player—he had been trained to be a concert pianist—and was so happy to see our old upright, and delighted that mother was willing for him to play it. After having visited for a few Sundays, he found the nerve to ask mother if he could make some spaghetti from his father's recipe—the original I found not too long ago. We had several soldiers visiting that Sunday, and the quantity of spaghetti—that was wonderful—was enough to feed several more. We did not hear from Baldini after the war, and felt sure he had not come home—he would have contacted my parents had he been able.

Another dear friend was John "Cherry" Briggs from North Carolina. There was an immediate connection between him and my family, and he very quickly became a member of the family, to the extent that when he could get a weekend pass, he didn't have to find out if he was welcome—he just came. That was in the days (unimaginable now!) when doors were not locked. We'd wake up and find him in "his" bed!

My birthday was coming up soon, and fell on a Saturday of a week when Cherry had Office of the Day duty, and could not get a pass to come to Manhattan. Instead, he invited us to come to the base and have dinner with him at the mess hall. We were eating when the announcement came over the radio that Pearl Harbor had been bombed. To this day, I cannot imagine being anywhere else, when the reality of what was to come for every young man in that mess hall was very apparent. It was definitely one of those moments that lives forever in memory.

Cherry had been posted to Fort Riley in 1938 or 1939, so we had him as a friend for several years before he was shipped out. He was a wonderful neighborhood attraction—very adept with a lariat! He could skip rope in a big vertical loop or in a smaller horizontal loop, to say nothing about being able to rope youngsters running around the yard. Needless to say, neighborhood kids for some distance were drawn to our yard like a magnet when they saw him with his lariat!

He stopped to see my parents after the war was over—he was with his parents and sister, driving cross county. He stayed in the service, until he retired as a Lieutenant Colonel. We would hear from him occasionally, but eventually lost track of him, partly because mother moved from Manhattan to live in Kingman, Kansas, with me. I came home one day to find a note from him stuck in my door—I nearly cried with disappointment but immediately wrote to him at the New Mexico address he had left. He went back east again in about ten days, so I did get to see him and meet his wife. He also took time to go to the nursing home to see mother. He had been able to get her address by going to the Methodist Church office in Manhattan. I was able to see him two or three more times when I was able to travel quite a bit. He had a stroke about 10-12 years ago and has since passed away.

The sequel to this story is that when I was a freshman at Kansas State University, in an

English class, we were asked to write an essay about where we were when we heard about Pearl Harbor. The instructor had been in the service and it had been a pivotal time in his life. He was stunned when he read and graded the papers, to find that only two people in the class had any memory at all of that day! I was one of the two!

My Australian War Bride Mom
By Ann Warner of Spearville, Kansas
Born 1947

I didn't realize how unique my upbringing was as a child until I was years older, but my mother was an Australian war bride who came over here from the shores of Brisbane around April 1, 1946, sailing on the USS Mariposa, dubbed a Red Cross ship, and arriving on the shores of San Francisco, California, somewhere around April 25th. She finished her practically around the world trek by train, coming into Newton, Kansas, on April 30th, where Daddy met her, and then arriving at her final destination, Protection, Kansas, on May 1, 1946, just in time for my cousin Diana's birthday. Aunt Bert had been sitting atop the ice cream churn so Uncle Gerald could crank it for the celebration planned for mom's arrival, and the jarring must have brought on the baby, because there was much excitement that day as they rushed to the hospital as well as awaited Mom's highly anticipated arrival!

She only weighed 98 pounds by that time, the days on the ship having brought terrible seasickness and the necessity to carry around her 13-month-old son Winton, born earlier in Australia on March 25, 1945, as he quit walking on the decks of the rolling ship during that trip! Many war brides came over on many different ships as the Red Cross helped them reach America to get settled wherever their husbands resided, most of these husbands having been discharged from the war and sent home before they were ever reunited with their wives and whatever children were left behind in Australia. She could never have done this if she hadn't been an extremely strong woman, as all these war brides must have been; to go sailing off into the wild blue yonder to goodness knew where, leaving family and security behind as they looked forward to a future with their husbands. Not all these marriages made it successfully, either, as many returned back to Australia in disillusionment, but my mom and dad remained blissfully happy for almost 50 years!

Her trip through the deserts from San Francisco to Kansas by train, in fact, made her fall in love with the desert, and every vacation we took went through that area somehow or other.

Mom came over from living in urban Brisbane, the capital of Queensland, to life on a farm near a very small town, which she loved dearly. There was quite a bit of excitement in that small town, too, as everyone wanted to meet the "war bride," and see whom George Teter, my father, had brought home to America to be his wife! Several folks thought she was going to be an Aborigine, which is a dark-skinned native of Australia, and years later one of my prankster cousins told his girlfriend his aunt was an Aborigine, waiting until they met to reveal the truth of the matter, that she was in fact Caucasian. Mom had a great sense of humor and none of these shenanigans ever bothered her.

I was born on that farm (well, actually in Ashland, Kansas, at the hospital there) January 16, 1947, and my brother and I grew up in the tranquility of the '50s when America was happy and healthy, really idyllic years for this generation of baby-boomers. Eventually we moved into Protection itself, then on to Dodge City in 1953, where mom lived the rest of her life until she came to live with me. She told us so many stories of growing up in Australia, naturally it was familiar to us through her, but everyone around was always amazed to know she was from another country. In Australia, she lived across the street from a huge Morton bay fig tree that collected the flying foxes, large bats that ate the figs, squabbling over them and making a huge racket. She had an emu for a pet once, and would fill our heads with visions of the lush tropical flowers and scents of her tropical home. The strange animals over there, the koala bears, kangaroos, kookaburras, also fascinated us, and our Grandma Bunny, Mom's mother who still lived over there, would send us boxes of books, shells, etc. that always thrilled us.

Sadly, she never made it back to Australia to visit, as she would never get on a boat again and flying terrified her; however, Grandma Bunny did come over and stay with us for two years when my brother and I were very young. In 1993, my brother and I finally made it over there to meet the family we'd never seen, and as my brother explained it, to see the other side of our faces. To meet all those aunts and uncles and cousins for the first time and to see all the places Mom had described to us so often was pretty amazing. Mom and Dad met in the Brisbane City Hall where the USO sponsored dances, and my dad said he fell in love with Mom when he saw her beautiful green eyes clear across that crowded room! They were married July 4 in the First Baptist Church there that covered a whole city block, and it's still there.

Of course, Mom had an accent, but we never noticed any because we were always used to the way she talked; however, people were always fascinated by that accent, without fail wanting to know where she was from! Mom was talented in so many ways; she could sing, play the piano, paint figurines, make clothes for herself and me, cook, garden, and grow the most amazing flowers. Her musical inclination came from her grandmother on her mom's side, who was a concert pianist and taught mom to play. She picked it up quickly and was able to play by ear, though that talent did not pass down to me or my brother. Several of her grandchildren are able to do this however. Our home was always the neighborhood center for children because she continued to be a stay-at-home mom when the after-war women first started working outside the home. Mom was always there, a comfort and constant in our lives and those of our friends, always cheerful and buoyant.

The war years were tense for the Brisbanites; always living under the fear they would be bombed, though the Japanese never got further south than around Darwin, with that agenda. However, they had blackouts in Brisbane and Mom remembered the stress of it, though as a lively young woman, it was exciting to her as well as terrifying because though she had two brothers at war, there was something happening all the time with all those soldiers in town, and there was a training center set up in the park across the way from her house. She would hear her mom praying for her brothers faithfully every day for a safe return, which, thank God, they did.

Mom was a great debater, not sure whether she took it in school, but she could argue that black was white if the need arose, and since my Grandpa Teter lived with us throughout our teen years, she and grandpa had a friendly disagreement every day, especially about politics—she always took the opposite opinion from him just to keep things interesting! When we visited over there, my uncles could still remember how she would argue with all of them about almost anything! She worked in downtown Brisbane after graduating from school, crossed the Story Bridge in high heels every day, about two miles, until she got married and had Winton.

Later, when I got married and moved to a ranch outside of Dodge City, she was so thrilled that I would live in the country again, which had always been her favorite place, so I was glad she was able to spend the last of her 94 years with me out in the country! Mom was an incredible woman. She passed along many wonderful traits to her nine grandchildren and 15 great-grandchildren; all of them loved her dearly, as well as Winton and myself and all of her nieces and nephews! I am so thankful to have had her as my mother; she and Daddy always were and remain a huge blessing in my life.

Riding the Bus
By Mrs. Pat Stapleton Van Dolah of Garden City, Kansas
Born 1955

School buses have always been part of my school life. What makes this experience more unique than for others is the ages of our bus drivers. Our one-room schoolhouse, located on my family's property, closed when I began school in the first grade. As this corner of Hodgeman County was so isolated—21 miles from three towns—no one wanted to annex the few families living there. Eventually Cimarron school district welcomed us. More importantly, they provided bus travel. This is where my story begins.

Throughout my 12 years of school, our bus route was always driven by high school students who lived on the route. During the 1960s and 1970s, no one wanted to have the challenge of driving this long, often precarious route besides young people wanting jobs. One family had four of their high-school-aged daughters drive the bus over the years.

My older brother was my first bus driver. A high school student, Harold held his first paying job to be our route's bus driver. As a child, I often remember sweeping the floors of the bus for a dime. I thought I was rich!

In grade school, I remember when a classmate rode our bus. He was spending the night with another classmate neighbor of mine. We begged my brother, then a senior, to "hit the bump!" This was an intersection where one side sloped far away. If you sat in the back of the bus, you flew off your seat when going across this country road. All three of us were in the very back. Harold drove over the "bump." We flew up. "Look, no hands!" We fell back to our seats. The visiting classmate, though, got more than he wanted. When he landed, he knocked out a front tooth by hitting the back of the seat ahead of him!

Later, when I was in high school, another classmate drove the bus for two years. Our senior year proved trying for Vaughn, but he stuck it out. The route from our farm took one hour, one way—on nice, normal days. The winter of 1973 was very wet. Southwestern Kansas received snow that season. Parts of our route were not sanded. There were weeks during that time that our bus never made it past those nasty, treacherous spots in the road. This was before CB radios. The bus picked my siblings and I up in the morning. Then, managing to make a few more stops, the bus picked up additional students. We attempted to continue to school…and never made it. Eventually, the head transportation man would trace our route, going from school. Sometimes our parents would become concerned and start looking for us. Between the two, the bus would be pulled out of the snow or the mud (whatever the case!) and everyone would be dropped off at their homes, because the school day was usually over at that point. It would start all over again the next day! The good thing was that we did not have to make up the missing schoolwork. The bad thing was staying on a cold bus with nothing to eat or drink all day. As I was the oldest girl, when one of the little girls had to use the restroom, I had to accompany her to the outside and find a shielded spot to do our business. No hand sanitizer back then!

Pat's brother, Harold Stapleton

Two more memorable accounts occurred during my senior year. One time when the bus was just rounding the curve on the highway at the east edge of Cimarron, a pheasant blasted through the passenger side of the large front window. We had met a semi-truck and the force of the wind current caused that to happen. Another time as we cleared the top of the hill (just to the north side of the grade school), one of the bus's front tires came loose and rolled on down to the houses down to the west. The bus screeched to a halt. It was exciting seeing the wheel rolling away from us and going down the hill. Since we were fairly close to the grade school, all of us got off the bus and walked to the building—to climb into another bus heading to the high school building (old building is gone now).

Generally the bus rides to and from school were very routine. I learned to enjoy reading when I was in high school. Sitting in the middle area over the wheel well, I discovered that it road pretty smoothly. Over the 12 years that I rode the bus, I felt safe at all times. I never thought it to be odd to have teenagers as bus drivers. That always had been part of my life.

Today I am a schoolteacher and, of course, there are the occasional bus rides for activities. I still feel safe on these trips. However, I know that I am comfortable on a bus thanks to those many young drivers from my past.

Burning Cow Chips
By Beauford Wilkerson of Manter, Kansas
Born 1936

I was born August 16, 1936 to Charles and Nellie (Von Hemel) Wilkerson in Manter, Stanton County, Kansas at my Granddad Peat and Grandma Bessie (Ward) Von Hemel's basement house. I was the fourth of six kids. My nickname is Tube; I have been called that all my life.

I started my first year of school in 1942 in a one-room school. There were eight grades in one room; it was the Lone Star School District #23 in Northwest Stanton County. I went there for four years. There were "out houses," one for the girls and one for the boys. There were no school buses for the kids to ride to school, my mother was one of the parents that picked up school kids and took them to school.

I got my share of spankings from the teachers when I went to Lone Star and I deserved everyone. This one teacher used a rubber hose to spank us, it never did hurt that bad. One day us boys in school started digging a hole in the school yard making, as we called it, a cave; it had a top that was made from old boards found in the school yard; it probably took us two months to dig during recess. We cut out a place to sit on in our cave. The teacher wanted to go down in our cave. We helped her down into it, then when she got ready to come out she needed help, we told her to hand us one end of the rubber hose and we would help her out. After she got out, she handed one of us the hose so she could brush her clothes off. We didn't give it back to her that day. Me and my brother took it home with us that day, but decided we better take it back to her because if our dad found out about it we would get a good spanking from him.

My family moved to Manter, Kansas when I was in the fourth grade and I went the rest of my grade school years and graduated from Manter High School in Manter in 1955; there were seven of us in my class.

My favorite teacher was my seventh grade teacher, Mr. Garrett. My desire after I got out of high school was to work. I helped my dad in his shop in Manter where he worked as a mechanic. He would work on whatever needed fixed.

I was offered a job from a farmer-driving tractor, taking care of cattle, and whatever needed done. I worked for $8 a day. I later was offered $200 a month and was glad as I was assured a steady income, as I didn't get paid when I wasn't working. I loved farming and was eventually able to farm for myself; my dad and brothers all farmed together.

I remember my mother washing our clothes on a washboard once a week. Sunday was bath night to get ready for school. The first kid's bath was pretty hot and the last one was pretty cold. Water was heated on the cook stove and the potbelly stove. The tub we took a bath in was the washtub my mother did laundry in. When we lived in the country, we milked cows and feed hogs. Us kids helped milk the cows and (as we called it) slopped the hogs and separated the milk all before going to school in the morning. The skimmed milk was fed to the hogs and the cream was taken to the Manter Train Depot for shipping by train to Dodge City, Kansas.

We had a wooden icebox; a block of ice was used to keep the food cold. We got our ice from the "ice house" in Johnson, Kansas. We didn't have to buy ice in the wintertime; we could get ice from the water tank. We finally was able to purchase a kerosene refrigerator in the early 1950s. My mother used coal for her cook stove and the house was heated with coal. We had kerosene lights as we didn't have electricity yet.

The place we lived in when we first moved on the farm northwest of Manter was an old place with three rooms that we used for a kitchen/living room, and two bedrooms. Another room was built on and was then used as a kitchen from the rest of the house we had to go outside. Our dad used to listen to a radio program called "Mr. District Attorney" every Wednesday night after we eat supper. Us kids like to listen with him, but we would be scared after listening to it and hated to go outside to get to our beds.

We also would listen to the radio on Saturday night, listening to "The Grand Ole

Opry." My folks also would listen to the news, to hear what was happening in World War II. Our radio was a battery radio, so we didn't listen that often, as it would run the battery down.

The first bad dirt storm I remember was February 19, 1954, it came up during the night and blowed all that day and thru the night; it kind of cleared by the next morning. When I got up that first morning I thought it was still night as it was as dark as night. My mom had blankets up to the windows and if you touched them, the dust would just fly. The cars', pickups', and tractors' motors were just blowed full of dirt. They had to all be cleaned out and a lot of them started using oil after that and the motors went out. I seen a lot of dirt storms rolling in from the northwest after that first bad blow. They usually rolled in during the afternoon. If you seen them coming you knew you better get home. It usually got real still right before it started blowing. Thistles blew up in fencerows and the dirt piled up, some of the fences blew away. Machinery and such also blew under with dirt.

Another bad storm was the blizzard of March 1957. It snowed and blew for two days and people were stranded in their cars. It didn't get that cold and most people stayed in their car. The snowdrifts were at least 12 feet high. You could get on a drift and walk on top of a house. You couldn't get anywhere by vehicle as drifts had roads closed. The Bear Creek Bridge north of Manter was completely drifted full and it took the County road department at least two days to get it opened up. Cattle strayed off and walked until their lungs filled up with water and they just killed over from exhaustion. A lot of the cattle died in corrals. It was a terrible loss for the cattleman.

When I was working for a farmer my brother and I were riding horses looking through his cattle and came upon two rattle snakes. They were wrapped around each other. My uncle was in a pickup and I motioned for him to come and he had a shovel and hit the snakes as they were about ready to enter a hole. Both snakes were killed and we noticed where one snake was broke open there was a sack-looking thing; we were thinking it was guts until it started moving. We open each sack up and there were baby snakes alive and ready to strike. We ended up killing baby snakes.

My Grandma Von Hemel would tell about riding on a sled picking up cow chips for burning for heat. It was pulled by a horse that was ridden by my uncle. My uncle kept making the horse go faster; grandma said she kept telling him to slow down, but he didn't and finally she upset and they had to pick the cow chips back up. She was pretty mad at him. She said sometimes they had to saw the tops off of the fence posts as they had ran out of anything to burn to keep warm and cooking.

Water
By Maxine Stapleton of Cimarron, Kansas
Born 1924

God willing, I will be 90 years old on July 20, 2014. I have seen so many changes in my lifetime. I could write stories of snakes, Dirty Thirties, homemade clothes and mattresses, one-room schools, school days, home remedies, first moon landing (which was on my birthday), washday, phones, puppy love, cooking from scratch, or games we played.

I decided to write about water. It is an essential necessity of life. I was born and spent my first ten years in Colorado. We lived 11 miles west of Delhi, which was between La Junta and Trinidad.

We had water, but it had alkali and was unfit for humans; it was alright for livestock to drink. We had a wooden slat barrel to catch the rainwater. Rainwater is soft, so it was good to wash clothes, dishes, and baths. We had a cement-walled cistern. We had to take a water tank to the spring, which was about 11 miles north of our house. We would fill the tank with fresh spring water and take it

Maxine Stapleton

Maxine's daughter, Shirley in 1957

home to the cistern. It was my job to go down in the cistern and clean it up before the water was emptied. I would stand in a bucket with my cleaning rags or brushes. Mom and Dad lowered me with a rope and pulley, and then pulled me back up with the rope and pulley. To get a bucket of water from the cistern, you put the bucket on the rope and used a pulley. When you reached water, you flipped it so it turned on its side and filled with water, and then you pulled it up.

Back in the late '20s or early '30s, the neighbors got together, and put cement around the boxed-in spring. The children put their footprints and their handprints in the wet cement. I wonder if there is any sign of them now.

We usually did our laundry outside. We carried buckets of water and filled a broiler to heat on the cook stove. Then you carried hot water outside to a tub. We did our laundry with a washboard and a bar of homemade lye soap. After the clothes, you used the water to mop the wooden floor before discarding the water.

Bath night, you started with a tub of clean, warm water. Same water for the whole family—one at a time. One night a week. We couldn't waste water.

In the house, we had a bucket of water with a dipper. Everyone drank from the dipper; and if you didn't drink it all, it went back in the bucket. We just couldn't waste water and I don't remember ever getting a bad disease from anybody.

We had a pond close to the house. The livestock drank from the pond, as long as it held water. When the pond would go dry, I can remember driving the horses, cattle, and goats to a water hole.

My dad did some trucking and would be gone some times. One neighbor was a bootlegger and for some reason he thought the folks had turned him in, so he was mad. One time when Dad was gone, this neighbor put our dog in our cistern. Of course, the water was ruined. We had to borrow some water from another neighbor, until we could get fresh water. We knew it was this neighbor that put the dog in the cistern because of the way the dog acted when it saw the neighbor.

My dad loved to dance. When he found out they were having dances on the west side of the Apishapa River in a country schoolhouse, we went often. One time the river was up. One lone guy was on the west side and he managed to wade across. He was convinced that Dad's car would make it across. We got almost across when the car were washed aside and was stopped by a big rock. The guy was able to move the rock with the help of the rushing water. Our group was the only one at the dance.

My dad passed away in 1935; he was 42 years old. Now I believe he was one of the first to have heart surgery. They just didn't know enough to keep him alive. We had to move. The mortgage company foreclosed. Mom didn't drive. She had three children to raise. So we moved to a farm close to Jetmore, Kansas, to be housekeeper and cook for my two bachelor uncles.

Oh boy! A windmill with nice, fresh water to drink—water to waste and there was an old, rusty can on a peg for everyone to drink from. A milk house made of limestone stood nearby—water was pumped through a trough to keep food cold. There was a big stock tank nearby to cool off in the summer.

We didn't have fish in our region Colorado. The Pawnee Creek had water and fish. In the spring, the fish would go upstream to lay their eggs. They often didn't make it back to the Pawnee before the Sand Creek went dry. My two brothers and I took gunnysacks and picked up fish from the house to the Pawnee. Oh! How stupid! We had to carry or drag the sacksful home.

When I started to high school, I found hot and cold running water. Just turn a faucet. It was so easy to wash clothes, take a bath, and do other things with water.

In 1951, we moved to the farm where I still live. There was no electricity yet. So none of the conveniences of town could be used. We learned to use a pump handle and a water bucket with a dipper again, but we still had an easy source of water.

We finally got REA so I have running water again. I hope we never run out of water or get it so polluted that we can't use it. Most of the creeks that had water and fish are dry now. I live on the Buckner Creek. It is dry, but I can remember lots of fun in the water, when the creek was full of water.

I think my generation appreciates things more because we had to "make DO" with what we had. As hard as people worked, they still had time for their neighbors.

Hometown Memories from the Good Ole Days
By Thane Baker of Granbury, Texas
Born 1931

Those of us that were residents of Southwest Kansas during the 1930s, considered some parts of those times good and some bad. Fortunately, we don't remember how bad the bad were and the good probably were not as good as we remember. Having said this, writing down what I remember will give others an insight as to why I would not call the 1930s the "Good Ole Days." All of us that lived during this time could probably write about the same stories. But, if we did not commit our individual memories to paper, then perhaps some interesting things would be left out.

Remembrances cannot be told in chronological order so the years will be spilled together. Two major circumstances define the 1930s, the Depression and dust storms. These were endured and you might say accepted, because everyone else was experiencing them. And, we couldn't do anything about them anyway.

The Depression came first and it was a great shock because of how good things were in the 1920s. (I was told.) Everyone had to change their way of life and some could not deal with it. Some families moved or broke up, and people just were gone one day. We lost track of almost everyone that left. Our family stayed, because my Father always had a job in Elkhart, Kansas, but his pay was continually reduced. As a mechanic, in the Ford garage, he mentioned how cars were repaired or salvaged for parts. Car owners never changed oil or did other maintenance care so cars broke down and often sat where they were for years. Appearances were not considered as long as cars ran.

As expected, food was a major concern. We always ordered one hundred baby chickens early every spring, raised them and ate them all summer and fall, kept about twenty hens to give us eggs the next winter. To feed the chickens, we cleaned up what was left from farmer's grain piles after they removed the clean grain they could sell. My Father made a small building to store all the grain collected for the next year.

Jack Rabbits were a source of food for us and others. In the evening after my Father's work, we would drive in the country with my father's single shot twenty-two, looking for the next day's meat. He seldom missed. Mother would cut up and fry young rabbits as you would a chicken but the old ones she cut up and put in soup or hash. Beans of all kinds were a good source of protein. Corn meal mush covered with homemade syrup, using maple flavoring, with a fried egg was not unusual at the table. One uncle would sometimes bring butter and eggs from his farm for us to sell for them. Mother sold them in town and gave him the money. In return, we got to keep some butter. We would go to an uncle's farm and help butcher a calf in the spring and a pig in the fall. We would buy (he wouldn't take regular price,) some of the meat. When we got back to town, the meat was cut up, fat cut off and cooked to get the lard, wrapped in butcher paper, marked what it was and taken to the local ice house where we rented a locker.

Clothes were "recycled." All my friends

and I wore overhauls until the seventh grade. They were patched front and back, sometimes very creatively. Mother made some shirts and repaired others. She would darn socks by reweaving or make a patch by using a light bulb inside the sock. We bought rubber soles over and over that were glued on the shoes until the tops wore out. Neighbors often traded their children's outgrown clothes.

Fortunately, I didn't get sick and miss school. I had perfect attendance for eleven of my twelve years of school in Elkhart and only missed two weeks as a freshman for a knee operation. I walked seven blocks to grade school and three blocks to high school. I remember one time in the fourth grade my Mother dropped me off at school. My classmates teased me about it. I asked her not to do it again.

I always went home for lunch. At lunch time, I would stand on the corner of the school ground and wait for the town noon whistle to blow. When it sounded, I ran for home. Mother would stand on the front porch and when she heard the whistle sound would look at her alarm clock for the time. It had no second hand. When I stepped in the yard, she would look at the clock, and tell me how long it took me to get home. Of course, I always tried to do better. I became a short distance sprinter later and have always thought I was the only sprinter that was ever timed with a wind up alarm clock.

A garden was planted in town by most people. Some years were better than others but we usually had onions, radishes, carrots, tomatoes, lettuce, peas, and sometimes strawberries. Mother canned everything she could. Neighbors traded garden vegetables so the variety was welcome. We put solid wood boards around two sides of the garden to protect it from the wind, but it mostly collected blown in dirt. The blown in dirt was very rich so we turned it into our soil. One of my jobs was to clean out the hen house and spread the removed product on the garden. Excellent fertilizer, but chasing feathers in neighbor's yards was also part of my job. On an uncles farm, we planted watermelon, cantaloupe, field corn (not what we call sweet corn now,) and popcorn. The field corn was eaten from the cob and canned when ready. There was only a short time it was edible before it got too hard so we had a busy week or two. Field corn was used because sweet corn did not do as well without much rain and when hard, it made better animal food. The popcorn was harvested by hand and shelled with a stationary combine. We sold about twenty big gunnysacks some years to a grocery store. The popcorn was a lot of work, but it resulted in cash. The coyotes ate some of the watermelons and snakes made the farm exciting.

The population of Elkhart, Kansas was reduced by about half during the 1930s because of the Depression and the dust storms. Many went west, including two of my uncles. When leaving, many came by the garage or our house to say goodbye and they said they would be back, but they almost never returned to live. They would take everything they could carry in a truck or trailer or on top of their cars and tell us to go by their house and help ourselves to anything they left. We did sometimes and found something we thought we would save for them when they came back. We found a foot pump organ one time and Mother played it. She wanted to take it but we had no place in our house for it. It was sad to see furniture, equipment, dishes, and tools just left. Scavengers appeared regularly in trucks to take everything from empty houses.

The Depression also meant problems with many things. Water in town was limited because of cost to us, and also the city told us not to water lawn grass. Of course, we could water the garden. Electricity failed with any storm because it came in on poles and wires that were not well maintained. We had a diesel-powered generator in the town but it could not always be started. It was turned over with saved compressed air, but many times the air ran out before it would start. All broken appliances and tools were repaired or salvaged. My Father fixed many things in the Ford garage that were not cars.

Now, about the dust storms. They only lasted a day or so usually. We placed wet gauze masks over our nose and mouth and went to the basement where there was less dust. The masks were black in a few hours. Wetting with egg whites worked well but didn't last long. Many people got dust pneumonia and some died. Dust would accumulate one-fourth to one-half inch thick on the windowsills in a day. We turned on the lights to read because it was so dark. When a storm was over, a train would show up with a snowplow on the front of the engine to bust through the dirt that was blocking the tracks. Town people came to watch as the engine backed up over and over to get up speed and hit the dune. The fine dirt flew up like snow.

One thing resulted from the storms that was entertaining. Or, as I have heard it said, it is an ill wind that does not blow some good. During a dust storm, the top soil would blow off a field to the depth it was plowed and leave a hard, dry and smooth surface. On a calm Sunday afternoon when the dust was temporarily relocated and resting quietly waiting for another wind, we would walk the fields picking up arrowheads and buffalo horns. We had several three pound coffee cans of broken ones and a cigar box full of perfect ones. Some were small as a nickel and others, several inches long. Interestingly, they were made of gray stone, red stone, a black glass like material, and even a few white ones. Aunt Fay, found a beautiful red six-inch long spear point. One of my uncles, found beads, pottery, and bones in a low spot. Some thought it was a ceremonial location and others an Indian burial ground. An expert was never called.

Every town needs a local hero. Elkhart's was a distance runner named Glenn Cunningham., that set a world record in the one mile run at a track meet in Chicago (in 1931, I think) while he was still in high school. The front page of the newspaper was framed and prominently mounted just inside the high school front door. He went to college and set more world records. The excitement of the 1930s for Elkhart was celebrating the return of Glenn from the 1936 Berlin Olympics where he placed second in the 1,500 meters. The band marched down Main Street and a few trucks with people on board drove by honking their horns. One activity was the children under eight got to try to catch a small turned loose greased pig. I had it cornered under a step but the Wagner boy got there and picked it up before I figured out how to do it. The big attraction was Glenn running down three blocks of the main street(from the Church of God to the Sinclair service station) in his Olympic uniform. As a young boy. I stood there mesmerized and told myself I wanted to run in the Olympics one day. I dreamed it for years, and sixteen years later, I did, in Helsinki, Finland.

I have good memories of family softball games, pitching horseshoes, making homemade ice cream at my uncles farm, playing paper dolls with my older sister(under protest) riding my second hand bike all over town with my dog on the handle bars, watching the town blacksmith, soaping the windows at Halloween, church picnics, shooting sparrows with my BB gun, and sleeping in a tent in the backyard. Other memories include weeding the garden, mowing the grass, and smelling the homemade beer in the basement where my room was.

I don't remember people complaining that much. We were all in the same circumstances and reminded each other it would be better one day. People helped each other without asking and didn't expect to be paid.

Summer with my Grandparents
By Marian Williams of Caldwell, Kansas
Born 1927

I grew up in the 1930s and loved spending the summer with my grandparents. These are a few of the special adventures and memories I hold close to my heart.

My Grandparents owned several lots on the outskirts of town with only a few neighbors close by. It was a "wonderful" land of flower gardens, vegetable gardens, fish pond, chickens, roosters, rabbits, milk cow, baby calf (all of which was raised to provide food for the family) as well as of course, a cat and a dog.

I loved helping grandma feed the chickens and gather the eggs each morning. The old hens intimidated me at first, but I soon learned to "out fox" them and quickly stick my hand

Memorial Day Parade in Caldwell, KS

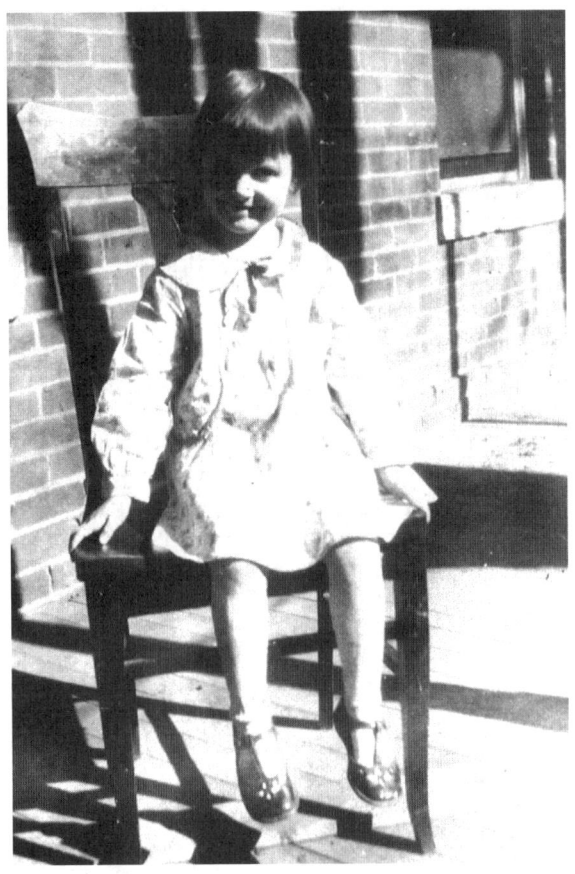

Marian Williams

underneath their roost to pull out the eggs.

Each Sunday we'd look forward to a fresh chicken dinner, whether fried up crispy or stewed with homemade noodles or dumplings. My tiny, loving grandma had no qualms about grabbing out one of those chickens, placing them on the old tree stump, and beheading it with a sharp corn knife she used just for that purpose. I watched with horrified fascination as those headless chickens, would flap around that old stump before grandma would grab them and begin plucking out their feathers.

I wasn't old enough to churn the cream into butter provided by the old milk cow but would watch my grandpa has he'd complete the cycle. The fresh buttermilk was a favorite drink of ours. Another favorite was when we'd spread the thick cream on a slice of homemade bread and sprinkle it with brown sugar. I remember my grandpa would take the cow. "Bessie" to the neighborhood community pastures to eat grass each morning before heading off to work. There would always be three or four other neighbors' cows staked in the pasture too. They'd spend the day grazing on the lush grass before the men would lead them back home at the end of the day.

I'd help in the garden too, weeding and picking potato bugs off the potato plants. I would earn five cents for every can of bugs I would pick. All the vegetables were cooked up fresh during the summer then later canned for the family to use in the winter. Grandpa would give me my own special plot to take care of, watering, and weeding. Too often, my big toe got in the way of the sharp garden hoe. Out would come the home remedy of bacon fat wrapped in white strips of cloth around my toe. Never once did I get any kind of infection!

The house was surrounded by a huge flower garden with flowers of every kind as well as different fruit trees. Every evening after work and supper, Grandpa and I would head out to tend the garden. I credit my Grandparents for my love of flowers and gardening that stayed with me my whole life.

Weekends were a special time in our small farming community of Caldwell, Kansas. There was a large group of farm families of Czech and German descent that would come to town each Saturday for supplies. Businesses stayed open until 9:00 p.m. to accommodate them. The ladies would do their shopping then congregate on the benches in front of the stores to visit while the men would

Marian with her grandparents and brother, Carl

"disappear" to what I later learned was the pool hall to play dominoes. I would walk up and down the street looking in the windows and listening to the ladies chat in their home country languages. Occasionally, I'd spend my hard-earned "potato bug" money on penny candy or an ice cream cone.

Soon, the lights in the businesses would start to disappear and parents would round up their kids and say their goodbyes until the next week. Grandpa would "reappear" to take Grandma and I home. He always had a bag of Grandma's favorite orange slices candy.

On especially hot summer nights, I got to sleep outside on my own folding cot under the trees. Lots of families did this as there was no air conditioning back then and the temperatures would stay up in the 80s even late into the night.

Although by today's standards, life seemed a lot tougher in those days—especially when it came to day to day living without modern conveniences. But I wouldn't trade one minute of growing up and experiencing those simpler ways of life of my Grandma and Grandpa.

You Better Not Tell
By Roger Roy Hoffman of Coldwater, Kansas
Born 1935

My name is Roger Hoffman. I am seventy-eight years and live in the Buttermilk Area just three-fourths mile from the home I grew up in, I was born on November 13, 1935 in a house three mile north and one-half mile west of the nearest town of Coldwater, Kansas; it was not any bigger than most living rooms in houses today. I lived there along with my parents Bill and Eunice and my two older brothers; Doyle, and Allen. Except for not having electricity or an indoor bathroom, I don't remember much about the time we lived there. I do remember that it was nice having cousins that lived right across the road from us. My Dad worked for a farmer, Otto Sherman, until he bought his own place and started farming on his own. He bought a one-half section of land at Buttermilk. Kansas in 1938 that had a house on it. The house was big, but in pretty bad shape, in fact the room that eventually became our bathroom was used for grain storage. In 1939, after he got the house fixed up, we moved there. Now we were twelve miles south of Coldwater and I remember Doyle & Allen, who were now twelve and eleven respectively, were not happy about the move and being so far from their friends; now I was only four so I adjusted fairly quickly. We still didn't have electricity or a bathroom, but it was a lot bigger. It's kind of funny; we still spent most of our time in one room, the kitchen, especially during the winter, because we got our heat from our potbelly stove there. The rest of the rooms were closed off most of the time, so our bedrooms were cold. We would take a hot brick to bed with us and put it under the covers at our feet for warmth. Mornings were usually pretty cold until Dad got the stove going, but we were always ready to get up because Mom would always have a great breakfast ready for us; biscuits, gravy, sausage and eggs. A lot of days after breakfast, you would find my Mom out at the chicken house catching and killing a chicken for dinner.

When I was five years old, I started the first grade at Avilla Country School, two miles from our home on Highway 1. Vera Griffith was my first grade teacher, then the next year, Elaine Coles became our teacher until the school closed in my Junior High years and I started attending school at Coldwater. Going from a one-room school to going to different rooms for each subject was quite a change for a ten year old. I was afraid at first that I would go to the wrong room. The Avilla School House consisted of one big room with a small room on each side. One small room was for our lunches and coats; I can still smell the aroma of oranges, apples, and other lunch items that permeated that room. The other room was for school supplies; these rooms were not heated. The big room was our classroom and had a wood and coal burning stove right in the middle of it. There was no bathroom in the school, it was outside about fifty, or sixty feet from the school building, but we were pretty uptown because we had two outhouses, one for the boys, and one for the girls.

School days at Avilla have a lot of good memories for me. At the beginning of each day, we would raise the flag up the flagpole and then say the Pledge of Allegiance. Sometime during the day, we would have music, our teacher would play the piano, and we would sing Patriotic songs together.

There were certain times for each class to be taught, but we all had to be still and listen even when it wasn't our turn. Because we listened to the older student's lessons, we learned some things earlier than usual; I think that is why I was able to stay up with my class clear through to my senior year even though I was the youngest in my class and was only seventeen when I graduated. Recesses were really fun times; mostly we played games such as softball, tag, crack the whip, run sheep run, antiover, and others. Sometimes since World War II was going on, we played war games, but we always planned this a day ahead so we could bring our favorite toy weapons to school. Oh boy! We would all probably be expelled in today's world; the games and weapons would be deemed too dangerous, but we had a great time and we all survived. The recess I remember the most, was the day my big brothers let me in their fort. Doyle, Allen, Jerry Guse, Russell Harness, and probably others I don't recall constructed a little structure in a corner of the school yard from scraps of firewood and straw. They allowed me in reluctantly, I found out they were smoking cigarettes and they swore me to secrecy. Well, when recess was over and we were back in the classroom, someone looked out the window, and saw their little 'smoke' house on fire. When Mrs. Coles asked how that happened no one seemed to know and eyes were saying to me, "You better not say anything,' of course I didn't because I valued my life.

Sometime in the late 1940s, the REA finally got 120-volt electricity to us, but for a few years before that, we had a wind charger on a tall tower outside our house that gave us twelve-volt electricity. We didn't even know what a TV was, but we had a radio, which is what we mostly used the electricity for because the charger didn't produce enough for the lights. We would sit by the light of the kerosene lamps and listen to shows like "Amos & Andy," "Fiber McGee and Molly," "Lum and Abner," and "The Shadow." I even remember listening to the fight when Joe Lewis lost his title, I cried. My folks listened to a Soap Opera; one day before it started the charger froze up leaving us with no electricity, so Mom heated some water in a teapot and Dad climbed up the icy tower with the teapot, poured the hot water on the charger until it thawed and began working; all so they could listen to the program, I still have that old radio today.

Most of my spare time was spent building Model Airplanes, mostly because B-17 Superfortress Bombers would fly in formation over our house on their way from the Boeing Factory to California and I had uncles in the war, I became very fascinated by airplanes. I really enjoyed building and flying the planes; most of them were equipped with a gas engine and were flown by control lines forty or fifty feet long. Several other kids made them too, so on Saturday or Sunday, if the weather was good and not too much wind, we would gather at the old Vic Stark Airport, northeast of Coldwater, to fly our planes. To fly the airplane, I held onto the control line, the plane would take off and fly in a circle with me turning round and round controlling it with the lines. In order to keep from crashing, it was important to bring it in for a landing before the fuel ran out, usually giving me about ten-fifteen minutes of flight time. I would get dizzy if I tried it now but back then, it didn't bother me at all. Sometimes the planes would crash, but usually I was able to rebuild them and try it again. Each one of us would take our turn, we usually drew a nice crowd to watch us, and it was always a lot of fun. I miss those times; I never lost my fascination for planes and worked on the real bombers while in the Air force for several years. Now I'm seventy-eight years old and I still love planes; I still have some of the planes I made back then, I guess that would make them sixty to sixty-five years old.

Life was much simpler and slower during the 1930s, 1940s, and 1950s, I thank God I was born on a farm in Kansas, near a small town with God fearing parents and two older brothers, who loved me and saved me from many mishaps.

On the Farm in the Artesian Valley
By Warrenetta Fisher of Garden City, Kansas
Born 1926

First of all, I don't remember this but I was told I was born on the Mayhan place and I was nine months old when Daddy and Mother (Warren and Feryl also known as W. W. Marrs) bought the place where I grew up. The house consisted of a kitchen, living room, a bedroom to the east of the living room and a long room on the north end of the house with two beds on each end and stairs leading up to the four rooms upstairs on the east end of the room. We had no clothes closets in out bedrooms, so Daddy put up a board on one wall and we put a curtain in front across to put our clothes, one in the north room downstairs and one in a bedroom upstairs, which later would be my bedroom with one of my sisters. We had no running water in the house and no bathroom. The outhouse was west of the house, north of the chicken house, with not even a door on it. We also had a party line phone. I was the middle of nine children. A large covered porch was on the southeast corner of the house and a trough, which was made from wood, had an artesian well running in it where we put milk, cream, butter, and anything that had to be kept cold. With nine kids, Mother, and Daddy there were not any leftovers after a meal. We cooked on a wood stove, heated water for laundry and baths on Saturday night in a round laundry tub and later we had a large oval tub. As each one would bathe, we just added a little more hot water.

The Marrs family in 1925

We celebrated Christmas by going down south of the barn as we had groves of trees all around south and west of the house. In one where a lot of trees were planted, there were some large pine trees so we would cut off a limb to make a Christmas tree for that Christmas. The tree was put in a corner of the living room, and we kids would string popcorn and make ornaments to hang on the tree. Mother would hang a white sheet up around the tree. We would put our presents around the tree as we never wrapped them/

I went to Western Gem School through the sixth grade. While attending country school we either walked to school or rode the horse, ole Babe. My school started with Elizabeth Wyatt, as my first grade teacher and Eldon McBee was my second thru sixth grade teacher. When the school closed for the next six years, I attended Fowler Grade School and graduated in 1944 from Fowler High School. The highlight of my high school years was having the lead roles in my junior and senior class plays. This was during WWII and gas, tires, and sugar were rationed and we were driving to school, as they hadn't started buses yet.

When the tires wore out on the 1929 Chevy car, we rented a house in Fowler and Mabel moved Leola, myself, LaVon, Betty, Virgil, Wendell, Elsie, and Delbert to town. That same year the red measles were going around. Virgil was the first one to go back to the country for Daddy to tend. As each one came down with the measles, we were taken to the farm for Daddy to keep us in the dark, because they affected the eyes. While living in Fowler, I celebrated my sixteenth birthday and had a surprise party. That is where I met my boyfriend that I dated until my senior year during the senior play.

As we each got old enough to do our share of the chores, we had to gather kindling to start the kitchen cook stove so breakfast could be cooked. I don't remember what birthday I was having, but I had come home from school at Western Glen and Mother was cleaning some clothes with gasoline and rubbing them together started a fire and burned her hands and she said to me, "Warrenetta, you aren't going to have a birthday cake this year."

Our laundry was done in a brick washhouse my Dad built over a large cellar with a Maytag wringer washing machine. The cellar was used to store the canning we would do during the summer.

Mother passed away on June 16, 1937, when I was ten and a half years old. That summer we older girls had to care for little Wendell, nineteen months, Virgil, almost three years old, and Betty. Cook, clean, wash, and iron, and anything else that had to be done- summer of 1937 thru 1939.

The reservoir had four artesian wells running in the pond. Daddy drilled an irrigation well to help fill the acre reservoir, which was just east of the house. It was stocked with catfish, sunfish, bass, crappie, and bluegill. It had two floodgates in the southeast and southwest corners of the pond. The pond was used to irrigate the alfalfa, milo, and also garden and corn that we canned. While drilling the well, Daddy got his overalls leg caught in the auger and pulled his overalls off, but he was not hurt. We also swam in the reservoir.

We milked Holstein cows and separated the cream and would take five and ten gallon cans of cream to the depot at Fowler and ship it to make butter. We did have a milking machine to use, when it was down, we milked by hand. In order to get some money we girls, when we could drive, would gather garden produce, tomatoes, roasting ears, watermelon, cantaloupe, and anything else we had plenty of and load the car and head to town, go up and down the streets selling our produce for spending money. When we lived in town, after school I got a job ironing for Ethel Meyers and ironed her husband's shirts.

During the war, when Alfred was called to the Army, we girls had to help Daddy with the farming. I helped clean the chicken house and stack hay, but didn't do machinery work. We were all in 4-H and I learned to sew from my Aunt Dessie and won Grand Champion in Style Review at the Meade County Fair and got to go to the Hutchinson State Fair. I was County Health Champion and attended the 4-H Days in Manhattan.

Mabel and her three children came to live with us just before school started in 1939.

My Mother instilled in my mind, if anything is worth doing, it's worth doing well. We were also told to get out work done before we played, but sometimes we did just the opposite! Guess what! We got in trouble.

Daddy and Mother did take the family in

Warrenetta Marrs

an Essex car we had to Dodge City to see the Barnum and Bailey Circus. Before going to the circus, Mother and Daddy went shopping and bought a pair of sheets for Aunt Ruth and Uncle Gene Flinn, which were left in the car and no locks on the car doors. When we got back to the car, someone had got in the car and took the sheets. Alleen's purse and other things that were left in the car.

We also got to go to Stonington, Colorado, where Aunt Verna, Mother's sister, and Uncle Frank Brown lived and visited one weekend. In those days, (as a whole family,) that was a big deal if Daddy and Mother went very far from home to visit.

My Dad was also hit by lightning when he was on a tractor, south of the house farming and a rainstorm came in. He walked from the tractor to the barn and up to the house. He was deaf in his right ear after that, and he did have a wound on his left chest above his nipple. Mother put him to bed and we heated bricks in the oven of the kitchen stove and put them around him to get him warm and to keep him from going into shock.

Even though our Mother was taken from us at an early age of thirty-seven years, we were never told that she loved us, but I think we took that for granted, as she was a wonderful mother. She was always sewing cute little dresses for us six girls for Easter of Memorial Day.

We had big blizzards that would blow down the driveway in eight-foot drifts that we had to climb over to get to the barn to do the chores. In the 1930s, there were also dust storms; my Mother would hang up wet sheets to the north windows and a door.

Daddy and some of us would help him plant the large garden and when ready to harvest, we would pick peas, beans, tomatoes, corn, make pickles from cucumbers, and make kraut from the cabbage. One time making, kraut, I was slicing the cabbage on a board and I sliced a part of my right thumb. My Dad used adhesive tape to put strips across the wound to close it, as it was on Friday night and the doctor's office was closed. I still have a large scar. I also was bitten by a water moccasin snake and had to have the top of my foot lanced.

We would can all summer long from the garden, so we would have food to eat. Daddy would butcher our meat and cure it and put it on the east side of the washhouse. The washhouse was built over the cellar where we stored our canned food and I have my Mother's large kraut jar that the kraut was put in. We never went to bed hungry, as we always had good meals. I learned to make homemade bread, making six to seven loaves at a time. All of us girls learned to sew, cook, clean house and help Mother do the washing from the washhouse just south of the house. We hung the clothes on the clothesline that was stretched from the mulberry tree on the bank of the reservoir to the other side of the yard to a walnut tree.

As a young girl, our neighbor, Opal Boyd, would take me to Sunday school and church to the Christian church and later when we could drive, we would go to the Methodist church in Fowler.

While living on the farm, I did not have an indoor bathroom and no running water in the house, until Daddy put it in for Mother's Day. We had an acre reservoir just outside our back door with four wells that ran all the time and the water that was in the house ran free all the time. They were called Artesian wells. We used kerosene lamps for lights.

In the fall of 1939, Mabel Fuhrman and her three children Elsie, Delbert, and Herman, came to live with us. In 1940, Daddy and she were married. After I graduated, they tore down the house and built a new one.

When growing up on the farm, I learned responsibility and how to do many things that I have used all of my life. My memories on the farm are good ones as we were taught to take care of what you had and to be a responsible person in life. My Mother and Dad were loving parents and after Mother passed away, Daddy had his hands full and had our interest at heart.

After graduating May 18, 1944, I helped to take care of several families that were in need of help. I also helped Daddy harvest wheat and Aileen sew flour sack dresses that summer. In the fall, I moved to Meade, got a job in a cleaning shop. Guin and I lived together until Bub came home from the service. All of this was before I turned eighteen in November 1944.

June 15, 1963: A Hot Time in the Prairie Town
By Jill Voran of Annapolis, Maryland
Born 1947

I was fifteen and bored by the excruciatingly slow progression of monotonous, hot summer days in Pretty Prairie, Kansas, my hometown of six-hundred plus. My neighborhood friend, Charlotte and I had spent the evening sitting in the middle of Main Street listening to the quiet whir of lawn sprinklers, inhaling the smell of freshly cut lawns, and hoping that a car would drive down the street. It didn't So far the only excitement of the summer had been generated when, after hearing the fire alarm go off in the fire station two blocks away, we watched the volunteer firemen assemble and subsequently convinced my Dad to follow the fire truck to the fire. (Luckily, the fire had been small and easily extinguished.)

After my evening in the middle of Main, I went home to watch one of our three television stations. Just after ten o'clock, I turned off the news and walked down the hall to my bedroom. As I was about to get into bed, I heard the deafening crash of a lightning bolt and found myself sitting on the floor in the dark hugging my knees. I realized that the electricity was off and was surprised to see a glow of light coming from the living room where I had just been watching television so I walked down the hall to investigate and saw an inflamed wall of curtains. I quickly surmised that lightning had come down the TV antenna and flashed across the living room igniting the curtains. In fact, this was the second time that lightning had struck our television antenna. However, the first time the electrical charge had simply blown the antenna cord out of the wall socket.

Seizing a chance to play a starring role in this memorable event, I sprang into action. "Mother, I screamed, "The house is on fire!' "I'll be right down," Mother replied. Now that wasn't the response I had anticipated. My words had obviously not had much effect on her. She sounded like she had just been informed that a neighbor had dropped by for coffee. So I tried again. "Mother the HOUSE is ON FIRE!' To which she repeated, "I'll be right down." Unbeknownst to me, Mother was in the shower wearing what Dad later described as "nothing more than a proverbial smile." She was sopping wet and unable to get her underwear on, so she simply gave up on the undergarments and pulled on her dress, thus perhaps becoming the first woman in our town to go bra-less in the 1960s.

Mother's tardy response to my alarm convinced me that I had to take matters into my own hands, so I began filling cooking pots at the kitchen sink and flinging water toward the wall of flames. However, the practically nonexistent water pressure in our kitchen made this process incredibly slow, and the heat of the flames as well as the smoke in the living room prevented me from getting close to the fire and rendered my efforts totally ineffectual.

Meanwhile, Mother had awakened Dad and my eleven-year-old brother, discovered that our phone was dead, and, fearing that the whole house was about to go up in flames, issued instructions for saving what was dearest to her. She told my brother and me to leave the house and ordered Dad to save himself and the family car from incineration by backing it out of the garage. Then, in the pouring rain, she dashed across the street to the home of our neighbor, Bones Chamberlain, to call the fire department.

After blindly, following Mom's instructions. My dad, my brother, and I found ourselves standing outside shivering in the pouring rain until it dawned on us that her reaction to the fire was a bit hyperbolic. We saw no flames flashing through the roof and no walls collapsing. Therefore, we decided to go back into the house where, because of the low water pressure, we formed a "coffee cup brigade." Mom returned from the neighbor's home, reported that the fire truck was on its way, scolded us for risking our lives by re-entering the house, and pronounced our firefighting attempts pitiful. Subsequently, Dad realized that the front door was locked, depriving the firefighters access to the burning room. So a Keystone Cops routine ensued as my thoroughly drenched mom, my bleary-eyed brother, and I tried to pull a garden hose through our garage, kitchen, and dining room and into her living room to spray water on Dad as he opened the front door to welcome the firemen who still hadn't arrived. Why was it taking so long to drive two blocks?

Suddenly we heard a loud pop, followed by the splintering of glass, and discovered that the heat of the fire had caused the living room picture window to shatter. By this time, the stuffed chairs in the room were burning and producing thick smoke that made breathing difficult. We were all starting to cough, and just as we heard the fire truck siren, Mother once again ordered out family to evacuate the house. While exiting, I belatedly remembered that Jackie, my beloved parakeet, was still in the kitchen. Dad bravely volunteered to enter the smoke-filled house and attempt to rescue Jackie. While Mom, my brother, and I stood outside waiting for Dad to return, I was consumed with feelings of guilt and dread. "Why had it taken me so long to remember that my only pet needed rescuing?" "What if my dad is injured while trying to rescue him?" The next few minutes seemed like hours. When Dad finally appeared carrying the birdcage, which was covered with the cloth I always, put over it at night, none of us knew what to expect. My hands were shaking as I lifted the cover off the cage, and I dreaded seeing my bird lying unconscious at the bottom of it. However, there was Jackie sitting on his perch as perky as ever, and he greeted us by uttering the only words we could ever teach the self-centered creature: "Jackie is a pretty bird." Then, surveying us carefully and noticing our bedraggled condition, he mocked us by giving his best imitation of the whistle usually used by construction workers while eyeing an attractive lady walking down the street.

When the local volunteer firefighters finally arrived, they dealt with the fire with impeccable dispatch. They simply doused the burning rug with water, picked up the smoldering chairs, carried them out of the house, and announced that they had put the fire out.

As I walked out onto our front lawn, I was shocked to see many friends and neighbors staring at us the way a theatre audience stares at actors on a stage. In fact, when the firefighters carried our smoldering living room chairs out onto the lawn, the townspeople actually applauded. I was temporarily delighted to realize that I had played a heroic part in this small town drama, of course, if I hadn't been awake, the lightning strike could have produced much more disastrous results. However, my self-satisfaction was quickly followed by a feeling of chagrin when I realized that wearing only my pink and rather ratty looking pajamas, I was standing in front of practically the whole town.

Years later, when I mentioned my role in the fire of 1963, my brother, who was always in charge of deflating my ego, was quick to remind me that I wasn't very heroic because I failed to awaken him and almost forgot about my pet parakeet. In retrospect, my brother was probably right; however, this hot time in the prairie town did have a lasting effect on me. It made me skeptical of the old saws touting the importance of "early to bed" and asserting that "Lightning never strikes in the same place twice." And it also fostered in me a quality which most Kansans share: a healthy respect for Mother Nature.

Eleanor's parents, Edna and Elmer Fox

My Life
By Eleanor M. Fox of Goddard, Kansas
Born 1934

My story begins on February 29, 1934. I was born in the friendly little town of Ashland, Kansas to the most wonderful parents any child could hope for, Edna and Elmer Fox. My Dad was a butcher with his own grocery store. Mom was City Clerk for thirty-three years. I was blessed to have a sister, Yvonne (Bonnie) who was twenty-one months older than I.

I had the happiest childhood filled with every joy and happenings only available during these years before television, I-phones, and computers.

After breakfast, it was "out the door to explore," and we did just that. Our imagination had no stopping point and we pushed it to the limit.

Ashland had the most wonderful swimming pool in the whole world. It was built in 1916 and was concrete. Its walls were tall and slanted and were not slick but rough, which played havoc with our swimming suit "bottoms."

We taught ourselves to swim and spent much too much time at the wonderful pool. There was no filter system but a large drain in the very deepest part, which emptied the pool once a week. By the end of the week, it needed it! We never noticed that the water had turned green and very warm. We loved it.

On the way to the pool was a very large mulberry tree that hung out over the road. We always stopped here to eat some of the biggest and most delicious berries, and by the time

Eleanor Mae Fox

we got to the pool, our feet (we went barefoot most of the time,) were purple on the bottom.

I developed the love of horses at a very young age. My dear Mom and I created the most wonderful "stick horse" in the whole world. We drew a horse's head on an 8x1 board and my dear, patient; Mom took her coping saw and sawed it out. If you have seen how slow a coping saw works, you know this was truly a labor of love. Two thinner boards connected to the head at one end and to a broom stick at the other end became a fine stick horse. But we were not finished. I took a nylon rope and after it was unbraided, it turned into the most beautiful mane to be attached to the neck. Finally after attaching the bridle and reins…Eureka! My almost alive stick horse. I rode that stick horse much longer than I care to admit.

A short distance to the East of Ashland down a dirt road was what we called "The Old Castle." It was built in 1888 by Dr. W.J. Workman. It really did resemble a castle since it had a round lookout on the North. By the time we went exploring it was empty and falling apart. In its glory, there were five bedrooms, two living rooms, and running water to a bathroom! We imagined that there was a "mad" scientist in a hidden laboratory somewhere. It was a fun place to poke around and I'm sure if we had been discovered we would have been shoo'd away.

At the east of Ashland was a fantastic area set apart from the city by a steep road down into the park. The road then circled the whole park with picnic tables at the south end around to the tennis courts, back around to where the same road we came down on gave us the exit where we shifted into "low gear" to climb the hill on our bikes.

Running along the east side of this wonderful park was a creek (Bear Creek.) It usually had very little water in it. But once after a big rain we discovered this creek had turned into a "river" or so we thought. The water was moving along quite rapidly. Boy! My sister and another friend quickly scrambled down into the water….clothes and all. When I think back now, how dangerous that was, but no one got injured. How stupid! WE NEVER TOLD MOM AND DAD!!!!

We collected tadpoles out of that creek and took a container of them home with us and placed them in our bathtub. Pets! Lucky for us, tadpoles turn into little frogs very quickly and were were able to set them free. What my dear Mom endured. She had the patience of a saint.

I enjoyed being a Girl Scout. We were so lucky to have a lovely rock building that was donated to the girl scouts. I keep a picture of that lovely building.

In our backyard was an area where no grass was growing, which had been our chicken pen. This was the perfect place to turn into a little town with houses, roads, trees for our little cars and trucks to run. And we never gave any thought as to the "leavings" of the chickens in that dirt. What fun!

We had an icebox in our home and the ice truck that delivered our ice was driven by "Pete the Ice Man." We watched for him as he always gave us little chunks of ice.

I remember Mom tying pennies into our little hankies to take our offerings to Sunday school. We attended the Methodist Church, and I did love singing in the Choir as soon as I was old enough.

Ashland was a safe, wonderful place to grow up in. I have been blessed. What more could any little girl ask for. Thank you, Ashland, for being "My Home Town."

Growing Up in the late 1940s
By Judy Schremmer Corby of Wichita, Kansas
Born 1943

Growing up in a small town in the middle of USA in the late 1940s was simple and quiet. The war was over, the soldiers were home, and the Great Depression was over. Our family consisted of four, Mother, Dad, my brother, and me. Times were still hard but manufacturing was improving and many changes were coming our way.

We lived in a three-bedroom house with large living and dining rooms and a moderate sized kitchen. Mother was always home, cooking, cleaning, washing, and raising children. Dad worked in the oil field as it was the best paying job around and he was strong and hard working. The home was the center of our lives back then.

We had a real "icebox," which later folks would probably call a cooler. Ours was a metal insulated, rectangular box that stood upright in the kitchen. Ice was kept in the bottom and milk and eggs, and cheese in the top. The grocery man would deliver a block of ice to our house along with a bottle of milk daily. We looked forward to his visit, as he was funny and always had a pink peppermint candy for each of us.

Milk came in glass bottles and the cream floated on top, leaving the "blue john," at the bottom. We would skim the cream and use part of it on our oatmeal for breakfast and keep the rest for making butter.

We made butter two ways. The first was easiest by pouring the cream into a glass container, adding salt, and attaching the lid with a paddle and turn wheel to churn the cream into butter. The other way was more tiring. The cream was placed into a glass Mason jar and lid attached securely then we would shake the jar until it turned into butter. The milk left after the clump of butter was lifted out was called buttermilk. It did not taste anything like the store bought kind. There was nothing as tasty as a toasted piece of homemade bread with homemade butter on it.

We had a brown heating stove standing in the corner of the dining room. It was made of metal and had a stovepipe coming out of the top going up into the chimney. Ours burned gas but some had wood burning stoves. It did not heat the whole house but kept the living room and dining room cozy. We had to be careful playing around it as the metal got very hot and would burn us.

There was no television, cell phones, or computers back then. We did have a small radio. Reception was poor so Dad hooked a wire to the back of the radio, ran it out the window and all the way to the back of the yard, and attached it to a metal piece on a telephone pole. Reception was great then and we would sometimes get a station from Del Rio, Texas, when the weather was just right. We gathered around the radio each evening and listened to shows like, "Amos and Andy," "The Shadow," "Dragnet," and "The Grand Ole Opry." We used our imaginations to picture the scenes they described as we children played with marbles and cards on the floor. We did not have a television until 1957. It was black and white and the only shows we could get were, "The Ed Sullivan Show," "The Price is Right," "Roy Rogers & Dale Evans," and "Gene Autry."

Washday was an all-day event. Mother would put a pot of beans on to cook early in the morning. After breakfast, she would fill the wringer washer and washtub with hot water. She poured soap in the washer and turned the agitator on. She separated the clothes into piles and washed whites first, and Dad's dirty work clothes last.

The wringer washer was electric. It had a large tub with an arm on one side where the ringer was attached. The wringer had two rubber rollers that manually separated then could be clamped down to wring the water out of the clothes. It could be very dangerous if fingers got too close while adding clothes as the wringer would grab them and pull them through. One boy got his hand in and it pulled him in clear to his elbow before he could get released. It left a lifetime scar.

While the clothes were agitating we would take clean rags and go wipe the clothesline. The clothesline was made of three wires stretched between three poles in the backyard. The clothes were hung with clothespins to the lines to dry in the sunshine and wind. Some clothespins were "u" shaped but they broke easily so our Uncle Bill, who lived in California, created the pinch clothespin. It was made of two straight pieces of wood with a pivot spring in the middle allowing it to clamp the clothes to the line and stay all day.

The dry clothes were gathered into a basket and each piece sprinkled damp with water and rolled into a roll then placed in the basket to be ironed the next day.

Times were simple and safe back then. Everyone knew everyone and parents disciplined their children at home. If a neighbor saw a child doing something wrong, the parents knew about it before the child got home. If Mother didn't get the results needed, she turned the discipline over to Dad when he got home from work. Kids were mischievous but not malicious and drugs, killings, and kidnapping were not heard of.

We played out in the yard from morning and into the night. There was so much to do and so many games to play. When we could get the neighbor kids together, we played baseball and basketball. We made up games like wood tag where you ran from tree to tree and one kid would try to tag you. We loved shadow tag on sunny days and at night. This game consisted of one person trying to tag others by stepping on their shadows. There were lots of giggling and roars of laughter. Boys whistled happy tunes and girls sang made up songs, as they would swing high in their swings. Sometimes we would get creative and make mud pies by gathering dirt in a pan, stirring water into it, and letting it set a bit then adding rose petals and pebbles to the top for decorations. Dolls and dogs got to eat these creations.

Dads took the boys fishing in the creek and the boys caught crickets and grasshoppers for bait. Girls learned to sew and make doll clothes, plant flowers, and design toy houses for their dolls with their Mother. Families prayed together, played together, and stayed together. It was a pleasant, peaceful time growing up in the late 1940s.

Life in Goddard
By Peggy J. Gammill of Wichita, Kansas
Born 1943

My name is Peggy Gammill. This story is about my Grandparents, Herbert and Hazel Means. Hazel Naomi Hummel was born April 20, 1896. Her sister, Josephine Eliza was born, March 17, 1898. They grew up in Monte

Hazel, Dolly, Herbert, Naomi Jo, and Dorothy Means

Ne, Arkansas. Hazel and Aunt Joe played in a band at Monte Ne, when they were young.

When Hazel and Aunt Joe were younger, their parents took twin boys from New York Orphans Train to raise. I think the twins were five years old. As it turned out, the boys were retarded. Grandpa always said he was glad they got them because some people might not have been good to them since they were retarded. When the boys were in their thirties or forties, one of the boys had to be put in an institution because he had become violent. Grandpa and Grandma tried everything but they couldn't manage him. The other boy was with the family until he died when he was in his seventies.

Aunt Joe and Aunt Berry were the best. Uncle Berry was part Indian and was a very good-looking man. They lived with Grandma Hummel after Grandpa Hummel passed away. They took over the store, post office, and other businesses. Aunt Joe and Uncle Berry never had any children of their own. But they had lots of foster children from the orphanage at Little Rock. Three of the children stayed until they were grown and were treated like they were their children. When these children married and had children, Aunt Joe and Uncle Berry were grandparents to them.

Aunt Joe loved to can food and she canned a lot. In the spring, she would tell some of the poor people to bring her empty jars and she's give them full jars. She'd empty out her food supply and get ready to can more.

They helped to build a little Baptist church down in the valley. In later years, a dam was built that caused the valley to flood where the church and store were. This is where Beaver Lake is located now. Aunt Joe and Uncle Berry bought property in Rogers and relocated the church there.

Herbert had four brothers, Delbert, Chester, Evert, and John. Delbert was a preacher and a teacher. Chester and Evert were farmers and John passed away of T. B in 1916, in these days they did not have ways of treating and preventing diseases like they do today.

Herbert and Hazel were married on Grandpa Hummel's birthday, August 12, 1915 at Grandma and Grandpa Hummel's home at Monte Ne, Arkansas. Grandpa and Grandma were having a party and Grandpa stopped the party and told everyone that something special was going to happen. Herbert and Hazel came out and were married at the party.

It was customary for the neighbors to have a Chivaree for newlyweds in those days. The Chivaree gang sometimes did some pretty ornery things. The neighbors sent some of their kids to keep the folks home until the Chivaree gang got there. Herbert and hazel knew why the kids were there, so they told to the kids to go look down the road to see if they were coming. The kids went to look and the folks sneaked out and hid in a cornfield near their home.

They didn't stay on the farm very long. They moved to Arkansas and lived with Hazel's folks. The family grew, now there were three children, Naomi, Jo, Dorothy, and Dolly. When Dolly was a baby, the folks moved from Arkansas to a farm five miles from Goddard, Kansas. Hazel hadn't lived on a farm, but I'm sure it didn't take her long to learn the ways of living on the farm. She would try anything even though she had children to care for she also did lots of farm work. The folks had seven more children after moving back to Kansas.

Herbert was a farmer and he farmed a half section of ground and always had a herd of cattle. The milk cows were a big source of income for the family. Hazel had a big, five-gallon churn and on Fridays, she churned butter. She molded it into one-pound molds and then took it to town to sell. She had a butter route in Wichita and sold butter and cream. She gave the buttermilk away to her customers. She also sold butter to two stores in Wichita.

As children growing up on a farm, we learned to milk cows, feed chickens, gather eggs, garden, shock wheat and oats and shuck corn. Kids nowadays wouldn't know what shocking wheat was because they don't use binders anymore. Back in those days, the farmers used binders instead of combines. The binder cut and bound the wheat and oats in bundles. The bundles were picked up and stood up in groups of several to hold them up. Several days later, a threshing machine would come and the binders would be brought in and threshed. It would make a large straw stack. The grain would be put in a wagon to be hauled to the elevator in town or put in the granaries' on the farm. Some would be used

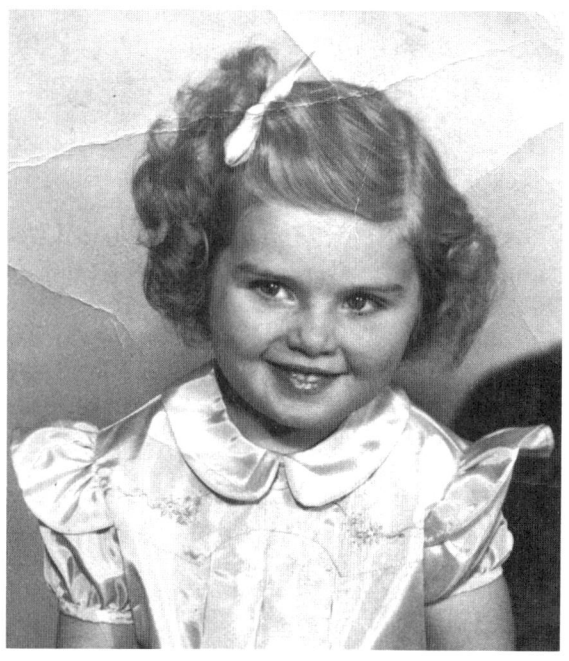

Peggy Champ Gammill

for seed for the next year's crop and some would be sold later. The farmers would all get together to work when the threshing machine came. It took lots of men to work when the wheat was threshed. It also meant lots of work for the women because of all the cooking for the Harvest crew. This was a very exciting event for the kids but a lot of work for the adults.

We lived in a five-room house. We had a living room, dining room, two bedrooms, and a kitchen. Our home was heated by a stove that was in the dining room. When it was real cold, Hazel would let the little ones sit on the table to play. The dining room table was used for everything. That is where we did our lessons and played games. We played a lot of Jacks on the table.

Hazel never had a large crib for her babies. She only had a small one and never mentioned needing a large one.

We had a telephone; we were on a party line with six or eight other people on the same line. There was only one phone for each house. The phone at each house had a different ring like two longs and a short or two short rings, etc. We all knew whose number was being rung and some people listened in on the conversations. You sure didn't talk about anything that you didn't want others to hear.

We had a pump organ but it wore out and Herbert made Hazel a chest out of it for clothes or whatever. Grandpa Hummel sent money to the folks to buy a piano. They bought a second hand piano and we really enjoyed it. I learned to play it and some church songs. I also learned to play a lot of songs by ear.

Our family had a model T. It had to be cranked to start it. Hazel drove that car and she cranked it to start it. It wasn't easy, most roads weren't hardtops then and when it rained, it was hard to drive on muddy roads. The cars didn't go very fast back then.

We always had lots of company; Hazel never knew when she was going to have extra people for a meal. I grew up during the Depression and money was very scarce. We didn't have fancy food. Everyone loved Hazel's homemade bread and biscuits in the summer; we had many meals where everything on the table came from the garden. We had cows so we always had plenty of milk. In the spring, we always looked forward to having lamb quarters, and greens. We picked them in our yard. Most people thought of them as weeds. Hazel would pick dandelion leaves and other wild plants from our yard. She was very particular and we had to look over every leaf and other wild plants from our yard. We loved the greens so we didn't complain.

We always had a large garden. We grew lots of potatoes, green beans, peas, cucumbers, onions, and tomatoes. Herbert would plow the garden and help plant the potatoes and them most of the rest of the garden work was left to Hazel and us kids. Hazel canned lots of green beans and pickles from the garden. She also canned lots of field corn. They planted the tomatoes and cucumbers around haystacks. We had to walk quite a ways to get to them. Sometimes, we had to carry the tomatoes, and cucumbers, back to the house in buckets.

In the spring, Hazel would order baby chicks and they would come by mail. Because they were cheaper, she would order baby roosters and always ended up with enough hens to keep us furnished with eggs. The roosters furnished us with fried chicken all summer. That was our main meat in the summer. We ate lots of fried chicken, chicken and noodles, and creamed chicken.

In summer, lots of people would camp on the road north of the house. Gypsies camped on it often and would come and buy farm products or trade for them. Once we talked Hazed into trading for two baby goats. When I was growing up, I think people helped each other more than they do these days.

The only brand new car that Herbert ever bought was a Ford Touring car. They had a bad wreck and he and Hazel were hurt real bad and ended up in the hospital. Dale Herbert was just six months and had a broken leg. The Higbees who lived about a mile from us, kept Dale for quite a while until Hazel was able to take care of him again, even though the Higbees had a large family of their own. Grandma Means and Grandpa Erskine stayed with the rest of us kids while the folks were in the hospital. Hazel washed our clothes on a washboard. It was hard work. Finally, she got a washing machine that required pulling a lever to agitate the clothes. Herbert rigged up a motor to run it and that was a big help. The wringer had to be turned by hand. It was really going first class when Hazel got her first Maytag washer. She let her friends come and use it sometimes. The folks were always ready to share anything they had.

We didn't have wash and wear clothes, so everything had to be ironed. At first, we ironed with a flat iron that was heated on the stove. What a delight when we got a gasoline iron. There was lots of ironing to do. The folks didn't have any electricity until after the kids were grown. Getting an electric stove, hot water heater, and some electric appliances was a real help for Hazel. They also got water piped into the house and built a bathroom out of some space from the back porch.

We didn't have a refrigerator. Hazel would put the butter in a bowl and then put the bowl in a kettle with a handle. She would tie a rope to the handle and drop it down into the well. The rope would be secured to something on the top of the well. It was great when she got an icebox.

A man came by every few days and Hazel would buy a hundred-pound block of ice for the icebox. It was really great to keep milk, butter, and other perishables in the icebox.

Dust Storm
By Dorl Rader of Larned, Kansas
Born 1927

I was born in 1927, on a farm, six miles southwest of Mullinsville, Kansas. There was no hospital in the area and the doctor drove from Greensburg, sixteen miles away. We had just experienced a bad rainstorm. The roads then had no paved surfaces or even gravel, just plain old black mud. They became impassable at times and the doctor just barely made it to our house. I was a breech birth, and we had no electricity or running water. The doctor just used the instruments he carried in his case. It's hard to envision a successful birth but he was successful.

The roads were so bad that the doctor did not attempt to return to Greensburg, but stayed all night. Several years later, after the doctor retired, our family encountered him on a trip to town. Mom asked him, "Do you remember Dorl?" The doctor replied, "Oh yes, he came butt first (The doctors own words.)"

One of my earliest memories was riding in a horse drawn wagon while Dad shucked corn. I was three years old and my brother was two years old. We hid in the wagon bed and Dad played games with us. When he shucked an ear, he would toss it in the wagon where he thought we were hiding. Now and then, he hit us with it. The horse drawn wagon was handy because no driver was required. When Dad needed the wagon moved forward, he spoke to the horses and they pulled it up and stopped when he said whoa.

In 1936, our family was heading to town in our 1928 Studebaker, when we looked behind us and saw an enormous dust cloud bearing down on us. What was fascinating to me was seeing thousands and thousands of birds flying in front of it. We hurried to a neighbor's house and just got inside when day turned to night. We couldn't see anything. Mom thought my four-year-old sister, Betty was with Dad, and Dad thought Mom had her. They called her name several times but no answer. We were about to panic. The neighbor lady finally got a lamp lit and we found Betty huddled in a corner, unhurt and scared to death but safe.

In our part of Kansas, we called that day Black Friday.

In the early 1930s, we had not electricity, icebox, or running water. Dad built a unique watering system in what we called The Well House next to the windmill. He put

Dorl Rader and his brother, Lyle in 1930

an old vinegar barrel on a stand inside the well house. He put a second barrel on the floor. The windmill pumped water into the top barrel, when it filled; it drained into the bottom barrel. When full the water drained into what we called the milk trough. This was a trough about two feet wide, ten feet long, and eighteen inches deep. When the trough filled. It drained into the stock tanks, which were, located about fifty yards downhill in the edge of the pasture, then into a pond below. Fresh water all the time!

The milk trough was where we stored milk, cream, butter, etc. This produce was put in jars or cans, then put in the fresh water and weighted down to hold them in the water.

An old cowboy named Henry Reed lived in a little hillside shack on the Laramore Ranch, about six miles south of us. He went everywhere on horseback, even to town for groceries. It was about twelve miles from his home to town and he went right through our yard. Henry was an old time cowboy with all the trappings: hat, boots, and big Mexican style spurs. My brother and I really admired him and vowed to grow up to be a cowboy (and we did.)

Once in a while, when he came by, Mom could give him some milk, butter or whatever he needed. If we were not home, Henry just helped himself and we would be missing some produce!

Mom didn't mind because she said we should help folks like that.

Before combines became common, most farmers used a grain binder to harvest their wheat, oats, and barley. This machine cut off and tied the standing crop into bundles that were put in shocks to dry.

In the fall, a man with a large threshing machine went from farm to farm. The machine separated the straw, putting the grain in a wagon, and blowing the straw into big round stacks. This straw was used in the winter to feed the cows.

Each farmer would help his neighbor, so very little extra help was needed. A banker in town owned quite a lot of land so the threshing machine was on his land for quite a while. One fall when I was a preschooler, (no kindergarten then) he hired me to drive the teams and wagon from shock to shock so the pitcher could load the bundles to haul to the machine. He said, "I'll pay you a dollar a day." Boy was I excited! One of the first things I learned was to drive on the down wing side of the shock. Those pitchers did not like to pitch bundles against the wind!

When the barge was full, the owner took the lines and drove to the machine; I rode the full one until an empty, came by, then jumped off, and caught the rear of the empty to ride back out to the field.

About every third or fourth load, I was allowed to go all the way in to get a drink. The water was kept in a five-gallon cream can with a dipper hanging on the side. We all drank out of the same dipper.

When I went to the bank to get paid, the banker told the employees that I had worked eleven days and did an excellent job. He then handed me a Ten-dollar bill. Being a youngster, I didn't say anything, that dollar short meant a lot to me and Mom had to work quite a while to convince me to forgive him.

Work Ethic
By E. Earl Kendrick of Scott City, Kansas
Born 1938

The word chores can have different meanings: A dictionary will say a daily, light work for household or farm. Some people might tell you of the physical exertion, the drudgery, or the demeaning quality of chores, or they might also tell you how they hated chores, but may I tell you my experiences with chores?

Born on a ranch in western Kansas in May 1938, World War II had not started yet, but there were rumors of its coming, and I was born into a time of worry, indecision, and hard work.

There was no electricity except for a few wind chargers, which were twenty-four volts and good only for lights and very, very few telephones on farms, especially when you lived thirty miles from town. Many of the cars were Model A Fords, or other makes of equal quality. Horses were for work, either cow horses or plow horses.

After World War II began, each American had an important role to play for the success of the family and nation. Family expenses were controlled by ration coupons, which were distributed each month. Everything was rationed such as sugar, gasoline, oil, shoes, tires, some food items, margarine replaced butter, mechanical parts were scarce or not available, and we patched our own tires. We endured these shortages/inconveniences for the good of America, and they just intensified our part in the war. As kids we, too, were involved enough to feel that we had a role to fulfill to "help the soldiers."

One of these soldiers was my oldest brother who was really one of three cousins, raised by my parents, but we were raised as a family. Through the years, death has thinned the ranks, but the remainders still call and consider each as brother and sister.

Chickens were a farms wife's contribution to a family's survival with meat and eggs (Which, could be sold or traded for groceries.) Milk cows paid their way with milk and cream, (Which was sold at the creamery,) and heifers for replacement milk cows. All this does not include the fried chicken, (a delicacy,) steers, hogs, goats, rabbits, (jack, cottontails, or tame,) that were food, and added to this was fruit from native wild plums, sand hill plums, chokecherries, mulberries, currants, rhubarb, and some other fruits, plus a garden with an ample supply of vegetables.

All this supplied our food requirements. Sounds like a lot of food. It was, but this had to feed a family of nine for at least a year, and though this sounds like a lot, there was no irrigation except rainfall, which cut down on the amount of food available but we never missed a meal. For years, I never knew that many people who lived in cities got their food from a soup line, but there was never enough. Though we lived a rough life, did without a lot of things, we were never hungry nor did we go without love!

Nearly everything was evaluated by the importance it played in maintaining life. So you can see the importance/purpose of chores/chorehands! As children/youth, we didn't understand all of this, but the parents had just gone through the "dirty thirties," and were very aware of what a food shortage was.

This is where we, the children, began to learn that living/doing were contributions to our family and neighbors. Neither our family, nor our neighbors, had money for frivolous things. We learned to prove our worth by helping do chores, and as we did our chores, (which were assigned to us,) we learned and accepted the responsibilities/values of these opportunities to help. These responsibilities consisted of: getting firewood each evening for the cook stove, making sure there was coal oil in the lamps before dark, milking cows, feeding the hogs, gathering eggs, plowing the garden, (With a horse pulling a one bottom plow,) planting and weeding the garden, then harvesting and canning the crops. We didn't do all of any of these chores, but were available and required, to do our part,

You might ask, "Where were your parents? Couldn't they help?"

With the exception of one milk cow, Dad's cow herd had perished in a blizzard in March, 1931, so he was rebuilding the herd and farming in the summer months, but since this was a ranch, the farming was very limited, but there was always fence to maintain, hay to harvest, and stack by hand, and he still had cows to care for.

Mom would be working in the garden at 4:00 a.m. when it was cooler, and it would soon be sun up. This let us kids sleep a little later when there was no school, but we knew when we got up that after breakfast there were chores to do, with no fussing,

Breakfast was a meal that would sustain you 'til the next meal, with no snacks. Dinner was at noon, but if we were working cattle, putting up hay, etc., it would be ready when we showed up, but we tried to be there at noon for Mom's benefit.

Mom took care of the one hundred fifty to two hundred hens and felt rewarded in doing this in that she always, had a few pets that she could pick up and carry around, talk to them and put them down. She knew more about chickens than anyone I knew. Our chores seldom varied, but started as soon as we left the house with milk buckets, headed for the barn.

On one side of an alley, which ran through the barn, were the horses used most often with hay mangers and grain troughs. On the other side of the alley were the stanchions, in which we latched the cows while milking, and gave them their grain. I can still visualize the cows as they came into the barn. Each cow had a .name and a stanchion, and if a cow got in the wrong stanchion, which was seldom but it did happen, there was butting to settle the conflict.

First was Crumpy, a cow that I milked, then Jersey, Blackie, Speck and Bawley. Probably a couple more that I forgot, this was seventy years ago.

After milking, the milk was carried to the house where it was separated using a hand-cranked separator. Separating was running the fresh milk through a centrifuge, leaving skimmed milk for us, cream for butter and to sell at the creamery.

After the milk was cared for, it was back outside to feed the hogs and chickens, feed the bucket calves, turn the milk cows out to pasture, curry, brush, and saddle the horses if we had cattle to work.

It was hard, daily work, but being kids we softened the work by having lots of fun as it got done. Dad, being Scot-Irish and a true pioneer, always enjoyed a laugh, though the work couldn't be slighted.

Life was dependent on everyone doing their part, and as young people we learned a work ethic that is still evident in our lives today.

The country school that Delorse's grandmother attended

My Love of Airplanes
By Delorse Lessenden of Cheney, Kansas
Born 1937

My name is Delorse; I was born at home, as were my two brothers. We lived in a small house, I slept in a dresser drawer, and my brothers had beds on shelves in a pantry. My first memories were when I was three or four years old. I had an earache, My Daddy came home and found me crying, I had an earache. He blew smoke in my ear and put a warm cloth on it.

My Dad worked on a ranch and he was my hero. My Mother was sick a lot and I was on my own a lot. My Dad gave me a spanking one time in my life. They were bringing cattle home for the winter, there was a fence and gate to keep them on the road and out of the yard. I wanted to watch so I climbed to the top of the gate; the cattle were shoving the gate as they crowded down the road. My Dad rode up on his horse, grabbed me off the gate, swatted my behind, and took me to the house, yelled at my mother for not watching me. If I had fell off, the cattle would have trampled me.

Later, I had a baby sister. She was so little; she slept in a baby bed. My Mother drove my brothers to meet their ride to school every day. She left me with a bottle of milk to feed the baby if she woke up. She woke up, drank all the milk, had a poopy diaper, and was crying. I had watched my Mom change her diaper and decided if I climbed in the bed (I was five-years-old,) I could change her, that worked out, she quit crying, and went back to sleep. My Mom came home and was not happy with me because I got the sheet dirty and she had to wash it.

Life was hard, no running water, a pump outside, you had to heat the water, and use a motorized washer. For small batches you, you used a tube with a washboard.

My Mom went to the hospital; my Grandparents took my baby sister home with them. They came on weekends to help bathe my brothers and I and wash our hair in the washtub, and do laundry.

My Dad had a lady come to watch me and cook meals, She just wiped off the dishes and pans, left them on the table and on the stove. My Dad was not happy. The lady didn't come to work, so I was alone. I wanted to help Dad by washing the dishes. I couldn't pick up the teakettle to heat water, so I determined I could put the dish pan on the stove, carry water and soap to it, and let it heat. I climbed on a chair, and was standing there washing the dishes when my Dad came to check on me, grabbed me off the chair, and explained I might have caught my dress on fire and burned up.

I remember Pearl Harbor, everyone was talking about the Japanese in airplanes bombing and killing people. I wondered how a little bitty plane could bomb and kill people.

I had only seen airplanes in the sky and did not realize how big they were. Shortly after this as I was playing in the yard, there came a little plane with a little man inside. I ran and hid in the woodpile so it wouldn't kill me. It was actually a boy from town who was flying his model plane. My Dad took us over to Boeing so we could see a real plane. When the Japanese surrendered, my brothers and I rode in the back of the truck to town, where everyone gathered to celebrate.

I followed my brothers everywhere. We had many adventures, my poor Dad.

There were many unbroken horses at the ranch. My brothers decided to try to ride one. They got one in the barn, put a bridle on it, and my brother didn't want to get his clothes dirty, so decided to put a gunnysack on the hors to keep clean. People didn't have a lot of clothes back then, only two or three changes. The sack wasn't a good idea, it could slide, the horse bucked him off and broke his arm. My Grandparents were there and we took him to get his arm set. A short time later, we were chasing a rabbit; it ran in a hole, they decided to chop him out with an axe. As one brother was swinging the axe, the other decided to look in the hole; the axe hit him and split his head open. MY Grandparents were there again, and we took him to the doctor. The doctor stitched his head, saying another one-fourth of an inch more would probably have killed him. My Grandparents had brought us new hats and gloves, we didn't get new things, very often and the only thing he was worried about was that his new hat was probably ruined. When we got home, my other brother went to get his hat for him, all was well, and the hat was fine; and may just have saved his life.

We were very fortunate living in the country, many people went to bed hungry and food was rationed. We had chickens to lay eggs and to eat, chicken and noodles or fried chicken are still my favorite foods. We had cows for milk, cream to make butter, homemade bread, lots of pancakes, fried mushif. We had sugar and ice for the icebox. We had homemade ice cream. Fruit or candy was hard to find. Bananas came in large wood crates packed in shredded paper, usually when we got there; all that was left was paper.

My brothers and I survived many more adventures and are living to a healthy old age. Unfortunately, our sister died of cancer before she was three years old. Our Grandparents had her until her death and she was surrounded by love and gentle care. My Grandparents were devastated by the loss of a beautiful little girl.

My Mother's health returned, my dear Father survived all our antics and they lived to a comfortable old age.

The Above Ground Swimming Pool
By E. Joan Rollins of Oklahoma City, Oklahoma
Born 1931

I was born in 1931 in the old Epworth Hospital in Liberal, Kansas. I didn't leave there until my husband joined the Air Force in 1952.

Liberal is located in the very southwest corner of Kansas and during those years was a very small, rural town. We always played outdoors during our free time with the other children in the neighborhood. After all, we had no TV.

There was a vacant lot in the block north of our home that had a very old, rusty, combine parked in the center of the lot. Weeds grew up around it but both boys and girls were free to play on it anytime. It could be a ship, a plane, or anything that our imaginations could conjure up.

I remember one of the older boys in the neighborhood taught me how to ride a bike and what fun I had doing that. We had sidewalks and many knees were skinned, and then covered with Mercurochrome, from roller-skating. Girls sat on the sidewalks to play Jacks. Other times we would play with paper dolls. My dolls were the two English Princesses Elizabeth and Margaret Rose.

When we came home after school, we would listen to the children's radio programs. I remember Jack Armstrong, the All American Boy, The Gene Autry program, and Little Orphan Annie. There were others, but I especially remember Little Orphan Annie because the sponsor was Ovaltine. I really wanted to try Ovaltine, but mother explained that our grocery budget couldn't stretch that far. This was my introduction to the Depression Era.

As a family, we listened to the radio in

the evening. It was a treat if I was allowed to stay up late enough to listen to "Lux Radio Theater" and "I Love a Mystery" with Jack Doc, and Reggie, if I remember those names correctly.

Our neighborhood was only a block from the swimming pool. Having nearly drowned in her youth, my mother was deathly afraid of water. She made sure that my brother and I took Red Cross swimming lessons at the pool and that's where we spent our summers.

We had a most unusual pool because it was above aground. It was like a big concrete box with the pool in the center. When you entered the door, you were in a perimeter hallway that ran around the pool. After you paid or showed your season ticket, you picked up your basket, then the girls went to the left to their dressing rooms, and the boys went to the right.

After we returned our baskets, we walked to the end of the dressing room hall; we walked through a shower, then stepped through a chlorinated footbath, and walked upstairs to the pool.

I've often wondered if there were any other towns that had this distinctive type of pool. I do hope there is a picture of it in the Coronado Museum in Liberal because it was eventually torn down, no longer exists, and is rather difficult to explain.

We spent our summers in that pool and I eventually was a lifeguard there the summer after my junior year at Liberal High School. To this day, I can still walk through that area in my mind as if it were yesterday.

Swimming became a big part of my life because of that old, unique pool. After my husband finished his four years in the Air Force, we moved just down Highway 54 to Guymon, Oklahoma. I eventually became certified as a Water Safety Instructor though the Red Cross and I taught swimming lessons in an outdoor pool in Guymon, Oklahoma, to both youth and adults for over 40 years.

But that's another story for another day.

My Memories

My Memories

Index A
By Name, Year of Birth, and Hometown

Name	Year	City	State	Page
Barbara Engelhardt	1928	Abilene	Kansas	136
Kyle Klenke	1975	Alpharetta	Georgia	124
Lavon Wiersig	1941	Alva	Oklahoma	215
Jill Voran	1947	Annapolis	Maryland	425
Shirlee Hoopes	1932	Anthony	Kansas	311
Pauline F. Hoopes	1934	Anthony	Kansas	179
L. K. Adams	1947	Anthony	Kansas	177
L. Marlene Roe	1935	Argonia	Kansas	30
Alvera Lacey	1938	Argonia	Kansas	406
Janice Merrill	1944	Argonia	Kansas	112
John "J. W." Minor	1922	Ashland	Kansas	119
Earleta Selm	1935	Attica	Kansas	54
Loretta (Rita) Casper	1949	Attica	Kansas	146
Karen Poynter	1940	Augusta	Kansas	51
Nell Moore	1929	Aurora	Colorado	35
Larry Schlotfeldt	1944	Bastrop	Texas	41
Richard L. Sandoval	1943	Beaufort	Missouri	357
Juanita Grantz	1946	Bel Aire	Kansas	53
Patty L. Craven	1937	Biloxi	Mississippi	176
Samuel Walter Scott	1923	Bloom	Kansas	213
Rev. Allen Smith	1952	Bloom	Kansas	39
Ellen Sullivan	1923	Branson	Missouri	280
Ruby A. (Bare) Swanson	1933	Brookings	South Dakota	293
Esther L. Schroeder	1922	Buhler	Kansas	110
Lois Schroeder	1934	Buhler	Kansas	67
Marlene Shirley Neufeld	1937	Buhler	Kansas	126
Carol Redd	1937	Buhler	Kansas	64
Lottie Harder	Unknown	Buhler	Kansas	51
Jim Hammeke	1934	Burns	Oregon	370
Jacka Penner	1930	Burrton	Kansas	149
Earl Polk	1945	Burrton	Kansas	144
Gregg A. Stone	1956	Burrton	Kansas	61
Gwendolyn E. Rice	1926	Caldwell	Kansas	231
Marian Williams	1927	Caldwell	Kansas	419
J. R. Jenista	1930	Caldwell	Kansas	104
Clara Cottle Ginn	1937	Caldwell	Kansas	84
Jim E. Quillin	1940	Caldwell	Kansas	175
Kathleen Risley	1946	Caldwell	Kansas	171
Suzie Yunker	1949	Caldwell	Kansas	181
Galen P. Yunker	1951	Caldwell	Kansas	232

Name	Year	City	State	Page
LuAnn Jamison	1953	Caldwell	Kansas	194
Walter Perrin	1941	Callam Bay	Washington	389
Dave Ackerman	1948	Canon City	Colorado	360
Flora Erickson	1926	Chanuk	Kansas	313
Naomi Chestnut	1933	Chanute	Kansas	35
Vernon McMinimy	1930	Charlottesville	Virginia	264
Jack Wolfe	1945	Chatham	Illinois	47
Eugena "Jean" Burdorf	1936	Cheney	Kansas	244
Delorse Lessenden	1937	Cheney	Kansas	436
Maxine Stapleton	1924	Cimarron	Kansas	415
Marilyn Small	1950	Cimarron	Kansas	57
Cleta Cornett	1928	Clearwater	Kansas	113
Joan Clayton	Unknown	Clovis	New Mexico	361
Marilyn Jean Davis	1936	Clyde Hill	Washington	374
Grace McLaughlin	1933	Coldwater	Kansas	281
Roger Roy Hoffman	1935	Coldwater	Kansas	421
Phyllis Hatltom	1936	Coldwater	Kansas	343
Mary Ann Buller	1942	Coldwater	Kansas	331
Bernice Steinmetz	1931	Colorado Springs	Colorado	81
Virginia C. Winter	1923	Conway Springs	Kansas	310
Alberta L. Kingsly	1929	Conway Springs	Kansas	197
Larue Lennen	1925	Coolidge	Kansas	27
Helen Green	1931	Costa Mesa	California	107
Jack Adams	1925	Deerfield	Kansas	63
Laura (Lorene Hunt) Hart	1934	Denver	Colorado	152
Milton B. Moore	1921	Derby	Kansas	79
Dortha Schroeder	1925	Derby	Kansas	42
Alfred Rohr	1930	Derby	Kansas	314
Elma Ash	1932	Derby	Kansas	401
Howard L. Underwood	1932	Derby	Kansas	211
Shirley A. Schwarz	1940	Derby	Kansas	158
Karen Matthews Parker	1943	Derby	Kansas	382
Roy F. Parker	1944	Derby	Kansas	76
Robert A. Strong	1930	Dighton	Kansas	53
Maurice B. Creghead	1926	Dodge City	Kansas	251
Vera Jean Swafford	1927	Dodge City	Kansas	52
Bob Hessman	1935	Dodge City	Kansas	282
Jim "Pete" Carmichael	1939	Dodge City	Kansas	43
Shirley Hoskinson	1947	Dodge City	Kansas	348
Richard D. Blackburn	1948	Dodge City	Kansas	35
Gwen Wilson Brooks	Unknown	Dodge City	Kansas	263
Jean Peintner	Unknown	Dodge City	Kansas	36
Kenneth Howe	1933	Dundee	Oregon	160
Maureen Grandon	1932	Eatonville	Washington	398
Marilyn Newman	1939	Elgin	S. Carolina	198
Shirley Kempke	1935	Ellsworth	Kansas	49

Name	Year	City	State	Page
Marlene L. Goertz	1931	Farmington	New Mexico	50
Leah Sellers	1944	Florence	Kansas	100
Larry Harsh	1935	Flrgonia	Kansas	173
Ruby Ashcraft Deaver	1930	Fowler	Kansas	264
Frances Elffner	Unknown	Fowler	Kansas	131
Ruby Waltner	1931	Freeman	South Dakota	210
Betty Elaine Koehn	1929	Galva	Kansas	261
Robert E. Barton	1922	Garden City	Kansas	147
Laverne Griggs-Hiemstra	1923	Garden City	Kansas	179
Warrenetta Fisher	1926	Garden City	Kansas	422
Jeanette Elder	1934	Garden City	Kansas	218
Gerald Speer	1938	Garden City	Kansas	407
Leonard Hitz	1942	Garden City	Kansas	238
Sue Knight	1943	Garden City	Kansas	302
Glenda Crone	1946	Garden City	Kansas	140
Sharilyn Reifschneider	1947	Garden City	Kansas	188
Arlie DeFreese, Jr.	1955	Garden City	Kansas	272
Pat Stapleton Van Dolah	1955	Garden City	Kansas	412
Judy Farris	Unknown	Garden City	Kansas	69
Stanley J. Smith	1929	Garden Plain	Kansas	115
Kathy Ast	1943	Garden Plain	Kansas	118
Cecil Roger Thomas, Jr.	1934	Garner	N. Carolina	161
George Roets, Sr.	1930	Goddard	Kansas	230
Eleanor M. Fox	1934	Goddard	Kansas	427
Anna Mae Pracht	1937	Goddard	Kansas	312
Letha Roets	1938	Goddard	Kansas	280
Erlene R. Unruh	1929	Goessel	Kansas	88
Thane Baker	1931	Granbury	Texas	417
Robert Peterson	1942	Grayson	Georgia	298
Sister Teresita Huse	1918	Great Bend	Kansas	96
Siser Alvina Miller, O.P.	1918	Great Bend	Kansas	214
Wilma Steadman	1928	Great Bend	Kansas	109
Sister C. Ann Stremel	1943	Great Bend	Kansas	288
Loren & Arlene Schamaun	1931/1932	Great Bend	Kansas	52
Edna Irene J. Butler	1926	Greeley	Colorado	34
Jim Gilger	1924	Greeley County	Kansas	20
Patrick Sandoval	1950	Greenwood Village	Colorado	253
Phyllis Yockey	1946	Grove	Oklahoma	87
Peg Koehn	1939	Halstead	Kansas	183
Gordon Beaushaw	1952	Halstead	Kansas	373
Beulah Simcox	1934	Hanston	Kansas	202
Frances Johnson	1930	Harper	Kansas	119
Shirley Ummel	1940	Harper	Kansas	29
Brian M. Ede	1948	Harper	Kansas	283
Dana Davidson	1954	Harper	Kansas	230
Doug Fisher	1927	Haven	Kansas	371

Name	Year	City	State	Page
Charlene Heim	1943	Haven	Kansas	187
Aden E. Nettie Keim	1949	Haven	Kansas	339
Dr. Herb Frazier	1939	Haviland	Kansas	177
Clement A. Smith	1924	Haysville	Kansas	71
Noah J. Lewis	1930	Haysville	Kansas	194
Henry Pauls	1943	Henderson	Nebraska	200
Mary Hershberger	1939	Hesston	Kansas	103
Elfreda Fast	1917	Hillsboro	Kansas	150
Arthur G. Green	1926	Holcomb	Kansas	154
Rita Anne Mills	1943	Hugoton	Kansas	256
Cathy Boles Amara	1956	Huntsville	Alabama	247
Cecil A. Unruh	1923	Hutchinson	Kansas	17
Marcketta Peak	1924	Hutchinson	Kansas	156
Alice R. Uphoff	1925	Hutchinson	Kansas	353
Marian Redford	1926	Hutchinson	Kansas	176
June M. Winslow	1927	Hutchinson	Kansas	163
Joan Irene Farney Dunn	1928	Hutchinson	Kansas	301
Joan Goering	1928	Hutchinson	Kansas	220
Joyce A. McMannis	1928	Hutchinson	Kansas	45
Peter J. Neufeld	1929	Hutchinson	Kansas	91
Geraldine Stufflebeam	1929	Hutchinson	Kansas	284
Mary E. Yoder	1930	Hutchinson	Kansas	341
Estol Coen	1931	Hutchinson	Kansas	346
Carroll M. Snell	1931	Hutchinson	Kansas	148
Geri Shafer	1932	Hutchinson	Kansas	108
Lolita Bonnie Baker	1933	Hutchinson	Kansas	349
Julane Ediger	1933	Hutchinson	Kansas	36
Doris Schroeder	1933	Hutchinson	Kansas	19
Mora L. Weber	1933	Hutchinson	Kansas	308
Don Graber	1934	Hutchinson	Kansas	65
Carol J. Stone	1934	Hutchinson	Kansas	326
Bob Metzler	1936	Hutchinson	Kansas	106
Richard Robl	1936	Hutchinson	Kansas	404
Elva Unruh Kunze	1938	Hutchinson	Kansas	184
Helen Normandin	1938	Hutchinson	Kansas	182
Beverly J. Davis Smith	1938	Hutchinson	Kansas	307
Wendel Chalfant	1939	Hutchinson	Kansas	267
Diane Berry	1943	Hutchinson	Kansas	360
Carolyn Arpin	1944	Hutchinson	Kansas	227
Marjorie Terrell	1944	Hutchinson	Kansas	108
Marilyn J. Albright	1945	Hutchinson	Kansas	282
Dale Klenke	1946	Hutchinson	Kansas	294
Martha Stroup	1947	Hutchinson	Kansas	321
Jackie C. Smith-Lamkin	1950	Hutchinson	Kansas	217
Linda Gering	1952	Hutchinson	Kansas	48
Connie O'Bleness	1933	Idaho Falls	Idaho	315

Name	Year	City	State	Page
Norma Caldwell	Unknown	Ingalls	Kansas	72
Shirley F. Knackstedt	1936	Inman	Kansas	40
Ellen Pulliam Young	1945	Isabel	Kansas	286
Albert Hanlon	Unknown	Jennings	Oklahoma	180
Anna Schlereth Looney	1947	Jetmore	Kansas	318
Evelyn Mace	1930	Johnson	Kansas	365
Lowell Wayne Jones	1934	Johnson	Kansas	260
Georgia Thomas	1930	Kansas City	Missouri	305
Anna Jane Goetz	1926	Kingman	Kansas	312
Maxine Kirkpatrick	1928	Kingman	Kansas	97
Vita M. Henning	1936	Kingman	Kansas	392
Olive Ann McCormick	1940	Kingman	Kansas	378
Helen Farney	1928	Kiowa	Kansas	234
Patsy K. Miller Wilson	1945	Kiowa	Kansas	344
Lorene P. Gnaedinger	1932	Lady Lake	Florida	316
Iris McIntosh	1938	Lakewood	Colorado	280
Tom Walters	1942	Lakin	Kansas	313
Linda Walters	1945	Lakin	Kansas	314
Justine Sullivan	Unknown	Lakin	Kansas	235
Sister Irene Hartman	1921	Larned	Kansas	130
Roger G. Fox	1926	Larned	Kansas	145
Dorl Rader	1927	Larned	Kansas	433
Rebecca Otter	1935	Larned	Kansas	304
Nancy Ashworth Douglas	1944	Larned	Kansas	288
Cyndee Huddleston	1948	Larned	Kansas	166
Helen Gilger Glenn	1926	Las Vegas	Nevada	299
Joel Voran	1952	Leawood	Kansas	28
Alice Kay Miller	1948	Lenexa	Kansas	396
Marie Fletcher	1928	Leoti	Kansas	38
Simon Korbe, jr.	1931	Leoti	Kansas	335
LaVern Gregg Thomas	1924	Liberal	Kansas	99
John H. Duncan	1933	Liberal	Kansas	385
Jean L. Regier	1935	Liberal	Kansas	122
Barbara C. Campbell	1942	Liberal	Kansas	269
Arlene Schuler Grinnell	1929	Longmont	Colorado	25
Paula J. Etrick	1938	Longmont	Colorado	31
Mariella Sawin	1928	Lyons	Kansas	274
Pat Williamson	1930	Lyons	Kansas	107
Jan Pinsince	1951	Manhattan	Kansas	155
Beauford Wilkerson	1936	Manter	Kansas	414
Larry L. Gates	1937	McPherson	Kansas	147
Mr. Leslie Groves	Unknown	McPherson	Kansas	22
June M. Henderson	1944	Meade	Kansas	128
Helen Sindelar	1928	Medford	Oklahoma	101
Trulin Kinser	1931	Medicine Lodge	Kansas	350
Wilma Kinser	1934	Medicine Lodge	Kansas	343

Charlotte Ringer	1935	Medicine Lodge	Kansas	55
John A. Harding	1940	Medicine Lodge	Kansas	230
Claire Ryta Thompson	1948	Milan	Kansas	296
Evelyn Olson	1923	Monte Vista	Colorado	345
Jeanette U. Nightengale	1941	Montezuma	Kansas	185
Bill Temaat	1939	Monument	Colorado	295
Marion W. Nattier	1923	Moundridge	Kansas	159
Gertrude Raple	1920	Mt. Hope	Kansas	402
Pat Reichenberger	1942	Mt. Hope	Kansas	394
Merrill R. Deck	1934	Muldrow	Oklahoma	80
Clara B. Thompson	1929	Mulvane	Kansas	112
Jeri Myers	1948	Mulvane	Kansas	236
Lois M. Theis	1936	Nashville	Kansas	33
Terrence Keenan	1945	Ness City	Kansas	68
Connie Taylor	1935	New Canaan	Connecticut	289
Elsie Reiger	1918	Newton	Kansas	287
Helen L. Murray	1923	Newton	Kansas	248
Verene V. Eason	1926	Newton	Kansas	280
Galen Rudiger	1926	Newton	Kansas	99
Betty Swendson	1927	Newton	Kansas	27
Clayton Sadowski	1928	Newton	Kansas	321
Aliene Bolton	1930	Newton	Kansas	180
Jean Hicks	1933	Newton	Kansas	277
Melvin D. Pauls	1936	Newton	Kansas	191
Nancy J. Pauls	1936	Newton	Kansas	184
Douglas R. Van Horn	1936	Newton	Kansas	120
Richard O. Stineman	1937	Newton	Kansas	138
Pat Curtis	1939	Newton	Kansas	169
Elinor Keesling	1992	Newton	Kansas	248
Rose Alderson	1943	Nickerson	Kansas	233
Marie Regehr	1924	North Newton	Kansas	172
Vernon Pauls	1930	North Newton	Kansas	48
Laura Ann Schrag	1931	North Newton	Kansas	246
Janice A. Pauls	1939	North Newton	Kansas	211
Nora Ellen Allender	1929	Norwich	Kansas	242
Mardia "Dinky" Meece	1953	Norwich	Kansas	205
Adolph Kuhn	1921	Oceanside	California	114
Evelyn Crockett	1932	Offerle	Kansas	359
Galen R. Boehme, Ph.D.	1944	Offerle	Kansas	329
Judy Konrade	1951	Oggerle	Kansas	121
E. Joan Rollins	1931	Oklahoma City	Oklahoma	437
Martha J. H. Wakefield	1949	Omaha	Nebraska	344
Martina Stegman	1933	Oxford	Michigan	250
Betty J. Lehr	1930	Park City	Kansas	208
Francis "Frank" Moore	1947	Pasco	Washington	285
Arlys Kraus	1941	Pheonix	Arizona	311

Name	Year	City	State	Page
Marilyn Goracke	1945	Phillipsburg	Kansas	21
Beulah Gleeson Ratzlaff	1934	Plains	Kansas	153
Dorathe Wiltshire	1922	Pratt	Kansas	231
Ivan Harris Phillips	1925	Pratt	Kansas	266
David G. Davis	1927	Pratt	Kansas	105
Joann Danley	1931	Pratt	Kansas	125
Calvin L. Barnhart	1946	Pratt	Kansas	325
Carol S. Blankenship	1948	Pratt	Kansas	93
Larry Popovich	1948	Pratt	Kansas	151
Melody Elsworth	1953	Pretty Prairie	Kansas	225
Joyce Murphey	1931	Protection	Kansas	137
Dell Spurgeon	1931	Protection	Kansas	290
Susan Edmonston	1947	Protection	Kansas	59
Chester I. Bare, Jr.	1925	Raytown	Missouri	116
Lesta Freeman Esser	1946	Riverton	Wyoming	362
Larry Miles	1941	Round Rock	Texas	281
James M. Hall	1934	Salina	Kansas	401
Mark McIver	Unknown	Santana	Kansas	310
Shauna Labo	1963	Saraland	Alabama	270
Margaret Surprise	1921	Scott City	Kansas	37
E. Earl Kendrick	1938	Scott City	Kansas	434
Art Gomez	1941	Scott City	Kansas	192
Carolyn Kay Mohler	1941	Scott City	Kansas	366
Liz Miller	1948	Scott City	Kansas	148
Garee Geist	1953	Scott City	Kansas	108
Gail Schroeder	1941	Sedgwick	Kansas	311
Robert C. Dick, Ph.D.	1938	Sedona	Arizona	111
Ruth B. Sanderson	1929	Shawnee	Kansas	410
Gene Hirst	1926	Shell Knob	Missouri	145
Marita McBride	1936	South Hutchinson	Kansas	121
Lloyd H. Yoder	1937	South Hutchinson	Kansas	260
Virginia L. Ryan	1930	Spearville	Kansas	178
Ann Warner	1947	Spearville	Kansas	411
Sister Diane Traffas	1935	St. Catharine	Kentucky	347
Michael Hathaway	1961	St. John	Kansas	62
Marion L. Hearn	1931	Stafford	Kansas	355
Darlene McMillion	1936	Stafford	Kansas	73
Jayne Smoot	1925	Sterling	Kansas	405
Elinor "Skip" Vasey	1932	Sylvia	Kansas	408
Pauline Fecht	1931	Syracuse	Kansas	105
Faye Klinge	1937	Syracuse	Kansas	247
Jennifer I. Beaver	1951	Tampa	Florida	165
Joyce Stark Morse	1943	Tempe	Arizona	195
Rachel Witte	1931	The Villages	Florida	233
Lester Seuser	1930	Timken	Kansas	317
Allan T. Kimmell	1925	Topeka	Kansas	250

Name	Year	City	State	Page
Galen Rapp	1935	Topeka	Kansas	89
Joy Kline Moser	1942	Topeka	Kansas	380
Kenneth Lipprand	1948	Topeka	Kansas	116
Colleen Lemman-Tarman	1936	Tribune	Kansas	133
Doloris Ungles	1932	Ulysses	Kansas	110
Eleanor Smith	1936	Ulysses	Kansas	106
Ralph E. Nutter, Sr.	1917	Valley Center	Kansas	222
Icel Lee Russell	1922	Valley Center	Kansas	402
Marie S. Clemence	1928	Valley Center	Kansas	42
Ruth Saranko	1931	Valley Center	Kansas	249
Mickie Gillette	1935	Valley Center	Kansas	62
Lavona Hobson	1941	Valley Center	Kansas	336
Jack Moser	1927	Vilas	Colorado	142
Christiana B. Bollig	1929	Wakeeney	Kansas	377
Hildred Schmidt	1932	Walton	Kansas	351
Jane Keel Sapone	1930	Wanchese	N. Carolina	66
Esley Schmidt	1926	Waverly	Kansas	401
Dorothy Richardson	1930	Wellington	Kansas	240
Diana Dry	1942	Wellington	Kansas	65
Ken Patterson	1944	Wellington	Kansas	319
Carla Rains	1944	Wellington	Kansas	98
Jolene Rice Roitman	1951	Wellington	Kansas	403
Gerold R. "Jerry" Falls	1952	Wellington	Kansas	83
Brian T. Lohrenz	1961	Wellington	Kansas	62
Katherine Becker Cruz	1925	Westminster	Colorado	387
Russell O. Vail	1941	White Lake	Michigan	157
Howard Hamilton	1922	Wichita	Kansas	363
Lorraine L. Lovette	1929	Wichita	Kansas	367
Cecile M. T. Shoemaker	1930	Wichita	Kansas	70
Mary Ann Rix	1931	Wichita	Kansas	150
Lois Timmermeyer	1932	Wichita	Kansas	334
Barbara Woodman	1933	Wichita	Kansas	144
Judy Schremmer Corby	1943	Wichita	Kansas	429
Peggy J. Gammill	1943	Wichita	Kansas	430
Jana Sibley Finkbiner	1944	Wichita	Kansas	74
Jane Keel Schmidt	1951	Wilmore	Kansas	338
Donald C. Lipprand	1935	Winfield	Kansas	259